Conversion Tables

Conversion Tables
Volume 3

Subject Headings
LC and Dewey

Third Edition

Mona L. Scott

LIBRARIES
UNLIMITED
A Member of the Greenwood Publishing Group

Westport, Connecticut • London

Library of Congress Cataloging-in-Publication Data

Scott, Mona L.
    Conversion tables / by Mona L. Scott.
      p. cm.
    ISBN 1-59158-348-9 (set : alk. paper) — ISBN 1-59158-315-2 (v. 1 :
    alk. paper) — ISBN 1-59158-346-2 (v. 2 : alk. paper)
    —ISBN 1-59158-347-0 (v. 3 : alk. paper)
    1. Classification, Library of Congress. 2. Classification,
    Dewey decimal. 3. Reclassification (Libraries) I. Title.
    Z696.U4S36 2006
    025.4'33—dc22   2005030846

British Library Cataloguing in Publication Data is available.

Library of Congress Catalog Card Number: 2005030846
ISBN: 1-59158-315-2 (Volume 1)
        1-59158-346-2 (Volume 2)
        1-59158-347-0 (Volume 3)
        1-59158-348-9 (Set)

First published in 2006

Libraries Unlimited, 88 Post Road West, Westport, CT 06881
A Member of Greenwood Publishing, Inc.
www.lu.com

Printed in the United States of America

The paper used in this book complies with the
Permanent Paper Standard issued by the National
Information Standards Organization (Z39.48–1984).

10   9   8   7   6   5   4   3   2   1

Contents

Introduction

The third edition of *Conversion Tables: LC-Dewey; Dewey-LC* contains extensive updates of Dewey numbers that reflect the 22nd edition of the Dewey Decimal Classification. Also included are almost one thousand additional sets of class numbers and corresponding Library of Congress (LC) subject headings. These include new subjects that reflect today's world, such as the September 11, 2001, Terrorist Attacks; the War on Terrorism; the Afghan War of 2001; and the Iraq War of 2003. There are also classification and subject sets that broaden areas that were found in the earlier editions, such as Druids and Druidism; World War, 1939–1945—Campaigns—Burma; 401(k) plans; Cosmic noise; Butterfly gardens; Anorexia; CPR (First aid); Computer art; and many ethnic groups found in Africa.

Materials referenced in the *Conversion Tables* are the 22nd edition of the Dewey Decimal Classification (DDC) and the most current editions of the various volumes of the Library of Congress classification schedules and LC Subject Headings available. Library of Congress authority files were consulted regularly to maintain the currency of country or nation names.

Conversion Tables was conceived as a cataloging tool or standard reference in any cataloging department for daily copy cataloging activities, the converting of classifications of individual MARC (machine readable cataloging) records from bibliographic utilities that include only one of the classifications. The LC subject heading table also can be used as call a number assigning tool for both LC and DDC classifications.

The LC and DDC classification schemes approach the organization of knowledge from different perspectives. This can be seen in how LC and Dewey view language and the literatures of each language. LC classes them together in the Ps, whereas Dewey separates them, placing language in the 400s and literature in the 800s. Similarly, LC places military and naval sciences in stand-alone classes, U for military science and V for naval sciences; Dewey places both in the so-called megaclass 300s, which includes virtually all of social and political sciences.

Becasue the two schemes differ so greatly in basic concepts, it was necessary to analyze the concepts of each order to select the corresponding numbers or alphanumeric notations to construct the tables. Ultimately, it involved assigning tens of thousands of class notations.

Structure of the Tables

This cataloging tool is arranged in three sections, each in its own volume: LC to Dewey, Volume 1; Dewey to LC, Volume 2; and Subject Headings with corresponding classifications, Volume 3. Thus each volume contains the same list of classifications in the two systems and corresponding subject headings but is arranged differently.

Example:

LC to Dewey tables

LC	Dewey	Subject Heading
DS79.76	956.70443	Iraq War, 2003

Dewey to LC tables

Dewey	LC	Subject Heading
956.70443	DS79.76	Iraq War, 2003

Subject Heading tables

Subject Heading	Dewey	LC
Iraq War, 2003	956.70443	DS79.76

The notation for a general concept such as Philosophy, which is 100 in Dewey and B in the Library of Congress Classification, will have divisions and subdivisions broken down into smaller concepts and thus more detailed notations ("Philosophy—Congresses" is 105 in Dewey and B20 in LC).

The differences just discussed also result in more than one notation corresponding to the other, or even a whole range of numbers and alphanumeric notations corresponding to the other. For example, 951.041 in the Dewey schedule under the history of China corresponds to seven LC notations in these tables, in the range DS773.83 to DS777.45.

Dates in the LC and Dewey schemes are a problem. The two schedules often do not agree on the date that an event occurred. For example, the LC classification indicates that the Time of Troubles in Russian history was from 1598–1613, but the Dewey scheme uses the date 1605–1613. In other places, however, the dates match perfectly, as in the history of Tunisia. To aid in the conversion, I have often used a range of dates from Table 1 in the Dewey Classification to indicate a century, rather than the single date.

The following conventions have been used:

- Diacritics have not been included in the subject headings.

- Within the class numbers and subject headings, "/" indicates a choice and is usually contained within parentheses or brackets.

- As in conventional cataloging rules, brackets [ ] contain words added by the author.

Instructions for Use of the Tables

To convert a classification from LC to Dewey or Dewey to LC, find the volume containing the table from which you wish to convert. Locate the classification from which you wish to convert in the left column. As indicated earlier, it may be included in a range of "numbers" or alphanumeric notations that correspond to the other classification, or it may fall between two classifications. In these cases, locate the class nearest in concept by using the Subject Headings. The classification to which you wish to convert is in the middle column, with the subject heading on the right.

The Subject Heading section provides a shortcut to the call-number assigning process. Using that section, you can search for the subject heading that reflects or approximates the subject matter of the item that is being cataloged and note the appropriate classifications next to it. This notation may be the classification that is needed, or it will lead you to the appropriate one in the schedules.

Subject Headings—Dewey and LC

Subject Heading	Dewey	LC	Subject Heading	Dewey	LC
35mm cameras	771.32	TR262	Abraham (Biblical patriarch) in the New Testament	225.92	BS580.A3
401(k) plans	332.0240145	HD7105.4-.45			
4-H clubs	630.6	S533.F66			
A stars	523.8	QB843.A12	Abscess	616.047	RD641
Aardvark	599.31	QL737.T8	Absentee mothers	306.8743	HQ759.3
Aaronic Priesthood (Mormon Church)	262.1	BX8659.5	Absentee voting	324.65	JF1033
			Absenteeism (Labor)	331.2598	HD5715-.2
Aatimna (Hindu deity)	294.52113	BL1225.A	Absolute, The	111.6	BD416
Abaca (Fiber)	633.571	SB261.M3	Absolution (Canon law)	262.933	BX1939.A
Abacus	513.0284	QA75	Absorption (Physiology)	612.38	QP165
Abalone culture	639.4832	SH371.5-.52	Absorption of light	535.326	QC437
Abalone fisheries	639.4832	SH371.5-.52	Absorption of sound	534.208	QC233
Abalones	594.32	QL430.5.H34	Abused lesbians	306.7663	HQ75.3-.6
Abandoned children	362.73	HV873-875.7	Abused parents	306.874	HQ755.85
Abandoned children—[By region or country]	362.7309(4-9)	HV880-887	Abused wives—Services for	362.8292	HV697-700.5
			Abused wives—Services for—[By region or country]	362.829209(4-9)	HV699-700
Abandoned children—United States	362.730973	HV880-885	Abused women—Pastoral counseling of	259.082	BV4445.5
Abazin language	499.962	PK9201.A2	Abyssinian cat	636.826	SF449.A28
Abbasids	953.80099	DS234-238	Abyssinian Expedition, 1867-1868	963.041	DT386.3
Abbeys	726.7	NA4800-6113			
Abbots (Canon law)	262.932	BX1939.A	Academic costume	378.28	LB2389
Abbreviations, Persian	491.5511	PK6395	Academic freedom	371.104	LC72-.5
Abbreviations, Romanian	459.11	PC785	Academic libraries	027.7	Z675.U5
Abdomen	611.95	QM543	Academies and learned societies	060	AS
Abdomen—Cancer	616.99495	RC280.A2			
Abdomen—Diseases	617.55	RC944	Acala (Buddhist deity)	294.34211	BQ4860.A4
Abdomen—Surgery	617.55059	RD540-548	Accelerometers	629.1352	TL589.2.A3
Abdomen—Tumors	616.99495	RC280.A2	Acceptances	332	HG1655
Abdomen—Wounds and injuries	617.55044	RD540-548	Accident law—England	344.42047	KD3510
			Accident law—United States	344.73047	KF3970
Abduction	364.154	HV6571-6574			
Abenaki Indians	974.0049734	E99.A13	Accidents—Prevention	363.107	HV675-677
Abent squirrel	599.36	QL737.R68	Acclimatization	578.42	QH543.2
Aberration	522.9	QB163	Accordion	788.8609	ML1083
Abhayagiri (Sect)	294.39	BQ8000-8049	Accordion music	788.86	M175.A4
Ability grouping in education	371.254	LB3061	Account books	657	HF5680-5681
			Accounting	657	HF5601-5689.8
Ability in children	155.4139	BF723.A25	Accounting machines	657.0284	HF5679
Ability in infants	155.42239	BF720.A24	Accounting—Study and teaching (Internship)	657.071	HF5630
Ability—Testing	153.93	BF431-433			
Abitibi Indians	974.004971	E99.A12	Accounts current	657.72	HF5681.A2
Abkhaz language	499.9623	PK9201.A3	Accounts payable	657.74	HF5681.A27
Abkhaz literature	899.9623	PK9201.A35-.A39	Accounts receivable	657.72	HF5681.A3
			Accounts receivable loans	332.7	HG3752.3
Abkhazo-Adyghian languages	499.962	PK9051	Accreditation (Education)	379.158	LB2810-.5
			Acetal resins	668.423	TP1180.A33
Abnormalities, Human	618.32043	RG626-629	Acetylene	547.413	QD305.H8
Abortion	342.084	RA1067	Acetylene compounds	547.413	QD305.H8
Abortion	363.46	HQ767-.52	Achaemenid dynasty, 559-330 B.C.	935.05	DS281-284.7
Abortion in the press	363.46	PN4784.A18			
Abortion in the press	363.460973	PN4888.A2	Achievement motivation	153.8	BF501-505
Abortion services	363.46	RG734-.5	Achievement tests	371.271	LB3060.3
			Acid mine drainage	628.42	TD899.M5

Subject Heading	Dewey	LC	Subject Heading	Dewey	LC
Acid precipitation (Meteorology)	551.5771	QC926.5-.57	Acute myelocytic leukemia in children	618.9299419	RJ416.A25
Acid rain	363.7386	QC926.5-.57	Acute renal failure in children	618.92614	RJ476.R46
Acid soils	631.42	S592.57-.575	Acute toxicity testing	615.907	RA1199.4.A38
Acid sulphate soils	631.42	S592.575	Adam (Biblical figure) in the Koran	297.122092	BP133.7.A3
Acidosis	616.3992	RB147	Adamawa languages	496.361	PL8024.A33
Acids	661.2	TP213-217	Adaptation (Biology)	578.4	QH546
Ackia, Battle of, 1736	976.202	F347.A25	Adaptation (Physiology)	578.4	QP82-.2
Acne	616.53	RL131	Addison's disease	616.45	RC659
Acoli language	496.5	PL8041	Addition	513.211	QA115
Acoustic microscopy	502.82	QH212.A25	Addition polymerization	547.28	QD281.P6
Acoustic nuclear magnetic resonance	538.362	QC762.6.A25	Adelie penguin	598.47	QL696.S473
Acoustical engineering	620.2	TA365-367	Adhesion	541.33	QC183
Acoustooptical devices	621.3828	TA1770	Adhesives	668.3	TP967-970
Acquisition of art catalogs	025.277	Z688.A7	Adhesives industry	338.476683	HD9999(.A4-.A44)
Acquisition of databases	025.284	Z692.D38	Adipose tissues	611.01827	QM565
Acquisition of maps	025.286	Z692.M3	Aditi (Hindu deity)	294.52114	BL1225.A4
Acquisition of medical literature	025.2761	Z688.M4	Adityas (Hindu deities)	294.52113	BL1225.A42
Acquisition of serial publications	025.28305	Z692.S5	Adjustment (Psychology)	155.24	BF335-337
Acquisitions (Libraries)	025.2	Z689-.8	Adlerian psychology	150.1953	BF175.5.A33
Acrobatics	796.47	GV551-553	Administrative law	342.066	K3400-3431
Acromegaly	616.47	RC658.3	Administrative law— United States	342.73066	KF5401-5425
Acrophobia	616.85225	RC552.A43	Administrative responsibility	352.35	JF1621
Acrostics	793.73	PN6366-6377	Administrators apostolic	262.02	BX1939.A3
Acrylic fiber industry	338.476774742	HD9929.5.A2 (7-74)	Admirals	359.331	VB190
Acrylic painting	751.426	ND1535	Adolescence	155.5	LB1135
Acting	792.028	PN2061-2071	Adolescence	305.235	GN483-484
Acting—Vocational guidance	792.023	PN2055	Adolescence	599.90835	GN63
Action research in education	370.72	LB1028.24	Adolescent analysis	618.928917	RJ503
			Adolescent gynecology	618.92098	RJ478-.5
Actions and defenses— United States	347.73053	KF8863-8865	Adolescent medicine	616.00835	RJ550
Actium, Battle of, 31 B.C.	937.05	DG269	Adolescent psychiatric nursing	616.8900835	RJ502.3
Active childbirth	618.4	RG662	Adolescent psychiatry	616.8900835	RJ503
Active galaxies	523.112	QB858.3	Adolescent psychology	155.5	BF724-.3
Active oxygen	546.721	QD181.O1	Adolescent psychopathology	616.8900835	RJ503
Active oxygen in the body	572.53	QP535.O1			
Activity coefficients	541.34	QD541-543	Adolescent psychotherapy	616.891400835	RJ503
Activity-based costing	657.42	HF5686.C8	Adolescent psychotherapy— Termination	616.891400835	RJ505.T47
Actors	792.028092	PN2205-2217	Adonis (Greek deity)	292.2113	BL820.A25
Actors—Professional ethics	174.97914	PN2056	Adoption	362.734	HV874.8-875.7
Actresses	792.028092	PN2205-2217	Adrenal cortex	612.45	QP188.A28
Acupressure	615.8222	RM723.A27	Adrenal glands	611.45	QM371
Acupressure for children	615.8222083	RJ53.A27	Adrenal glands	618.9245	RJ420.A27
Acupuncture	615.892	RM184-.5	Adrenal glands	612.45	QP188.A3
Acupuncture for children	615.892083	RJ53.A27	Adrenal glands—Diseases	616.45	RC659
Acupuncture points	615.892	RC73.2	Adrenalectomy	617.44	RD599.5.A37
Acute abdomen	617.55	RD540-548	Adrenaline	573.46	QP572.A27
Acute hemorrhagic conjunctivitis	617.773	RE320	Adrenergic alpha blockers	616.1206	RC634
			Adrenergic beta blockers	616.1206	RC684.A35
Acute leukemia	616.99419	RC643	Adrianople, Battle of, 378	949.501	DF559
			Adult children of alcoholics	362.2923	HV5132

Subject Heading	Dewey	LC	Subject Heading	Dewey	LC
Aeronautics, Commercial—Israel	387.7095694	HE9868.45	Aesthetics	701.17	N61-79
Aeronautics, Commercial—Italy	387.70945	HE9851	Aesthetics, Ancient	111.850901	BH91-116
			Aesthetics, Byzantine	111.8509495	BH221.B
Aeronautics, Commercial—Japan	387.70952	HE9877	Aesthetics, Canadian	111.850971	BH221.C
Aeronautics, Commercial—Mexico	387.70972	HE9816	Aesthetics, Medieval	111.850902	BH131-137
			Aesthetics, Medieval	701.170902	N61
Aeronautics, Commercial—Middle East	387.70956	HE9868.2-.95	Aesthetics, Modern	111.850903	BH151-208
Aeronautics, Commercial—Philippines	387.709599	HE9876	Aesthetics, Modern—16th century	111.8509031	BH161-168
Aeronautics, Commercial—Russia	387.70947	HE9855	Aesthetics, Modern—16th century	701.1709031	N61
Aeronautics, Commercial—South America	387.7098	HE9830-9841	Aesthetics, Modern—17th century	111.8509032	BH171-178
Aeronautics, Commercial—Spain	387.70946	HE9861	Aesthetics, Modern—17th Century	701.1709032	N61
Aeronautics, Commercial—Switzerland	387.709494	HE9863	Aesthetics, Modern—18th century	111.8509033	BH181-188
Aeronautics, Commercial—United States	387.70973	HE9803-9814	Aesthetics, Modern—18th century	701.1709033	N61
Aeronautics, Commercial—West Indies	387.709729	HE9824-9829.9	Aesthetics, Modern—19th century	111.8509034	BH191-198
Aeronautics, Commercial—Freight	387.744	TL720.7	Aesthetics, Modern—19th century	701.1709034	N61
Aeronautics, Commercial—History	387.709	HE9774-9775	Aesthetics, Modern—20th century	111.850904	BH201-208
Aeronautics, Commercial—Passenger traffic	387.742	HE9787-.5	Aesthetics, Modern—20th century	701.170904	N61
Aeronautics, Commercial—Periodicals	387.705	HE9761-.9	Aesthetics, Oriental	111.85095	BH101-102
			Aesthetics—Congresses	111.8506	BH19
Aeronautics, Military	358.4	UG630-670	Aesthetics—Dictionaries	111.8503	BH56
Aeronautics—Abbreviations	629.1300148	TL509	Aesthetics—History	111.8509	BH81-208
Aeronautics—Biography	629.130092	TL539-540	Aesthetics—Periodicals	111.8505	BH1-8
Aeronautics—Communication systems	629.135	TL692-696	Aesthetics—Study and teaching	111.85071	BH61-62
Aeronautics—Congresses	629.13006	TL505	Aetolia (Greece)	938.3	DF261.A2
Aeronautics—Flights	629.13	TL721	Afar language	493.5	PJ2465
Aeronautics—History	629.13009	TL515-532	Affective disorders	616.8527	RC537-545
Aeronautics—Law and legislation	343.097	K4091-4124	Affective disorders in children	618.928527	RJ506.D4
Aeronautics—Patents	629.1300272	TL513	Affinity credit cards	332.178	HG1643
Aeronautics—Pictorial works	629.1300222	TL549	Affirmative action programs	331.133	HF5549.5.A34
Aeronautics—Safety measures	629.1300289	TL553.5	Afforestation	634.956	SD409
			Afghan hounds	636.7533	SF429.A4
Aeronautics—Sanitation	629.1344	RA615.2	Afghan War, 2001—Prisoners and prisons American	958.1047	DS371.414
Aeronautics—Societies, etc.	629.13006	TL500-504			
Aerosols	363.7392	QC882.4-.46	Afghanistan—Census	315.81	HA4570.6
Aerospace engineering	629.1	TL500-4050	Afghanistan—Civilization	958.1	DS354
Aerospace industries	338.4762912	HD9711.5	Afghanistan—Civilization	939.6	DS354
Aerospace telemetry	629.437	TL694.T35	Afghanistan—Description and travel	913.9604	DS352
Aerostatics	533.61	QC168	Afghanistan—Description and travel	915.8104	DS352
Aerotherapy	615.836	RM824-827	Afghanistan—Economic conditions	330.9581	HC416-420
Aesculapius (Greek deity)	292.2113	BL820.A4	Afghanistan—Gazetteers	913.96003	DS351
			Afghanistan—Gazetteers	915.81003	DS351
			Afghanistan—History	958.1	DS355-371.2

Subject Heading	Dewey	LC	Subject Heading	Dewey	LC
Afghanistan—History	939.6	DS355-371.2	Africa, West—History—1884-1960	966.03(12-26)	DT476.2-.23
Afghanistan—History—1989-	958.104(5-6)	DS371.3	Africa, West—History—1960-	966.03(26-3)	DT476.5-.523
Afghanistan—History—Soviet occupation, 1979-1989	958.1045	DS371.2	Africa, West—Maps	912.66	G2640-2714
Afghanistan—Maps	912.581	G2265-2269	Africa—Armed Forces—Supplies and stores	355.8096	UC247-253
Afghanistan—Maps	912.581	G7630-7634	Africa—Biography	920.06	CT1920-2750
Afghanistan—Politics and government	320.9581	JQ1760-1769	Africa—Church history	276	BR1359-1470
Africa	960	DT	Africa—Civilization	960	DT14
Africa, Central—Church history	276.7	BR1430	Africa—Climate	551.696	QC991
Africa, Central—History—To 1884	967.0(1-2)	DT352.65	Africa—Colonization	325.6	JV246
Africa, Central—History—1884-1960	967.03(1-26)	DT352.7	Africa—Commerce	381.096	HF3871-3937
Africa, Central—Maps	912.67	G2590-2639	Africa—Description and travel	916.04	DT6.5-12.25
Africa, East	967.6	DT365-469	Africa—Economic conditions	330.96	HC800-1085
Africa, East—Church history	276.76	BR1440-1445	Africa—Emigration and immigration	325.(26) or (6)	JV8790-9024.5
Africa, East—History	967.6	DT365.5-.8	Africa—Gazetteers	916.003	DT2
Africa, East—History—To 1886	967.601	DT365.65	Africa—Genealogy	929.107206	CS1550-1779
Africa, East—Maps	912.676	G2500-2559	Africa—History	960	DT17-39
Africa, North	961	DT160-177	Africa—History—To 1498	960.(1-21)	DT25
Africa, North	939.7	DT160-177	Africa—History—To 1884	960.(1-23)	DT24-28
Africa, North—Church history	276.1	BR1369-1415	Africa—History—1884-1918	960.(23-314)	DT29
Africa, North—Description and travel	913.9704	DT163-165.2	Africa—History—1884-1960	960.(23-326)	DT29-30.2
Africa, North—Description and travel	916.104	DT163-165.2	Africa—History—1960-	960.3(26-3)	DT30.5
Africa, North—History	961	DT160-176	Africa—Manufactures	670.96	TS115-119
Africa, North—History	939.7	DT160-176	Africa—Maps	912.6	G2445-2739
Africa, North—History—To 647	939.701	DT168-171	Africa—Maps	912.6	G8200-8202
Africa, North—History—647-1517	961.0(22-45)	DT172	African buffalo	599.642	QL737.U53
Africa, North—History—1882-	961.0(3-5)	DT176	African drama (English)	822	PR9343
Africa, North—Maps	912.61	G2455-2499	African drama (English)	822.08	PR9347
Africa, North—Maps	912.61	G8220-8222	African elephant	599.674	QL737.P98
Africa, North—Religion	299.3	BL2462	African essays	089.96	AC177-189
Africa, Northwest	964	DT179.2-.9	African fiction (English)	823	PR9344
pnumAfrica, Northwest	939.7	DT179.2-.9	African fiction (English)	823.09	PR9347.5
Africa, Southern—Church history	276.8	BR1446-1458	African fish eagle	598.942	QL696.F32
Africa, Southern—History—Mfecane period, 1816-ca. 1840	968.0009034	DT1123	African gray parrot	598.71	QL696.P7
Africa, West	966	DT470-671	African languages	496	PL
Africa, West—Church history	276.6	BR1460-1463	African languages	496	PL8000-8008
Africa, West—History—To 1884	966.02	DT476	African languages—Grammar	496.5	PL8008
			African languages—Study and teaching	496.071	PL8004
			African literature	896	PL8010-8014
			African literature (English)	820.9	PR9340-9408
			African literature (French)	840	PQ3980-3989.2
			African literature (Portuguese)	869	PQ9900-9948
			African periodicals	079.6	PN5450-5499
			African poetry (English)	821.08	PR9346-.5
			African poetry (English)	821.09	PR9342

Subject Heading	Dewey	LC	Subject Heading	Dewey	LC
African trypanosomiasis	616.9363	RC186.T82	Afro-Americans—Biography	920.009296073	E185.96-.97
African violets	583.95	QK495.G4	Afro-Americans—Civil rights	323.1196073	E185.61
African wild ass	599.665	QL737.U62	Afro-Americans—Communication	302.208996073	P94.5.A37
Africander cattle	636.28	SF199.A3			
Africanized honeybee	595.799	QL568.A6	Afro-Americans—Crimes against	362.8808996073	HV6250.4.E75
Africa—Politics and government	320.96	JQ	Afro-Americans—Economic conditions	330.9730896073	E185.8
Africa—Politics and government	320.96	JQ1870-3981	Afro-Americans—Education	371.82996073	LC2701-2853
Africa—Religion	299.6	BL2400-2490	Afro-Americans—Education (Elementary)	372.182996073	LC2771
Afrikaans drama	839.36208	PT6570			
Afrikaans drama	839.36209	PT6520	Afro-Americans—Education (Higher)	378.1982996073	LC2781
Afrikaans fiction	839.36308	PT6570	Afro-Americans—Education (Secondary)	373.182996073	LC2779
Afrikaans fiction	839.36309	PT6525			
Afrikaans language	439.36	PF861-884	Afro-Americans—Health and hygiene	613.08996073	RA448.5.N4
Afrikaans literature	839.36	PT6500-6593.36			
Afrikaans poetry	839.36108	PT6545	Afro-Americans—History	973.0496073	E185.18-.98
Afrikaans poetry	839.36108	PT6560	Afro-Americans—History—To 1863	973.(1-7) + 0496073	E185.18
Afrikaans poetry	839.36109	PT6515			
Afrikaans prose literature	839.36808	PT6525	Afro-Americans—History—1863-1877	973.(7-82) + 0496073	E185.2
Afrikaans prose literature	839.36808	PT6590			
Afrikaans prose literature	839.36808	PT6570	Afro-Americans—History—1877-1964	973.(83-923) + 0496073	E185.6
Afrikaans wit and humor	839.367	PN6222.S			
Afro-American artists	700.08996073	N6538.N5	Afro-Americans—History—1964-	973.92(3-9) + 0496073	E185.615
Afro-American authors	810.9896073	PS153.N5			
Afro-American Catholics	282.08996073	BX1407.N4	Afro-Americans—Housing	363.5908996073	HD7288.72
Afro-American children	305.2308996073	E185.86	Afro-Americans—Medical care	362.108996073	RA448.5.N4
Afro-American children's games	394.308996073	GR103			
Afro-American decorative arts	745.08996073	NK839.3.A35	Afro-Americans—Mental health	616.89008996 + 073	RC451.5. + N4
			Afro-Americans—Mortality	304.6408996073	HB1323.B5
Afro-American engineers	620.008996073	TA157	Afro-Americans—Professional education	378.01308996 + 073	L2785
Afro-American Episcopalians	283.7308996073	BX5979			
			Afro-Americans—Psychology	155.8496073	E185.625
Afro-American families	306.850896073	E185.86			
Afro-American freemasonry	366.108996073	HS875-895	Afro-Americans—Scholarships, fellowships, etc.	371.22308996 + 073	LC2707
Afro-American lawyers	349.730899 + 6073	KF299.A35			
Afro-American mass media	302.2308996 + 073	P94.5.A37	Afro-Americans—Segregation	305.896073	E185.61
			Afro-Americans— Services for	362.8496073	HV3181-3185
Afro-American Methodists	287.8	BX8435-8473			
Afro-American newspapers	070.484	PN4882.5	Afro-Americans—Social conditions	973.0496073	E185.86
Afro-American nurses	615.7308996073	RT83.5			
Afro-American pharmacists	615.108996073	RS122.5	Afro-Americans—Social life and customs	390.089 + (960 73)	E185.86
Afro-American press	070.484	PN4882.5			
Afro-American prints	769.08996073	NE539.3.A35	Afro-Americans—Social life and customs	973.04	E185.86
Afro-American psychologists	150.8996073	BF109			
			Afro-Americans—Suffrage	324.6208996073	JK1924-1929
Afro-American theater	792.08996073	PN2270.A35	Afro-Americans—Vocational education	370.11308996 + 073	LC2780
Afro-Americans	973.0496073	E185			
Afro-Americans and mass media	302.2308996 + 073	P94.5.A37	Afroasiatic languages	492	PJ990
			Afro-Brazilian cults	299.891	BL2590.B7
Afro-Americans in business	338.790896073	E185.8	AGATE (Computer war game)	355.480285	U310
Afro-Americans in dentistry	617.6008996073	RK60.45			
Afro-Americans in mass media	302.2308996 + 073	P94.5.A37	Agates	622.387	TN997.A35
Afro-Americans in medicine	610.8996073	R695			

Subject Heading	Dewey	LC
Agave	584.352	QK495.A26
Agave products industry	338.173577	HD9019.A43- + .A434
Age distribution (Demography)	305.2	HB1531-1738
Age distribution (Demography)—[United States, By state]	305.2097(4-9)	HB1565
Age distribution (Demography)—United States	305.20973	HB1545-1567
Age distribution—[By region or country]	305.209(4-9)	HB1541-1737
Aged	305.26	HQ1060-1064
Aged	362.6	HV1450-1494
Aged in mass media	305.26	P96.A38
Aged in the Bible	220.0846	BS680.A34
Aged—[By region or country]	362.609(4-9)	HV1457-1494
Aged—Anthropometry	599.940846	GN59.A35
Aged—Crimes against	362.880846	HV6250.4.A34
Aged—Diseases	618.97	RC952-954.6
Aged—Dwellings	728.0846	NA7195.A4
Aged—Education	374	LC5451-5493
Aged—Employment	331.398	HD6279-6283
Aged—Mental health services	362.20846	RC451.4.A5
Aged—Psychology	155.67	BF724.8-.85
Aged—Recreation	790.1926	GV184
Aged—Religious life	248.85	BV4580
Aged—Sexual behavior	306.70846	HQ30
Aged—Surgery	617.97	RD145
Agency (Law)—Canada	346.7102	KE1328-1332
Agency (Law)—United States	346.73029	KF1341-1348
Aggada	296.19	BM516-.5
Aggressiveness (Psychology)	155.232	BF575.A3
Aggressiveness (Psychology) in adolescence	155.51247	BF724.3.A34
Aggressiveness (Psychology) in youth	155.51247	BF724.3.A34
Aggressiveness in children	155.418232	BF723.A35
Agincourt, Battle of, 1415	944.026	DC101.5.A2
Aging	571.878	QH529
Agnosticism	211.7	BL2700-2790
Agnus Dei (Sacramental)	264.0209	BX2310.A
Agoraphobia	616.85225	RC552.A44
Agrammatism	616.8552	RC425.5
Agricultural chemistry	631.41	S583-587.5
Agricultural colleges	630.711	S537-539
Agricultural conservation	631.451	S604.5-.64
Agricultural cooperative credit associations	332.31	HG2041-2051
Agricultural credit	332.71	HD1439-1440
Agricultural ecology	577.55	S441-482
Agricultural education	630.7	S530-539
Agricultural engineering	631	S671-760
Agricultural exhibitions	630.74	S550-559
Agricultural experimental stations	630.724	S541-543
Agricultural extension work	630.715	S544-545
Agricultural geography	630.9(4-9)	S439-481
Agricultural implements	631.3	S676-.3
Agricultural implements, Prehistoric	630.901	GN799.A4
Agricultural instruments	631.3	S676.5
Agricultural laborers	331.763	HD1521-1542
Agricultural laws and legislation—Canada	343.71076	KE1671-1745
Agricultural laws and legislation—England	343.42076	KD2241-2295
Agricultural laws and legislation—United States	343.73076	KF1681-1755
Agricultural machinery	631.3	S671-760
Agricultural machinery	631.3	TJ1480-1496
Agricultural machinery industry	338.76313	HD9486-.6
Agricultural mechanics	631.3	S675.3
Agricultural museums	630.74	S549
Agricultural pests	632.(6-7)	SB599-999
Agricultural pests—Congresses	632.(6-7)06	SB599.2
Agricultural pests—Control	632.6	SB950-.5
Agricultural physics	631.43	S589-.6
Agricultural pollution	577.273	TD195.A34
Agricultural prices	338.13	HD1447
Agricultural productivity	338.16	S494.5.P75
Agricultural surveys	630.723	S441-451
Agricultural surveys	630.723	S494.5.E8
Agricultural systems	630.11	S439-481
Agricultural wages	331.283	HD4966.A29
Agricultural wastes as feed	636.08556	SF99.A37
Agriculture	630-638	S
Agriculture	630-638	S1-954
Agriculture and energy	631.37	S494.5.E5
Agriculture, Cooperative	334.683	HD1483-1491.5
Agriculture, Prehistoric	630.901	S421-431
Agriculture—History	630.9	S419-481
Agriculture—International cooperation	338.181	HD1428-1431
Agriculture—Origin	630.901	GN799.A4
Agriculture—Periodicals	630.5	S1-19
Agriculture—Research	630.72	S539.5-542
Agriculture—Rome	630.945632	S431
Agriculture—Safety measures	630.289	S565
Agriculture—Societies, etc.	630.6	S20
Agriculture—Study and teaching	630.71	S531-539
Agriculture—Vocational guidance	630.23	S494.5.A4
Agroforestry	634.99	S494.5.A45

Subject Heading	Dewey	LC	Subject Heading	Dewey	LC
Agropastoral systems	630	S494.5.A47	Airplane ambulances	362.188	RA996.5
Aid to families with dependent children	362.713	HV697-700	Airplanes	629.13334	TL670-723
			Airplanes, Company	387.7	HE9795-9796
AIDS (Disease)	616.9792	RA644.A25	Airplanes, Military	358.4183	UG1240-1242
AIDS (Disease)	616.9792	RC607.A26	Airplanes, Military	623.746	TL685.3
AIDS (Disease) in adolescence	616.979200835	RJ387.A25	Airplanes, Military—Turrets	359.94834	VG90-95
			Airplanes, Military—Turrets	623.746	UG630-635
AIDS (Disease) in children	618.929792	RJ387.A25	Airplanes—Air conditioning	629.13442	TL681.A5
AIDS (Disease) in infants	618.929792	RJ387.A25	Airplanes—Electronic equipment	629.1355	TL693-696
AIDS (Disease) in mass media	362.1969792	P96.A39	Airplanes—Flight testing	629.13453	TL671.7
AIDS (Disease) in pregnancy	618.3	RG580.A44	Airplanes—Fuel	629.134351	TL704.7
			Airplanes—Inspection	629.13452	TL671.7
Aids to air navigation	629.1351	TL695-696	Airplanes—Jet propulsion	629.134353	TL709-.5
Aids to navigation	387.155	VK381-397	Airplanes—Landing	629.1325213	TL711.L3
Aids to navigation	387.155	VK1000-1249	Airplanes—Landing gear	629.134381	TL682-683
AIDS vaccines	615.372	QR189.5.A33	Airplanes—Motors	629.13435	TL701-704.7
AIDS-related complex	614.599392	RA644.A25	Airplanes—Nuclear power plants	629.134355	TL708
Aikido	796.8154	GV1114.35	Airplanes—Oxygen equipment	629.1344	TL697.O8
Ailanthus moth	595.78	QL561.S2			
Ainu	952.004946	DS832	Airplanes—Piloting	629.13252	TL710-713.5
Ainu language	494.6	PL495	Airplanes—Pressurization	629.13442	TL681.P7
Air	533.6	QC161-166.5	Airplanes—Radio equipment	629.1355	TL693.R2
Air bag restraint systems	629.276	TL159.5			
Air conditioning	697.93	TH7687-7688	Airplanes—Take-off	629.1325212	TL711.T3
Air defenses	358.414	UG730-735	Airplanes—Turbine-propeller engines	629.1343532	TL709.3.T8
Air forces	358.4	UG622-1425			
Air forces—Congresses	358.4006	UG623	Airplanes—Turbojet engines	629.1343533	TL709.3.T83
Air forces—History	358.4009	UG625			
Air forces—Insignia	358.414	UG1180-1185	Airplanes—Turbojet engines—Air intakes	629.134353	TL709.5.I5
Air forces—Societies, etc.	358.4006	UG622			
Air interdiction	358.41422	UG700	Airplanes—Wings	629.13432	TL672-673
Air mail service	383.144	HE6238	Airplanes—Wings, Swept-back	629.13432	TL673.S9
Air masses	551.5512	QC880.4.A5			
Air pilots	629.13252	TL712	Air—Pollution	628.53	TD881-890
Air pilots, Military	358.40092	UG626-.2	Airport buildings	725.39	NA6300-6307
Air quality	628.53	TD883	Airport buildings	629.136	TL725.3.B8
Air raid shelters	690.5	TH1097	Airport control towers	629.1366	TL725.3.C64
Air traffic control	629.1366	TL725.3.T7	Airport slot allocation	387.7364	HE9797.4.S56
Air traffic controllers	629.1366092	HD8039.A425	Airports	387.736	HE9797-.5
Air warfare	358.4	UG630	Airports	629.136	TL725-733
Airborne infection	616.9	RA642.A5	Airports—Visibility	629.136	TL557.V5
Airborne warning and control systems	358.414	UG730-735	Airships	629.13324	TL650-668.1
			Airways	387.72	TL725-733
Air-brakes	625.25	TF420-430	Aisne, Battle of the, France, 1917	940.431	D545.A5
Air-compressors	621.51	TJ990-992			
Aircraft accidents	363.124	TL553.5	Aisne, Battle of the, France, 1918	940.434	D545.A5
Aircraft cabins	629.13445	TL681.C3			
Aircraft carriers	359.9435	V874-875	Akan language	496.3385	PL8046.A63
Aircraft gas-turbines—Combustion chambers	629.134353	TL709.5.C55	Akkadian language	492.1	PJ3101
			Alabama	976.1	F321-355
Aircraft industry	338.4738773	HD9711-.2	Alabama—Gazetteers	917.61003	F324
Airdrop	355.83	UC330-335	Alabama—History—To 1819	976.105	F326
Airframes	629.13431	TL671.6			
Airlift, Military	355.83	UC330-335	Alabama—History—1819-1950	976.10(5-63)	F326
Airlines	387.7	HE9761-9990			
Airlines—Rates	387.712	HE9783-.75			

Subject Heading	Dewey	LC	Subject Heading	Dewey	LC
Alabama—History—1951-	976.106(3-4)	F330-.3	Albanian philology	491.991	PG9501-9513
Alabama—Maps	912.761	G3970-3974	Albania—Periodicals	949.65005	DR901
Alabama—National Guard	355.3709761	UA50-59	Albania—Periodicals	939.8005	DR901
Alabama—Periodicals	976.1005	F321	Alberta—Gazetteers	917.123003	F1075.4
Alaska	979.8	F901-951	Alberta—History	971.23	F1075-1080
Alaska—Gazetteers	917.98008	F902	Alberta—Maps	912.7123	G3500-3504
Alaska—History—To 1867	979.80(1-2)	F907	Alberta—Periodicals	971.23005	F1075
Alaska—History—1867-1959	979.80(3-4)	F908-909	Albinos and albinism	599.945	GN199
			Alchemy	540.112	QD13
Alaska—History—1959-	979.805	F910-.7	Alchemy	540.112	QD23.3-26.5
Alaska—Maps	912.798	G4370-4374	Alcohol	663.1	TP593
Alaska—National Guard	355.3709798	UA60-69	Alcohol as fuel	662.6692	TP358
Alaska—Periodicals	979.8005	F901	Alcoholic liver diseases	616.3624	RC848.A42
Albania	949.65	DR901-998	Alcoholic psychoses	616.861	RC525-527
Albania	939.8	DR901-998	Alcoholics' spouses	362.2923	HV5132
Albania—Biography	920.0398	DR928-934	Alcoholics—Family relationships	362.2923	HV5132
Albania—Biography	920.04965	DR928-934			
Albania—Census	314.965	HA1620.5	Alcoholism	362.292	HV5001-5722
Albania—Civilization	949.65	DR922	Alcoholism	616.861	RC564.7-565.9
Albania—Civilization	939.8	DR922	Alcoholism and crime	362.292	HV5053-5055
Albania—Congresses	949.65006	DR903.5	Alcoholism and employment	658.3822	HF5549.5.A4
Albania—Congresses	939.8006	DR903.5			
Albania—Description and travel	913.9804	DR914-918	Alcoholism counseling	362.29286	HV5275-5283
			Alcoholism—[By region or country]	362.29209(4-9)	HV5285-5722
Albania—Description and travel	914.96504	DR914-918			
			Alcoholism—United States	362.2920973	HV5285-5298
Albania—Economic conditions	330.94965	HC402	Alcoholism—[Other countries]	362.29209(4-9)	HV5301-5722
Albania—Gazetteers	913.98003	DR907	Alcoholism—Periodicals	362.29205	HV5001-5002
Albania—Gazetteers	914.965003	DR907	Alcoholism—Psychological aspects	616.8610019	HV5045
Albania—History	949.65	DR927-977.25			
Albania—History	939.8	DR927-977.25	Alcohol—Law and legislation	344.042	K3651-3654
Albania—History—To 1501	949.6501	DR954-960.5			
Albania—History—To 1501	939.8	DR954-960.5	Alcohol—Law and legislation—England	344.42042	KD3466-3480
Albania—History—Turkish War, 15th century	949.6501	DR959-960.5			
			Alcohol—Law and legislation—United States	344.7305	KF3901-3925
Albania—History—1501-1 912	949.6501	DR961-969			
			Aleut language	497.19	PM31-34
Albania—History—1840-1912	949.6501	DR965.9-969	Aleutian Islands (Alaska)	979.84	F951
			Aleuts	979.80049719	E99.A34
Albania—History—1878-1912	949.6501	DR966	Alexandrine War, 48-47 B.C.	932.021	DT92-.7
Albania—History—1912-1944	949.6502	DR970-975			
			Alfalfa	633.31	SB205.A4
Albania—History—Uprising, 1912	949.6502	DR969	Alfalfa as feed	636.0855	SF99.A5
			Algae	579.8	QK564-580.5
Albania—History—Peasant Uprising, 1914-1915	949.6502	DR972	Algebra	512	QA150-272.5
			Algebra, Abstract	512.02	QA162
Albania—History—June Revolution, 1924	949.6502	DR973	Algebra, Boolean	511.324	QA10.3
			Algebra, Universal	512	QA251
Albania—History—Axis occupation, 1939-1944	949.6502	DR975	Algebraic fields	512.3	QA247-.45
			Algebraic functions	512.74	QA341
Albania—History—1944-1990	949.6503	DR976-977.25	Algebraic logic	511.324	QA10-.3
			Algebras, Linear	512.5	QA184
Albania—History—1990-	949.650(3-4)	DR976-977.25	Algebra—Study and teaching	512.0071	QA159
Albanian language	491.991	PG9501-9599			
			Algeria	965	DT271-299
Albanian literature	891.991	PG9601-9665	Algeria	939.71	DT271-299

Subject Heading	Dewey	LC	Subject Heading	Dewey	LC
Algeria—Census	316.5	HA4683	Allegory	808.8015	PN56.A5
Algeria—Civilization	965	DT282	Allergy	571.972	QR188
Algeria—Civilization	939.71	DT282	Allergy	614.5993	RA645.A44
Algeria—Description and travel	913.97104	DT277.8-280.2	Allergy	616.97	RC583-598
			Allergy in children	618.9297	RJ386-.5
Algeria—Description and travel	916.504	DT277.8-280.2	Allied health personnel	610.737	R697.A4
			Alligator farming	639.3984	SF515.5.A44
Algeria—Economic conditions	330.965	HC815	Alligator hunting	799.27984	SK305.A
			Alligators	597.984	QL666.C925
Algeria—Gazetteers	913.971003	DT274	Alloys	669.95	TN690
Algeria—Gazetteers	916.5003	DT274	Alluvial plains	551.453	GB591-598
Algeria—History	965	DT283-299	Almanacs	551.6365	QC999
Algeria—History	939.71	DT283-299	Almanacs, American	031	AY67.N5
Algeria—History—To 647	939.71	DT288	Almanacs—America	031	AY51-381
Algeria—History—647-1516	965.022	DT289	Almanacs—Australia	032.0994	AY1600-1636
			Almanacs—Canada	031.0971	AY410-425
Algeria—History—1516-1830	965.024	DT291-292	Almanacs—Germany	033.1	AY850-860
			Almanacs—Great Britain	032	AY830-839
Algeria—History—1830-1962	965.03	DT294-295.3	Almanacs—History	030.9	AY30-39
			Almanacs—Italy	035.1	AY890-899
Algeria—History—1945-1962	965.04	DT295-.3	Almanacs—Portugal	036.9	AY1010-1019
			Almanacs—Spain	036.1	AY1000-1009
Algeria—History—Expedition of Charles V, 1541	965.024	DT292	Almshouses	362.585	HV61
			Aloe	633.88	SB295.A45
			Alpenhorn music	788.92	M110
Algeria—History—English Expedition, 1620-1621	965.024	DT291	Alpha rays	539.7232	QC793.5.A22-+ .A229
Algeria—History—Spanish Expedition, 1775	965.024	DT291	Alphabets	411	P211-214
Algeria—History—English Expedition, 1816	965.024	DT291	Alpine gardens	635.9528	SB459
			Alps	949.47	DQ820-829
Algeria—History—French Expedition, 1830	965.03	DT294	Alps—Maps	912.4947	G6035-6036
			Altaic languages	494	PL1-9
Algeria—History—Revolution, 1954-1962	965.046	DT295	Altars	247.1	BV195-196
			Altars	726.5291	NA5060
Algeria—History—1962-	965.05	DT295.5-.55	Altars, Buddhist	294.3437	BQ5070-5075
Algeria—Maps	912.65	G8240-8244	Altered states of consciousness	154.4	BF1045.A48
Algiers, Battle of, 1816	965.024	DT291	Alternative medicine	615.5	R733
Algonquian Indians	970.00497	E99.A35	Alternative schools	371.04	LC46-.8
Algonquian languages	497.3	PM600-609	Alternatives to imprisonment	364.68	HV9276.5
Algonquin Indians	974.004973	E99.A349			
Alien labor	331.62	HD6300	Altitude, Influence of	571.49	QP82.2.A4
Aliens—England	342.42083	KD4130-4139	Alto horn music	788.974	M110
Aliens—United States	342.73083	KF4800-4848	Alto trombone music	788.974	M90-94
Alimentary canal	611.3	QM301-367	Altruism	171.8	BJ1474
Alkali lands	631.42	S595	Aluminum alloys	620.186	TA480.A6
Alkalies	546.38	QD172.A4	Aluminum, Structural	620.186	TA480.A6
Alkalies	661.03	TP222-223	Aluminum—Metallurgy	669.722	TN775
Alkalies	669.725	TN895-897	Alvars	294.5213	BL1171
Alkaloids	547.7	QD421-.7	Alzheimer's disease	616.831	RC523-.2
Alkaloids	615.321	RM666.A4	Amateur circus	791.3	GV1838
All Saints' Day	263.98	BV67	Amateur plays	792.0222	PN6119.9
All Souls' Day	263.9	BV50.A4	Amateur radio stations	621.38416	TK9956
All Souls' Day	394.264	GT4995.A4	Amateur theater	792.0222	PN3151-3171
All terrain cycling	796.63	GV1056	Amazons	292.13	BL820.A6
All terrain vehicles	388.34	TL235.6-.7	Amazons	305.409	HQ1139
Allegiance	323.6	JC328			

Subject Heading	Dewey	LC
Amber	622.339	TN885
Ambition	302.54	BJ1533.A4
Ambivalence	152.4	BF575.A45
Ambulance service	362.188	RA995-996
Ambulances	629.22234	TL235.8
Ambulatory blood pressure monitoring	616.132075	RC683.5.A43
Ambulatory electrocardiography	616.1207547	RC683.5.A45
Ambulatory electroencephalography	616.8047547	RC386.6.A45
Ambulatory surgery	617.024	RD110-.5
Ambushes and surprises	355.422	U167
Amebiasis	614.516	RA644.A57
Amebiasis	616.936	RC121.A5
America	970	E
America	980	E
America—Biography	920.07	E17
America—Biography	920.08	E17
America—Colonization	325.(7-8)	JV221-231
America—Discovery and exploration	970.01	E101-135
America—Discovery and exploration	980.01	E101-135
America—Gazetteers	917.003	E14
America—Gazetteers	918.003	E14
America—History	970	E16-18.85
America—History	970-989	F
America—History	980	E16-18.85
America—Maps	912.7	G3290-5669
American beaver	599.37	QL737.R632
American bison	599.643	QL737.U53
American bison	636.292	SF401.A45
American bison hunting	799.27643	SK297
American diaries	818.03	PS409
American diaries	818.3	PS669
American drama	812.08	PS623-635
American drama	812.09	PS330-351
American drama (Comedy)	812.052309	PS336.C7
American drama (Tragedy)	812.051209	PS336.T7
American drama—Study and teaching	812.071	PS335
American essays	081	AC1-8
American essays	814.08	PS680-688
American essays	814.09	PS420-428
American fiction	813	PZ1
American fiction	813.09	PS371-379
American letters	816.08	PS670-678
American letters	816.09	PS410-418
American literature	810	PS
American literature— 1783-1850	810.(2-3)09	PS208
American literature—19th century	810.309	PS201-214
American literature—20th century	810.509	PS221-228

Subject Heading	Dewey	LC
American literature— Afro-American authors	810.80896073	PS508.N3
American literature— Colonial period, ca. 1600-1775	810.109	PS185-191
American literature— History and criticism	810.9	PS153-490
American literature— Revolutionary period, 1775-1783	810.209	PS193
American literature— Women authors	810.809287	PS508.W7
American literature— Women authors	810.99287	PS147-151
American loyalists	973.314	E277
American newspapers	051	PN4840-4899
American periodicals	071	PN4840-4900
American poetry	811	PS
American poetry—Colonial period, ca. 1600-1775	811.109	PS312
American poetry— Revolutionary period, 1775-1783	811.209	PS314
American poetry— 1783-1850	811.209	PS319
American poetry—19th century	811.309	PS316-321
American poetry—20th century	811.509	PS324
American poetry—Afro-American authors	811.0080896 + 073	PS591.N4
American poetry—Study and teaching	811.071	PS306-.5
American poetry—Women authors	811.00809287	PS589
American prose literature	818.08	PS642-659.2
American prose literature	818.0809	PS360-379
American prose literature— Colonial period, ca. 1600-1775	818.08109	PS366
American prose— Revolutionary period, 1775-1783	818.08209	PS367-369
American saddlebred horse	636.13	SF293.A5
American Samoa	996.13	DU819.A1
American Samoa—Census	319.613	HA4018.5
American wit and humor	817.008	PN6157-6162
American wit and humor	817.09	PS430-438
Americanism (Catholic controversy)	282.73	BX1407.A5
Americanization	323.60973	JK1758
America—Periodicals	970.005	E11
America—Periodicals	980.005	E11
Amines in the body	572.548	QP801.A48
Amino acid sequence	572.633	QP551
Amino acids	547.75	QD431-.7
Amino acids	572.65	QP561-563

Subject Heading	Dewey	LC	Subject Heading	Dewey	LC
Amino acids in human nutrition	613.282	QP561	Anemia	616.152	RC641-.7
Amino acids in nutrition	613.282	QP551	Anesthesia	615.781	RD78.3-87.3
Amish	289.73092	BX8129.A5-.A6	Anesthesia in dentistry	617.9676	RK510-512
Ammonia	546.7112	QD181.N1	Anesthesia in obstetrics	617.9682	RG732-733
Ammunition	358.1282	UF700-770	Anesthetics	615.781	RD78.3-87.3
Amnesia	616.85232	RC394.A5	Aneurysms	616.133	RC693
Amniocentesis	618.3204275	RG628.3.A48	Angels	202.15	BL477
Amniotic liquid	571.86	QL975	Angels	235.3	BT960-968
Amniotic liquid	611.013	QM611	Angels (Islam)	297.215	BP166.89
Amoeba	579.432	QL368.A5	Anger	152.47	BF575.A5
Amon (Egyptian deity)	299.31	BL2450.A45	Anger	152.47	RC569.5.A53
Amphibians	597.8	QL641-669.3	Anger	179.8	BJ1535.A6
Amphibious warfare	355.46	U261	Angina pectoris	616.122	RC685.A6
Amphitheaters	725.827	NA313	Angiocardiography	616.1207572	RC683.5.A5
Amplifiers (Electronics)	621.381535	TK7871.2-.58	Angiography	616.1307572	RC691.6.A53
Amplifiers (Electronics)	621.38412	TK6565.A55	Angioplasty	617.413	RD598.5
Amputation	617.58059	RD553	Angiosperms	580	QK495.A1
Amsterdam (Netherlands)	949.2352	DJ411.A5-59	Angiosperms, Fossil	561	QE980-983
Amulets	398.45	GR600	Anglican Communion	283	BX5001-5009
Amulets (Buddhism)	294.3437	BQ4570.A4	Anglican Communion—History	283.09	BX5005
Amulets (Islam)	297.39	BP190.5.A5	Anglican Communion—Sermons	252.03	BX5008
Amusement parks	791.068	GV1851-186	Anglican orders	255.83	BX5178
Amusements—Law and legislation—England	344.42099	KD3523	Anglo-Dutch War, 1664-1667	949.204	DJ180-182
Amusements—Law and legislation—United States	344.73099	KF3987	Anglo-Dutch War, 1780-1784	949.204	DJ205-206
Amycus (Greek mythology)	292.13	BL820.A63	Anglo-French War, 1666-1667	940.252	D274.5-.6
Anabaptists	284.3	BX4929-4946	Anglo-Saxon race	941.0042	CB216-220
Anaerobic bacteria	579.3149	QR89.5	Anglo-Saxons	941.0892	DA150-162
Anagrams	793.734	GV1507.A5	Anglo-Saxons	942.017	DA150-162
Analgesics	615.783	RM319	Anglo-Spanish War, 1718-1748	941.072	DA498-499
Analog-to-digital converters	621.39814	TK7887.6	Anglo-Spanish War, 1718-1748	946.055	DP194
Analogy	169	BD190	Anglo-Spanish War, 1762-1763	941.073	DA505-512
Analogy (Religion)	210	BL210	Anglo-Spanish War, 1762-1763	946.057	DP199
Analysis of variance	519.538	QA279-.2	Angola—Census	316.73	HA4710
Analytic functions	515.73	QA331	Angola—Civilization	967.3	DT1302
Analytical biochemistry	572.36	QP519.7-.9	Angola—Description and travel	916.7304	DT1282-1286
Analytical toxicology	615.907	RA1221-1223	Angola—Economic conditions	330.9673	HC950
Anarchism	335.83	HX821-970.7	Angola—Gazetteers	916.73003	DT1264
Anarchism—[By region or country]	335.8309(4-9)	HX841-970.7	Angola—History	967.3	DT1314-1436
Anatolian languages	491.998	P1001	Angola—History—To 1482	967.301	DT1357
Anatomical museums	611.0074	QM51	Angola—History—1482-1648	967.301	DT1357-1369
Anatomy, Artistic	743.49	NC760-783.8	Angola—History—1648-1885	967.302	DT1373-1382
Anatomy, Comparative	571.3	QL801-950.9	Angola—History—1885-1961	967.30(2-3)	DT1385-1396
Anatomy, Surgical and topographical	611.9	QM531-549			
Ancestor worship	202.13	BL467			
Anchors	623.862	VM791			
Andean condor	598.92	QL696.F33			
Andorra	946.79	DC921-930			
Androgens	612.61	QP572.A5			
Androgyny (Psychology)	155.334	BF692.2			
Andrology	616.65	RC875-899.5			
Anecdotes	808.882	PN6259-6268			

Subject Heading	Dewey	LC	Subject Heading	Dewey	LC
Angola—History—Revolution, 1961-1975	967.303	DT1398-1417	Anniversaries	394.268	AS7
Angola—History—Civil War, 1975-	967.304	DT1428	Annuals (Plants)	635.9312	SB422
			Annuities	368.37	HG8790-8793
Angola—Maps	912.673	G8640-8644	Anorexia	616.85262	RB150.A65
Anguilla	972.973	F2033	Anorexia nervosa	616.85262	RC552.A5
Anguilla—Maps	912.72973	G5045-5049	Antacids	615.73	RM365
Animal behavior	591.5	QL750-795	Antarctica	319.89	HA4020-.5
Animal biotechnology	636.0821	SF140.B54	Antarctica	919.89	G845-890
Animal breeding	636.082	SF105-109	Antarctica—Maps	912.989	G3100-3102
Animal burrowing	591.5648	QL756.15	Antarctica—Maps	912.989	G9800-9804
Animal communication	591.59	QL776	Antelopes	599.64	QL737.U53
Animal culture	636	SF	Antennas (Electronics)	621.3824	TK7871.6
Animal defenses	591.47	QL759	Anthems	782.265	M2038-2099
Animal ecology	591.7	QH540-549.5	Anthologies	808.8	PN6010-6065
Animal experimentation	590.724	HV4905-4959	Anthracite coal	622.335	TN820-823
Animal feeding	636.084	SF94.5-99	Anthrax	636.0896956	SF787
Animal fibers	677.3	TS1545-1548	Anthrax	616.956	RC121.A6
Animal flight	573.798	QP310.F5	Anthrax—Russia (Federation)—Epidemiology	614.5610947	RA644.A6
Animal genetics	591.35	QH432			
Animal health	636.0893	SF600-1100	Anthropologists	301.092	GN20-21
Animal intelligence	591.513	QL785	Anthropology	301	GN
Animal locomotion	612.76	QP301-310	Anthropology—Methodology	301.01	GN33-34.3
Animal navigation	573.87	QL782			
Animal nutrition	636.085	SF94.5-99	Anthropology—Research	301.072	GN42-46
Animal populations	591.788	QL752	Anthropometry	599.94	GN51-59
Animal products	664.9	TS1950-1982	Anthropomorphism	211	BL215
Animal psychology	591.5	QL785-.27	Anthroposophy	299.935	BP595-597
Animal rights	179.3	HV4701-4890.7	Antiaircraft guns	358.1382	UF625
Animal sculpture	731.832	NB1940-1942	Antiallergic agents	616.97	RC588.C45
Animal sounds	591.594	QL765	Antibacterial agents	615.329	RM409
Animal tracks	591.479	QL768	Antibiotics	615.329	RM265-267
Animal training	791.32	GV1829-1831	Antibiotics in animal nutrition	636.08557	SF98.A5
Animal traps	639.1	SK283.2			
Animal weapons	591.47	QL940	Antibiotics in veterinary medicine	636.0895329	SF918.A5
Animal welfare	636.0832	HV4701-4959			
Animal worship	202.12	BL439-443	Antichrist	236	BT985
Animals as carriers of disease	636.089456	SF740	Antidepressants	615.78	RM332-.3
			Antietam, Battle of, Md., 1862	973.733	E474.65
Animals as carriers of disease	614.43	RA639-641			
			Antifertility vaccines	613.9432	RG136.85
Animals in art	743.6	NC780-783.8	Antigen-antibody reactions	571.9677	QR187-.3
Animals in art	758.3	ND1380-1383	Antigens	571.9645	QR186.5-.6
Animals, Fossil	560	QE760.8-899.2	Antigua	972.974	F2035
Animals, Mythical	398.369	GR820-830	Antigua—Maps	912.72974	G5050-5054
Animals—Diseases	636.0896	SF600-1100	Antilles, Greater	972.9(1-5)	F1741-1991
Animals—Food	591.5(3-4)	QL756.5-.57	Antilles, Lesser	972.9(7-8)	F2001-2151
Animals—Habitations	591.564	QL756-.15	Antimony	546.716	QD181.S3
Animals—War use	355.8	UH87-100	Anti-Nazi movement	943.086	DD256.3-.4
Animated films	741.58	NC1765-1766	Antineoplastic agents	616.99406	RC271.C5
Animated films	741.58	PN1997.5	Antiprotons	539.72123	QC793.5.P72-.P729
Animation (Cinematography)	778.5347	TR897.5-.75			
			Antiques	745.1	NK
Animism	202.1	GN471	Antiques—Dictionaries	745.103	NK30
Annapolis (Md.)	975.256	F189.A6	Antiques—Encyclopedias	745.103	NK28
Annihilation reactions	539.75	QC794	Antiques—Exhibitions	745.1074	NK512-520
Annihilationism	236.23	BT930	Antiques—Periodicals	745.105	NK1-9

Subject Heading	Dewey	LC
Antiques—Private collections	745.1074	NK530-570
Antiques—Reproduction	745.102872	NK1128
Antiques—Study and teaching	745.1071	NK50-440
Antiquities—Collection and preservation	930.10288	CC135-137
Anti-Semitism	305.8924	DS145-146
Antisocial personality disorders	616.858	RC555
Antisubmarine aircraft	358.4283	UG1242.A25
Anti-submarine warfare	359.93	V214-.5
Antitank weapons	358.12	UF628
Antitoxins	615.37	RM278
Antitrust law—England	343.420721	KD2218-2220
Ants	595.796	QL568.F7
Antwerp, Battle of, 1944	940.542193222	D763.B42.A
Anu (Assyro-Babylonian deity)	299.21	BL1625.A5
Anxiety	152.46	BF575.A6
Anxiety	616.8522	RC531
Anxiety in children	155.41246	BF723.A5
Anxiety in children	618.9285223	RJ506.A58
Aorta	611.13	QM191
Aorta—Diseases	616.138	RC691
Aortic aneurysms	616.138	RC693
Apache (Attack helicopter)	358.4383	UG1233
Apache Indians	979.0049725	E99.A6
Apartment houses	728.314	NA7860-7863
Apartment houses	647.92	TX957-959
Apes	599.88	QL737.P96
Aphasia	616.8552	RC425-.7
Aphorisms and apothegms	398.9	PN6269-6278
Aphrodisiacs	615.7669	RM386
Apnea	616.209	RC737-.5
Apocalyptic literature	220.046	BS646
Apocryphal books (New Testament)	229	BS2831-2970
Apologetics	239	BT1095-1255
Apologetics—Early church, ca. 30-600	230.1	BT1115
Apologetics—History	239.09	BT1109-1115
Apostles	225.92	BS2440
Apostolic Fathers	270.1092	BR60-67
Appalachian dulcimer music	787.75	M142.A7
Apparitions	133.1	BF1444-1486
Appellate courts—England	347.4203	KD7132-7216
Appellate courts—Scotland	347.41103	KDC110-113
Appellate procedure	347.035	K5495
Appellate procedure—United States	347.7305	KF8741-8752
Appendectomy	617.5545	RD542
Appendix (Anatomy)	611.345	QM345
Apperception	153.73	BF321-323
Apperception	153.73	LB1067
Appetizers	641.812	TX740
Apples	583.73	QK495.R78
Apples	634.11	SB363-.6
Application software	005.5	QA76.76.A65
Applications for positions	650.142	HF5383
Applied human geography	304.2	GF24
Applied sociology	360	HN29.5
Appomattox Campaign, 1865	973.738	E477.67
Apprentices	331.55	HD4881-4885
Approximation theory	512.924	QA221-224
April Fools' Day	394.262	GT4995.A6
Aquaculture	639.8	SH20.5-191
Aquaculture—[By region or country]	639.809(4-9)	SH34-133
Aquaculture—History	639.809	SH21
Aquariums	597.073	SF456-458.83
Aquariums, Public	597.073	QL78-79
Aquarius (Astrology)	133.5276	BF1727.7
Aquatic animals	591.77	QL120-149
Aquatic animals—Antarctic Ocean	591.777	QL126.5
Aquatic animals—Arctic Ocean	591.7732	QL126
Aquatic animals—Atlantic Ocean	591.773	QL127-135
Aquatic animals—Indian Ocean	591.775	QL137
Aquatic animals—Pacific Ocean	591.774	QL138
Aquatic biology	578.76	QH90-100
Aquatic ecology	577.6	QH541.5.W3
Aquatic exercises	613.71	RA781.17
Aquatic exercises	613.716	GV838.53.E94
Aquatic plants	581.76	QK102-105
Aquatic plants	581.76	QK930-935
Aquatic sports	797	GV771-840
Aquatint	766.3	NE2230
Aqueducts	628.15	TD398
Arab countries	909.04927	DS36-39.2
Arab countries—Civilization	909.04927	DS36.77-.88
Arab countries—History	909.04927	DS37-39.2
Arab countries—History—1517-1918	909.09749270 + (5-821)	DS38.8
Arab countries—History—1798-	909.097492708	DS38.9
Arab countries—History—20th century	909.0974927082	DS39
Arab countries—History—Arab Revolt, 1916-1918	909.0974927 + 0821	DS39
Arab countries—Politics and government	320.9174927	JQ1850
Arabic alphabet	492.711	PJ6123
Arabic drama	892.72008	PJ7665
Arabic drama	892.72009	PJ7565
Arabic essays	089.927	AC105-106
Arabic language	492.7	PJ6001-7144
Arabic language—Dialects	492.77	PJ6701-6901

Subject Heading	Dewey	LC	Subject Heading	Dewey	LC
Arabic language—Dialects—Arabian Peninsula	492.77	PJ6841-6880	Archaeology—Directories	930.1025	CC120-125
			Archaeology—Methodology	930.101	CC73-75
Arabic language—Dialects—Egypt	492.77	PJ6771-6799	Archaeology—Periodicals	930.105	CC1-15
			Archaeology—Philosophy	930.101	CC72-81
Arabic language—Dialects—Iraq	492.77	PJ6821-6830	Archaeology—Societies, etc.	930.106	CC20-39
Arabic language—Dialects—Lebanon	492.77	PJ6810	Archdeacons	262.02	BX1911
			Archdeacons	262.03	BX5179
Arabic language—Dialects—Palestine	492.77	PJ6805-6808	Archdeacons	262.12	BX5179
			Archery	799.32	GV1185-1189
Arabic language—Dialects—Spain	492.77	PJ6751-6760	Arches	721.41	NA2880
Arabic language—Dialects—Syria	492.77	PJ6811-6820	Architects—Professional ethics	174.972	NA1995
Arabic language—Dictionaries	492.73	PJ6031	Architectural acoustics	729.29	NA2800
			Architectural design	721	NA2750-2793
Arabic language—Etymology	492.72	PJ6172-6199	Architectural drawing	720.222	NA2700-2780
			Architectural models	720.22	NA2790
Arabic language—Grammar	492.75	PJ6101-6599	Architectural photography	778.94	TR659
Arabic language—Study and teaching	492.7071	PJ6065-6069	Architecture	720	NA
			Architecture and the handicapped	720.87	NA2545
Arabic literature	892.7	PJ7501-8518			
Arabic literature—Africa	892.7	PJ8195-8390	Architecture, American	720.9(7-8)	NA702.5-939
Arabic literature—America	892.7	PJ8500-8517	Architecture, Ancient	722	NA210-340
Arabic literature—Asia	892.7	PJ8025-8190	Architecture, Assyro-Babylonian	722.51	NA220-221
Arabic literature—Europe	892.7	PJ8395-8490	Architecture, Baroque	724.16	NA590
Arabic literature—Middle East	892.7	PJ8030-8129	Architecture, Colonial	724.1	NA707
			Architecture, Domestic	728	NA7100-7882
Arabic philology	492.7	PJ6001-6071	Architecture, Domestic—[By region and country]	728.09(4-9)	NA7201-7333
Arabic poetry	892.71008	PJ7631-7661			
Arabic poetry	892.71009	PJ7541-7561	Architecture, Domestic—Designs and plans	728.0222	NA7127-7135
Arabic prose literature	892.7808	PJ7571-7577			
Arabic prose literature	892.7808	PJ7671-7677	Architecture, Egyptian	720.962	NA1581-1585.3
Arab-Israeli conflict	956.04	DS119.7-.76	Architecture, Egyptian	722.2	NA215-216
Arachnida	595.4	QL451-459.2	Architecture, Etruscan	722.62	NA300-301
Aramaic language	492.2	PJ5201-5329	Architecture, Georgian	724.19	NA640
Arapaho Indians	978.00497354	E99.A7	Architecture, Gothic	723.5	NA440-489
Arapaho language	497.354	PM635	Architecture, Greek	722.8	NA270-290
Arbitration and award—Canada	347.7109	KE8618	Architecture, Industrial	725.4	NA6400-6589
			Architecture, Italian	722.70937	NA295-340
Arbitration and award—England	347.4209	KD7645-7647	Architecture, Medieval	723	NA350-497
			Architecture, Modern	724	NA500-680
Arbitration and award—United States	347.7309	KF9085-9086	Architecture, Modern—18th century	724.19	NA627-640
Arbitration, Industrial	331.89143	HD5481-5630.7	Architecture, Modern—19th century	724.5	NA645-670
Arbitration, Industrial—[By region or country]	331.8914309 + (4-9)	HD5501-5630.7	Architecture, Modern—20th century	724.6	NA673-682
Arbovirus infections	571.992562	QR201.A72	Architecture, Norman	723.4	NA423-429
Arboviruses	579.2562	QR398	Architecture, Oriental	720.95	NA1460-1579
Arc measures	526.30287	QB291	Architecture, Primitive	722	GN414
Arch dams	627.8	TC547	Architecture, Primitive	722	NA205-207
Archaeological geology	930.1028	CC77.5	Architecture, Queen Anne	720.94209033	NA630
Archaeological surveying	930.1028	CC73-75	Architecture, Renaissance	724.12	NA510-575
Archaeologists	930.1092	CC110-115	Architecture, Rococo	724.19	NA590
Archaeology	930	CC	Architecture, Roman	722.7	NA310-340
Archaeology	930.1	GN700-890			
Archaeology—Dictionaries	930.103	CC70			

Subject Heading	Dewey	LC	Subject Heading	Dewey	LC
Architecture, Romanesque	723.4	NA390-419	Architecture—French Guiana	720.9882	NA897
Architecture, Spanish	720.946	NA1301-1313.3	Architecture—Germany	720.943	NA1061-1089
Architecture—Aesthetics	720.1	NA2500	Architecture—Great Britain	720.941	NA961-981
Architecture—Biography	720.92	NA40	Architecture—Greece	720.9495	NA1091-1103
Architecture—Competitions	720.79	NA2335-2360	Architecture—Guatemala	720.97281	NA776-778
Architecture—Composition, proportion, etc.	729.11	NA2760	Architecture—Guyana	720.9881	NA895
Architecture—Conservation and restoration]	720.288	NA105-112	Architecture—Haiti	720.97294	NA806-808
			Architecture—Honduras	720.97283	NA779-781
Architecture—Designs and plans	720.222	NA2600-2635	Architecture—Hungary	720.9439	NA1012-1022
Architecture—Details	721	NA2835-3060	Architecture—Iceland	720.94912	NA1241-1253.3
Architecture—Directories	720.25	NA50-60	Architecture—India	720.954	NA1501-1510.3
Architecture—Encyclopedias	720.3	NA31	Architecture—Indonesia	720.9598	NA1526-.8
			Architecture—Iran	720.955	NA1480-1489
Architecture—History	722-724	NA190-1555.5	Architecture—Iraq	720.9567	NA1467-1469
Architecture—Periodicals	720.5	NA1-9	Architecture—Israel	720.95694	NA1477-1479
Architecture—Societies, etc.	720.6	NA10-17	Architecture—Italy	720.945	NA1111-1123.3
			Architecture—Jamaica	720.97292	NA809-811
Architecture—Study and teaching	720.71	NA2000-2320	Architecture—Japan	720.952	NA1550-1559.6
Architecture—Afghanistan	720.9581	NA1492-.3	Architecture—Jordan	720.95695	NA1479.6-.8
Architecture—Africa	720.96	NA1580-1599	Architecture—Korea	720.9519	NA1560-1570.3
Architecture—Africa, East	720.9676	NA1597-.6	Architecture—Laos	720.9594	NA1516-.3
Architecture—Africa, West	720.966	NA1598-1599	Architecture—Lebanon	720.95692	NA1476.6-.8
Architecture—Algeria	720.965	NA1588-.3	Architecture—Libya	720.9612	NA1589-.3
Architecture—Argentina	720.982	NA830-839	Architecture—Malaysia	720.9595	NA1525-.8
Architecture—Arid regions	720.9154	NA2542.A73	Architecture—Mexico	720.972	NA750-759
Architecture—Asiatic Russia	720.957	NA1492.6-1499	Architecture—Morocco	720.964	NA1590-.3
			Architecture—Netherlands	720.9492	NA1141-1153.3
Architecture—Australia	720.994	NA1600-1605.3	Architecture—New Zealand	720.993	NA1606-1608
Architecture—Austria	720.9436	NA1001-1011.6	Architecture—Nicaragua	720.97285	NA782-784
Architecture—Bahamas	720.97296	NA800-802	Architecture—Norway	720.9481	NA1261-1273.3
Architecture—Belgium	720.9493	NA1161-1173.3	Architecture—Oceania	720.99(5-6)	NA1610-1613
Architecture—Bolivia	720.984	NA840-849	Architecture—Pakistan	720.95491	NA1510.7-.73
Architecture—Brazil	720.981	NA850-859	Architecture—Panama	720.97287	NA785-787
Architecture—Bulgaria	720.9499	NA1381-1393.3	Architecture—Paraguay	720.9892	NA900-909
Architecture—Burma	720.9591	NA1512-.3	Architecture—Peru	720.985	NA910-919
Architecture—Cambodia	720.9596	NA1515-.3	Architecture—Philippines	720.9599	NA1527-1529
Architecture—Canada	720.971	NA740-749.5	Architecture—Poland	720.9438	NA1466.P6
Architecture—Central America	720.9728	NA760-790	Architecture—Portugal	720.9469	NA1321-1333.3
			Architecture—Puerto Rico	720.97295	NA812-814
Architecture—Chile	720.983	NA860-869	Architecture—Romania	720.9498	NA1421-1433.3
Architecture—China	720.951	NA1540-1549.6	Architecture—Russia	720.947	NA1181-1199
Architecture—Colombia	720.9861	NA870-879	Architecture—Saudi Arabia	720.9538	NA1470-1472
Architecture—Costa Rica	720.97286	NA773-775	Architecture—Scandinavia	720.948	NA1201-1293.3
Architecture—Cuba	720.97291	NA803-805	Architecture—South America	720.98	NA820-939
Architecture—Czechoslovakia	720.9437	NA1023-1034.5			
			Architecture—Southern Africa	720.968	NA1591.7-1596.6
Architecture—Denmark	720.9489	NA1211-1223.3	Architecture—Spain	720.946	NA1301-1313.3
Architecture—Ecuador	720.9866	NA880-889	Architecture—Sri Lanka	720.95493	NA1510.6-.63
Architecture—El Salvador	720.97284	NA788-790	Architecture—Surinam	720.9883	NA896
Architecture—Ethiopia	720.963	NA1586-.3	Architecture—Sweden	720.9485	NA1281-1293.3
Architecture—Europe	720.94	NA950-1455	Architecture—Switzerland	720.9494	NA1341-1353.3
Architecture—Finland	720.94897	NA1455.F5	Architecture—Syria	720.95691	NA1489.6-.8
Architecture—France	720.944	NA1041-1059	Architecture—Thailand	720.9593	NA1521-1523
			Architecture—Tunisia	720.9611	NA1591-.3

Subject Heading	Dewey	LC	Subject Heading	Dewey	LC
Architecture—Turkey	720.9561	NA1361-1375	Archives—Russia	027.047	CD1710-1739.5
Architecture—United States	720.973	NA705-738	Archives—South America	027.08	CD4000-4279.5
			Archives—Spain	027.046	CD1850-1879.5
Architecture—Uruguay	720.9895	NA920-929	Archives—Sweden	027.0485	CD1830-1849.5
Architecture—Venezuela	720.987	NA930-939	Archives—Switzerland	027.0494	CD1900-1929.5
Architecture—Vietnam	720.9597	NA1514-.63	Archives—United States	027.073	CD3020-3615
Architecture—West Indies	720.9729	NA791-815	Archives—[United States, By state]	027.07(4-9)	CD3070-3609
Architecture—Yugoslavia	720.9497	NA1441-1453.3			
Archive buildings	725.15	CD981-986.5	Arctic Ocean—Maps	912.19632	G3055-3064
Archives	027	CD	Arctic regions	330.998(1-8)	HC731-740
Archives	027	CD921-4280	Arctic regions	919.8	G600-839
Archives, Medical	026.61	R119.8	Arctic regions—American	917.98(6-7)	G725-770
Archives, Technical	026.6	T11.9	Arctic regions—Norwegian	914.843	G778-787
Archives—Dictionaries	027.003	CD945	Arctic regions—Siberian	915.7	G820-839
Archives—Directories	027.0025	CD941	Ardennes, Battle of the, 1944-1945	940.542131	D756.5.A7
Archives—History	027.009	CD995-4280			
Archives—Law and legislation—England	344.42092	KD3753-3755	Area measurement	526.3	GA23
			Argentina	982	F2801-3021
Archives—Law and legislation—United States	344.73092	KF4325	Argentina—Census	318.2	HA941-960
			Argentina—Civilization	982	F2810
Archives—Methodology	027.0028	CD973	Argentina—Description and travel	918.204	F2811-2817
Archives—Periodicals	027.005	CD921			
Archives—Philosophy	027.001	CD947	Argentina—Economic conditions	330.982	HC171-180
Archives—Study and teaching	027.0071	CD987-988			
			Argentina—Emigration and immigration	325.(282) or (82)	JV7440-7449
Archives—[By region or country]	027.0(4-9)	CD1000-4280			
			Argentina—Gazetteers	918.2003	F2804
Archives—Africa	027.06	CD2300-2491	Argentina—Manufactures	670.982	TS36-37
Archives—Asia	027.05	CD2001-2291	Argentina—Maps	912.82	G5350-5354
Archives—Australia	027.094	CD2500-2529.5	Argentina—Periodicals	982.005	F2801
Archives—Austria	027.0436	CD1120-1149.5	Argentina—Politics and government	320.982	JL2000-2099
Archives—Balkan Peninsula	027.0496	CD1930-1989.5			
			Argentina—History	982	F2827-2849.22
Archives—Belgium	027.0493	CD1670-1689.5	Argentina—History—To 1810	982.0(1-24)	F2841
Archives—Canada	027.071	CD3620-3649.6			
Archives—Caribbean area	027.0729	CD3860-3985	Argentina—History—1515-1535	982.0(1-22)	F2841
Archives—Central America	027.0728	CD3690-3859.5			
Archives—China	027.051	CD2030-2059.5	Argentina—History—1535-1617	982.02(2-3)	F2841
Archives—Czechoslovakia	027.0437	CD1150-1169.5			
Archives—Denmark	027.0489	CD1770-1789.5	Argentina—History—1617-1776	982.023	F2841
Archives—Europe	027.04	CD1000-2000			
Archives—France	027.044	CD1190-1219.5	Argentina—History—1776-1810	982.023	F2841
Archives—Germany	027.043	CD1220-1243.5			
Archives—Great Britain	027.041	CD1040-1199.5	Argentina—History—19th century	982.04	F2843
Archives—Hungary	027.0439	CD1170-1189.5			
Archives—Iceland	027.04912	CD1790-1809.5	Argentina—History—English Invasions, 1806-1807	982.024	F2845
Archives—India	027.054	CD2080-2099.5			
Archives—Israel	027.05694	CD2010-2919.5	Argentina—History—1810-	982.0(3-7)	F2843
Archives—Italy	027.045	CD1400-1658	Argentina—History—War of Independence, 1810-1817	982.03	F2845
Archives—Japan	027.052	CD2160-2189.5			
Archives—Mexico	027.072	CD3650-3679.5	Argentina—History—1817-1860	982.0(3-4)	F2846
Archives—Netherlands	027.0492	CD1690-1733.3			
Archives—New Zealand	027.093	CD2570-2789.5	Argentina—History—Revolution, 1833	982.04	F2846
Archives—Norway	027.0481	CD1810-1829.5			
Archives—Oceania	027.09(5-6)	CD2795	Argentina—History—1860-1910	982.0(4-5)	F2847
Archives—Poland	027.0438	CD1740-1759.5			
Archives—Portugal	027.0469	CD1880-1899.5			

Subject Heading	Dewey	LC	Subject Heading	Dewey	LC
Argentina—History—Revolution, 1890	982.05	F2847	Armenia	947.56	DS161-195.5
Argentina—History—1910-1943	982.061	F2848	Armenia—Civilization	947.56	DS171
			Armenia—Description and travel	914.75604	DS165
Argentina—History—Revolution, 1930	982.061	F2848	Armenia—History	947.56	DS173-195.5
Argentina—History—1943-	982.0(61-7)	F2849-.22	Armenia—History—To 428	947.56	DS181-184
Argentina—History—1943-1955	982.06(1-2)	F2849	Armenia—History—Arsacid (Arshakuni) dynasty, 66-428	947.56	DS181-184
Argentina—History—Revolution, 1955	982.063	F2849.2	Armenia—History—428-1522	947.56	DS186-188
Argentina—History—1955-1983	982.06(3-4)	F2849.2	Armenia—History—428-640	947.56	DS186-188
Argentina—History—Peronist Revolt, 1956	982.063	F2849.2	Armenia—History—Arab period, 640-885	947.56	DS186-188
Argentina—History—Coup d'etat, 1966	982.063	F2849.2	Armenia—History—Turkic Mongol Domination, 1045-1522	947.56	DS186-188
Argentina—History—1983-	982.0(64-7)	F2849.2			
Argentine literature	860	PQ7600-7798.36	Armenia—History—1522-1800	947.5607	DS191-193
Argon	546.753	QD181.A6	Armenia—History—1801-1900	947.560(7-83)	DS194-.5
Argonne, Battle of the, 1915	940.424	D545.A6	Armenia—History—1901-	947.5608(3-6)	DS195-.3
			Armenia—History—Revolution, 1917-1920	947.560841	DS195.5
Argonne, Battle of the, 1918	940.434	D545.A63	Armenia (Republic)	947.56	DK680-689.5
Arianism	273.4	BT1350	Armenia (Republic)—History— Uprising, 1921	947.560841	DS195.5
Arid regions	551.415	GB611-618			
Arid regions agriculture	630.9154	S612-619	Armenian Church	281.62	BX120-129
Arid regions climate	551.69154	QC993.7	Armenian essays	089.91992	AC132-133
Arid soils	631.49154	S592.17.A73	Armenian language	491.992	PK8001-8454
Aries (Astrology)	133.5262	BF1727	Armenian literature	891.992	PK8501-8835
Aristocracy (Social class)	305.52	HT647-653	Armenian literature—Europe	891.992	PK8601-8661
Arithmetic	513	GN476.1			
Arithmetic	513	QA101-141.8	Armenian literature—United States	891.992	PK8681-8689
Arithmetic—Foundations	513	QA248-.5			
Arizona	979.1	F806-820	Armenian massacres, 1915-1923	947.560(83-841)	DS195.5
Arizona—Gazetteers	917.91003	F809			
Arizona—Maps	912.791	G4330-4334	Armies	355.31	UA
Arizona—National Guard	355.3709791	UA70-79	Armies, Colonial	355.352	UA14
Arizona—Periodicals	979.1005	F806	Armies, Cost of	355.622	UA17
Arizona—History—To 1912	979.10(1-4)	F811	Armies—Commissariat	355.62	UC700-780
Arizona—History—1912-1950	979.105(2-3)	F811	Armies—Equipment	355.81	UC460-465
			Armies—Officers	355.332	UB410-415
Arizona—History—1951-	979.105(3-4)	F815-.3	Arminianism	284.9	BX6195-6197
Arkansas	976.7	F406-420	Armor	623.4409	U800-897
Arkansas—Gazetteers	917.67003	F409	Armor, Ancient	623.4410901	U805
Arkansas—Maps	912.767	G4000-4004	Armor—[By region or country]	623.44109(4-9)	U818-823.5
Arkansas—National Guard	355.3709767	UA80-89			
Arkansas—Periodicals	976.7005	F406	Armored personnel carriers	358.1883	UG446.5
Arm	611.97	QM548	Armored trains	623.63	UG345
Arm wrestling	796.812	GV1196.5	Armored vessels	359.32	V799-800
Armada, 1588	942.055	DA360	Armor—Exhibitions	623.441074	U804
Arm—Amputation	617.574059	RD557	Armories	355.75	UA
Armatures	621.316	TK2477	Army ants	595.796	QL568.F7
Armed forces—Mobilization	355.28	UA910-915	Arnhem, Battle of, 1944	940.54219218	D763.N4
Armed forces—Procurement	355.6212	UC260	Aromatherapy	615.3219	RM666.A68
			Aromatic compounds	547.6	QD330-341

Subject Heading	Dewey	LC	Subject Heading	Dewey	LC
Aromatic plants	633.81	SB301-303	Art—Austria—History	709.436	N6805-6808.5
Aroostook War, 1839	973.57	E398	Art—Belgium—History	709.493	N6967-6973
Arraignment—United States	345.73072	KF9645-9650	Art—Canada—History	709.71	N6540-6545.5
			Art—Central America—History	709.728	N6573.2-6582.5
Arras, Battle of, 1917	940.431	D545.A7	Art—Czechoslovakia—History	709.437	N6828-6831.5
Arras, Battle of, 1940	940.5421	D756.5.A78			
Arrest (Police methods)	363.232	HV8080.A6	Art—Greece—History	709.495	N6897-6898.5
Arrest—United States	345.730527	KF9625	Art—Hungary—History	709.439	N6819-6820.5
Arrhythmia	616.128	RC685.A65	Art—Italy—History	709.45	N6915-6923
Arrowheads	623.441	GN498.B78	Art—Mexico—History	709.72	N6555-.5
Arroyos	551.442	GB561-568	Art—Portugal—History	709.469	N7125-7128.5
Arsenals	355.7	UF540-545	Art—Scandinavia—History	709.48	N7007-7088
Arson	364.164	HV6638-.5	Art—South America—History	709.8	N6635-6735.5
Arson—[By region or country]	364.16409(4-9)	HV6638.5	Art—Spain—History	709.46	N7105-7108.5
Art, Abstract	709.04052	N6490	Art	700	N
Art, Ancient	709.01	N5315-5899	Art and mythology	704.947	N7760-7763
Art, Arab	709.394	N5470	Art and photography	770	N72.P5
Art, Classical	709.38	N5603-5896.3	Art and technology	700.105	N72.T4
Art, Early Christian	704.9482	N7832	Art as an investment	332.63	N8600
Art, Egyptian	709.32	N5350-5351	Art criticism	701.18	N7475-7485
Art, Greek	709.38	N5630-5720	Art dealers	381.457(3-6)	N8610-8660
Art, Medieval	709.02	N5940-6320	Art deco	709.04012	N6494.A7
Art, Modern	709.03	N6350-6494	Art metal-work	739	NK6400-8459
Art, Modern—17th century	709.032	N6410-6415	Art museums	708	N400-3990
Art, Modern—18th century	709.033	N6420-6425	Art museums—Belgium	708.93	N1750-1850
Art, Modern—19th century	709.034	N6450-6465	Art museums—Europe	708.(2-9)	N1010-3690
Art, Modern—20th century	709.04	N6480-6494	Art museums—France	708.4	N2010-2180
Art, Oriental	709.5	N7260-7355.5	Art museums—Germany	708.3	N2210-2406
Art, Prehistoric	700.901	GN799.A	Art museums—Great Britain	708.2	N1020-1560
Art, Prehistoric	709.011	N5310-5313			
Art, Primitive	709.011	N5310-5313	Art museums—Greece	708.95	N2410-2430
Art, Renaissance	709.024	N6370-6375	Art museums—Italy	708.5	N2510-3065
Art, Rococo	709.0332	N6410	Art museums—Netherlands	708.92	N2450-2505
Art, Roman	709.37	N5760-5763	Art museums—Russia	708.7	N3310-3382
Art, Romanesque	709.0216	N6280	Art museums—Spain	708.6	N3410-3499
Art, Sumerian	709.35	N5370	Art museums—United States	708.1(3-9)	N510-880
Art, Syrian	709.3943	N5460			
Art, Turkish	709.392	N5480-5560	Art objects, Ancient	745.0901	NK610-685
Art—Biography	709.2	N40-43	Art objects, Classical	745.0938	NK665-680
Art—Congresses	706	N21	Art objects—[By region or country]	745.09(4-9)	NK801-1094.5
Art—Conservation and restoration	702.88	N8554-8585			
			Art objects—Catalogs	745.0294	NK1133-.26
Art—Dictionaries	703	N33	Art objects—Collectors and collecting	745.075	NK1125-1130
Art—Directories	702.5	N50-55			
Art—Exhibitions	707.4	N4390-5098	Art schools	707.1	N325-335
Art—History	709	N5300-7418	Art schools—Europe	707.104	N332
Art—Periodicals	705	N1-9.9	Art schools—United States	707.1073	N328-330
Art—Philosophy	701	N61-75	Art therapy	616.891656	RC489.A7
Art—Private collections	708	N5198-5299	Art thieves	364.162	N8795
Art—Private collections—Europe	708.(2-8)	N5240-5280	Arterial catheterization	617.413	RD598.5
			Arteries	573.185	QL835
Art—Private collections—United States	708.1(3-9)	N5215-5220	Arteries	611.13	QM191
			Arteries—Diseases	616.13	RC691-697
Art—Societies, etc.	706	N10-17	Arthritis	616.13	RC694.5.I53
Art—Study and teaching	707.1	N81-390	Arthritis	616.722	RC933
Art—Technique	702.8	N7429.7-7433			

Subject Heading	Dewey	LC
Arthropoda	595	QL434-599.82
Arthropoda, Fossil	565	QE815-832
Articulation disorders	616.855	RC424.7
Artificial arms	617.574	RD756.2-.22
Artificial corneas	617.7190592	RE336
Artificial flowers	745.5943	TT890-894
Artificial hip joints	617.4720592	RD549
Artificial horizons (Nautical instruments)	527.0284	VK584.A7
Artificial insemination	636.08245	SF105.5
Artificial insemination, Human	618.178	RG134
Artificial intelligence	006.3	Q334-342
Artificial knee	617.5820592	RD561
Artificial larynx	617.5330592	RF538
Artificial legs	617.58	RD756.4-.42
Artificial limbs	617.58	RD756-.42
Artificial minerals	666.86	TP870
Artificial reefs	639.92	SH157.85.A7
Artificial respiration	617.1806	RC87.9
Artificial satellites	384.51	HE9719-9721
Artificial satellites	629.46	TL796-798
Artificial satellites in navigation	623.893	VK562
Artificial satellites in telecommunication	621.3825	TK5104-.2
Artillery	358.12	UF
Artillery, Coast	358.16	UF450-455
Artillery, Field and mountain	358.12	UF400-445
Artillery—[By region or country]	358.1209(4-9)	UF21-124
Artillery—Africa	358.12096	UF115-119
Artillery—Argentina	358.120982	UF36-37
Artillery—Asia	358.12095	UF99-113
Artillery—Australia	358.120994	UF121-122
Artillery—Canada	358.120971	UF26-27
Artillery—Central America	358.1209728	UF30-31
Artillery—Chile	358.120983	UF43-44
Artillery—China	358.120951	UF101-102
Artillery—Colombia	358.1209861	UF45-46
Artillery—Europe	358.12094	UF55-95
Artillery—France	358.120944	UF71-72
Artillery—Germany	358.120943	UF73-74
Artillery—Great Britain	358.120941	UF57-64
Artillery—Greece	358.1209495	UF75-76
Artillery—India	358.120954	UF103-104
Artillery—Italy	358.120945	UF79-80
Artillery—Japan	358.120952	UF105-106
Artillery—Mexico	358.120972	UF28-29
Artillery—New Zealand	358.120993	UF122.5
Artillery—Oceania	358.12099(5-6)	UF123-124
Artillery—Portugal	358.1209469	UF83-84
Artillery—Russia	358.120947	UF85-86
Artillery—Scandinavia	358.120948	UF86.5
Artillery—South America	358.12098	UF34-54
Artillery—Spain	358.120946	UF87-88
Artillery—United States	358.120973	UF23-25
Artillery—Venezuela	358.120987	UF54
Artillery—West Indies	358.1209729	UF32-33
Artillery—Dictionaries	358.1203	UF9
Artillery—History	358.1209	UF15
Artillery—Societies, etc.	358.12006	UF1
Artillery drill and tactics	358.124	UF157-302
Artists	700.92	N40
Artists' materials	700.284	N8530-8540
Artists' models	702.8	N7574
Artists' tools	702.84	N8543
Arts	700	NX
Arts and crafts movement	745	NK1135-1149.5
Arts, Islamic	704.9489	NX688
Arts—[By region or country]	700.9(4-9)	NX501-596.3
Arts—Afghanistan	700.9581	NX575.6
Arts—Africa	700.96	NX587-589.8
Arts—Africa, East	700.9676	NX588.8-.9
Arts—Africa, North	700.961	NX587.6-588.6
Arts—Africa, Southern	700.968	NX589.7-.8
Arts—Africa, West	700.966	NX589-.6
Arts—Argentina	700.982	NX531
Arts—Asia	700.95	NX572-586
Arts—Asiatic Russia	700.957	NX575.7
Arts—Australia	700.994	NX590
Arts—Austria	700.9436	NX548
Arts—Bahamas	700.97296	NX524
Arts—Balkan Peninsula	700.9496	NX566-569
Arts—Belgium	700.9493	NX555
Arts—Bolivia	700.984	NX532
Arts—Brazil	700.981	NX533
Arts—Cambodia	700.9596	NX578.6.C3
Arts—Canada	700.971	NX513-.3
Arts—Central America	700.9728	NX515-522
Arts—Chile	700.983	NX534
Arts—China	700.951	NX583
Arts—Colombia	700.9861	NX535
Arts—Costa Rica	700.97286	NX517
Arts—Cuba	700.97291	NX525
Arts—Denmark	700.9489	NX558
Arts—Ecuador	700.9866	NX536
Arts—Egypt	700.962	NX588-.3
Arts—El Salvador	700.97284	NX522
Arts—Ethiopia	700.963	NX588.7
Arts—Europe	700.94	NX542-571
Arts—France	700.944	NX549
Arts—Germany	700.943	NX550-.6
Arts—Great Britain	700.941	NX543-547.6
Arts—Greece	700.9495	NX551
Arts—Guatemala	700.97281	NX518
Arts—Haiti	700.97294	NX526
Arts—Honduras	700.97283	NX519
Arts—Iceland	700.94912	NX559
Arts—India	700.954	NX576
Arts—Indonesia	700.9598	NX580

Subject Heading	Dewey	LC	Subject Heading	Dewey	LC
Arts—Iran	700.955	NX574	Ashanti War, 1873-1874	966.23	DT507
Arts—Israel	700.95694	NX573.7	Ashanti War, 1895-1896	966.31	DT507
Arts—Italy	700.945	NX552	Asia	950	DS
Arts—Jamaica	700.97292	NX527	Asia, Central	958	DK845-860
Arts—Japan	700.952	NX584	Asia, Central	958	DS327-329.4
Arts—Korea	700.9519	NX584.6-.7	Asia, Central	939.6	DS327-329.4
Arts—Laos	700.9594	NX578.6.L3	Asia, Central—Commerce	381.0958	HF3770.22-.27
Arts—Malaysia	700.9595	NX579	Asia, Southeastern—	275.9	BR1178-1261
Arts—Mexico	700.972	NX514	Church history		
Arts—Middle East	700.956	NX573-.7	Asia, Southeastern—	959	DS524-526.7
Arts—Netherlands	700.9492	NX554	History		
Arts—New Zealand	700.993	NX593	Asia, Southeastern—	299.5	BL2050-2150
Arts—Nicaragua	700.97285	NX520	Religion		
Arts—Norway	700.9481	NX560	Asia—Armed Forces—	355.8095	UC234-245
Arts—Oceania	700.99(5-6)	NX595-596	Supplies and stores		
Arts—Pakistan	700.95491	NX576.7	Asia—Biography	920.05	CT1498-1919
Arts—Panama	700.97287	NX521	OAsia—Church history	275	BR1060-1357
Arts—Paraguay	700.9892	NX538	Asia—Climate	551.695	QC990
Arts—Peru	700.985	NX539	Asia—Description and	915.04	DS5.95-10
Arts—Philippines	700.9599	NX581	travel		
Arts—Portugal	700.9469	NX563	Asia—Economic conditions	330.95	HC411-495
Arts—Puerto Rico	700.97295	NX528	Asia—Emigration and	325.(25) or (5)	JV8490-8758
Arts—Russia	700.947	NX556	immigration		
Arts—Scandinavia	700.948	NX557-561	Asia—Gazetteers	915.03	DS4
Arts—South America	700.98	NX530-541	Asia—Genealogy	929.107205	CS1080-1549.5
Arts—Spain	700.946	NX562	Asia—History	950	DS31-35.2
Arts—Sri Lanka	700.95493	NX576.6	Asia—History—1945-	950.4(2-3)	DS35.2
Arts—Sweden	700.9485	NX561	Asia—History—20th	950.4	DS35-.2
Arts—Switzerland	700.9494	NX564	century		
Arts—Thailand	700.9593	NX578.7	Asia—Maps	912.5	G2200-2444
Arts—Turkey	700.9561	NX565	Asia—Maps	912.5	G7400-8198.54
Arts—United States	700.973	NX503-512.3	Asian flu	616.203	RC150
Arts—Uruguay	700.9895	NX540	Asian periodicals	079.5	PN5360-5449
Arts—Venezuela	700.987	NX541	Asians—Education	371.82995	LC3001-3501
Arts—Vietnam	700.9597	NX578.6.V5-.V55	Asia—Periodicals	950.05	DS1
Arts—West Indies	700.9729	NX523-529	Asia—Politics and	320.95	JQ
Arts—Dictionaries	700.3	NX80	government		
Arts—Encyclopedias	700.3	NX70	Asia—Politics and	320.95	JQ21-1825
Arts—Endowments	700.79	NX700-750	government		
Arts—Forgeries	702.874	NX636	Asiatic Russia—	670.957	TS109-110
Arts—Periodicals	700.5	NX1-9	Manufactures		
Aruba—Maps	912.72986	G5170-5174	Asparagus	635.31	SB325
AS (Coin)	737.4937	CJ937	Asphalt	622.337	TN853
Asbestos	622.3672	TN930	Asphyxia	617.18	RA1071-1082
Ascension Day	263.93	BV57	Asphyxia	617.18	RC87.3
Ascension Day	394.266	GT4995.A8	Asphyxia neonatorum	618.922	RJ256
Asceticism	204.47	BJ1491	Aspirin	338.476153137	HD9675.A7-.A74
Asceticism	204.47	BL625	Aspirin	615.3137	RM666.A82
Asceticism	248.47	BV5015-5068	Assamese language	491.451	PK1550-1599
Asceticism—Buddhism	294.34447	BQ6200-6240	Assassination	364.1524	HV6278
Asceticism—History—Early	248.470901	BV5023	Assassination	364.1524	HV6499-6535
church, ca. 30-600			Assassins (Ismailites)	297.822	BP195.A8
Asceticism—History—	248.470902	BV5025	Assault and battery	364.1555	HV6618
Middle Ages, 600-1500			Assault rifles	356.1182425	UD390-395
Asceticism—Islam	297.576	BP190.5.A75	Assaying	669.92	TN550-580
Ashanti War, 1822-1831	966.23	DT507	Assaying	669.92	HG325-329
			Assertiveness training	158.2	RC489.A77

Subject Heading	Dewey	LC	Subject Heading	Dewey	LC
Asses	599.665	QL737.U62	Astronomy—Periodicals	520.5	QB1
Assimilation (Sociology)	303.482	JV6342	Astronomy—Philosophy	520.1	QB14.5
Assisted suicide	179.7	R726	Astronomy—Study and teaching	520.71	QB61-62.7
Associate clergy	262.14	BV674			
Association of ideas	153.2	BF365-395	Astronomy in the Bible	220.852	BS655
Associations, institutions, etc.—Law and legislation—United States	346.7306	KF1355-1480	Astrophysics	523.01	QB460-466
			Asylum, Right of	323.631	HV8652-8654
Assyro-Babylonian literature	892.1	PJ3601-3953	Atheism	211.8	BL2700-2790
			Athena (Greek deity)	292.2114	BL820.M6
Assyro-Babylonian religion	299.21	BL1620-1625	Athens (Greece)	949.512	DF915-936
Asteroids	523.44	QB377-379	Athletes	796.092	GV697
Asteroids	523.44	QB516	Athletic clubs	796.068	GV563
Asteroids	523.44	QB651	Athletic fields	796.068	GV411-416
Asthma	616.238	RB150.A87	Athletics	796	GV561-749.5
Asthma	616.238	RC591	Athletics—Equipment and supplies	796.0284	GV743-749
Asthma in children	618.92238	RJ436.A8			
Astigmatism	617.755	RE932	Atlanta (Ga.)	975.8231	F294.A8
Astral projection	133.95	BF1389.A7	Atlanta Campaign, 1864	973.7371	E476.7
Astrodynamics	629.4	TL1050-1060	Atlantic Ocean—Maps	912.1963	G2805-2839
Astrographic catalog and chart	520.216	QB6	Atlantic States—Maps	912.7(4-5)	G3709.3-3933
			Atlantic Wall (France and Belgium)	940.5421	D756.3
Astrology	133.5	BF1651-1729			
Astrology	520	QB25-26	Atmosphere	551.5	QC851-999
Astrology and politics	133.5832	BF1729.P6	Atmosphere, Upper	551.514	QC879-.59
Astrology, Arab	133.593927	BF1714.A6	Atmosphere, Upper—Rocket observations	551.514	QC879
Astrometry	522	QB807			
Astronautical charts	629.453	TL1070	Atmospheric chemistry	551.511	QC879.6-.85
Astronautical instruments	629.474	TL1082	Atmospheric circulation	551.517	QC880.4.A8
Astronautics	629.4	TL787-4050	Atmospheric density	551.5	QC880
Astronautics— Experiments	629.40724	TL794.3	Atmospheric electricity	551.563	QC960.5-969
Astronautics—Study and teaching	629.4071	TL845-848	Atmospheric ionization	551.561	QC966.7.A84
			Atmospheric nucleation	551.5741	QC921.6.C6
Astronomers—Biography	520.92	QB35-36	Atmospheric pressure	551.54	QC885-896
Astronomical clocks	522.5	QB107	Atmospheric pressure—Physiological effect	571.437	QP82.2.P7
Astronomical geography	525	QB630-638.8			
Astronomical instruments	522.2	QB84.5-115			
Astronomical models	520.228	QB67	Atmospheric radiation	551.5273	QC912.3
Astronomical observatories	522.29	QB81-84	Atmospheric radio refractivity	551.51	QC973.4.R35
Astronomical photography	522.63	QB121-.5			
Astronomical photometry	522.62	QB135	Atmospheric radioactivity	551.5276	QC913-.2
Astronomical spectroscopy	522.67	QB465	Atmospheric temperature	551.525	QC901-912.2
Astronomy	520	QB	Atmospheric thermodynamics	551.52	QC880.4.T5
Astronomy, Ancient	520.901	QB16-22			
Astronomy, Assyro-Babylonian	520.935	QB19	Atmospheric tides	551.464	QC883.2.A8
			Atmospheric turbulence	551.55	QC880.4.T8
Astronomy, Chinese	520.931	QB17	Atomic absorption spectroscopy	535.84	QC454.A8
Astronomy, Greek	520.938	QB21			
Astronomy, Medieval	520.902	QB23-26	Atomic mass	541.242	QC173
Astronomy, Prehistoric	520.901	GN799.A8	Atomic mass	541.242	QD466
Astronomy, Renaissance	520.90(23-31)	QB29	Atomic structure	539.14	QC173.4.A87
Astronomy—Charts, diagrams, etc.	529.223	QB65	Atomic theory	541.2	QD461
			Atomic weights	541.242	QD463-464
			Atomism	146.5	BD646
Astronomy—Encyclopedias	520.3	QB14	Atomism	182	B193
Astronomy—History	520.9	QB15-34	Atoms	539.7	QC173
Astronomy—Mathematics	520.151	QB47	Atonement	234.5	BT263-268
Astronomy—Observations	522.1	QB4-.9	Atopic dermatitis	616.5	RL242-249

Subject Heading	Dewey	LC	Subject Heading	Dewey	LC
Attack helicopters	358.4383	UG1230-1235	Australia—Maps	912.94	G8960-8964
Attack planes	358.43	UG1242.A28	Australian aborigines—Antiquities	994.01	GN871-875
Attention	153.1532	LB1065			
Attention	153.733	BF321-323	Australian aborigines—Ethnic identity	305.89915	GN666
Attention in newborn infants	155.42221532	BF720.A85	Australian languages	499.15	PL7001-7101
Attention-deficit hyperactivity disorder	618.928589	RJ506.H9	Australian literature	820	PR9600-9619.3
			Australian periodicals	079.94	PN5510-5590
Attics	643.5	TH3000	Austria	943.6	DB1-879
Attitude (Psychology)	152.4	BF327	Austria	936.3	DB1-879
Attribute (Philosophy)	111.8	BD352	Austria	943.(6, 7, 9)	DB
Atum (Egyptian deity)	299.31	BL2450.A89	Austria—Biography	920.0363	DB36-.7
Auction bridge	795.414	GV1282	Austria—Biography	920.0436	DB36-.7
Auctions	381.17	HF5476-5477	Austria—Census	314.36	HA1171-1190
Audiences	302.23	P96.A83	Austria—Civilization	943.6	DB30
Audiology	617.8	RF286-320	Austria—Civilization	936.3	DB30
Audiology—Instruments	617.800284	RF298-310	Austria—Description and travel	913.6304	DB21-27.5
Audiology—Societies, etc.	617.8006	RF286			
Audiometry	612.85	RF294-.5	Austria—Description and travel	914.3604	DB21-27.5
Audio-visual education	371.335	LB1043-1044.9			
Auditing	657.45	HF5667-5668.25	Austria—Economic conditions	330.9436	HC261-270
Auditing, Internal	657.458	HF5668-.25			
Auditoriums	725.83	NA6815	Austria—Emigration and immigration	325.(2436) or (436)	JV7800-7899
Augmentation mammaplasty	618.190592	RD539.8			
			Austria—Gazetteers	914.36003	DB14
Augustinians	255.4	BX2901-2956	Austria—Historiography	943.60072	DB36.8-.9
Aura	133.892	BF1389.A8	Austria—Historiography	936.30072	DB36.8-.9
Auroras	538.768	QC970-972.5	Austria—History	943.6	DB46-99.2
Auschwitz (Poland : Concentration camp)	940.5318538	D805.P7	Austria—History	936.3	DB46-99.2
			Austria—History, Military	355.009436	DB42-44
			Austria—History, Naval	359.009436	DB45
Australia—Armed Forces—Supplies and stores	355.80994	UC255-256	Austria— History—To 1273	943.602	DB51-57
			Austria—History—To 1273	936.3	DB51-57
			Austria—History—1273-1519	943.60(25-3)	BD57-59
Australia—Biography	920.0994	CT2800-2808			
Australia—Census	319.4	HA3001-3010	Austria—History—1519-1740	943.60(25-31)	DB65.2-77
Australia—Church history	279.4	BR1480-1483			
Australia—Climate	551.6994	QC992	Austria—History—Revolution, 1848-1849	940.284	DB83
Australia—Commerce	381.0994	HF3941-3950			
Australia—Description and travel	919.404	DU97-5-105.2	Austria—History—1918-1938	943.6051	DB96-99.2
			Austria—History—1938-1945	943.6052	DB99
Australia—Economic conditions	330.994	HC601-610			
			Austria—History—1955-	943.6053	DB99.2
Australia—Emigration and immigration	325.(294) or (94)	JV9100-9199	Austria—Manufactures	670.9436	TS65-.2
			Austria—Maps	912.436	G1935-1939
Australia—Gazetteers	919.4003	DU90	Austria—Maps	912.436	G6490-6494
Australia—Genealogy	929.1072094	CS2000-2009	Austrian Succession, War of, 1740-1748	940.2532	D291-294
Australia—History	994	DU108-117.2			
Australia—History—To 1788	994.01	DU98.1	Austrian Succession, War of, 1740-1748	940.2532	DB72
			Austria—Periodicals	943.6005	DB1
Australia—History—1788-1851	994.02	DU115	Austria—Periodicals	936.3005	DB1
			Austria—Politics and government	320.9436	JN1601-2041
Australia—History—1788-1900	994.0(2-3)	DU114-115.2			
			Austroasiatic languages	495.93	PL4281-4587
Australia—History—20th century	994.04	DU116-117.2	Austro-Italian War, 1866	945.084	DG558
Australia—Manufactures	670.994	TS121-122			
Australia—Maps	912.94	G2750-2793			

Subject Heading	Dewey	LC	Subject Heading	Dewey	LC
Austronesian languages	499.2	PL5021-6571	Automobiles—Electric equipment	629.2548	TL272
Austro-Prussian War, 1866	943.076	DD436-440	Automobiles—Encyclopedias	629.22203	TL9
Austro-Sardinian War, 1848-1849	945.083	DG553-.5	Automobiles—Heating and ventilation	629.2772	TL271-.5
Austro-Turkish War, 1716-1718	956.10153	DR545	Automobiles—History	629.22209	TL15
Austro-Turkish War, 1737-1739	956.10153	DR548	Automobiles—Maintenance and repair	629.287	TL152-.2
Autarchy	338.9	HD82-85	Automobiles—Marketing	381.45388342	HD9710-.37
Authoritarianism (Personality trait)	155.232	BF698.35.A87	Automobiles—Models	629.221	TL237-.2
Authority	303.36	HM271-276	Automobiles—Motors	629.252	TL210-.7
Authority—Religious aspects	262.8	BT88-92	Automobiles—Museums	629.222074	TL7
Authors and publishers—United States	070.520973	KF3084	Automobiles—Periodicals	629.22205	TL1-5
			Automobiles—Pollution control devices	629.25	TL214.P6
Authorship	808.02	PN101-249	Automobiles—Testing	629.282	TL285-295
Authorship—Marketing	381.45808	PN161	Automobiles—France	629.2220944	TL71-72.5
Autism	616.85882	RC553.A88	Automobiles—Germany	629.2220943	TL73-74.5
Autism in children	618.928982	RJ506.A9	Automobiles—Great Britain	629.2220941	TL57-64
Autoantibodies	571.973	QR186.82-.83	Automobiles—Japan	629.2220952	TL105-106
Autobiographies	920	CT101	Automobiles—Russia	629.2220947	TL85-86
Autobiography	920	CT25	Automobiles—United States	629.2220973	TL23-25
Autoerotic asphyxia	616.8583	RC560.A97			
Autographs	929.88	Z41-42.5	Autopsy	614.1	RA1063.4
Autoharp music	787.75	M175.A8	Autopsy	616.0759	RB57
Autoimmune diseases	616.978	RC600	Auxiliary sciences of history	900	C
Autoimmunity	571.973	QR188.3	Auxiliary sciences of history—Congresses	906	C3
Automatic control	629.8	TA165	Auxiliary sciences of history—Periodicals	905	C4
Automatic machinery	629.8	TJ212.2-225	Auxiliary sciences of history—Societies, etc.	906	C2
Automatic meteorological stations	551.63	QC875	Avalanches	551.307	QC929.A8
Automatic pilot (Airplanes)	629.1326	TL589.5	Avant-garde (Aesthetics)	700.411	BH301.A94
Automation	670.427	T59.5	Avarice	178	BJ1535.A8
Automobile drivers	629.283092	TL152.5-.55	Aversion therapy	616.89142	RC489.B4
Automobile driving	629.283	TL152.5-.55	Avestan language	491.52	PK6101-6109
Automobile engineers—Biography	629.222092	TL139-140	Aviaries	598.073	QL677.8
Automobile parking	629.283	TL154	Aviation medicine	616.980213	RC1050-1097
Automobile racing drivers	796.72092	GV1032	Aviculture	636.6	SF461
Automobile rallies	796.73	GV1029.2	Avionics	629.135	TL695-696
Automobile theft investigation	363.25962	HV8079.A98	Avitaminosis	616.39	RC623.7
			Avulsion fractures	617.15	RD104.A95
Automobile travel	796.7	GV1021-1025	Axioms	516.	QA481
Automobiles	629.222	TL1-230.5	Azerbaijan	947.54	DK690-699.5
Automobiles, Military	623.7472	UG615-620	Azerbaijani language	494.361	PL311-314
Automobiles, Racing	629.228	TL236	Azimuth	526.63	QB207
Automobiles, Steam	629.2292	TL200	Azimuth	526.63	TA597
Automobiles—Aerodynamics	629.231	TL245	Azimuth	527	VK563
Automobiles—Bodies	629.26	TL255-256.5	Azores—Census	314.699	HA2280
Automobiles—Catalogs	629.2220294	TL12	Azores—Maps	912.4699	G9130-9134
Automobiles—Congresses	629.22206	TL6	Aztec mythology	299.78452013	F1219.76.R45
Automobiles—Conservation and restoration	629.287	TL152.2	Aztecs	972.00497452	F1219.73-.75
			B stars	523.8	QB843.B12
Automobiles—Design and construction	629.23	TL240-278	B-52 bomber	358.42830973	UG1242.B6
			Baal (Deity)	299.26	BL1671

Subject Heading	Dewey	LC
Babism	297.92	BP340
Baby books	305.232	HQ779-.5
Babysitting	649.10248	HQ769.5
Baccalaureate addresses	252.68	BV4255
Bachelor of arts degree	378.2	LB2383
Bachelor parties	392.5	GV1472.7.B33
Bachelorette parties	392.5	GV1462.7.B33
Bachelors	305.8152	HQ800.3
Bacillus (Bacteria)	579.362	QR82.B3
Bacitracin	615.329	RM666.B2
Back	612.9	QM540
Backache	617.564	RD771.B217
Backpacking	796.51	GV199.6
Backyard gardens	635	SB473
Bacon's Rebellion, 1676	975.502	F229
Bacteria	579.3	QR75-99.5
Bacteria cell surfaces	571.629	QR77.35
Bacteria—Evolution	579.3138	QR81.7
Bacterial antigens	571.9645	QR186.6.B33
Bacterial diseases	571.993	QR201.B34
Bacterial diseases	616.92	RC115-116
Bacterial diseases in children	618.9292	RJ406.B32
Bacterial vaccines	615.372	QR189.5.B33
Bacteriological laboratories	579.3072	QR64-.8
Bacteriology	579.3	QR
Bacteriology, Agricultural	579.31755	QR111
Bacteriology, Agricultural	579.31755	QR351
Bacteriology—Technique	579.3028	QR65-69
Bacteriophages	579.26	QR342-.2
Badges	929.6	CR67-69
Bagpipe music	788.49	M145
Bahai faith	297.93	BP300-395
Bahai meditations	297.93435	BP380
Bahamas	972.96	F1650-1660
Bahamas—Civilization	972.96	F1654
Bahamas—Description and travel	917.29604	F1651
Bahamas—Gazetteers	917.296003	F1650.7
Bahamas—History	972.96	F1655.3-1657.2
Bahamas—Maps	912.7296	G4980-4984
Bahamas—Periodicals	972.96005	F1650
Bahamas—Politics and government	320.97296	JL610-619
Bahrain—Census	315.365	HA4568
Bahrain—Economic conditions	330.95365	HC415.38
Bahrain—Maps	912.5365	G7590-7594
Bahrain—Politics and government	320.95365	JQ1846
Bailments—Canada	346.71025	KE970-972
Bailments—England	346.42025	KD1679-1685
Bailments—United States	346.73025	KF939-951
Bail—United States	345.73056	KF9632
Bait	799.10284	SH448
Bait fishing	799.122	SH455.4
Bakers and bakeries	338.47641815	HD9057-9058
Bakers and bakeries	641.815	HD8039.B2
Bakers and bakeries	664.02	TX761-799
Baking	664.02	TX761-778
Baking powder	338.4766468	HD9330.B2-.B23
Balalaika music	787.875	M142.B2
Balance beam	796.44	GV512
Balance of payments	332.152	HG3882-3890
Balance of power	327.112	D217
Balance of trade	382.17	HF1014
Balconies	721.84	NA3070
Balcony gardening	635.9671	SB419.5
Bald eagle	598.943	QL696.F32
Balder (Norse deity)	293.2113	BL870.B3
Baldness	616.546	RL155-.5
Balinese (Indonesia people)	959.80049922	DS632.B25
Balinese language	499.22	PL5221-5224
Balkan Peninsula	949.6	DR
Balkan Peninsula—Biography	920.0496	DR33
Balkan Peninsula—Biography	920.0496	CT1399-1458
Balkan Peninsula—Civilization	949.6	DR22-23
Balkan Peninsula—Congresses	949.6006	DR1.5
Balkan Peninsula—Description and travel	914.9604	DR11-16
Balkan Peninsula—Economic conditions	330.9496	HC401-407
Balkan Peninsula—Gazetteers	914.96003	DR5
Balkan Peninsula—History	949.6	DR32-48.5
Balkan Peninsula—Manufactures	670.9496	TS95.A2
Balkan Peninsula—Periodicals	949.6005	DR1
Balkan Peninsula—Politics and government	320.9496	JN9600-9689
Ball games	796.3	GV861
Ballads	782.43	M1627
Ball-bearings	621.822	TJ1071-1073
Ballet	781.55609	ML3460
Ballet	792.84	GV1787
Ballet dancing	792.84	GV1788
Ballet slippers	792.8028	GV1789.2
Ballet—Costume	792.8026	GV1789.2
Ballista	355.8241	U875
Ballistic instruments	623.510284	UF830
Ballistic missile defenses	358.171	UG740-745
Ballistic missiles	358.1754	UG1312.B34
Ballistics	623.51	UF820-840
Ballistics—Tables	623.51021	UF820
Ballistics—Tables	623.51021	VF550
Balloon ascensions	629.13322	TL620
Balloon decorations	745.5941	TT926
Balloon racing	797.51	GV763
Ballooning	797.51	GV762-763

Subject Heading	Dewey	LC	Subject Heading	Dewey	LC
Balloons	629.13322	TL609-639	Bankruptcy	332.75	HG3760-3769
Ballot	324.65	JF1091-1177	Bankruptcy—Canada	346.71078	KE1491-1506
Ballot	324.650973	JK2214-2217	Bankruptcy—England	346.42078	KD2141-2164
Ballroom dancing	793.33	GV1751	Bankruptcy—United States	346.73078	KF1501-1548
Balls (Parties)	793.38	GV1746-1750	Banks and banking	332.1	HG1501-3550
Balls (Parties)	793.38	GV1757	Banks and banking, Cooperative	334.2	HG2032-2039
Balls (Sporting goods)	796.30284	GV749.B34	Banks and banking— Accounting	657.8333	HG1706-1708
Ball's Bluff, Battle of, 1861	973.731	E472.63	Banks and banking— Computer programs	332.10285	HG1709
Baltic Entente, 1934-1940	947.0842	DK511.B3	Banks and banking— Customer services	332.17	HG1616.C87
Baltic States	947.9	DK502.3-.7	Banks and banking—[By region or country]	332.109(4-9)	HG2401-3542.7
Baltic States—History	947.9	DK502.7	Banks and banking— United States	332.10973	HG2401-2626
Baltimore (Md.)	975.26	F189.B1	Bantams	636.5871	SF489.B2
Baltimore, Battle of, 1814	973.523	E356.B2	Bantu languages	496.39	PL8025
Bamboo	584.9	QK495.G74	Baptism	265.1	BV803-814
Bananas	584.39	QK495.M98	Baptism (Canon law)	262.933	BX1939.B3
Bananas	634.772	SB379.B2	Baptism for the dead	265.1	BV814
Band music	784	M1200-1268	Baptism in the Holy Spirit	234.13	BT123
Band music—Analysis, appreciation	784.117	MT125	Baptismal water	264.02036	BX2307.3
Bandages and bandaging	617.93	RD113-.4	Baptisteries	726.4	NA4910
Bandonion music	788.84	M175.B2	Baptists	286.(1-5)	BX6201-6495
Bands (Music)	784.09	ML1300-1354	Baptists—Biography	286.1092	BX6493-6495
Bangladesh—Census	315.492	HA4590.6	Baptists—Catechisms	238.6(1-5)	BX6336
Bangladesh—Civilization	954.92	DS393.8	Baptists—Creeds	238.6	BX6335
Bangladesh—Civilization	934	DS393.8	Baptists—Dictionaries	286.(1-5)03	BX6211
Bangladesh—Economic conditions	330.95492	HC440.8	Baptists—Doctrines	230.6(1-5)	BX6330-6331.2
Bangladesh—Gazetteers	915.492003	DS393.3	Baptists—Education	268.86(1-5)	BX6219-6227
Bangladesh—Gazetteers	934.003	DS393.3	Baptists—Government	262.06(1-5)	BX6340-6346.3
Bangladesh—History	954.92	DS394.5-395.7	Baptists—History	286.(1-5)09	BX6231-6328
Bangladesh—History	934	DS394.5-395.7			
Bangladesh—History— Revolution, 1971	954.92051	DS395.5	Baptists—Liturgy	264.06(1-5)	BX6337
Bangladesh—Maps	912.5492	G2275-2279	Baptists—Sermons	252.06(1-5)	BX6333
Bangladesh—Maps	912.5492	G7645-7649	Baptists—Societies, etc.	286.(1-5)06	BX6205
Bangladesh—Politics and government	320.95492	JQ630-639	Baptists—Africa	286.(1-5)6	BX6320-6322
Banjo	787.8807	MT560-570	Baptists—Asia	286.(1-5)5	BX6315-6316
Banjo Music	787.88	M120-122	Baptists—Australia	286.(1-5)94	BX6325-6326
Bank accounts	332.1752	HG1660	Baptists—Canada	286.(1-5)71	BX6251-6253
Bank buildings	725.24	NA6240-6245	Baptists—Europe	286.(1-5)4	BX6275-6310
Bank capital	332.1	HG1616.C34	Baptists—Oceania	286.(1-5)9(5-6)	BX6327-6328
Bank credit cards	332.178	HG1643	Baptists—South America	286.(1-5)8	BX6271-6273
Bank deposits	332.1752	HG1660	Baptists—United States	286.(1-5)73	BX6235-6249
Bank investments	332.1754	HG1616.I5	Bar Mitzvah	296.4424	BM707.4
Bank loans	332.1753	HG1641-1643	Barbados	972.981	F2041
Bank mergers	332.16	HG1722	Barbados—Census	317.2981	HA865
Bank notes	332.4044	HG348-353.5	Barbados—Maps	912.72981	G5140-5144
Bank notes	332.40440973	HG607-610	Barbecue cookery	641.5784	TX840.B3
Bank reserves	332.1	HG1656	Barbering	646.724	TT950-979
Bank stocks	332.6722	HG1723	Barbershop quartets	783.14	M1580.4
Banking law	346.082	HG1725-1778	Barbershop quartets	783.14	M1594
Banking law	346.082	K1066-1088	Barbershop quartets	783.14	M1604
Banking law—Canada	346.71082	KE991-1026	Barbershop singing	783.14	M3516
Banking law—England	346.42082	KD1715-1737	Barbiturates	615.7821	RM325
Banking law—United States	346.73082	KF966-1032			

26

Subject Heading	Dewey	LC	Subject Heading	Dewey	LC
Barges	623.829	VM466.B3	Bear River Massacre, Idaho, 1863	979.60(1-2)	E83.863
Baritone music	788.975	M90-94	Beard	391.5	GT2320
Bark	581.47	QK648	Beard	616.546	RL91
Barley	633. 16	SB191.B2	Bearings (Machinery)	621.822	TJ1061-1073.7
Barnacles	595.35	QL444.C58	Bears	599.78	QL737.C27
Barns	728.922	NA8230	Beatitudes	226.93	BT382
Barometers	551.540284	QC886-887	Beauty culture	646.7042	TT950-979
Barracks	355.71	UC400-440	Beauty, Personal	391	GT49
Barrel racing	791.84	GV1834.45.B35	Bedrooms	747.77	NK2117.B4
Bartending	641.874	TX951	Beds (Gardens)	635	SB423.7-.75
Baryton music	787.6	M59	Bedsores	616.545	RL675
Basal cell carcinoma	616.99477	RC280.S5	Bee culture	638.1	SF521-539
Base measuring	526.3	QB303	Bee pollen	615.36	RM666.B375
Baseball	796.357	GV862-880.6	Bee pollen	638.16	SF539
Baseball cards	796.357075	GV875.3	Bee products	638.16	SF539
Baseball fields	976.357068	GV879.5	Beechcraft (Airplanes)	629.13334	TL686.B36
Baseball players	796.357092	GV865	Beecher Island, Battle of, 1868	978.802	E83.868
Baseball—Records	796.357	GV877	Beef	641.362	TX556.B4
Basements	643.5	TH3000.B36	Beef cattle	636.213	SF207
Bashfulness	155.232	BF575.B3	Beer	663.42	TP568-587
Basic education	370	LC1035-.8	Bees	595.799	QL563-569.4
Basket making	746.412	GN431	Beeswax	638.17	TP678
Basket making	746.412	TT879.B3	Beet sugar	664.123	TP390-391
Basketball	796.323	GV885	Beetles	595.76	QL571-597.2
Basketball players	796.323092	GV884	Begging	364.256	HV6174
Basketwork	746.412	NK3649.5-.55	Begonias	583.627	QK495.B4
Basque language	499.92	PH5001-5259	Begonias	635.933627	SB413.B4
Basque literature	899.92	PH5280-5490	Behavior disorders in children	618.92858	RJ506.B44
Basque philology	499.92	PH5001-5022	Behavior modification	153.85	BF637.B4
Bas-relief	731.54	NB1280-1291	Behavior modification	370.1528	LB1060.2
Bass clarinet music	788.65	M70-74	Behavior therapy	616.89142	RC489.B4
Bass fishing	799.1758	SH681	Behaviorism (Psychology)	150.1943	BF199
Bass guitar music	787.87	M125-129	Beheading	364.66	HV8552-8555
Bassoon	788.5807	ML953	Beijing (China)—History	951.156	DS795.23-.3
Bassoon music	788.58	M75-79	Bektashi	297.48	BP189.7.B4-.B42
Bastille Day	394.2635	DC167			
Bat Mitzvah	296.4434	BM707-.4	Belarus	947.8	DK507-.95
Bataan, Battle of, Philippines, 1942	940.5425991	D767.4	Belarus—Gazetteers	914.78003	DK507.18
Bathrooms	696.182	TH6485-6500	Belarus—History	947.8	DK507.37-.78
Bathrooms	747.78	NK2117.B33	Belfort, Battle of, 1871	944.0812	DC305.22
Baths	613.41	RA780	Belgian literature (French)	840	PQ3810-3858
Bathtubs	696.182	TH6493	Belgium	949.3	DH401-811
Batik	746.662	TT852.5	Belgium	936.4	DH401-811
Battle cruisers	359.3253	V820-.5	Belgium—Biography	920.0364	DH513-516
Battles	355.4	D25	Belgium—Biography	920.0493	DH513-516
Battleships	359.8352	V815-.5	Belgium—Census	314.93	HA1391-1410
Bayonets	356.118241	UD340-345	Belgium—Civilization	949.3	DH471
Bayonets	356.118241	UD400	Belgium—Civilization	936.4	DH471
Bazaars (Charities)	361.7	HV544	Belgium—Description and travel	913.6404	DH431-435
Beach volleyball	796.325	GV1015.5.B43	Belgium—Description and travel	914.9304	DH431-435
Beaches	796.53	GV454.B3	Belgium—Economic conditions	330.9493	HC311-320
Beacons	623.8944	VK1000-1249			
Beadwork	745.582	NK3650-.5			
Beadwork	745.582	TT860			
Bear hunting	799.2778	SK295			

Subject Heading	Dewey	LC	Subject Heading	Dewey	LC
Belgium—Emigration and immigration	325.(2493) or (493)	JV8160-8169	Beltways	388.122	HE336.E94
			Benediction	264.13	BV197.B5
Belgium—Gazetteers	913.64003	DH414	Benediction	264.13	BX2048.B5
Belgium—Gazetteers	914.93003	DH414	Beneficial birds	632.96	SB995-996
Belgium—History, Military	355.009493	DH540-545	Beneficial insects	638	SF517-562
Belgium—History, Naval	359.309493	DH551	Benelux countries	949.(2-3)	DH
Belgium—History—To 1555	949.30(1-2)	DH571-584	Benelux countries	912.492	G1850-1874
Belgium—History—To 1555	936.4	DH571-584	Benelux countries—Colonies	325.3492	JV2500-2899
Belgium—History—1555-1648	949.302	DH585-606	Benelux countries—Commerce	381.09492	HF3591-3620.5
Belgium—History—Charles V, 1506-1555	949.302	DH584	Benelux countries—Genealogy	929.10720492	CS780-839
Belgium—History—1648-1794	949.302	DH607-619	Bengali (South Asian people)	954.0049144	DS432.B4
Belgium—History—1794-1814	949.302	DH620-631	Bengali language	491.44	PK1651-1695
Belgium—History—Revolution, 1789-1790	949.302	DH616-618.5	Benin—Census	316.683	HA4722
			Benin—Civilization	966.83	DT541.4
Belgium—History—Revolution, 1830-1839	949.303	DH650-665	Benin—Description and travel	916.68304	DT541.27
Belgium—History—Leopold II, 1865-1909	949.303	DH671-676	Benin—History	966.83	DT541.5-.845
			Benin—History—To 1894	966.8301	DT541.65-.67
Belgium—History—Albert I, 1909-1934	949.3041	DH681-685	Benin—History—Coup d'etat, 1977	966.83051	DT541.845
Belgium—History—German occupation, 1914-1918	949.3041	DH682	Benin—Maps	912.6683	G8750-8754
			Bennington, Battle of, 1777	973.333	E241.B4
Belgium—History—German occupation, 1940-1945	949.3042	DH687	Benzene	547.611	QD341.H9
			Berber languages	493.3	PJ2340-2349
Belgium—History—Baudoiun I, 1951-	949.304(3-4)	DH690-692	Berber languages	493.3	PJ2369-2399
			Berber languages—Dictionaries	493.33	PJ2349
Belgium—Manufactures	670.9493	TS67-68	Berber languages—Etymology	493.32	PJ2347
Belgium—Maps	912.493	G6010-6014			
Belgium—Periodicals	949.3005	DH401	Berber languages—Grammar	493.35	PJ2345
Belgium—Periodicals	936.4005	DH401			
Belgium—Politics and government	320.9493	JN6101-6371	Berbers	961.004933	DT193.5.B45
			Berga (Germany: Concentration Camp)	940.531853	D805.G3
Belief and doubt	121.5	BD215			
Belief and doubt	121.6	BD215	Bergen-Belsen (Germany: Concentration camp)	940.5318535954	D805.G3
Belize	972.82	F1441-1457			
Belize—Census	317.282	HA791-800	Berlin (Germany)	943.155	DD851-900
Belize—Civilization	972.82	F1443.8	Berlin, Battle of, 1945	940.54213155	D757.9
Belize—Description and travel	917.28204	F1444-.3	Bermuda Islands	972.99	F1630-1640
			Bermuda Islands—Census	317.299	HA921-930
Belize—History	972.82	F1445.5-1448	Bermuda Islands—Civilization	972.99	F1633
Belize—Maps	912.7282	G4820-4824			
Belize—Periodicals	972.82005	F1441	Bermuda Islands—Description and travel	917.29904	F1631
Belize—Politics and government	320.97282	JL670-679			
			Bermuda Islands—Gazetteers	917.299003	F1630.7
Belladonna (Drug)	615.323952	RM666.B4			
Belladonna (Plant)	583.952	QK495.S7	Bermuda Islands—History	972.99	F1635-1637
Belleau Wood, Battle of, 1918	940.434	D545.B4	Bermuda Islands—Periodicals	972.99005	F1630
Bells	786.8848	CC200-255	Bermuda Islands—Politics and government	320.97299	JL590-599
Belmont (Mo.), Battle of, 1861	973.731	E472.28			
			Bernese mountain dog	636.73	SF429.B47
Belts and belting	621.852	TJ1100-1119	Berries	634.7	SB381-386

Subject Heading	Dewey	LC	Subject Heading	Dewey	LC
Bessarabia (Moldova and Ukraine)	947.(6-7)	DK509.1-.95	Bible—Chronology	220.9	BS637
Bessemer process	669.1423	TN736-738	Bible—Commentaries	220.7	BS482-498
Beta decay	539.7523	QC793.5.B425	Bible—Concordances	220.(4-5)	BS420-429
Betrothal	392.4	GN484.43	Bible—Criticism, interpretation, etc.	220.6	BS500-534.8
Betrothal	392.4	GT2650	Bible—Devotional use	242	BS617.8
Beverages	641.2	TX951	Bible—Evidences, authority, etc.	220.1	BS480
Beverages	641.87	TX815-817	Bible—Examinations, questions, etc.	220.076	BS612
Beverages	663	TP500-660	Bible—History	220.09	BS445-460
Bhagavatas	294.5924	BL1245.B5	Bible—History of Biblical events	220.9	BS635-636
Bhakti	294.5211	BL1214.32.B53	Bible—Inspiration	220.13	BS480
Bhutan—Census	315.498	HA4590.3	Bible—Language, style	220.(4-5)	BS537
Bhutan—Description and travel	915.49804	DS491.5	Bible—Parables	226.8	BS680.P3
Bhutan—Maps	912.5498	G7780-7784	Bible—Prayers	242.5	BS680.P64
Biak Island (Indonesia), Battle of, 1944	940.542598	D767.7	Bible—Prophecies	220.15	BS647-649
Biathlon	796.932	GV854.B5	Bible—Study and teaching	220.071	BS585-613
Bible	220	BS	Bible—Theology	230.041	BS543
Bible as literature	809.93522	BS535-537	Bible—Versions	220.4	BS450-460
Bible stories	220.9505	BS546-559	Bible—Versions	220.5	BS450-460
Bible. English	220.52	BS135-198	Biblical cosmology	231.765	BS651-652
Bible. N.T.	225-228	BS1901-2970	Bibliography	010	Z1001-9000
Bible. N.T. Acts	226.6	BS26S20-2628	Bibliography, National	015	Z1201-4980
Bible. N.T. Epistles	227	BS2630-2815.5	Bibliography, National—Africa	015.6	Z3501-3975
Bible. N.T. Gospels	226	BS2549	Bibliography, National—Armenia	015.4756	Z3461-3465
Bible. N.T. Pauline Epistles	227	BS2640-2815.5	Bibliography, National—Asia	015.5	Z3126-3415
Bible. N.T.—Commentaries	225.7	BS2333-2348	Bibliography, National—Asia, Southeastern	015.59	Z3221-3415
Bible. N.T.—Concordances	225.(4-5)	BS2301-2308	Bibliography, National—Asiatic Russia	015.47	Z3401-3409
Bible. N.T.—Criticism, interpretation, etc.	225.6	BS2350-2393	Bibliography, National—Australia	015.94	Z4001-4439
Bible. N.T.—History	225.09	BS2315-2318	Bibliography, National—Canada	015.71	Z1365-1401
Bible. N.T.—Study and teaching	225.071	BS2525-2544	Bibliography, National—Europe	015.4	Z2000-2959
Bible. N.T.—Theology	230	BS2397	Bibliography, National—Iran	015.55	Z3366-3370
Bible. N.T.—Versions	225.(4-5)	BS1901	Bibliography, National—Israel	015.5694	Z3476-3480
Bible. O.T. Apocrypha	229	BS1691-1830	Bibliography, National—Lebanon	015.5692	Z3466-3470
Bible. O.T. Greek	221.48	BS737-765	Bibliography, National—Mexico	015.72	Z1411-1431
Bible. O.T. Latin	221.47	BS767-815	Bibliography, National—Middle East	015.56	Z3013-3028
Bible. O.T. Pentateuch	222.1	BS1221-1285.5	Bibliography, National—South America	015.8	Z1601-1939
Bible. O.T. Psalms	223.2	BS1419-1450	Bibliography, National—Syria	015.5691	Z3481-3485
Bible. O.T. Song of Solomon	223.9	BS1481-1490	Bibliography, National—United States	015.73	Z1215-1363
Bible. O.T.—Biography	221.092	BS580			
Bible. O.T.—Commentaries	221.7	BS1143-1158			
Bible. O.T.—Concordances	221.(4-5)	BS1121-1128			
Bible. O.T.—Criticism, interpretation, etc.	221.6	BS1160-1191.5			
Bible. O.T.—Harmonies	221.65	BS1104			
Bible. O.T.—History	221.09	BS1130-1134			
Bible. O.T.—Study and teaching	221.071	BS1193-1195			
Bible. O.T.—Theology	230.0411	BS1192.5			
Bible. O.T.—Versions	221.(4-5)	BS701-1013			
Bible. Polyglot	220.51	BS1-3			
Bible—Abridgments	220.5	BS405-408			
Bible—Biography	220.092	BS570-580			

Subject Heading	Dewey	LC
Bibliography, National—West Indies	015.729	Z1501-1595
Bibliotherapy	615.8516	RC489.B48
Bicycle racing	796.62	GV1049
Bicycle touring	796.64	GV1044-1046
Bicycle trails	625.88	TE301
Bicycles	388.3472	HE5736-5739
Bicycles	629.2272	TL410-438
Bicycles	796.6(2-4)	GV1040-1058
Biela's comet	523.6	QB723.B5
Big band music	784.48	M1366
Big bang theory	523.18	QB991.B54
Big Bethel, Battle of, 1861	973.731	E472.14
Big Blue, Battle of the, Mo., 1864	973.737	E477.16
Big business	338.644	HD2350.8-2356
Big game fishing	799.12	SH457.5
Big game hunting	799.26	SK295-305
Big sagebrush	583.99	QK495.C74
Bile	573.38379	QP197
Bile acids	573.38379	QP752.B54
Bile ducts	573.38	QL867
Bile ducts	573.38	QM351
Bile ducts—Surgery	617.5567	RD546-547
Bill drafting	328.373	JF525
Billboards	659.1342	HF5843
Billiards	794.72	GV891
Bills of exchange	332.77	HG1689
Bills, Legislative—United States	348.7301	KF16-22
Bingo	795.3	GV1311.B5
Binoculars	681.4125	QC373.B55
Binomial theorem	512.9422	QA161.B5
Bioadhesive drug delivery systems	615.19	RS201.B54
Biochemical engineering	660.63	TP248.3
Biochemistry	572	QD415-436
Biochemistry	572	QH345
Biochemistry	572	QP501-801
Bioclimatology	577.22	QH543-.2
Bioethics	174.957	QH332
Biofertilizers	631.847	S654.5
Biogas	665.776	TP359.B48
Biogeochemistry	577.14	QH343.7-344
Biogeography	578.09	QH84-198
Biographical preaching	251	BV4235.B56
Biography	920	CT
Biography as a literary form	809.93592	CT21-22
Biography—To 500	920.00901	D55
Biography—Middle Ages, 500-1500	920.00902	D107-110.5
Biography—Middle Ages, 500-1500	920.00902	D115
Biography—20th century	920.00904	D1070-1075
Bioinorganic chemistry	572.51	QP531-535
Biological apparatus and supplies	570.284	QH324
Biological control systems	571.7	QH508
Biological diversity	333.95	QH541.15.B56
Biological diversity conservation	333.95	QH75-77
Biological invasions	577.18	QH353
Biological laboratories	570.72	QH321-323.2
Biological models	570.228	QH324.8
Biological pest control agents	632.96	SB975
Biological productivity	577.15	QH541.3
Biological rhythms	571.77	QH527
Biological rhythms	571.77	QP84.6
Biological rhythms in plants	571.772	QK761
Biological rhythms—Effect of space flight on	612	RC1151.B54
Biological transport	571.64	QH509
Biological warfare	358.38	UG447.8
Biological weapons—Soviet Union	358.38820947	UG447.8
Biologists	570.92	QH26-31
Biology	570	QH301-705
Biology—Data processing	570.285	QH324.2
Biology—History	570.9	QH305-.2
Biology—Philosophy	570.1	QH331
Biology—Research	570.72	QH315-320
Biology—Study and teaching	570.71	QH315-320
Bioluminescence	572.4358	QH641
Biomagnetism	154.72	QH504
Biomathematics	570.151	QH323.5
Biomechanics	571.43	QH513
Biomedical engineering	610.28	R856-857
Bionics	003.5	Q317-321
Bioorganic chemistry	572	QP550-801
Biophysics	571.4	QH505
Biosphere reserves	333.95	QH75-77
Biotechnology	660.6	TP248.13-.65
Bioterrorism	613.6	RC88.9.T47
Biplanes	629.133343	TL684.4
Bipolar transistors	621.381528	TK7871.96.B55
Bird attracting	639.978	QL676.5-.57
Bird dogs	636.752	SF428.5
Bird navigation	573.87	QL698.8
Bird pests	632.68	SB995
Bird refuges	333.958	QL676.5-.57
Bird trapping	799.258	SK319
Birdhouses	636.50831	QL676.5-.57
Birds	598	QL671-699
Birds, Protection of	333.95816	SK351-579
Birds—Flight	598.1479	QL698.7
Birds—Geographical distribution	598.09(4-9)	QL678-695.5
Birdsongs	598.1594	QL698.5
Birth control	304.666	HQ763-767.52
Birth control—Moral and ethical aspects	363.96	HQ766.2-.4
Birth customs	392.12	GN482.1

Subject Heading	Dewey	LC	Subject Heading	Dewey	LC
Birth customs	392.12	GT2460-2465	Blocks (City planning)	711.41	NA9053.B58
Birth weight, Low	618.9201	R281	Blood	612.11	QP91-99.5
Bisa language	496.391	PL8025	Blood banks	362.1784	RM172
Biscuits	641.815	TX770.B55	Blood circulation disorders	616.1	RB144-.5
Bisexuality	306.765	HQ74-.2	Blood coagulation disorders	616.157	RC647.C55
Bismarck Sea, Battle of the, 1943	940.5426	D774.B57	Blood coagulation factors	612.115	QP93.5-.7
			Blood coagulation factors	615.39	RM171.5
Bismuth ores	622.347	TN490.B6	Blood diseases in pregnancy	618.3261	RG580.H47
Bits (Bridles)	636.10837	SF309.9			
Bitumen	622.33	TN850	Blood groups	612.11825	QP98
Bitumen	625.85	TE210.5.B5	Blood plasma	612.116	QP99
Bituminous materials	625.85	TE221	Blood plasma substitutes	615.399	RM171.7
Bka'-rgyud-pa (Sect)	294.39	BQ7669	Blood platelet disorders	616.15	RC647.B5
Black death	616.9232	RC171-179	Blood platelets—Transfusion	615.39	RM177
Black Hand (United States)	364.10660973	HV6448			
Black Hawk War, 1832	977.303	E83.83	Blood pressure	612.14	QP105-.4
Black holes (Astronomy)	523.8875	QB843.B55	Blood products	615.39	RM171.4-.45
Black Muslims	297.87	BP221-223	Blood substitutes	615.399	RM171.7
Black Patch War, 1906-1909	976.9041	F456	Blood—Analysis	616.07561	RB45-15
			Blood—Coagulation	612.115	QP93.5-.7
Black Sea Coast	947.7	DJK61-66	Blood—Diseases	616.15	RC633-647.5
Black Sea Mutiny, 1919	947.0841	DK265.42.F8	Blood—Parasites	616.96	RC226-248
Black theology	230.08996	BT82.7	Blood—Transfusion	615.39	RM171-174
Blackberries	634.713	SB386.B6	Blood-vessels	573.18	QL835
Blackleg in cattle	636.208969	SF962	Blood-vessels	611.13	QM191
Blacks in medicine	610.8996073	R695	Blood-vessels—Diseases	616.13	RC691-701
Blacks in motion pictures	791.4308996 + 073	PN1995.9.N4	Blood-vessels—Diseases—Diagnosis	616.13075	RC691.5-.6
Blacks—Education	371.82996073	LC2699-2913	Blood-vessels—Surgery	617.413	RD598.5-.7
Bladder	573.49	QL872	Bloodborne infections	616.94	RA642.B56
Bladder	611.62	QM411	Blowpipe	542.4	QD87
Bladder—Diseases	616.62	RC919-921	Blue and white transfer ware	738.27	NK4277
Bladder—Diseases	616.62	RG484-485			
Bladder—Surgery	617.462059	RD580-581	Blue and white ware	738.27	NK4399.B58
Bladensburg, Battle of, 1814	973.523	E356.B5	Blue crab	595.386	QL444.M33
			Blue Licks, Battle of the, Ky., 1782	973.338	F454
Blasphemy	205.695	BV4627.B6			
Blast furnaces	669.0282	TN677-.5	Blueberries	634.737	SB386.B7
Blast furnaces	669.1413	TN713-718	Bluegrass music	784.164209	ML3519-3520
Blasting	622.23	TN279	Blueprinting	686.42	TR415
Blasting	624.1526	TA748	Blueprinting	686.42	TR921
Bleaching	667.14	TP894-895	Blueprints	604.25	T379
Blind	362.41	HV1571-2349	Blues (Music)	784.164309	ML3521
Blind aged	362.6	HV1597.5	Blunt trauma	617.1	RD96.15
Blind, Apparatus for the	362.418	HV1701	Board games	794	GV1312-1469
Blind, Music for the	780.87107	MT38	Boards of trade	381.06	HF294-343
Blind—[By region or country]	362.4109(4-9)	HV1783-2220.5	Boards of trade—History	381.0609	HF351-499
			Boat living	643.2	GV777.7
Blind—United States	362.410973	HV1783-1796	Boatbuilding	623.82	VM320-361
Blind—[Other regions or places]	362.4109(4-9)	HV1801-2220.5	Boats and boating	797.1	GV771-836.15
			Boats and boating—Electronic equipment	623.8504	VM325
Blind—Education	371.911	HV1618-1782			
Blind—Employment	331.1250871	HV1652-1658			
Blind-deaf—Services for	362.41	HV1597-.2	Boats, Prehistoric	623.821	GN799.B62
Blindness	617.712	RE91-95	Bobsledding	796.95	GV856
Blinds	690.182	TH2276	Bodhisattva stages (Mahayana Buddhism)	294.344	BQ4330
Block books	092	Z240-241.5			

Subject Heading	Dewey	LC	Subject Heading	Dewey	LC
Body fluids—Analysis	616.0756	RB52	Bolivia—History—Revolution, 1952	984.052	F3326
Body language	153.69	BF637.N66	Bolivia—History—Revolution, 1964	984.052	F3326
Body marking	391.65	GN419.15			
Body piercing	391.7	GN419.25	Bolivia—History—Coup d'etat, 1979	984.052	F3326
Body snatching	393	GT3353			
Body surface mapping	616.12075	RC683.5.B63	Bolivia—History—Coup d'etat, 1980	984.052	F3326
Body temperature	612.01426	QP135			
Body temperature	616.0754	RC75	Bolivia—History—1982-	984.052	F3327
Body, Human (Philosophy)	128	B105.B64	Bolivia—Manufactures	670.984	TS38-39
Body, Human—Microbiology	616.9041	QR46-48	Bolivia—Maps	912.84	G5320-5324
			Bolivia—Periodicals	984.005	F3301
Bodybuilding	613.713	GV546.5-.56	Bolivia—Politics and government	320.984	JL2200-2299
Bog ecology	577.687	QH541.5.B63			
Bogs	551.41	GB621-628	Bolivian literature	860	PQ7801-7820
Bohemia (Czech Republic)—History—To 1526	943.71023	DB2080-2133	Bolts and nuts	621.882	TJ1330-1333
			Bombing and gunnery ranges	355.5	U300-305
Bohemia (Czech Republic)—History—1526-1618	943.710232	DB2135-2151			
			Bombings	364.164	HV6640
			Bonaire	972.986	F2048
Bohemia (Czech Republic)—History—1618-1848	943.7102	DB2155-2162	Bonaire—Maps	912.72986	G5175-5179
			Bonapartism	321.030944	JC359
			Bond transfer	332.6323	HG4028.B6
Bohemia (Czech Republic)—History—1848-1918	943.71024	DB2165-2182	Bonds	332.6323	HG4651
			Bone carving	736.6	NK6020-6022
			Bone carving	745.58	TT288
Boiler-plates	621.194	TJ290-291	Bone diseases in children	618.9271	RJ482.B65
Boilers	697.07	TH7538	Bone marrow	611.41	QM569
Boilers	697.507	TH7588	Bone marrow—Transplantation	617.4410592	RD123.5
Boiling (Cookery)	641.73l	TX685			
Boiling water reactors	621.4834	TK9203.B6	Bone wiring (Orthopedics)	617.471	RD103.B65
Bok choy	583.64	QK495.C9	Bone-grafting	617.4710592	RD123
Bok choy	635.3	SB351.C53	Bone-meal	631.85	S659
Bolivia	984	F3301-3359	Bones	573.76	QL821
Bolivia—Census	318.4	HA961-970	Bones	611.71	QM101-117
Bolivia—Civilization	984	F3310	Bones—Diseases	616.71	RC930-931
Bolivia—Description and travel	918.404	F3311-3315	Bones—Surgery	617.471059	RD684
			Bonpo (Sect)	294.39	BQ7960-7989
Bolivia—Economic conditions	330.984	HC181-185	Bonpo incantations	294.343	BQ7982.4
			Bonsai	635.9772	SB433.5
Bolivia—Emigration and immigration	325.(284) or (84)	JV7450-7459	Bonus system	331.2164	HD4928.B6
			Book burning	323.445	Z657-659
Bolivia—Gazetteers	918.4003	F3304	Book clubs	070.5	Z549
Bolivia—History	984	F3320.3-3327	Book clubs	070.5	Z1008
Bolivia—History—To 1809	984.0(1-3)	F3322	Book collecting	026.1	Z987-997.2
Bolivia—History—Wars of Independence, 1809-1825	984.041	F3323	Book selection	025.21	Z689-.5
			Book thefts	025.82	Z702
Bolivia—History—1825-1879	984.04(2-5)	F3324	Bookbinders	686.30092	Z269-.3
			Bookbinding	686.3	Z266-276
Bolivia—History—1879-1938	984.0(45-51)	F3324-3325	Bookkeeping	657.2	HF5601-5689.8
			Books—Conservation and restoration	025.7	Z700.9-701.5
Bolivia—History—1938-	984.05(1-2)	F3326-3327			
Bolivia—History—1938-1982	984.05(1-2)	F3326	Books—Deacidification	025.84	Z701.3.D4
			Books and reading	028	Z1003-.5
Bolivia—History—Coup d'etat, 1943	984.051	F3326	Books of hours	242.802	BX2080
			Booksellers and bookselling	381.45002	Z278-550
Bolivia—History—Revolution, 1946	984.051	F3326	Boots	685.31	TS989-1025

Subject Heading	Dewey	LC	Subject Heading	Dewey	LC
Borax	338.27633	HD9585.B67-.B674	Botswana—Civilization	968.83	DT2452
Borax	622.3633	TN917	Botswana—Description and travel	968.8304	DT2448
Bordeaux Raid, 1942	940.54214	D772.B	Botswana—Gazetteers	916.883003	DT2434
Borderline personality disorder	616.85852	RC569.5.B67	Botswana—History	968.83	DT2464-2502
Bores (Tidal phenomena)	551.464	GC376	Botswana—History—To 1966	968.830(1-2)	DT2483-2493
Boring	622.24	TN281	Botswana—History—1966-	968.8303	DT2496-2502
Boring	628.114	TD412	Botswana—Maps	912.6883	G8600-8604
Boron	553.6	QD181.B1	Bottles	666.192	TP866
Boroughs	352.16	JS261	Bottling	663	TP866
Bosnia and Hercegovina	949.742	DR1652-1785	Bottom fishing	799.122	SH455.6
Bosnia and Hercegovina	939.8	DR1652-1785	Bougainvillea	583.53	QK495.N9
Bosnia and Hercegovina—History	949.742	DR1697-1785	Bougainvillea	635.93353	SB413.B65
Bosnia and Hercegovina—Maps	912.49742	G6860-6863	Bound states (Quantum mechanics)	530.12	QC174.17.B6
Boston (Mass.)	974.461	F73-.9	Boundaries	320.12	JC323
Boston Massacre, 1770	973.3113	E215.4	Boundary layer	532.051	QA913
Boston Tea Party, 1773	973.3115	E215.7	Boundary layer	629.13237	TL574.B6
Botanical chemistry	572.2	QK861-899	Boundary stones	320.12	CC600-605
Botanical gardens	580.73	QK71-73	Bow and arrow	355.8241	U877-878
Botanical pesticides	632.9	SB951.145.B68	Bow and arrow	623.441	GN498.B78
Botanists	580.92	QK26-31	Bowhead whale	599.5276	QL737.C423
Botany	580	QK	Bowhunting	799.215	SK36
Botany, Economic	338.1	SB107-109	Bowling	794.6	GV901-909
Botany, Medical	581.634	QK99	Bowling alleys	794.6	GV907
Botany—Anatomy	575	QK641-707	Boxing	796.83	GV1115-1137
Botany—Classification	580.12	QK91-97	Boy Scouts	369.43	HS3312-3316
Botany—Dictionaries	580.3	QK9	Boycotts	331.893	HD5461
Botany—Exhibitions	580.74	QK79-.5	Boys	369.42	HV877-878
Botany—Folklore	398.368	GR780	Boys	649.132	HQ775
Botany—Nomenclature	580.14	QK96	Boys—Prayer-books and devotions	242.82	BV283.B7
Botany—Pictorial works	580.222	QK98	Boys—Societies and clubs	369.42	HS3301-3325
Botany—Societies, etc.	580.6	QK1	Boys—Societies and clubs	369.42	HV878
Botany—Study and teaching	580.71	QK51-57	Boys as soldiers	355.3308351	UB418.B69
Botany—Terminology	580.14	QK10	Boy's clothing	646.40608341	TT603
Botany—Africa	580.96	QK381-424	Brackish water biology	578.77	QH95.9
Botany—Antarctica	580.9989	QK474.4	Braddock's Campaign, 1755	973.26	E199
Botany—Arctic regions	580.998	QK474-.3	Brahmanism	294.5	BL1100-1245
Botany—Asia	580.95	QK341-379	Brahmans	294.5	BL1241.46
Botany—Asia, Southeastern	580.959	QK360-368	Braids (Hairdressing)	646.7247	TT975
Botany—Australia	580.994	QK431-461	Brain	599.948	GN181-190.5
Botany—Canada	580.971	QK201-203	Brain	612.82	QP376-430
Botany—Central America	580.9728	QK215-222	Brain death	616.078	RA1063.3
Botany—Europe	580.94	QK281-339	Brain—Cancer	616.99481	RC280.B7
Botany—Mexico	580.972	QK211	Brain-damaged children	618.928043	RJ496.B7
Botany—Middle East	580.956	QK353	Brain—Degeneration	616.8	RC394.D35
Botany—South America	580.98	QK241-274	Brain—Diseases	616.8(1-4)	RC386-395
Botany—Turkey	581.9561	QK376	Brain—Surgery	617.481059	RD594-.15
Botany—United States	580.973	QK115-195	Brain—Tumors	616.99481	RD663
Botany—[United States, By state]	580.97(4-9)	QK145-195	Brainwashing	153.853	BF633
Botany—West Indies	580.9729	QK225-231	Brain—Wounds and injuries	617.481044	RD594-.15
Botswana—Census	316.883	HA4706	Braising (Cookery)	641.77	TX686
			Branding (Punishment)	364.67	HV8609

Subject Heading	Dewey	LC	Subject Heading	Dewey	LC
Brandy	663.53	TP599	Brazil—History—Contestado Insurrection, 1912-1916	981.05	F2537
Brandywine, Battle of, 1777	973.333	E241.B8	Brazil—History—Revolution, 1922	981.05	F2537
Brass	673.3	TS564-589	Brazil—History—Revolution, 1924-1925	981.05	F2537
Brass band music	784.9	M1200-1269	Brazil—History—1930-1945	981.061	F2538
Brass ensembles	785.9	M955-959			
Brass instrument music	788.9	M111	Brazil—History—Revolution, 1930	981.05	F2538
Brass instruments	788.907	MT418	Brazil—History—Uprising, 1935	981.061	F2538
Brazil	981	F2501-2656			
Brazil—Census	318.1	HA971-990	Brazil—History—Revolution, 1938	981.061	F2538
Brazil—Civilization	981	F2510	Brazil—History—1945-1954	981.061	F2538
Brazil—Description and travel	918.104	F2511-2517	Brazil—History—1954-1964	981.062	F2538.2-.22
Brazil—Economic conditions	330.981	HC186-190	Brazil—History—Revolution, 1964	981.063	F2538.2
Brazil—Emigration and immigration	325.(281) or (81)	JV7460-7469	Brazil—History—1964-1985	981.063	F2538.25-.27
Brazil—Gazetteers	918.1003	F2504	Brazil—History—1985-	981.064	F2538.3-.5
Brazil—History	981	F2520.3-2538.5	Brazil—Manufactures	670.981	TS41-42
Brazil—History—To 1822	981.0(1-33)	F2526-2534	Brazil—Maps	912.81	G5400-5404
Brazil—History—1500-1548	981.03(1-2)	F2526	Brazil—Periodicals	981.005	F2501
Brazil—History—1548-1580	981.032	F2528	Brazil—Politics and government	320.981	JL2400-2499
Brazil—History—1549-1762	981.032	F2528	Brazilian literature	869	PQ9500-9699
Brazil—History—French colony, 1555-1567	981.032	F2529	Brazing	745.56	TT267
Brazil—History—1580-1640	981.032	F2530	Bread	641.815	TX769-770
Brazil—History—Dutch Conquest, 1624-1654	981.032	F2532	Break dancing	793.3	GV1796.B74
Brazil—History—War of the Emboabas, 1707-1709	981.032	F2528	Break-even analysis	658.1554	HD47.25
			Breakfasts	641.52	TX733
Brazil—History—1763-1822	981.033	F2534	Breakwaters	627.24	TC333
Brazil—History—1822-	981.0(4-6)	F2535-2538.5	Breast	611.49	QM495
Brazil—History—United Kingdom, 1815-1822	981.033	F2534	Breast feeding	613.269	RJ216
			Breast—Diseases	618.19	RG491-499
Brazil—History—Empire, 1822-1889	981.04	F2536	Breathing exercises	613.192	RA782
Brazil—History—Declaration of Independence, 1822	981.033	F2536	Breeding	636.082	S494
			Bremsstrahlung	539.7222	QC484.3
Brazil—History—Revolution, 1842	981.04	F2536	Breton language	491.68	PB2800-2849
			Breton language—Grammar	491.685	PB2811-2847
Brazil—History—Canudos Campaign, 1893-1897	981.05	F2537	Breton language—Study and teaching	491.68071	PB2807
Brazil—History—Naval Revolt, 1893-1894	981.05	F2537	Breton literature	891.68	PB2856-2932
Brazil—History—Quebra Quilos' Revolt, 1874	981.04	F2536	Breviaries	264.024	BX2000-.68
			Breweries	663.3	TP569-587
Brazil—History—1889-1930	981.05	F2537	Brewing	663.3	TP568-587
			Bribery	364.1323	HV6301-6321
Brazil—History—Naval Revolt, 1910	981.05	F2537	Bribery—[By region or country]	364.132309(4-9)	HV6303-6321
			Bribery—United States	364.13230973	HV6306-6316
			Brick houses	728	NA7150
			Brick walls	690.12	TH2243

Subject Heading	Dewey	LC
Bricklaying	693.1	TH5501
Brickmaking	666.737	TP826-833
Bricks	666.737	TP826-833
Bricks	691.4	TA432-433
Bridal price	392.4	GN480.1
Bridge whist	795.415	GV1281
Bridges	388.132	HE374-377
Bridges	624.2	TG
Bridges (Dentistry)	617.692	RK666
Bridges, Arched	624.225	TG327-340
Bridges, Brick	624.225	TG330
Bridges, Cantilever	624.219	TG385
Bridges, Concrete	624.22	TG335-340
Bridges, Continuous	624.21	TG413-416
Bridges, Stone	624.225	TG330
Bridges, Truss	624.217	TG375-380
Bridges, Wooden	624.218	TG365
Bridges, Wooden	624.218	TG375
Bridges—Abutments	624.28	TG325
Bridges—[By region or country]	624.209(4-9)	TG21-127
Bridges—Congresses	624.206	TG5
Bridges—Design and construction	624.25	TG300-304
Bridges—Floors	624.283	TG325.6
Bridges—Foundations and piers	624.284	TG320
Bridges—History	624.209	TG15-20
Bridges—Maintenance and repair	624.20288	TG315
Bridges—Periodicals	624.205	TG1-4
Bridles	636.10837	SF309.9
pnumBrief psychotherapy	616.8914	RC480.55
Brigands and robbers	364.1552	HV6441-6453
Bright's disease	616.612	RC907
Briquets (Fuel)	662.65	TP323
British Columbia—Gazetteers	917.11003	F1086.4
British Columbia—History	971.1	F1086-1089.7
British Columbia—Maps	912.711	G3510-3514
British Columbia—Periodicals	971.1005	F1086
British literature	820	PN849.G
British Virgin Islands	972.9725	F2129
British Virgin Islands—Maps	912.729725	G5020-5024
Brittany spaniel	636.7524	SF429.B78
Brittleness	620.1126	TA418.16
Broad jump	796.432	GV1077
Broadband amplifiers	621.381535	TK7871.58.B74
Broadcasting	384.54	PN1990-1992.92
Broad-banded copperhead	597.96	QL666.069
Brody (Ukraine), Battle of, 1944	940.542177	D764.3.B73
Broiling	641.76	TX687
Brokers	381.2092	HF5419-5422
Bromides	632.95	SB952.B7
Bronchi—Diseases	616.23	RC778
Bronchitis	616.234	RC778
Bronze	673.3	TS570
Bronze age	930.15	GN777-778
Bronze sculpture	731.456	NB135-143
Brook trout	597.554	QL638.S2
Brooms and brushes	679.6	TS2301.B8
Brotherhoods	267	BV950-1220
Brown algae	579.88	QK569.P5
Brown bear	599.784	QL737.C27
Brownian movements	530.475	QC183
Brunei—Civilization	959.55	DS650.4
Brunei—Description and travel	915.95504	DS650.35
Brunei—Gazetteers	915.955003	DS650.2
Brunei—History	959.55	DS650.44-.83
Brush drawing	741.26	ND2460
Brushes, Carbon	621.316	TK2484
Brushwork	751.4	ND1505
Brussels (Belgium)	949.332	DH802-809.95
Bryophytes	588	QK532.4-563.87
Brythonic languages	491.6	PB
Brythonic languages	491.6	PB2001-2060
Brythonic languages—Etymology	491.6(2-8)2	PB2021
Brythonic languages—Grammar	491.6(2-8)5	PB2009-2015
Brythonic languages—Lexicography	491.6(2-8)3028	PB2023
Brythonic languages—Study and teaching	491.6(2-8)071	PB2005
Brzeziny, Battle of, 1914	940.422	D552.B7
Buccaneers	910.45092	F2161
Buccaneers	910.45092	G535-537
Buchenwald (Germany: Concentration camp)	940.5318532241	D805.G3
Buckling (Mechanics)	620.112	TA410
Buckling (Mechanics)	624.252	TG265
Buckshot War, Harrisburg, Pa., 1838	974.803	F153
Budapest (Hungary)	943.912	DB981-999
Buddha (The concept)	294.363	BQ4180
Buddhas	294.363	BQ4670-4690
Buddhism	294.3	BQ
Buddhism	294.3	BQ1-9999
Buddhism	294.3923	BQ7530-7950
Buddhism—Apologetic works	294.342	BQ4050
Buddhism—Catechisms	294.32	BQ4170
Buddhism—Charities	294.3378	BQ5851-5899
Buddhism—Creeds	294.32	BQ4170
Buddhism—Customs and practices	294.344	BQ4965-5030
Buddhism—Doctrines	294.342	BQ4061-4570
Buddhism—Doctrines	294.342	BQ5485-5530

Subject Heading	Dewey	LC
Buddhism—Doctrines—History	294.34209	BQ4080-4125
Buddhism—History	294.309	BQ251-799
Buddhism—History—To ca. 100 A.D.	294.30901	BQ287-296
Buddhism—Liturgical objects	294.3437	BQ5070-5075
Buddhism—Missions	294.372	BQ5901-5975
Buddhism—Periodicals	294.305	BQ1-10
Buddhism—Prayer-books and devotions	294.34433	BQ5535-5594
Buddhism—Psychology	294.3375	BQ4570.P76
Buddhism—Relations	294.3372	BQ4600-4610
Buddhism—Rituals	294.3438	BQ4965-5030
Buddhism—Sacred books	294.382	BQ1100-3340
Buddhism—Societies, etc.	294.365	BQ12-93
Buddhism—Africa	294.3096	BQ710-719
Buddhism—America	294.309(7-8)	BQ720-760
Buddhism—Asia, Central	294.30958	BQ570-609
Buddhism—Burma	294.3309591	BQ416-439
Buddhism—Canada	294.30971	BQ740-749
Buddhism—China	294.30951	BQ620-649
Buddhism—East Asia	294.3095	BQ610-699
Buddhism—Europe	294.3094	BQ700-709
Buddhism—India	294.30954	BQ330-349
Buddhism—Indonesia	294.309598	BQ510-539
Buddhism—Japan	294.30952	BQ670-699
Buddhism—Korea	294.309519	BQ650-669
Buddhism—Malaysia	294.309595	BQ540-549
Buddhism—Nepal	294.3095496	BQ380-396
Buddhism—[New Zealand/Australia/Oceania]	294.3099(3-6)	BQ770-799
Buddhism—Sri Lanka	294.3095493	BQ350-379
Buddhism—Thailand	294.309593	BQ550-568
Buddhism—United States	294.30973	BQ730-739
Buddhism and social problems	294.33783	BQ5851-5899
Buddhist astrology	133.59443	BF1714.B7
Buddhist education	294.375	BQ141-209
Buddhist education of children	294.375	BQ171-199
Buddhist ethics	294.35	BJ1289
Buddhist pilgrims and pilgrimages	294.34351	BQ6400-6495
Buddhist precepts	294.342	BQ5485-5530
Buddhist sects	294.39	BQ8000-9800
Buddhist shrines	294.3435	BQ6300-6388
Buddhists—Biography	294.3092	BQ840-845
Budding (Plant propagation)	631.53	SB123.65
Budget	352.48	HJ2005-2216
Budget—Law and legislation—England	343.42034	KD5292
Budget—Law and legislation—United States	343.73034	KF6221-6227
Buffalo meat	641.36292	TX556.B8
Buffaloes	599.642	QL737.U5
Building	690	TH
Building fittings	696-697	TH6010-6013
Building management	647	TX955
Building materials	620.1(2-9)	TA401-492
Building stones	691.2	TA426-428
Building, Adobe	721.04422	NA4145.A35
Building, Bombproof	693.854	TH1097
Building, Brick	693.21	TH1301
Building, Fireproof	693.82	TH1061-1093
Building, Ice and snow	693.91	TH1431
Building, Iron and steel	624.182	TA684-695
Building, Iron and steel	693.71	TH1610-1635
Building, Stone	693.1	TH1201
Building—[By region or country]	690.09(4-9)	TH21-127
Building—United States	690.0973	TH23-25
Building—Accidents	690.22	TH443
Building—Congresses	690.06	TH5
Building—Details	690.1	TH2025-3000
Building—Directories	690.025	TH12-13
Building—Equipment and supplies	690.0284	TH915
Building—Estimates	692.5	TH434-437
Building—History	690.09	TH15-19
Building—Periodicals	690.05	TH1-4
Building—Study and teaching	690.071	TH165-213
Buildings, Prefabricated	693.97	TH1098
Buildings, Prefabricated	721.04497	NA8480
Buildings—Additions	690.24	TH4816.2
Buildings—Earthquake effects	693.852	TH1095
Buildings—Environmental engineering	697	TH6014-6085
Buildings—Joints	690.1	TH2060
Buildings—Maintenance	690.24	TH3351-3361
Buildings—Remodeling for other use	690.24	TH3401-3411
Buildings—Repair and reconstruction	690.24	TH3401-3411
Buildings—Specifications	692.3	TH425
Bulgaria	949.9	DR
Bulgaria	949.9	DR51-98
Bulgaria	939.8	DR51-98
Bulgaria—Biography	920.0398	DR66
Bulgaria—Biography	920.0499	DR66
Bulgaria—Census	314.99	HA1621-1630
Bulgaria—Civilization	949.9	DR63
Bulgaria—Civilization	939.8	DR63
Bulgaria—Description and travel	913.9804	DR57-61
Bulgaria—Description and travel	914.9904	DR57-61
Bulgaria—Directories	949.90025	DR53.7
Bulgaria—Economic conditions	330.9499	HC403
Bulgaria—Gazetteers	913.98003	DR53
Bulgaria—Gazetteers	914.99003	DR53

Subject Heading	Dewey	LC	Subject Heading	Dewey	LC
Bulgaria—Historiography	949.90072	DR66.7-.97	Burkina Faso—Maps	912.6625	G8805-8809
Bulgaria—Historiography	939.80072	DR66.7-.97	Burlesques	792.7	PN6231.B84
Bulgaria—History	949.9	DR65-93.34	Burma—Census	315.91	HA4570.7
Bulgaria—History	939.8	DR65-93.34	Burma—Civilization	959.1	DS527.9
Bulgaria—History—To 681	949.9013	DR74.3	Burma—Description and travel	915.9104	DS527.5-.7
Bulgaria—History—To 681	939.8	DR74.3	Burma—Economic conditions	330.9591	HC422
Bulgaria—History—681-1018	949.9013	DR74.5	Burma—History—To 1824	959.102	DS527.2-.3
Bulgaria—History—1018-1185	949.9014	DR79	Burma—History—1824-1948	959.10(2-4)	DS529.7-530.32
Bulgaria—History—1393-1878	949.9015	DR82-.5	Burma—History—Peasant Uprising, 1931	959.104	DS530
Bulgaria—History—1878-1944	949.902	DR84.9-.8	Burma—History—Japanese occupation, 1942-1945	959.104	DS530
Bulgaria—History—1944-	949.90(2-3)	DR89.9-93.34	Burma—History—1948-	959.105	DS530.4
Bulgaria—History, Military	355.009499	DR70	Burma—Maps	912.591	G2285-2289
Bulgaria—Maps	912.499	G2040-2044	Burma—Maps	912.591	G7720-7724
Bulgaria—Maps	912.499	G6890-6894	Burma—Politics and government	320.9595	JQ751
Bulgaria—Periodicals	949.9005	DR51	Burmese language	495.8	PL3921-3969
Bulgaria—Periodicals	939.8005	DR51	Burmese literature	895.8	PL3970-3988
Bulgarian language	491.81	PG801-993	Burn care teams	617.11	RD96.4-.55
Bulgarian language—Dictionaries	491.813	PG975-984	Burn out (Psychology)	158.723	BF481
Bulgarian language—Grammar	491.815	PG831-925	Burns and scalds	617.11	RD96.4-.55
Bulgarian literature	891.8109	PG1000-1146	Burr Conspiracy, 1805-1807	973.48	E334
Bulgarian philology	491.81	PG801-823	Bursitis	616.76	RC935.B8
Bulimia	616.85263	RC552.B84	Burundi—Census	316.7572	HA4696
Bulk carrier cargo ships	623.8245	VM393.B7	Burundi—Civilization	967.572	DT450.63
Bull Run, 1st Battle of, Va., 1861	973.731	E472.18	Burundi—Description and travel	916.757204	DT450.6
Bull Run, 2nd Battle of, Va., 1862	973.732	E473.77	Burundi—Economic conditions	330.967572	HC880
Bullfights	791.82	GV1107-1108.6	Burundi—Gazetteers	916.7572003	DT450.515
Bullmastiff	636.73	SF429.B86	Burundi—History	967.572	DT450.66-.855
Bumblebees	595.799	QL568.A6	Burundi—Maps	912.67572	G8435-8439
Bungee jumping	797.5	GV770.27	Bus drivers	629.22233092	TL232.3
Bunker Hill, Battle of, 1775	973.3312	E241.B9	Bus lanes	388.12	HE336.B8
Bunkers (Fortification)	623.1	UG405.15	Bus lines	388.322	HE5601-5725
Buoys	623.8944	VK1000-1246	Bus stops	388.33	HE5620.B87
Buoys—[By region or country]	623.8944	VK1150-1246	Business	338.7	HF5001-6182.2
Burglar alarms	643.16	TH9739	Business—Forms	651.29	HF5371
Burglary	364.162	HV6646-6665	Business cards	741.685	NE965-.3
Burglary protection	643.16	TH9701-9745	Business communication	651.7	HF5717-5734.7
Burial	393.1	GN486	Business consultants	658.46	HD69.C6
Burial	393.1	GT3150-3390.5	Business cycles	338.542	HB3711-3840
Burial	614.6	RA625-630	Business cycles—[By region or country]	338.54209(4-9)	HB3741-3840
Burkina Faso—Census	316.625	HA4728	Business education	650.071	HF1101-1186
Burkina Faso—Civilization	966.25	DT555.4	Business education—[By region or country]	650.0710 (4-9)	HF1131-1186
Burkina Faso—Description and travel	916.62504	DT555.27	Business education—Africa	650.07106	HF1176
Burkina Faso—Gazetteers	916.625003	DT555.15	Business education—Asia	650.07105	HF1171
Burkina Faso—History	966.25	DT555.52-.83	Business education—Australia	650.071094	HF1181-1182
Burkina Faso—History—Coup d'etat, 1987	966.25053	DT555.8			

Subject Heading	Dewey	LC	Subject Heading	Dewey	LC
Business education—Europe	650.07104	HF1140-1165	Byzantine Empire—History—Justinian I, 527-565	949.5013	DF572-.8
Business education—Latin America	650.07108	HF1135	Byzantine Empire—History—Justine II, 565-578	949.5013	DF573
Business education—United States	650.071073	HF1131-1134	Byzantine Empire—History—Tiberius II, 578-582	949.5013	DF573.2
Business enterprises—Finance	338.6041	HG4001-4285	Byzantine Empire—History—Maurice, 582-602	949.5013	DF573.5
Business ethics	174.4	HF5387	Byzantine Empire—History—Heraclius, 610-641	949.5013	DF574
Business etiquette	395.52	HF5389			
Business failures	332.75	HG3760-3769	Byzantine Empire—History—Constans II, 641-668	949.5013	DF575.3
Business forecasting	338.544	HD30.27			
Business intelligence	658.47	HD38.7	Byzantine Empire—History—Leo III the Isaurian, 717-741	949.502	DF582
Business law	346.07	K1010-1014			
Business law—United States	346.7307	KF1970-2105	Byzantine Empire—History—Constantine V Copronymus, 741-775	949.502	DF583
Business libraries	027.69	Z675.B8			
Business logistics	658.5	HD38.5	Byzantine Empire—History—Irene, 797-802	949.502	DF586
Business mathematics	650.01513	HF5691-5716			
Business meetings	658.456	HF5734.5	Byzantine Empire—History—Basil I, 867-886	949.502	DF589
Business names—England	346.42048	KD1450			
Business relocation	338.7	HC79.D5	Byzantine Empire—History—Leo VI, 886-911	949.502	DF592
Business report writing	651.74	HF5719			
Business writing	651.74	HF5718.3-5734	Byzantine Empire—History—Romanus II, 959-963	949.502	DF594
Busing for school integration	379.263	LC214.5-.53			
Busts	731.74	NB1300	Byzantine Empire—History—1081-1453	949.50(3-4)	DF604-649
Butter	637.2	SF263-269.5			
Butterflies	595.789	QL541-562.4	Byzantine Empire—History—Alexius I Comnenus, 1081-1118	949.503	DF605
Butterfly gardens	638.5789	QL544.6			
Buzzards	598.94	QL696.F3	Byzantine Empire—History—John II Comnenus, 1118-1143	949.503	DF606
Byzantine drama	882.208	PA5190-5194			
Byzantine drama	882.209	PA5160-5163	Byzantine Empire—History—Manuel I Comnenus, 1143-1180	949.503	DF607
Byzantine Empire	949.50(13-3)	DF501-649			
Byzantine Empire—Biography	920.0495	DF506-.5	Byzantine Empire—History—Lascarid dynasty, 1208-1259	949.504	DF625
Byzantine Empire—Congresses	949.50(13-3)006	DF501.5			
Byzantine Empire—Geography	914.95	DF518	Byzantine Empire—History—John V Palaeologus, 1341-1391	949.504	DF638
Byzantine Empire—Historiography	949.50 (13-3) + 0072	DF505-.7	Byzantine Empire—History, Military	355.009495	DF543
Byzantine Empire—History	949.50(13-3)	DF550-649	Byzantine Empire—History, Naval	359.309495	DF544
Byzantine Empire—History—To 527	949.5013	DF553.5-568	Byzantine Empire—Periodicals	949.50(13-3)005	DF501
Byzantine Empire—History—Arcadius, 395-408	949.5013	DF561	Byzantine Empire—Politics and government	320.9495	JC91-93
Byzantine Empire—History—Theodosius II, 408-450	949.5013	DF562			
Byzantine Empire—History—Leo I, 457-474	949.5013	DF564			
Byzantine Empire—History—Leo II, 474	949.5013	DF565			
Byzantine Empire—History—Zeno, 474-491	949.5013	DF566			

Subject Heading	Dewey	LC	Subject Heading	Dewey	LC
Byzantine Empire—Study and teaching	949.50 (13-3) + 0071	DF505.8-.82	Calisthenics	613.714	GV481-510
Byzantine literature	880.8002	PA5170-5198	Calligraphy	745.61	NK3600-3640
Byzantine literature	880.9002	PA5101-5167	Calligraphy	745.61	Z43-45
Byzantine poetry	881.208	PA5180-5189	Calorimeters	536.6	QC290-297
Byzantine poetry	881.209	PA5150-5155	Calvinism	284.2	BX9401-9640
Byzantine prose literature	888.08	PA165	Calvinism—Periodicals	284.205	BX9401
Byzantine prose literature	888.08	PA5195-5196	Calvinistic Methodists	287	BX8901-9225
Cab and omnibus service	388.413214	HE5601-5725	Cambodia—Census	315.96	HA4600.3
Cabala	135.47	BF1585-1623	Cambodia—Civilization	959.6	DS554.42
Cabala	296.16	BM525	Cambodia—Description and travel	915.9604	DS554.34-.382
Cabinet officers	352.240973	JK610-616	Cambodia—Economic conditions	330.9596	HC442
Cabinet system	352.24	JF331-341	Cambodia—Gazetteers	915.96003	DS554.25
Cabinetwork	684.16	TT197	Cambodia—History	959.6	DS554.5-.842
Cables, Submarine	384.1	TK5601-5681	Cambodia—History—To 800	959.601	DS554.6-.64
Cables, Submarine	384.1	HE7709-7741	Cambodia—History— 800-1444	959.602	DS554.6-.64
Cabooses (Railroads)	625.22	TF485	Cambodia—History— 1444-1863	959.603	DS554.6-.64
Cacao	633.74	SB267	Cambodia—History— 1863-1953	959.60(3-41)	DS554.7-.73
Cache memory	621.397	TK7895.M4	Cambodia—History— 1953-1975	959.604(1-2)	DS554.8-.83
Cactus	634.775	SB317.C2	Cambodia—History—Civil War, 1970-1975	959.6042	DS554.84
Cactus	635.93356	SB438-.34	Cambodia—History— 1975-	959.6042	DS554.84-.842
Cafeteria benefit plans	331.255	HD4928.N6	Cambodia—Maps	912.596	G2374.3-.34
Caffeine habit	362.299	RC567.5	Cambodia—Maps	912.596	G8010-8014
Cage birds	636.68	SF461	Cambodia—Politics and government	320.9596	JQ930-939
Cairn terriers	636.755	SF429.C3	Camcorders	384.558	TR882.3
Cake	641.8653	TX771-.2	Camels	599.6362	QL737.U54
Cake decorating	641.86539	TX771.2	Camels	636.295	SF401.C2
Calais, Battle of, 1940	940.542142	D756.5.C	Cameos	736.222	NK5720-5722
Calcification	572.516	RB138	Cameras	771.3	TR250-265
Calcium	572.516	QP535.C2	Cameroon—Census	316.711	HA4719
Calcium in the body	572.516	QP535.C2	Cameroon—Civilization	967.11	DT569.5
Calculators	510.284	QA75	Cameroon—Description and travel	916.71104	DT566-568
Calculators	681.145	HF5688-5689	Cameroon—Economic conditions	330.96711	HC995
Calculus	515	QA303-316	Cameroon—Gazetteers	916.711003	DT563
Calculus of variations	515.64	QA315-316	Cameroon—History	967.11	DT572-578.4
Calendar, Assyro-Babylonian	529.0935	CE33	Cameroon—History—Coup d'etat, 1984	967.1102	DT578
Calendar, Islamic	529.327	CE59	Cameroon—Maps	912.6711	G8730-8734
Calendar, Jewish	529.326	CE35	Camouflage (Military science)	355.41	UG449
Calendar, Julian	529.42	CE75	Camouflage (Military science)	359.41	V215
Calendar, Roman	529.309376	CE46	Camp sites, facilities, etc.	796.54	GV198.L3
Calendars	529.3	CE73	Campaign funds	324.780973	JK1991-.5
Calico cats	636.8	SF449.C34	Campaign insignia	737.223	CJ5806
California	979.4	F856-870	Campaign literature	324.70973	JK2251-2391
California, Southern	979.49	F867			
California—Gazetteers	917.94003	F859			
California—History—To 1846	979.40(1-3)	F864			
California—History— 1846-1850	979.40(3-4)	F865			
California—History— 1850-1950	979.40(4-53)	F866			
California—History—1950-	979.405(3-4)	F866.2-.4			
California—Maps	912.794	G4360-4364			
California—National Guard	355.3709794	UA90-99			
California—Periodicals	979.4005	F856			
Caliphs	953.80099	DS234-238			

Subject Heading	Dewey	LC	Subject Heading	Dewey	LC
Camping	796.54	GV191.68-198.9	Canada—Maps	912.71	G3400-3612
Camp-meetings	269.24	BV3798-3799	Canada—Periodicals	971.005	F1001
Camp-meetings	269.24	BX8475-8476	Canada—Politics and government	320.971	JL
Camps	796.54	GV192-198	Canada—Politics and government	320.971	JL1-500
Camps for the handicapped	796.542087	GV197.H3	Canada—Politics and government—To 1763	320.971090 + (1-33)	JL41-45
Campus parking	371.61	LB3253	Canada—Politics and government—1763-1791	320.97109033	JL48
Campus police	363.289	HV8290-8291	Canada—Politics and government—1791-1841	320.9710903 + (3-4)	JL53
Canaanites	933.004926	DS121.4	Canada—Politics and government—1841-1867	320.97109034	JL55
Canaanites	956.004926	DS121.4	Canada—Politics and government—1867-	320.971090 + (34-511)	JL65
Canada	971	F1001-1040	Canadian football	796.33	GV948
Canada. Parliament	342.7105	KE4533-4665	Canadian Invasion, 1775-1776	973.33(1-2)	E231
Canada. Parliament	354.7299	JL131-179	Canadian periodicals	051	PN4901-4920
Canada—Armed forces—Supplies and stores	355.80971	UC90-93	Canal-boats	623.829	TC765
Canada—Biography	920.071	CT280-310	Canals	386.4	HE526
Canada—Census	317.1	HA741-750	Canals	627.13	TC601-791
Canada—Civilization	971	F1021-.2	Canals, Interoceanic	386.42	HE528-545
Canada—Climate	551.6971	QC985-.5	Canals, Interoceanic	627.1	TC601-791
Canada—Commerce	381.0971	HF3221-3230	Canals—Lifts	627.1353	TC763
Canada—Constitutional law	342.71	KE4125-4775	Canals—Steam-navigation	623.89229	TC769
Canada—Description and travel	917.104	F1012-1017	Canaries	636.68625	SF463-.7
Canada—Economic conditions	330.971	HC111-120	Canary Islands—Census	316.49	HA2287
Canada—Emigration and immigration	325.(271) or (71)	JV7200-7299	Canary Islands—Maps	912.649	G9150-9154
Canada—Foreign relations—Law and legislation	342.710412	KE4310	Cancer	616.994	RC261-282
			Cancer (Astrology)	133.5265	BF1727.3
Canada—Gazetteers	917.1003	F1004	Cancer—Etiology	616.994071	RC268.48
Canada—Genealogy	929.1072071	CS80-90	Cancer—Genetic aspects	616.994042	RC268.4-.44
Canada—History, Military	355.00971	F1028	Cancer—Homeopathic treatment	616.99406	RX261.C3
Canada—History, Naval	359.30971	F1028.5	Cancer—Hormone therapy	616.99406	RC271.H55
Canada—History—To 1763 (New France)	971.01	F1030-.9	Cancer—Immunotherapy	616.99406	RC271.I45
Canada—History—1755-1763	971.0188	F1030.9	Cancer—Nursing	616.9940231	RC266
Canada—History—1763-1867	971.02(2-49)	F1032	Cancer—Prevention	616.99405	RC268-.15
Canada—History—1763-1791	971.02	F1031	Cancer—Radiotherapy	616.9940642	RC271.R3
Canada—History—1775-1783	971.024	F1032	Cancer—Research	616.9940072	RC267
Canada—History—1791-1841	971.03	F1032	Cancer—Surgery	616.994059	RD651-678
Canada—History—Rebellion, 1837-1838	971.038	F1032	Cancer—Treatment	616.99406	RC270.8-271
Canada—History—1841-1867	971.04(2-8)	F1032	Candles	665.1	TP993
			Candlesticks	745.5933	NK3685
Canada—History—Fenian Invasions, 1866-1870	971.049	F1033	Candlewicking (Embroidery)	746.44	TT778.C24
Canada—History—Confederation, 1867	971.05	F1033	Candy	641.853	TX783-793
			Cannabis	615.7827	RM666.C266
Canada—History—1914-1945	971.06(12-32)	F1034	Cannabis	616.8635	RC568.C2
			Canned foods	641.612	TX552
Canada—History—1945-	971.0(632-7)	F1034.2-.3	Cannibalism in animals	591.53	QL756.57
Canada—Manufactures	670.971	TS26-27	Canning and preserving	641.4	TX599-612
Canada—Maps	912.71	G1115-1193	Canoe racing	797.14	GV786
			Canoes and canoeing	386.229	GN440.2
			Canoes and canoeing	797.122	GV781-785

Subject Heading	Dewey	LC	Subject Heading	Dewey	LC
Canon law—Early church, ca. 30-600	262.90901	BV761	Carcinogens	616.994071	RC268.6-.7
Canonization	235.24	BX576	Card games	795.4	GV1232-1299
Canonization	235.24	BX2330	Card system in business	651.53	HF5735-5746
Cantatas, Sacred	782.24	M2020-2036	Card tricks	793.85	GV1549
Cantatas, Secular	782.48	M1530-1546.5	Cardiac arrest	616.123025	RC685.C173
Cantatas, Secular (Unison)	782.5	M1609	Cardiac catheterization	617.412	RD598.35.C35
Canteens (Establishments)	355.341	UC750-755	Cardiac intensive care	616.12028	RC684.C36
Cantonese dialects	495.1727	PL1731-1740	Cardiac pacemakers	617.4120645	RC684.P3
Cantors (Judaism)	296.462	BM658.2	Cardiac pacing	617.4120645	RC684.P3
Canvas embroidery	746.442	TT778.C3	Cardinal virtues	241.4	BV4645
Canvassing	381	HF5446-5456	Cardinals	262.17092	BX4663-4665
Cape Verde—Census	316.658	HA2289	Cardinals (Birds)	598.883	QL696.P2438
Cape Verde—Civilization	966.58	DT671.C23	Carding	676.02821	TS1485-1487
Cape Verde—Description and travel	916.65804	DT671.C22	Cardiogenic shock	616.12	RC685.C18
Cape Verde—History	966.58	DT671.C25-.C28	Cardiologists	616.10092	RC666.7-.72
Cape Verde—History—To 1975	966.580(1-2)	DT671.C265	Cardiomyoplasty	617.412	RD598.35.C37
Cape Verde—History—1975-	966.5803	DT671.C28	Cardiotonic agents	615.71	RM349
			Cardiovascular agents	615.71	RM345-349
Cape Verde—Maps	912.6658	G9160-9164	Cardiovascular pharmacology	615.71	RM345-349
Capillaries	573.187	QP106.6	Cardiovascular system	573.1	QL835-841
Capital	332.041	HB501	Cardiovascular system	611.1	QM178-197
Capital	332.041	HC79.C3	Cardiovascular system—Abnormalities	616.1043	RC701
Capital	658.152	HD39-40.7	Cardiovascular system—Diagnosis	616.1075	RC670-.5
[Other countries]—Capital and capitol	725.1109(4-9)	NA4415	Cardiovascular system—Diseases	616.1	RC666-701
Capital gains tax	336.2424	HJ4639	Cardiovascular system—Diseases—Eclectic treatment	616.106	RV251-256
Capital gains tax	336.24240973	HJ4653.C3			
Capital investments	332.0414	HG4028.C4	Cardiovascular system—Diseases—Homeopathic treatment	616.106	RX311-316
Capital movements	332.042	HG3891			
Capital punishment—United States	345.730773	KF9725	Cardiovascular system—Diseases—Nursing	616.10231	RC674
Capitalism	330.122	HB501	Cardiovascular system—Surgery	617.41	RD597-598.7
Capitols	725.11	NA4410-4417	Career changes	650.14	HF5384
Capricorn (Astrology)	133.5275	BF1727.65	Career development	650.1	HF5381-5382.5
Capstan	621.864	VM811	Career development	658.3	HF5549.5.C35
Capsules (Pharmacy)	615.19	RS201.C3	Career education	370.113	LC1037-.8
Captive wild animals	636.9	SF408-.6	Career plateaus	650.1	HF5384.5
Captive wild birds	636.6	SF462.5	Cargo handling	387.544	VK235
Capuchin monkeys	599.85	QL737.P925	Cargo ships	623.8245	VM391-395
Car pools	388.413212	HE5620.C3	Caribbean Area	972.9	F2155-2191
Carabobo, Battle of, 1821	973.54	F2324	Caribbean Area—Church history	277.29	BR655
Caravels	623.821	VM311.C27			
Carbohydrates	547.78	QD320-327	Caribbean Area—History	972.9	F2173-2191
Carbohydrates	572.56	QP701-702	Caribbean Area—Maps	912.729	G1535-1537
Carbon	661.0681	TP245.C4	Caribbean Area—Maps	912.729	G4390-4392
Carbon dioxide	546.6812	QD181.C1	Caribbean Area—Politics and government	320.9729	JL
Carbon dioxide—Physiological effect	612.22	QP913.C1			
Carbon monoxide	615.91	RA1247.C17	Caricatures and cartoons	741.5	NC1300-1766
Carbon steel	620.17	TA479.C37	Caricatures and cartoons—[By region or country]	741.59(4-9)	NC1400-1762
Carbonated beverages	663.62	TP628-636			
Carbuncle	616.523	RL221			
Carburetors	621.437	TJ787			
Carcinogenesis	616.994071	RC268.5-.7			

Subject Heading	Dewey	LC	Subject Heading	Dewey	LC
Caricatures and cartoons—Exhibitions	741.5074	NC1310-1312	Caste	305.5122	HT713-725
Caricatures and cartoons—Periodicals	741.505	NC1300	Caste	305.51220954	DS422.C3
Carillon music	786.64	M172	Casting (Fishing)	799.124	SH454-.9
Carnations	635.93353	SB413.C3	Cast-iron	620.17	TA474-475
Carnivals	394.26	GT4180-4299	Cast-iron	669.1413	TN710
Carnivals	791.1	GV1834.7-1835.56	Castles	728.81	NA7710-7786
			Castor oil	615.32369	RM666.C375
Carnivals	791.1	GV1835	Castor oil	665.353	TP684.C275
Carnivora	599.7	QL737.C2	Castration	617.463059	RD572
Carnivorous plants	583.75	QK917	Castration complex	150.195	BF175.5.C37
Carnivorous plants	635.93375	SB432.7	Casual labor	331.544	HD5855-5856
Caroline Islands	996.6	DU560-568	Cat breeds	636.8	SF449
Caroline Islands—History	996.6	DU565-567	Cat flea	636.808696	SF986.C37
Caroline Islands—Maps	912.966	G9420-9424	Catacombs	937.6	DG807.4
Carolingians	943.014	DD129-134.9	Catacombs	945.632	DG807.4
Carolingians	949.401	DQ85-87	Catalan language	449.9	PC3801-3899
Carpal tunnel syndrome	616.856	RC422.C26	Catalan language—Etymology	449.92	PC3883-3886
Carpathian Mountains	947.79	DJK71-76			
Carpentry	338.47694	HD9716 + (.C3-.C33)	Catalan language—Grammar	449.95	PC3819-3873
			Catalan language—Lexicography	449.93028	PC3887-3895
Carpentry	694	TH5601-5695			
Carpentry drafting	694.1	TH5611	Catalan literature	849.9	PC3900-3976
Carpets	677.643	TS1772-1779.5	Catalogs, Booksellers'	017.4	Z998-1000.5
Carpets	747.5	NK2775-2898	Catalogs, Union	025.31	Z695.83
Carriage and wagon-making	688.6	TS2001-2035	Catalysis	541.395	QD505
			Catalysts	541.395	QD501
Carrier proteins	572.696	QP552.C34	Catalysts	660.2995	TP159.C3
Carriers—Law and legislation—Canada	343.71093	KE1099-1135	Catalytic cracking	665.533	TP690.4
			Catamarans	623.822	VM311.C3
Carriers—Law and legislation—England	343.42093	KD1800-1847	Catamarans	797.1246	GV811.57
			Catapult	355.8241	U875
Carriers—Law and legislation—United States	343.73093	KF1091-1137	Catapults (Aeronautics)	623.441	TL732
			Cataract	617.742	RE451
Cartels	338.87	HD2757.5	Catboats	623.8203	VM311.C33
Cartilage	611.0183	QM567	Catechetics	238	BX8068-8070
Cartography	526	GA	Catechetics	268.82	BX1968
Cartography	526	GA101-1999	Catechetics (Canon law)	262.933	BX1939.C3
Cartography—History	526.09	GA201-246	Catechisms	238	BT1029-1040
Cartography—United States	526.0973	GA405	Caterers and catering	642.4	TX901-921
			Cathedrals	726.6	NA4830
Cartography—[United States, By state]	526.097(4-9)	GA409-460	Cathode ray oscilloscope	621.3815483	TK7878.7
			Cathode ray tubes	537.0284	QC544.C3
Cartons	658.7884	HF5770	Catholic Church	282	BX800-4795
Cartridges	358.128255	UF740-745	Catholic Church—Apologetic works	230.2	BX1752
Carving (Meat, etc.)	642.6	TX885			
Carzano, Battle of, 1917	940.432	D569.C	Catholic Church—Biography	282.092	BX4650-4705
Cascade Range	979.5	F851.7			
Cash discounts	658.82	HG3752	Catholic Church—Bishops	262.122	BX1905
Cash management	658.15244	HG4028.C45	Catholic Church—Byzantine rite	281.5	BX4711.11-.995
Cashew nut	634.57	SB401			
Casinos	364.17206	HV6711	Catholic Church—Byzantine rite, Greek	281.509495	BX4711.231-.2395
Cassava	641.33682	SB211.C3			
Casserole cookery	641.821	TX693	Catholic Church—Catechisms	238.2	BX1958-1968
Castanet music	786.873	M175.C35			
Caste	305.5122	GN491.4	Catholic Church—Clergy	262.142	BX1912-1914.5

Subject Heading	Dewey	LC
Catholic Church—Clergy—Sexual behavior	253.252	BX1912.9
Catholic Church—Dictionaries	282.03	BX841
Catholic Church—Doctrines	230.2	BX1746-1755
Catholic Church—Education	268.82	BX895-939
Catholic Church—Finance	254.8	BX1950
Catholic Church—Government	262.02	BX1800-1920
Catholic Church—History	270	BX940-1745
Catholic Church—History	282.09	BX940-1745
Catholic Church—Liturgy	264.02	BX1970.A7-.Z
Catholic Church—Liturgy—Texts	264.02 (1-9)	BX1999.8-2047
Catholic Church—Liturgy—Theology	264.02	BX2347-2348
Catholic Church—Missions	266.2	BV2130-2300
Catholic Church—Periodicals	282.05	BX800-806
Catholic Church—Prayer-books and devotions	242.802	BX2050-2155
Catholic Church—Sermons	252.02	BX1756
Catholic Church—Societies, etc.	282.06	BX808-816
Catholic Church—[By region or country]	282.73	BX4600-4644
Catholic Church—Africa	282.6	BX1675-1682
Catholic Church—Asia	282.5	BX1615-1673
Catholic Church—Canada	282.71	BX1419-1424
Catholic Church—Central America	282.728	BX1432-1447
Catholic Church—East Asia	282.5	BX1662-1670.7
Catholic Church—Europe	282.4	BX1490-1612
Catholic Church—France	282.44	BX1528-1533
Catholic Church—Germany	282.43	BX1534-1539
Catholic Church—Great Britain	282.41	BX1491-1514
Catholic Church—Italy	282.45	BX1543-1548
Catholic Church—Mexico	282.72	BX1427-1431
Catholic Church—Middle East	282.56	BX1617-1636
Catholic Church—[New Zealand or Australia]	282.9(3 or 4)	BX1685-1692
Catholic Church—Russia	282.47	BX1558-1560
Catholic Church—South America	282.8	BX1460-1489
Catholic Church—Spain	282.46	BX1583-1588
Catholic Church—United States	282.73	BX1404-1418
Catholic Church—West Indies	282.729	BX1448-1459
Catholic universities and colleges	378.07122	LC487
Cats	636.8	SF441-450
Cats—Diseases	636.80896	SF985-986
Cats—Pedigrees	636.80822	SF443
Cats—Training	636.80835	SF446.6
Cattle	636.2	SF191-219
Cattle brands	636.20812	SF101-103.5
Cattle breeds	636.2(2-8)	SF198-199
Cattle stealing	364.1552	HV6646-6665
Cattle trade	381.4162	HD9433
Cattle—Diseases	636.20886	SF961-967
Cattle—Infections	636.208969	SF961-967
Cattle—Transportation	385.24	HE2321.L7
Cattle—Transportation	387.5448	HE595.L7
Caucasian languages	499.96	PK9001-9201
Caucasian race	305.8034	GN537
Caucasian race	305.8034	HT1575-1577
Caucus	324.52	JF2085
Causation	122	BD530-595
Causation (Buddhism)	294.34	BQ4240
Cavalry	357	UE
Cavalry—History	357.09	UE15
Cavalry—Societies, etc.	357.06	UE1
Cavalry—Uniforms	357.04144	UE440-445
Cavalry—[By region or country]	357.09(4-9)	UE21-124
Cavalry—Africa	357.096	UE115-119
Cavalry—Argentina	357.0982	UE36-37
Cavalry—Asia	357.095	UE99-113
Cavalry—Australia	357.0994	UE121-122
Cavalry—Canada	357.0971	UE26-27
Cavalry—Central America	357.09728	UE30-31
Cavalry—Chile	357.0983	UE43-44
Cavalry—China	357.0951	UE101-102
Cavalry—Colombia	357.09861	UE45-46
Cavalry—Europe	357.094	UE55-95
Cavalry—France	357.0944	UE71-72
Cavalry—Germany	357.0943	UE73-74
Cavalry—Great Britain	357.0941	UE57-64
Cavalry—Greece	357.09495	UE75-76
Cavalry—India	357.0954	UE103-104
Cavalry—Italy	357.0945	UE79-80
Cavalry—Japan	357.0952	UE105-106
Cavalry—Mexico	357.0972	UE28-29
Cavalry—Oceania	357.099(5-6)	UE123-124
Cavalry—Portugal	357.09469	UE83-84
Cavalry—Russia	357.0947	UE85-86
Cavalry—Scandinavia	357.0948	UE86.5
Cavalry—South America	357.098	UE34-54
Cavalry—Spain	357.0946	UE87-88
Cavalry—United States	357.0973	UE23-25
Cavalry—Venezuela	357.0987	UE54
Cavalry—West Indies	357.09729	UE32-33
Cavalry drill and tactics	357.184	UE157-302
Cave animals	591.7584	QL117
Cave bear	569.78	QE882.C15
Cave dwellings	930.1	GN783-784
Cave mapping	796.525	GB601.52.M34
Caves	551.447	GB601-608
Caves	930.1	GN783-.5
Caving	796.525	GV200.6-.66

Subject Heading	Dewey	LC	Subject Heading	Dewey	LC
Cavitation	620.1064	TA357.5.C38	Central African Republic—Civilization	967.41	DT546.34
Cayman Islands	972.921	F2048.5			
Cayman Islands—Maps	912.72921	G4965-4969	Central African Republic—Gazetteers	916.741003	DT546.315
Cayman Islands—Politics and government	320.972921	JL629.5	Central African Republic—History	967.41	DT546.348-.384
CD-ROMs	621.39767	TK7895.C39			
Cedar Creek (Va.), Battle of, 1864	973.737	E477.33	Central African Republic—History—To 1960	967.410(1-3)	DT546.365-.37
Ceilings	690.17	TH2531-2533	Central African Republic—History—1960-	967.4105	DT546.375-.384
Ceilings	721.7	NA2950			
Celesta music	786.83	M175.C44	Central African Republic—History—Coup d'etat, 1979	967.4105	DT546.38
Celestial mechanics	521	QB349-421			
Celibacy	253.25	BV4390	Central African Republic—Maps	912.6741	G8710-8714
Celibacy	306.732	HQ800.15			
Cell culture	571.638	QH585.2-.45	Central America	972.8	F1421-1577
Cell death	571.939	QH671	Central America—Armed Forces—Supplies and stores	355.809728	UC98-99
Cell differentiation	571.835	QH607			
Cell division	571.844	QH605-.3			
Cell membranes	571.64	QH601-602	Central America—Biography	920.0728	CT570-638
Cell metabolism	572.4	QH634.5			
Cell nuclei	571.66	QH595	Central America—Church history	277.28	BR620-625
Cell physiology	571.6	QH631-647			
Cell respiration	572.47	QH633	Central America—Civilization	972.8	F1430
Cells	571.6	QH573-671			
Cells—Effect of radiation on	571.6345	QH652-.7	Central America—Commerce	381.09728	HF3241-3310
Cellular radio	384.53	HE9713-9715	Central America—Description and travel	917.2804	F1431-1433.2
Celluloid	668.44	TP1180.C5			
Cellulose	668.44	TP1180.C6	Central America—Economic conditions	330.9728	HC141-148
Celtic Church	274.4	BR748			
Celtic Church	274.4	BR794	Central America—Gazetteers	917.28003	F1424
Celtic harp music	787.95	M142.C44			
Celtic languages	491.6	PB	Central America—Genealogy	929.10720728	CS120-199
Celtic languages	491.6	PB1001-1095			
Celtic languages—Etymology	491.6(2-8)2	PB1083-1085	Central America—History	972.8	F1435.4-1439.5
			Central America—Manufactures	670.9728	TS30-31
Celtic languages—Grammar	491.6(2-8)5	PB1019-1071			
			Central America—Maps	912.728	G1550-1594
Celtic languages—Lexicography	491.6(2-8)3028	PB1087-1089	Central America—Maps	912.728	G4800-4884
			Central America—Periodicals	972.8005	F1421
Celtic languages—Study and teaching	491.6071	PB1011			
			Central America—Politics and government	320.9728	JL
Celtic philology	491.6	PB1001-1095			
Celts	941.089916	DA140-143	Central nervous system depressants	615.782	RM330
Celts—History	936.4	D70	Centrifuges	542	QD54.C4
Cement	622.368	TN945	Centurion (Tank)	358.1883	UG446.5
Cemeteries	363.75	RA626-630	Ceramic tableware	738.38	NK4695.T33
Cemeteries	393.1	GT3320	Cereals as food	641.331	TX393
Censers	264	BV196.C	Cereals, Prepared	641.331	TX395
Census	310	HA175-4737	Cereals, Prepared	664.756	TP434-435
Centaurs	292.13	BL820.C	Cerebral palsied children	618.92836	RJ496.C4
Centers for the performing arts	725.83	PN1585-1589	Cerebellum	573.86	QL937
			Cerebellum	611.81	QM455
Centipedes	595.62	QL449.5-.55	Cerebellum	612.827	QP379
Central African Republic—Census	316.741	HA4717	Cerebral cortex	612.825	QP383-.17
			Cerebral infarction	616.81	RC394.I5

Subject Heading	Dewey	LC	Subject Heading	Dewey	LC
Cerebral palsied	616.836	RC388	Chants (Buddhist)	294.3438	BQ5035-5065
Cerebral palsy	614.59836	RA645.C47	Chants (Hindu)	294.538	BL1226.2
Cerebrovascular disease	616.81	RC388.5	Chaotic behavior in systems	003.857	Q172.5.C45
Ceres (Roman deity)	292.2114	BL820.C5	Chaparral	578.738	SD397.C47
Ceres (Roman deity)	292.2114	BL820.C5	Chaparral ecology	577.38	QH541.5.C5
Certainty	121.63	BD171	Chapels	726.5	NA4870
Cervical syndrome	616.73	RC422.C4	Chaplains	355.347	UH20-25
Cervical vertebrae	611.711	QM111	Chaplains, Military	359.347	VG20-25
Cervix erosion	618.14	RG314	Character	155.2	BF818-839
Cervix uteri—Diseases	618.14	RG310-315	Character	370.114	LC251-301
Cesarean section	618.86	RG761	Character tests	155.2076	BF818-839
Cesium	546.385	QD181.C8	Charades	793.24	PN6366-6377
Cesium	661.0385	TP245.C25	Charcoal	662.74	TP331
Cha-cha (Dance)	793.33	GV1796.C2	Charcoal drawing	741.22	NC850
Chad—Census	316.743	HA4718	Chariot racing	798	GV33
Chad—Civilization	967.43	DT546.44	Charisma (Personality trait)	155.232	BF698.35.C45
Chad—Description and travel	916.74304	DT546.427	Charities	361.7	HV1-4959
Chad—Economic conditions	330.96743	HC990	Charities, Medical	361.7	HV687-694
			Charity	241.4	BV4639
Chad—History	967.43	DT546.457-.483	Charity organization	361.7	HV40-69
Chad—History—1960-	967.4304	DT546.48-.483	Charleston (Dance)	793.33	GV1796.C4
Chad—History—Civil War, 1965-	967.4304(1-4)	DT546.48	Charm	646.76	BJ1609-1610
			Charms	398.45	GR600
Chad—Maps	912.6743	G8720-8724	Charms (Buddhism)	294.3437	BQ4570.A4
Chafing dish cookery	641.585	TX825	Chastity	176	BJ1533.C4
Chain stores	381.12	HF5468	Chastity	241.66	BV4647.C5
Chair caning	684.130288	TT199	Chastity belts	392.5	GT2810
Chairs	684.13	TS880	Chateauguay, Battle of, 1813	973.523	E356.C4
Chalices	739.2282	NK7215-7230			
Chalk	338.2768	HD9999.C36	Chattanooga (Tenn.), Battle of, 1863	973.7359	E475.97
Chalk Bluff (Ark. and Mo), Battle of, 1863	973.734	E474.9			
			Chattanooga Railroad Expedition, 1862	973.731	E473.55
Chamber music	785	M177-990			
Chamber music—History and criticism	785.009	ML1100-1165	Check collection systems	332.76	HG1692
			Check credit plans	332.178	HG1643
Chameleons	597.956	QL666.L23	Check float	332.76	HG1692
Chameleons as pets	639.3956	SF459.C45	Checkers	794.2	GV1461-1463
Champ (Monster)	001.944	QL89.2.C53	Checking accounts	332.1752	HG1691-1704
Champagne (Wine)	663.224	TP555	Cheddar cheese	637.354	SF272.C5
Champagne, Battles of, 1914-1917	940.4(2-3)	D545.C37	Cheek	611.92	QM535
			Cheerfulness	179.9	BJ1477-1486
Champlain, Lake, Battle of, 1814	973.523	E356.C	Cheerfulness	179.9	BJ1533.C5
			Cheerleading	791.64	LB3635
Chance	123.3	BC141	Cheese	637.3	SF270-274
Chance	123.3	BD595	Cheesecake (Cookery)	641.8653	TX773
Chance	519.2	QA273-274.8	Chemical apparatus	542	QD53-54
Chance compositions	781.3	M1470	Chemical burns	617.11	RD96.45
Chancellorsville (Va.), Battle of, 1863	973.733	E475.35	Chemical carriers (Tankers)	623.8245	VM455.3
			Chemical elements	540	QD466-467
Chandeliers	749.63	NK8360	Chemical engineering	660	TP155-156
Change	116	BD373	Chemical engineering— Equipment and supply	660.283	TP157-159
Channeling (Spiritualism)	133.91	BF1281-1315			
Channels (Hydraulic engineering)	532.54	TC175-.2	Chemical engineering laboratories	660.072	TP165-183
			Chemical equilibrium	541.392	QD501
Chantilly (Va.), Battle of, 1862	973.732	E473.77	Chemical fire engines	628.9259	TH9375
			Chemical industry	338.4766	HD9650-9660

Subject Heading	Dewey	LC	Subject Heading	Dewey	LC
Chemical laboratories	540.72	QD51-64	Chest—Diseases—Eclectic treatment	617.5406	RV293
Chemical oceanography	551.465	GC109-149			
Chemical plants	660.28	TP155.5-.6	Chest—Diseases—Homeo pathic treatment	617.5406	RX360
Chemical processes	660.281	TP155.7-.75			
Chemical reaction, Conditions and law of	541.39	QD501-505.5	Chests	684.16	TT197
			Cheyenne Indians	978.00497353	E99.C53
Chemical senses	612.86	QP455-458	Chicago (Ill.)	977.311	F548-.9
Chemical spills	628.16836	TD196.C45	Chickamauga (Ga.), Battle of, 1863	973.73(4-5)	E475.81
Chemical warfare	358.34	UG447-.65			
Chemical weapons	358.3482	UG447.5-.65	Chickenpox	616.914	RC125
Chemicals	661	TP200-248	Chickens	636.5	SF481-513
Chemicals—Safety measures	660.2804	TP149	Child abuse	364.15554	HV6626.5-.54
			Child abuse	616.858223	RC569.5.C55
Chemistry	540	QD	Child abuse—Investigation	363.2595554	HV8079.C46
Chemistry, Analytic	543	QD71-142	Child analysis	618.928917	RJ504.2
Chemistry, Analytic—Periodicals	543.05	QD71	Child care	649.1	HQ778.5-.7
			Child development	155.4	LB1101-1139
Chemistry, Analytic—Qualitative	543	QD81-98	Child development	612.65	GN63
			Child development	612.65	RJ131-137
Chemistry, Analytic—Quantitative	543.1	QD101-117	Child mental health	155.4	BF721-723
			Child mental health	618.9289	RJ499-507
Chemistry, Forensic	363.25	HV8073-8077.5	Child psychiatry	618.9289	RJ499-520
Chemistry, Forensic	614.12	RA1057	Child psychology	155.4	BF721-723
Chemistry, Inorganic	546	QD146-197	Child psychopathology	618.9289	RJ499-520
Chemistry, Inorganic—Societies, etc.	546.06	QD146	Child psychopathology—Research	618.9289027	RJ500.2
Chemistry, Organic	547	QD241-441	Child psychotherapy	618.928914	RJ504-505
Chemistry, Organic—Periodicals	547.005	QD241	Child rearing	649.1	HQ768-777.95
			Child sexual abuse	616.85836	RC560.C46
Chemistry, Physical and theoretical	541	QD450-801	Child sexual abuse	616.85836	RJ506.C48
			Child sexual abuse—Investigation	363.2595554	HV8079.C48
Chemistry, Physical and theoretical—Societies, etc.	541.06	QD450			
			Child welfare	362.7	HV701-1420.5
Chemistry, Technical	660	TP	Child welfare—Periodicals	362.705	HV701
Chemistry, Technical—Congresses	660.06	TP5	Child welfare—[By region or country]	362.709(4-9)	HV741-804
Chemistry, Technical—Encyclopedias	660.03	TP9	Child welfare—United States	362.70973	HV741-743
Chemistry, Technical—History	660.09	TP15-20	Child welfare—[Other countries]	362.709(4-9)	HV745-804
Chemistry, Technical—Periodicals	660.05	TP1	Childbirth at home	618.4	RG661.5
			Children	305.23	HQ767.8-792.2
Chemistry—Dictionaries	540.3	QD4-5	Children—Diseases	618.92	RJ
Chemistry—Experiments	540.724	QD43	Children—Diseases—Eclectic treatment	618.9206	RV375-377
Chemistry—History	540.9	QD11-18			
Chemistry—Nomenclature	540.14	QD7	Children—Diseases—Homeopathic treatment	618.9206	RX501-531
Chemistry—Societies, etc.	540.6	QD1			
Chemistry—Study and teaching	540.71	QD40-49	Children—Diseases—Treatment	615.542	RJ52-53
Chemists	540.92	QD21-22	Children—Employment	331.31	HD6228-6250.5
Chemotherapy	615.58	RM260-263	Children—Growth	612.65	RJ131-137
Cherokee Indians	975.00497557	E99.C5	Children—History	305.2309	HQ767.87
Cherokee language	497.557	PM781-784	Children—Metabolism	618.92716	RJ128
Chess	794.1	GV1313-1457	Children—Mortality	304.64083	HB1323.C5
Chest pain	617.54	RC941	Children—Nutrition	612.3	RJ206-235
Chest—Diseases	617.54	RC941	Children—Physiology	612.0083	RJ125-137
			Children—Sexual behavior	306.7083	HQ784.S45

Subject Heading	Dewey	LC	Subject Heading	Dewey	LC
Children—Surgery	617.98	RD137-139	Chile—Politics and government	320.983	JL2600-2699
Children of alcoholics	362.2923	HV5132	Chilean literature	860	PQ7900-8098.36
Children of interracial marriage	306.843083	HQ777.9	Chili powder	641.3384	TX407.C
Children's clothing	646.406	TT635-645	Chime music	786.848	M172
Children's literature	808.068	PZ5-90	Chimneys	690.15	TH2281-2288
Children's museums	069.083	AM8	Chimneys	721.5	NA3040
Children's parties	793.21	GV1205	Chimpanzees	599.885	QL737.P96
Children's sermons	252.53	BV4315	Chin	611.92	QM535
Children's songs	782.42083	GV1215	China	931	DS701-799.9
Children's songs	782.42083	M1990-1998	China	951	DS701-799.9
Chile	983	F3051-3285	China—Armed Forces	355.00951	UA835
Chile—Census	318.3	HA991-1010	China—Armed Forces—Management	355.60951	UB101-102
Chile—Civilization	983	F3060	China—Census	315.1	HA4631-4640
Chile—Description and travel	918.304	F3061-3065	China—Church history	275.1	BR1280-1297
Chile—Economic conditions	330.983	HC191-195	China—Civilization	931	DS721-727
Chile—Emigration and immigration	325.(283) or (83)	JV7470-7479	China—Civilization	951	DS721-727
Chile—Gazetteers	918.3003	F3054	China—Commerce	381.0951	HF3831-3840
Chile—History	983	F3081-3098	China—Description and travel	913.104	DS707-712
Chile—History—To 1565	983.0(1-3)	F3091	China—Description and travel	915.104	DS707-712
Chile—History—To 1810	983.0(1-3)	F3091	China—Economic conditions	330.951	HC426-430
Chile—History—1565-1810	983.03	F3091	China—Emigration and immigration	325.(251) or (51)	JV8700-8709
Chile—History—1810-	983.0(4-6)	F3093	China—Gazetteers	915.1003	DS705
Chile—History—War of Independence, 1810-1824	983.04	F3094	China—Gazetteers	931.003	DS705
Chile—History—1824-1920	983.0(4-63)	F3095	China—History—To 221 B.C.	931.0(1-3)	DS741-747.23
Chile—History—Insurrection, 1851	983.05	F3095	China—History—Spring and Autumn period, 722-481 B.C.	931.01	DS747.15
Chile—History—Insurrection, 1859	983.05	F3095	China—History—Warring States, 403-221 B.C.	931.01	DS747.2
Chile—History—War with Spain, 1865-1866	983.061	F3095	China—History—221 B.C.-960 A.D.	931.04	DS747.28-749.7
Chile—History—Revolution, 1891	983.062	F3098	China—History—221 B.C.-960 A.D.	951.01	DS747.28-749.7
Chile—History—20th century	983.064	F3099	China—History—Ch'in dynasty, 221-207 B.C.	931.04	DS747.5-.9
Chile—History—1920-1970	983.06(3-45)	F3099	China—History—Han dynasty, 202 B.C.-220 A.D.	931.04	DS748-.164
Chile—History—Naval Revolt, 1931	983.0641	F3099	China—History—220-589	931.04	DS748.17-.76
Chile—History—Uprising, 1938	983.0642	F3099	China—History—Three Kingdoms, 220-265	931.04	DS748.2-.29
Chile—History—1970-1973	983.0646	F3100	China—History—Chin dynasty, 265-419	931.04	DS748.4-.44
Chile—History—Coup d'etat, 1973	983.065	F3100	China—History—Five Hu & the Sixteen kingdoms, 304-439	931.04	DS748.45-.48
Chile—History—1973-1988	983.065	F3100	China—History—Northern and Southern dynasties, 386-589	951.015	DS748.5-.76
Chile—History—1988-	984.06(5-6)	F3100			
Chile—Manufactures	670.983	TS43-44	China—History—Northern Wei dynasty, 386-534	931.04	DS748.7-.76
Chile—Maps	912.83	G5330-5334			
Chile—Periodicals	983.005	F3051			

Subject Heading	Dewey	LC	Subject Heading	Dewey	LC
China—History—Northern Wei dynasty, 386-534	951.015	DS748.7-.76	China—History—Revolution, 1911-1912	951.036	DS773.32-.6
China—History—Liu Sung dynasty, 420-479	951.015	DS748.6-.66	China—History—Republic, 1912-1949	951.04	DS773.83-777.5
China—History—Ch'i dynasty, 479-502	951.015	DS748.6-.66	China—History—1912-1928	951.041	DS776.4-777.46
China—History—Liang dynasty, 502-557	951.015	DS748.6-.66	China—History—Revolution, 1913	951.041	DS777.2
China—History—Northern Ch'i dynasty, 550-577	951.015	DS748.7-.76	China—History—Revolution, 1915-1916	951.041	DS777.25
China—History—Ch'en dynasty, 557-589	951.015	DS748.7-.76	China—History—Warlord period, 1916-1928	951.041	DS777.36
China—History—Northern Chou dynasty, 557-581	951.015	DS748.7-.76	China—History—May Fourth movement, 1919	951.041	DS777.43
China—History—An Lu shan Rebellion, 755-763	951.017	DS749.46	China—History—May Thirtieth movement, 1925	951.041	DS777.45
China—History—Huang Ch'ao Rebellion, 874-884	951.017	DS749.47	China—History—1928-1937	951.042	DS777.47-.514
China—History—Five dynasties and the Ten kingdoms, 907-979	951.0(18-24)	DS749.5-.76	China—History—Tsinan Incident, 1928	951.042	DS777.462
China—History—Earlier Shu kingdom, 907-925	951.018	DS749.7-.76	China—History—Long March, 1934-1935	951.042	DS777.5132-.51
China—History—Southern Han kingdom, 917-971	951.0(18-24)	DS749.7-.76	China—History—December Ninth Movement, 1935	951.042	DS777.51393
China—History—Later Shu kingdom, 934-965	951.018	DS749.7-.76	China—History—December Ninth Movement, 1935	951.042	DS775
China—History—Southern T'ang kingdom, 937-975	951.0(18-24)	DS749.7-.76	China—History—Sian Incident, 1936	951.042	DS777.514
China—History—Liao dynasty, 947-1125	951.0(18-24)	DS751.72-.78	China—History—1937-1945	951.042	DS777.518-.531
China—History—Hsi Hsia dynasty, 1038-1227	951.024	DS751.82-.88	China—History—Southern Anhui Incident, 1941	951.042	DS777.534
China—History—Chin dynasty, 1115-1234	951.024	DS751.92-.98	China—History—Civil War, 1945-1949	951.042	DS777.535-.544
China—History—Li Tzu ch'eng Rebellion, 1628-1645	951.026	DS753.65	China—History—1949-	951.05	DS777.545-779
			China—History—1949-1976	951.05(5-7)	DS777.55
China—History—White Lotus Rebellion, 1796-1804	951.033	DS756.3-.37	China—History—Hundred Flowers Campaign, 1956	951.055	DS778.4
China—History—Opium War, 1840-1842	951.033	DS757.4-.7	China—History—Antirightist Campaign, 1957-1958	951.055	DS778.5
China—History—Taiping Rebellion, 1850-1864	951.034	DS758.7-759.4	China—History—Cultural Revolution, 1966-1969	951.056	DS778.7
China—History—Nien Rebellion, 1853-1868	951.034	DS759.5	China—History—1976-	951.0(57-6)	DS779.15-.29
China—History—1861-1912	951.03(4-6)	DS763.5-773.6	China—History—Tiananmen Square Incident, 1989	951.058	DS779.32
China—History—Self-strengthening movement, 1861-1895	951.03(4-5)	DS763.65	China—History, Military	355.00951	DS777.65
			China—History, Military—1912-1949	355.00951	DS775.4
China—History—Boxer Rebellion, 1899-1901	951.035	DS770-772.3	China—Manufactures	670.951	TS101-102
China—History—20th century	951.0(35-59)	DS774	China—Maps	912.51	G2305-2321
			China—Maps	912.51	G7820-7824
China—History—Hsuan t'ung, 1908-1912	951.035	DS773-.6	China—Politics and government	320.951	JQ1500-1519
			China—Religion	299.51	BL1800-1975
			Chincoteague pony	636.16	SF315.2.C4

Subject Heading	Dewey	LC
Chinese drama	895.12008	PL2566-2603
Chinese drama	895.12009	PL2356-2393
Chinese essays	089.951	AC149-150
Chinese essays	895.14008	PL2606-2623
Chinese essays	895.14009	PL2395-2413
Chinese fiction	895.13008	PL2625-2653
Chinese fiction	895.13009	PL2415-2443
Chinese language	495.1	PL1001-2244
Chinese language—To 600	495.17	PL1077
Chinese language—Ancient Chinese, 600-1200	495.17	PL1079
Chinese language—Middle Chinese, 1200-1919	495.17	PL1081
Chinese language—Modern Chinese, 1919-	495.17	PL1083
Chinese language—Dialects	495.17	PL1501-1940
Chinese language—Dictionaries	495.13	PL1420-1498
Chinese language—Etymology	495.12	PL1281-1315
Chinese language—Grammar	495.15	PL1099-1241
Chinese language—Lexicography	495.13028	PL1401-1498
Chinese language—Phonology	495.115	PL1201-1219
Chinese literature	895.1	PL2250-3207
Chinese literature—To 221 B.C.—History and criticism	895.1109	PL2280
Chinese literature—221 B.C.-960 A.D.—History and criticism	895.10900(2-3)	PL2283
Chinese literature—220-589—History and criticism	895.109002	PL2284.5
Chinese literature—Three kingdoms, 220-265—History and criticism	895.109002	PL2285
Chinese literature—Chin dynasty, 265-419—History and criticism	895.109002	PL2286
Chinese literature—Liu Sung dynasty, 420-479—History and criticism	895.109002	PL2287
Chinese literature—Sui dynasty, 581-618—History and criticism	895.1090024	PL2290
Chinese literature—Yüan dynasty, 1260-1368—History and criticism	895.1090044	PL2294
Chinese literature—Ming dynasty, 1368-1644—History and criticism	895.1090046	PL2296
Chinese literature—Ch'ing dynasty, 1644-1912—History and criticism	895.1090048	PL2297
Chinese poetry	895.11008	PL2517-2565.8
Chinese poetry	895.11009	PL2306-2355.8
Chinese-Japanese War, 1894-1895	951.035	DS764.4-767.6
Chinook (Military transport helicopter)	358.4483	UG1232.T72
Chinook salmon	597.56	QL638.S2
Chinook winds	551.5185	QC939.F6
Chiropractic	615.534	RZ
Chiropractic	615.534	RZ201-275
Chiropractic clinics	362.12	RZ242
Chiropractic schools	615.534	RZ237-238
Chiropractic—Congresses	615.53406	RZ213
Chiropractic—History	615.53409	RZ221-225
Chiropractic—Periodicals	615.53405	RZ211
Chiropractic—Societies, etc.	615.53406	RZ201
Chiropractic—Study and teaching	615.534071	RZ237-238
Chiropractors—Biography	615.534092	RZ231-232
Chiropractors—Directories	615.534025	RZ233
Chloroform	615.781	RD86.C5
Choctaw (Military transport helicopter)	358.4483	UG1232.T72
Choctaw Indians	976.00497387	E99.C8
Choirs (Music)	782.507	MT88
Cholera	614.514	RA644.C3
Cholera	616.932	RC126-134
Cholesterol	572.5795	QP752.C5
Choral music	782.509	ML1500-1554
Choral singing	782.507	MT875
Chordata	596	QL605-739.8
Choruses, Secular	782.5	M1547-1610
Christian art and symbolism	704.9482	BV150-168
Christian art and symbolism	704.9482	N7810-8189.6
Christian biography	270.092	BR1690-1725
Christian communities	262.26	BV4405-4406
Christian denominations	280	BX
Christian education of children	268.432	BV1474-1475.2
Christian ethics	241	BJ1188.5-1278
Christian ethics	241	BV4625-4780
Christian ethics	241	BJ1188.5-1278
Christian giving	254.8	BV772
Christian leadership	262.1	BV652.1
Christian life	248.4	BV4500-4595
Christian pilgrims and pilgrimages	263.04	BX2323
Christian saints	235.2	BX380
Christian saints	235.2	BX575-577.5
Christian saints	270.092	BX2325-2333
Christian Science	289.5	BX6901-6997
Christian Science—Biography	289.5092	BX6990-6996

Subject Heading	Dewey	LC	Subject Heading	Dewey	LC
Christian Science—Congresses	289.506	BX6905-6907	Church buildings—Interdenominational use	254.7	BV636
Christian Science—Education	268.895	BX6917	Church calendar	529.44	CE81-83
Christian Science—Government	262.095	BX6958	Church camps	796.5422	BV1650
			Church camps—Baptists	269.24	BX6475-6476
Christian Science—History	289.509	BX6931-6935	Church charities	361.75	HV530
Christian Science—Liturgy	264.095	BX6960	Church colleges	378.071	LC427-629
Christian Science—Societies, etc.	289.506	BX6903	Church controversies	250	BV652.9
			Church decoration and ornament	726.51	NA5000
Christian sects	280	BR157	Church decoration and ornament	747.86	NK2190-2192
Christian shrines	263.042	BX2320-2321	Church etiquette	395.53	BJ2018-2019
Christian union	280.042	BX1-9.5	Church finance	254.8	BV770-777
Christianity	230	BR	Church fund raising	254.8	BV772.5
Christianity	230	BR1-129	Church growth	254.5	BV652.25
Christianity and other religions	261.2	BR127-128	Church history—[By date]	270.(1-8)	BR160-481
Christianity—Early church, ca. 30-600	270.(1-2)	BS2410	Church history—Primitive and early church, ca. 30-600	270.(1-2)	BR160-240
Christmas	394.2663	GT4985	Church history—Middle Ages, 600-1500	270.3	BR160-270
Christmas cookery	641.5686	TX739.2.C45			
Christmas sermons	252.615	BV4257	Church history—Modern period, 1500-	270.(5-8)	BR290-481
Christmas trees	394.2663	GT4989	Church history—Biography	270.092	BR1690-1725
Chromolithography	764.2	NE2500-2529	Church history—Congresses	270.06	BR41-43
Chromosomes	572.87	QH600-.6			
Chronic active hepatitis	616.3623	RC848.C4	Church history—Dictionaries	270.03	BR95
Chronic diseases	616.044	RB156			
Chronic diseases	616.044	RC108	Church history—Periodicals	270.05	BR1-9
Chronic encephalitis	616.832	RC390	Church history—Philosophy	270.01	BR138
Chronic fatigue syndrome	616.0478	RB150.F37	Church history—Societies, etc.	270.06	BR21-29
Chronic lymphocytic leukemia	616.99419	RC643			
Chronic renal failure	616.614	RC918.R4	Church libraries	027.67	Z675.C5
Chronology	529	CE	Church management	254	BV652-.9
Chronology, Assyro-Babylonian	529.30935	CE33	Church membership	254.5	BV820
			Church music	781.71009	ML3000-3190
Chronology, Greek	529.30938	CE42	Church music	781.71017	ML3869
Chronology, Historical	900	D11-.5	Church music—Catholic Church	782.3222009	ML3002-3051
Chronology, Oriental	529.325	CE31-39.5			
Chronology—Congresses	529.06	CE1.5	Church music—Catholic Church (Byzantine rite)	782.32215009	ML3060
Chronology—Dictionaries	529.03	CE4	Church music—Church of England	782.3223009	ML3166
Chronology—History	529.09	CE6			
Chronology—Periodicals	529.05	CE1	Church music—Episcopal Church	782.3223009	ML3166
Chronometers	522.5	QB107			
Church	262	BV590-640	Church music—Protestant churches	782.3224009	ML3100-3188
Church and social problems	261.83	HN30-39	Church of England—Biography	283.0972092	BX5619-5620
Church and state	261.7	BV629-631			
Church and state	322.1	K3280-3282	Church of England—Biography	283.42092	BX5197-5199
Church and state—Catholic Church	261.7	BX1790-1795	Church of England—Clergy	262.03	BX5175-5182.5
Church and state—United States	342.730852	KF4865-4869	Church of England—Directories	283.42025	BX5031
Church architecture	726.5	NA4790-6113			
Church attendance	254.5	BV4523	Church of England—Doctrines	230.342	BX5137-5140
Church buildings	726.5	NA4790-5095			

Subject Heading	Dewey	LC
Church of England—Government	262.0342	BX5150-5182.5
Church of England—History	283.4209	BX5051-5101
Church of England—Liturgy	264.0342	BX5140.5-5147
Church of England—Parties and movements	283.42	BX5115-5126
Church of England—Periodicals	283.4205	BX5011
Church of England—Prayer-Books and devotions	264.03	BX5145
Church of England—Relations	283.42	BX5127-5129.8
Church of England	283.42	BX5011-5740
Church of England—[New Zealand/Australia]	283.9(3 or 4)	BX5701-5720.8
Church of England—Africa	283.6	BX5681-5700.9
Church of England—Asia	283.5	BX5661-5680.7
Church of England—Canada	283.72	BX5601-5620
Church of England—Canada—History	283.72	BX5610-5613
Church of England—Oceania	283	BX5721-5740
Church of England—Wales	283.429	BX5596-5598
Church of Ireland	283.415	BX5410-5595
Church of Ireland—Biography	283.415092	BX5590-5595
Church of Ireland—History	283.41509	BX5500-5510
Church of Scotland	285.233	BX9075-9095
Church officers	262.1	BV705
Church orders, Ancient	255.00901	BV761.A1-.A5
Church publicity	254.4	BV652.95-657
Church renewal	262.0017	BV600
Church schools	371.071	LC427-629
Church Slavic language	491.81701	PG601-698
Church Slavic language—Grammar	491.817015	PG661-698
Church Slavic literature	891.81	PG700-716
Church societies	267	BV900-1450
Church vestments	391.04204	BV167
Church vestments	391.04282	BX1925
Church vestments	391.04282	BX2790
Church vestments	391.04283	BX5180
Church work with prostitutes	362.809(4-9)	HQ301-440.7
Church year	263.9	BV30-135
Church—Authority	262.8	BT91
Church—Catholicity	261	BV601.3
Cigarette boats	623.8231	VM341
Cigarette habit	362.296	HV5740-5745
Cigars	679.72	TS2260
Cinematography	778.53	TR845-899.5
Cinematography—Special effects	778.5345	TR858
Cipher and telegraph codes	384.14	HE7669-7679
Circle	516.152	QA484
Circle—Religious aspects	203.7	BL604.C5
Circular DNA	572.86	QP624.5.C57
Circumcision	392.1	GN484
Circumcision	617.463	RD590
Circumpolar medicine	616.9881	RC955-958
Circus	791.3	GV1800-1831
Cities and towns	307	HT101-395
Cities and towns	364.22	HV6177
Cities and towns, Ancient	307.76093	HT114
Cities and towns, Medieval	307.760902	D134
Cities and towns, Medieval	307.760902	HT115
Citizens band radio	621.38454	TK6570.C5
Citizenship	323.6	JF801
Citizenship—England	342.42083	KD4050-4058
Citizenship—United States	342.73083	KF4700-4720
Citrus	583.77	QK495.R98
Citrus	634.304	SB369-370
Citrus fruits	634.3	SB369
City children	305.23091732	HT206
City churches	250.91732	BV637
City clergy	262.14091732	BV637.5
City halls	725.13	NA4430-4437
City noise	620.23	TD891-893
City planning	307.1216	HT165.5-169.5
City planning	711	NA9000-9284
City planning and redevelopment law—United States	346.73045	KF5691-5710
City planning—[By region or country]	307.121609(4-9)	HT167-169.54
City planning—[By region or country]	711.09(4-9)	NA9101-9285
City planning—United States	307.12160973	HT167-168
City-states	321.06	JC352
Civil defense	363.35	UA926-929
Civil defense—Law and legislation—England	344.420535	KD6340
Civil defense—Law and legislation–United States	344.730535	KF7685
Civil disobedience	322.4	JC328.3
Civil engineering	624	TA
Civil law	346	K623-968
Civil law—Canada	347.71	KE495
Civil law—England	347.42	KD720-721
Civil procedure	347.05	K2201-2385
Civil procedure—United States	347.7305	KF8810-9075
Civil rights	323	JC571-628
Civil rights	342.085	K3236-3268
Civil rights—Canada	342.71085	KE4381-4430
Civil rights—England	342.42085	KD4080-4119
Civil rights—Religious aspects	201.72	BL65.C58
Civil service	342.068	K3440-3460
Civil service	351	JF1501-1521
Civil service	351.73063	JK631-868

Subject Heading	Dewey	LC	Subject Heading	Dewey	LC
Civil service	352.63	HD8001-8013	Classical antiquities—Study and teaching	938.0071	DE15-.5
Civil service	352.63	JS148-153	Classical biography	920.0937	DE7
Civil service, Colonial	353.15	JV443	Classical biography	920.0938	DE7
Civil service—Canada	352.630971	JL106-111	Classical drama	882.008	PA3461-3466
Civil service—Pensions	353.549	JF1671	Classical drama—History and criticism	882.009	PA3024-3029
Civil service—Personnel management	352.63	JK765-770	Classical education	373.242	LC1001-1021
Civil service—United States	342.73068	KF5336-5398	Classical geography	913.(7-8)	DE23-31
Civil service reform	352.630973	JK681	Classical geography	913.(7-8)	G87
Civilian-based defense	355.45	UA10.7	Classical languages	480	PA
Civilization	900	CB	Classical languages—Dictionaries	480.03	PA31
Civilization	909	HM101	Classical languages—Grammar, Comparative	485	PA111
Civilization, Ancient	930	CB311			
Civilization, Arab	909.04927	DS36.77-.88	Classical literature	880.8	PA3301-3671
Civilization, Arab—20th century	909.04927082	DS36.88 .B36	Classical literature—Appreciation	880.01	PA3013
Civilization, Assyro-Babylonian	935	DS70.7	Classical literature—History and criticism	880.09	PA3001-3045
Civilization, Christian	230	BR115.C5	Classical philology	480	PA1-199
Civilization, Classical	937	DE46-61	Classical poetry	881	PA3431-3459
Civilization, Classical	938	DE46-61	Classical poetry	881.009	PA3019-3022
Civilization, Germanic	943	CB213-214	Classicism	808.80142	PN56.C6
Civilization, Hindu	909.097645	DS423-425	Classroom management	371.1024	LB3013
Civilization, Islamic	909.0976701	DS35.62	Clavichord	786.309	ML649.8-747
Civilization, Medieval	909.07	CB351-355	Clavichord music	786.3	M20-39
Civilization, Modern	909.08	CB357-430	Clavicle	611.717	QM101
Civilization, Oriental	950	CB253-256	Clay	552.5	QE471.3
Civilization, Western	909.09812	CB245	Clay	622.361	TN941-943
Civilization—Dictionaries	903	CB9	Clay	666.3	TP811
Civilization—Extraterrestrial influences	001.94	CB156	Clay pot cookery	641.589	TX825.5
			Clay soils	631.42	S592.367
Civilization—Historiography	907.2	CB15-18	Clean rooms	620.86	TH7694
Civilization—Periodicals	905	CB3	Cleaning compounds	667.1	TP990-992.5
Civilization—Philosophy	901	CB19	Clearcutting	634.92	SD387.C58
Civilization—Pictorial works	902.22	CB13	Clearing of land	631.61	S607
Civilization—Study and teaching	907.1	CB20	Clearinghouses (Banking)	332.12	HG2301-2351
			Cleft lip	617.522	RD524
Civil-military relations	322.5	JF195	Clergy	262.14	BV659-683
Clamming	639.44	SH400.5.C53	Clergy (Canon law)	262.932	BX1939.C665
Clams	594.4	QL430.6-.7	Clergy couples	262.14	BV675.7
Clapps Mill, Battle of, N.C., 1781	973.337	E241.C56	Clergy—Divorce	253.2	BV4395.5
			Clergy—Family relationships	253.22	BV4396
Clarinet	788.6207	MT380-388			
Clarinet music	788.62	M70-74	Clergy—Pensions	331.252912532	BV4382
Clark's Expedition to the Illinois, 1778-1779	973.334	E234	Clergy—Political activity	253.2	BV4327
			Clerks (Retail trade)	381.1092	HD8039.M39
Class reunions	371.8	LB3618	Client/server computing	004.36	QA76.9.C55
Class size	371.251	LB3013.2	Client-centered psychotherapy	616.8914	RC481
Classical antiquities	937	DE			
Classical antiquities	938	DE	Cliff-dwellers	978.9004974	E99.P9
Classical antiquities—Periodicals	937.005	DE1	Climacteric, Male	616.693	RC884
			Climatic changes	551.5253	QC981.8.C5
Classical antiquities—Periodicals	938.005	DE1	Climatic changes	551.5253	QC982.8-994.9
			Climatology	551.6	QC851-999
Classical antiquities—Study and teaching	937.0071	DE15-.5	Clinical biochemistry	616.0756	RB112.5

Subject Heading	Dewey	LC	Subject Heading	Dewey	LC
Clinical chemistry	616.0756	RM40	Coaling	387.54044	VK361
Clinical medicine	616	RC31-80	Coal-tar	661.803	TP953
Clinical pharmacology	615	RM301.28	Coast defenses	355.45	UG410-442
Clinical psychology	616.89	RC466.8-467.95	Coast defenses	355.45	UG448
Clinical trials	615.50724	R853.C55	Coastal ecology	577.69	QH541.5.C65
Clinics	362.12	RA966	Coastal surveillance	359.984	VG50-55
Cloaks	687.147	TT530-535	Coasts	551.457	GB450-460
Clock and watch making	681.11(3-4)	TS540-549	Coastwise shipping	387.524	HE730-943
Clocks and watches	338.4768111	HD9999.C6	Coating processes	667.9	TP156.C57
Clocks and watches	681.11(3-4)	TS540-549	Coats	687.141	TT595-600
Clocks and watches	739.3	NK7480-7499	Coats	687.142	TT530
Cloning	660.65	QH442.2	Cobalt ores	622.3483	TN490.C6
Close and open communion	264.36	BV820	Cobras	597.96	QL666.O64
			Coca	583.79	QK495.E92
Closed-circuit television	384.556	TK6680	Coca	615.32379	RS165.C5
Clothes moths	595.78	QL561.T55	Cocaine habit	362.298	HV5810
Clothing and dress	391	GN418-419	Cocaine habit	616.8647	RC568.C6
Clothing and dress	391	GT500-2350	Cochlear implants	617.8820592	RF305
Clothing and dress	646.3	TX340	Cockatoos	598.71	QL696.P7
Clothing and dress	687	TT507	Cockatoos	636.6865	SF473.C63
Clothing and dress—Alteration	646.408	TT550	Cockroaches	595.728	QL505.5-.82
Clothing and dress—Repairing	646.2	TT720-730	Cockroaches as carriers of disease	614.432	RC641.C6
Clothing and dress—Social aspects	391	GT525	Cocktails	641.874	TX951
			Cocoa	641.877	TX817.C5
Clothing factories	687	TT498	Coconut	634.61	SB401
Clothing trade	687	TT490-695	Coconut oil	665.355	TP684.C7
Clothing trade—Periodicals	646.05	TT490	Codependency	616.8619	RC569.5.C63
Cloture	328.34	JF538	Coelenterata	593.5	QL375-379
Cloud forest ecology	577.34	QH101-198	Coevolution	576.87	QH372
Cloud forest ecology	577.34	QH541.5.C63	Coffee	394.12	GT2918
Clouds	551.576	QC920.7-924	Coffee	633.73	SB269
Clowns	791.33	GV1811	Coffee	641.3373	TX415
Clubhouses	728.4	NA7910-7977	Coffee	663.93	TP645
Clubs	367	HS2501-3371	Coffee cakes	641.8659	TX771
Clubs—[By region or country]	367.9(4-9)	HS2721-3200	Coffee habit	616.8526	RC567.5
			Coffeehouses	647.95	TX901-910
Clubs—United States	367.973	HS2721-2725	Coffer-dams	624.157	TC198
Clubs—[Other regions or countries]	367.9(4-9)	HS2731-3200	Cogeneration of electric power and heat	621.3121	TK1041-1078
Clubs—Directories	367.025	HS2507-2515	Cognition	153	BF309-499
Clubs—Periodicals	367.05	HS2501-2503	Cognition in animals	591.513	QL785
Cluster headache	616.84913	RC392	Cognition in children	155.413	BF723.C5
Coach horses	636.14	SF312	Cognitive balance	153	BF337.C62
Coaching	388.228	HE5746-5749	Cognitive psychology	153	BF201
Coaching	388.341	SF304.5-307	Cognitive styles	153	BF311
Coaching (Athletics)	796.077	GV711	Cognitive therapy	616.89142	RC489.C63
Coal	338.2724	HD9540-9559	Cognitive-analytic therapy	616.89142	RC489.C6
Coal	622.334	TN799.9-844.7	Coherence (Optics)	535.2	QC403
Coal gasification	665.772	TP759	Cohesion	541.33	QC183
Coal mine accidents	622.8	TN311-320	Coho salmon	597.56	QL638.S2
Coal mines and mining	622.334	TN799.9-844.7	Coin tricks	793.8	GV1559
Coal mines and mining—Safety measures	622.8	TN295	Coinage	332.4042	HG261-315
			Coinage	332.40420973	HG551-566
Coal slurry pipelines	388.57	TJ898.5	Coinage, International	332.45	HG381-421
Coal trade	381.422	HD9540-9559	Coins	737.4	CJ1-4625

Subject Heading	Dewey	LC	Subject Heading	Dewey	LC
Coins, African	737.496	CJ3920-4389	Collectors and collecting—[By region or country]	069.509(4-9)	AM301-396
Coins, American	737.4973	CJ1800-2449	Collectors and collecting—Africa	069.5096	AM387-389
Coins, Ancient	737.493	CJ201-1397	Collectors and collecting—Asia	069.5095	AM372-385
Coins, Ancient [By region or country]	737.493	CJ1021-1144	Collectors and collecting—Australia	069.50994	AM390-391
Coins, Ancient—Africa	737.496	CJ1071-1085	Collectors and collecting—Canada	069.50971	AM313
Coins, Ancient—Asian	737.49396	CJ1087-1099	Collectors and collecting—Central America	069.509728	AM315-322
Coins, Ancient—Europe	737.4936	CJ1101-1147	Collectors and collecting—Europe	069.5094	AM342-371
Coins, Ancient—Europe	737.49398	CJ1101-1147	Collectors and collecting—France	069.50944	AM349
Coins, Ancient—Italy	737.4937	CJ1021-1070	Collectors and collecting—Germany	069.50943	AM350
Coins, Australian	737.4994	CJ4400-4419	Collectors and collecting—Great Britain	069.50941	AM343-347
Coins, Byzantine	737.49398	CJ1201-1291	Collectors and collecting—Mexico	069.509728	AM314
Coins, Canadian	737.4971	CJ1860-1879	Collectors and collecting—New Zealand	069.50993	AM393
Coins, European	737.494	CJ2450-3369	Collectors and collecting—Oceania	069.5099(5-6)	AM395-396
Coins, Greek	737.4938	CJ301-763	Collectors and collecting—Portugal	069.509469	AM363
Coins, Greek	737.4938	CJ425-763	Collectors and collecting—Russia	069.50947	AM356
Coins, Italian	737.4937	CJ517-542	Collectors and collecting—South America	069.5098	AM330-341
Coins, Latin American	737.498	CJ1889-2449	Collectors and collecting—Spain	069.50946	AM362
Coins, Medieval	737.40902	CJ1601-1715	Collectors and collecting—United States	069.50973	AM303-311
Coins, Medieval—[By region or country]	737.49(4-9)	CJ1800-4625	Collectors and collecting—West Indies	069.509729	AM323-329
Coins, Oriental	737.49396	CJ1301-1397	College administrators	378.111	LB2341
Coins, Oriental	737.495	CJ3370-3893	College applications	378.1616	LB2351.5-.52
Coins, Roman	737.4937	CJ801-1147	College athletes—Recruiting	796.043	GV350.5
Coins—Congresses	737.406	CJ27	College buildings	727.3	NA6600-6605
Coins—Errors	737.4	CJ125	College costs	378.38	LB2342-.2
Coins—Exhibitions	737.4074	CJ39-41	College credits	378.1618	LB2359.5
Coins—Grading	737.4	CJ101	College sports	796.043	GV346-350
Coins—History	737.409	CJ59	College students—Employment	331.34	HD6276.5-.52
Coins—Periodicals	737.405	CJ1-9	College teachers	378.12	LB1778
Coins—Philosophy	737.401	CJ53	Collisions (Nuclear physics)	539.757	QC794.6.C6
Coins—Societies, etc.	737.406	CJ14-23	Collisions at sea—Prevention	623.8884	VK371-378
Cold (Disease)	616.205	RF361	Colloquial language	418	P408
Cold regions agriculture	630.911	S604.33	Collotype	686.2325	TR930-937
Cold regions agriculture	630.911	SB109.7	Colombia	986.1	F2251-2299
Cold storage	664.02852	TP372.2	Colombia—Census	318.61	HA1011-1020
Cold storage on shipboard	623.8535	VM485	Colombia—Civilization	986.1	F2260
Cold waves (Meteorology)	551.5512	QC981.8.A5			
Cold weather clothing	391	GT529			
Cold—Physiological effect	571.464	QP82.2.C6			
Colic	618.9233	RJ267			
Colic in horses	636.1089755	SF959.C6			
Colitis	616.3447	RC862.C6			
Collagen diseases in children	618.9277	RJ520.C64			
Collars in heraldry	929.6	CR41.C5			
Collectibles as an investment	332.63	AM237			
Collections	080	AC			
Collective bargaining	331.89	HD6971.5-.65			
Collective farms	334.683	HD1492-.5			
Collectivism	335	HX			
Collectivization of agriculture	334.683	HD1492-.5			
Collectors and collecting	069	AM			
Collectors and collecting	069.5	AM200-401			
Collectors and collecting—History	069.509	AM221			

Subject Heading	Dewey	LC	Subject Heading	Dewey	LC
Colombia—Description and travel	918.6104	F2261-2264.2	Colorado	978.8	F771-785
			Colorado—Gazetteers	917.88003	F774
Colombia—Economic conditions	330.9861	HC196-200	Colorado—History—To 1876	978.80(1-2)	F780
Colombia—Emigration and immigration	325.(2861) or (861)	JV7480-7489	Colorado—History—1876-1950	978.803(1-3)	F781
Colombia—Gazetteers	918.61003	F2254	Colorado—History—1951-	978.803(3-4)	F781.2-.3
Colombia—Guidebooks	918.6104	F2259.5	Colorado—Maps	912.788	G4310-4314
Colombia—History	986.1	F2270.3-2279.22	Colorado—Periodicals	978.8005	F771
Colombia—History—To 1810	986.10(1-2)	F2272	Color-printing	686.23042	Z258
Colombia—History—Insurrection of the Comuneros, 1781	986.102	F2272	Color—Psychological aspects	535.6019	BF789.C7
			Color—Therapeutic use	615.8312	RM840
Colombia—History—19th century	986.105	F2273	Color—Therapeutic use	615.8312	RZ414.6
			Colors	535.6	QC494-496.9
Colombia—History—1810-	986.10(3-6)	F2273	Colors, Liturgical	246.6	BV165
Colombia—History—War of Independence, 1810-1822	986.10(3-4)	F2274	Columbia River Valley	979.7	F853
			Columbus Day	394.264	E120
Colombia—History—1822-1832	986.104	F2275	Columns	690.13	TH2252-2253
			Columns, Corinthian	721.3	NA2860-2875
Colombia—History—1832-1886	986.105(2-61)	F2276	Columns, Ionic	721.3	NA2860
			Coma	616.849	RB150.C6
Colombia—History—Civil War, 1860-1862	986.1053	F2276	Comanche Indians	976.4004974572	E99.C85
Colombia—History—1886-1903	986.1062	F2276.5	Combat survival	355.4	U225
Colombia—History—Revolution, 1899-1903	986.1062	F2276.5	Combat—Psychological aspects	616.85212	RC550
			Combinations	511.64	QA165
Colombia—History—1903-1946	986.106(2-31)	F2277	Combinatorial analysis	511.6	QA164-167.2
Colombia—History—Coup d'etat, 1953	986.10632	F2278	Combined operations (Military science)	355.46	U260
Colombia—History—1946-1974	986.1063(2-3)	F2278	Combustion	541.361	QD516
			Combustion chambers	621.43	TJ254.7
Colombia—History—1974-	986.1063(4-5)	F2279-.22	Combustion, Spontaneous	622.82	TN313-315
Colombia—Manufactures	670.9861	TS45-46	Comets	523.6	QB717-732
Colombia—Maps	912.861	G5290-5294	Comets—Orbits	523.63	QB357
Colombia—Periodicals	986.1005	F2251	Comic books, strips, etc.	070.444	PN6700-6790
Colombia—Politics and government	320.9861	JL2800-2899	Command of troops	355.33041	UB210
			Commander Islands (Russia), Battle of, 1943	940.54217	D764.3
Colombian literature	860	PQ8160-8180.36	Commandments of the church	241.5	BV4720-4730
Colon (Anatomy)	611.347	QM345			
Colon—Cancer	616.994347	RC280.C6	Commando troops	355.422	U262
Colon—Diseases	616.34	RC860-862	Commerce	381	HF
Colonies	321.08	JV	Commerce	395.52	GT6010-6070
Colonies—Administration	353.15	JV412-461	Commerce—Directories	381.025	HF54
Colonies—History	325.309	JV61-151	Commerce—Encyclopedias	381.03	HF1001-1002.5
Colonies—Law and legislation	341.28	K3375	Commerce—Periodicals	381.05	HF1-53
			Commercial art	741.6	NC997-1003
Colonization	325.3	JV1-5399	Commercial art—Periodicals	741.605	NC997.A1
Color	535.6	QC494-496.9			
Color blindness	617.759	RE921	Commercial art—Study and teaching	741.6071	NC1000
Color of man	599.945	GN197			
Color photography	778.6	TR510-545	Commercial associations	381.06	HF294-343
Color prints	769	NE1850-1879	Commercial buildings	725.2	NA6210-6280
Color television	621.38804	TK6670	Commercial buildings—Design and construction	690.52	TH4311-4315
Color vision—Testing	617.759075	RE918-921			

Subject Heading	Dewey	LC	Subject Heading	Dewey	LC
Commercial catalogs	659.133	HF5861-5863	Community centers— United States	790.06873	HN43-45
Commercial correspondence	651.75	HF5721-5734	Community colleges	378.1543	LB2328
Commercial credit	332.742	HG3751-3754.5	Community development	307.14	HN49.C6
Commercial geography	381.09	HF1021-1027	Community health nursing	610.7343	RT98
Commercial law	343.07	K3840-4375	Community life	307	HM131-134
Commercial law	346.07	K1001-1388	Community psychiatry	362.22	RC455
Commercial law—Canada	343.7107	KE1935-1999	Community psychology	362.22	RA790.55
Commercial law—England	343.4207	KD2455-2530	Community service (Punishment)	364.68	HV9277.5
Commercial law—Ireland	343.41507	KDK550-769	Community-based corrections	365.34	HV9279
Commercial law—Northern Ireland	343.41607	KDE235-282	Comoro Islands—Census	316.94	HA2303
Commercial law—United States	343.7307	KF1600-2940	Comoro Islands—Maps	912.694	G9210-9214
Commercial loans	332.1753	HG1641-1643	Compact disc players	621.38932	TK7881.75
Commercial policy	381.3	HF1410-1411	Compact discs	621.3976	TK7882.C56
Commercial products	381.4	HF1040-1044	Comparative law	340.2	K583-591
Commercial statistics	381.7021	HF1016-1017	Comparative linguistics	410	P123
Commission merchants	381.2092	HF5422	Compass	623.8932	VK577
Commodity exchanges	332.644	HG6046-6051	Compassion (Buddhism)	294.342	BQ4360
Commodity exchanges— Law and legislation— United States	343.7308	KF1085-1087	Compensatory education	370.111	LC213-.3
			Competition	338.6048	HD41
Commodity futures	332.6328	HG6046-6051	Competition	338.6048	HF1414
Commons	333.2	HD1286-1289	Competition (Biology)	577.83	QH546.3
Commonwealth countries	349.42	KD5020-5025	Competition, Imperfect	338.6048	HB238
Commonwealth countries—Economic conditions	330.917241	HC246	Competition, Unfair— England	343.42072	KD2225-2226
			Competition, Unfair— United States	343.73072	KF1601-1611
Commonwealth countries—History	909.0971241	DA10-18.2	Competition, Unfair— United States	343.73072	K3195-3198
Communal living	307.774	HQ970-975.7	Compilers (Computer programs)	005.453	QA76.76.C65
Communicable diseases	614.5	RA643-644			
Communicable diseases	616.9(01-6)	RC109-216	Complement (Immunology)	571.9688	QR185.8.C6
Communicable diseases in animals	636.08969	SF781-809	Complex carbohydrate diet	613.283	RM237.58
			Complexes (Psychology)	154.2	RC569.5.C68
Communication	302.2	P87-96	Composite materials	620.118	TA418.9.C6
Communication policy	302.2	P95.8	Composition (Art)	701.8	N7429.7-7433
Communication, Prehistoric	302.2	GN799.T73	Composition (Music)	781.307	MT40-67
Communications software	005.3	TK5105.9	Composition (Music)	781.309	ML430-455
Communications, Military	355.85	UA940-945	Compost	363.728	TD796.5
Communications, Military	623.8567	VG70-85	Compost	631.875	S661
Communicative disorders	616.855	RC423-428.8	Compressed air	621.51	TJ981-1009
Communion of saints	262.73	BT972	Compressed air— Therapeutic use	615.836	RM827
Communion sermons	252	BV4257.5			
Communism	335.43	HX1-780.9	Compressibility	536.4	QC284
Communism and agriculture	334.683	HX550.A37	Compressors	621.51	TJ990-992
			Compromise (Ethics)	179.9	BJ1430-1438
Communist countries	940.54217	D847-.2	Compromise of 1850	973.64	E423
Communist ethics	171.7	BJ1390-.5	Compromise of 1850	973.7113	E423
Communist leadership	335.43092	HX518.L4	Compulsive behavior	616.8584	RC533
Communist state	321.92	JC474	Compulsive eating	616.8526	RC552.C65
Communities	307	HT	Compulsive gambling	616.85841	RC569.5.G35
Community centers	790.068	HN41-46	Computer algorithms	005.1	QA76.9.A43
Community centers—[By region or country]	790.068(4-9)	HN43-46	Computer architecture	004.22	QA76.9.A73
			Computer art	776	N7433.8
			Computer chess	794.172	GV1449.3

Subject Heading	Dewey	LC	Subject Heading	Dewey	LC
Computer crimes	364.168	HV6772-6773.3	Confederate Memorial Day	394.26975	E645
Computer crimes—Investigation	363.25968	HV8079.C65	Confederate States of America	973.713	E482-489
Computer engineering	621.39	TK7885-7895	Confederate States of America	975	E482-489
Computer games	794.8	GV1469.15-.25	Confederate States of America. Army	355.30975	UA580-585
Computer graphics	006.6	T385	Confederate States of America. Army—	355.620975	UC85-86
Computer interfaces	621.398	TK7887.5	Commissariat		
Computer literacy	004	QA76.9.C64	Confederate States of America. Army—Field	355.350975	U173.5
Computer networks	004.6	TK5105.5-.9	service		
Computer security	005.8	QA76.9.A25	Confederate States of America. Army—Firearms	355.82420975	UD383.5
Computer simulation	003.3	QA76.9.C65	Confederate States of America. Army—Prisons	973.771	E611-612
Computer software	005.3	QA76.75-.9	Confederate States of America. Navy—History	359.30975	E591-600
Computer stores	381.45004	HF5468.2	Confederate States of America. Navy— Ordnance	359.80975	VA393-395
Computer terminals	621.3985	TK7887.8.T4	and ordnance stores		
Computer viruses	005.84	QA76.76.C68	Confederate States of America—Defenses	355.450975	UA580-585
Computer war games	355.480285	U310	Confederate States of America—History	973.713	E487-488
Computer-aided engineering	620.00420285	TA345	Confederate States of America—History	975	E487-488
Computer-assisted instruction	371.334	LB1028.5-.7	Confederate States of America—History, Military	973.742	E470.2
Computers	004	QA75.5-.95	Confederate States of America—History, Military	973.742	E545
Computers	621.39	TK7885-7895	Confederate States of America—History, Naval	359.30975	E591-600
Computers—Dictionaries	004.03	QA76.15	Confederate States of America—Politics and	320.0975	JK9661-9993
Computers—History	004.09	QA76.17	government		
Computers—Maintenance and repair	621.390288	TK7887	Confederate States of America—Social conditions	973.713	E487
Conception	612.63	QP251-281	Confederate States of America—Social conditions	975	E487
Conception	618.2	RG133	Confession	234.166	BX5949.C6
Concertina music	788.84	M154	Confession	264.020862	BX2262-2267
Concord, Battle of, 1775	973.3311	E241.C7	Confession	264.03562	BX5149.C6
Concrete	620.136	TA439-446	Confession	265.62	BV845-847
Concrete blocks	666.894	TP885.C7	Confirmation	265.2	BV815
Concrete blocks	693.5	TH1491	Confirmation (Buddhist rite)	294.3438	BQ5005
Concrete construction	624.1834	TA680-683.94	Confirmation (Canon law)	262.933	BX1939.C72
Concrete construction	693.5	TH1461-1501	Confirmation (Jewish rite)	296.4424	BM707-.4
Concrete construction	721.0445	NA4125	Conflict of laws	342.042	K7000-7720
Concrete dams	627.82	TC547	Conflict of laws—Arbitration	347.09	K7690
Concrete houses	728	NA7160	and award		
Concrete products	666.894	TP885	Conflict of laws—Banking	340.982	K7380-7384
Concrete sculpture	731.2	NB1215	Conflict of laws—Commercial law	340.97	K7340-7512
Concrete walls	624.1834	TA683.5.W34	Conflict of laws—Contracts	340.92	K7265-7305
Concrete walls	690.12	TH2245	Conflict of laws—Contracts	340.97	K7350-7444
Condensation (Meteorology)	551.574	QC921.6.C6			
Condensation products (Chemistry)	547.2	QD341			
Condensed matter	530.41	QC173.45-.458.U54			
Condensed milk	637.142	SF259			
Condensers (Steam)	621.197	TJ557-565			
Condiments	394.12	GT2870			
Condiments	641.3382	TX819			
Conditional immortality	236.23	BT919-925			
Conduct disorders in children	618.9289	RJ506.C65			
Conduct of life	170.44	BJ1545-1697			
Conducting	781.4507	MT85			
Confectionery	641.853	TX783-799			

Subject Heading	Dewey	LC	Subject Heading	Dewey	LC
Conflict of laws—Copyright licenses	340.9482	K7555-7557	Congregational churches—Creeds	238.58	BX7235-7236.2
Conflict of laws—Corporations	340.966	K7490-7495	Congregational churches—Education	268.858	BX7119-7127
Conflict of laws—Domestic relations	340.915	K7155-7197	Congregational churches—Government	262.058	BX7240-7246
Conflict of laws—Guardian and ward	340.918	K7197	Congregational churches—History	285.809	BX7131-7228
Conflict of laws—Industrial property	340.948	K7570-7582	Congregational churches—Liturgy	264.058	BX7237
Conflict of laws—Inheritance and succession	340.952	K7230-7245	Congregational churches—Sermons	252.058	BX7233
Conflict of laws—Insurance	340.986	K7470	Congregational churches—Societies, etc.	285.806	BX7105
Conflict of laws—Intellectual property	340.948	K7550-7582	Congregational churches—Africa	285.86	BX7220-7222
Conflict of laws—Juristic persons	340.913	K7145-7148	Congregational churches—Asia	285.85	BX7215-7216
Conflict of laws—Maritime law	343.096	K7449-7460	Congregational churches—Australia	285.894	BX7225-7226
Conflict of laws—Negotiable instruments	340.996	K7360-7370	Congregational churches—Canada	285.871	BX7151-7153
Conflict of laws—Obligations	340.92	K7260-7335	Congregational churches—Europe	285.84	BX7175-7210
Conflict of laws—Parent and child	340.917	K7181-7197	Congregational churches—United States	285.873	BX7135-7149
Conflict of laws—Persons	340.912	K7120-7197	Congregationalism	285.8	BX7101-7260
Conflict of laws—Property	340.94	K7200-7218	Congregationalist—Biography	285.8092	BX7259-7260
Conflict of laws—Quasi contracts	340.929	K7310	Congresses and conventions	060	AS6
Conflict of laws—Sales	340.972	K7350	Congruences (Geometry)	516.2	QA608
Conflict of laws—Torts	340.93	K7315-7335	Congruences and residues	512.72	QA242-244
Conflict of laws—Canada	342.71042	KE470-474	Conifers	585	QK494
Conflict of laws—England	342.42042	KD680-685	Conifers	634.974	SD397.C7
Conflict of laws—United States	342.73042	KF410-418	Conjunctiva—Diseases	617.773	RE310-326
Conformal mapping	515.9	QA360	Conjunctivitis	617.773	RE321
Conformal mapping	515.9	QA646	Conjunctivitis, Infantile	618.92097773	RJ296
Confucianism	299.512	BL1830-1875	Conjuring	793.8	GV1541-1561
Congenital heart disease	616.12043	RC687	Connecticut—Gazetteers	917.46003	F92
Conglomerate corporations	338.8042	HD2756-.2	Connecticut—History	974.6	F91-105
Congo (Brazzaville)—Census	316.724	HA4716	Connecticut—History—Colonial period, ca. 1600-1775	974.60(1-2)	F97
Congo (Brazzaville)—Civilization	967.24	DT546.24	Connecticut—History—1775-1865	974.60(2-3)	F99
Congo (Brazzaville)—Economic conditions	330.96724	HC980	Connecticut—History—1865-1950	974.604(1-3)	F100
Congo (Brazzaville)—Gazetteers	916.724003	DT546.215	Connecticut—History—1951-	974.604(3-4)	F101
Congo (Brazzaville)—History	967.24	DT546.25-.283	Connecticut—Maps	912.746	G3780-3784
Congo (Brazzaville)—History—To 1960	967.240(1-3)	DT546.265-.275	Connecticut—National Guard	355.3709746	UA100-109
Congo (Brazzaville)—Maps	912.6724	G8700-8704	Connecticut—Periodicals	974.6005	F91
Congo River—Description and travel	916.75104	DT639	Connective tissue diseases in children	618.9277	RJ482.C65
Congregational churches	285.8	BX7101-7260	Connective tissues	611.74	QM563
Congregational churches—Congresses	285.806	BX7106-7109			

Subject Heading	Dewey	LC	Subject Heading	Dewey	LC
Connective tissues—Diseases	616.77	RC924-.5	Consumption (Economics)	339.47	HC79.C6
Conscience	170	BJ1471	Contact dermatitis	616.51	RL244
Conscience	241.1	BV4615	Contact lenses	617.7523	RE977.C6
Conscience, Examination of	241.1	BX2377	Container gardening	635.986	SB418-.4
Conscientious objectors	355.224	UB341-342	Containers	688.8	TS197.5
Consciousness	153	BF309-499	Containers—Law and legislation—England	343.42075	KD2230-2231
Consecration	265.92	BV4501	Contemplation	248.34	BV5091.C7
Consecration of virgins	264.02092	BX2305	Contempt of court	364.1340973	JK1543
Conservation of natural resources	333.72	S900-954	Continuing education	374	LC5201-6660
Conservation of natural resources—United States	346.73044	KF5505-5510	Contraception	613.94	RG136-137.6
			Contraceptive drugs	613.9432	RG137.4-.6
Conservative Judaism	296.8342	BM197.5	Contraceptives	613.9432	RG137-.6
Consolation	242.4	BV4900-4911	Contraceptives, Vaginal	613.9435	RG137.2
Consolation (Judaism)	296.72	BM729.C6	Contract labor	331.542	HD4871-4875
Consolidation and merger of corporations	338.83	HD2746.5-.55	Contracting out	331.542	HD2365-2385
			Contracts	346.02	K840-917
Consolidation and merger of corporations	338.83	HG4028.M4	Contracts	346.02	K1024-1132
Consolidation of land holdings	333.33	HD1334-1335	Contracts for work and labor—United States	344.7301542	KF898-905
Conspiracies	364.1	HV6275	Contracts, Aleatory—United States	344.730542	KF1241
Constables	363.2	HV7981			
Constellations	523.1	QB63	Contracts—Canada	346.7102	KE850-1225
Constipation	616.3428	RC861	Contracts—England	346.4202	KD1554-1920
Constitutional amendments—United States	342.73032	KF4555-4558	Contracts—Ireland	346.41502	KDK370-437
			Contracts—United States	346.7302	KF801-1241
Constitutional conventions	342.0292	JF71-99	Contradiction	165	BC199.C6
Constitutional conventions	342.73024	JK301	Control theory	515.642	QA402.3-.37
Constitutional history	342.029	K3161	Controlled fusion	539.764	QC791.7-.775
Constitutional law	342	K3154-3367	Convection oven cookery	641.58	TX840.C65
Constitutional law—United States	342.73	KF4501-5130	Convenience stores	381.147	HF5469.25-.55
			Convention facilities	725.91	NA6880-.5
Constitutions, State	342.0297(4-9)	JK2413-2428	Conversation	395.59	BJ2120-2128
Construction equipment	690.0284	TH900-915	Conversion	248.24	BR110
Construction industry	338.47624	HD9715-9717.5	Conversion	248.24	BT780
Construction industry—Law and legislation	343.42078624	KD2435	Conversion	248.24	BV4912-4950
			Converts	248.24	BV4930-4935
Construction industry—Law and legislation	343.71078624	KE1915	Conveying machinery	621.867	TJ1385-1418
			Convict labor	365.65	HV8888-8931
Construction industry—Law and legislation—United States	343.73078624	KF1950	Convulsions	616.845	RC394.C77
			Cook Islands—Census	319.623	HA4017.5
			Cook Islands—Maps	912.9623	G9600-9604
Consumer affairs departments	381.3	HF5415.5	Cookery	641.5	TX642-840
			Cookery (Canned foods)	641.612	TX821
Consumer cooperatives	334.5	HD3271-3575	Cookery (Eggs)	641.675	TX813.C7
Consumer cooperatives—[By region or country]	334.509	HD3281-3410.9	Cookery (Fish)	641.692	TX747
			Cookery (Meat)	641.66	TX749-.5
			Cookery (Pasta)	641.822	TX809.M17
Consumer credit	332.743	HG3755-3756	Cookery (Poultry)	641.665	TX750-.5
Consumer education	640.73	TX335	Cookery (Seafood)	641.692	TX747
Consumer price indexes	338.528	HB225	Cookery (Vegetables)	641.65	TX801-807
Consumer satisfaction	658.812	HF5415.5	Cookery, French	641.5944	TX719-.2
Consumers	339.47092	HC79.C6	Cookery, German	641.5943	TX721
Consumers' leagues	334.5	HD3271-3575	Cookery, Japanese	641.5952	TX724.5.J3
Consumption (Economics)	339.47	HB801-843	Cookery, Marine	641.57	VC370-375
			Cookery, Mexican	641.5972	TX716.M4

Subject Heading	Dewey	LC	Subject Heading	Dewey	LC
Cookery, Military	641.57	UC720-735	Cornish language—Grammar	491.675	PB2511-2547
Cookery—History	641.509	TX645			
Cookery—Study and teaching	641.5071	TX661-669	Cornish language—Study and teaching	491.67071	PB2507
Cookery for the sick	641.563	RM219	Cornish literature	891.67	PB2551-2621
Cookies	641.8654	TX772	Coronary artery bypass	617.413	RD598.35.C67
Cooks	641.5092	TX649	Coronary care units	362.1961204	RA975.5.C6
Cooling towers	621.197	TJ563	Coronary circulation	612.17	QP108
Cooperation	334	HD2951-3575	Coronary heart disease	616.123	RC685.C6
Cooperation—History	334.09	HD2956	Coronations	321.6	JC391
Cooperation—Societies, etc.	334.06	HD2952	Coronations	394.4	D127
			Coronations	394.4	GT5050
Coopers and cooperage	331.287482	HD4966.C82	Corporal punishment	355.13325	UB810-815
Coopers and cooperage	338.4767482	HD9750-9769	Corporal punishment	359.13325	VB910
Coopers and cooperage	674.82	TS890	Corporal punishment	364.67	HQ770.4
Copenhagen (Denmark)	948.913	DL276	Corporal punishment	364.67	HV8609-8621
Copper	620.182	TA480.C7	Corporal works of mercy	241.4	BV4647.M4
Copper age	930.15	GN777-778	Corporate divestiture	658.164	HD2746.6
Copper—Metallurgy	669.3	TN780	Corporate governance	658.4	HD2741-2749
Copper mines and mining	622.343	TN440-449	Corporate image	338.74	HD59.2
Copperhead	597.963	QL666.069	Corporate state	321.94	HD3611-4730.9
Copra	634.61	SB401	Corporate state	321.94	JC478
Coptic language	493.2	PJ2001-2187	Corporation law—Canada	346.71066	KE1369-1465
Coptic language—Etymology	493.22	PJ2161	Corporation law—England	346.42066	KD2057-2127
Coptic language—Grammar	493.25	PJ2029-2113	Corporation law—United States	346.73066	KF1384-1480
Coptic language—Lexicography	493.23028	PJ2181	Corporations	338.74	HD2709-2932
			Corporations, Government	338.749	HD3850
Coptic language—Study and teaching	493.2071	PJ2019	Corporations, Government	352.266	HD3850
Coptic literature	893.2	PJ2190-2199	Corporations, Government—Law and legislation—United States	346.73067	KF1480
Copying processes	686.4	Z48			
Copyright	346.0482	K1411-1485	Corporations, Government—United States	352.2660973	HD3881-4420.8
Copyright	351.824	Z551-656			
Copyright—England	346.420482	KD1281-1325			
Copyright—Transfer	346.0482	Z649.T7	Corporations, Government—[Other countries]	352.26609(4-9)	HD4001-4420.7
Copyright—United States	346.730482	KF2986-3080			
Coral fisheries	639.32	SH399.C6	Corporations—Accounting	657.95	HF5686.C7
Coral reef biology	578.7789	QH95.8	Corporations—Corrupt practices	364.168	HV6763-6771
Coral reef ecology	577.789	QH541.5.C7			
Coral reefs and islands	551.424	GB461-468	Corporations—Finance	338.74	HG4001-4285
Coral reefs and islands	551.424	QE565-566	Corporations—Investor relations	338.74	HD59
Coral Sea, Battle of the, 1942	940.5426	D774.C			
			Corporations—Law and legislation—United States	346.73066	KF1396-1477
Coral snakes	597.9644	QL666.064			
Cordage	677.71	TS1784-1787	Corporations—Taxation	336.207	HD2753
Cordage, Prehistoric	623.8620901	GN799.C49	Corporations—[By region or country]	338.7409	HD2770-2930.7
Corinthian League	938.0(1-8)	DF233.2			
Corn	584.92	QK495.G74	Corporations—Africa	338.74096	HD2917-2929.3
Corn	633.15	SB191.M2	Corporations—Australia	338.740994	HD2930
Corn as feed	633.255	SF99.C59	Corporations—Benelux countries	338.7409492	HD2865.5-2873.5
Corn products	664.724	TP435.C67			
Cornea—Diseases	617.719	RE336-340	Corporations—Canada	338.740971	HD2807-2810
Cornet music	788.96	M85-89	Corporations—Central America	338.7409728	HD2813.5-2819
Cornish language	491.67	PB			
Cornish language	491.67	PB2501-2549	Corporations—China	338.740951	HD2910

Subject Heading	Dewey	LC
Corporations—Europe	338.74094	HD2844-2891.84
Corporations—France	338.740944	HD2853-2856
Corporations—Germany	338.740943	HD2857-2860.5
Corporations—Great Britain	338.740941	HD2845-2847.5
Corporations—Greece	338.7409495	HD2891.83
Corporations—India	338.740954	HD2897-2900
Corporations—Indonesia	338.7409598	HD2904
Corporations—Iran	338.740955	HD2892.56
Corporations—Iraq	338.7409567	HD2892.55
Corporations—Israel	338.74095694	HD2892.2
Corporations—Italy	338.740945	HD2862-2865
Corporations—Japan	338.740952	HD2907
Corporations—Mexico	338.740972	HD2811
Corporations—Philippines	338.7409599	HD2905
Corporations—Portugal	338.7409469	HD2889
Corporations—Russia	338.740947	HD2874-2877
Corporations—South America	338.74098	HD2827-2843
Corporations—Spain	338.740946	HD2885-2888
Corporations—Turkey	338.7409561	HD2891.93
Corporations—United States	338.740973	HD2771-2798.5
Corporations—West Indies	338.7409729	HD2820.5-2825.9
Correlation (Statistics)	310.72	HA31.3
Correlation (Statistics)	519.537	QA273-281
Corrosion and anti-corrosives	620.11223	TA418.74-.76
Corrosion resistant alloys	620.16	TA486
Corsets	391.42	GT2075
Corsica (France)—History	944.945	DC611.C8-.C839
Cosmetics	391.63	GT2340-2341
Cosmetics	668.55	TP983-986
Cosmic dust	523.1125	QB791
Cosmic magnetic fields	538.7	QC809.M25
Cosmic noise	551.5276	QC809.C6
Cosmic physics	550	QC801-809
Cosmic physics	551.5276	QC883.2.S6
Cosmic ray showers	539.7223	QC485.8.S5
Cosmic rays	539.7223	QC484.8-485.9
Cosmochemistry	523.02	QB450-.5
Cosmogony	523.12	QB980-991
Cosmology	113	BD493-708
Cosmology	523.1	QB980-991
Cosmology, Ancient	113.0901	BD495
Cosmology, Medieval	113.0902	BD495.5
Cosmology—History	113.09	BD494-497
Cost accounting	657.42	HF5686.C8
Cost and standard of living	339.42	HD6977-7080
Cost control	658.1552	HD47.3
Cost effectiveness	658.1554	HD47.4
Costa Rica	972.86	F1541-1557
Costa Rica—Census	317.286	HA801-810
Costa Rica—Civilization	972.86	F1543.8
Costa Rica—Description and travel	917.28604	F1544

Subject Heading	Dewey	LC
Costa Rica—Emigration and immigration	325.(27286) or (7286)	JV7413
Costa Rica—Gazetteers	917.286003	F1542
Costa Rica—History—To 1821	972.860(1-3)	F1547
Costa Rica—History—1821-1948	972.8604	F1547.5
Costa Rica—History—Uprising, 1932	972.86044	F1547.5
Costa Rica—History—1948-1986	972.86051	F1548
Costa Rica—History—1986-	972.86052	F1548.2-.23
Costa Rica—Maps	912.7286	G4860-4864
Costa Rica—Periodicals	972.86005	F1541
Costa Rica—Politics and government	320.97286	JL1440-1459
Costa Rican literature	860	PQ7480-7489.2
Costume	391	GT500-2370
Costume, Jewish	391.0088296	GT540
Costume—History	391.0090(1-5)	GT530-596
Costume—History—To 500	391.00901	GT530-560
Costume—History—Medieval, 500-1500	391.00902	GT575
Costume—History—16th century	391.009031	GT585
Costume—History—17th century	391.009032	GT585
Costume—History—18th century	391.009033	GT585
Costume—[By region or country]	391.009(4-9)	GT601-1605
Costume—Africa	391.0096	GT1580-1589
Costume—Asia	391.0095	GT1370-1570
Costume—Australia	391.00993	GT1590-1593
Costume—Europe	391.0094	GT720-1330
Costume—New Zealand	391.00994	GT1595
Costume—North America	391.0097	GT603-648
Costume—Oceania	391.00996	GT1597-1599
Costume—South America	391.0098	GT675-716
Costume jewelry	745.5942	NK4890.C67
Cote d'Ivoire—Census	316.668	HA4725
Cote d'Ivoire—Civilization	966.68	DT545.4
Cote d'Ivoire—Description and travel	916.66804	DT545.27
Cote d'Ivoire—Economic conditions	330.96668	HC1025
Cote d'Ivoire—Gazetteers	916.668003	DT545.15
Cote d'Ivoire—History	966.68	DT545.52-.83
Cote d'Ivoire—Maps	912.6668	G8780-8784
Cottage industries	338.634	HD2336.2-.25
Cottages	728.37	NA7551-7555
Cotton	677.21	TS1542
Cotton growing	338.17351	HD9070-9093
Cotton trade	381.41351	HD9070-9089
Cotton trade	381.41351	HD9870-9889
Cotton-picking machinery	631.37	S715.C64

Subject Heading	Dewey	LC	Subject Heading	Dewey	LC
Councils and synods	262.(4-5)	BV710	Covenants—Judaism	296.31172	BM612.5
Councils and synods, Episcopal (Catholic)	262.52	BX820-838	Coverlets	746.46	TT835
Counseling	158.3	BF637.C6	Cowbirds	598.874	QL696.P2475
Counted thread embroidery	746.442	TT778.C65	Cowboys	636.213092	F596
Counterfeits and counterfeiting	332.490973	HG641-645	Cowgirls	636.213092	F596
			Cows	636.2	SF191-219
Counterfeits and counterfeiting	332.90973	HG335-341	Coyote trapping	636.0839	SK341.C65
Counterinsurgency	355.0218	U241	CPR (First aid)	616.1025	RC87.9
Counter-Reformation	270.6	BR430	Crab culture	639.56	SH380.4-.45
Counter-Reformation	943.03	D220-271	Crab fisheries	639.56	SH380.4-.45
Counter-Reformation	943.03	DD176-189	Crabbing	639.56	SH400.5.C7
Counterrevolutions	321.09	JC492	Crabgrass	584.92	QK495.G74
Countertransference (Psychology)	616.8914	RC489.C68	Crabs	595.386	QL444.M33
			Crack (Drug)	362.298	HV5810
Counting	513.211	QA113	Crack (Drug)	616.8647	RC568.C6
Counting-out rhymes	398.8	GR485	Crackers	641.815	TX769
Country life	390.091734	GT3470	Cracking process	665.533	TP690.4
Country music	784.164209	ML3523-3524	Cradles	645.4	GN415.C8
Country swing (Dance)	793.3	GV1796.C68	Crane Island, Battle of, 1813	973.523	E356.C8
Country-dance	793.3	GV1763			
County agricultural agents	630.715092	S533-534	Cranes, derricks, etc.	621.87	TJ1363-1365
County government— United States	352.150973	JS411	Craniology	599.948	GN71-131
			Craniotomy	617.514	RD529
County school systems	379.123	LB2813	Craniotomy	618.88	RG781
Couple-owned business enterprises	338.7	HD62.27	Crape myrtle, Common	583.76	QK495.L9
			Crates	674.82	TS900
Couplings	621.825	TJ183	Crayfish	595.384	QL444.M33
Coups d'etat	321.09	JC494	Crayon drawing	741.23	NC855-875
Courage	179.6	BJ1533.C8	Crayons	741.23	NC870
Court dances	793.38	GV1747	aspnumCreameries	637.148	SF266
Court rules—United States	347.73051	KF8816-8821	Cream-separators	637.148	SF247
Court tennis	796.342	GV1003	Creation	213	BL224-226
Courtesy	177.1	BJ1520-1688	Creation	231.765	BS651-652
Courtesy	177.1	BJ1533.C9	Creation (Literary, artistic, etc.)	153.35	BF408-426
Courthouses	725.15	NA4470-4477			
Courtly love	392.4	GT2620	Creation (Literary, artistic, etc.)	153.35	BH301.C84
Courts—Canada	347.7101	KE4775			
Courts—Canada	347.7101	KE8200-8605	Creationism	231.7652	BS651-652
Courts—England	347.4201	KD4645	Creative ability	153.3	BF408
Courts—United States	347.7301	JK1606	Creative ability in children	155.4133	BF723.C7
Courts—United States	347.7301	KF101-153	Creative activities and seat work	371.3	LB1027.25
Courts—United States— Officials and employees	347.731(4-6)	KF8771-8807			
			Creative activities and seat work	371.3	LB1140.35.C74
Courts—Wales	347.42901	KD9480-9484			
Courts and courtiers	390.23	GT3510-3530	Creative activities and seat work	371.3	LB1537
Courts of honor	355.13	UB880			
Courts of love	396.70944	DC611.P961	Creative thinking	153.3	BF408-426
Courts-martial and courts of inquiry	343.0143	UB850-857	Creative thinking	370.157	LB1062
			Credit	332.7	HG3691-3769
Courts-martial and courts of inquiry	343.0143	VB800-807	Credit control	332.75	HG3705-3711
			Credit ratings	332.7	HG3751.5-.9
Courts-martial and courts of inquiry—United States	343.730143	KF7625-7659	Credit unions	334.22	HG2032-2039
			Creeds	238	BT990-1010
Covenant theology	231.76	BT155	Creeds, Ecumenical	238	BT990
Covenants (Church polity)	262	BT1010	Creek War, 1813-1814	975.803	E83.813
			Creek War, 1836	975.803	E83.836
			Creepers (Birds)	598.82	QL696.P23

Subject Heading	Dewey	LC	Subject Heading	Dewey	LC
Cremation	393.2	GT3330	Criminal statistics—Central America	364.09728021	HV7317-7323
Cremation	614.6	RA631-636.7	Criminal statistics—China	364.0951021	HV7378
Crematoriums	363.75	RA636-.7	Criminal statistics—Europe	364.094021	HV7342-7367.7
Creole dialects	447.9	PM7831-7875	Criminal statistics—France	364.0944021	HV7348
Crests	929.6	CR55-57	Criminal statistics—Germany	364.0943021	HV7349-.5
Crete (Greece)—History	949.59	DF901.C78-.C89	Criminal statistics—Great Britain	364.0941021	HV7343-7345.5
Cretinism	616.858848043	RC657	Criminal statistics—India	364.0954021	HV7371
Cribs (Children's furniture)	645.4083	TS886.5.C74	Criminal statistics—Italy	364.0945021	HV7351
Cricket	796.358	GV911-929.3	Criminal statistics—Japan	364.0952021	HV7377
Crickets	595.726	QL508.G8	Criminal statistics—Mexico	364.0972021	HV7316
Crime	364	HV6001-7220.5	Criminal statistics—Russia	364.0947021	HV7355
Crime analysis	363.256	HV7936.C88	Criminal statistics—South America	364.098021	HV7330-7341
Crime and age	364.24	HV6163	Criminal statistics—Spain	364.0946021	HV7361
Crime in mass media	364	P96.C74	Criminal statistics—United States	364.0973021	HV7245-7300
Crime prevention	364.4	HV7431	Criminal statistics—West Indies	364.09729021	HV7324-7329.9
Crime stoppers programs	364.4	HV7936.C58	Criminals	364.3	HV6001-7220.5
Crimean War, 1853-1856	956.10154	DR567	Criminals	390.406927	GT6550-6710
Crimean Tatar language	494.388	PL65.C74	Criminals—[By region or country]	364.309(4-9)	HV6774-7220.5
Crimean War, 1853-1856	947.0738	DK214-215	Criminals—[Other countries]	364.309(4-9)	HV6801-7220.5
Crimes of passion	364.1	HV6053	Criminals—Identification	363.258	HV6065-6079
Crimes without victims	364.1	HV6705-6738	Criminals—Rehabilitation	364.601	HV9261-9430.7
Criminal anthropology	364.2	HV6001-6197	Criminals—United States	364.30973	HV6774-6795
Criminal behavior—Genetic aspects	364.24	HV6047	Criminology	364	HV
Criminal investigation	363.25	HV8073-8079.3	Criminology	364	HV6001-7220.5
Criminal jurisdiction	345.01	K5036-5048	Criminology—History	364.09	HV6021-6023
Criminal jurisdiction	345.01	K5423	Criminology—Periodicals	364.05	HV6001-6006
Criminal justice, Administration of	345.05	HV7231-9960	Criminology—Research	364.072	HV6024.5
Criminal justice, Administration of	345.050973	HV9950	Criminology—Study and teaching	364.071	HV6024
Criminal justice, Administration of—[By region or country]	345 0509(4-9)	HV9950-9960	Crinolines	391.42	GT2075
Criminal law	345	K5011-5316	Crisis management	658.4056	HD49-.6
Criminal law—Canada	345.71	KE8801-9112	Critical care medicine	616.028	RC86-88.9
Criminal law—England	345.42	KD7850-8090	Critical phenomena (Physics)	530.474	QC173.4.C74
Criminal law—Ireland	345.415	KDK1750-1782	Criticism, Textual	801.959	P47
Criminal law—Scotland	345.411	KDC910-920	Criticism, Textual	880.9	PA47
Criminal law—United States	345.73	KF9201-9479	Croatia	939.8	DR1502-1645
Criminal law—Wales	345.429	KD9490	Croatia	949.72	DR1502-1645
Criminal liability	345.04	K5064-5083	Croatia—History	939.8	DR1547-1598
Criminal procedure	345.05	K5401-5570	Croatia—History	949.72	DR1547-1598
Criminal procedure—England	345.4205	KD8220-8464	Croatia—Maps	912.4972	G2030-2032
Criminal procedure—Northern Ireland	345.41675	KDE550-557	Croatia—Maps	912.4972	G6870-6873
Criminal psychology	364.3	HV6080-6113	Crocheting	746.434	TT820-829
Criminal statistics—[By region or country]	364.09(4-9)021	HV7245-7400	Crocodiles	597.982	QL666.C925
Criminal statistics—Africa	364.096021	HV7382-7388.4	Cro-Magnon man	569.98	GN286.3
Criminal statistics—Asia	364.0995021	HV7368-7381	Crop improvement	631.52	SB106.I47
Criminal statistics—Australia	364.0994021	HV7389	Crop insurance	368.121	HG9968
			Crop rotation	631.582	S603
Criminal statistics—Canada	364.0971021	HV7315	Crop science literature	630	SB45.65
			Crops	630	SB

Subject Heading	Dewey	LC	Subject Heading	Dewey	LC
Crops—Congresses	630.6	SB16	Cryptography	652.8	Z102.5-104.5
Crops—Effect of acid precipitation on	632.19	SB745	Crystal gazing	133.322	BF1335
			Crystal growth	548.5	QD921-926
Crops—Effect of air pollution on	632.19	SB745	Crystalline lens— Diseases	617.742	RE401-461
			Crystallization	548.5	QD901-999
Crops—Evolution	631.52	SB106.074	Crystallography	548	QD901-999
Crops—Genetic engineering	631.5233	SB123.57	Crystallography, Mathematical	548.7	QD911-919
Crops—Periodicals	630.5	SB1-13	Ctenophora	593.8	QL380-.8
Crops—Research	630.72	SB51-56	Cuba	972.91	F1751-1854.9
Croquet	796.354	GV931-933	Cuba—Civilization	972.91	F1760
Cross, Sign of the	264.9	BV197.S5	Cuba—Description and travel	917.29104	F1761-1765.3
Cross-country running	796.428	GV1063			
Cross-country ski racing	796.932	GV855.5.R33	Cuba—Emigration and immigration	325.(27291) or (7291)	JV7370-7379
Cross-country skiing	796.932	GV855-.5			
Cross-cousin marriage	306.81	GN480.4	Cuba—Gazetteers	917.291003	F1754
Cross-cultural orientation	303.482	GN345.65	Cuba—History	972.91	F1751-1849
Crosses	203.37	BL406.C7	Cuba—History—To 1810	972.910(1-4)	F1779
Crosses	246.558	BV160	Cuba—History—1810-1899	972.9105	F1783
Crosses	246.558	CC300-350			
Crossword puzzles	793.732	GV1507.C7	Cuba—History—British occupation, 1762-1763	972.9103	F1781
Croup	616.201	RC746			
Crow Indians	978.004975272	E99.C92	Cuba—History—Black Eagle Conspiracy, 1830	972.9105	F1783
Crow language	497.5272	PM1001			
Crowds	302.33	HM281-283	Cuba—History—Negro Conspiracy, 1844	972.9105	F1783
Crowns	929.7	CR4480.C7			
Crowns (Dentistry)	617.6922	RK666	Cuba—History—Insurrection, 1849-1851	972.9105	F1783
Crows	598.864	QL696.P2367			
Crucifixion	364.66	HV8569	Cuba—History—Insurrection, 1868-1878	972.9105	F1785
Cruelty	179	BJ1535.C7			
Cruise missiles	358.42	UG1312.C7	Cuba—History—1878-1895	972.9105	F1785
Crusades	940.18	D151-173	Cuba—History—Revolution, 1879-1880	972.9105	F1785
Crusades—Biography	940.18092	D156-.5			
Crusades—Historiography	940.18072	D156.58	Cuba—History—1895-	972.910(5-6)	F1786-1788.22
Crusades—First, 1096-1099	940.182	D161-.5	Cuba—History—Revolution, 1895-1898	972.9105	F1786
Crusades—Second, 1147-1149	940.182	D162-.5	Cuba—History—1899-1906	972.9106(1-2)	F1787
Crusades—Third, 1189-1192	940.182	D163-.5	Cuba—History—American occupation, 1906-1909	972.91062	F1787
Crusades—Fourth, 1202-1204	940.184	D164-.5	Cuba—History—1909-1933	972.91062	F1787
Crusades—Fifth, 1218-1221	940.184	D165	Cuba—History—Revolution, 1933	972.91063	F1787.5
Crusades—Sixth, 1228-1229	940.184	D166	Cuba—History—Moncada Barracks Attack, 1953	972.91063	F1787.5
Crusades—Seventh, 1248-1250	940.184	D167	Cuba—History—Revolution, 1959	972.91064	F1788
Crusades—Eighth, 1270	940.184	D168	Cuba—History—Invasion, 1961	972.91064	F1788
Crusades—Later 13th, 14th, and 15th centuries	940.19	D171-173	Cuba—Maps	912.7291	G4920-4924
Crushing machinery	621.914	TJ1345	Cuba—Periodicals	972.91005	F1751
Crustacea	595.3	QL435-445.2	Cuba—Politics and government	320.97291	JL1000-1019
Crutches	617.9	RD756			
Cryobiology	571.4645	QH324.9.C7	Cuban literature	860	PQ7370-7390
Cryochemistry	541.3686	QD515	Cuban Missile Crisis, 1962	973.922	E841.W49
Cryptogams	586	QK504-635	Cultivators	631.3	S683-685

Subject Heading	Dewey	LC	Subject Heading	Dewey	LC
Cultivators	631.510284	TJ1482	Czech language	491.86	PG4601-4771
Culture	306	GN400-406	Czech language—Dialects	491.867	PG4700-4771
Culture	306	HM101-121	Czech language— Dictionaries	491.863	PG4625-4693
Culverts	625.7342	TE213	Czech literature	891.86	PG5000-5146
Cuneiform inscriptions, Sumerian	499.9511	PJ4051-4075	Czech philology	491.86	PG4001-4771
Cuneiform writing	492.111	PJ3191-3225	Czechoslovakia	943.7	DB2000-3150
Curacao	972.986	F2049	Czechoslovakia—Census	314.37	HA1191-1200
Curacao—Maps	912.72986	G5180-5184	Czechoslovakia— Civilization	943.7	DB2035
Curacao—Politics and government	320.972986	JL770-779	Czechoslovakia— Congresses	943.7006	DB2003
Curbs	625.888	TE298	Czechoslovakia— Description and travel	914.37(04)	DB2018-2022
Cushitic languages	493.5	PJ2401-2413	Czechoslovakia— Directories	943.70025	DB2009
Cushitic languages— Dialects	493.57	PJ2425-2594	Czechoslovakia— Economic conditions	330.9437	HC270.2-.295
Cushitic languages— Dictionaries	493.53	PJ2413	Czechoslovakia— Gazetteers	914.37003	DB2007
Cushitic languages— Etymology	493.52	PJ2409	Czechoslovakia—History	943.7	DB2044-2232
Cushitic languages— Grammar	493.55	PJ2405	Czechoslovakia—History	943.7	DB2185-2232
Customer relations	658.812	HF5415.5-.55	Czechoslovakia—History— 1918-1939	943.7032	DB2195-2202
Customs administration	352.448	HJ6603-7390	Czechoslovakia—History— 1938-1945	943.7033	DB2205-2211
Customs administration— [By region or country]	352.44809(4-9)	HJ6622-7390	Czechoslovakia—History— 1945-1992	943.704	DB2215-2232
Customs administration— United States	352.4480973	HJ6622-6731	Czechoslovakia—History— Coup d'etat, 1948	943.7042	DB2222
Customs administration— [Other countries]	352.44809(4-9)	HJ6750-7390	Czechoslovakia—History— 1968-1989	943.7043	DB2225-2232
Cut glass	748.6	NK5200-5205	Czechoslovakia—History— Intervention, 1968	943.7042	DB2232
Cutlery	683.82	TS380-.4	Czechoslovakia— Manufactures	670.9437	TS65.3-.4
Cutting machines	621.93	TJ1230-1240	Czechoslovakia—Maps	912.437	G1945-1949
Cybernetics	003.5	Q300-390	Czechoslovakia—Maps	912.437	G6510-6514
Cybernetics—Dictionaries	003.503	Q304	Czechoslovakia— Periodicals	943.7005	DB2000
Cybernetics—History	003.509	Q305	Czechoslovakia—Politics and government	320.9437	JN2210-2229
Cybernetics—Study and teaching	003.5071	Q316	D document (Biblical criticism)	220.6	BS1181.17
Cycling	796.6	GV1040-1059	D region	538.7672	QC881.2.D2
Cyclone forecasting	551.64513	QC951	Daba language	493.7	PL8117
Cyclones	551.5513	QC940.6-959	Dachau (Germany: Concentration camp)	940.53185336	D805.G3
Cymbal music	786.873	M146	Dachshunds	636.7538	SF429.D25
Cyprus—Census	315.693	HA4557	Dacian War, 1st, 101-102	937.07	DG59.D3
Cyprus—Civilization	939.37	DS54.35	Dacian War, 2nd, 105-106	937.07	DG59.D3
Cyprus—Civilization	956.93	DS54.35	Dacians	949.8004	D90.D
Cyprus—Description and travel	913.93704	DS54.A4-Z	Dadaism	709.04062	N6494.D3
Cyprus—Description and travel	915.69304	DS54.A4-Z	Dadaism	709.04062	NX600.D3
Cyprus—History	939.37	DS54.5-.9	Daedalus (Greek mythology)	292.13	BL820.D25
Cyprus—History	956.93	DS54.5-.9			
Cyprus—Maps	912.5693	G2215-2219			
Cyprus—Maps	912.5693	G7450-7454			
Cyprus—Politics and government	320.95693	JQ1811			
Cystic fibrosis	616.37	RC858.C95			
Cytology	571.6	QH573-671	Daffodils	584.34	QK495.A484
Cytology—Research	571.6072	QH583-.2	Daffodils	635.93434	SB413.D12

Subject Heading	Dewey	LC	Subject Heading	Dewey	LC
Daghestan languages	499.964	PK9051	Dam safety	627.80684	TC550
Daghestan literature	899.964	PK9051.5-.8	Damage control (Warships)	623.888	V810
Daguerreotype	772.12	TR365	Dampness in buildings	693.892	TH9031
Dahlias	635.93399	SB413.D13	Dams	627.8	TC540-558
Daiichi Togyo Kabushiki Kaisha Strike, 1970-1975	331.89280952	HD5427	Dams—Design and construction	627.8	TC540
Daikokuten (Japanese deity)	299.56	BL2211.D33	Dams—Earthquake effects	627.8	TC542.5
Dairy barns	690.8922	TH4930	Damselflies	595.733	QL520-.42
Dairy barns	728.922	NA8280	Dam-tshig-rdo-rje (Buddhist deity)	294.34211	BQ4890.D33-.D334
Dairy cattle	636.2142	SF208	Dan literature	896.34	PL8123.5-.9
Dairy farming	636.2142	SF221-250	Dance	792.8	GV1580-1799.4
Dairy farms	636.2142	SF221-250	Dance—Biography	792.8092	GV1785
Dairy inspection	637.12	SF255	Dance criticism	792.809	GV1600
Dairy processing	637.14	SF250.5-275	Dance for children	793.083	GV1799
Dairy products	637	SF250.5-275	Dance for the aged	793.0846	GV1799.3
Dairy products industry	338.47637143	HD9275-9283.7	Dance for the handicapped	793.087	GV1799.2
Dairy products—Drying	637.143	SF259	Dance in art	704.9497928	N8217.D3
Dairy products—Marketing	381.417	HD9275-9283.7	Dance music—History and criticism	781.55409	ML3400-3451
Dairy products—Marketing	381.417	SF261	Dance of death	700.4548	N7720
Dairy schools	636.21420711	SF241-245	Dance therapy	616.891655	RC489.D3
Dairying	636.2142	SF221-250	Dance therapy for children	615.85155083	RJ505.D3
Dairying—Accounting	636.21420681	SF261	Dance-orchestra music	784.48	M1356
Dairying—Equipment and supplies	636.21420284	SF247	Dance-orchestra music	784.4809	ML3518
Dairying—Study and teaching	636.2142071	SF241-245	Dancing mice	599.35	QL737.R6
Daisies	583.99	QK495.C74	Dandelions	583.99	QK495.C74
Daisies	635.93399	SB413.D2	Dandie Dinmont terrier	636.755	SF429.D33
Daisy Girl Scouts	369.463	HS3359	Dandruff	616.546	RL91
Dajo, Mount, Battle of, 1906	959.9032	DS685	Dangerous animals	591.65	QL100
Dakini (Buddhist deity)	294.34211	BQ4750.D33	Dangerous birds	598.165	QL677.75
Dakota Indians	978.004975243	E99.D1	Dangerous fishes	597.165	QL618.7
Dakota Indians—Wars, 1862-1865	978.302	E83.86	Dangerous marine animals	591.6509162	QL100
Dakota Indians—Wars, 1862-1865	978.402	E83.86	Dangerous reptiles	597.9165	QL645.7
Dakota Indians—Wars, 1876	978.302	E83.876	Danish Americans	973.043981073	E184.S19
Dakota Indians—Wars, 1876	978.402	E83.876	Danish drama	839.81208	PT7999-8020
Dakota Indians—Wars, 1876	978.403031	E83.876	Danish drama	839.81209	PT7800-7832
Dakota Indians—Wars, 1890-1891	978.303031	E83.89	Danish fiction	839.81308	PT8022-8024
Dakota language	497.5243	PM1021-1024	Danish fiction	839.81309	PT7835-7862
Dalai lamas	294.361	BQ7930	Danish language	439.81	PD3001-3929
Dall Porpoise	599.53	QL737.C434	Danish language—Dialects	439.817	PD3700-3929
Dallas (Tex.)	976.42812	F394.D21	Danish language—Dictionaries	439.813	PD3625-3693
Dalmatia (Croatia)—Maps	912.4972	G2025-2027	Danish language—Etymology	439.812	PD3571-3599
Dalmatian dog	636.72	SF429.D3	Danish language—Grammar	439.815	PD3101-3400
Dalmatian language (Romance)	457.994972	PC890	Danish language—Lexicography	439.813028	PD3601-3693
Dalmatian poetry	891.821008	PG1654-.5	Danish language—Slang	439.817	PD3901-3929
Dalmatian poetry	891.821009	PG1650-.5	Danish language—Study and teaching	439.81071	PD3065
Dalton laboratory plan	371.382	LB1029.L3	Danish letters	839.81608	PT8030
			Danish letters	839.81609	PT7866
			Danish literature	839.81	PT7601-8260
			Danish literature—To 1500	839.811	PT7721-7737

Subject Heading	Dewey	LC	Subject Heading	Dewey	LC
Danish literature—18th century	839.814	PT7741-7747	Day care centers	362.712	HQ778.5-.7
Danish literature—19th century	839.816	PT7751-7756	Day care centers for the aged	362.68	HV1455-.2
Danish literature—20th century	839.817	PT7760	Day care centers for the handicapped	362.48	HV1568.7-.8
Danish literature—Study and teaching	839.81071	PT7640-7644	Daylighting	729.28	NA2794
			Daylilies	584.32	QK495.L72
Danish newspapers	078.489	PN5281-5289	Days	398.33	GR930
Danish periodicals	058.81	PN5281-5290	Daytona International Speedway Race	796.72068759	GV1033.5.D
Danish philology	439.81	PD3001-3071			
Danish poetry	839.811	PT7770-7795	Daza language	496.5	PL8127
Danish poetry	839.81108	PT7975-7994	De facto school segregation	379.263	LC212.6-.63
Danish prose literature	839.81808	PT7835-7862			
Danish prose literature	839.81808	PT8021-8024	Deaconesses	262.14	BV4423-4425
Dano-Swedish War, 1643-1645	948.9701	DL190	Deacons	262.02	BX1912
			Deacons	262.14	BV680
Dano-Swedish Wars, 1657-1660	948.9701	DL192	Dead	393	GR455
			Dead	393	GT3150-3390
Danube River Valley	943.3	DJK76.2-.8	Dead	614.6	RA619-640
Dardanelles, Battle of the, 1656	956.10153	DR534.5.D3	Dead loads (Mechanics)	624.172	TA648.2
			Deadly sins	241.3	BV4626
Dardic languages	491.499	PK7001-7070	Deaf	362.42	HV2350-2990.5
Dargwa language	499.964	PK9201.D3	Deaf—[By region or country]	362.4209(4-9)	HV2510-2990.5
Dargwa literature	899.964	PK9201.D35-+ .D39			
			Deaf—Education	371.912	HV2417-2500
Dari language	491.56	PK6871-6879	Deaf—Marriage	306.810872	HQ1040
Dark matter (Astronomy)	523.1126	QB791.3	Deaf—United States	362.420973	HV2510-2561
Darters (Fishes)	597.75	QL638.P4	Deafness	617.8	RF286-320
Darts (Game)	794.3	GV1564-1565	Deafness, Noise induced	617.8	RF293.5
Data compression (Computer science)	005.746	QA76.9.D33	Deans (Education)	371.4	LB2341
			Death	306.9	HQ1073-.5
Data recovery (Computer science)	005.86	QA76.9.D348	Death	393	GR455
			Death	393	GT3150-3390.5
Data tape drives	621.3976	TK7887.55	Death	571.936	QH671
Data transmission systems	621.38216	TK5105-.42	Death	571.939	QP87
Database design	005.74	QA76.9.D26	Death	616.078	RA1063-.5
Database industry	338.4702504	HD9696.D36-.D364	Death, Apparent	616.078	RA1063
			Death—Causes	616.078	RA1063
Database management	005.74	QA76.9.D3	Death—Proof and certification	353.596	RA405
Database marketing	381.1	HF5415.126			
Database security	005.8	QA76.9.D314	Death—Psychological aspects	155.937	BF789.D4
Databases	005.74	QA76.9.D32			
Date	634.62	SB364	Death instinct	155.937	BF175.5.D4
Date palm	584.5	QK495.P17	Death marches	940.547	D804.7.D43
Date palm	634.62	SB364	Deathbed hallucinations	133.9013	BF1063.D4
Dating violence	306.73	HQ801.83	Debates and debating	808.53	PN4177-4191
Dattatreya (Hindu deity)	294.52113	BL1225.D3	Debit cards	332.76	HG1710.5
Dauntless (Dive bomber)	358.42	UG1242.A28	Debris avalanches	551.307	QE599
David, King of Israel, in the Koran	297.122092	BP133.7.D38	Debts, External	336.34	HJ8003-8899
			Debts, Public	336.34	HJ8001-8899
Davits	623.86	VM801	Debts, Public—[By region or country]	336.3409(4-9)	HJ8101-8899
Davits	623.86	VM831			
Dawah (Islam)	297.74	BP170.85	Debts, Public—Law and legislation—England	343.42037	KD5300
Dawn redwood	585.5	QK494.5.T3			
Dawn redwood	634.9758	SD397.D37	Debts, Public—Law and legislation—United States	343.73037	KF6241-6245
Day camps	796.5423	GV197.D3			
			Decadrachma	737.4938	CJ359

Subject Heading	Dewey	LC	Subject Heading	Dewey	LC
Decalcomania	745.74	NK9510	Deductive databases	006.33	QA76.9.D32
Decapoda (Crustacea)	595.38	QL444.M33	Deep diving	797.23	GV840.S78
Decay schemes (Radioactivity)	539.752	QC793.3.D4	Deep-sea drilling ships	623.828	VM453
Decay schemes (Radioactivity)	539.752	QC795.8.D4	Deep-sea ecology	577.7	QH541.5.D35
Decca navigation	623.89	VK560	Deep-sea temperature	551.4653	GC175
Decentralization in government	352.283	JS113	Deepwater rice	584.9	QK495.G74
Decentralization in management	658.402	HD50	Deer	599.65	QL737.U55
			Deer farming	636.29401	SF401.D3
Decidability (Mathematical logic)	511.3	QA9.65	Deer hunting	799.2765	SK301
			Defecation disorders	616.342	RC866.D43
Decimal fractions	513.265	QA242	Defense industries	338.47355	HD9743-9744
Decimal system	332.404	HG393	Defense industries—Employees	338.47355092	HD8039.M9
Decimal system	530.812	QC90.8-94			
Decision-making	153.83	BF448	Defense Mechanisms Inventory	155.2	RC473.D43
Decision-making	519.542	QA279.4-.7	Deferred tax	657.46	HF5681.D39
Decision-making	658.403	HD30.23	Deficiency diseases	616.39	RC623.5-627
Decision-making	658.5036	T57.95	Deflation (Finance)	332.41	HG229-.5
Decision-making—Psychic aspects	133.3	BF1045.D42	Deformations (Mechanics)	620.11232	TA417.6
			Deglutition disorders	616.32	RC815.2
Deck machinery	623.86	VM781	Deglutition disorders	641.5631	RM221.D4
Decks (Architecture, Domestic)	690.893	TH4970	Degree of freedom	530.143	QC174.52.D43
			Degrees, Academic	378.2	LB2381-2391
Decomposition method	518	QA402.2	Delaware Indians	974.00497345	E99.D2
Decompression sickness	616.9894	RC103.C3	Delaware—Gazetteers	917.51003	F162
Decoration and ornament	745.4	NK1160-1590	Delaware—History	975.1	F161-175
Decoration and ornament, Ancient	745.442	NK1180-1250	Delaware—History— Revolution, 1775-1783	975.10(2-3)	E263.D3
Decoration and ornament, Architectural	729	NA3310-4050	Delaware—History—War of 1812	975.103	E359.5.D3
Decoration and ornament, Baroque	745.443	NK1345	Delaware—History—Civil War, 1861-1865	975.103	E500
Decoration and ornament, Buddhist	745.40882943	NK1676	Delaware—History—1865-1950	975.14(1-3)	F169
Decoration and ornament, Byzantine	745.442	NK1652.25	Delaware—History—1951-	975.104(3-4)	F170
Decoration and ornament, Gothic	745.442	NK1295	Delaware—Maps	912.751	G3830-3834
			Delaware—National Guard	355.3709751	UA110-119
Decoration and ornament, Islamic	745.442088297	NK1270-1275	Delaware—Periodicals	975.1005	F161
Decoration and ornament, Medieval	745.442	NK1260-1295	Delegation of authority	658.402	HD50-.5
			Delegation of powers	352.283	JF225
Decoration and ornament, Primitive	745.441	NK1177	Delftware	738.37	NK4295-.5
			Delirium tremens	616.861	RC526
Decoration and ornament, Renaissance	745.443	NK1330	Delivery of goods	658.788	HF5761-5780
Decoration and ornament, Rococo	745.443	NK1355	Delmarva Peninsula—History— Revolution, 1775-1783	975.210(2-3)	E263.D3
Decoration and ornament, Romanesque	745.442	NK1285	Delphian oracle	133.32480938	DF261.D35
Decorations of honor	355.1342	UB430-435	Delphinium	635.93334	SB413.D4
Decorations of honor	929.81	CR4501-6305	Deltas	551.456	GB591-598
Decoys (Hunting)	745.5936	TT199.75	Deluge	222.11	BS658
Decoys (Hunting)	799.2028	SK335	Demand for money	332.414	HG226.5
Dedekind rings	512.4	QA251.3	Deme	320.938	JC75.D
Dedication services	265.92	BV199.D4	Dementia	616.83	RC521-524
			Demeter (Greek deity)	292.2114	BL820.C5
			Demidoff's galago	599.83	QL737.P93
			Democracy	321.8	JC421-423
			Democratic centralism	335.43	HX77

Subject Heading	Dewey	LC	Subject Heading	Dewey	LC
Demographic anthropology	304.6	GN33.5	Demography—Congo (Brazzaville)	304.6096724	HB3665
Demographic libraries	026.3046	Z675.D28	Demography—Cook Islands	304.6099623	HB3693.65
Demographic surveys	304.60723	HB849.49	Demography—Costa Rica	304.6097286	HB3537-3538
Demographic transition	304.6	HB887	Demography—Cote d'Ivoire	304.6096668	HB3666
Demography	304.6	HB	Demography—Cuba	304.6097291	HB3549-3550
Demography	304.6	HB848-3697	Demography—Curacao	304.60972986	HB3557.37
Demography—Biography	304.6092	HB855-865	Demography—Cyprus	304.6095693	HB3633.5
Demography—Periodicals	304.605	HB848	Demography—Czechoslovakia	304.609437	HB3592.3
Demography— Afghanistan	304.609581	HB3636.6	Demography—Denmark	304.609489	HB3611-3612
Demography—Albania	304.6094965	HB3626.5	Demography—Djibouti	304.6096771	HB3662.3
Demography—Algeria	304.60965	HB3661.4	Demography—Dominica	304.609729841	HB3556.93
Demography—American Samoa	304.6099613	HB3693.7	Demography—Dominican Republic	304.6097293	HB3552
Demography—Angola	304.609673	HB3664.4	Demography—Ecuador	304.609866	HB3569-3570
Demography—Anguilla	304.60972973	HB3556.72	Demography—Egypt	304.60962	HB3661.7
Demography—Antigua	304.60972974	HB3556.74	Demography—El Salvador	304.6097284	HB3544
Demography—Arctic Regions	304.60998	HB3695	Demography—England and Wales	304.60942(9)	HB3585-3586
Demography—Argentina	304.60982	HB3559-3560	Demography—Equatorial Guinea	304.6096718	HB3664.6
Demography—Aruba	304.60972986	HB3557.35	Demography—Ethiopia	304.60963	HB3662
Demography—Australia	304.60994	HB3675-3676	Demography—Falkland Islands	304.6099711	HB3671
Demography—Austria	304.609436	HB3591-3592	Demography—Fiji	304.6099611	HB3693.5
Demography—Azores	304.6094699	HB3667.5	Demography—Finland	304.6094897	HB3608.3
Demography—Bahamas	304.6097296	HB3547-3548	Demography—France	304.60944	HB3593-3594
Demography—Bahrain	304.6095365	HB3635.9	Demography—French Guiana	304.609882	HB3572.7
Demography—Bangladesh	304.6095492	HB3640.6	Demography—French Polynesia	304.609962	HB3693.9
Demography—Barbados	304.60972981	HB3556.57	Demography—Gabon	304.6096721	HB3664.9
Demography—Belgium	304.609493	HB3603-3604	Demography—Gambia	304.6096651	HB3667
Demography—Belize	304.6097282	HB3535-3536	Demography—Germany	304.60943	HB3595-3596.5
Demography—Benin	304.6096683	HB3665.7	Demography—Ghana	304.609667	HB3666.8
Demography—Bermuda Islands	304.6097299	HB3668	Demography—Greece	304.609495	HB3632.5
Demography—Bhutan	304.6095498	HB3640.3	Demography—Greenland	304.609982	HB3696
Demography—Bolivia	304.60984	HB3561-3562	Demography—Grenada	304.609729845	HB3556.95
Demography—Bonaire	304.60972986	HB3557.36	Demography—Guadeloupe	304.60972976	HB3557.7
Demography—Botswana	304.6096883	HB3663.9	Demography—Guam	304.609967	HB3692.7
Demography—Brazil	304.60981	HB3563-3564	Demography—Guatemala	304.6097281	HB3539
Demography—Bulgaria	304.609499	HB3627-3628	Demography—Guinea	304.6096652	HB3666.2
Demography—Burkina Faso	304.6096625	HB3666.4	Demography—Guinea-Bissau	304.6096657	HB3667.3
Demography—Burma	304.609591	HB3636.7	Demography—Guyana	304.609881	HB3572.3
Demography—Burundi	304.60967572	HB3662.8	Demography—Haiti	304.6097294	HB3551
Demography—Cambodia	304.609596	HB3644.3	Demography—Honduras	304.6097283	HB3540
Demography—Cameroon	304.6096711	HB3665.4	Demography—Hong Kong	304.6095125	HB3657
Demography—Canada	304.60971	HB3529-3530	Demography—Hungary	304.609439	HB3592.5
Demography—Canary Islands	304.609649	HB3669	Demography—Iceland	304.6094912	HB3613-3614
Demography—Cape Verde	304.6096658	HB3669.5	Demography—India	304.60954	HB3639-3640
Demography—Central African Republic	304.6096741	HB3665.2	Demography— Indonesia	304.609598	HB3647-3648
Demography—Chad	304.6096743	HB3665.3	Demography—Iran	304.60955	HB3636.4
Demography—Chile	304.60983	HB3565-3566	Demography—Iraq	304.609567	HB3636.3
Demography—China	304.60951	HB3654	Demography—Ireland	304.609415	HB3589-3590
Demography—Colombia	304.609861	HB3567-3568	Demography—Israel	304.6095694	HB3634
Demography—Comoro Islands	304.609694	HB3672.5			

Subject Heading	Dewey	LC	Subject Heading	Dewey	LC
Demography—Italy	304.60945	HB3599-3600	Demography—Portugal	304.609469	HB3621-3622
Demography—Jamaica	304.6097292	HB3553-3554	Demography—Qatar	304.6095363	HB3635.7
Demography—Japan	304.60952	HB3651-3652	Demography—Reunion	304.6096981	HB3673.5
Demography—Jordan	304.6095695	HB3634.3	Demography—Romania	304.609498	HB3631-3632
Demography—Kenya	304.6096762	HB3662.5	Demography—Russia	304.60947	HB3607-3608.2
Demography—Kerguelen Islands	304.609699	HB3674	Demography—Rwanda	304.60967571	HB3662.7
Demography—Kiribati	304.6099681	HB3692.9	Demography—Saba (Netherlands Antilles)	304.60972977	HB3557.38
Demography—Korea	304.609519	HB3652.5-.6	Demography—Saint Eustatius (Netherlands Antilles)	304.60972977	HB3557.385
Demography—Kuwait	304.6095367	HB3636			
Demography—Laos	304.609594	HB3644.4			
Demography—Lebanon	304.6095692	HB3633.9	Demography—Saint Helena	304.609973	HB3670
Demography—Lesotho	304.6096885	HB3663.7			
Demography—Liberia	304.6096662	HB3667.2	Demography—Saint Kitts and Nevis	304.60972973	HB3556.78
Demography—Libya	304.609612	HB3661.6			
Demography—Liechtenstein	304.60943648	HB3592.9	Demography—Saint Lucia	304.609729843	HB3556.97
			Demography—Saint Martin	304.60972977	HB3557.39
Demography—Luxembourg	304.6094935	HB3606.5	Demography—Saint Vincent	304.609729844	HB3556.99
Demography—Macao	304.6095126	HB3655			
Demography—Madagascar	304.609691	HB3663.2	Demography—Sao Tome and Principe	304.6096715	HB3664.7
Demography—Madeira Islands	304.6094698	HB3668.5			
			Demography—Saudi Arabia	304.609538	HB3634.7
Demography—Malawi	304.6096897	HB3664	Demography—Scotland	304.609411	HB3587-3588
Demography—Malaysia	304.609595	HB3644.6	Demography—Senegal	304.609663	HB3666.5
Demography—Maldives	304.6095495	HB3671.5	Demography—Seychelles	304.609696	HB3672
Demography—Mali	304.6096623	HB3666.3	Demography—Sierra Leone	304.609664	HB3666.9
Demography—Martinique	304.60972982	HB3557.9	Demography—Solomon Islands	304.6099593	HB3693
Demography—Mauritania	304.609661	HB3666.6			
Demography—Mauritius	304.6096982	HB3673	Demography—Somalia	304.6096773	HB3662.2
Demography—Mexico	304.60972	HB3531-3532	Demography—South Africa	304.60968	HB3663.4
Demography—Monaco	304.60944949	HB3594.5	Demography—Spain	304.60946	HB3619-3620
Demography—Mongolia	304.609517	HB3652.8	Demography—Sri Lanka	304.6095493	HB3636.8
Demography—Montserrat	304.60972975	HB3556.76	Demography—Sudan	304.609624	HB3661.8
Demography—Morocco	304.60964	HB3661.3	Demography—Surinam	304.609883	HB3572.5
Demography—Mozambique	304.609679	HB3663	Demography—Swaziland	304.6096887	HB3663.8
Demography—Namibia	304.6096881	HB3664.2	Demography—Sweden	304.609485	HB3617-3618
Demography—Nepal	304.6095496	HB3636.9	Demography—Switzerland	304.609494	HB3623-3624
Demography—Netherlands	304.609492	HB3605-3606	Demography—Syria	304.6095691	HB3633.7
Demography—New Caledonia	304.6099597	HB3693.3	Demography—Taiwan	304.60951249	HB3656
			Demography—Tanzania	304.609678	HB3662.9
Demography—New Zealand	304.60993	HB3692.5	Demography—Thailand	304.609593	HB3644.55
			Demography—Togo	304.6096681	HB3665.8
Demography—Nicaragua	304.6097285	HB3541	Demography—Tonga	304.6099612	HB3693.6
Demography—Niger	304.6096626	HB3665.9	Demography—Trinidad and Tobago	304.60972983	HB3557
Demography—Nigeria	304.609669	HB3666.7			
Demography—Northern Ireland	304.609416	HB3588.5	Demography—Tristan da Cunha	304.609973	HB3670.5
Demography—Norway	304.609481	HB3615-3616	Demography—Tunisia	304.609611	HB3661.5
Demography—Oman	304.6095353	HB3635.3	Demography—Turkey	304.609561	HB3633.4
Demography—Pakistan	304.6095491	HB3640.5	Demography—Uganda	304.6096761	HB3662.6
Demography—Panama	304.6097287	HB3542-3543	Demography—United Arab Emirates	304.6095357	HB3635.5
Demography—Papua New Guinea	304.609953	HB3692.8			
			Demography—United States	304.60973	HB3505-3527
Demography—Paraguay	304.609892	HB3573-3574			
Demography—Peru	304.60985	HB3575-3576	Demography—[United States, By State]	304.6097(4-9)	HB3525
Demography—Philippines	304.609599	HB3649-3650			
Demography—Poland	304.609438	HB3608.7			

Subject Heading	Dewey	LC
Demography—[United States, By City]	304.6097(4-9)	HB3527
Demography—Uruguay	304.609895	HB3577-3578
Demography—Vanuatu	304.6099595	HB3693.4
Demography—Venezuela	304.60987	HB3579-3580
Demography—Vietnam	304.609597	HB3644.5
Demography—Virgin Islands of the United States	304.609729722	HB3556.3
Demography—Western Sahara	304.609648	HB3667.4
Demography—Western Samoa	304.6099614	HB3693.8
Demography—Yemen	304.609533	HB3634.9-3635
Demography—Yugoslavia	304.609497	HB3628.5
Demography—Zaire	304.6096751	HB3664.5
Demography—Zambia	304.6096894	HB3663.6
Demolition, Military	358.23	UG370
Demoniac possession	133.426	BF1555
Demonology	133.42	BF1501-1562
Demonology	202.16	BL480
Demonology	398.45	GR540
Demonology, Islamic	297.216	BP166.89
Demurrage (Car service)	385.22	HE1826
Demythologization	225.68	BS2378
Dendrobium	635.9344	SB409
Dengue	614.58852	RA644.D4
Dengue	616.91852	RC137
Denkyira (Kingdom)	966.68	DT532.12
Denmark—History—Christian III, 1534-1559	948.903	DL187
Denmark— History—The Count's War, 1534-1536	948.903	DL187
Denmark—Census	314.89	HA1471-1490
Denmark—Civilization	936.3	DL131-133
Denmark—Civilization	948.9	DL131-133
Denmark—Colonies	325.3489	JV3300-3399
Denmark—Description and travel	913.6304	DL115-120
Denmark—Description and travel	914.8904	DL115-120
Denmark—Economic conditions	330.9489	HC351-360
Denmark—Emigration and immigration	325.(2489) or (489)	JV8200-8209
Denmark—Gazetteers	913.63003	DL105
Denmark—Gazetteers	914.89003	DL105
Denmark—History	936.3	DL101-291
Denmark—History—To 1241	948.9015	DL162-173.8
Denmark—History—1241-1397	948.90(1-2)	DL174-183.9
Denmark—History—Waldemar IV, 1340-1375	948.9015	DL176
Denmark—History—1397-1448	948.902	DL179-181.6
Denmark—History—1448-1660	948.90(2-3)	DL182-192.3
Denmark—History—Frederick I, 1523-1533	948.903	DL185-192.8
Denmark—History— Coup d'etat, 1536	948.903	DL187
Denmark—History—Frederick II, 1559-1588	948.903	DL188-.8
Denmark—History—Christian IV, 1588-1648	948.903	DL189-.5
Denmark—History—Frederick III, 1648-1670	948.903	DL191.8
Denmark—History—Coup d'etat, 1660	948.903	DL192.3
Denmark—History—Christian V, 1670-1699	948.903	DL195-.8
Denmark—History—Fredrick IV, 1699-1730	948.903	DL196-.8
Denmark—History—18th century	948.903	DL197-199
Denmark—History—Coup d'etat, 1784	948.903	DL199-.8
Denmark—History—19th century	948.904	DL201-249
Denmark—History—War of 1807-1814	948.903	DL206
Denmark—History—Frederick VI, 1808-1839	948.904	DL205-208
Denmark—History—Christian VIII, 1839-1848	948.904	DL209-212
Denmark—History—Frederick VII, 1848-1863	948.904	DL213-228
owidctlparDenmark—History—1849-1866	948.904	DL217-241
Denmark—History—Christian IX, 1863-1906	948.904	DL234-249
Denmark—History—1900-	948.90(4-6)	DL248-263
Denmark—History—Christian X, 1912-1947	948.9051	DL255-257
Denmark—History—German occupation, 1940-1945	948.9051	DL256.5-257
Denmark—Manufactures	670.9489	TS69-70
Denmark—Maps	912.489	G2055-2059
Denmark—Maps	912.489	G6920-6924
Denmark—Periodicals	948.9005	DL101
Denmark—Politics and government	320.9489	JN7101-7367
Densitometer (Meteorological instrument)	551.50284	QC880
Density matrices	530.122	QC174.17.D44
Dental adhesives	617.695	RK652.7-.8
Dental amalgams	617.675	RK519.A4
Dental anthropology	599.943	GN209
Dental auxiliary personnel	617.60233	RK60.5
Dental bonding	617.69	RK652.7-.8
Dental calculus	617.6	RK328
Dental caries	617.67	RK331

Subject Heading	Dewey	LC	Subject Heading	Dewey	LC
Dental cavity preparation	617.672	RK515	Dentures	617.692	RK656-666
Dental cements	617.695	RK652.7-.8	Dentures, Immediate	617.692	RK656-666
Dental ceramic metals	617.675	RK653.5	Denver (Colo.)	978.883	F784.D4
Dental ceramics	617.675	RK655	Department stores	381.141	HF5460-5469.5
Dental clinics	362.11	RK3-.5	Dependency (Psychology)	155.232	BF575.D34
Dental clinics—[By region or country]	362.1109(4-9)	RK3.5	Dependency (Psychology)	155.232	RC569.5.D47
Dental deposits	617.6	RK328	Deposit insurance	368.854	HG1662
Dental drilling	617.672	RK515	Depository libraries	025.26	Z675.D4
Dental enamel microabrasion	617.634	RK320.E53	Depreciation	657.73	HF5681.D5
			Depression in adolescence	616.852700835	RJ506.D4
Dental enamel—Diseases	617.634	RK340-341	Depression in children	618.928527	RJ506.D4
Dental ethics	174.2	RK52.7	Depression in infants	618.928527	RJ506.D4
Dental health education	617.60071	RK60.8	Depression in old age	616.852700846	RC537.5
Dental instruments and apparatus	617.600284	RK681-686	Depression, Mental	616.8527	RC537-545
			Depressions	338.542	HB3711-3840
Dental jurisprudence	614.18	RA1062	Depth charges	359.8251	VF509
Dental libraries	026.6176	Z675.D3	Dermatoglyphics	599.945	GN192
Dental materials	617.695	RK652.5-655	Dermatologic nursing	616.50231	RL125
Dental metallurgy	617.675	RK653	Dermatologists	616.50092	RL46.2-.3
Dental plaque	617.6	RK328	Dermatologists—Directories	616.50025	RL43
Dental prophylaxis	617.601	RK60.7-.8			
Dental public health	614.5996	RK52-.45	Dermatology	616.5	RL
Dental surveys	617.600723	RK52-.45	Dermatology	616.506	RV381-391
Dental therapeutics	617.606	RK318-320	Dermatology	616.506	RX561-581
Dentistry	617.6	RK	Dermatology, Experimental	616.5027	RL79
Dentistry, Ancient	617.60901	RK31	Dermatology—Apparatus and instruments	616.500284	RL55
Dentistry, Naval	359.345	VG280-285			
Dentistry, Operative	617.605	RK501-519	Dermatology—Congresses	616.5006	RL31
Dentistry, Operative—Complications	617.605	RK513	Dermatology—History	616.5009	RL46
			Dermatology—Periodicals	616.5005	RL26
Dentistry, Operative—Positioning	617.605	RK503	Dermatology—Societies, etc.	616.5006	RL1
Dentistry—Congresses	617.6006	RK21	Dermatology—Study and teaching	616.50071	RL77
Dentistry—Examinations, questions, etc.	617.60076	RK57			
			Dermatology—Terminology	616.50014	RL39
Dentistry—Formulae, receipts, prescriptions	617.606	RK701-715	Dermis	573.5	QL941-943
			Dermis	573.5	QP88.5
Dentistry—History	617.60901	RK29-34	Dermis	611.77	QM484
Dentistry—Periodicals	617.6005	RK16	Description (Rhetoric)	820.8022	PE1427
Dentistry—Practice	617.6023	RK58-59.3	Description (Rhetoric)	820.8022	PR1285
Dentistry—Psychological aspects	617.60019	RK53	Descriptive cataloging	025.32	Z693-695.83
			Desensitization (Psychotherapy)	616.8914	RC489.D45
Dentistry—Research	617.60072	RK80			
Dentistry—Societies, etc.	617.6006	RK1	Desert animals	591.754	QL116
Dentistry—Study and teaching	617.60071	RK71-231	Desert biology	578.754	QH88
			Desert ecology	577.54	QH541.5.D4
Dentistry—Study and teaching—[By region or country]	617.600710(4-9)	RK86-231	Desert gardening	635.9525	SB427.5
			Desert kangaroo rat	599.35987	QL737.R66
			Desert locust	595.726	QL508.A2
Dentistry—Study and teaching—United States	617.6071073	RK91-97	Desert plants	581.754	QK922
			Desert plants	581.754	QK938.D4
Dentistry—Terminology	617.60014	RK28	Desert plants	635.9525	SB427.5
Dentistry—Vocational guidance	617.60023	RK60-.5	Desert reclamation	333.736153	HD1711-1741
			Desert reclamation	333.736153	TC801-957
Dentists—Directories	617.60025	RK37	Desert reclamation	631.6	S612-619
Denture attachments	617.69	RK656	Desert soils	631.49154	S592.17.D47
			Desert soils	631.49154	S599-.9

Subject Heading	Dewey	LC	Subject Heading	Dewey	LC
Desert tortoise	597.92	QL666.C584	Developing countries—Population	304.6091724	HB884
Desertification	551.415	GB611-618	Development banks	332.28	HG1975-1976
Desertification—Control	551.415	GB611-618	Developmental immunology	571.9638	QR184.5
Desertion and non-support	306.88	HQ805	Developmental psychology	155	BF712-724.85
Desertion, Military	355.1334	UB788	Developmental reading	418.4	LB1050.53
Desertion, Naval	359.1334	VB870-875	Developmentally disabled	362.1968	HV1570-.5
Desertion—[Other countries]	306.8809(4-9)	HQ837-960.9	Developmentally disabled children	362.1968	HV891-901
Desertion—United States	306.880973	HQ833-836	Deventer, Surrender of, 1587	949.203	DH199.D4
Deserts	551.415	GB611-618	Device drivers (Computer programs)	005.713	QA76.76.D49
Deserts	578.754	QH88	Devices (Heraldry)	929.6	CR67-69
Deserts—Maps	912.1954	G1046.C813	Devil	133.422	BF1546-1561
Design	745.4	NC703	Devil	202.16	BL480
Design	745.4	NK1160-1590	Devil	235.4	BT980-981
Design protection—England	346.420484	KD1345	Devil (Islam)	297.216	BP166.89
Design protection—United States	346.730484	KF3086	Devil in literature	808.8038291 + 216	PN57.D4
Designer drugs	616.86	RM316	Devon cattle	636.226	SF199.D38
Design—Study and teaching	745.4071	NK1170	Devotion	242	BV4815
Desirade (Guadeloupe)	972.976	F2050	Devotion (Buddhism)	294.344	BQ5595-5630
Desks	684.14	TS880	Devotional calendars	242.3	BV4810-4812
Desks	684.14	TT197.5.D4	Devotional exercises	248	BV4800-4897
Desktop publishing	686.22544416	Z253.53-.532	Devotional literature	242	BV4800-4895
Desktop publishing	686.22544416	Z286.D47	Devotional literature	242	BX2177-2198
Despotism	321.6	JC375-392	Dew	551.5744	QC929.D5
Desserts	641.86	TX773	Dewar flasks	542	QD535
Destroyers (Warships)	359.3254	V825-.5	Dew-ponds	628.13	TD395
Detective and mystery plays	808.82527	PN6120.M9	Dexter cattle	636.225	SF199.D4
Detective and mystery stories	808.83872	PZ1-3	Dextrose	547.78	QD321
Detective and mystery stories	809.3872	PN3448.D4	Dge-lugs-pa (Sect)	294.39	BQ7530-7950
Detective and mystery stories—Technique	809.3872	PN3377.5.D4	Dharma (Buddhism)	294.34	BQ4195-4250
Detectives	363.25092	HV7551-8077	Dhat al-Sawari, Battle of, 655	956.013	DS38.1
Detectives in mass media	363.25092	P96.D4	Dhows	623.8226	VM371
Detergent pollution of rivers, lakes, etc.	628.1682	TD427.D4	Diabetes	614.59462	RA645.D5
Determinants	512.9432	QA191	Diabetes	616.462	RC658.5
Determination (Personality trait)	155.234	BF698.35.D48	Diabetes	616.462	RC660-662.4
Determinism (Philosophy)	123	B105.D47	Diabetes clinics	362.12	RC660.7
Deterrence (Strategy)	355.0217	U162.6	Diabetes in adolescence	616.46200835	RJ420.D5
Detonation waves	532.593	QC168.85.D46	Diabetes in children	618.92462083	RJ420.D5
Detroit (Mich.)	977.434	F574.D4	Diabetes in pregnancy	618.326	RG580.D5
Detroit (Mich.)—Surrender to the British, 1812	973.523	E356.D4	Diabetes in youth	618.92462083	RJ420.D5
Deuterium	546.212	QD181.H1	Diabetic retinopathy	617.735	RE661.D5
Deuteron magnetic resonance spectroscopy	538.362	QC762	Diagnosis	616.075	RC71-78.7
Devanagari alphabet	491.(2-4)	PK119	Diagnosis, Differential	616.075	RC71.5
Devanarayana (Hindu deity)	294.52113	BL1225.D48	Diagnosis, Fluoroscopic	616.07572	RC78.7.F5
Developing countries—History	909.09724	D880-888	Diagnosis, Laboratory	616.075	RB37-56.5
			Diagnosis, Noninvasive	616.075	RC71.6
			Diagnosis, Radioscopic	616.0757	RC78-.5
			Diagnosis, Ultrasonic	616.07543	RC78.7.U4
			Diagnostic equipment industry	338.47681761	HD9995 .D54-.D544
			Diagnostic imaging	616.0754	RC78.7.D53
			Dialectical materialism	146.32	B809.8

Subject Heading	Dewey	LC	Subject Heading	Dewey	LC
Dialing	529.7	QB215	Differentiable dynamical systems	515.39	QA614.8
Dialogue	808.8026	PN1551	Differential Aptitude Tests	153.94	BF432.5.D53
Dialogue sermons	252	BV4307.D5	Differential equations	515.35	QA370-380
Diamagnetism	538.42	QC771	Differential equations	620.00151	TA347.D45
Diamond Necklace Affair, France, 1785	944.035	DC137.15	Differential equations, Linear	515.354	QA372
Diamonds	549.27	QE393	Differential equations, Partial	515.353	QA374-377
Diamonds	622.382	TN990-994	Differential forms	515.37	QA381
Diamonds	739.27	NK7658-7663	Differential invariants	515.37	QA381
Diamonds	739.27	TS753-.5	Differential relays	621.317	TK2861
Diamonds as an investment	332.63	HD9677	Differential topology	514.72	QA613.6-.66
Diamonds, Artificial	666.88	TP873.5.D5	Differential-algebraic equations	512.56	QA372.5
Diamonds, Industrial	621.9	TJ1193	Differential-difference equations	515.38	QA373
Diaphragm	573.26	QL851	Diffraction	535.4	QC414.8-417
Diaphragm	611.26	QM265	Diffusion	530.475	QC185
Diaphragm	612.2	QP121	Diffusion processes	519.233	QA274.75
Diarrhea	616.3427	RC862.D5	Digambara (Jaina sect)	294.493	BL1380.D
Diarrhea Infantile	618.923427	RJ456.D5	Digestion	612.3	QP145-159
Diarrhea—Homeopathic treatment	616.306	RX336.D5	Digestive enzymes	573.347	QP609.D52
Diathermy	615.8323	RM874	Digestive organs	573.3	QL856-867
Diatomaceous earth	622.36	TN948.D5	Digestive organs	611.3	QM301-367
Dice	795.1	GV1303	Digestive organs—Cancer	616.99434	RC280.D5
Dice games	795.1	GV1303	Digestive organs—Diseases	616.3	RC799-869
Dicetyledons, Fossil	561.3	QE983	Digestive organs—Diseases—Eclectic treatment	616.306	RV271-276
Dicotyledons	583	QK108-474.5			
Dicotyledons	583	QK495.A12	Digestive organs—Diseases—Homeopathic treatment	616.306	RX331-336
Dictating machines	651.74	HF5548			
Dictators	321.9092	JC495			
Dictionaries, Polyglot	413	P361	Digestive organs—Radiography	616.307572	RC804.A5
Dictionaries, Polyglot	413	PB331			
Dictograph	651.74	HF5548	Digestive organs—Surgery	617.55059	RD540-547
Didgora Mountain (Georgia), Battle of, 1121	947.02	DK511.G44	Digital audiotape recorders and recording	621.3883	TK7881.65
Diegueno Indians	979.40049757	E99.D5	Digital cameras	771.33	TR256
Dielectric measurements	537.240287	QC584	Digital communications	621.382	TK5103.7-.8
Dielectrics	537.24	QC584-585.8	Digital computer industry	338.47004	HD9696.D54-.D544
Dien Bien Phu (Vietnam), Battle of, 1954	959.7042	DS553.3.D5			
Dieppe Raid, 1942	940.54214	D756.5.D5	Digital integrated circuits	621.395	TK7874-.8
Dies (Metal-working)	621.984	TS253	Digital mapping	526.0285	GA139
Diesel fuels	665.5384	TP343	Digital photography	775	TR267
Diesel fuels industry	338.476655384	HD9579.D5-.D54	Digital subtraction angiography	618.92107572	RJ423.5.D54
Diesel locomotives	625.266	TJ619-.7	Digital television	621.38807	TK6678
Diesel motor	621.436	TJ795	Digital video	621.388332	TK6680.5-6687
Diet	613.2	RA784	Digitalis	615.711	RM666.D5
Diet	641.563	TX551-560	Digitalis	615.711	RS165.D5
Diet in disease	615.854	RM214-258	Dikes (Engineering)	627.24	TC337
Diet kitchens	363.883	HV694	Dikes (Geology)	551.88	QE611-.5
Diet therapy	615.854	RM214-258	Diktynna (Greek deity)	292.2114	BL820.D54
Diet therapy for children	618.9200654	RJ53.D53	Dill	583.849	QK495.U48
Dietaries	641.563	TX551-560	Diluted magnetic semiconductors	537.6223	QC611.8.M25
Dietetics	615.854	RM214-258			
Difference algebra	512.56	QA247.4			
Difference equations	515.625	QA431			

Subject Heading	Dewey	LC	Subject Heading	Dewey	LC
Dining room furniture	684.13	TT197.5.D5	Disaster relief—[By region or country]	363.34809(4-9)	HV555
Dining room furniture	747.76	NK2117.D5	Disaster relief—Law and legislation—United States	344.7305348	KF3750
Dining rooms	643.4	TX855-859	Disasters in the press	904	PN4784.D57
Dining rooms	747.76	NK2117.D5	Disasters—Psychological aspects	155.935	BF789.D5
Dinka (African people)	962.4004965	DT155.2.D56	Disbudding	631.54	SB125
Dinka language	496.5	PL8131	Discernment of spirits	248.29	BV5083
Dinners and dining	641.54	TX737	Discernment of spirits (Islam)	297.21	BP166.89
Dinosaurs	567.9	QE862.D5	Disciples of Christ	286.6	BX7301-7343
Dinosaurs in mass media	567.9	P96.M6	Discipline of children	371.5	LB3025
Dinwiddie Court House, Battle of, Dinwiddie, Va.1865	973.738	E477.67	Discipline of children	649.64	HQ770.4
Diocesan pastoral councils	262.3	BX838	Disco dancing	793.33	GV1796.D57
Diodes, IMPATT	621.381522	TK7871.89.A94	Discount	332.84	HG1651-1654
Diodes, Switching	621.381522	TK7871.89.S95	Discount brokers	332.62	HG4621
Diola (African people)	966.30049632	DT549.45.D56	Discount houses (Finance)	332.84	HG1651-1654
Diola language	496.32	PL8134	Discount houses (Retail trade)	381.149	HF5429.2-.215
Dionysia	292.2113	BL820.B2	Discourse analysis	401.41	P302-.87
Diophantine analysis	512.74	QA242	Discoverer (Artificial satellite)	629.434	TL796.5.U6D
Diophantine equations	512.72	QA242	Discoveries in geography	910.9	G200-336
Diorama	751.74	ND2880-.5	Discoveries in science	509	Q180.55.D57
Diorite	552.3	QE462.D56	Discrete-time systems	003.83	QA402
Diphtheria	616.9313	RC138-.9	Discretion	241.4	BV4647.D6
Diphtheria—Prevention	614.5123	RA644.D6	Discriminate analysis	519.535	QA278.65
Diplomatics	327.2	CD	Discrimination in education	379.26	LC212-.863
Diplomatics	327.2	CD1-724	Discrimination in employment	331.133	HD4903-.5
Diplomatics—[By region or country]	327.2090(1-5)	CD50-79	Discrimination in housing	363.51	HD7288.75-.76
Diplopia	617.762	RE738	Discrimination in mortgage loans	332.72	HG2040.2
Dippers (Birds)	598.832	QL696.P235	Diseases and history	616.009	R702
Direct broadcast satellite television	384.552	TK6677	Diseases—Chiropractic treatment	615.534	RZ260-275
Direct costing	657.42	HF5686.C8	Diseases—Reporting	614.4	RA404
Direct current amplifiers	621.381535	TK7871.58.D5	Disfigured children	362.4083	HV903-907
Direct energy conversion	621.3124	TK2896	Disguise	391	GT1747-1748
Direct marketing	381.1	HF5415.126	Disguised unemployment	331.137	HD5708.7-.75
Direct reactions (Nuclear physics)	539.76	QC794.8.D57	Disinfection and disinfectants	614.48	RA761-767
Direct taxation	336.294	HJ3863-3925	Disinfection markings (Philately)	769.56	HE6184.D56
Direct taxation—[By region or country]	336.29409(4-9)	HJ3925.A-.Z	Dislocations	617.16	RD106
Directories	011.7	AY2001	Dislocations in crystals	548.842	QD945
Directories	030	AY	Disorderly conduct	364.143	HV6486-6491
Directors of corporations	658.422	HD2745	Dispensaries	362.12	RA960-993
Directors of religious education	268.3	BV1531	Dispensatories	615.13	RS151.2-.9
Disability evaluations	616.075	RA1055.5	Dispensatories, Eclectic	615.53	RV431
Disability evaluations	616.075	RC963.4	Dispersion	535.4	QC431-435
Disability retirement	306.38	HD7105.2-.25	Displacement (Ships)	623.81	VM157
Disability studies	362.4072	HV1568.2-.25	Display of merchandise	659.152	HF5845-5849
Disappeared persons	362.87	HV6322-.7	Displays in education	371.33	LB1043.6
Disappointment	152.4	BF575.D57	Disposal tableware industry	338.4767634	HD9971.5(.T32-.T324)
Disarmament—Inspection	327.1747	UA12.5			
Disaster hospitals	362.11	RA975.D57			
Disaster nursing	610.7349	RT108			
Disaster relief	363.348	HV553-639			

Subject Heading	Dewey	LC	Subject Heading	Dewey	LC
Dissecting aortic aneurysms	617.413	RD598.5	Divorce therapy	616.89156	RC488.6
Dissecting aortic aneurysms	617.413059	RC693	Divorced fathers	306.874208653	HQ756
Disseminated intravascular coagulation	616.157	RC647.D5	Dixieland music	781.653	M1366
			Dixieland music	784.165309	ML3505.8-3509
Dissenters, Religious—England	280.40941	BX5200-5207	Diyari (Australian people)	994.0049915	DU125.D59
Dissertations, Academic	378.242	LB2369	Djibouti	967.71	DT411-.9
Dissociation	541.364	QD517	Djibouti—Census	316.771	HA4691
Dissociation	541.3722	QD562.I65	Djibouti—Civilization	967.71	DT411.4
Dissociative disorders	616.8523	RC553.D5	Djibouti—Description and travel	916.77104	DT411.27
Distance education	371.35	LC5800-5808	Djibouti—Gazetteers	916.771003	DT411.15
Distances—Tables	910.21	G109-110	Djibouti—History	967.71	DT411.5-.83
Distemper	636.70896	SF991.D5	DNA	572.86	QP624-.75
Distillation	542.4	QD63.D6	DNA Ligases	572.86	QP619.D53
Distillation	660.28425	TP156.D5	DNA topoisomerase I	572.86	QP616.D56
Distilled water	623.854	VM505	DNA topoisomerase II	572.86	QP616.D56
Distilleries	690.54	TH4532	DNA viruses	579.24	QR394.5
Distillers feeds	636.0855	SF99.D5	Doberman pinschers	636.736	SF429.D6
Distilling industries	338.4766316	HD9390-9395	Docks	387.15	HE550-560
Distinguished Conduct Medal (Great Britain)	355.13420941	UB435.G	Docks	387.15	HE951-953
			Docks	387.15	VK361-365
Distinguished Service Cross (U.S.)	355.13420973	UB433	Docks	627.31	TC355-365
			Doctor of philosophy degree	378.2	LB2386
Distributed artificial intelligence	006.3	Q337	Doctrinal theology	230	BT
Distributed databases	005.758	QA76.9.D3	Doctrine and covenants stories	289.32	BX8628.A5
Distributed operating systems (Computers)	005.4476	QA76.76.O63	Documentary credit	332.7	HG3746
			Documentary hypothesis (Pentateuchal criticism)	222.106	BS1225
Distribution (Probability theory)	519.24	QA273.6	Documentary photography	070.49	TR820.5
Ditch, Battle of the, 627	953.802	DS232	Documents on microfilm	686.43	Z265-.5
Ditches	627.54	TC970	Dodder	583.94	QK495.C98
Diuretics	615.761	RM377	Dodo	598.65	QL696.C67
Diuretics	615.761	RS431.D58	Dog breeders	636.7082	SF422.7-.86
Dive bombers	358.4283	UG1242.A28	Dog collars	636.70837	SF427.15
Divehi language	491.487	PK1836	Dog grooming industry	381.41670833	SF427.55
Divergence (Meteorology)	551.515	QC880.4.D5	Dog industry	381.4167	SF434.5-435
Diversification in industry	338.6	HD2756-.2	Dog Mass	264.02	BX2015.5.H
Diversity in the workplace	658.3008	HF5549.5.M5	Dog owners	636.708	SF422.7-.82
Dividend reinvestment	332.63221	HG4028.D5	Dog race betting	798.8	SF440.2
Divination	133.3	BF1745-1779	Dog racing	798.8	SF439.5-440.2
Divination	203.2	BL613	Dog rescue	636.0832	HV4746
Divine right of kings	321.6	JC389	Dog shows	636.70811	SF425-.8
Diving	797.24	GV837	Dog walking	636.7083	SF427.46
Diving bells	623.827	VM987	Dogfish	597.36	QL638.9
Diving for men	797.24081	GV838.62.M45	Dogger Bank, Battle of the, 1915	940.455	D582.D6
Diving for women	797.24082	GV838.62.W65	Dogma	230	BT19-33
Diving—Jackknife dive	797.24	GV838.65.J32	Dogmatism	155.232	BF698.35.D64
Diving—Swan dive	797.24	GV838.65.S84	Dogon (African people)	966.004963	DT530.5.D64
Division	513.214	QA115	Dogon (African people)	966.23004963	DT551.45.D64
Division algebras	512.3	QA247.45	Dogs	398.3699772	GR720
Division of labor	338.6	HD51	Dogs	599.77	QL737.C2
Divorce	306.89	HQ811-960.7	Dogs	636.7	SF421-440.2
Divorce—[By region or country]	306.8809(4-9)	HQ831-960.7	Dogs as carriers of disease	614.56	RA641.D6
			Dogs—Diseases	636.70896	SF991-992

Subject Heading	Dewey	LC	Subject Heading	Dewey	LC
Dogs—Obedience trials	636.70811	SF425.7	Dominican Republic—Civilization	972.93	F1935
Dogs—Pedigrees	636.70822	SF423	Dominican Republic—Description and travel	917.29304	F1936-.3
Dogs—Training	636.70835	SF431	Dominican Republic—Emigration and immigration	325.(27293) or (7293)	JV7395
Dolgan dialect	494.332	PL364.Z9.D			
Doll clothes—Patterns	745.5922	TT175.7			
Doll furniture	745.5923	TT175.5	Dominican Republic—Gazetteers	917.293003	F1932
Doll industry	338.476887221	HD9993 .D65-.D654	Dominican Republic—History	972.93	F1937-1938.58
Dollhouses	745.5923	NK4891.3-4894.4	Dominican Republic—History—To 1844	972.930(1-4)	F1938.3
Dollhouses	745.5923	TT175.3	Dominican Republic—History—1844-1930	972.930(4-52)	F1938.4
Dollhouses	790.133	GV1220	Dominican Republic—History—American occupation, 1916-1924	972.93052	F1938.45
Dolls	688.7221	TS2301.T7			
Dolls	745.59221	NK4891.3-4894.4	Dominican Republic—History—1930-	972.9305(3-5)	F1938.5-.58
Dolls	745.59221	TT175-.7	Dominican Republic—History—1930-1961	972.93053	F1938.5
Dolls	790.133	GV1219	Dominican Republic—History—Invasion, 1959	972.93053	F1938.5
Dolomite	549.782	QE391.D6	Dominican Republic—History—1961-	972.9305(4-5)	F1938.55-.58
Dolomite	552.58	QE471.15.D6	Dominican Republic—History—Coup d'etat, 1963	972.93054	F1938.55
Dolomite	622.3516	TN967			
Dolphins	599.53	QL737.C432			
Dolphins, Fossil	569.5	QE882.C5	Dominican Republic—History—Revolution, 1965	972.93054	F1938.55
Domain-referenced tests	371.271	LB3060.32.D65	Dominican Republic—History—Revolution, 1973	972.93054	F1938.55
Domes	690.146	TH2170-.7	Dominican Republic—History—Uprising, 1984	972.93054	F1938.55
Domes	721.46	NA2890			
Domestic animals	636	GN407.6-.7	Dominican Republic—Maps	912.7293	G4950-4954
Domestic animals—Diseases	636.0896	SF600-1100	Dominican Republic—Periodicals	972.93005	F1931
Domestic animals—Genetic engineering	636.0821	SF756.5	Dominican Republic—Politics and government	320.97293	JL1120-1139
Domestic animals—Parasites	636.089696	SF810	Dominican sisters	255.972	BX4337-.5
Domestic asses	636.1	SF360.6-361.75	Dominican-Haitian Conflict, 1937	972.93053	F1938.5
Domestic drama, English	822.09	PR635.D45	Dominicans	255.2	BX3501-3556
Domestic relations	346.015	K670-709	Dominion theology	230.046	BT82.25
Domestic relations—Canada	346.71015	KE531-606	Dominoes	795.32	GV1467
Domestic relations—England	346.42015	KD750-785	Donati's Comet	523.6	QB723.D
Domestic relations—United States	346.73015	KF501-553	Donation of organs, tissues, etc.	362.1783	RD129.5
Domestication	392.3	GT5870-5899	Donation of Pepin	943.0(13-25)	DD126.5
Domestication	636.082	SF41	Donatists	273.4	BT1370
Domestics	640.46	TX331-334	Dong Khe (Vietnam), Battle of, 1950	959.7041	DS553.3
Domestics	640.46	HD6072-.2			
Domestics	640.46	HD8039.D5	Doniphan's Expedition, 1846-1847	973.6242	E405.2
Dominica	972.9841	F2051			
Dominica—Maps	912.729841	G5100-5104	Donkey breeders	636.182092	SF361
Dominica, Battle of, 1782	973.35	E271	Donkeys	636.182	SF361
Dominican Americans	973.04687293 + 073	E184.D6			
Dominican literature	860	PQ7400-7409.2			
Dominican poetry	861	PQ7402			
Dominican poetry	861	PQ7406			
Dominican Republic	972.93	F1931-1941			

Subject Heading	Dewey	LC
Door fittings	690.1822	TH2279
Doors	690.1822	TH2278
Doorways	721.822	NA3010
Doped semiconductors	537.6223	QC611.8.D66
Doppler echocardiography	616.1207543	RC683.5.U5
Doppler radar	621.3848	TK6592.D6
Dorians	938.01004	DF136.D6
Doric Greek dialect	480	PA530-539
Dormancy in plants	571.782	QK761
Dormice	599.3596	QL737.R656
Dormitories	371.871	LB3226-3229
Dornach, Battle of, 1499	949.403	DQ107.S8
Dorr Rebellion, 1842	974.503	F83.4
Double bass	787.5107	MT320-334
Double cropping	631.58	S603.7
Double descent (Kinship)	306.83	GN480
Double flowers	575.6	QK653
Double flowers	575.6	QK830
Double pinochle	795.416	GV1295.P6
Double salts	546.34	QD191
Double stars	523.841	QB421
Double stars	523.841	QB821-830
Double-bass music	787.5	M55-58
Doubloons	737.4946	CJ3188
Douglas airplanes	629.13334	TL686.D65
Douglas fir	585.2	QK494.5.P66
Douglas fir	634.9754	SD397.D7
Douglas fir beetle	595.76	QL596.S35
Douglas transport planes	629.13334	TL686.D65
Dovecotes	728.927	NA8370
Downhill ski racing	796.935	GV854.9.R3
Downhill skiing	796.935	GV854-.87
Down's syndrome	616.858842	RC571
Down's syndrome	618.92858842	RJ506.D68
Downsizing of organizations	658.3134	HF5549.5.D55
Downsizing of organizations	658.406	HD58.85
Downy mildew diseases	632.446	SB741.D68
Dowry	392.4	HQ1017
Dowsers	133.323	BF1628
Dowsing	133.323	BF1628
Doxology	242.72	BV194.D
Doxorubicin	616.994061	RC271.D68
Doyayo (African people)	967.1100496361	DT571.D68
Draft	355.22363	UB340-355
Draft	355.225	UB350-355
Draft animals	636.0882	SF180
Draft horses	636.15	SF311-.3
Draft Riot, New York, N.Y., 1863	322.4.099747	F128.44
Draft Riot, New York, N.Y., 1863	974.703	F128.44
Draft-gear	625.21	TF413
Drafts	332.55	HG1685-1704
Drag racing	796.72	GV1029.3
Dragonflies	595.733	QL520-.42
Dragons	398.469	GR830.D7
Drainage	627.54	TC970-978
Drainage	631.62	S621
Drainage, House	628.742	TD929
Drainage, House	696.13	TH6571-6675
Drain-gages	631.62	S594
Drain-tiles	620.14	TA447
Drain-tiles	666.733	TP839
Drama	808.2	PN1600-1861
Drama—Collections	808.82	PN6110.5-6120
Drama—History and criticism	809.2	PN1720-1861
Drama—Study and teaching	808.20071	PN1701
Drama—Technique	808.2	PN1660-1692
Drama in Christian education	268.67	BV1534.4
Dramatic criticism	809.2	PN1707
Dramatic music	781.552	ML3857-3862
Dramatic music	782.1	M1500-1527.8
Dramatic music	782.109	ML1699-2100
Drapery	646.21	TT390
Drapery	746.94	NK3175-3296.3
Drapery in art	743.4	NC775
Drapery in interior decoration	747.5	NK2115.5.D73
Drapery industry	338.476453	HD9939
Dravidian languages	494.8	PL4601-4794
Dravidian philology	494.8	PL4601
Drawbacks	382.7	HF1715-1718
Drawbridges	624.24	TG420
Drawing	741	NC
Drawing, Medieval	741.0902	NC70-75
Drawing, Renaissance	741.09024	NC85
Drawing—17th century	741.09032	NC86
Drawing—18th century	741.09033	NC87-.5
Drawing—19th century	741.09034	NC90-.5
Drawing—20th century	741.0904	NC95-.5
Drawing—Catalogs	741.0294	NC37-38.5
Drawing—Copying	741.217	NC1920-1940
Drawing—Exhibitions	741.074	NC15-17
Drawing—Periodicals	741.05	NC1
Drawing—Private collections	741.074	NC30-33
Drawing—Study and teaching	741.071	NC390-670
Drawing—Technique	741.2	NC730-758
Drawing—[By region or country]	741.09(4-9)	NC101-377
Drawing—Afghanistan	741.09581	NC324.6
Drawing—Africa	741.096	NC360-368.6
Drawing—Africa, East	741.09676	NC366-6
Drawing—Africa, North	741.0961	NC361-365.6
Drawing—Africa, Southern	741.0968	NC368-.6
Drawing—Africa, West	741.0966	NC367-.6
Drawing—Argentina	741.0982	NC192-194
Drawing—Asia	741.095	NC315-359
Drawing—Asiatic Russia	741.0957	NC325

Subject Heading	Dewey	LC	Subject Heading	Dewey	LC
Drawing—Australia	741.0994	NC369-371	Drawing—Thailand	741.09593	NC335
Drawing—Bahamas	741.097296	NC171-173	Drawing—Turkey	741.09561	NC294-296
Drawing—Balkan Peninsula	741.09496	NC297-308	Drawing—United States	741.0973	NC105-139.3
Drawing—Bolivia	741.0984	NC195-197	Drawing—Uruguay	741.09895	NC219-221
Drawing—Brazil	741.0981	NC198-200	Drawing—Venezuela	741.0987	NC222-224
Drawing—Cambodia	741.09596	NC334.C3	Drawing—Vietnam	741.09597	NC334.V5-.V55
Drawing—Canada	741.0971	NC141-143.3	Drawing—West Indies	741.09729	NC168-186
Drawing—Central America	741.09728	NC147-167	Drawing ability in children	155.4133	BF723.D7
Drawing—China	741.0951	NC348-350	Drawing instruments	604.20284	T375-377
Drawing—Colombia	741.09861	NC204-206	Drawing instruments	741.2	NC845-915
Drawing—Costa Rica	741.097286	NC153-155	Drawing-room management	604.2068	T352
Drawing—Cuba	741.097291	NC174-176			
Drawing—Denmark	741.09489	NC273-275	Drawing-room practice	604.24	T352
Drawing—Ecuador	741.09866	NC207-209	Dreams	135.3	BF1074-1099
Drawing—Egypt	741.0962	NC363-.3	Dreams	154.63	RC499.D7
Drawing—El Salvador	741.097284	NC167	Dredges	627.73	TC188
Drawing—Ethiopia	741.0963	NC365.7	Dredging	627.73	TC187-188
Drawing—Europe	741.094	NC225-312	Dredging spoil	627.73	TC187
Drawing—France	741.0944	NC246-248	Dresden, Battle of, 1813	940.27	DC236.7.D8
Drawing—Germany	741.0943	NC249-251.6	Dresden, Peace of, 1745	943.054	DD407.5
Drawing—Great Britain	741.0941	NC228-242	Dressage	798.23	SF309.48-.658
Drawing—Greece	741.09495	NC252-254	Dressage horses	636.13	SF309.65-.653
Drawing—Guatemala	741.097281	NC156-158	Dressmaking	687.112	TT500-560
Drawing—Haiti	741.097294	NC177-179	Dried flower arrangement	745.92	SB449.3.D7
Drawing—Honduras	741.097283	NC159-161	Dried foods	641.44	TX609
Drawing—Iceland	741.094912	NC276-278	Dried milk	637.143	SF259
Drawing—India	741.0954	NC327-329	Dried milk industry	338.7637143	HD9282
Drawing—Indonesia	741.09598	NC339-341	Dried skim milk	641.37143	TX556.M5
Drawing—Iran	741.0955	NC321-323	Drift indicator	629.1352	TL589.2.D7
Drawing—Israel	741.095694	NC320	Driftwood sculpture	731.2	NB1250
Drawing—Italy	741.0945	NC255-257	Drill (Agricultural implement)	631.3	S687-689
Drawing—Jamaica	741.097292	NC180-182			
Drawing—Japan	741.0952	NC351-353	Drill presses	621.952	TJ1260
Drawing—Korea	741.09519	NC353.6-.7	Drilling and boring	621.952	TJ1260-1270
Drawing—Laos	741.09594	NC334.L3	Drilling muds	622.3381	TN871.27
Drawing—Malaysia	741.09595	NC336-338	Drinking and traffic accidents	363.12514	HE5620.D7
Drawing—Mexico	741.0972	NC144-146			
Drawing—Middle East	741.0956	NC318-320	Drinking cups	394.12	GT2940-2947
Drawing—New Zealand	741.0993	NC372-374	Drinking cups	394.13	GT2940-2947
Drawing—Nicaragua	741.097285	NC162-164	Drinking customs	394.1	GT2850-2930
Drawing—Norway	741.09481	NC279-281	Drinking glasses	748.83	NK5440.D75
Drawing—Oceania	741.099(5-6)	NC375-376	Drinking vessels	748.83	NK4895
Drawing—Pakistan	741.095491	NC331	Driveways	625.889	TE279.3
Drawing—Panama	741.097287	NC165	Driving of horse-drawn vehicles	388.341	SF304.5-307
Drawing—Paraguay	741.09892	NC213-215			
Drawing—Peru	741.0985	NC216-218	Driving ranges	796.35206	GV975-.5
Drawing—Philippines	741.09599	NC342-344	Drone aircraft	623.7469	UG1242.D7
Drawing—Portugal	741.09469	NC288-290	Droop Mountain (W. Va.), Battle of, 1863	973.735	E475.76
Drawing—Puerto Rico	741.097295	NC183-185			
Drawing—Russia	741.0947	NC267-269	Dropouts	371.2913	LC142-145
Drawing—Scandinavia	741.0948	NC270-284	Drought forecasting	551.64773	QC929.2-.28
Drawing—South America	741.098	NC189-224	Droughts	363.34929	HV625-626
Drawing—Spain	741.0946	NC285	Droughts	551.5773	QC929.2-.28
Drawing—Sri Lanka	741.095493	NC330	Drought-tolerant plants	635.9525	SB439.8
Drawing—Sweden	741.09485	NC282-284	Drowning	617.18	RA1076
Drawing—Switzerland	741.09494	NC291-293	Drug abuse	362.29(3-8)	HV5800-5840

Subject Heading	Dewey	LC	Subject Heading	Dewey	LC
Drug abuse—[By region or country]	362.29(3-8) 09 + (4-9)	HV5825-5840	Dry-goods	677	TS1760-1770
Drug abuse—United States	362.29(3-8)0973	HV5825-5833	Drying apparatus—Food	641.44	TX609
Drug abuse—[Other countries]	362.29(3-8) 09 + (4-9)	HV5840	Dry-point	767.3	NE2220-2225
Drug abuse—Prevention	362.29(3-8)7	HV5800-5840	Duala (African people)	967.11004 + 963962	DT571.D83
Drug abuse in pregnancy	618.3268	RG580.D76	Duala language	496.3962	PL8141
Drug activation	615.7045	RM301.56	Dualism	147.4	B812
Drug allergy	616.9758	RC598.D7	Dualism (Religion)	211.33	BL218
Drug delivery devices	615.19	RS210	Dualism (Religion)	211.33	BL218
Drug delivery systems	615.19	RS199.5-210	Duality (Logic)	160	BC199.D8
Drug development	615.19	RM301.25	Dual-purpose cattle	636.226	SF211
Drug factories	690.54	TH4541	Dubbing of motion pictures	791.4302	TR886.7
Drug interactions	615.7045	RM302-.4	Duchenne muscular dystrophy	618.92748	RJ482.D78
Drug resistance in microorganisms	616.9041	QR177	Duck shooting	799.244	SK333.D8
Drug stability	615.1	RS424	Duckpin bowling	794.6	GV910.5.D8
Drug testing	362.29363	HV5823-.5	Ducks	598.41	QL696.A52
Drug traffic—Investigation	363.25977	HV8079.N3	Ducks	636.597	SF504.7-505.63
Drugged driving	364.147	HE5620.D65	Dude ranches	796.56	GV198.945-.975
Drugs	615.1	RM300-671.5	Dudley's Defeat, 1813	973.523	E356.D8
Drugs, Nonprescription	615.1	RM671-.5	Dueling	394.8	CR4571-4595
Drugs—Administration	615.6	RM147-180	Duets	785.12	M177-298.5
Drugs—Analysis	615.1901	RS189-190	Dugout canoes	386.229	GN440.2
Drugs—Controlled release	615.19	RS201.C64	Dugout canoes	623.8202	VM353
Drugs—Dosage forms	615.14	RS200-201	Dukhobors	289.9	BX7433
Drugs—Law and legislation—Canada	344.7104233	KE3714-3725	Dulcimer	787.7409	ML1015-1018
Drugs—Law and legislation—England	344.4204233	KD3460-3462	Dulcimer music	787.74	M142.D8
Drugs—Packaging	615.18	RS159.5	Dumbbells	613.7130284	GV547.4
Drugs—Prescribing	615.14	RM138	Dump trucks	629.224	TL230
Drugs—Preservation	615.18	RS159	Dumping (International trade)	382.6	HF1425
Drugs—Psychic aspects	154.4	BF1045.D76	Dune buggies	629.222	TL236.7
Drugs—Side effects	615.7042	RM302.5	Dune buggy racing	796.72	GV1029.9.D8
Drugs—Standards	615.10128	RS189	Dunes, Battle of the, 1658	944.033	DC124.45
Drugs—Testing	615.1901	RM301.27	Dung beetles	595.7649	QL596.S3
Drugs—Vehicles	615.19	RS201.V43	Dunkerque (France), Battle of, 1940	940.5421428	D756.5.D8
Drugs and employment	658.3822	HF5549.5.D7	Dunmore's Expedition, 1774	975.502	E83.77
Drugs in motion pictures	791.43655	PN1995.9.D78	Duodecimal system	513.5	QA141.5
Drugs of abuse	615.78	RM316	Duodenoscopy	616.3407545	RC804.D79
Drugs of abuse	615.78	RS190.D77	Duodenum	573.378	QL863
Drugstore employees	615.1092	HD8039.D7	Duodenum	611.341	QM345
Druids and Druidism	299.16	BL910	Duodenum	612.33	QP156
Drum	786.909	ML1035	Duodenum—Radiography	616.3407572	RC804.R6
Drum Point Lighthouse (Md.)	623.894209 + 16347	VK1025.D	Duplex ultrasonography—Diagnostic use	616.07543	RC78.7.D86
Drunk driving	364.147	HE5620.D7	Duplex ultrasonography—Diagnostic use	616.1307543	RC691.6.D87
Drunk driving—Investigation	363.25947	HV8079.D76	Duplicate contract bridge	795.415	GV1282.8.D86
Drunkenness (Philosophy)	362.29201	B105.D78	Duplicate whist	795.413	GV1283
Druzes	297.85	BL1695	Durazzo, Battle of, 48 B.C.	937.05	DG266
Dry cleaning	667.12	TP932-.6	Durazzo, Battle of, 1918	940.458	D589.U7
Dry docks	627.31	TC361	Durga (Hindu deity)	294.52114	BL1225.D8
Dry farming	631.586	SB110	Durga-puja (Hindu festival)	294.536	BL1213.D87
Dry slope skiing	796.93	GV854.9.D78	Durmast oak	583.46	QK495.F14
Dryads	292.13	BL820.D	Durmast oak	634.9721	SD397.D87

Subject Heading	Dewey	LC	Subject Heading	Dewey	LC
Durnstein, Battle of, 1805	940.27	DC227.5.D8	Dutch poetry	839.31108	PT5470-5488
Duroc Jersey swine	636.483	SF393.D9	Dutch poetry	839.31109	PT5201-5245
Durum wheat	584.9	QK495.G74	Dutch prose literature	839.31808	PT5300-5336
Durum wheat	633.11	SB191.W5	Dutch prose literature	839.31808	PT5517-5547
Durum wheat industry	338.17311	HD9049.W3-.W5	Dutch rabbits	636.9322	SF455.D8
Dusky seaside sparrow	598.883	QL696.P2438	Dutch War, 1672-1678	940.252	D277-278.5
Dust	551.5113	QC882.5	Dutch War, 1672-1678	949.204	DJ190-191
Dust storms	551.559	QC958-959	Dutch wit and humor	839.317008	PN6222.N
Dutch	839.31	PT	Dutch wit and humor	839.31708	PT5541
Dutch Americans	973.043931073	E184.D9	Dutch wit and humor	839.31709	PT5346
Dutch drama	839.31208	PT5490-5515	Duty	170	BJ1450-1458
Dutch drama	839.31209	PT5250-5295	Dwarf ale glasses	748.83	NK5440.D85
Dutch essays	083	AC16-19	Dwarf children	599.949083	HQ773.65
Dutch essays	839.31408	PT5539	Dwarf Galaxies	523.112	QB858
Dutch fiction	839.31308	PT5520-5530	Dwarf hamsters	599.356	QL737.R638
Dutch fiction	839.31309	PT5320-5336	Dwarf hamsters as pets	636.93560887	SF459.H3
Dutch language	439.31	PF1-979	Dwarf irises	584.38	QK495.I75
Dutch language	439.31	PF1001-1184	Dwarf irises	635.93438	SB413.I8
Dutch language—Dialects	439.317	PF700-979	Dwarf Novae	523.8446	QB843.D85
Dutch language—Dictionaries	439.313	PF620-693	Dwarf pelargoniums	635.93379	SB413.G35
Dutch language—Dictionaries	439.313	PF1175-1184	Dwarf rabbits	636.9322	SF455.D85
Dutch language—Etymology	439.312	PF1161-1167	Dwarf sea horse	597.6798	QL638.S9
Dutch language—Etymology	439.32	PF571-599	Dwarf stars	523.88	QB843.D9
Dutch language—Grammar	439.315	PF97	Dwarf trees	635.9772	SB435-.8
Dutch language—Grammar	439.315	PF1033-1125	Dwarfism, Pituitary	618.9247	RJ420.P58
Dutch language—History	439.3109	PF51-60	Dwarfs	599.949	GN69.3-.5
Dutch language—History	439.3109	PF1015	Dwellings	392.36	GR490-497
Dutch language—Lexicography	439.313028	PF601-693	Dwellings	392.36	GT165-476
Dutch language—Morphology	439.315	PF171-197	Dwellings	690.8	TH4805-4890
Dutch language—Parts of speech	439.315	PF199-335	Dwellings	728	NA7100-7884
Dutch language—Phonology	439.3115	PF131-168	Dwellings—Air conditioning	697.938	TH7688.H6
Dutch language—Rhetoric	808.043931	PF410-497	Dwellings—Social aspects	392.36	GT170
Dutch language—Slang	439.317	PF951-979	Dwellings—[By region or country]	392.3609(4-9)	GT201-384
Dutch language—Study and teaching	439.31071	PF65-69	Dwellings—Africa	392.36096	GT373-377
Dutch language—Study and teaching	439.31071	PF1019	Dwellings—Argentina	392.360982	GT261-262
Dutch literature	839.31	PT5001-5980	Dwellings—Asia	392.36095	GT343-372
Dutch literature—To 1500	839.3109	PT5121-5137	Dwellings—Asia	392.36095	GT349-350
Dutch literature—1500-1800	839.31(2-4)09	PT5141-5165	Dwellings—Australia	392.360994	GT379-380
Dutch literature—19th century	839.31509	PT5170-5175	Dwellings—Austria	392.3609436	GT295-296
Dutch literature—20th century	839.31609	PT5180-5185	Dwellings—Bahamas	392.36097296	GT249-250
Dutch literature—Study and teaching	839.31071	PT5040-5044	Dwellings—Balkan Peninsula	392.3609496	GT331-341
Dutch periodicals	053.931	AP14-17	Dwellings—Belize	392.36097282	GT235-236
Dutch philology	439.31	PF1-979	Dwellings—Bolivia	392.360984	GT263-264
			Dwellings—Brazil	392.360981	GT265-266
			Dwellings—Canada	392.360971	GT228-229
			Dwellings—Chile	392.360983	GT267-268
			Dwellings—China	392.360951	GT365-366
			Dwellings—Colombia	392.3609861	GT269-270
			Dwellings—Costa Rica	392.36097286	GT237-238
			Dwellings—Cuba	392.36097291	GT251-252
			Dwellings—Denmark	392.3609489	GT315-316
			Dwellings—Ecuador	392.3609866	GT271-272
			Dwellings—Egypt	392.360962	GT375-376
			Dwellings—El Salvador	392.36097284	GT246-.5

Subject Heading	Dewey	LC	Subject Heading	Dewey	LC
Dwellings—France	392.360944	GT297-298	Dynamics of a particle	531.16	QA851-855
Dwellings—Germany	392.360943	GT298.9-300.5	Dynamite	662.27	TP285
Dwellings—Great Britain	392.360941	GT285-294	Dynix (Computer system)	025.3132	Z678.93.D85
Dwellings—Greece	392.3609495	GT301-302	Dysentery	616.935	RC140
Dwellings—Guatemala	392.36097281	GT239-240	Dyslexia	371.9144	LB1050.5
Dwellings—Haiti	392.36097294	GT253-254	Dyslexia	616.8553	RC394.W6
Dwellings—Honduras	392.36097283	GT241-242	Dyslexic children	371.9144	LC4708-4710
Dwellings—Hungary	392.3609439	GT296.5-.6	Dyslexic children	618.928553	RJ496.A5
Dwellings—Iceland	392.36094912	GT317-318	Dysmenorrhea	618.172	RG181
Dwellings—India	392.360954	GT351-352	Dyula (African people)	966.6800496345	DT545.45.D85
Dwellings—Indonesia	392.3609598	GT359-360	Dzongkha language	495.4	PL3651.D96
Dwellings—Iran	392.360955	GT347-348	E document (Biblical criticism)	220.6	BS1181.2
Dwellings—Iraq	392.3609567	GT346.5-.6	E region	551.5145	QC881.2.E2
Dwellings—Ireland	392.3609415	GT294.5-.6	Eagle dance	299.7138	E98.D2
Dwellings—Italy	392.360945	GT303-304	Eagles	598.942	QL696.F32
Dwellings—Jamaica	392.36097292	GT255-256	Ear	573.89	QL948
Dwellings—Japan	392.360952	GT367-368	Ear	611.85	QM507
Dwellings—Korea	392.3609519	GT369-370	Ear	612.85	QP460-471.2
Dwellings—Malaysia	392.3609595	GT357-358	Ear, External	573.89	QL948
Dwellings—Mexico	392.360972	GT231-232	Ear, External	611.85	QM507
Dwellings—Netherlands	392.3609492	GT307-308	Ear—Diseases	617.8	RF110-320
Dwellings—New Zealand	392.360993	GT381-382	Ear—Surgery	617.8059	RF126-127
Dwellings—Nicaragua	392.36097285	GT243-244	Ear—Tumors	616.99485	RC280.E2
Dwellings—Norway	392.3609481	GT319-320	Ear training	781.424	MT35
Dwellings—Oceania	392.36099(5-6)	GT383-384	Eared dove	598.65	QL696.C63
Dwellings—Panama	392.36097287	GT245-.5	Eared seals	599.79	QL737.P63
Dwellings—Paraguay	392.3609892	GT275-276	Early childhood education	372.21	LB1139.2-.4
Dwellings—Peru	392.360985	GT277-278	Early childhood educators	372.11	LB1775.6
Dwellings—Philippines	392.3609599	GT361-362	Early retirement	306.38	HD7110-.5
Dwellings—Portugal	392.3609469	GT325-326	Early stars	523.88	QB843.E2
Dwellings—Puerto Rico	392.36097295	GT257-.5	Earrings	391.7	GT2265
Dwellings—Russia	392.360947	GT311-312	Earth	525	QB630-638.8
Dwellings—Spain	392.360946	GT323-324	Earth—Age	551.701	QE508
Dwellings—Sri Lanka	392.36095493	GT352.5-.6	Earth—Internal structure	551.11	QE509
Dwellings—Sweden	392.3609485	GT321-322	Earth—Origin	523.12	QB632
Dwellings—Switzerland	392.3609494	GT327-328	Earth—Rotation	525.35	QB633
Dwellings—Syria	392.36095691	GT344-.2	Earth construction	690.8370473	TH1421
Dwellings—Thailand	392.3609593	GT355-356	Earth currents	538.748	QC845
Dwellings—Turkey	392.3609561	GT345-346	Earth dams	627.83	TC543
Dwellings—United States	392.360973	GT205-227	Earth houses	690.8370473	TH4818.A3
Dwellings—Uruguay	392.3609895	GT279-280	Earth movements	551.307	QE598-600.3
Dwellings—Venezuela	392.360987	GT281-282	Earth science instruments	550.284	QE49.5
Dye industry	338.4754786	HD9660.D84-.D844	Earth sheltered houses	690.8370473	TH4819.E27
Dye lasers	621.3664	TA1690	Earth sheltered houses	728.370473	NA7531
Dye plants	581.636	QK98.7	Earth temperature	551.12	QE509
Dye plants	633.86	SB285-287	Earthmoving machinery	624.1520284	TA725
Dyes and dyeing	667.2	TP897-929	Earthquake engineering	624.1762	TA654.6
Dyes and dyeing	746.6	TT853-854.5	Earthquake resistant design	624.1762	TA658.44
Dyes and dyeing—Chemistry	667.2	TP890-929	Earthquakes	363.3495	HV599-600
Dynamic meteorology	551.5	QC880-.4	Earthquakes	551.22	QE531-541
Dynamic personality inventory	155.283	BF698.8.D9	Earths, Rare	546.41	QD172.R2
			Earthwork	624.152	TA715-772
Dynamics	531.11	QA845-871	Earthworks (Archaeology)	930.1028	GN789
Dynamics, Rigid	531.11	QA861-863	Earthworm culture	639.75	SF597.E3
			Earthworms	592.64	QL391.A6

Subject Heading	Dewey	LC	Subject Heading	Dewey	LC
East Armenian dialect	491.9927	PK8451-8499	Eclipsing binaries—Orbits	523.8444	QB835.E4
East Asia	950	DS501-519	Ecological heterogeneity	577	QH541.15.E24
East Asia—History—1945-	950.4(2-3)	DS518.1	Ecological surveys	577.0723	QH541.15.S95
East Asia—Strategic aspects	355.03305	UA830	Ecology	577	QH540-549.5
East Asian literature	895	PL491-494	Econometric models	330.011	HB141
East Coast fever	636.208969	SF967.E3	Econometrics	330.015195	HB139-141
East European Americans	973.04917073	E184.E17	Economic anthropology	306.3	GN448-450.7
East Indian Americans	973.04914073	E184.E2	Economic development	338.9	HD72-88
East Prussian cattle	636.23	SF199.E2	Economic development—Methodology	338.901	HD108-.8
East-West trade	382	HF4050	Economic forecasting	330.0112	HB3730
Easter	263.93	BV55	Economic geography	330.9	HF1021-1027
Easter	394.2667	GT4935	Economic history	330.9	HC
Easter	529.44	CE83	Economic history—Medieval, 500-1500	330.0902	HC41-42
Easter—Sermons	252.63	BV4259	Economic history—20th century	330.0904	HC54-60.5
Easter cookery	641.568	TX739.2.E37	Economic history—1945-	330.09044	HC59-60.5
Easter decorations	745.59416	TT900.E2	Economic policy	338.9	HD87-88
Easter Island	996.18	F3169	Economic sanctions	327.117	HF1413.5
Easter lily	584.32	QK495.L72	Economic stabilization	339.5	HB3732
Easter Offensive, 1972	959.704342	DS557.8.E23	Economics	330	HB
Eastern bluebird	598.842	QL696.P288	Economics	330	HB1-130
Eastern chipmunk	599.364	QL737.R68	Economics—Congresses	330.06	HB21
Eastern churches	281.5	BX100-189	Economics—Dictionaries	330.03	HB61
Eastern diamondback rattlesnake	597.96	QL666.069	Economics—Directories	330.025	HB63
Eastern Hemisphere	910.021811	G680-700	Economics—History	330.09	HB75-130
Eastern Hemisphere—History	909.09811	D890-893	Economics—History—To 1800	330.090(1-33)	HB77-83
Eastern Hemisphere—Maps	912.19811	G1780-2799	Economics—History—19th century	330.09034	HB85
Eastern hemlock	585.2	QK494.5.P66	Economics—History—20th century	330.0904	HB87
Eastern hemlock	634.9753	SD397.E27	Economics—Periodicals	330.05	HB1-9
Eastern hemlock	635.97752	SB413.E27	Economics—Sociological aspects	306.3	HM35
Eastern Indians, Wars with, 1722-1726	974.02	E83.72	Economics—Statistical methods	330.0727	HB137
Eastern question (Far East)	950.(3-41)	DS740.6-.63	Economics in the Bible	220.8330	BS670
Eastern red cedar	585.4	QK494.5.C975	Ecotones	577	QH514.15.E27
Eastern tent caterpillar	595.78139	QL561.L3	Ecstasy	204.2	BL626
Eating disorders	616.8526	RC552.E18	Ecstasy	248.29	BV5091.E3
Eating disorders in adolescence	616.852600835	RJ506.E18	Ectoparasitic infestations	616.968	RC119.5
Ebisu (Japanese deity)	299.56	BL2211.E24	Ectopic pregnancy	618.31	RG586
Ecclesiastical geography	262.009	BR97-99	Ecuador	986.6	F3701-3799
Ecclesiastical law	262.9	BV759-763	Ecuador—Census	318.66	HA1021-1030
Echinococcosis	616.964	RC184.T6	Ecuador—Civilization	986.6	F3710
Echinococcosis	636.0896964	SF810.H8	Ecuador—Description and travel	918.6604	F3711-3716
Echinodermata	593.9	QL381-385.2	Ecuador—Economic conditions	330.9866	HC201-204.5
Echo	534.204	QC233	Ecuador—Emigration and immigration	325.(2866) or (866)	JV7490-7499
Echo sounding	623.8938	VK584.S6	Ecuador—Gazetteers	918.66003	F3704
Echocardiography	616.1207543	RC683.5.U5	Ecuador—History	986.6	F3723.3-3738.4
Echocardiography	618.326107543	RG628.3.E34	Ecuador—History—To 1809	986.60(1-2)	F3733
Echocardiography	618.921207543	RJ423.5.U46			
Eclampsia	618.7	RG576			
Eclectic psychotherapy	616.8914	RC489.E24			
Eclecticism	148	B814			
Eclecticism	186.3	B271			
Eclipses	523.99	QB175-185			

Subject Heading	Dewey	LC	Subject Heading	Dewey	LC
Ecuador—History—Wars of Independence, 1809-1830	986.60(2-4)	F3734	Education, Minoan	370.938	LA77
Ecuador—History—1830-1895	986.60(5-6)	F3736	Education, Preschool	372.21	LB1140-.5
			Education, Primary	372	LB1501-1547
Ecuador—History—1895-1944	986.60(6-72)	F3737	Education, Primary—Activity programs	372.11	LB1537
Ecuador—History—Revolution, 1895	986.606	F3736	Education, Rural	370.91734	LC5146-5148
			Education, Urban	370.91732	LC5101-5143
Ecuador—History—20th century	986.6071	F3737	Education—Aims and objectives	370.1	LB41
Ecuador—History—Coup d'etat, 1925	986.6072	F3737	Education—Congresses	370.6	L106-107
			Education—Curricula	375	LB1570-1571
Ecuador—History—1944-	986.607(2-5)	F3738	Education—Data processing	371.334	LB1028.43
Ecuador—History—Coup d'etat, 1944	986.6072	F3738	Education—Directories	370.25	L900-991
Ecuadorian fiction	863	PQ8212	Education—Experimental methods	371.3	LB1027.3
Ecuadorian fiction	863	PQ8216.F5	Education—Finance	371.206	LB2824-2830
Ecuadorian literature	860	PQ8200-8220.36	Education—Finance—Law and legislation—United States	344.73076	KF4125-4143
Ecuadorian poetry	861	PQ8210			
Ecuadorian poetry	861	PQ8214-.5	Education—Forecasting	370.112	LB41.5
Ecuador—Manufactures	670.9866	TS47	Education—Graduate work	378.155	LB2372.E3
Ecuador—Maps	912.866	G5300-5304	Education—History	370.9	LA
Ecuador—Periodicals	986.6005	F3701	Education—History	370.9 (1-5)	LA190-2284
Ecuador-Peru Conflict, 1941	986.6072	F3737	Education—Museums	370.74	L797-898
			Education—Periodicals	370.5	L7-101
Ecuador-Peru Conflict, 1981	986.6074	F3738	Education—Philosophy	370.1	LB125-875
			Education—Research	370.72	LB1028-.25
Ecuador—Politics and government	320.9866	JL3000-3099	Education—Simulation methods	371.397	LB1029.S53
Ecumenical liturgies	264	BV186.7	Education—[By region or country]	370.9(4-9)	L111-791
Ecumenical movement—African influences	280.042	BX9.5.A37	Education—Africa	370.96	L651-742
Ecumenists	262.0011092	BX6.7-.8	Education—Asia	370.95	L561-642
Eczema	616.51	RL251	Education—Australia	370.994	L750-792, 757-775
Eczema in children	618.92521	RJ516.E35			
Eddy currents (Electric)	621.31042	TK2271	Education—Austria	370.9436	L361-366
Edema	616.047	RB144-.5	Education—Belgium	370.9493	L431-436
Eden	222.11	BS1237	Education—Bulgaria	370.9499	L541-542
Edible dormouse	599.3596	QL737.R656	Education—Canada	370.971	L221-223
Editing	808.027	PN162	Education—Central America	370.9728	L231-249
Education	370	L			
Education	370	LB	Education—China	370.951	L571-573
Education, Ancient	370.901	LA31-81	Education—Czechoslovakia	370.9437	L385-387
Education, Bilingual	370.1175	LC3701-3743	Education—Denmark	370.9489	L471-476
Education, Compulsory	379.23	LC129-139	Education—Developing countries	370.91724	LC2601-2611
Education, Egyptian	370.932	LA37	Education—Europe	370.94	L341-551
Education, Elementary	372	LB1555-1601	Education—France	370.944	L391-396
Education, Greek	370.938	LA75	Education—Germany	370.943	L401-410
Education, Higher	378.009	LA173-186	Education—Great Britain	370.941	L341-359
Education, Higher—Law and legislation—United States	344.73074	KF4225-4257	Education—Greece	370.9495	L411-416
			Education—Hungary	370.9439	L381-383
Education, Humanistic	370.112	LC1001-1024	Education—Iceland	370.94912	L481
Education, Humanistic	370.11209024	LA106-108	Education—India	370.954	L577-578
Education, Medieval	370.902	LA91-98	Education—Indochina	370.959(4-7)	L585-586
Education, Medieval	378.00902	LA177	Education—Indonesia	370.9598	L597-598

Subject Heading	Dewey	LC
Education—Iran	370.955	L615-616
Education—Iraq	370.9567	L627-628
Education—Ireland	370.9415	L346-348
Education—Israel	370.95694	L631-632
Education—Italy	370.945	L421-426
Education—Japan	370.952	L611-612
Education—Korea	370.9519	L613-614
Education—Mexico	370.972	L227-229
Education—Netherlands	370.9492	L441-446
Education—New Zealand	370.993	L754-755
Education—Norway	370.9481	L491-496
Education—Oceania	370.99(5-6)	L777-791
Education—Pakistan	370.95491	L578.5-.6
Education—Portugal	370.9469	L521-526
Education—Romania	370.9498	L545-546
Education—Russia	370.947	L451-466
Education—Siberia	370.957	L617-620
Education—South America	370.98	L291-335
Education—Spain	370.946	L511-516
Education—Sweden	370.9485	L501-506
Education—Switzerland	370.9494	L531-536
Education—Turkey	370.9561	L539-540
Education—United States	370.973	L111-219
Education—[United States, By state]	370.97(4-9)	L116-219
Education—West Indies	370.9729	L251-267
Education—Yugoslavia	370.9497	L549-550
Education and crime	364.25	HV6166
Education and state	379	LC71-188
Education in mass media	370	P96.E29
Education in the Bible	220.837	BS680.E3
Education in the Bible	221.837	BS1199.E38
Education of princes	371.82621	JC393
Educational acceleration	371.28	LC1049-.8
Educational accountability	379.158	LB2806.22
Educational anthropology	306.43	LB45
Educational counseling	371.4	LB1027.5-.8
Educational equalization	379.26	LC213-.3
Educational evaluation	379.158	LB2822.75
Educational exchanges	370.116	LB2283-2286
Educational exchanges	378.016	LB2375-2378
Educational fund raising	371.206	LC241-245
Educational fund raising	378.106	LB2335.95-2337
Educational games	371.337	LB1029.G3
Educational innovations	371.3	LB1027
Educational law and legislation	344.07	K3740-3762
Educational law and legislation	344.4207	KD3600-3689
Educational law and legislation—Canada	344.7107	KE3805-3917
Educational law and legislation—United States	344.7307	KF4101-4257
Educational law and legislation—United States	344.7307	KF4195-4223
Educational leave	331.25763	HD5257-.2
Educational planning	371.207	LC71.2

Subject Heading	Dewey	LC
Educational psychology	370.15	LB1051-1091
Educational sociology	306.43	LC189-214.53
Educational statistics	370.21	LB2846
Educational surveys	370.723	LB2823
Educational tests and measurements	371.271	LB3051-3060.87
Educational toys	371.337	LB1029.T6
Educators	370.92	LA2301-2397
Educators	370.92	LB51-875
Eel fisheries	639.2743	SH351.E4
Eel fishing	799.1743	SH691.E4
Eels	597.43	QL637.9.A5
Efik (African people)	966.9004963642	DT515.45.E34
Efik language	496.3642	PL8147
Egba (African people)	966.900496333	DT515.45.E35
Egg decoration	745.5944	TT896.7
Eggbeaters	641.589	TX657.E35
Egg-free diet	613.26	RM232
Eggplant	583.952	QK495.S7
Eggplant	635.646	SB351.E5
Eggs	636.5142	SF490-.8
Eggs—Incubation	636.5082	SF495
Eggs—Production	636.5142	SF490-.8
Ego (Psychology)	155.2	BF175.5.E35
Ego Function Assessment	154.2	RC473.E36
Egoism	171.9	BJ1474
EGPS (Computer program language)	005.13	QA76.5
Egungun (Cult)	299.6869	BL2480.Y6
Egypt in the Koran	297.12209	BP134.E5
Egypt—Census	316.2	HA4686
Egypt—Civilization	932	DT70
Egypt—Civilization	962	DT70
Egypt—Description and travel	913.204	DT49.98-56
Egypt—Description and travel	916.204	DT49.98-56
Egypt—Economic conditions	330.962	HC830
Egypt—Gazetteers	913.2003	DT45
Egypt—Gazetteers	916.2003	DT45
Egypt—History	932	DT43-154
Egypt—History	962	DT43-154
Egypt—History—To 332 B.C.	932.0(1-2)	DT83-91
Egypt—History—To 640 A.D.	932	DT83-93
Egypt—History—Eighteenth dynasty, ca. 1570-1320 B.C.	932.014	DT87-.5
Egypt—History—332-30 B.C.	932.021	DT92-.7
Egypt—History—Greco Roman period, 332 B.C.-640 A.D.	932.02	DT92-93
Egypt—History—30 B.C.-640 A.D.	932.02(2-3)	DT93

Subject Heading	Dewey	LC
Egypt—History—640-1882	962.0(2-3)	DT95-107.4
Egypt—History—640-1250	962.02	DT95-.88
Egypt—History—Saladin, 1171-1193	962.02	DT95.8-.88
Egypt—History—Invasion of Saint Louis, 1249	962.02	DT95.8
Egypt—History—1250-1517	962.02	DT96-.7
Egypt—History—1517-1882	962.03	DT97-107.4
Egypt—History—1798-	962.0(3-55)	DT100-107.87
Egypt—History—French occupation, 1798-1801	962.03	DT103
Egypt—History—Mohammed Ali, 1805-1849	962.03	DT104
Egypt—History—Ismail, 1863-1879	962.03	DT106
liOEgypt—History—Tewfik, 1879-1892	962.0(3-4)	DT107-.4
Egypt—History—British occupation, 1882-1936	962.0(4-51)	DT107.3-.8
Egypt—History—Fuad, 1917-1936	962.0(4-51)	DT107.8
Egypt—History—1919-	962.0(4-55)	DT107.8-.87
Egypt—History—Insurrection, 1919	962.04	DT107.8
Egypt—History—1952-	962.05(3-5)	DT107.821-.87
Egypt—History—Revolution, 1952	962.052	DT107.82
Egypt—History—Intervention, 1956	962.053	DT107.83
Egypt—Manufactures	670.962	TS117-118
Egypt—Maps	912.62	G8300-8304
Egypt—Politics and government	320.932	JC66
Egypt—Religion	299.31	BL2420-2460
Egyptian drama	893.12	PJ1571
Egyptian fiction	893.13	PJ1487
Egyptian language	493.1	PJ1001-1479
Egyptian language—Demotic, ca. 650 B.C.-450 A.D.	493.1	PJ1801-1921
Egyptian language—Dictionaries	493.13	PJ1031
Egyptian language—Dictionaries	493.13	PJ1423-1439
Egyptian language—Etymology	493.12	PJ1350-1371
Egyptian language—Grammar	493.15	PJ1121-1201
Egyptian language—Inscriptions	493.111	PJ1501-1819
Egyptian language—Lexicography	493.13028	PJ1401-1439
Egyptian language—Papyri	493.111	PJ1501-1921
Egyptian language—Writing	493.111	PJ1051-1109
Egyptian language—Writing, Demotic	493.111	PJ1107
Egyptian language—Writing, Hieratic	493.11	PJ1105
Egyptian language—Writing, Hieroglyphic	493.111	PJ1091-1097
Egyptian literature	893.1	PJ1481-1989
Egyptian philology	493.1	PJ1001-1109
Egyptology	932	DT57-154
Eider	598.415	QL696.A52
Eidetic imagery	153.32	BF367
Eighth house (Astrology)	133.52	BF1716.28
Eight-hour movement	331.25723	HD5106-5267
Eileithyia (Greek deity)	292.2114	BL820.E5
Ejector pumps	621.6	TJ901
El Alamein, Battle of, Egypt, 1942	940.5423	D766.9
El Caney, Battle of, 1898	973.893	E717.1
El Ebano, Battle of, 1915	972.0816	F1234
El Jigue (Cuba), Battle of, 1958	972.91063	F1787.5
El Nino Current	551.462	GC296.8.E
El Salvador	972.84	F1481-1497
El Salvador—Census	317.284	HA841-850
El Salvador—Civilization	972.84	F1483.8
El Salvador—Description and travel	917.28404	F1484-.3
El Salvador—Emigration and immigration	325.(27284) or (7284)	JV7423
El Salvador—Gazetteers	917.284003	F1482
El Salvador—History	972.84	F1485.5-1488.53
El Salvador—History—To 1838	972.840(1-42)	F1487
El Salvador—History—1838-1944	972.840(4-52)	F1487.5
El Salvador—History—Revolution, 1944	972.84052	F1487.5
El Salvador—History—1944-1979	972.84052	F1488
El Salvador—History—Revolution of 1948	972.84052	F1488
El Salvador-Honduras Conflict, 1969	972.84052	F1488
El Salvador—History—1979-	972.8405(3-4)	F1488.3-.53
El Salvador—History—1979-1992	972.84053	F1488.3
El Salvador—History—1992-	972.8405(3-4)	F1488.5-.53
El Salvador—Maps	912.7284	G4840-4844
El Salvador—Periodicals	972.84005	F1481
El Salvador—Politics and government	320.97284	JL1560-1579
Elamite language	499.93	P943
Elands	599.642	QL737.U5
Elastic plates and shells	531.382	QA935
Elastic solids	531.382	QA935

Subject Heading	Dewey	LC	Subject Heading	Dewey	LC
Elastic solids	531.382	QC191	Electric engineering—[By region or country]	621.309(4-9)	TK21-127
Elastic tissue	611.0182	QM563	Electric engineering—Congresses	621.306	TK5
Elastic waves	531.382	QA935	Electric engineering—Dictionaries	621.303	TK9
Elastic waves	531.382	QC191	Electric engineering—Directories	621.3025	TK12
Elastic waves	551.22	QE539	Electric engineering—History	621.309	TK15-18
Elasticity	531.382	QA931-939	Electric engineering—Museums	621.3074	TK6
Elasticity	531.382	QC191	Electric engineering—Periodicals	621.305	TK1-4
Elastomer industry	338.47678	HD9662.E42-.E423	Electric engineering—Study and teaching	621.3071	TK165-213
Elbow—Fractures	617.157	RD558	Electric furnaces	541.370284	QD277
Elchingen, Battle of, 1805	940.27	DC227.5.E6	Electric furnaces	546.0284	QD157
Election (Theology)	234	BT809-810.2	Electric furnaces	621.4028	TK4661
Election sermons	252.68	BV4260-4261	Electric furnaces	669.028	TN687
Elections	324	JF1001-1048	Electric generators	621.313	TK2411-2491
Elections	324.620973	JK1965-2217	Electric guitar music	787.87	M142.E4
Elections—Corrupt practices	324.66	JF1081-1083	Electric heating	621.402	TK4601-4661
Elections—Corrupt practices	324.66	JK1994	Electric industries	381.456213121	HD9697
Elections—Corrupt practices	324.660941	JN1088	Electric insulators and insulation	621.31937	TK3331-3441
Elections—Corrupt practices	324.660973	JK2249	Electric inverters	621.3815322	TK2699
Electors (Kurfursten)	324.630943	JN3250.C83	Electric inverters	621.3815322	TK7872.I65
Electric alarms	621.38928	TK7241	Electric laboratories	537.072	QC541
Electric apparatus and appliances	537.0284	QC543-544	Electric lamps	621.32	TK4310-4399
Electric apparatus and appliances	610.284	RM889	Electric lamps, Arc	621.325	TK4321-4335
Electric arc	537.52	QC705	Electric lamps, Portable	622.473	TN307
Electric batteries	621.31242	TK2896-2986	Electric light fixtures	621.320284	TK4198
Electric boats	623.8726	VM345-347	Electric lighting	621.32	TK4125-4399
Electric cables	621.31934	TK3301-3351	Electric lighting—[By region or country]	621.3209(4-9)	TK4134-4156
Electric charge and distribution	537.21	QC581.E4	Electric lighting, Arc	621.325	TK4311-4335
Electric circuit-breakers	621.317	TK2842	Electric lighting, Incandescent	621.326	TK4341-4367
Electric circuits	621.3192	TK3001-3521	Electric lines	621.3192	TK3201-3261
Electric conductivity	537.62	QC610.3-635	Electric lines—Poles and towers	621.3192	TK3242-3243
Electric conductors	621.3193	TK3301-3351	Electric locomotives	625.263	TF975
Electric contactors	621.317	TK2861	Electric machinery	621.31042	TK2000-2891
Electric controllers	621.33	TF930	Electric machinery—Alternating current	621.3133	TK2711-2799
Electric controllers	629.8043	TK2851	Electric machinery—Direct current	621.3132	TK2611-2699
Electric countershock	616.120645	RC684.E4	Electric measurements	537.0287	QC535-537
Electric cranes	621.873	TJ1363-1365	Electric measurements	621.37	TK275-399
Electric current converters	621.313	TK2796	Electric meters	621.373	TK301-399
Electric current rectifiers	621.3137	TK7872.R35	Electric motors	621.46	TK2511-2541
Electric currents	537.6	QC601-641	Electric motors	621.46	TK2681
Electric currents, Alternating	537.6	QC641	Electric motors	621.46	TK2781-2789
Electric currents, Alternating	621.31913	TK1141-1168	Electric motors, Alternating current	621.46	TK2781-2789
Electric currents—Heating effects	537.6	QC623	Electric motors—Design and construction	621.46	TK2435
Electric detonators	358.1282	UF780			
Electric drafting	621.30221	TK431			
Electric driving	629.2293	TK4058-4059			
Electric engineering	621.3	TK			

Subject Heading	Dewey	LC	Subject Heading	Dewey	LC
Electric network topology	621.3192	TK454.2	Electrical burns	617.12	RD96.5
Electric networks	621.3192	TK3226	Electrical injuries	617.12	RA1091
Electric networks, Active	621.3192	TK454.2	Electricians	537.092	QC514-515
Electric networks, Passive	621.3192	TK454.2	Electricians	621.31924092	TK139-140
Electric power	621.31	TK1001-1841	Electricity	537	QC501-721
Electric power	621.31	TK3001-3511	Electricity in aeronautics	629.1354	TL690-691
Electric power	621.31	TK4001-9971	Electricity in military	623.76	UG480
Electric power distribution	621.319	TK3001-3521	engineering		
Electric power distribution—Alternating current	621.31913	TK3141-3171	Electricity in mining	622.48	TN343
			Electricity—Experiments	537.0724	QC527
			Electricity—Experiments	537.0724	QC533-534
Electric power distribution—Direct current	621.31912	TK3111	Electro-acoustics	621.3828	TK5981-5990
			Electrocardiography	616.1207547	RC683.5.E5
Electric power distribution—High tension	621.31913	TK3144	Electrochemical analysis	543.4	QC115-116
			Electrochemistry	541.37	QD273
Electric power factor	621.31	TK153	Electrochemistry	541.37	QD551-575
Electric power failures	621.319	TK3091	Electrochemistry, Industrial	660.297	TP250-261
Electric power production	621.3121	TK1001-1841	Electroconvulsive therapy	616.89122	RC485
Electric power transmission	621.319	TK3001-3521	Electroculography	617.707547	RE79.E39
Electric power transmission—Alternating current	621.31913	TK3141-3171	Electrocution	364.66	HV8696
			Electrodes	541.3724	QD571-572
			Electrodiagnosis	616.07547	RC77-.5
Electric power-plants	621.3121	TK1191-1841	Electro-diesel locomotive	625.263	TF980
Electric power-plants—Testing	621.31210287	TK1831	Electrodynamics	537.6	QC630-648
			Electroencephalography	616.8047547	RC386.6.E43
Electric railroads	388.42	HE5351-5600	Electrohomeopathy	615.532	RZ420
Electric railroads, Miniature	625.19	TF857	Electroluminescence	535.357	QC480
Electric railroads—[By region or country]	621.3309(4-9)	TF1021-1127	Electrolysis in medicine	615.845	RM886
			Electrolysis in surgery	617.05	RD33.5
Electric railroads—Brakes	625.25	TF949.B7	Electrolyte therapy	615.854	RD52.F59
Electric railroads—Cars	625.2	TF920-952	Electrolytes	541.372	QC541-543
Electric railroads—Design and construction	621.33	TF863-952	Electrolytes	541.372	QD549
			Electrolytes	541.372	QD553-585
Electric railroads—Equipment and supplies	621.330284	TF920-952	Electrolytes—Conductivity	541.372	QD565
			Electrolytic corrosion	628.15	TD491
Electric railroads—Freight	385.24	TF970	Electrolytic oxidation	541.393	QD63.O9
Electric railroads—Rails	625.15	TF872			
Electric railroads—Third rail	625.15	TF890	Electrolytic oxidation	547.23	QD281.O9
Electric railroads—Wires and wiring	621.33	TF880-900	Electrolytic reduction	541.393	QD63.R4
			Electrolytic reduction	547.23	QD281.R4
Electric railway motors	621.33	TF935	Electromagnetic fields	539.2	QC665.E4
Electric resistance	537.62	QC611	Electromagnetic interactions	539.7546	QC794.8.E4
Electric resistors	621.384133	TK6565.R426			
Electric rheostats	621.317	TK2851	Electromagnetic theory	537	QC669-675.8
Electric rocket engines	629.4755	TL783.54-.63	Electromagnetic waves—Diffraction	539.2	QC665.D5
Electric shavers	646.724	TT967			
Electric signs	621.3229	TK4399.S6	Electromagnetic waves—Transmission	539.2	QC665.T7
Electric substations	621.3126	TK1751			
Electric switchgear	621.317	TK2821-2846	Electromagnetism	537	QC759.6-761.3
Electric testing	621.37	TK401	Electromagnets	538	QC760-.3
Electric transformers	621.314	TK2551	Electrometallurgy	669.0284	TN681-687
Electric utilities	333.7932	HD9685-9695	Electron accelerators	539.73	QC787.E39
Electric waves	537.534	QC660.5-665	Electron beams—Therapeutic use	615.845	RM862.E4
Electric welding	671.521	TK4660			
Electric wire	621.31933	TK3301-3351	Electron microscopes	570.2825	QH212.E4
Electric wiring	621.31933	TK3201-3285	Electron microscopic immunocytochemistry	616.0758	RB46.7
Electric wiring, Interior	621.31933	TK3271-3285			

Subject Heading	Dewey	LC	Subject Heading	Dewey	LC
Electron microscopy	570.2825	QH212.E4	Electronics—Congresses	621.38106	TK7801
Electron optics	537.56	QC793.5.E62-.E629	Electronics—Graphic methods	621.3810728	TK7825
Electron paramagnetic resonance	538.364	QC763	Electronics—Periodicals	621.38105	TK7800
Electron Tubes	621.38151	TK7871.7-.84	Electronics—Research	621.381072	TK7855
Electronic analog computers	621.3919	TK7888	Electronics in military engineering	623.043	UG485
Electronic apparatus and appliances	621.3810284	TK7869-7872	Electronics in navigation	623.893	VK560
Electronic behavior control	153.85	BF210	Electronics in rocketry	629.470284	TL784.E4
Electronic circuits	621.3815	TK7867-7868	Electronics in sanitary engineering	648	TH6025
Electronic counter-countermeasures	623.043	UG485	Electrons	539.72112	QC793.5.E462-.E4629
Electronic countermeasures	623.043	UG485	Electrons—Polarization	539.72112	QC793.5.E628
Electronic data interchange	651.8	HF5548.33	Electrooptical devices	623.7314	TA1750
Electronic data processing documentation	004	QA76.9.D6	Electrophoresis	541.372	QD79.E44
Electronic data processing—Backup processing alternatives	005.86	QA76.9.B32	Electrophoresis	541.372	QD117.E45
			Electrophoresis	541.372	QD272.E43
Electronic data processing—Data entry	005.72	QA76.9.D337	Electrophotography	686.44	TR1035-1050
			Electrophysiology	572.437	QH517
Electronic data processing—Data preparation	005.72	QA76.9.D345	Electrophysiology	572.437	QP341
			Electrophysiology of plants	572.4372	QK845
Electronic data processing—Distributed processing	004.36	QA76.9.D5	Electroplating	671.732	TS670-693
			Electroretinography	617.707547	RE79.E4
			Electroslag process	669.0284	TN686.5.E4
Electronic digital computers	621.39	TK7888.3-.4	Electroslag welding	671.521	TK4660
Electronic digital computers—Circuits	621.395	TK7888.4	Electrostatic accelerators	539.732	QC787.E4
			Electrostatic microphone	621.38284	TK5986
Electronic digital computers—Programming	004.1	QA76.6-.66	Electrostatics	537.2	QC570-596.9
			Electrotherapeutics	615.845	RM869-890
Electronic drafting	621.3810221	TK7866	Electrotyping	686.221	Z252
Electronic filing systems	651.53	HF5738	Elementary school administration	372.12	LB2822.5
Electronic funds transfer	332.10285	HG1710-.5			
Electronic games	794.8	GV1469.2	Elementary school dropouts	372.12913	LC145.5-.8
Electronic harpsichord music	786.4	M20-32			
			Elementary school principals	372.12012	LB2831.9-.976
Electronic instruments	621.3810284	TK7870			
Electronic keyboard (Synthesizer)	786.7409	ML1092	Elementary school teachers	372.11	LB1776
			Elephant hunting	799.2767	SK305.E3
Electronic mail systems	004.692	TK5105.73	Elephant seals	599.794	QL737.P64
Electronic mail systems	384.34	HE7551	Elephant shrews	599.336	QL737.M242
Electronic measurements	621.3810287	TK7878-7879.4	Elephantiasis	616.9652	RC142.5
Electronic news gathering	070.435	PN4784.E53	Elephants	599.67	QL737.P98
Electronic office machine industry	338.476816	HD9801	Eles (Firm) Strike, Bleidenstadt, Ger., 1975	331.89280943	HD5379.C6
Electronic organ music	786.59	M14.8	Elevators	621.877	TJ1370-1380
Electronic surveillance	621.38928	TK7882.E2	Elevators (Airplanes)	629.13433	TL677.E6
Electronic systems	621.381	TK7870	Elixirs	615.19	RS201.E4
Electronic traffic controls	625.794	TE228	Elk	599.657	QL737.U55
Electronic transformers	621.314	TK7872.T7	Elk farming	636.965701	SF401.E4
Electronics	621.381	TK7800-8360	Elk hunting	799.27657	SK303
Electronics—Charts, diagrams, etc.	621.3810223	TK7866	Elliptic functions	515.983	QA343
			Elvas, Linhas de, Battle of, 1659	946.9032	DP635
			Embalming	393.3	GT3340
			Embankments	624.162	TA760-772
			Embankments	627.133	TC759

Subject Heading	Dewey	LC	Subject Heading	Dewey	LC
Embankments	627.24	TC337	Emotions in children	155.412	BF723.E6
Embankments	627.42	TC533	Emotions in infants	155.42224	BF720.E45
Embargo, 1807-1809	973.48	E336.5	Empathy	152.41	BF575.E55
Embarrassment	152.4	BF575.E53	Emperor penguin	598.47	QL696.S473
Embassy buildings	725.17	NA4440-4447	Emperor worship	202.13	BL465
Embellishment (Music)	781.247	MT80	Emperor worship, Rome	291.2130937	DG124
Embellishment (Vocal music)	781.247	MT80	Emperor worship—Japanese	299.56	BL2211.E46
Embezzlement	364.162	HV6675-6685	Emperors	920.00902	D107
Emblems	203.7	BL603	Emperors—Byzantine Empire	949.50 (13-3) + 0099	DF506-.5
Emblems	246.55	BV150-155	Emperors—Rome	937.0099	DG270-365
Emblems	704.946	N7740	Emphysema, Pulmonary	616.248	RC776.E5
Emblems, National—England	344.4209	KD4650	Empiricism	146.44	B816
Emblems, National—United States	344.7309	KF5150	Employee assistance programs	331.255	HF5549.5.E42
Embolism	616.135	RC691	Employee discounts	331.255	HD4928.E4
Embroidery	677.77	TS1783	Employee fringe benefits	331.255	HD4928.N6
Embroidery	746.44	NK9200-9315	Employee fringe benefits—Accounting	657.742	HF5681.N65
Embroidery	746.44	TT769-778	Employee morale	658.314	HF5549.5.M6
Embroidery, Hmong	746.44	NK9206.4.H56	Employee motivation	658.314	HF5549.5.M63
Embryology	571.86	QL951-991	Employee orientation	658.31242	HF5549.5.I53
Embryology, Experimental	571.860724	QL961	Employee ownership	338.69	HD5650-5660
Embryology, Human	611.013	QM601-695	Employee rights	331.011	HD6971.8
Emeralds	622.386	TN997.E5	Employee selection	658.3112	HF5549.5.S38
Emergency management	363.34068	HV551.2-639	Employee stock options	331.2164	HD4928.S74
Emergency management	658.477068	HD49	Employee theft	658.473	HF5549.5.E43
Emergency medical personnel	616.025	RA645.5-.8	Employees—Counseling of	658.3151	HF5549.5.C8
Emergency medical services	362.18	RA645.5-.9	Employees—Drug testing	658.3112	HF5549.5.D7
Emergency medical technicians	616.025	RA645.5-.7	Employees-Rating of	658.3125	HF5549.5.R3
Emergency medicine	616.025	RC86-88.9	Employees—Recruiting	658.3111	HF5549.5.R44
Emergency nursing	616.025	RT120.E4	Employees' buildings and facilities	725.4	NA6598
Emery-wheels	621.923	TJ1290	Employer-supported day care	658.3	HF5549.5.D39
Emetics	615.73	RM359	Employment (Economic theory)	331.125	HD5701.5-.75
Emigration and immigration	325.(2 or 1)	JV6001-9500	Employment agencies	331.128	HD5860-6000.7
Emigration and immigration—Economic aspects	325.(2 or 1)	JV6118	Employment agencies—[By region or country]	331.12809(4-9)	HD5871-6000.7
Emigration and immigration—History	325.(2 or 1) + 090(1-5)	JV6021-6032	Employment forecasting	331.1250112	HD5701.55
Emin Pasha Relief Expedition, 1887-1889	967.0312	DT363	Employment interviewing	658.31124	HF5549.5.I6
Eminent domain	343.0252	K3511-3512	Employment references	650.14	HF5549.5.R45
Eminent domain—England	343.420252	KD1185-1189	Employment tests	658.3112	HF5549.5.E5
Eminent domain—United States	343.730252	KF5599	Emporia (Va.)—History—Civil War, 1861-1865	975.503	F234.E
Emission spectroscopy	535.84	QC454.E46	Emulsions	660.294514	TP156.E6
Emotional problems of children	155.4	BF723.E598	Emulsions (Pharmacy)	615.19	RS201.E5
Emotions	128.37	B815	Emus	598.53	QL696.C34
Emotions	152.4	BF511-593	Enamel and enameling	738.4	NK4997-5024
Emotions (Philosophy)	128.37	B105.E3	Enameled glass	748.6	NK5439.E5
Emotions in adolescence	155.512	BF724.3.E5	Encaustic painting	751.46	ND2480
Emotions in children	155.412	BF720.E45	Encke's comet	523.6	QB723.E3
			Encyclicals, Papal	262.91	BX860
			End of the universe	523.19	QB991.E53
			End of the world	236.9	BT875-891

Subject Heading	Dewey	LC
End play (Football)	796.3322	GV951.25
Endangered ecosystems	578.68	QH75-77
Endangered plants	581.68	QK86
Endangered species	578.68	QH75-77
Endangered species	578.68	QL81.5-84.77
Endemic goiter in children	618.92442	RJ420.G65
Endocarditis	616.11	RC685.E5
Endocrine glands	573.4	QL868
Endocrine glands	611.4	QM371
Endocrine glands	611.4	QM576
Endocrine glands	612.4	QP187-.6
Endocrine glands—Diseases	616.4	RC648-665
Endocrine gynecology	618.17	RG159-208
Endocrine manifestations of general diseases	616.047	RB48.5
Endocrinology	612.4	QP187-.6
Endocrinology	616.4	RC648-665
Endocrinology, Comparative	573.4	QL868
Endocrinology, Comparative	612.4	QP187-.6
Endodontics	617.6342	RK351-356
Endogamy and exogamy	306.82	GN480.3
Endometrium—Diseases	618.1	RG316
Endoscopic surgery	617.057	RD33.53
Endoscopic ultrasonography	618.107543	RG107.5.E48
Endoscopy	616.07545	RC78.7.E5
Endowment of research	001.40681	Q180.55.G7
Endowments	378.106	LB2336-2337
Endpapers	686.3	Z272
Endurance sports	796.425	GV749.5
Energy conservation	531.62	QC73.8.C6
Energy levels (Quantum mechanics)	539.725	QC795.8.E5
Energy metabolism	572.43	QP176
Energy minerals	333.79	TN263.5
Energy policy	333.79	HD9502-.5
Enfield rifle	356.1182425+ 973	UD395.E
Engagement (Philosophy)	392.4	B105.E5
Engineering	620	TA
Engineering—Congresses	620.006	TA5
Engineering—Dictionaries	620.003	TA9
Engineering—Equipment and supplies	620.00284	TA213-215
Engineering—Graphic methods	620.00728	TA337-338
Engineering—History	620.009	TA15-19
Engineering—Management	620.0068	TA190-194
Engineering—Notation	620.00148	TA11
Engineering—Periodicals	620.005	TA1-4
Engineering—Research	620.0072	TA160-.6
Engineering—Specifications	620.00212	TA180-182
Engineering—Statistical methods	620.00727	TA340
Engineering—Supplies	620.00284	T13
Engineering—[By region or country]	620.009(4-9)	TA21-127
Engineering—Africa	620.0096	TA115-119
Engineering—Arctic regions	620.00998	TA125-.5
Engineering—Argentina	620.00982	TA36-37
Engineering—Asiatic Russia	620.00957	TA109-110
Engineering—Australia	620.00994	TA121-122
Engineering—Austria	620.009436	TA65-.2
Engineering—Balkan Peninsula	620.009496	TA95.A2
Engineering—Belgium	620.009493	TA67-68
Engineering—Bolivia	620.00984	TA38-39
Engineering—Brazil	620.00981	TA41-42
Engineering—Canada	620.00971	TA26-27
Engineering—Central America	620.009728	TA30-31
Engineering—Chile	620.00983	TA43-44
Engineering—China	620.00951	TA101-102
Engineering—Colombia	620.009861	TA45-46
Engineering—Czechoslovakia	620.009437	TA65.3-.4
Engineering—Denmark	620.009489	TA69-70
Engineering—Ecuador	620.009866	TA47
Engineering—Egypt	620.00962	TA117-118
Engineering—Finland	620.0094897	TA95.F5
Engineering—France	620.00944	TA71-72.5
Engineering—French Guiana	620.009882	TA50
Engineering—Germany	620.00943	TA73-74.5
Engineering—Great Britain	620.00941	TA57-64
Engineering—Greece	620.009495	TA75-76
Engineering—Guyana	620.009881	TA48
Engineering—Hungary	620.009439	TA65.5-66
Engineering—India	620.00954	TA103-104
Engineering—Indonesia	620.009598	TA113.I55
Engineering—Iran	620.00955	TA107-108
Engineering—Iraq	620.009567	TA113.I7
Engineering—Israel	620.0095694	TA113.I75
Engineering—Italy	620.00945	TA79-80
Engineering—Japan	620.00952	TA105-106
Engineering—Mexico	620.00972	TA28-29
Engineering—Netherlands	620.009492	TA77-78
Engineering—New Zealand	620.00993	TA122.5-.6
Engineering— Norway	620.009481	TA81-82
Engineering—Oceania	620.0099(5-6)	TA123-124
Engineering—Pakistan	620.0095491	TA104.5-.6
Engineering—Paraguay	620.009892	TA51
Engineering—Peru	620.00985	TA52
Engineering—Philippines	620.009599	TA113.P6
Engineering—Portugal	620.009469	TA83-84.5
Engineering—Russia	620.00947	TA85-86
Engineering—Scandinavia	620.00948	TA88.5
Engineering—Spain	620.00946	TA87-88
Engineering—Sri Lanka	620.0095493	TA104.7-.8
Engineering—Surinam	620.009883	TA49
Engineering—Sweden	620.009485	TA89-90

Subject Heading	Dewey	LC	Subject Heading	Dewey	LC
Engineering—Switzerland	620.009494	TA91-92	English diaries	828.03	PR908
Engineering—Turkey	620.009561	TA111-112	English diaries	828.03	PR1330
Engineering—United States	620.00973	TA23-25	English drama	822.08	PR1241-1273
Engineering—Uruguay	620.009895	TA53	English drama	822.09	PR621-739
Engineering—Venezuela	620.00987	TA54	English drama (Comedy)	822.052308	PR1248
Engineering—West Indies	620.009729	TA32-33	English drama (Comedy)	822.052309	PR631
Engineering—Yugoslavia	620.009497	TA95.Y8	English drama (Tragedy)	822.051208	PR1257
Engineering design	620.0042	TA174	English drama (Tragedy)	822.051209	PR633
Engineering economy	620.00681	TA177.4-185	English drama—To 1500	822.(1-2)08	PR1260
Engineering ethics	174.962	TA157	English drama—To 1500	822.(1-2)09	PR641-644
Engineering experiment stations	620.0072	TA416-417	English drama—Early modern and Elizabethan, 1500-1600	822.(2-3)08	PR1262-1263
Engineering firms	620.006	TA157	English drama—Early modern and Elizabethan, 1500-1600	822.(2-3)09	PR646-658
Engineering firms	620.006	TA216-217	English drama—17th century	822.408	PR1265.3-1266
Engineering firms—Directories	620.0025	TA12	English drama—17th century	822.409	PR671-698
Engineering geology	624.151	TA703-705.4	English drama—18th century	822.508	PR1269
Engineering geology—[By region or country]	624.15109(3-4)	TA705.2-.4	English drama—18th century	822.509	PR701-719
Engineering inspection	620.0044	TA191	English drama—19th century	822.808	PR1271
Engineering instruments	620.00284	TA165	English drama—19th century	822.809	PR721-734
Engineering laboratories	620.0072	TA416-417	English drama—20th century	822.909	PR736-739
Engineering mathematics	620.00151	TA329-348	English drama—20th century	822.9108	PR1272
Engineering models	620.00228	TA177	English essays	824.009	PR921-927
Engineers	620.0023	TA157-158.3	English essays	824.08	PR1361-1369
Engineers—Biography	620.0092	TA139-140	English fiction	823.08	PR1281-1309
Engines	621.4	TJ250-255	English fiction	823.09	PR821-888
England	936.2	DA20-690	English fiction—20th century	823.9109	PR881-888
England	942	DA20-690	English fiction—Women authors	823.00809287	PZ1
England. Royal Air force	358.400942	DA89.5	English language	420	PE1001-3729
England—Church history—449-1066	274.109021	BR749	English language— Old English, ca. 450-1100	429	PE101-299
England—Church history—1066-1485	274.10902	BR745-754	English language— Old English, ca. 450-1100—Grammar	429.5	PE129-231
England—Church history—1485-	274.10903	BR750	English language— Old English, ca. 450-1100—Dialects	429.7	PE287-299
England—Church history—16th century	274.109031	BR755-757	English language— Old English, ca. 450-1100—Dictionaries	429.3	PE275-285
England—Church history—17th century	274.109032	BR756	English language—Old English, ca. 450-1100—Etymology	429.2	PE261-269
England—Church history—20th century	274.10904	BR759	English language— Old English, ca. 450-1100—Lexicography	429.3028	PE274-285
England—Constitutional history	342.42029	KD3931-3966			
England—Constitutional law	342.42	KD3931-4645			
England—Description and travel	914.204	DA600-632			
England—Economic conditions	330.942	HC251-260			
England—Foreign relations—Law and legislation	342.420412	KD4030			
England—Maps	912.42	G5750-5754			
England—Periodicals	936.2005	DA20			
England—Periodicals	942.005	DA20			
English cocker spaniel	636.7524	SF429.E47			

Subject Heading	Dewey	LC	Subject Heading	Dewey	LC
English language—Old English, ca. 450-1100—Philology	429	PE101-123	English literature	820	PR
			English literature	820	PR1-9680
English language— Middle English, 1100-1500	427.02	PE501-685	English literature—Old English, ca. 450-1100	829.09	PR171-236
English language— Middle English, 1100-1500—Dialects	427.027	PE688	English literature—Middle English, 1100-1500	820.(1-2)09	PR251-369
English language— Middle English, 1100-1500—Dictionaries	427.023	PE575-585	English literature—Middle English, 1100-1500	820.(1-2)08	PR1119-1131
English language— Middle English, 1100-1500—Etymology	427.022	PE561-569	English literature—Early modern, 1500-1700	820.(2-4)09	PR401-439
English language— Middle English, 1100-1500—Grammar	427.025	PE29-531	English literature— Early modern, 1500-1700	820.(2-4)08	PR1119-1131
English language— Middle English, 1100-1500—Lexicography	427.023028	PE574-585	English literature—18th century	820.508	PR1134-1139
English language— Middle English, 1100-1500—Philology	427.02	PE524-531	English literature—18th century	820.509	PR441-449
			English literature—19th century	820.808	PR1143-1145
English language—Early modern, 1500-1700	427.00903(1-2)	PE1079-1081	English literature—19th century	820.808	PR1301-1304
English language—18th century	427.009033	PE1083	English literature—19th century	820.809	PR451-469
English language—19th century	427.009034	PE1085	English literature—20th century	820.909	PR471-479
English language—Dialects	427	PE1700-3601	English literature—20th century	820.908	PR1149
English language—Dictionaries	423	PE1704	English literature—Catholic authors	820.809222	PR1110.C3
English language—Etymology	422	PE1571-1599	English literature—Criticism, Textual	820.9	PR57-78
English language—Grammar	425	PE1097-1105	English literature—Dictionaries	820.3	PR19
English language—Grammar—1950-	425	PE1112	English literature—History and criticism	820.9	PR1-978
English language—History	427.9	PE1079-1087	English literature—Irish authors	820.809415	PR8831-8893
English language—Lexicography	423.028	PE1601-1693	English literature—Irish authors	820.99415	PR8700-8821
English language—Morphology	425	PE1171	English literature—Japanese authors	820.80952	PR9900.J
English language—Parts of speech	425	PE1199-1359	English literature—Outlines, syllabi, etc.	820.0202	PR87
English language—Phonology	421.5	PE1133-1168	English literature—Scottish authors	820.809411	PR8631-8693
English language—Phonology, Historical	421.509	PE1133	English literature—Scottish authors	820.99411	PR8500-8621
English language—Rhetoric	808.042	PE1402-1497	English literature—Study and teaching	820.71	PR31-55
English language—Slang	427.09	PE3701-3729	English literature—Welsh authors	820.809429	PR8900-8997
English language—Study and teaching	420.71	PE1065-1069	English literature—Women authors	820.809287	PR1110.W6
English language—Synonyms and antonyms	423.1	PE1591	English literature—Women authors	820.99287	PR111-119
English language—United States	427.73	PE2801-3102	English newspapers	072.(1-8)	PN5111-5129
			English oak	583.46	QK495.F14
English letters	826.009	PR911-917	English oak	634.9721	SD397.E54
English letters	826.08	PR1341-1349	English periodicals	052	PN5111-5130

Subject Heading	Dewey	LC	Subject Heading	Dewey	LC
English periodicals	052	AP2-9	English prose literature—Scottish authors	828.08	PR8672-8687
English philology	420	PE			
English poetry	821	PR1170-1227	English saddles	636.13037	SF309.9
English poetry	821.9	PR500-611	English springer spaniels	636.7524	SF429.E7
English poetry—Old English, ca. 450-1100	829.1	PR1490-1508	English West Indian Expedition, 1654-1655	972.903	F1621
English poetry—Old English, ca. 450-1100	829.109	PR201-217	English West Indian Expedition, 1695	972.903	F1621
English poetry, Middle English, 1100-1500	821.(1-2)09	PR311-369	English West Indian Expedition, 1739-1742	986.102	F2272.5
English poetry—Early modern, 1500-1700	821.(3-4)08	PR1204-1213	English West Indian Expedition, 1759	972.903	F2151
English poetry—Early modern, 1500-1700	821.(3-4)09	PR521-549	English West Indian Expedition, 1793-1794	972.903	F1621
English poetry—18th century	821.508	PR1215-1219	English West Indian Expedition, 1795-1796	972.903	F1621
English poetry—18th century	821.509	PR551-579	English wit and humor	827	PN931-937
English poetry—19th century	821.808	PR1221-1224	English wit and humor	827.008	PN6173-6175
English poetry—19th century	821.809	PR581-599	English wit and humor	827.009	PR931-937
English poetry—20th century	821.9109	PR601-609	English wit and humor, Pictorial	741.5942	NC1470-1479
English poetry—20th century	821.9108	PR1224-1227	English-horn music	788.53	M110.E5
English poetry—History and criticism	821.9	PR500-609	Engravers	769.92	NE800
			Engravers' marks	760.278	NE820
English poetry—Irish authors	821.00809415	PR8848-8863	Engraving	760	NE
English poetry—Scottish authors	821.00809411	PR8649-8663	Engraving (Metal-work)	765	NE2700-2710
			Engraving—14th century	760.09023	NE1638
English poetry—Scottish authors	821.0089411	PR8561-8581	Engraving—15th century	760.09024	NE1655-1656
			Engraving—16th century	760.09031	NE1665-1666
English poetry—Welsh authors	821.00809429	PR8955-8969	Engraving—17th century	760.09032	NE1670-1690
English poetry—Welsh authors	821.00909429	PR8926-8932	Engraving—18th century	760.09033	NE1710-1719
			Engraving—19th century	760.09034	NE1720.5-1739
English poetry—Women authors	821.00809287	PR1177	Engraving—20th century	760.0904	NE1740-1749
			Engraving—Exhibitions	760.074	NE1410-1412
English poetry—Women authors	821.0099287	PR111-119	Engraving—Printing	760	NE2800-2890
			Engraving—Themes, motives	760.04	NE886
English prose literature	828.08	PR750-888			
English prose literature	828.08	PR1281-1300	Enki (Sumarian deity)	299.9295	BL1616.E54
English prose literature—Old English, ca. 450-1100	829.80809	PR221-236	Enlightenment	190	B802
			Ensemble playing	785.143807	MT728
English prose literature—Early modern and Elizabethan, 1500-1600	828.08(2-3)	PR1293-1295	Entebbe Airport Raid, 1976	956.94054	DS119.7
			Enteritis	616.344	RC862.E5
English prose literature—Early modern, 1500-1700	828.08(2-3)09	PR767-769	Enterobacterial vaccines	615.372	QR189.5.E53
			Entertainers in motion pictures	791.4092	PN1995.9.E77
English prose literature—18th century	828.08509	PR769	Entertainers—Diseases	616.0088791	RC965.P46
			Entertaining	395.3	BJ2021-2078
English prose literature—18th century	828.085	PR1297	Entertaining	642.(6-8)	TX851-885
			Entertaining	642.4	TX731-739
English prose literature—Scottish authors	828.08	PR8597-8607	Entertaining	793.2	GV1470-1521
			Enthusiasm	153.1533	BF575.E6
			Enthusiasm	248.2	BR112
			Entitlement spending	336.39	HJ7543
			Entomology—Research	595.7072	QL468.5
			Entrees (Cookery)	641.82	TX740
			Entrepreneurship	338.04	HB615

Subject Heading	Dewey	LC	Subject Heading	Dewey	LC
Enuresis	616.849	RC569.5.E5	Epigrams	808.882	PN1441
Enuresis	618.92849	RJ476.E6	Epigrams	808.882	PN6279-6288
Envelopment (Military science)	355.422	U167.5.E57	Epigrams, French	848.02	PN6282
Environmental auditing	363.7	TD194.7	Epilepsy	616.853	RC372-374.5
Environmental chemistry	577.14	TD193-.5	Epilepsy in adolescence	616.85300835	RJ496.E6
Environmental degradation	363.7	GE140-160	Epilepsy in children	618.92853	RJ496.E6
Environmental education	333.7071	GF70-90	Epilepsy in pregnancy	618.3268	RG580.E64
Environmental education	333.72071	S946	Epinal (France), Battle of, 1870	944.0812	DC309.E8
Environmental education	577.071	QH541.2-.264	Epiphany	263.915	BV50.E7
Environmental impact analysis	363.7	TD194.6	Epirus (Greece and Albania)	949.53	DF261.E65
Environmental impact statements	363.7	TD194.5-.58	Episcopacy	262.12	BV669-670.2
Environmental indicators	363.7	GE140-160	Episcopacy	262.12	BX5176-5178
Environmental management	333.7	GE300-350	Episcopal Church	264.035	BX5949
Environmental monitoring	363.7063	QH541.15.M64	Episcopal Church—Creeds	238.373	BX5939
Environmental protection	628	TD169-171.8	Episcopal Church—Creeds	238.373	BX6074
Environmental psychology	155.9	BF353-.5	Episcopal Church—Doctrines	230.373	BX5929-5930.2
Environmental quality	363.7	GE140-160	Episcopal Church—Education	268.8373	BX5850-5876
Environmental sampling	363.7064	GE45.S25	Episcopal Church—Education	268.8373	BX6061-6064.5
Environmental sciences	333.7	GE	Episcopal Church—Government	262.0373	BX5950-5968
Environmental sciences	363.7	GE	Episcopal Church—Government	262.0373	BX6076
Environmental testing	363.7064	TA171	Episcopal Church—History	283.7309	BX5879-5919
Environmental toxicology	615.902	RA1226	Episcopal Church—History	283.7309	BX6065-6069
Environmentalism	333.72	GE195-199	Episcopal Church—Liturgy	264.03	BX5940-5948
Environmentally induced diseases	616.98	RB152	Episcopal Church—Liturgy	264.03	BX6075
Enzymes	572.7	QP601-619	Episcopal Church—Missions	266.373	BX5969
Eoliths	930.11	GN775-776	Episcopal Church—Periodicals	283.7305	BX6051
Ephedra	633.8858	SB295.E63	Episcopal Church—Prayer-books and devotions	264.03	BX5943-5945
Ephemerides	528	QB7-9	Episcopal Church—Relations	283.73	BX5926-5928.5
Epic literature, French	841.03209	PQ201-205	Episcopal conferences (Catholic)	262.3	BX837.5
Epic poetry	808.8132	PN1301-1333	Episcopalians	283.73092	BX5800-6093
Epic poetry	808.8132	PN6110.E6	Episcopalians—Biography	283.73092	BX5990-5995
Epic poetry, English	821.03209	PR321-347	Episcopalians—Biography	283.73092	BX6091-6093
Epic poetry, German	831.03208	PT1411-1418	Epistemics	121	B820.3
Epic poetry, Greek	881.03208	PA3437-3439	Epitaphs	929.50937	CN528.E6
Epic poetry, Greek	881.03209	PA3105-3107.5	Epitaphs	929.50938	CN375.E6
Epic poetry, Latin	871.032108	PA6125	Epizootic catarrh in sheep	636.308969	SF969.E
Epidemic encephalitis	614.59832	RA644.E52	Epoxy resins	668.374	TP1180.E6
Epidemic encephalitis	614.832	RC141.E6	Epsom Derby, England (Horse race)	798.400942	SF357.E67
Epidemics	614.4	RA648.5-654	Epstein-Barr virus diseases	571.992	QR201.E75
Epidemics—[By region or country]	614.42(4-9)	RA650-650.9	Epstein-Barr virus diseases	616.91	RC141.5
Epidemics—Africa	614.426	RA650.8	Equality	305	HM146
Epidemics—America	614.42(7-8)	RA650-.55	Equality	323.42	JC575-578
Epidemics—Asia	614.425	RA650.7	Equality—Religious aspects	200.8	BL65.E68
Epidemics—Australia	614.4294	RA650.9.A8	Equations	512.94	QA211-218
Epidemics—Europe	614.424	RA650.6			
Epidemiology	614.4	RA648.5-653.5			
Epidermis	573.5	QL941-943			
Epidermis	573.5	QP88.5			
Epidermis	611.77	QM484			
Epidermis	611.77	QM561			
Epiglottis	611.22	QM255			

Subject Heading	Dewey	LC
Equations, Abelian	512.25	QA215
Equations, Binomial	512.9422	QA245
Equations, Cubic	512.9422	QA215
Equations, Quadratic	512.94222	QA161
Equations, Quartic	512.9422	QA215
Equations, Theory of	512.94	QA211-218
Equatorial Guinea—Census	316.718	HA4712
Equatorial Guinea—Civilization	967.18	DT620.4
Equatorial Guinea—Description and travel	967.1804	DT620.27
Equatorial Guinea—Gazetteers	916.718003	DT620.15
Equatorial Guinea—History	967.18	DT620.46-.83
Equatorial Guinea—Maps	912.6718	G8660-8664
Equestrian statues	731.81	NB1312-1313
Equilibrium	531.11	QC131
Equilibrium	531.12	QA821-835
Equilibrium (Economics)	339.5	HB145
Equity—Canada	346.71004	KE457
Equity—England	346.42004	KD674
Equity—United States	346.73004	KF398-400
Equus	599.665	QL737.U62
Ergodic theory	514	QA611.5
Ergodic theory	515.48	QA313
Erie, Lake, Battle of, 1813	973.5254	E356.E6
Erinyes (Greek mythology)	292.13	BL820.F8
Eritrea—History—1962-1993	963.5071	DT397
Eritrea—History—1993-	963.5072	DT397.3
Erosion	551.302	QE571-597
Erotic art	704.9428	N8217.E6
Erotic drawing	743.828	NC825.E76
Erotic literature	808.803538	PN6071.E7
Erotic literature	809.933538	HQ450-472
Error	121	BD171
Error analysis (Mathematics)	511.43	QA275
Errors, Popular	001.96	AZ999
Escalators	621.8676	TJ1376
Escapes	365.641	HV8657-8658
Eschatology	202.3	BL500-547
Eschatology	236	BT819-891
Eschatology, Buddhist	294.3423	BQ4475-4525
Eschatology, Islamic	297.23	BP166.8
Eskimo dogs	636.73	SF429.E8
Eskimo languages	497.1	PM50-94
Eskimos	979.8004971	E99.E7
Esophageal varices	616.32	RC815.7
Esophagectomy	617.548	RD539.5
Esophagus	573.359	QL861
Esophagus	611.32	QM331
Esophagus	612.315	QP146
Esophagus—Abnormalities	616.32043	RC815.7
Esophagus—Atresia	618.9232	RJ456.E83
Esophagus—Cancer	616.99432	RC280.E8
Esophagus—Diseases	616.32	RC815.7

Subject Heading	Dewey	LC
Esophagus—Foreign bodies	616.32	RF545
Esophagus—Surgery	617.548059	RD539.5
Esophagus—Tumors	616.99432	RC280.E8
Esophagus—Wounds and injuries	617.548044	RD539.5
Esopus Indians—Wars, 1655-1660	974.702	E83.655
Esopus Indians—Wars, 1663-1664	974.702	E83.663
Esperanto	499.992	PM8201-8298
Espionage, West German	327.1243	UB271.G
Espionage—History	327.1209	JF1525.I6
Essay	808.4	PN4500
Essays	808.84	PN6141-6145
Essays and proofs (Philately)	769.56	HE6184.D4
Essence and essential oils	661.806	TP958-959
Essenes	296.814	BM175.E8
Essential fatty acids	572.57	QP752.E84
Essential hypertension	616.132	RC685.H8
Estate planning—England	346.4205	KD1497
Estates (Law)—England	346.420432	KD841-960
Estill's Defeat, 1782	976.902	F454
Estimation theory	519.544	QA276.8
Estonia	947.98	DK503-.95
Estonia—Gazetteers	914.798003	DK503.18
Estonia—History—1944-1991	947.98	DK503.75-.77
Estonia—History—1991-	947.9808	DK503.8-.85
Estonia—Maps	912.4798	G7030-7033
Estonian language	494.545	PH601-629
Estonian literature	894.545	PH630-671
Estuaries	551.4618	GC96-97.8
Estuarine ecology	577.786	QH541.5.E8
Estuarine oceanography	551.4618	GC96-97.8
Estuarine plants	581.7786	QK108-474.5
Estuarine plants	581.7786	QK938.E
Etchers	767.2092	NE2110
Etching	767.2	NE1940-2232.5
Etching—[By region or country]	767.209(4-9)	NE2001-2096.3
Etching—18th century	767.209033	NE1990-1992
Etching—19th century	767.209034	NE1994-1995
Etching—20th century	767.20904	NE1997-1998
Etching—Catalogs	767.20294	NE1960
Etching—Exhibitions	767.2074	NE1950-1955
Etching—History	767.209	NE1980-2055.5
Eternity	236.21	BT910-912
Ether (Anesthetic)	617.96	RD79-86
Ethical culture movement	171	BJ10.E8
Ethics	170	BJ
Ethics, Assyro-Babylonian	170.935	BJ136-138
Ethics, Chinese	170.95	BJ116-118
Ethics, Chinese	170.951	BJ965-968
Ethics, Evolutionary	171.7	BJ1298-1335
Ethics, French	170.944	BJ701-704
Ethics, Germanic	170.943	BJ751-759

Subject Heading	Dewey	LC	Subject Heading	Dewey	LC
Ethics, Greek	170.938	BJ160-224	Ethnic groups—North America	305.80097	GN550-560
Ethics, Greek	170.9495	BJ801-804	Ethnic groups—Oceania	305.80099(5-6)	GN662-671
Ethics, Indic	170.954	BJ121-123	Ethnic groups—South America	305.80098	GN562-564
Ethics, Japanese	170.952	BJ969-971			
Ethics, Jewish	296.36	BJ1279-1287	Ethnic mass media	302.23089	P94.5.M55
Ethics, Korean	170.9519	BJ973-976	Ethnic radio broadcasting	384.54089	PN1991.8.E84
Ethics, Medieval	170.902	BJ231-255	Ethnic relations	305.8	GN496-498
Ethics, Modern	170.903	BJ301-982	Ethnic schools	371.829	LC3800-3806
Ethics, Modern—18th century	170.9033	BJ311	Ethnicity	305.8	GN495.6
Ethics, Modern—19th century	170.9034	BJ315	Ethnohistory	305.8009	GN345.2
			Ethnological museums and collections	305.80074	GN35-41
Ethics, Modern—20th century	170.904	BJ319	Ethnology	305.8	GN301-673
Ethics, Oriental	170.95	BJ961-977	Ethnology	305.8	GN325
Ethics, Polish	170.9438	BJ847-850	Ethnology in the Bible	220.83058	BS661
Ethics, Positivist	171.2	BJ1365-1385	Ethnology—Afghanistan	939.6004	DS354.5-.6
Ethics, Renaissance	170.90(23-31)	BJ271-285	Ethnology—Afghanistan	958.1004	DS354.5-.6
Ethics—Congresses	170.6	BJ19	Ethnology—Africa	960.04	DT15-16
Ethics—Dictionaries	170.3	BJ63	Ethnology—Albania	939.8004	DR923-925
Ethics—History	170.9	BJ71-982	Ethnology—Albania	949.65004	DR923-925
Ethics—Outlines, syllabi, etc.	170.202	BJ1075-1077	Ethnology—Algeria	939.71004	DT283-.6
			Ethnology—Algeria	965.004	DT283-.6
Ethics—Periodicals	170.5	BJ1-8	Ethnology—Angola	967.3004	DT1304-1308
Ethics—Philosophy	170.1	BJ37-60	Ethnology—Armenia	947.56004	DS172
Ethics—Societies, etc.	170.6	BJ10-11	Ethnology—Asia	950.04	DS13-28
Ethics—Study and teaching	170.71	BJ66-68	Ethnology—Australia	994.004	DU120-125
Ethics—Textbooks	170	BJ991-1185	Ethnology—Austria	936.3004	DB33-34.5
Ethics in the Bible	220.817	BS680.E84	Ethnology—Austria	943.6004	DB33-34.5
Ethiopia	963	DT371-398	Ethnology—Balkan Peninsula	949.6004	DR24-27
Ethiopia—Census	316.3	HA4689			
Ethiopia—Civilization	963	DT379.5	Ethnology—Bangladesh	934.004	DS393.82-.83
Ethiopia—Description and travel	916.304	DT375-378.3	Ethnology—Bangladesh	954.92004	DS393.82-.83
			Ethnology—Belgium	936.4004	DH491-492
Ethiopia—Economic conditions	330.963	HC845	Ethnology—Belgium	949.3004	DH491-492
			Ethnology—Benin	966.83004	DT541.42-.45
Ethiopia—Gazetteers	916.3003	DT371.5	Ethnology—Botswana	968.83004	DT2454-2458
Ethiopia—History	963	DT380.5-387.95	Ethnology—Brunei	959.55004	DS650.42-.43
Ethiopia—History—To 1490	963.0(1-2)	DT383	Ethnology—Bulgaria	939.8004	DR64
			Ethnology—Bulgaria	949.9004	DR64
Ethiopia—History—1490-1889	963.0(2-4)	DT384-386.73	Ethnology—Burkina Faso	966.25004	DT555.42-.45
			Ethnology—Burma	959.1004	DS528-.2
Ethiopia—History—1889-1974	963.0(43-6)	DT387-.92	Ethnology—Burma	959.1004	DS538-539
			Ethnology—Burundi	967.572004	DT450.64-.65
Ethiopia—History—Rebellion, 1928-1930	963.054	DT387.7-.8	Ethnology—Byzantine Empire	949.50(13-3)004	DF542-.4
Ethiopia—History—Coup d'etat, 1960	963.06	DT387.9	Ethnology—Cambodia	959.6004	DS554.44-.46
			Ethnology—Cameroon	967.11004	DT570-571
Ethiopia—Maps	912.63	G8330-8334	Ethnology—Cape Verde	966.58004	DT671.C242-.C2
Ethiopian languages	492.8	PJ8991-8999	Ethnology—Central African Republic	967.41004	DT546.342-.345
Ethiopic language	492.81	PJ9001-9087			
Ethiopic literature	892.81	PJ9090-9101	Ethnology—Chad	967.43004	DT546.422-.445
Ethnic groups	305.8	GN495.4	Ethnology—China	931.004	DS730-731
Ethnic groups—Africa	305.80096	GN643-661	Ethnology—China	951.004	DS730-731
Ethnic groups—Asia	305.80095	GN625-635	Ethnology—Congo (Brazzaville)	967.24004	DT546.242-.245
Ethnic groups—Europe	305.80094	GN575-585			
			Ethnology—Cote d'Ivoire	966.68004	DT545.42-.45

Subject Heading	Dewey	LC	Subject Heading	Dewey	LC
Ethnology—Cyprus	939.37004	DS54.4-.44	Ethnology—Madagascar	969.1004	DT469.M276-.M277
Ethnology—Cyprus	956.93004	DS54.4-.44	Ethnology—Malawi	968.97004	DT3189-3192
Ethnology—Czechoslovakia	943.7004	DB2040-2043	Ethnology—Malaysia	959.5004	DS595-.2
Ethnology—Denmark	936.3004	DL141-142	Ethnology—Mali	966.23004	DT551.42-.45
Ethnology—Denmark	948.9004	DL141-142	Ethnology—Mauritania	966.1004	DT554.42-.45
Ethnology—Djibouti	967.71004	DT411.42-.45	Ethnology—Mauritius	969.82004	DT469.M442-.M445
Ethnology—Egypt	932.004	DT71-72	Ethnology—Morocco	939.71004	DT313-.6
Ethnology—Egypt	962.004	DT71-72	Ethnology—Morocco	964.004	DT313-.6
Ethnology—Equatorial Guinea	967.18004	DT620.42-.45	Ethnology—Mozambique	967.9004	DT3324-3328
Ethnology—Ethiopia	963.004	DT380-.4	Ethnology—Namibia	968.81004	DT1554-1558
Ethnology—Europe	940.55004	D1056-.2	Ethnology—Nepal	954.96004	DS493.8-.9
Ethnology—Europe, Central	943.004	DAW1026-1028	Ethnology—Netherlands	936.3004	DH91-92
Ethnology—Europe, Eastern	947.0004	DJK26-28	Ethnology—Netherlands	936.3004	DJ91-92
Ethnology—Finland	948.97004	DL1018-1020	Ethnology—Netherlands	949.2004	DH91-92
Ethnology—France	936.4004	DC34-.5	Ethnology—Netherlands	949.2004	DJ91-92
Ethnology—France	944.004	DC34-.5	Ethnology—New Zealand	993.004	DU422.5-424.5
Ethnology—Gabon	967.21004	DT546.142-.145	Ethnology—Niger	966.26004	DT547.42-.45
			Ethnology—Nigeria	966.9004	DT515.42-.45
Ethnology—Gambia	966.51004	DT509.42-.45	Ethnology—Norway	936.3004	DL441-442
Ethnology—Germany	943.004	DD73-78	Ethnology—Norway	948.1004	DL441-442
Ethnology—Ghana	966.7004	DT510.42-.43	Ethnology—Pakistan	934.004	DS380.A1-.A2
Ethnology—Great Britain	936.1004	DA120-125	Ethnology—Pakistan	954.91004	DS380.A1-.A2
Ethnology—Great Britain	941.004	DA120-125	Ethnology—Poland	943.8004	DK4120-4122
Ethnology—Greece	938.004	DF135	Ethnology—Portugal	936.6004	DP533-534.5
Ethnology—Greece	949.50(4-9)004	DF745-747	Ethnology—Portugal	946.9004	DP533-534.5
Ethnology—Greece	949.5004	DF135	Ethnology—Reunion	969.81004	DT469.R38-.R39
Ethnology—Guinea	966.52004	DT543.42-.45	Ethnology—Romania	939.8004	DR213-214
Ethnology—Guinea-Bissau	966.57004	DT613.42-.45	Ethnology—Romania	949.8004	DR213-214
Ethnology—Hawaii	996.9004	DU624.6-.7	Ethnology—Russia (Federation)	947.004	DK33-35
Ethnology—Hungary	939.8004	DB919-.2			
Ethnology—Hungary	943.9004	DB919-.2	Ethnology—Rwanda	967.571004	DT450.24-.25
Ethnology—Iceland	949.12004	DL331-334	Ethnology—Sao Tome and Principe	967.15004	DT615.42-.45
Ethnology—India	934.004	DS430-432.5	Ethnology—Saudi Arabia	939.49004	DS218-219
Ethnology—India	954.004	DS430-432.5	Ethnology—Saudi Arabia	953.8004	DS218-219
Ethnology—Indonesia	959.8004	DS631-632	Ethnology—Scandinavia	936.3004	DL41-42
Ethnology—Iran	935.004	DS268-269	Ethnology—Scandinavia	948.004	DL41-42
Ethnology—Iran	955.004	DS268-269	Ethnology—Senegal	966.3004	DT549.42-.45
Ethnology—Iraq	935.004	DS70.8	Ethnology—Seychelles	969.6004	DT469.S442-.S443
Ethnology—Iraq	956.7004	DS70.8	Ethnology—Sierra Leone	966.4004	DT516.42-.45
Ethnology—Israel	933.004	DS113.2-.8	Ethnology—Slovakia	943.73004	DB2740-2743
Ethnology—Israel	956.94004	DS113.2-.8	Ethnology—Somalia	967.73004	DT402.3-.45
Ethnology—Italy	937.004	DG455-457	Ethnology—South Africa	968.004	DT1754-1770
Ethnology—Italy	945.004	DG455-457	Ethnology—Spain	936.6004	DP52-53
Ethnology—Japan	952.004	DS830-832	Ethnology—Spain	946.004	DP52-53
Ethnology—Jordan	933.004	DS153.5-.55	Ethnology—Sri Lanka	954.93004	DS489.2-.25
Ethnology—Jordan	956.95004	DS153.5-.55	Ethnology—Sudan	962.4004	DT155-.2
Ethnology—Kenya	967.62004	DT433.542-.545	Ethnology—Swaziland	968.87004	DT2744-2746
Ethnology—Korea	951.9004	DS904.5-.7	Ethnology—Sweden	936.3004	DL639-641
Ethnology—Laos	959.4004	DS555.44-.45	Ethnology—Sweden	948.5004	DL639-641
Ethnology—Lebanon	939.44004	DS80.5	Ethnology—Switzerland	936.4004	DQ48-49
Ethnology—Lebanon	956.92004	DS80.5	Ethnology—Switzerland	949.4004	DQ48-49
Ethnology—Lesotho	968.85004	DT2592-2596	Ethnology—Syria	939.43004	DS94.7-.8
Ethnology—Liberia	966.62004	DT630-.5	Ethnology—Syria	956.91004	DS94.7-.8
Ethnology—Libya	961.2004	DT223-.2			

Subject Heading	Dewey	LC	Subject Heading	Dewey	LC
Ethnology—Taiwan	931.004	DS799.42-.43	Europe, Eastern—Congresses	947.0006	DJK1.5
Ethnology—Taiwan	951.249004	DS799.42-.43	Europe, Eastern—Description and travel	914.7004	DJK11-18
Ethnology—Tanzania	967.8004	DT443-.3	Europe, Eastern—Gazetteers	914.70003	DJK6
Ethnology—Thailand	959.3004	DS569-570	Europe, Eastern—Historiography	947.00072	DJK32-34
Ethnology—Togo	966.81004	DT582.42-.45	Europe, Eastern—History—1918-1945	947.000904(1-4)	DJK49
Ethnology—Tunisia	939.73004	DT253-.2	Europe, Eastern—History—1945-	947.00090(44-5)	DJK50
Ethnology—Tunisia	961.1004	DT253-.2	Europe, Eastern—History—1945-1989	947.000904(4-8)	DJK50
Ethnology—Turkey	939.2004	DR434-435	Europe, Eastern—History—1989-	947.00090(48-5)	DJK51
Ethnology—Turkey	956.1004	DR434-435	Europe, Eastern—Periodicals	947.0005	DJK1
Ethnology—Uganda	967.61004	DT433.242-.245	Europe, Eastern—Study and teaching	947.00071	DJK35-36
Ethnology—United States	973.04	E184-185.98	Europe—Armed Forces—Supplies and stores	355.8094	UC158-233
Ethnology—Vietnam	959.7004	DS556.44-.45	Europe—Biography	920.04	CT759-1495
Ethnology—Yugoslavia	939.8004	DR1229-1230	Europe—Census	314	HA1107-1650
Ethnology—Yugoslavia	949.7004	DR1229-1230	Europe—Civilization—18th century	940.2(526-7)	CB411
Ethnology—Zaire	967.51004	DT649.5-650	Europe—Civilization—19th century	940.2(7-87)	CB204
Ethnology—Zambia	968.94004	DT3054-3058	Europe—Climate	551.694	QC989
Ethnology—Zimbabwe	968.91004	DT2910-2913	Europe—Commerce	381.094	HF3491-3750.7
Ethnomethodology	305.8001	HM24	Europe—Description and travel	914	D901-980
Ethnomusicology	780.89	ML3797.7-3799	Europe—Economic conditions	330.94	HC240-407
Ethnophilosophy	305.8001	GN468	Europe—Foreign relations—1989-	327.4	D2009
Ethnopsychology	155.82	GN270-279	Europe—Genealogy	929.107204	CS410-1059
Ethnopsychology	155.82	GN502-517	Europe—Historical geography—Maps	911.4	G1791-1799
Ethologist	590.92	QL26-31	Europe—History	940	D900-1075
Etiquette	395	BJ1801-2195	Europe—History—1789-1815	940.27	D301-309
Etiquette for men	395.142	BJ1855	Europe—Intellectual life—19th century	940.2(7-87)	CB204
Etiquette for women	395.144	BJ1856	Europe—History—1945-	940.5(5-6)	D1050-1075
Etiquette—Dictionaries	395.03	BJ1815	Europe—History—1945- —Periodicals	940.5(5-6)005	D1050
Etiquette—History	395.09	BJ1821	Europe—Intellectual life—20th century	940.(288-559)	CB203-231
Etiquette—Periodicals	395.05	BJ1801	Europe—Maps	912.4	G5700-7153
Etruscan language	499.94	P1078	Europe—Politics and government	354.094	JN
Etruscans—Religion	299.9294	BL740-760	Europe—Politics and government—1989-	320.940948	D2009
Eucalyptus	583.766	QK495.M9	Europe—Politics and government—20th century	320.94	JN12
Eucalyptus	634.973766	SD397.E8	Europe—Religion	200.94	BL690-980
Eucharistic congresses	264.02036	BX2215.A1	European Americans	973.04(2-8)073	E184.E95
Euclid's Elements	516.21	QA451-469			
Eugenics	363.92	HQ750-755.5			
Euler's numbers	515.52	QA246			
Euphonium	788.97509	ML99L0.E			
Euphonium music	788.975	M110.B33			
Euro-bond market	337.14	HG3896			
Europa Cup (Soccer)	796.33466	GV943.5			
Europe, Central	943	DAW			
Europe, Central—Civilization	943	DAW1024			
Europe, Central—Congresses	943.0006	DAW1004			
Europe, Central—Description and travel	914.304	DAW1014-1015			
Europe, Central—History	943	DAW1031-1051			
Europe, Central—Periodicals	943.0005	DAW1001			
Europe, Eastern	947	DJK			
Europe, Eastern—Biography	920.047	DJK31			
Europe, Eastern—Civilization	947	DJK24			

Subject Heading	Dewey	LC	Subject Heading	Dewey	LC
European Economic Community literature	341.2422	HC241.2-.25	Examinations	371.271	LB3050-3060
European federation	321.04094	D1060	Examinations	378.013076	LC1070-1071
European federation	321.04094	JN15	Examinations	378.241	LB2366-2367
European periodicals	073-078	PN5110-5355	Examinations—Design and construction	371.27	LB3060.65
Eustachian tube	573.89	QL948	Examinations—Questions	371.271	LB3051-3059
Eustachian tube	611.85	QM507	Examinations—Scoring	371.27	LB3060.77
Eustachian tube	612.854	QP461	Examinations—Study guides	371.27	LB3060.57
Eustachian tube—Diseases	617.86	RF230	Exanthemata	616.9	RC106
Eutaw Springs, Battle of, 1781	973.337	E241.E	Excavating machinery	621.865	TA735-747
Euthanasia	179.7	R726	Excavation	624.152	TA730-748
Evacuation Day, Nov. 25, 1783	973.339	E239	Excavation	624.152	TH5101
Evangelical academies	269.2	BV4487.E9	Excavations (Archaeology)	930.10283	CC75
Evangelical Revival	274.109033	BR758	Excavations (Archaeology)	930.10283	CC165
Evangelicalism and Christian union	280.042	BX9.5.E94	Excess profits tax	336.24320973	HJ4653.E8
Evangelicalism—Episcopal Church	269.2	BX5925	Excise tax	336.271	HJ5730-5731
Evangelistic invitations	269.2	BV3793	Excise tax—Law and legislation	343.0553	K4572-4580
Evangelistic sermons	252.3	BV3797	Excision of ankle	617.584059	RD562
Evangelistic work	269.2	BV3750-3799	Exciton theory	530.416	QC176.8.E9
Evangelists	269.2092	BV3780-3785	Excretion	612.46	QP159
Evaporation	536.44	QC304	Excretion	612.46	QP211
Evaporation (Meteorology)	551.572	QC915-917	Excretory organs	573.49	QL872-875
Evapotranspiration	551.572	QC915.5-.7	Execution sermons	252.68	BV4262
Evapotranspiration	575.8	QK873	Executions and executioners	364.66	HV8551-8586
Even language	494.1	PL481.E92	Executive ability	658.409	HD38.2-.25
Evening and continuation schools	374.8	LC5501-5560	Executive departments—Canada	347.71	JL87-111
Evenki language	494.1	PL451-459	Executive departments—Confederate States of America	351.75	JK9720-9770
Event horses	636.10811	SF295.7			
Evergreens	635.9775	SB435	Executive departments—United States	342.7306	KF5050-5125
Everlasting flowers	635.973	SBS428.5			
Everlasting flowers	635.973	SB447	Executive power	342.062	K3332-3351
Evidence	121.65	BC171-173	Executive power	352.235	JF251-289
Evidence (Law)—United States	347.7306	KF8931-8969	Exercise	613.71	GV460-548
Evidence preservation	363.24	HV7936.E85	Exercise	613.71	QP301-336
Evidence, Criminal	345.06	K5465-5490	Exercise	613.71	RA781-.85
Evidence, Criminal—United States	345.7306	KF9660-9678	Exercise—Physiological aspects	612.044	QP301-310
Evil eye	133.425	BF1553	Exercise for men	613.71081	GV482.5
Evil eye	133.425	GN475.6	Exercise therapy	615.82	RM725-727
Evil, Non-resistance to	241.3	BR115.W2	Exercise therapy for children	618.920062	RJ53.E95
Evolution	146.7	B818	Exercise therapy for the aged	615.820846	RC953.8.E93
Evolution (Biology)	576.8	QH359-425			
Evolution—Religious aspects	213	BL263	Exgot alkaloids	615.321	RS431.E73
Ewe (African people)	966.7004 + 963374	DT510.43.E94	Exhibition buildings	725.91	NA6750-6751
			Exhibitions	607.34	T391-999
Ewe (African people)	966.81004 + 963374	DT582.45.E93	Existential ethics	171.2	BJ1340
			Existential phenomenology	142.78	B818.5
Ewe language	496.3374	PL8161-8164	Existential psychology	150.192	BF204.5
Ex-monks	255.(1-7)	BX4668.2-.3	Existential psychotherapy	616.8914	RC489.E93
Examinations	370.711	LB1762-1765	Existentialism	142.78	B819
			Exocrine glands	612.4	QP187.7

Subject Heading	Dewey	LC	Subject Heading	Dewey	LC
Eyes, Artificial	617.79	RE986-988	Fallacies (Logic)	165	BC175
Eyestrain	617.75	RE51	Fallopian tubes	611.65	QM421
Eyestrain	617.755	RE48	Fallopian tubes—Diseases	618.12	RG421-433
F region	551.5145	QC879	Falls Fight, 1676	974.402	E83.67
Fava bean	633.3	SB205.F3	Familial behavior in	591.563	QL761.5
Facades	729.1	NA2840-2841	animals		
Face	611.92	QM535	Family	306.8	HQ503-1064
Face	743.42	NC770	Family	306.85	GN480-.65
Face—Surgery	617.52059	RD523-527	Family	306.85	HQ
Face—Wounds and injuries	617.52044	RD523	Family	306.85	HQ734
Facelift	617.520592	RD119.5.F33	Family	392	GT2420
Facing heads	737.4	CJ161.F3	Family demography	304.63	HQ759.98
(Numismatics)			Family in dreams	154.63	BF1099.F34
Facsimile transmission	621.38235	TK6710-7620	Family psychotherapy	616.89156	RC488.5-.6
Factor analysis	519.5354	QA278.5	Family recreation	790.191	GV182.8
Factor tables	513.23021	QA51	Family size	304.63	HQ760-767.7
Factories	338.4767	HD7406-7510	Family size—[By region or	304.6309(1-9)	HQ762
Factories	690.54	TH4511-4591	country]		
Factories	725.4	NA6396-6589	Family violence	364.1555(3-4)	HV6626-.23
Factories—Air conditioning	697.9354	TH7684.F2-.F3	Family violence	616.85822	RC569.5.F3
Factories—Design and	690.54	TH4511-4591	Family—Biblical teaching	220.830685	BS680.F3
construction			Family—Health and	613.04	RA418.5.F3
Factories—Soundproofing	693.834	TH1725	hygiene		
Factors (Algebra)	512.923	QA161.F3	Family-owned business	338.7	HD62.25
Factors (Algebra)	512.923	QA242	enterprises		
Factory and trade waste	628.51	TD896-899	Family—Religious life	249	BV200
Factory inspection	658.568	HD3656-3790.9	Famine compact, 1765	330.944	HC275
Factory inspection—[By	658.56809(4-9)	HD3661-3790.9	Famines	363.8	HC79.F3
region or country]			Famines	363.8	HV630-635
Factory sanitation	628.51	TD895	Famines in the Bible	220.83638	BS680.F32
Factory system	338.65	HD2350.8-2356	Fanaticism	248.2	BR114
Faculty advisors	378.194	LB2343	Fanconi's anemia	616.152	RC641.7.F36
Fafnir (Germanic	293.13	BL870.F28	Fancy work	746.4	TT740-897
mythology)			Fang language	496.396	PL8167.F3
Failure to thrive syndrome	618.92	RJ135	Fans	391.44	GT2150
Fairies	398.21	BF1552	Fans	745.594	NK4870
Fairies	398.45	GR549-552	Fans (Machinery) industry	338.4762161	HD9705.5.F35-
Fairness doctrine	384.54	HE8689.7.F34			.F354
(Broadcasting)			Fantasy in children	155.41332	BF723.F28
Fairs	381.1	HF5469.7-5481	Fantasy in mass media	154.3	P96.F36
Fairs	381.1	HF5481	Fanti language	496.3385	PL8167.F4
Fairs	394.6	GT4580-4699	Far ultraviolet radiation	535.014	QC459.5
Fairy tales	398.2	GR550-552	Farce	808.825232	PN1940-1949
Fairy tales	398.2	PZ8	Farces	808.825232	PN6120.F3
Faith	234.23	BT770-772	Farm buildings	690.892	TH4911-4935
Faith	241.4	BV4637	Farm buildings	728.92	NA8200-8260
Faith (Islam)	297.22	BP166.78	Farm equipment	631.3	S671-760
Faith (Judaism)	296.32	BM729.F3	Farm life	305.963	HT421
Falconry	799.232	SK321	Farm life	390.463	S521
Falcons	598.96	QL696.F34	Farm management	630.68	S560-572
Falkland Islands, Battle of	940.454	D582.F2	Farm manure	631.861	S655
the, 1914			Farm produce	338.17	HD9000-9019
Falkland Islands—Census	319.71	HA2295	Farm produce—Marketing	381.41	HD9000-9019
Falkland Islands—Maps	912.9711	G9175-9179	Farm produce—Marketing	381.41	S571-.5
Falkland Islands—Politics	320.99711	JL690-699	Farm tractors	629.2252	TL233-.8
and government			Farm tractors	631.372	S711-713
Fall of man	233.14	BT710	Farm trucks	631.373	S711-713

Subject Heading	Dewey	LC	Subject Heading	Dewey	LC
Farmer's lung	616.24	RC776.F33	Feast of the Sacred Heart	263.97	BV64.S3
Farmhouses	690.86	TH4920	Feathers	598.147	QL697
Farmhouses	728.6	NA8208-8210	Feathers as feed	636.0855	SF99.F37
Farms	338.16	HD1401-2210	Febrile convulsions	618.92845	RJ496.C7
Farms	630	S560-575	Fecal incontinence	616.342	RC866.D43
Farms, Size of	338.16	HD1470-1476	Fecal incontinence in	618.92342	RJ456.F43
Farms—Valuation	333.76	HD1393	children		
Faroese language	439.699	PD2483	Federal aid to education	379.121	LB2825-2826.6
Fasciae (Anatomy)	611.74	QM563	Federal government	321.02	JC355
Fascism	320.533	JC481	Federal government	321.02	K3285
Fascism	945.091	DG571	Federal government—	342.73042	KF4600-4629
Fashion	391	GT500-2370	United States		
Fashion drawing	741.672	TT509	Federal Reserve banks	332.110973	HG2559-2565
Fashion merchandising	381.45391	HD9940-9949.5	Feed additives	636.08557	SF98.A2
Fashoda Crisis, 1898	962.403	DT156.6	Feed mills	664.76	TS2158
Fast draw pistol shooting	799.31	GV1175.5	Feedback control systems	629.83	TJ216
Fast-day sermons	252.6	BV4270	Feedback oscillators	621.381533	TK7872.07
Fasteners	621.88	TJ1320-1340	Feedlot runoff	628.16846	TD930.2
Fasting	248.47	BV5055	Feeds	636.0855	SF94.5-99
Fasting	613.25	RM226-228	Feeds—Fiber content	636.0855	SF98.F
Fasting (Hinduism)	294.5447	BL1215.F3	Feeds—Flavor and odor	636.0855	SF97.7
Fasting (Islam)	297.53	BP179	Fehmarn, Battle of, 1644	948.9701	DL190
Fastnet Yacht Race	797.14091631	GV832	Fehrbellin, Battle of, 1675	943.044	DD394.3
Fasts and feasts	203.8	BL590	Feldspar	549.68	QE391.F3
Fasts and feasts	263.9	BV30-135	Felt	677.6(2-3)	TS1825
Fasts and feasts	263.9	CE81	Feminist theology	230.082	BT83.55
Fasts and feasts	394.2	GT3920-4995	Feminist theory	305.42	HQ1190
Fasts and feasts—Buddhism	294.3438	BQ5700-5720	Femur	611.718	QM117
Fasts and feasts—Hinduism	294.538	BL1239.72-.82	Fencers	796.86092	GV1144-.2
Fasts and feasts—Islam	297.53	BP186	Fences	631.27	NA8390-8392
Fasts and feasts—Jainism	294.438	BL1355.5	Fences	631.27	S790-.3
Fasts and feasts—Judaism	296.43	BM690-720	Fencing	796.86	GV1143-1150.6
Fasts and feasts—Samaritan religion	296.43	BM970	Feng-shui	133.3337	BF1779.F4
			Fenians	941.7081	DA954
Fatherhood	306.8742	HQ756-.7	Feral children	155.4567	GN372
Fathers	306.8742	HQ756-.7	Feral children	155.4567	RJ507.F47
Fathers of the church	270.092	BR60-67	Fermat's theorem	512.74	QA244
Fathers of the church	270.092	BR1705	Fermented foods	664.024	TP371.44
Fatigue	152.1886	BF482	Fermions	539.721	QC793.5.F42-.F429
Fatigue	612.744	QP321			
Fatigue	658.544	T57.72	Ferns, Ornamental	635.9373	SB429
Fatigue testing machines	620.11260287	TA413-.5	Ferreting	799.23	SK293
Fatty acids	572.57	QP752.F35	Ferries	386.6	HE5751-5870
Fatty acids in human nutrition	572.57	QP752.F35	Ferroelectric devices	621.3815	TK7872.F44
			Ferroelectricity	537.2448	QC596-.9
Faults (Geology)	551.872	QE606-.5	Fertility, Human	304.632	HB901-1108
Fear	152.46	BF575.F2	Fertility, Human—[By	304.63209(4-9)	HB901-1108
Fear in children	155.412	BF723.F4	region or country]		
Feast of Jesus Christ the King	263.97	BV64.J4	Fertility, Human—Developing countries	304.632091724	HB1108
Feast of the Assumption of the Blessed Virgin	263.97	BV50.A7	Fertilization (Biology)	571.864	QH485
			Fertilization in vitro, Human	618.178059	RG135
Feast of the Holy Innocents	263.97	BV50.H6	Fertilization of plants	571.8642	QK828
Feast of the Immaculate Conception	263.97	BV50.I6	Fertilization of plants by insects	571.8642	QK926
			Fertilizers	631.8	S631-667
			Fescue	584.9	QK495.G74

Subject Heading	Dewey	LC	Subject Heading	Dewey	LC
Festival-day sermons	252.6	BV4254.3	Fig	634.37	SB365
Festivals	394.26	GT3930-4995	Fighter pilots	358.43092	UG626-.2
Fetal death	618.32	RG631-633	Fighter plane combat	358.434	UG700-705
Fetal growth disorders	618.32	RG629.G75	Fighter plane combat—United States	358.430973	UG703
Fetal growth retardation	618.32	RG629.G76	Fighter planes	358.4383	UG1242.F5
Fetal heart rate monitoring	618.3261075	RG628.3.H42	Fighter planes	623.7464	TL685.3
Fetal heart—Abnormalities	618.3261043	RJ269	Figure drawing	743.4	NC765-778
Fetal malnutrition	618.32	RG627.6.M34	Figure painting	751.42242	ND2190-2192
Fetal monitoring	618.32075	RG628-.3	Figure painting	757	ND1290-1293
Fetal presentation	618.42	RG671-693	Figure sculpture	731.82	NB1930-1936
Fetishism	202.1	GN472	Figureheads of ships	623.84	VM308
Fetishism (Sexual behavior)	306.77	HQ79	Fiji	996.11	DU600
Fetterman Fight, Wyo., 1866	978.701	F761	Fiji—Census	319.611	HA4016
			Fiji—Maps	912.9611	G9380-9384
Fetus	618.32	RG600-650	Fijian language	499.5	PL6235
Fetus—Abnormalities	618.32043	RG626-629	Filariasis	614.5552	RA644.F5
Fetus—Diseases	618.32	RG626-629	Filariasis	616.9652	RC142.5
Fetus—Effect of drugs on	618.32	RG627.6.D79	File organization (Computer science)	005.741	QA76.9.F5
Fetus—Growth	612.647	RG613	File processing (Computer science)	005.74	QA76.9.F53
Fetus—Immunology	618.32	RG613.7			
Fetus—Metabolism	618.326	RG615	Fili (Irish poets)	891.621009	PB1321
Fetus—Physiology	612.647	RG610-621	Filibusters (Political science)	328.34	JF519
Fetus—Respiration and cry	618.4	RG620			
Fetus—Ultrasonic imaging	618.3207543	RG628.3.U58	Filing systems	651	HF5735-5746
Feudal law—England	340.550942	KD834-839	Filipino Americans	973.049921073	E184.F4
Feudalism	321.3	D131	Fillings (Dentistry)	617.675	RK517-519
Feudalism	321.3	JC109-121	Filmstrips in education	371.3352	LB1043.8
Fever	616.047	RB129	Filters and filtration	542.6	QD63.F5
Fever therapy	615.832	RM868-.5	Filters and filtration	628.164	TD441-449
Fever—Eclectic treatment	616.04706	RV211	Filters and filtration	660.284245	TP156.F5
Fever—Homeopathic treatment	616.04706	RX211	Finance	332	HG
			Finance, Personal	332.024	HG179
Few-body problem	521.4	QB362.F47	Finance, Public	336	HJ
Few-body problem	530.14	QC174.17.P7	Finance, Public—Accounting	657.61	HJ9701-9995
Fiber in animal nutrition	636.0852	SF98.F	Finance, Public—Auditing—Law and legislation—United States	343.73034	KF6231-6239
Fiber in human nutrition	613.263	TX553.F53			
Fiber optics	621.3692	QC447.9-448.2			
Fiber plants	633.5	SB241-261	Finance, Public—History	336.090(1-5)	HJ210-240
Fiberglass craft	731.2	NB1270.G5	Finance, Public—Law and legislation	343.03	K4430-4675
Fibrin	612.115	QP91			
Fibromyalgia	616.723	RC927.3	Finance, Public—Law and legislation—Canada	343.7103	KE5600-6328
Fibrous dysplasia of bone	616.71	RC931.F5			
Fibula (Archaeology)	611.718	CC400	Finance, Public—Law and legislation—England	343.4203	KD5280-5752
Fiction	808.3	PN3311-3503			
Fiction—History and criticism	809.3	PN3329-3503	Finance, Public—Law and legislation—Ireland	343.41503	KDK1430-1526
			Finance, Public—Law and legislation—Scotland	343.41103	KDC807-825
Fictions, Theory of	165	BC199.F5			
Fictions, Theory of	210	BL51	Finance, Public—Law and legislation—United States	343.7303	KF6200-6795
Fiction—Technique	808.3	PN3355-3383			
Field theory (Physics)	530.14	QC173.68-.75	Finance, Public—Periodicals	336.005	HJ9-99.8
Fielding (Baseball)	796.35724	GV870			
Fife	788.3307	MT356	Finance, Public—United States	336.73	HJ241-785
Fife music	788.33	M60-62			
Fifth generation computers	004.1	QA76.85			
Fifth Monarchy Men	941.063	DA420-429			
Fig	583.45	QK495.M73			

Subject Heading	Dewey	LC
Finance, Public—[United States, By state]	336.7(4-9)	HJ285-785
Finance—Congresses	332.06	HG63
Finance—Directories	332.025	HG64-96
Finance—Encyclopedias	332.03	HG151
Finance—History	332.09	HG171
Finance—Periodicals	332.05	HG1-61
Finance—Statistics	332.021	HG176-.5
Finance—Study and teaching	332.071	HG152-.5
Financial crises	338.542	HB3722-3725
Financial futures	332.6452	HG6024.3-.9
Financial institutions	332	HG1-9999
Financial planners	332.024092	HG179.5
Financial statements	657.3	HF5681.B2
Financial statements, Unaudited	657.3	HF5667.65
Fines (Penalties)	364.68	HV9277
Finger spelling	419	HV2477-2480
Fingerprints	363.24	HV6074
Fingerprints	599.945	GN192
Fingers	611.97	QM548
Finish carpentry	694.6	TH5640-5695
Finishes and finishing	677.02825	TP934-945
Finite element method	620.00151535	TA347.F5
Finite, The	111.6	BD411
Finland	948.97	DL1002-1180
Finland—Biography	920.04897	DL1024
Finland—Census	314.897	HA1450.5
Finland—Civilization	948.97	DL1017
Finland—Congresses	948.97006	DL1004
Finland—Description and travel	914.89704	DL1015-.4
Finland—Gazetteers	914.897003	DL1007
Finland—Historiography	948.970072	DL1025
Finland—History—To 1523	948.9701	DL1050-1052.9
Finland—History—1523-1611	948.9701	DL1055-1141.6
Finland—History—Gustavus II Adolphus, 1611-1632	948.9701	DL1058-1063
Finland—History—Charles X Gustavus, 1654-1660	948.9701	DL1060-.5
Finland—History—18th century	948.9701	DL1063-.9
Finland—History—1809-1917	948.9702	DL1065-.8
Finland—History—Revolution, 1917-1918	948.97031	DL1070-1075
Finland—History—1918-1939	948.97031	DL1084
Finland—History—1939-	948.9703(2-4)	DL1090-1105
Finland—History—20th century	948.970(2-3)	DL1066-1141.6
Finland—Manufactures	670.94897	TS95.F5
Finland—Maps	912.4897	G2075-2079
Finland—Maps	912.4897	G6960-6964
Finland—Periodicals	948.97005	DL1002
Finland—Politics and government	320.94897	JN7390-7399
Finnic languages	494.54	PH91-98
Finnish Americans	973.0494541073	E184.F5
Finnish language	494.541	PH101-293
Finnish language—Grammar	494.5415	PH131-225
Finnish literature	894.54109	PH300-405
Finnish philology	494.541	PH101-123
Finno-Ugric essays	089.945	AC80-85
Finno-Ugric languages	494.5	PH
Finno-Ugric languages—Grammar	494.55	PH21-41
Finno-Ugric languages—Study and teaching	494.5071	PH11
Finno-Ugric philology	494.5	PH1-11
faautoFins	597.1479	QL639
Finsler spaces	516.375	QA689
Fir	585.2	QK494.5.P66
Fir	634.9754	SD397.F5
Fire	660.2961	TP265-267
Fire-clay	620.143	TA455.F5
Fire-clay	622.367	TN941-943
Fire-escapes	628.922	TH2274
Fire-worshipers	202.12	BL453
Fire alarms	628.9225	TH9271-9275
Fire ants	595.796	QL568.F7
Fire control (Gunnery)	623.558	UF848-856
Fire control (Gunnery)—Optical equipment	623.5580284	UF849
Fire control (Naval gunnery)	359.422	VF520-530
Fire detectors	628.9225	TH9271
Fire doors	690.1822	TH2278
Fire engines	628.9259	TH9371-9377
Fire extinction	628.925	TH9111-9599
Fire extinction—Chemical systems	628.9254	TH9338
Fire extinction—Water-supply	628.9252	TH9311-9334
Fire extinguishers	628.9254	TH9362
Fire fighters—Physical training	363.37092	TH9128
Fire insurance claims adjusters	368.11014	HG9711-9715
Fire lookout stations	634.93	SD421.375
Fire prevention	693.82	TH9111-9599
Fire prevention—Law and legislation—United States	344.7305377	KF3975-3977
Fire prevention—Research	628.922072	TH9120
Fire resistant materials	693.82	TH1065
Fire sprinklers	628.9252	TH9336
Firearms	356.1182	UD380-415
Firearms	359.824	VD360-390
Firearms	683.4	TS532-537.5
Firearms—Identification	363.2565	HV8077
Firearms—Sights	356.1182	UD390

Subject Heading	Dewey	LC	Subject Heading	Dewey	LC
Firearms—Sights	623.46	UF854	Fisheries—Netherlands	639.209492	SH275-276
Firearms industry and trade	338.476834	HD9744	Fisheries—New Zealand	639.20993	SH318.5
		.F55-.F554	Fisheries—Norway	639.209481	SH279-280
Firearms ownership	683.4	HV8059	Fisheries—Oceania	639.2099(5-6)	SH319
Fireboats	628.9259	TH9391	Fisheries—Pacific Ocean	639.209164	SH214-215
Firecrackers	662.1	TP300-301	Fisheries—Portugal	639.209469	SH281-282
Firedamp	622.82	TN305-306	Fisheries—Russia	639.20947	SH283-284
Fireplaces	697.1	TH7421-7434.7			
Fireplaces	721.8	NA3050-3055	Fisheries—South America	639.2098	SH234-251
Fireproofing	693.82	TH1061-1093	Fisheries—Spain	639.20946	SH285-286
Fires	363.37	HV620	Fisheries—Sweden	639.209485	SH287-288
Fires	628.92	TH9448-9449	Fisheries—Turkey	639.209561	SH291-292
Fires—Casualties	617.11	RA1085	Fisheries—United States	639.20973	SH221-222
Fireworks	662.1	TP300-301	Fisheries—West Indies	639.209729	SH233
First aid for animals	636.08960252	SF914.3	Fisheries navigation	623.89	SH343.8
First aid in illness and injury	616.0252	RC86-88.9	Fisheries subsidies	338.3727	SH334
First communion	264.02036	BX2237	Fishers	639.2092	HD8039.F65
First day covers (Philately)	769.56	HE6184.F57	Fishers	799.1092	SH414-415
First of June, 1794, Battle of	941.073	DA87.5 1794	Fishery conservation	639.977	SH327.7
First-born children	306.87	HQ777.2	Fishery law and legislation—Canada	343.7107692	KE1760-1765
Fish as food	641.392	TX385	Fishery law and legislation—England	343.4207692	KD2310-2315
Fish culturists	639.2092	SH20	Fishery law and legislation—United States	343.7307692	KF1770-1773
Fish decoys	799.10284	SH451.3	Fishery management	639.2068	SH328-329
Fish habitat improvement	639.92	SH157.8-.85	Fishery processing	664.94	SH334.9-336.5
Fish inspection	363.1929064	SH335	Fishery products—Preservation	641.494	TX612.F5
Fish kills	639.96	SH171-179	Fishery products—Preservation	664.94(1-8)	SH335-337
Fish meal as feed	636.0855	SF99.F5	Fishery research stations	639.2072	SH332-.2
Fish oils	665.2	TP676	Fishery research vessels	338.372072	SH343.4
Fish populations	597.1788	QL618.3	Fishery resources	333.7	SH327.5
Fish traps	639.20284	SH344.6.T67	Fishery schools	639.2071	SH332-.2
Fish-culture	639.3	SH151-179	Fishery technology	639.2028	SH334.5-344.8
Fisheries	639.2	SH	Fishes	597	QL614-639.8
Fisheries—Congresses	639.206	SH3	Fishes—Classification	597.012	QL618
Fisheries—Equipment and supplies	639.20284	SH344-.8	Fishes—Diseases	639.964	SH171-179
			Fishes—Folklore	398.3697	GR745
Fisheries—History	639.209	SH211	Fishes—Genetics	597.135	QL638.99
Fisheries—Periodicals	639.305	SH1	Fishes—Geographical distribution	597.09(4-9)	QL619-637
Fisheries—Safety measures	639.20289	SH343.9	Fishes—Infections	639.964	SH171-179
Fisheries—Asia	639.2095	SH295-307	Fishes—Locomotion	597.1479	QL639.4
Fisheries—Atlantic Ocean	639.209163	SH213-.77	Fishes—Migration	597.1568	QL639.5
Fisheries—Australia	639.20994	SH317-318	Fishes—Parasites	639.96	SH175
Fisheries—Canada	639.20971	SH223-229	Fishes—Pathogens	639.964	SH171-179
Fisheries—Central America	639.209728	SH232	Fishes—Research	597.072	QL618.5-.55
Fisheries—China	639.20951	SH297-298	Fishes—Spawning	597.562	QL639.2
Fisheries—Denmark	639.209489	SH267-268	Fishhooks	639.20284	SH344.8.H6
Fisheries—Europe	639.2094	SH253-293	Fishhooks	799.10284	SH452.9.H
Fisheries—Great Britain	639.20941	SH255-260	Fishing	394.3	GT5904-5905
Fisheries—Greece	639.209495	SH273-274	Fishing	799.12	SH401-691
Fisheries—Greenland	639.209982	SH268.G83	Fishing—Equipment and supplies	799.10284	SH447-453
Fisheries—Indian Ocean	639.209165	SH216-.55			
Fisheries—Ireland	639.209415	SH261-262			
Fisheries—Italy	639.20945	SH277-278			
Fisheries—Japan	639.20952	SH301-302			
Fisheries—Korea	639.209519	SH302.5-.7			
Fisheries—Mexico	639.20972	SH231			

Subject Heading	Dewey	LC	Subject Heading	Dewey	LC
Fishing—History	799.109	SH421	Floodplains	551.442	GB561-568
Fishing—Periodicals	799.1205	SH401	Floods	363.34938	HV609-610
Fishing—Canada	799.10971	SH571-572	Floods	551.489	GB1399-.5
Fishing—North America	799.1097	SH462	Floods	634.9617	SD425
Fishing—United States	799.10973	SH463-565	Floor traders (Finance)	332.642	HG4621
Fishing—West Indies	799.1209729	SH577-578	Flooring	690.16	TH2521-2529
Fishing knots	799.1028	SH452.9.K6	Floors	721.6	NA2970
Fishing nets	639.20284	SH344.8.N4	Floriculture	635.9	SB403-450.87
Fishing ports	387.1	SH337.5	Florida—Gazetteers	917.59003	F309
Fishing rods	799.10284	SH452-.2	Florida—History	975.9	F306-320
Fishing tackle	799.10284	SH447-453	Florida—History—To 1565	975.901	F314
Fishways	639.92	SH153	Florida—History—To 1821	975.90(1-3)	F314
Five Civilized Tribes	976.603004973	E78.I5	Florida—History—Huguenot colony, 1562-1565	975.901	F314
Five Civilized Tribes	976.604004975	E78.O45	Florida—History—Spanish colony, 1565-1763	975.901	F314
Five Precepts (Buddhism)	294.342	BQ5485-5525	Florida—History—English colony, 1763-1784	975.90(2-3)	F314
Fjords	551.44	GB454.F5	Florida—History—Spanish colony, 1784-1821	975.903	F314
Flag Day	394.26973	JK1761	Florida—History—Cession to the United States, 1819	975.903	F314
Flagella (Microbiology)	571.672	QR78	Florida—History—1821-1865	975.90(4-5)	F315
Flagellata	579.82	QL368.F5	Florida—History—1951-	975.906(3-4)	F316.2-.23
Flagellation	364.67	HV8613-8621	Florida—History—Civil War, 1861-1865	975.905	E558.1-.9
Flags	355.15	UC590-595	Florida—History—1865-	975.906	F316-.23
Flags	359.15	V300-305	Florida—Maps	912.759	G3930-3934
Flags	929.92	CR101-115	Florida—National Guard	355.3709759	UA140-149
Flags—United States	359.150973	V303-304	Florida—Periodicals	975.9005	F306
Flags—[Other countries]	359.1509(4-9)	V305	Florists	381.4159092	SB442.8-445
Flame	541.361	QD516	Flossenburg (Germany: Concentration camp)	940.531853	D805.G3
Flaps (Airplanes)	629.13433	TL673.F6	Flour	641.331	TX393
Flat roofs	690.15	TH2409	Flour	664.7207	TS2120-2159
Flax	677.11	TS1700-1735	Flour-mills	664.7207	TS2120-2159
Flea markets	381.192	HF5482.15	Flow meters	532.510284	TC177
Fleet ballistic missile weapons systems	359.981782	V990-995	Flower arrangement	745.92	SB449-450.87
Flemish drama	839.31208	PT6350-6360	Flower gardening	635.9	SB403-450.87
Flemish literature	839.31	PT6000-6466.36	Flower language	302.222	GR780-790
Flemish literature—Study and teaching	839.31071	PT6040	Flower shows	635.9074	SB441-.75
Flemish periodicals	053.931	AP14-17	Flowering woody plants	635.97713	SB435-437
Flemish poetry	839.31108	PT6330-6348	Flowers	635.9	SB403-450
Flemish poetry	839.31109	PT6140	Flowers—Anatomy	575.633	QK653-661
Flemish prose literature	839.31808	PT6365-6397	Flowers—Morphology	575.633	QK653-661
Fleurus, Battle of, 1794	940.27	DC222.F6	Flowers in heraldry	929.6	CR41.F6
Flexible weapons (Hand-to-hand fighting)	355.824	U167.5.H3	Flue gases	628.532	TD885
Flexure	624.252	TG265	Flugelhorn	788.9707	MT493
Flight	629.13	TL570-578	Flues	697.8	TH2281-2288
Flight training	629.1325071	TL712-.8	Fluid copying processes	686.4	Z48
Flights around the world	910.41	G445	Fluid dynamic measurements	620.10640287	TA357.5.M43
Floating batteries	359.32	V890	Fluid dynamics	530.42	QA911-930
Floating bodies	532.25	QA907	Fluid dynamics	532.5	QC150-159
Floating bodies	532.25	QC147	Fluid dynamics	620.106	TA357-359
Floating harbors	623.83	TC363			
Flodden, Battle of, 1513	941.104	DA784.6			
Flood dams and reservoirs	627.4	TC167			
Flood dams and reservoirs	627.8	TC540-558			
Flood forecasting	551.4890112	GB1399.2			
Flood routing	551.489	GB1203			

Subject Heading	Dewey	LC	Subject Heading	Dewey	LC
Fluid therapy for children	618.9200653	RJ53.F5	Folk songs	782.42162	M1627
Fluidization	660.284292	TP156.F65	Folklore	398	GR
Fluidized-bed furnaces	697.07	TH7140	Folklore—[By region or country]	398.09(4-9)	GR100-390
Fluids	532	QA901-930	Folklore—Africa	398.096	GR350-360
Fluids	532	QC138-168.86	Folklore—Asia	398.095	GR265-345
Flumes	627.52	TC933	Folklore—Australia	398.0993	GR365-370
Fluorescence	535.352	QC477-.4	Folklore—Europe	398.094	GR135-263
Fluorescent lamps	621.3273	TK4386	Folklore—New Zealand	398.0994	GR375-376
Fluorine	546.731	QD181.F1	Folklore—North America	398.097	GR101-118
Fluorine	661.0731	TP245.F6	Folklore—Oceania	398.0996	GR380-385
Flute	788.307	MT340-348	Folklore—Performance	398	GR72.3
Flute music	788.3	M60-64	Folklore—South America	398.098	GR130-133
Flutter (Aerodynamics)	629.132362	TL574.F6	Folklorists	398.092	GR50
Fly casting	799.124	SH454.2	Fon dialect	496.337	PL8164.Z9
Fly fishing	799.124	SH456-.2	Fonts	726.5291	NA5070
Flying-machines	629.13334	TL670-724	Food	641.3	TX341-641
Foals	636.101	SF277-359.7	Food	641.592	GN407-411.5
Focal infection, Dental	617.63	RK305	Food—Bacteriology	664.001579	QR115-129
Focal infection, Dental	617.63	RK351	Food—Biotechnology	664.024	TP248.65.F66
Focused group interviewing	361.322	H61.28	Food—Caloric content	613.23	TX551
Fog	551.575	QC929.F7	Food—Carbohydrate content	613.283	TX553.C28
Fog—Control	629.1324	TL557.F6	Food—Cholesterol content	613.284	TX553.C43
Folds (Geology)	551.875	QE606-.5	Food—Drying	641.44	TX609
Foliage plants	635.975	SB431	Food—Preservation	641.4	TX599-613
Foliations (Mathematics)	514.72	QA613.62	Food—Toxicology	615.954	RA1258-1260
Folk art	745	N5312-5313	Food additives	641.3	TX553.A3
Folk dancing	793.31	GV1580-1799	Food adulteration and inspection	363.192	HD9000.9
Folk literature	398.2	GR72-390	Food adulteration and inspection	363.192064	TX501-597
Folk literature, Afrikaans	398.2043936	PT6540-6545	Food allergy	616.975	RC596
Folk literature, American	398.20973	PS451-478	Food allergy in children	618.92975	RJ386.5
Folk literature, Arabic	398.204927	PJ7580	Food allergy in infants	618.92975	RJ386.5
Folk literature, Arabic	398.204927	PJ7680	Food allergy—Diet therapy	616.9750654	RC588.D53
Folk literature, Chinese	398.204951	PL2445-2446	Food crops	635	SB175-177
Folk literature, Danish	398.2043981	PT7900-7930	Food crops	641.303	SB175
Folk literature, Dutch	398.2043931	PT5351-5395	Food habits	394.1	GT2850-2960
Folk literature, English	398.2042	PR951-981	Food in the Koran	297.12286413	BP134.F58
Folk literature, Flemish	398.2043931	PT6200-6230	Food law and legislation	344.04232	K3626-3633
Folk literature, French	398.20441	PQ781-841	Food law and legislation—Canada	344.7104232	KE1867-1906
Folk literature, German	398.20431	PT881-951	Food law and legislation—England	343.4207833 + 847664	KD2405-2430
Folk literature, Greek	398.2048	PA3285	Food law and legislation—United States	344.7304232	KF1900-1944
Folk literature, Hebrew	398.204924	PJ5048	Food of animal origin	394.12	GT2865-2866
Folk literature, Icelandic	398.20439691	PT7420-7438	Food of animal origin	641.36	TX743-759.5
Folk literature, Italian	398.20451	PQ4186-4199	Food preservatives	641.4	TX599-612
Folk literature, Japanese	398.204956	PL748-749	Food processor cookery	641.5892	TX840.F6
Folk literature, Korean	398.204957	PL968.2-.4	Food relief	363.883	HV696.F6
Folk literature, Low German	398.204394	PT4829-4830	Food service	388.476-4795	TX901-946.5
Folk literature, Norwegian	398.2043982	PT8600-8635	Food service management	338.476. 4795068	TX911.3.M27
Folk literature, Persian	398.2049155	PK6426	Food stamps	363.882	HV696.F6
Folk literature, Portuguese	398.20469	PQ9121-9128	Food supply	363.8	HD9000-9019
Folk literature, Scandinavian	398.204395	PT7088-7089			
Folk literature, Spanish	398.20461	PQ6155-6167			
Folk literature, Swedish	398.204397	PT9509-9542			
Folk literature—History and criticism	398.209	PN905-1008			
Folk poetry	398.2	PN1341-1347			

Subject Heading	Dewey	LC	Subject Heading	Dewey	LC
Food warmers	738.8	NK4695.F6	Forest reserves	333.7511	SD426-428
Foodborne diseases	614.5	RA601.5	Forest reserves—Recreational use	333.784	GV191.67.F6
Foot	611.98	QM549			
Foot—Abnormalities	617.585043	RD781-789	Forest roads	625.709152	TE229.5
Foot—Amputation	617.5850592	RD563	Forest thinning	634.953	SD396.5
Foot—Diseases	617.585	RC951	Forestry schools and education	634.9071	SD250-381.5
Foot—Dislocation	617.585044	RD781			
Foot—Examination	617.585075	RD563	Forests and forestry	634.9	SD
Foot—Reimplantation	617.5850592	RD563	Forests and forestry—Research	634.9072	SD356-.54
Foot—Surgery	617.585059	RD563			
Foot—Wounds and injuries	617.585044	RD563	Forests and forestry—Safety measures	634.93	SD411
Foot washing (Rite)	265.9	BV873.F7			
Football	796.332	GV937-960	Forests and forestry—Societies, etc.	634.906	SD1
Football—Defense	796.3322	GV951.18			
Football—Offense	796.3322	GV951.8	Forests and forestry—[By region or country]	634.909(4-9)	SD11-115
Football—Rules	796.33202022	GV955			
Football for children	796.332083	GV959.55.C45	Forests and forestry—United States	634.90973	SD11-12
Football players	796.332092	GV939			
Footprints	363.2562	HV8077.5.F6	Forests and forestry—[United States, By state]	634.9097(4-9)	SD12
Forage plants	633.2	SB193-207			
Forbes Expedition against Fort Duquesne, 1758	973.26	E199	Forgery	332.9	HG1696-1698
			Forgery	364.163	HV6675-6685
Forbidden fruit	222.11	BS1237	Forgery of antiquities	364.163	CC140
Force and energy	531.6	QC72-73.8	Forging	671.332	TS225
Forcing (Model theory)	511.34	QA9.A7	Forgiveness	177.7	BJ1476
Forearm	611.97	QM548	Forgiveness of sin	234.5	BT795
Forecasting	003.2	CB158-161	Forms (Law)—England	347.42055	KD318
Foreign exchange	332.45	HG3810-4000	Forms (Mathematics)	512.944	QA201
Foreign exchange futures	332.6452	HG3853	Forms (Mathematics)	512.944	QA243
Foreign exchange—Encyclopedias	332.4503	HG3810.5	Fornovo, Battle of, 1495	945.06	DG541
			Fort Harrison (Va.), Battle of, 1864	973.737	E477.21
Foreign exchange—History	332.4509	HG3811-3815			
Foreign exchange—Law and legislation—England	343.42032	KD5288	Fort Henry (Tenn.), Battle of, 1862	973.731	E472.96
			Fort Oswego (Oswego, N.Y.)—Capture, 1756	973.26	E199
Foreign exchange—[By region or country]	332.4509(4-9)	HG3901-4000			
			Fort William Henry (N.Y.)—Capture, 1757	973.26	E199
Foreign films	791.43	PN1995.9.F67			
Foreign trade promotion	382	HF1417.5	Fortification	623.1	UG400-442
Forensic ballistics	363.2562	HV8077	Fortification, Field	623.1	UG403
Forensic pathology	614.1	RA1063.4	Fortuna (Roman deity)	292.2114	BL820.F7
Forensic psychiatry	614.15	RA1151-1152	Fortune-telling	133.3	BF1845-1891
Forest animals	591.73	QL112	Forums (Discussion and debate)	371.396	LC6501-6560
Forest conservation	634.9	SD411-428			
Forest ecology	577.3	QH541.5.F6	Fossil man	569.9	GN282-286.7
Forest ecology	581.73	QK938.F6	Fossils—Collection and preservation	560.75	QE718
Forest fire detection	634.9618	SD421			
Forest fires	634.9618	SD420.5-421.5	Foundation garments	687.22	TT677
Forest fires—Prevention and control	634.9618	SD421	Foundations	624.15	TA775-787
			Foundations	690.11	TH2101
Forest genetics	634.956	SD399.5	Foundations	690.11	TH5201
Forest insects	634.96	SB761	Founding	671.2	TS228.97-239
Forest landscape design	719.33	SB475.9.F67	Founding	671.2	TS228.99-240
Forest machinery	634.90284	SD388	Foundlings	362.73	HV835-847
Forest plants	581.73	QK108-474.5	Fountains	714	NA9400-9425
Forest plants	581.73	QK938.F6	Four Horsemen of the Apocalypse	228	BS2820-2827
Forest products	338.17498	HD9750-9769			
Forest protection	634.93	SD411-428			

Subject Heading	Dewey	LC	Subject Heading	Dewey	LC
Fourier analysis	515.2433	QA403.5-404.5	France—History—Charles IX, 1560-1574	944.029	DC116-118
Fowling	799.24	SK311-335	France—History—War of the Huguenots, 1562-1598	944.0(29-3)	DC116-118
Fox hunting	799.259775	SK284-287			
Foxes	599.775	QL737.C22	France—History—Henry III, 1574-1589	944.029	DC119-120
Fractions	513.26	QA117			
Fractions—Study and teaching	513.26071	QA135-139	France—History— Henry IV, 1589-1610	944.031	DC122-.9
Fracture mechanics	620.1126	TA409	France—History—Bourbons, 1589-1789	944.03	DC120.8-138
Fractures	617.15	RD101-104			
Fractures, Spontaneous	617.15	RD101	France—History—Louis XIII, 1610-1643	944.032	DC123-.9
Fractures in animals	636.089715	SF914.4	France—History—Louis XIV, 1643-1715	944.033	DC124.5-130
Fragile X syndrome	618.928588	RJ506.F73			
Framing (Building)	694.2	TH2301-2311	France—History—Louis XV, 1715-1774	944.034	DC133-135
France	944	DC			
France—Biography	920.0364	DC36-.8	France—History—Louis XVI, 1774-1793	944.035	DC136-137.5
France—Biography	920.044	DC36-.8			
France—Census	314.4	HA1211-1230	France—History—Revolution, 1789-1799	944.04(1-2)	DC139-190.8
France—Church history	274.4	BR840-849			
France—Civilization	936.4	DC33-.9	France—History—Consulate and First Empire, 1799-1815	944.0(46-5)	DC191.2-249
France—Civilization	944	DC33-.9			
France—Colonies	325.344	JV1800-1899			
France—Commerce	381.0944	HF3551-3560	France—History—Louis XVIII, 1814-1824	944.05	DC256-260
France—Description and travel	913.6404	DC21-29.3			
			France—History—Louis Philip, 1830-1848	944.063	DC265-269
France—Description and travel	914.404	DC21-29.3			
			France—History—July Revolution, 1830	944.063	DC261-262
France—Description and travel—1945-1974	914.4040904	DC29			
			France—History—Second Republic, 1848-1852	944.07	DC271.5-274.5
France—Directories	944.0025	DC15			
France—Economic conditions	330.944	HC271-280	France—History—Coup d'etat, 1851	944.07	DC274-.5
			France—History—Second Empire, 1852-1870	944.07	DC275-292
France—Emigration and immigration	325.(244) or (44)	JV7900-7999			
			France—History—Third Republic, 1870-1940	944.081	DC342.8-396
France—Gazetteers	913.64003	DC14			
France—Gazetteers	914.4003	DC14	France—History—German occupation, 1914-1918	944.0814	DC385
France—History	936.4	DC35-423			
France—History	944	DC35-423	France—History—German occupation, 1940-1945	944.0816	DC397
France—History—To 987	944.01	DC60-81.5			
France—History—14th century	944.02(4-6)	DC97.5-101.7	France—History—1945-	944.08(2-4)	DC398-423
			France—Manufactures	670.944	TS71-72.5
France—History—Charles VI, 1380-1422	944.026	DC101-.7	France—Maps	912.44	G1837-1844.24
			France—Maps	912.44	G5830-5834
France—History—Cabochien Uprising, 1413	944.026	DC101.5.C33	France—Periodicals	936.4005	DC1
			France—Periodicals	944.005	DC1
France—History—Charles VII, 1422-1461	944.026	DC102-105.9	France—Politics and government	320.944	JN2301-3007
France—History—Louis XI, 1461-1483	944.027	DC106-.9	France—Politics and government—1969-1974	944.083(6-7)	DC421
France—History—Charles VIII, 1483-1498	944.027	DC107-.2	France—Politics and government—1974-1981	944.083(7-8)	DC422
France—History—Louis XII, 1498-1515	944.027	DC108-109	France—Politics and government—1981-	944.0838	DC423
France—History—Francis I, 1515-1547	944.028	DC113-.5	France—History, Military	355.00944	DC44-47
			France—History, Naval	359.00944	DC49-53
France—History—Henry II, 1547-1559	944.028	DC114-.5			
France—History—Francis II, 1559-1560	944.028	DC115			

Subject Heading	Dewey	LC	Subject Heading	Dewey	LC
Franciscans	255.3	BX3601-3656	French Guiana	988.2	F2441-2471
Franciscans	255.973	BX4361-4364	French Guiana—Census	318.82	HA1037
Franco-Provencal dialects	449	PC3081-3148	French Guiana—Civilization	988.2	F2449.8
Franco-Prussian War, 1870-1871	944.0812	DC281-326.5	French Guiana—Description and travel	918.8204	F2450-2452
Franco-Spanish War, 1635-1659	944.03(2-3)	DC124.45	French Guiana—Gazetteers	918.82003	F2444
Franking privilege	383.1202	HE6148	French Guiana—History	988.2	F2460.3-2464
Franking privilege—United States	383.12020973	HE6448	French Guiana—Manufactures	670.9882	TS50
Franks	945.02	DG515-519	French Guiana—Maps	912.882	G5270-5274
Fraud	364.163	HV6691-6699	French Guiana—Periodicals	988.2005	F2441
Fraud investigation	363.25963	HV8079.F7	French Guiana—Politics and government	320.9882	JL810-819
Fredericksburg (Va.), Battle of, 1862	973.733	E474.85	French language	440	PC2001-3761
Free choice of employment	331.702	HD4903-.5	French language—Dialects	447	PC2700-3761
Free electron lasers	621.366	TA1693	French language—Etymology	442	PC2571-2591
Free enterprise	330.122	HB95	French language—Etymology	442	PC2761
Free love	306.73	HQ961-967	French language—Grammar	445	PC2721-2746
Free love	306.73	HX546	French language—Grammar	445	PC2101-2400
Free piston engines	621.4335	TJ779	French language—Lexicography	443.028	PC2620-2693
Free ports and zones	387.13	HF1418-.5	French language—Lexicography	443.028	PC2766
Free radicals (Chemicals)	541.224	RB170	French language—Morphology	445	PC2171-2175
Free radicals (Chemistry)	541.224	QD471	French language—Parts of speech	445	PC2201-2321
Free radicals (Chemistry)	541.224	QP527	French language—Phonology	441.5	PC2131-2151
Free schools	371.04	LB1029.F7	French language—Readers	448.6	PC2113-2117
Free will and determinism (Islam)	297.227	BP166.3	French language—Study and teaching	440.71	PC2065
Freedom of religion	323.442	BL640	French language—To 1500	447.0(1-2)	PC2801-2896
Freedom of religion	323.442	BV741	French language—To 1500—Etymology	447.01(1-2)2	PC2883-2886
Freedom of the seas	940.45	D580	French language—To 1500—Grammar	447.0(1-2)5	PC2821-2873
Freedom Train	353.00074	JK4	French language—To 1500—Lexicography	447.0(1-2)3028	PC2887-2895
Freehand technical sketching	604.2	T359	French literature	840	PQ1-3999
Freemasonry	366.1	HS351-929	French literature—To 1500	840.(1-2)08	PQ1300-1595
Freemasonry—Rituals	366.12	HS455-459	French literature—To 1500	840.(1-2)09	PQ151-221
Freemasons	366.1	HS351-929	French literature—16th century	840.308	PQ1121-1125
Freemasons—[By region or country]	366.109(4-9)	HS501-680.7	French literature—16th century	840.309	PQ230-239
Freemasons—United States	366.10973	HS503-539	French literature—17th century	840.408	PQ1126-1130
Freemasons—[Other countries]	366.109(4-9)	HS557-680.7	French literature—17th century	840.409	PQ241-251
Freemasons—Directories	366.1025	HS381-390	French literature—18th century	840.508	PQ1131-1135
Freemasons—History	366.109	HS403-420	French literature—18th century	840.509	PQ261-276
Freemasons—Periodicals	366.105	HS351-359			
Freeze fracturing	570.2827	QH236.2			
Freight and freightage	385.24	HE2301-2547			
Freight and freightage	387.544	HE593-597			
Freight and freightage	388.044	HE199-.5			
French drama	842.08	PQ1211-1241			
French drama—To 1500	842.(1-2)08	PQ1341-1385			
French essays	084.1	AC20-25			
French fiction	843.009	PQ631-671			
French fiction	843.08	PQ1261-1279			
French fiction—20th century	843.909	PQ671			

Subject Heading	Dewey	LC	Subject Heading	Dewey	LC
French literature—19th century	840.708	PQ1136-1139	Frisians	949.213	DJ401.F5-.F59
French literature—19th century	840.709	PQ281-299	Frog culture	639.3789	SH185
French literature—20th century	840.9108	PQ1141	Frogs	597.89	QL668.E2-.E275
French literature—20th century	840.9109	PQ301-307	Frontal sinus	611.21	QM505
			Fronts (Meteorology)	551.5512	QC880.4.F7
French literature—Foreign countries	840	PQ3809	Frost	551.38	QC929.H6
			Frozen foods	641.453	TX610
French literature—Study and teaching	840.71	PQ51-65	Frozen foods	664.02853	TP372.3
			Fructose	547.78	QD321
French periodicals	054.1	AP20-28.7	Fruit	634	SB354-399
French periodicals	054.1	PN5171-5790	Frustration	152.47	BF575.F7
French philology	440	PC2001-2071	Frustration in children	155.41247	BF723.F7
French poetry	841.08	PQ1160-1193	Fuel	662.6	TP315-360
French poetry—To 1500	841.(1-2)08	PQ1300-1391	Fuel cells	621.312429	TK2931
French poetry—16th century	841.309	PQ416-418	Fuelwood	662.65	TP324
			Fula language	496.322	PL8181-8184
French poetry—17th century	841.409	PQ421-423	Fuladu (Kingdom)	966.3	DT532.128
			Fuladu (Kingdom)	966.51	DT532.128
French poetry—18th century	841.509	PQ426-428	Fumigation	614.48	RA761-767
			Fumigation	632.94	SB955
French poetry—19th century	841.709	PQ431-439	Functional analysis	515.7	QA319-329.9
			Functionalism (Linguistics)	410.18	P147
French poetry—20th century	841.910	PQ441-443	Functions	515.25	QA331-355
			Functions of complex variables	515.92	QA331.7
French poetry—History and criticism	841.09	PQ400-491	Functions of real variables	515.8	QA331.5
French prose literature	848.08	PQ601-657	Functions, Zeta	515.56	QA351
French prose literature	848.08	PQ1243-1279	Fund raising	361.70681	HV41.2-.9
French prose literature—To 1500	848.(1-2)08	PQ151-216	Fund raising	658.15224	HG177-.5
			Fundamental education	370.111	LC5161-5163
French-Canadian literature	840	PQ3900-3919.2	Fundamentalism	270.82	BT82.2
French-Canadians	971.004114	F1027	Funds-flow statements	657.3	HF5681.B2
Freshwater animals	591.76	QL141-149	Funeral orations	885.008	PA3482
Freshwater biology	578.76	QH96-100	Funeral rites and ceremonies	393	GN486
Freshwater ecology	577.6	QH541.5.F7			
Freshwater microbiology	579.176	QR105.5	Funeral rites and ceremonies	393	GT3150-3390.5
Freshwater plants	581.76	QK105			
Freshwater plants	581.76	QK932-.7	Funeral rites and ceremonies, Ancient	393.0901	GT3170
Friars	255.(2-3)	BX2820			
Friction	531.1134	QC197	Funeral rites and ceremonies, Buddhist	294.3438	BL1477.8.F8
Friendly fire (Military science)	355.422	U167	Funeral rites and ceremonies, Islamic	297.385	BP184.9.F8
			Funeral sermons	252.1	BV4275
Friendly societies	334.7	HG9201-9245	Funeral service	265.85	BV199.F8
Friendly societies	334.7	HS1501-1510	Fungal diseases of plants	632.4	SB733
Friendship	158.25	BF575.F66	Fungal viruses	579.27	QR343
Friendship	177.62	BJ1533.F8	Fungi	579.5	QK600-635
Friendship	302.34	GN486.3	Fungi—Genetics	579.5135	QK602
Friendship—Sociological aspects	302.34	HM132.5	Fungi, Edible	635.8	SB353-.5
			Fungi in agriculture	632.4	SB733
Friendship in children	302.34083	HQ784.F7	Fungicides	632.952	SB951.3
Fries Rebellion, 1798-1799	973.44	E326	Fur	675.3	TS1060-1070
			Fur farming	636.9701	SF402-405
Frisian language	439.2	PF1401-1497	Fur garments	685.24	TT525
Frisian language—Philology	439.2	PF1401-1411	Fur-bearing animals	636.97	SF403-405
Frisian literature	839.2	PF1501-1541	Fur-bearing animals	799.2597	SK283-.6

Subject Heading	Dewey	LC	Subject Heading	Dewey	LC
Furies (Roman mythology)	292.13	BL820.F8	Galician literature	869	PQ9450-9469.2
Furnaces	621.183	TJ320-358	Gallbladder	573.38	QL867
Furnaces	697.07	TH7400	Gallbladder	611.36	QM352
Furniture	392.36	GT450	Gallbladder	612.35	QP185
Furniture	684.1	TS880-889	Gallbladder—Diseases	616.365	RC849-853
Furniture	684.104	TT194-199.4	Gallbladder—Surgery	617.5565	RD546-547
Furniture	749	NK2200-2750	Galleys	365.3	HV8647-8649
Furniture—[By region or country]	749.09(4-9)	NK2401-2694.5	Gallo-Italian dialects	457	PC1851-1874
			Galls (Botany)	632.2	SB767
Furniture—Exhibitions	747.074	NK2210-2211	Galois theory	512.32	QA171
Furniture—Private collections	749.074	NK2220	Galois theory	512.32	QA211
			Galois theory	512.32	QA214
Furniture—Repairing	684.100288	TT199	Gambai dialect	496.5	PL8197
Furniture—Styles	749	NK2235	Gambia—Census	316.651	HA4734
Furniture making	684.1	TS880-889	Gambia—Civilization	966.51	DT509.4
Furniture making	684.1	TT194-199.4	Gambia—Description and travel	916.65104	DT509.27
Furuncle	616.523	RL221			
Fusion	536.42	QC303	Gambia—History	966.51	DT509.5-.83
Fusion reactors	621.484	TK9204	Gambia—History—Coup d'etat, 1981	966.51031	DT509.8
Future life	202.3	BL535-547			
Future life	236.2	BT899-940	Gambia—Maps	912.6651	G8870-8874
Futures	332.6452	HG6024-6051	Gambling	306.482	GN454.6
Ga language	496.3378	PL8191	Gambling	364.172	HV6708-6722
Gables	721.5	NA2920	Gambling	795	GV1301-1311
Gabon—Census	316.721	HA4715	Gambling systems	795	GV1302
Gabon—Civilization	967.21	DT546.14	Gambling—Law and legislation—England	344.42099	KD3527
Gabon—Description and travel	916.72104	DT546.127-.128			
			Game and game-birds, Dressing of	799.24	SK36.2
Gabon—Economic conditions	330.96721	HC975			
			Game bird culture	636.63082	SF508-510
Gabon—Gazetteers	916.721003	DT546.115	Game fowl	636.63	SF502.8-503.52
Gabon—History	967.21	DT546.15-.183	Game reserves	639.95	SK357
Gabon—History—1839-1960	967.2102	DT546.165-.175	Game theory	519.3	QA269-272.5
			Game theory	519.3	T57.92
Gabon—History—1960-	967.2104	DT546.18-.183	Games	394.3	GN454.8-455
Gabon—History—To 1839	967.2101	DT546.165	Games	394.3	GR480-485
Gabon—Maps	912.6721	G8690-8694	Games	790.1	GV1199-1570
Gadaba language (Dravidian)	494.82	PL4627	Games—Rules	790.102022	GV1201.42
			Games of chance (Mathematics)	519.27	QA273
Gaelic language	491.6(2-3)	PB1501-1599			
Gaelic language—Etymology	491.6(2-3)2	PB1583-1584	Gamma functions	515.52	QA353.G3
			Gamma ray bursts	522.6862	QB471.7.B85
Gaelic language—Grammar	491.6(2-3)5	PB1521-1573	Gamma ray sources	539.7222	QC793.5.G322
Gaelic language—Lexicography	491.6(2-3)3028	PB1587-1595	Ganda language	496.3957	PL8201
			Gang rape	364.1532	HV6558-6569
Gaelic language—Lexicography	491.6(2-3)3028	PB1187-1189	Gangrene	616.047	RD153
			Gangrene	616.047	RD628
Gaelic language—Study and teaching	491.6(2-3)071	PB1511	Gangs	364.106	HV6437-6439
			Gantry cranes	621.873	TJ1365
Gaelic literature	891.63	PB1605-1709	Garage sales	381.195	HF5482.3
Gaelic philology	491.6(2-3)	PB1101-1113	Garages	725.38	NA8348
Gaelic philology—Study and teaching	491.6(2-3)071	PB1111	Garden cities	307.76	HT161-165
			Garden ecology	577.554	QH541.5.G37
Gain sharing	331.2164	HD4928.G34	Garden fertilizers	631.8	S633
Gaita	788.4909	ML980	Garden lighting	621.3229	SB476
Galaxies	523.112	QB856-858.8	Garden ornaments and furniture	645.8	SB473.5
Galician dialect	469.794	PC5411-5414			

Subject Heading	Dewey	LC	Subject Heading	Dewey	LC
Garden pests	635.92	SB603.5	Gastrointestinal system	612.3	QP151-156
Garden pests—[By region or country]	632.09(4-9)	SB605	Gastrointestinal system	616.33	RC799-869
Garden tools	635.0284	SB454.8	Gastrointestinal system—Motility—Disorders	616.31	RC811
Gardening	635	SB450.9-467.8	Gastronomy	641.013	TX631-641
Gardening in the shade	635.9543	SB434.7	Gastroscopy	616.3307545	RC804.G3
Gardens	635	SB450.9-467	Gastrostomy	617.553059	RD540.5
Gardens, Miniature	635.9772	SB433.5	Gates	631.27	S723
Gardner machine-gun	359.82424	VF410.G2-.G24	Gatling guns	359.82424	VF410.G3-.G34
Garment cutting	687.043	TT520	Gauchos	980.0099	F2217
Garment cutting	687.043	TT590	Gaugamela, Battle of, 331 B.C.	938.07	DF234.5
Garnet	549.62	QE391.G37	Gauge fields (Physics)	530.1435	QC793.3.F5
Garnet	622.387	TN997.G3	Gaul—History	936.4	DC62-63
Garnishes (Cookery)	641.819	TX740.5	Gaul—History—Gallic Wars, 58-51 B.C.	936.402	DC62
Garo language	495.4	PL4001.G2	Gaul—History—Gallic Wars, 58-51 B.C.	937.05	DG264
Garrisons	355.35	U370-375	Gaulish language	491.6	PB3001-3029
Gas	665.7	TP700	Gautama Buddha—Date of death	294.363	BQ938
Gas	665.7	TP751-764	Gautama Buddha—Enlightenment	294.363	BQ935
Gases, Asphyxiating and poisonous	615.91	RA577	Gautama Buddha—Footprints	294.363	BQ922
Gases, Asphyxiating and poisonous	615.91	RA1245-1247	Gautama Buddha—Shrines	294.3435	BQ6460
Gases, Asphyxiating and poisonous—War use	358.34	UG447-.5	Gay liberation movement	306.766	HQ76.5-.8
Gas—Heating and cooking	697.043	TH7453-7457	Gay men	306.7662	HQ75.8
Gas as fuel	665.75	TP345-350	Gaza, Battles of, 1917	940.433	D568.7
Gas chromatography	543.85	QD79.C45	Gbandi language	496.348	PL8204
Gas chromatography	543.85	QD117.C515	Gbaya language	496.361	PL8205
Gas distribution	665.744	TP757	Gcod (Bonpo rite)	294.3438	BQ7982.3
Gas dynamics	533.2	QA930	Gcod (Buddhist rite)	294.3438	BQ7699.G36
Gas dynamics	533.2	QC167.5-168.86	Gdansk (Poland)	943.82	DK4650-4685
Gas engineering	622.3385	TN880-884	Gearing	621.833	TJ184-204
Gas gangrene	616.047	RC144.G3	Gearing, Bevel	621.8332	TJ193-196
Gas lasers	621.3663	TA1695	Gearing, Spiral	621.8333	TJ192
Gas manufacture and works	665.7	TP700-764	Gearing, Worm	621.8333	TJ200
Gas masks	622.80284	TN297	Geiger-Muller counters	539.774	QC787.G4
Gas tubes	621.381513	TK7871.8-.84	Geishas	390.0952	GT3412
Gas wells	622.3385	TN880-884	Gemini (Astrology)	133.5264	BF1727.25
Gas-burners	696.2	TH6880	Gems	391.7	GT2250-2280
Gas-fitting	696.2	TH6840	Gems	739.27	TS747-770
Gas-fixtures	621.3240284	TH7960-7967	Gene mapping	572.8633	QH445.2
Gas-lighting	621.324	TH7910-7970	Gene therapy	616.042	RB155.8
Gas-pipes	665.744	TP757	Genealogy	929.1	CS
Gas-turbines	621.433	TJ778	[By region or country]—Genealogy	929.10720(4-9)	CS42-2209
Gases	533	QC161-166.5	Genealogy in the Bible	220.9	BS569
Gases from plants	575.8	QK876	Genealogy—Congresses	929.106	CS2
Gasohol	662.6692	TP358	Genealogy—Dictionaries	929.103	CS6
Gasoline	665.53827	TP692.2	Genealogy—Directories	929.1025	CS5
Gasoline locomotives	622.66	TN338	Genealogy—Periodicals	929.105	CS1
Gasoline, Synthetic	662.66	TP692.2	General Convention of the Christian Church	286.63	BX6751-6793
Gastrectomy	617.553059	RD540.5-.57	General semantics	121.68	B820
Gastric juice	612.32	QP193			
Gastritis	616.333	RC831			
Gastroenteritis	616.33	RC840.G3			
Gastrointestinal agents	615.73	RM355-365			
Gastrointestinal system	611.3	QM301-367			

Subject Heading	Dewey	LC	Subject Heading	Dewey	LC
General strike, Great Britain, 1926	331.89250941	HD5366	Geographical myths	398.32	GR940-941
General strike, Northern Ireland, 1974	331.892509416	HD5368	Geography	910	G
General strikes	331.8925	HD5307	Geography	910	G128
Generalized spaces	514.3	QA689	Geography	910	GN476.4
Generals	355.0092	U51-55	Geography, Ancient	913	G83-88
Generals	940.3092	D507	Geography, Medieval	911.0902	G89-95
Generals—United States –Biography	358.40092	UG626.2.D66	Geography—History	910.9	G80-99
			Geography—Methodology	910.01	G70-.4
Generating functions	515.55	QA164.8	Geography—Societies, etc.	910.6	G2-55
Generating functions	515.55	QA353.G44	Geography—Study and teaching	910.71	G72-76.5
Generations, Alternating	571.884	QH489	Geological modeling	551.0228	QE43
Generative organs	573.6	QL876-881	Geological museums	551.074	QE51
Generative organs	611.6	QM416-421	Geological surveys	551.0723	QE61-350.62
Generative organs	612.6	QP251-285	Geological time	551.701	QE508
Generative organs, Female	573.66	QL881	Geologists	551.092	QE21-22
Generative organs, Female	611.65	QM421	Geology	551	QE
Generative organs, Female	612.62	QP259-281	Geology, Economic	553	TN260
Generative organs, Female—Surgery	618.145	RG104-.7	Geology, Stratigraphic	551.7	QE640-699
			Geology, Stratigraphic—Cenozoic	551.78	QE690-699
Generative organs, Male	573.65	QL878	Geology, Stratigraphic—Mesozoic	551.76	QE675-688
Generative organs, Male	611.63	QM416			
Generative organs, Male	612.61	QP253-257	Geology, Stratigraphic—Paleozoic	551.72	QE654-674
Generative organs—Abnormalities	616.65043	RC881.5-883.5	Geology—Computer programs	551.0285	QE48.8
Genes	572.86	QH447-.8	Geology—History	551.09	QE11-13
Genetic disorders	616.042	RB155.5-.8	Geology—Maps	551.0223	QE36
Genetic disorders in children	618.920042	RJ47.3-.4	Geology—Societies, etc.	551.06	QE1
			Geology—Study and teaching	551.071	QE40-48
Genetic engineering	660.65	TP248.6	Geology—Terminology	551.014	QE7
Genetic engineering	660.65	QH442-.6	Geology—Africa	556	QE320-339
Genetic psychology	155.7	BF699-711			
Genetic recombination	572.877	QH443-450.6	Geology—Antarctica	559.89	QE350
Genetic regulation	572.865	QH450-.6	Geology—Arctic regions	559.8(1-2)	QE70
Genetic transcription	572.8845	QH450.2	Geology—Asia	555	QE289-319
Genetic translation	572.645	QH450.5	Geology—Australia	559.4	QE340-348
Genetics	576.5	QH426-470	Geology—Canada	557.1	QE185-199
Geneva (Switzerland)—History—1536-1603	949.451	DQ458	Geology—Central America	557.28	QE210-217
			Geology—Europe	554	QE260-288
Genius	153.98	BF412-426	Geology—Mexico	557.2	QE201-203
Genoa (Italy)	945.182	DG631-645	Geology—North America	557	QE71-217
Genocide	364.151	HV6322.7	Geology—South America	558	QE230-251
Genomes	572.86	QH447	Geology—United States	557.3	QE72-182
Genre painting	754	ND1450-1452	Geology—[United States, By state]	557.(4-9)	QE81-182
Gentry	305.5232	HT657			
Geochemistry	551.9	QE514-516.5	Geology—West Indies	557.29	QE220-226
Geodesy	526.1	QB275-343	Geomagnetic observatories	538.79	QC818
Geodesy—Computer programs	526.10285	QB297	Geomagnetism	538.7	QC811-849
			Geomagnetism—Maps	538.70223	QC822
Geodesy—Encyclopedias	526.103	QB279	Geometry	516	QA440-699
Geodesy—History	526.109	QB280.5	Geometry, Algebraic	516.35	QA564-609
Geodetic astronomy	526.6	QB201-205	Geometry, Analytic	516.3	QA551-563
Geodetic satellites	629.46	TL798.G4	Geometry, Descriptive	516.6	QA501-521
Geodynamics	551.(2-3)	QE500-639.5	Geometry, Differential	516.36	QA641-672
Geographers—Biography	910.92	G67-69			
Geographical myths	398.32	GR650-690			

Subject Heading	Dewey	LC	Subject Heading	Dewey	LC
Geometry, Infinitesimal	516.36	QA615-639	German fiction—19th century	833.708	PT1332
Geometry, Modern	516.04	QA473-475	German fiction—19th century	833.709	PT763-771
Geometry, Plane	516.22	QA451-485	German fiction—20th century	833.908	PT1334
Geometry, Solid	516.23	QA457	German fiction—20th century	833.909	PT772
Geometry, Solid	516.23	QA491	German language	430	PF3001-5999
Geomorphology	551.41	GB400-649	German language— Old High German, 750-1050	437.01	PF3801-3991
Geophysics	550	QC801-809	German language— Old High German, 750-1050— Grammar	437.015	PF3831-3931
Geophysics	550	QE500-511.7	German language—Old High German, 750-1050— Philology	437.01	PF3801-3823
Geopolitics	320.12	JC319-323	German language—Middle High German, 1050-1500	437.02	PF4043-4350
Georgia	975.8	F281-295	German language—Middle High German, 1050-1500—Dictionaries	437.023	PF4333-4345
Georgia (Republic)	947.58	DK670-679.5	German language—Middle High German, 1050-1500— Grammar	437.025	PF4061-4171
Georgia—Gazetteers	917.58003	F284			
Georgia—History—1775-1865	975.80(2-3)	F290	German language—Middle High German, 1050-1500—Lexicography	437.023028	PF4327-4345
Georgia—History—Revolution, 1775-1783	975.80(2-3)	E263.G3	German language—Early modern, 1500-1700	437.090(1-2)	PF4501-4596
Georgia—History—War of 1812	975.803	E359.5.G4	German language— Dialects	437	PF5000-5951
Georgia—History—Civil War, 1861-1865	975.803	E503	German language— Dictionaries	433	PF3620-3693
Georgia—History—Civil War, 1861-1865	975.803	E559	German language— Etymology	432	PF3571-3599
Georgia—History—1865-	975.804	F291-.3	German language— Grammar	435	PF3097-3400
Georgia—Maps	912.758	G3920-3924	German language—History	437	PF3051-3060
Georgia—National Guard	355.3709758	UA150-159	German language— Lexicography	433.028	PF3601-3693
Georgia—Periodicals	975.8005	F281	German language— Morphology	435	PF3171-3197
Georgian language	499.969	PK9101-9151	German language—Parts of speech	435	PF3199-3335
Georgian language— Grammar	499.965	PK9106-9115	German language— Phonology	431.5	PF3131-3168
Georgian literature	899.969	PK9160-9169	German language— Rhetoric	808.0431	PF3410-3497
Gergovie, Battle of, 52 B.C.	936.402	DC62	German language—Slang	437.09	PF5971-5999
Geriatric anesthesia	617.9600846	RD145	German language—Study and teaching	430.71	PF3065-3069
Geriatric nursing	618.970231	RC954	German language dictionaries	830.3	PT41
Geriatric pharmacology	615.10846	RC953.7			
Geriatric psychiatry	618.9789	RC451.4.A5	German letters	836.009	PT811
Geriatrics	618.97	RC952-954.6	German letters	836.08	PT1348-1352
German	830	PT	German literature	830	PT1-1021
German American literature (German)	830	PT3900-3919	German literature	830.8	PT1100-1479
German drama	832.08	PT1251-1299			
German drama	832.09	PT605-709			
German drama (Comedy)	832.052308	PT1275-1277			
German drama (Tragedy)	832.051208	PT1271-1273			
German essays	083.1	AC30-35			
German essays	834.09	PT831			
German essays	834.08	PT1354			
German Expedition to China, 1900-1901	951.035	DS771.5			
German fiction	833.08	PT1314-1340			
German fiction	833.09	PT741-772			
German fiction—Early modern, 1500-1700	833.(4-5)09	PT753-756			
German fiction—18th century	833.608	PT1315			
German fiction—18th century	833.609	PT759			

Subject Heading	Dewey	LC	Subject Heading	Dewey	LC
German literature—Old High German, 750-1050	830.109	PT183	German prose literature	838.08	PT1301-1340
German literature—Old High German, 750-1050	839	PF3985-3991	Germanic fiction	839.3009	PN836
German literature—Middle High German, 1050-1500	830.(2-3)	PT175-230	Germanic languages	430	PD
German literature—Middle High German, 1050-1500	830.208	PT1375-1479	Germanic languages	430	PF
German literature—Early modern, 1500-1700	830.(4-5)08	PT1121-1126	Germanic languages—Dialects	430.047	PD700-777
German literature—Early modern, 1500-1700	830.(4-5)09	PT238-281	Germanic languages—Dictionaries	430.043	PD625-660
German literature—18th century	830.608	PT1131	Germanic languages—Etymology	430.042	PD571-599
German literature—18th century—History and criticism	830.609	PT285-321	Germanic languages—Grammar	430.045	PD99-321
German literature—19th century	830.708	PT1136	Germanic languages—History	437	PD51-60
German literature—19th century—History and criticism	830.709	PT341-395	Germanic languages—Lexicography	430.043028	PD601-660
German literature—20th century	830.909	PT401-403	Germanic languages—Periodicals	430.05	PD1-9
German literature—20th century	830.908	PT1141	Germanic languages—Study and teaching	430.071	PD65-69
German literature—Congresses	830.6	PT31	Germanic peoples	305.83	GN549.G4
German literature—Czechoslovakia	830	PT3830-3837.5	Germanic peoples—Religion	293	BL830-875
German literature—Foreign countries	830	PT3808-3809	Germany	943	DD
German literature—Study and teaching	830.71	PT51-65	Germany (East)	943.1087	DD280-289
German periodicals	053.1	PN5201-5220	Germany (West)	943.087	DD258-262
German periodicals	053.1	AP30-36.7	Germany—Armed Forces—Management	355.60943	UB73-74
German poetry	831.09	PT500-597	Germany—Armed Forces—Supplies and stores	355.80943	UC180-183
German poetry	831.08	PT1151-1241	Germany—Biography	920.0363	DD85-.8
German poetry—Middle High German, 1050-1500	831.(2-3)08	PT1391-1429	Germany—Biography	920.043	CT1050-1099.8
German poetry—Middle High German, 1050-1500	831.(2-3)09	PT175-227	Germany—Biography	920.043	DD85-.8
German poetry—Early modern, 1500-1700	831.(4-5)08	PT1163-1165	Germany—Census	314.3	HA1231-1349
German poetry—Early modern, 1500-1700	831.(4-5)09	PT525-531	Germany—Church history	274.3	BR850-856.35
German poetry—18th century	831.608	PT1167-1169	Germany—Civilization	936.3	DD60-68
German poetry—18th century	831.609	PT533-535	Germany—Civilization	943	DD60-68
German poetry—19th century	831.708	PT1171-1173	Germany—Commerce	381.0943	HF3561-3570.5
German poetry—19th century	831.709	PT541-547	Germany—Description and travel	913.6304	DD21.5-43
German poetry—20th century	831.908	PT1174-1175	Germany—Description and travel	914.304	DD21.5-43
German poetry—20th century	831.909	PT551-553	Germany—Directories	943.0025	DD15.5
German prose literature	838.08	PT711-871	Germany—Economic conditions	330.943	HC281-290.795
			Germany—Emigration and immigration	325.(243) or (43)	JV8000-8099
			Germany—Gazetteers	913.63003	DD14
			Germany—Gazetteers	914.3003	DD14
			Germany—Genealogy	929.1072043	CS610-699
			Germany—Historiography	936.30072	DD86-.7
			Germany—Historiography	943.0072	DD86-.7
			Germany—History	936.3	DD84-257.4
			Germany—History	943	DD84-257.4
			Germany—History—To 843	936.3	DD121-134.2
			Germany—History—To 843	943.01	DD121-134.2

Subject Heading	Dewey	LC	Subject Heading	Dewey	LC
Germany—History—843-918	943.021	DD134.3-135	Germany—Maps	912.43	G6080-6428
Germany—History—Saxon House, 919-1024	943.022	DD136-140.7	Germany—Politics and government	320.943	JN3201-4944
Germany—History—Franconian House, 1024-1125	943.023	DD141-144	Germination	571.862	QK740
			Gerrymander	328.33455	JK1347-1343
Germany—History—Hohenstaufen, 1138-1254	943.024	DD145-155	Gestalt psychology	150.1982	BF203
Germany—History—1273-1517	943.02(6-9)	DD156-174.6	Gettysburg (Pa.), Battle of, 1863	973.7349	E475.53
Germany—History—1618-1648	943.041	DD188-.5	Geysers	551.23	GB1198.5-.8
			Ghana—Census	316.67	HA4732
Germany—History—1648-1740	943.0(43-52)	DD190-.8	Ghana—Civilization	966.7	DT510.4
Germany—History—18th century	943.05	DD191-199	Ghana—Description and travel	916.6704	DT510.2
Germany—History—1789-1900	943.0(57-84)	DD197-231	Ghana—History	966.7	DT510.5-512.34
			Ghana—History—To 1957	966.70(1-3)	DT511-.3
Germany—History—1815-1866	943.07	DD206-214	Ghana—History—Portuguese rule, 1469-1637	966.7016	DT511
Germany—History—Revolution, 1848-1849	940.284	DD207-209	Ghana—History—Danish Settlements, 1659-1850	966.701(6-8)	DT511
Germany—History—1866-1871	943.081	DD214-216	Ghana—History—1957-	966.705	DT512-.34
Germany—History—1871-1918	943.08(3-4)	DD217-231	Ghana—History—Coup d'etat, 1966	966.7051	DT512
Germany—History—William I, 1871-1888	943.083	DD223-.9	Ghana—History—Coup d'etat, 1972	966.7051	DT512
Germany—History—William II, 1888-1918	943.084	DD228-231	Ghana—History—Coup d'etat, 1979	966.7052	DT512.32
Germany—History—Frederick III, 1888	943.084	DD224-226	Ghana—History—Coup d'etat, 1981	966.7052	DT512.32
Germany—History—20th century	943.08(4-79)	DD232-257.4	Ghana—Maps	912.667	G8850-8854
			Ghosts	133.1	BF1444-1486
Germany—History—Allied occupation, 1918-1930	943.085	DD650.M5	Ghosts	398.47	GR580
Germany—History—Revolution, 1918	943.085	DD248	Ghouls and ogres	398.45	GR525
			Ghouls and ogres	398.45	GR560
Germany—History—Kapp Putsch, 1920	943.085	DD249	Gifted children	155.455	BF723.G5
Germany—History—March Uprising, 1921	943.085	DD249	Gifted children	371.8279	LC3991-4000
			Gifted children	649.155	HQ773.5
Germany—History—Beer Hall Putsch, 1923	943.085	DD249	Gifts	394	GT3050
Germany—History—1933-1945	943.086	DD253-256.5	Gifts, Spiritual	234.13	BT767.3
			Gingivitis	617.632	RK410
Germany—History—Night of the Long Knives, 1934	943.086	DD247.R56	Ginseng	583.84	QK495.A6853
			Ginseng	633.88384	SB295.G5
Germany—History—1945-1955	943.087(4-5)	DD257-.4	Giraffe	599.638	QL737.U56
Germany—History—1990-	943.088	DD257.4	Girders	624.17723	TA492.G5
Germany—History—Unification, 1990	943.0881	DD257-.4	Girders	624.21	TG350-362
			Girders, Continuous	624.21	TG355
Germany—History, Military	355.00943	DD99-104	Girl Scouts	369.463	HS3353.G5
Germany—History, Naval	359.00943	DD106	Girls	369.46	HV879-887
Germany—Manufactures	670.943	TS73-74.5	Girls	390.08342	GT2540
Germany—Maps	912.43	G1907-1924	Gisu language	496.395	PL8207.G55
			Glacial epoch	551.792	QE697-698
			Glacial erosion	551.313	QE575-579
			Glacial landforms	551.315	GB581-588
			Glaciers	551.312	GB2401-2598
			Gladiators	796.8092	GV35
			Glands	573.4	QL865-868
			Glands	611.4	QM325-371

Subject Heading	Dewey	LC	Subject Heading	Dewey	LC
Glands	612.4	QP186-246	Gods, Egyptian	299.31	BL2450.G6
Glass	620.144	TA450	Going concern (Accounting)	657	HF5681.G55
Glass	748	NK5100-5440	Going public (Securities)	658.15224	HG4028.S7
Glass, Optical	666.156	QC375	Goiter	616.442	RC656-.3
Glass-workers	666.1092	HD8039.G5	Gold	332.4042	HG289
Glass blowing and working	666.122	TP859	Gold	332.40420973	HG551
Glass construction	693.96	TH1560	Gold—Metallurgy	669.22	TN760-769
Glass construction	721.04496	NA4140	Gold—Minting	332.4042	HG321
Glass engraving	748.62	NE2690	Gold alloys	617.675	RK653
Glass manufacture	666.1	TP845-869	Gold dredging	622.3422	TN422
Glass painting and staining	748.50282	NK5300-5430	Gold mines and mining	338.2741	HD9536
Glass sculpture	731.2	NB1270.G4	Gold mines and mining	622.3422	TN410-429
Glass shoes	748.8	NK5440.S49	Gold ores	622.3422	TN420-429
Glassware	666.19	TP865-868	Gold standard	332.4222	HG297
Glassware	748.2	NK5100-5440	Golden Horde	950.04942	DS22.7
Glaucoma	617.741	RE871	Golden rule	241.54	BV4715
Glazes	666.427	TP812	Golden rule	296.36	BJ1286.G64
Glazes	666.427	TP823	Golf	796.352	GV961-987
Glazing	698.5	TH8251-8275	Good and evil	170	BJ1400-1408.5
Gleaning	338.163	HD1549	Good Friday	263.925	BV95
Gliders (Aeronautics)	629.13333	TL760-769	Good Samaritan (Parable)	226.8	BT378.G6
Gliding and soaring	797.55	GV764-766	Gorgons (Greek mythology)	292.13	BL820.G7
Global analysis (Mathematics)	514.74	QA614-.97	Gorilla	599.884	QL737.P96
Global warming	551.5253	QC981.8.G56	Gospel music	782.254	M2198-2199
Glockenspiel music	786.843	M147	Gossip	177.2	BJ1535.G6
Glory of God	231	BT180.G6	Gothic language	439.9	PD1101-1211
Glottis	611.22	QM255	Gothic language—Dictionaries	439.93	PD1193
Gloves	391.412	GT2170	Gothic language—Grammar	439.95	PD1119-1167
Gloves	685.4	TS2160			
Glucose	547.78	QD321	Gout	616.3999	RC629-.5
Glue	668.3	TP967-970	Government liability	352.885	JF1621
Glue-sniffing	362.299	HV5822.G5	Government libraries	027.5	Z675.G7
Glycerin	338.476682	HD9660.G58-.G6	Government ownership	338.749	HD3840-4420.8
Glycerin	614.48	RA766.G6	Government ownership	352.266	HD3840-4420.8
Glycerin	668.2	TP973	Government property	343.02	K3558-3560
Gnosticism	273.1	BT1390	Government property	352.5	JF1525.P7
Goats	636.39	SF380-388	Government property—Canada	343.7102	KE5105-5420
Gobi Desert (Mongolia and China)—Description and travel	915.17304	DS793.G6	Government property—England	343.4202	KD1034-1107
God	231	BT98-180	Government property—United States	343.7302	KF5500-5865
God (Greek religion)	184	B398.G6	Government publications—[By region or country]	025.173409(4-9)	CD101-392
God (Hinduism)	294.5211	BL1200-1225	Government publications—Africa	025.1734096	CD255-269
God (Islam)	297.211	BP166.2	Government publications—Asia	025.1734095	CD221-254
God (Judaism)	296.311	BM610	Government publications—Australia	025.1734094	CD271-272
God—Attributes	231.4	BT130-157	Government publications—Canada	025.17340971	CD331-332
God—Biblical teaching	231	BT99	Government publications—Caribbean Area	025.173409729	CD351-362
God—Goodness	231.8	BT137	Government publications—Central America	025.173409728	CD335-350
God—History of doctrines	231.09	BT98			
God—Omnipotence	231.4	BT133			
God—Omniscience	231.4	BT131			
God—Proof, Cosmological	231.765	BT98-102			
God—Proof, Ontological	231.042	BT98-101			
Goddesses, Hindu	294.52114	BL1216			
Gods	202.1	BL473			

Subject Heading	Dewey	LC	Subject Heading	Dewey	LC
Government publications— Europe	025.1734094	CD101-215	Gravimeters (Geophysical instruments)	526.0284	QB331
Government publications— Mexico	025.17340972	CD333-334	Gravitation	526.7	QB341
Government publications— Oceania	025.1734099	CD291	Gravitation	531.14	QC178
Government publications— South America	025.1734098	CD365-392	Gravitational fields	531.14	QC178
Government publications— United States	025.17340973	CD309-311	Gravity	526.7	QB330-339
Government securities	332.63232	HG4701-4726	Gravity	571.435	QP82.2.G7
Government securities— United States	332.632320973	HG4931-4955	Gravity	571.63435	QH657
Government, Resistance to	323.044	JC328.3	Gravity waves	532.59	QA927
Governors—United States	352.232130973	JK2447-2454	Graz (Austria), Battle of, 1809	940.27	DC234.65
Grace (Theology)	234	BT760-769	Grazing	333.740973	HD241
Grace at meals	242.2	BV283.G7	Great Awakening	277.3081	BR520
Graces, The	292.13	BL820.G8	Great Britain. Parliament	328.41	JN500-678
Grading and marking (Students)	371.272	LB3051-3063	Great Britain. Parliament.	342.4105	KD4190-4381
Grafting	631.54	SB123.65	Great Britain. Royal Navy	359.80941	VC184-187
Grain	633.1	SB189-192	Great Britain—Armed Forces—Supplies and stores	355.80941	UC184-187
Grain trade	381.4131	HD9030-9049			
Grain trade	381.41331	HF2651.G8	Great Britain—Biography	920.0361	DA28-.9
Grammar, Comparative and general	415	P151-299	Great Britain—Biography	920.041	CT770-858
			Great Britain—Biography	920.041	DA28-.9
Gramme dynamos	621.3132	TK2441	Great Britain—Census	314.1	HA1121-1170
Granada (Kingdom)— History	946.82	DP115-118	Great Britain—Church history	274.1	BR740-799
Granada—Maps	912.729845	G5130-5134	Great Britain—Civilization	936.1	DA110-115
Granaries	728.92	NA8240	Great Britain—Civilization	941	DA110-115
Granaries—Design and construction	690.53	TH4461	Great Britain—Colonies	325.341	JV1000-1099
			Great Britain— Commerce	381.0941	HF3501-3530.5
Grand Alliance, War of the, 1689-1697	940.2525	D279-280.5	Great Britain—Emigration and immigration	325.(241) or (41)	JV7600-7699
Grand National Handicap Steeplechase	798.450942753	SF359.7.G7	Great Britain—Gazetteers	914.1003	DA640
			Great Britain—Genealogy	929.1072041	CS410-479.5
Grand Prix racing	796.73	GV1029	Great Britain—Historical geography—Maps	911.41	G5741
Grand unified theories (Nuclear physics)	530.142	QC794.6.G7	Great Britain—History	936.1	DA28-690
Grandparenting	306.8745	HQ759.9	Great Britain—History	941	DA
Granite	552.3	QE462.G7	Great Britain—History	941	DA28-690
Granite	622.352	TN970	Great Britain—History—To 1066	936.2	DA134-162
Grapefruit	634.32	SB370.G7			
Grapes	583.86	QK495.V84	Great Britain—History—To 1066	941.01	DA134-162
Grapes	634.8	SB387-399			
Graph theory	511.5	QA166-.24	Great Britain—History—To 1485	941.0(2-46)	DA170-260
Graphology	137	BF889-905	Great Britain—History— Modern period, 1485-	941.0(5-8)	DA300-591
Graphology	155.282	RC473.G7			
Grasses	584.9	QK495.G74	Great Britain—History— Tudors, 1485-1603	941.05	DA310-360
Grasses	633.2	SB197-202	Great Britain—History— History—Henry VIII, 1509-1547	941.052	DA331-339
Grassland ecology	577.4	QH541.5.P7			
Grassland fauna	591.74	QL115.3-.5			
Grasslands	577.4	QH541.5.P7	Great Britain—History— Elizabeth, 1558-1603	941.055	DA350-360
Grasslands	581.74	QK938.P7	Great Britain—History— Early Stuarts, 1603-1649	941.06	DA370-419.5
Gratitude	179.9	BJ1533.G8			
Graves' disease	616.443	RC657.5.G7	Great Britain—History— Civil War, 1642-1649	941.062	DA410-429

Subject Heading	Dewey	LC	Subject Heading	Dewey	LC
Great Britain—History—1660-1714	941.06(6-9)	DA430-463	Greece—History—Persian Wars, 500-449 B.C.	938.03	DF225-226
Great Britain—History—George I, 1714-1727	941.071	DA499	Greece—History—Ionian Revolt, 499-494 B.C.	938.03	DF225.3
Great Britain—History—George II, 1727-1760	941.072	DA500	Greece—History—Athenian supremacy, 479-431 B.C.	938.04	DF227-228
Great Britain—History—George III, 1760-1820	941.073	DA505-522	Greece—History—Peloponnesian War, 431-404 B.C.	938.05	DF229-230
Great Britain—History—George IV, 1820-1830	941.074	DA537-538	Greece—History—Spartan & Theban Supremacies, 404-362 B.C.	938.0(5-6)	DF231-232
Great Britain—History—William IV, 1830-1837	941.075	DA539-542	Greece—History—Expedition of Cyrus, 401 B.C.	938.05	DF231.32
Great Britain—History—Victoria, 1837-1901	941.081	DA550-565	Greece—History—Macedonian Expansion, 359-323 B.C	938.07	DF232.5-234.9
Great Britain—History—20th century	941.082	DA566-592	Greece—History—Third Sacred War, 355-346 B.C.	938.07	DF233.4
Great Britain—History, Military	355.00941	DA49-69.3	Greece—History—Macedonian Hegemony, 323-281 B.C.	938.08	DF235.3-.85
Great Britain—History, Naval	359.00941	DA70-89.1	Greece—History—281-146 B.C.	938.08	DF236-238.9
Great Britain—Kings and rulers	352.2330941	JN331-389	Greece—History—Galatian Invasion, 279-278 B.C.	938.08	DF236.4
Great Britain—Manufactures	670.941	TS57-64	Greece—History—Chremonidean War, 267-262 B.C.	938.08	DF236.5
Great Britain—Maps	912.41	G1805-1829.24	Greece—History—146 B.C.-323 A.D.	938.09	DF239-241
Great Britain—Maps	912.41	G5740-5814	Greece—History—146 B.C.-323 A.D.	949.501	DF239-241
Great Britain—Politics and government	320.941	JN101-1371	Greece—History—Geometric period, ca. 900-700 B.C.	938.01	DF221.5
Great Britain—Politics and government—1066-1485	320.9410902 + (1-4)	JN137-158	Greece—History—Dorian Invasions, ca. 1125-1025 B.C.	938.01	DF221-.3
Great Britain—Politics and government—1485-	320.941090 + (3-511)	JN175-231	Greece—History—1453-1821	949.505	DF801-.9
Great circle sailing	387.52	VK571	Greece—History—1821-	949.50(6-76)	DF802-854.32
Great Pyrenees	636.73	SF429.G75	Greece—History—Otho I, 1832-1862	949.5072	DF823-.7
Great supper (Parable)	226.8	BT378.G7	Greece—History—Acarnanian Revolt, 1836	949.5072	DF823.6
Great White Brotherhood	299.93	BP605.G68	Greece—History—Revolution, 1848	940.284	DF823.65
Grebo language	496.33	PL8221	Greece—History—Arta Revolt, 1854	949.5072	DF823.68
Greece	949.5	DF	Greece—History—George I, 1863-1913	949.5072	DF825-832
Greece	949.50(4-9)	DF701-854.32	Greece—History—Coup d'etat, 1909	949.5072	DF831.5
Greece—Census	314.95	HA1351-1359	Greece—History—Constantine I, 1913-1917	949.5072	DF837-841
Greece—Commerce	381.09495	HF3750.5	Greece—History—Civil War, 1944-1949	949.5074	DF849.5-.58
Greece—Description and travel	913.804	DF27-30			
Greece—Description and travel	914.9504	DF27-30			
Greece—Description and travel	914.9504	DF721-728			
Greece—Economic conditions	330.9495	HC291-300			
Greece—Emigration and immigration	325.(2495) or (495)	JV8110-8119			
Greece—History	949.50(4-9)	DF750-854.32			
Greece—History—To 146 B.C.	938.0(1-8)	DF218-238.9			
Greece—History—Age of Tyrants, 7th-6th centuries, B.C.	938.01	DF222-224			

Subject Heading	Dewey	LC	Subject Heading	Dewey	LC
Greece—History—1950-1967	949.5074	DF850-852.5	Greek language, Modern—Study and teaching	489.3071	PA1041-1049
Greece—History—1967-1974	949.5075	DF853-.5	Greek language, Modern—Syntax	489.35	PA1091-1097
Greece—History—Coup d'etat, 1967 (April 21)	949.5075	DF853	Greek language—Dialects	489	PA500-581
Greece—History—Coup d'etat, 1967 (Dec. 13)	949.5075	DF853	Greek language—Dictionaries	489.33	PA441-465
Greece—History—Coup d'etat, 1973 (May 22-23)	949.5075	DF853	Greek language—Etymology	489.32	PA421-430
Greece—History—1974-	949.5076	DF854-.32	Greek language—Grammar	489.35	PA251-379
Greece—History, Military	355.009495	DF765	Greek language—Lexicography	489.33028	PA431-465
Greece—Manufactures	670.9495	TS75-76	Greek language—Morphology	489.35	PA283-287
Greece—Maps	912.495	G2000-2004	Greek language—Parts of speech	489.35	PA303-361
Greece—Maps	912.495	G6810-6814	Greek language—Phonology	489.315	PA265-281
Greece—Periodicals	938.005	DF10	Greek language—Study and teaching	489.3071	PA231-241
Greece—Periodicals	949.5(4-9)005	DF701	Greek language—Style	889.309	PA401-407
Greece—Periodicals	949.5005	DF10	Greek language— Syntax	489.35	PA367-379
Greece—Politics and government	320.9495	JN5001-5191	Greek letter societies	371.85	LJ
Greece—Politics and government—To 146 B.C.	320.938	JC71-75	Greek literature	880	PA3051-4505
Greece—Religion	292.08	BL780-795	Greek literature	880.8	PA3300-3516
Greek drama	882	PA3461-3468	Greek literature, Hellenistic	880	PA3081-3084
Greek drama	882.009	PA3131-3239	Greek literature, Hellenistic—Criticism, Textual	880.9	PA3527
Greek drama (Comedy)	882.052308	PA3465-3466			
Greek drama (Comedy)	882.052309	PA3161-3199	Greek literature, Hellenistic—Criticism, Textual	881.09	PA3537-3543
Greek drama (Tragedy)	882.051208	PA3461-3463			
Greek drama (Tragedy)	882.051209	PA3131-3159	Greek literature, Modern	889	PA5201-5660
Greek drama, Modern	889.2008	PA5290-5294	Greek literature, Modern—History and criticism	889.09	PA5230-5269
Greek drama, Modern	889.2009	PA5260-5263	Greek literature, Modern—1453-1800	889.08001	PA5301-5395
Greek language	489.3	PA201-1179			
Greek language, Biblical	487.4	PA695-895	Greek literature—Criticism, Textual	880.9	PA3520-3564
Greek language, Biblical—Dictionaries	487.43	PA881			
Greek language, Biblical—Grammar	487.45	PA813-857	Greek periodicals	059.89	AP85
			Greek poetry	881.009	PA3092-3125
Greek language, Hellenistic (300 B.C.-600 A.D.)	487.4	PA600-895	Greek poetry, Modern	889.1008	PA5280-5289
			Greek poetry, Modern	889.1009	PA5259-5255
Greek language, Medieval and late	489	PA1000-1179	Greek prose literature	888.08	PA3255-3273
			Greek prose literature	888.08	PA3473-3475
Greek language, Modern	489.3	PA1000-1179	Greek prose literature, Modern	888.08	PA5265
Greek language, Modern—Dialects	489.37	PA1151-1159			
Greek language, Modern—Dictionaries	489.33	PA1031	Greek prose literature, Modern	889.808	PA5295
			Green manuring	631.874	S661
Greek language, Modern—Dictionaries	489.33	PA1123-1145	Green movement	333.72	GE195-199
			Green movement	333.72	JA75.8
Greek language, Modern—Etymology	489.32	PA1111-1114.5	Green Revolution	333.7316	S439-481
Greek language, Modern—Grammar	489.35	PA1051-1099	Greenbacks	332.40440973	HG604
			Greenhouse gardening	635.9823	SB415
Greek language, Modern—Morphology	489.35	PA1076	Greenhouse gases	628.532	TD885.5.G73
rinOGreek language, Modern—Parts of speech	489.35	PA1081-1089	Greenhouse plants	635.9823	SB414.6-416.3
Greek language, Modern—Phonology	489.315	PA1061-1072	Greenhouses	631.583	SB415-416.3

Subject Heading	Dewey	LC	Subject Heading	Dewey	LC
Greenland—Census	319.82	HA740	Guatemala—History—1821-1945	972.810(4-52)	F1466.45
Greenland—Economic conditions	330.9982	HC110.5	Guatemala—History—1945-1985	972.81052	F1466.5
Greenland—Maps	912.982	G1110-1114	Guatemala—History—1985-	972.8105(2-3)	F1466.7
Greenland—Maps	912.982	G3380-3384	Guatemala—Maps	912.7281	G4810-4814
Greenland—Politics and government	320.9982	JN7380-7389	Guatemalan literature	860	PQ7490-7499.2
Grenada	972.9845	F2056	Guatemala—Periodicals	972.81005	F1461
Grenada—Politics and government	320.9729845	JL629.6	Guatemala—Politics and government	320.97281	JL1480-1499
Grenades	358.1282	UF765	Guava	583.765	QK495.M9
Grievance procedures	331.8896	HD6972.5	Guernsey cattle	636.224	SF199.G8
Grievance procedures	658.3155	HF5549.5.G7	Guerrilla warfare	355.0218	U240
Grinding and polishing	621.92	TJ1280-1298	Guerrillas	355.0218	D25.5
Groceries	641	TX341-357	Guide dog schools	362.418071	HV1780-.6
Ground controlled approach	629.1325213	TL696.L33	Guides (Spiritualism)	133.9	BF1275.G85
Ground support systems (Astronautics)	629.478	TL4000-4050	Guidons	355.15	UC590-595
Groundhog Day	394.261	GT4995.G	Guild socialism	335.15	HD6479
Groundwater	551.49	GB1001-1199.8	Guilford Court House, Battle of 1781	973.337	E241.G9
Groundwater—Pollution	628.168	TD426-.8	Guillotine	364.66	HV8555
Group counseling	158.35	BF637.C6	Guilt	152.4	BF575.G8
Group extensions (Mathematics)	512.4	QA171	Guinea (Coin)	737.4941	CJ2484
Group homes for children	362.732	HV862-866	Guinea—Census	316.652	HA4726
Group marriage	306.842	HQ981-996	Guinea—Civilization	966.52	DT543.4
Group ministry	262.14	BV675	Guinea—Description and travel	916.65204	DT543.27
Group psychoanalysis	616.8917	RC510	Guinea—Economic conditions	330.96652	HC1030
Group psychotherapy	616.89152	RC488-.6	Guinea—History	966.52	DT543.5-.827
Group theory	512.2	QA174-183	Guinea—History—Portuguese Invasion, 1970	966.52051	DT543.8
Growth	571.8	QH511	Guinea—History—Coup d'etat, 1984	966.52052	DT543.822
Growth	612.6	QP84	Guinea—Maps	912.6652	G8790-8794
Growth (Plants)	571.82	QK731-745	Guinea-Bissau—Census	316.657	HA4736
Growth disorders	616.47	RB140-.5	Guinea-Bissau—Civilization	966.57	DT613.4
G-spaces	516.375	QA689	Guinea-Bissau—Description and travel	916.65704	DT613.2
Guadeloupe	972.976	F2066	Guinea-Bissau—History	966.57	DT613.5-.83
Guadeloupe—Census	317.2976	HA918.7	Guinea-Bissau—History—Revolution, 1963-1974	966.5702	DT613.78
Guadeloupe—Maps	912.72976	G5070-5074	Guinea-Bissau—History—Coup d'etat, 1980	966.5703	DT613.8
Guadeloupe—Politics and government	320.972976	JL820-829	Guinea-Bissau—Maps	912.6657	G8890-8894
Guam—Census	319.67	HA4012	Guinea pigs	599.3592	QL737.R634
Guaranteed annual wage	331.236	HD4928.A5	Guinea pigs	636.93592	SF401.G85
Guard duty	355.422	U190-195	Guitar	787.8707	MT580-588
Guard troops	355.35	UA12.8	Guitar music	787.87	M125-129
Guatemala	972.81	F1461-1477	Gujarati language	491.47	PK1841-1847
Guatemala—Census	317.281	HA811-820	Gujarati literature	891.47	PK1850-1888
Guatemala—Civilization	972.81	F1463.5	Gulf States—History	976	F296
Guatemala—Description and travel	917.28104	F1464-.3	Gulf Stream	551.462	GC296.G9
Guatemala—Emigration and immigration	325.(27281) or (7281)	JV7416	Gums—Diseases	617.632	RK401-410
Guatemala—Gazetteers	917.281003	F1462	Gums and resins	547.8434	QD419-.7
Guatemala—History	972.81	F1465-1466.7	Gums and resins	633.895	SB289-291
Guatemala—History—To 1821	972.810(1-3)	F1466.4			

Subject Heading	Dewey	LC
Gums and resins	668.37	TP977-979.5
Gums and resins, Synthetic	668.374	TP977-979.5
Gun control	363.33	HV7435-7439
Gunantuna (Melanesian people)	305.8995	GN671.B5
Guncotton	662.26	TP276
Gunnery	623.55	UF800-805
Gunpowder	662.26	TP272
Gunpowder Plot, 1605	941.061	DA392-.1
Gunshot wounds	617.145	RD96.3
Gunsmithing	683.4	TS535-.4
Gurjara-Pratihara dynasty	954.02	DS451.8
Gushers	622.3382	TN871
Guyana	988.1	F2361-2391
Guyana—Census	318.81	HA1033
Guyana—Civilization	988.1	F2369.8
Guyana—Gazetteers	918.81003	F2364
Guyana—History	988.1	F2380.3-2391
Guyana—History—To 1803	988.101	F2383
Guyana—History—1803-1966	988.10(1-31)	F2384
Guyana—History—1966-	988.1032	F2385
Guyana—Manufactures	670.9881	TS48
Guyana—Maps	912.881	G5250-5254
Guyana—Periodicals	988.1005	F2361
Guyana—Politics and government	320.9881	JL680-689
Guyanese literature	820	PR9320-.9
Gymnasiums	796.068	GV403-405
Gymnastics	796.44	GV461-475
Gymnosperms	585	QK494-.5
Gymnosperms, Fossil	561.5	QE975-978
Gynecologic emergencies	618.1025	RG158
Gynecologic examination	618.1075	RG107-.5
Gynecologic nursing	618.10231	RG105
Gynecologic pathology	618.07	RG77
Gynecologists	618.1092	RG71-76
Gynecologists—Directories	618.10025	RG32-33
Gynecology	618.1	RG
Gynecology—Congresses	618.1006	RG31
Gynecology—History	618.1009	RG51-67
Gynecology—Periodicals	618.1005	RG26
Gynecology—Psychological aspects	618.10019	RG103.5
Gynecology—Societies, etc.	618.1006	RG1
Gynecology—Terminology	618.10014	RG47
Gynoplasty	618.1059	RG104.5
Gypsies	909.0491497	DX
Gypsies—Biography	920.009291497	DX125-127
Gypsies—Education	371.82991497	LC3503-3520
Gypsies—History	909.0491497	DX135-145
Gypsum	622.3635	TN946
Gyro compass	623.8932	VK577
Gyro compass	629.1352	TL589.2.C58
Gyroscopes	531.34	QA862.G9
Habit	152.33	BF335-337

Subject Heading	Dewey	LC
Habit breaking	152.33	BF337.B74
Haciendas	333.335	HD1471
Hacksaws	621.93	TJ1233
Hadith	297.124	BP135
Hadith (Shiites)	297.124	BP193.25-.28
Hadrons	539.7216	QC793.5.H32-.H329
Hague, Treaty of, 1717	940.253	D283.5
Hail	551.5787	QC929.H15
Hailstorms	551.554	QC929.H15
Hair	573.58	QL942
Hair	611.78	QM488
Hair—Dyeing and bleaching	646.724	TT973
Hair preparations	646.7240284	TT969
Hairweaving	646.724	TT975
Haiti	972.94	F1900-1930
Haiti—Civilization	972.94	F1916
Haiti—Description and travel	917.29404	F1917
Haiti—Emigration and immigration	325.(27294) or (7294)	JV7393
Haiti—Gazetteers	917.294003	F1913
Haiti—History	972.94	F1918-1939
Haiti—History—To 1791	972.940(1-3)	F1923
Haiti—History—Revolution, 1791-1804	972.9403	F1923
Haiti—History—1804-1844	972.9404	F1924
Haiti—History—Revolution, 1843	972.9404	F1924
Haiti—History—1844-1915	972.9404	F1926
Haiti—History—American occupation, 1915-1934	972.9405	F1927
Haiti—History—1934-1986	972.940(6-72)	F1927-1928
Haiti—History—1986-	972.94073	F1928.2-.23
Haiti—History—Coup d'etat, 1991	972.94073	F1928.2
Haiti—Maps	912.7294	G4940-4944
Haiti—Periodicals	972.94005	F1900
Haiti—Politics and government	320.97294	JL1080-1099
Half-dollar	737.4973	CJ1835
Half-life (Nuclear physics)	539.752	QC795.8.H3
Half-timbered houses	728	NA7175
Half-track vehicles, Military	358.1883	UG446.5
Halide minerals	549.4	QE389.4
Hall effect	537.6	QC612.H3
Halley's comet	523.642	QB723.H2
Halloween	394.2646	GT4965
Hallucinations and illusions	154.4	BF491-493
Hallucinations and illusions	616.8634	RC553.H3
Hallucinogenic drugs	615.7883	RM324.8
Halocarbons	628.532	TD887.H3
Halogen compounds	546.73	QD165

Subject Heading	Dewey	LC	Subject Heading	Dewey	LC
Halogen compounds	547.62	QD412	Hare hunting	799.259328	SK341.H3
Hamiltonian systems	515.39	QA614.83	Harmonic analysis	515.2433	QA403-.3
Hammerhead sharks	597.3	QL638.95.S7	Harmonic functions	515.53	QA405
Hammers	621.973	TJ1201.H3	Harmonica	788.8209	ML1088
Hammond organ	786.509	ML597	Harmonica music	788.82	M175.M8
Hampton Roads (Va.), Battle of, 1862	973.752	E473.2	Harmony	781.25	ML3815
			Harmony	781.25	ML3836
Hamsters	599.356	QL737.R666	Harmony	781.25	ML3852
Hand	133.6	BF908-940	Harmony (Aesthetics)	701.8	BH301.H3
Hand	611.97	QM548	Harmony of the spheres	113	BD645
Hand—Surgery	617.575059	RD778-.5	Harness racehorses	636.12	SF343
Hand-to-hand fighting	796.81	GV1111-1141	Harness racing	798.46	SF338.7-345
Hand spinning	746.12	TT847	Harp music	787.9	M115-119
Hand weaving	746.14	TT848-849.2	Harpsichord music	786.4	M20-39
Handbell music	786.88485	M147	Harvest festivals	394.26	GT4380-4499
Handbell ringing	786.8848507	MT710	Harvesting	390.463	GT5810-5856.995
Handcuffs	363.20284	HV7936.E7			
Handgun hunting	799.213	SK39.3	Harvesting	631.55	SB129
Handicapped	362.(3-4)	HV1551-3024	Harvesting time	631.55	S600.7.H37
Handicapped children—Education	371.91	LC4001-4100	Harvesting time	631.55	SB185.8
			Hashish	616.8635	RC568.C2
Handicapped children—Services for	362.(3-4)	HV888-907	Hashish	633.79	RS165.H3
			Hasidism	296.8332	BM198
Handicapped parents	306.874087	HQ759.912	Hastings, Battle of, 1066	941.021	DA196
Handicapped—Marriage	306.81087	HQ1036-1043	Hate	152.4	BF575.H3
Handicapped—Sexual behavior	306.70816	HQ30.5	Hats	391.43	GT2110
			Haunted houses	133.122	BF1475
Handicraft	745.5	TT	Hawaii—Civilization	996.9	DU624.5
Handicraft—[By region or country]	745.509(4-9)	TT15-127	Hawaii—Gazetteers	919.69003	DU622
			Hawaii—History	996.9	DU625-629
Handicraft—Encyclopedias	745.503	TT9	Hawaii—Maps	912.969	G4380-4384
Handicraft—Exhibitions	745.5074	TT6	Hawaii—National Guard	355.3709969	UA159.1-.9
Handicraft—Periodicals	745.505	TT1	Hay fever	616.202	RC590
Handicraft—Therapeutic use	615.85156	RM735.7.H35	Hazardous occupations	363.11	T54
			Hazardous substances	604.7	T55.3.H3
Hanging	364.66	HV8579-8581	Hazing	355.0071073	U410.E9
Hanging baskets	635.986	SB418-.4	Hazing	371.8	LB3604-3615
Hankel functions	515.53	QA408	Head	611.91	QM535
Hanukkah	296.435	BM695.H3	Head—Diseases	617.51	RC936
Hanukkah cookery	641.5676435	TX739.2.H35	Head—Diseases—Eclectic treatment	617.5106	RV291
Hanukkah lamp	296.435	BM657.H3			
Happiness	152.42	BF575.H27	Head-gear	391.43	GT2110
Happiness	170	BJ1480-1486	Headache	616.8491	RB128
Harbor of Refuge Lighthouse	623.894209751	VK1025.H	Headache	616.8491	RC392
			Heads of state	352.23	JF251-289
Harbors	387.1	HE550-560	Heads of state—Succession	321.8042	JF285
Harbors	387.1	TC203-327			
Harbors	387.1	VK321-369.8	Heads of state—Term of office	352.23	JF286
Harbors	627.2	TC353-365			
Harbors—Law and legislation	343.0967	K4198-4200	Healers	615.851092	RZ407-408
			Healing gods	203.1	BL325.H4
Harbors of refuge	387.1	VK369-.8	Health	613	RA773-790
Hard materials	620.1126	TA418.45	Health boards	353.606	RA10-388
Hard-core unemployed	331.137	HD5708.8-.85	Health boards—Africa	353.60606	RA345-352
Hardanger fiddle music	787.6	M59	Health boards—Asia	353.60605	RA303-340
Hardness	620.1126	TA418.42	Health boards—Australia	353.606094	RA371-372
Hardware	683	TS400-455	Health boards—Canada	353.606071	RA184-186

Subject Heading	Dewey	LC	Subject Heading	Dewey	LC
Health boards—Central America	353.6060728	RA191	Hebrew language—Lexicography	492.43028	PJ4934-4937
Health boards—Europe	353.60604	RA239-299	Hebrew language—Morphology	492.45	PJ4601-4677
Health boards—Mexico	353.606072	RA187-188	Hebrew language—Phonology	492.415	PJ4576-4583
Health boards—South America	353.60608	RA198-235	Hebrew literature	892.4	PJ5001-5060
Health boards—United States	353.606073	RA11-182	Hebrew literature, Medieval	892.408002	PJ5037
Health boards—[United States, By city]	353.60607(4-9)	RA15-182	Hebrew literature, Medieval	892.409002	PJ5016
Health maintenance organizations	362.104258	RA413-.7	Hebrew literature, Modern	892.408003	PJ5038
			Hebrew literature, Modern	892.409003	PJ5017-5021
Health promotion	613	RA427.8	Hebrew literature—Study and teaching	892.4071	PJ5007
Health resorts	613.122	RA794-954	Hebrew philology	492.4	PJ4501-4541
Health surveys	614.42	RA407.3-408	Hebrew poetry, Biblical	223	BS1401-1405.5
Hearing	152.15	BF251-.5	Hedges	635.976	SB437
Hearing	612.85	QP460-469.3	Hedonism	171.4	BJ1491
Hearing aids	617.89	RF300-310	Hedonism	183	B279
Hearing disorders	617.8	RF286-320	Heisenberg uncertainty principle	530.122	QC174.17.H4
Hearing impaired	362.42	HV2350-2990.5	Helicopters	629.133352	TL716-.9
Heart	612.17	QP111-114	Heliograph	623.7312	UG582.H4
Heart—Anatomy	573.17	QL838	Helium	546.751	QD181.H4
Heart—Anatomy	611.12	QM181	Helium	665.822	TP245.H4
Heart—Diseases	616.12	RC681-688	Hell	202.3	BL545
Heart—Surgery	617.412	RD598-.35	Hell	236.25	BT834-838
Heart—Transplantation	617.4120592	RD598.35.T7	Hell	292.28	BL735
Heart, Artificial	617.4120592	RD598.35.A78	Helmets	355.81	U825
Heart valves—Diseases	616.125	RC685.V2	Help-wanted advertising	659.19658311	HF6125.5
Heat	536	QC251-338.5	Helplessness (Psychology)	155.232	BF575.H4
Heat—Transmission	536.2	QC319.8-338.5	Helsinki	948.971	DL1175-.95
Heat pumps	621.4025	TJ262	Hematological oncology	616.99419	RC280.H47
Heat pumps	697.3	TH7638	Hematology, Experimental	616.15027	RB145
Heat-engines	621.4025	TJ255-265	Hematology, Experimental	616.15027	RC636
Heating	392.36	GT420-425	Hemoglobin	612.1111	QP96.5
Heating	697	TH7005-7699	Hemophilia	616.1572	RC642
Heating plants	697.03	TH7461	Hemorrhage	616.157	RB144-.5
Heaven	236.24	BT844-849	Hemorrhoids	616.352	RC865
Heavy ions	539.7234	QC702.7.H42	Hepatitis	616.3623	RC848.H42
Heavy water reactors	621.4834	TK9203.H4	Hepatitis, Neonatal	618.923623	RJ272
Hebrew essays	089.924	AC101-102	Heracles (Greek mythology)	292.13	BL820.H5
Hebrew language	492.4	PJ4501-4937	Heraldry	929.6	CR
Hebrew language, Talmudic	492.47	PJ4901-4950	Heraldry, Ornamental	929.6	CR29-69
Hebrew language—Dialects	492.47	PJ4855-4937	Heraldry—Congresses	929.606	CR2
Hebrew language—Dictionaries	492.43	PJ4825-4847	Heraldry—Dictionaries	929.603	CR13
Hebrew language—Dictionaries	492.43	PJ4935-4937	Heraldry—Directories	929.6025	CR11
Hebrew language—Etymology	492.42	PJ4801-4819	Heraldry—Exhibitions	929.6074	CR9
Hebrew language—Etymology	492.42	PJ4931-4933	Heraldry—History	929.609	CR151-159
Hebrew language—Grammar	492.45	PJ4553-4731	Heraldry—Periodicals	929.605	CR1
Hebrew language—Grammar	492.475	PJ4911-4925	Heraldry—Philosophy	929.601	CR14-16
Hebrew language—Lexicography	492.43028	PJ4820-4847	Heralds	394.23	GT5020
			Heralds	929.6	CR183-185
			Herb gardens	635.7	SB351.H5
			Herbal teas	641.357	TX415
			Herbaria	580.74	QK75-77
			Herbicides	632.954	SB951.4
			Herbs	635.7	SB351.H5

Subject Heading	Dewey	LC	Subject Heading	Dewey	LC
Herbs	641.657	TX406-407	Hinduism	294.5	BL1100-1270
Herbs—Therapeutic use	615.321	RM666.H33	Hinduism	294.5	BL2000-2030
Heredity	304.5	HM121	Hinduism—Doctrines	294.52	BL1213.32-1215
Heredity	364.24	HV6121-6125	Hindustani language	491.43	PK1931-1937
Heresies, Christian	262.8	BT20-30	Hindustani literature	891.43	PK2030-2142
Hermaphroditism	616.694	RC883	Hinomoto (Sect)	299.5619	BL2222.H5
Hermeneutics	121.68	BD240-241	Hip joint—Dislocation, Congenital	617.71043	RD772
Hernia	617.559059	RD621-626	Hippocampus (Brain)	573.86	QL938.H56
Heroin	362.293	HV5822.H4	Hippocampus (Brain)	611.81	QM455
Herpes genitalis	614.547	RA644.H45	Hispanic Americans	973.0468073	E184.S75
Herpes genitalis	616.9518	RC203.H45	Hispanic Americans—Education	370.8968073	LC2667-2688
Heterocyclic compounds	547.59	QD399-406	Histochemistry	572	QH613
Hewitt-Nachbin spaces	514.3	QA611.234	Histology	571.5	QL807
Hibernation	591.565	QL755	Histology	611.018	QM550-577.8
Hibiscus	583.685	QK495.M27	Historians	907.202	D14-15
Hibiscus	635.933685	SB413.H6	Historic buildings—Law and legislation—United States	344.73094	KF4310-4312
Hides and skins	338.176	HD9778-.5	Historical fiction	809.381	PN3441
Hides and skins	675.2	TS967	Historical geography	911	G141
Hieroglyphic Bibles	220.49	BS560	Historical geology	551.09	QE28.3
Hieroglyphics	493.1	PJ1091	Historical lexicology	401.409	P326
Hieroglyphics	493.111	PH1091-1097	Historical linguistics	417.7	P140
High Holiday sermons	296.4731	BM746	Historical models	902.28	D16
High Holidays	296.431	BM693.H5	Historical sociology	301.09	HM104
High occupancy vehicle lanes	388.12	HE336.B8	Historicism	901	D16.9
High school dropouts	373.12913	LC146.5-.8	Historiography	907.2	D13-15
High school enrollment	373.1219	LC146	Historiography	909.08072	D206
High school equivalency certificates	373.238	LB1627.7	History	900	D
			History (Theology)	230	BR115.H5
High school principals	373.12012	LB2831.9-.976	History, Ancient	930	D51-95
High school teachers	373.11	LB1777-.4	History, Ancient—Dictionaries	930.03	D54
High schools	373.238	LB1603-1694	History, Ancient—Historiography	930.072	D56-.52
High schools—United States	373.73	LD7501	History, Ancient—Periodicals	930.05	D51
High temperatures	536.57	QC276-277	History, Modern	909.08	D204-725
High-calcium diet	613.285	RM237.56	History, Modern	940.2	D101-110.5
High-carbohydrate diet	613.283	RM237.59	History, Modern—16th century	909.5	D219-234
High-fiber diet	613.263	RM237.6	History, Modern—17th century	909.6	D242-283.5
High-frequency ventilation (Therapy)	616.206	RC735.H54	History, Modern—1945-	909.08	D839-850
High-protein diet	613.282	RM237.65	History, Modern—1945- —Periodicals	909.8(24-3)05	D839
Highway capacity	388.314	HE336.H48	History, Modern—20th century	909.82	D410-893
Highway engineering	625.7	TE	History, Modern—Dictionaries	909.0803	D205
Highway law	343.0942	K3492			
Highway law	343.0942	K4028-4042	History—Congresses	906	D3
Highway law—England	343.420942	KD1040-1048	History—Dictionaries	903	D9
Highway law—United States	343.730942	KF5521-5536	History—Methodology	901	D16-.18
Hiking	796.51	GV199-.5	History—Periodicals	905	D1
Hillside planting	631.455	S627.H5	History—Philosophy	901	D16.7-.9
Hindi language	491.43	PK1931-1939			
Hindu astrology	133.59445	BF1714.H5			
Hindu pilgrims and pilgrimages	294.5351	BL1239.32			
Hindu saints	294.5213	BL1171			
Hindu sects	294.55	BL1245.A1			
Hinduism	181.4	B130-133			

Subject Heading	Dewey	LC	Subject Heading	Dewey	LC
History—Study and teaching	907.1	D16.2-.5	Homeopathic physicians—Biography	615.532092	RX61-66
Hittite language	491.998	P945	Homeopathic physicians—Directories	615.532025	RX46
HIV (Viruses)	616.979201	QR414.6.H58	Homeopathy	615.532	RX
Hobbies	790.13	GV1201	Homeopathy—Attenuations, dilutions, and potencies	615.532	RX81
Hockey	796.962	GV847	Homeopathy—Congresses	615.53206	RX21
Hodgkin's disease	616.99446	RC644	Homeopathy—History	615.53209	RX51
Hoisting machinery	621.862	TJ1350-1383	Homeopathy—Hospitals and dispensaries	362.11	RX6-.5
Hokan-Coahuiltecan languages	497.57	PM1343	Homeopathy—Materia medica and therapeutics	615.532	RX601-675
Holding patterns (Aeronautics)	629.13252	TL711.H65	Homeopathy—Periodicals	615.53205	RX11
Holiday cookery	641.568	TX739-.2	Homeopathy—Societies, etc.	615.53206	RX1
Holiday pay	331.2576	HD4928.H	Homeopathy—Study and teaching	615.532071	RX91-101
Holidays	394.26	GT3930-4995	Homeostasis	571.75	QP90.4
Holiness	234.8	BT767	Homeowners' associations	363.506	HD7287.8-.82
Holocaust, Jewish (1939-1945)—Personal narratives	940.5318092	D804.3	Homeowner's insurance	368.096	HG9986
			Homestead law—United States	343.730253	KF5670-5673
Holography	774.0153	QC449-.3	Homework	371.30281	LB1048
Holy Cross	232.963	BT465	Homo erectus	569.97	GN284-.7
Holy Roman Empire—History	943.02	DD125-198.7	Homo habilis	569.9	GN283.9
Holy Shroud	232.966	BT587.S4	Homogenized milk	637.141	SF259
Holy Spirit	231.3	BT117-123	Homology theory	514.23	QA612.3-.77
Holy Week	232.96	BT414	Homosexuality	306.766	HQ75-76.95
Holy Week	263.925	BT414	Homosexuality	616.8583	RC558-.5
Holy Week	263.925	BV90-95	Honduran literature	860	PQ7500-7509.2
Holy Week	394.2667	GT4930	Honduras	972.83	F1501-1517
Home	306.8	HQ503-1064	Honduras—Census	317.283	HA821-830
Home	392.3	GT2420	Honduras—Civilization	972.83	F1503.8
Home banking services	332.17	HG1711-1712	Honduras—Description and Travel	917.28304	F1504
Home care services	362.14	RA645.3-.37	Honduras—Emigration and immigration	325.(27283) or (7283)	JV7419
Home economics	640	TX			
Home economics—[By region or country]	640.9(4-9)	TX21-127	Honduras—Gazetteers	917.283003	F1502
			Honduras—History	972.83	F1505.5-1508.33
Home economics—Congresses	640.6	TX5	Honduras—History—To 1838	972.830(1-4)	F1507
Home economics—Encyclopedias	640.3	TX11	Honduras—History—1838-1933	972.8305(1-2)	F1507.5
Home economics—Equipment and supplies	640.284	TX298-299	Honduras—History—Coup d'etat, 1904	972.83051	F1507.5
Home economics—History	640.9	TX15-19	Honduras—History—Revolution, 1919	972.83051	F1507.5
Home economics—Periodicals	640.5	TX1	Honduras—History—1933-1982	972.8305(2-3)	F1508-.22
Home economics—Study and teaching	640.71	TX165-286	Honduras—History—1982-	972.83053	F1508.3-.33
Home equity loans	332.722	HG2040.45	Honduras—Maps	912.7283	G4830-4834
Home improvement loans	332.722	HG2040.4	Honduras—Periodicals	972.83005	F1501
Home labor	338.634	HD2331-2336.35	Honduras—Politics and government	320.97283	JL1520-1539
Home missions	266.022	BV2650			
Home ownership	363.5	HD7287.8-.82			
Home schooling	371.042	LC40	Honesty	179.9	BJ1533.H7
Home-based businesses	338.634	HD2331-2336.35	Honey	638.16	SF539
Homelands (South Africa)	968.29	DT1760	Honey	641.38	TX560.H7
Homeless students	371.826942	LC5144-.3			

Subject Heading	Dewey	LC	Subject Heading	Dewey	LC
Honeybee	595.799	QL568.A6	Hospitals—United States	362.110973	RA981-982
Honeybee	638.12	SF521-539	Hostages—Lebanon— Biography	956.92044092	DS87.2.C4
Hong Kong—Census	315.125	HA4651-4655	Hostility (Psychology)	152.47	BF575.H6
Hong Kong—Maps	912.5125	G7940-7944	Hot air balloons	629.13322	TL638
Hopi Indians	979.100497458	E99.H7	Hot springs	551.23	GB1198-.4
Hopi language	497.458	PM1351	Hot springs	551.23	QE528
Hormone therapy	615.36	RM283-298	Hot-air heating	697.3	TH7601-7635
Hormones	573.44	QP801.H7	Hot-water heating	697.4	TH7511-7549
Hormones, Sex	612.405	QP572.S4	Hot-water supply	696.6	TH6551-6568
Horology	681.11(3-4)	TS540-549	Hotels	395.53	GT3770-3896
Horse farms	636.1	SF290-291	ctlparHotels	728.5	NA7800-7853
Horse racing	798.4	SF321-359.7	Hotels	910.46	TX901-946
Horse railroads	625.1	TF16	Hotels—Personnel management	910.460683	TX911.3.P4
Horse railroads	625.66	TF830	Hounds	636.753	SF429.H6
Horse shows	636.10811	SF294.5-297.7	Hour-glasses	529.7	QB214
Horse sports	798	SF294.2-294.35	Hours of labor	331.257	HD5106-5267
Horsemanship	357.2	UE460-475	Hours of labor, Flexible	331.25724	HD5109-.2
Horsemanship	798.2	SF309	Hours of labor, Staggered	331.25724	HD5108-.2
Horses	357.2	UC600-695	House cleaning	648.5	TX324
Horses	357.2	UE460-475	House construction	690.8	TH4805-4890
Horses	364.187	HV4749-4755	House painting	698.1	TT320-324
Horses	636.1	SF277-359.7	House plants	635.965	SB419-.3
Horticultural crops	635	SB317.5-319.77	Houseboats	728.78	VM335
Hosiery	391.413	GT2128	Houseboats	797.129	GV836
Hosiery	687.3	TT679-695	Household appliances, Electric	643.6	TK7018-7301
Hospice care	616.029	RT87.T45	Household ecology	577.554	QH541.5.H67
Hospices (Terminal care)	362.1756	R726.8	Househusbands	640.92	HQ756.6
Hospital libraries	027.662	Z675.H7	Houses (Astrology)	133.52	BF1716-.28
Hospitality	395.3	BJ2021-2028	Housing	363.5	HD7285-7391
Hospitals	362.11	RA960-996	Housing, Cooperative	334.1	HD7287.7-.72
Hospitals, Gynecologic and obstetric	362.11	RG12-16	Housing, Rural	363.5091734	HD7289
Hospitals, Medieval	362.110902	RA964	Housing—Law and legislation—United States	344.73063635	KF5721-5740
Hospitals, Naval and marine	359.72	VG410-450	Housing—[By region or country]	363.509(4-9)	HD7291-7391
Hospitals, Ophthalmic and aural	362.11	RF5-6	Housing—Africa	363.5096	HD7372-7378.4
Hospitals, Ophthalmic and aural —[By region or country]	362.1109(4-9)	RF6	Housing—Asia	363.5095	HD7359.6
			Housing—Australia	363.50994	HD7379
Hospitals—Administration	362.11068	RA971-.8	Housing—Benelux countries	363.509492	HD7342-7344.5
Hospitals—Emergency service	362.18	RA975.5.E5	Housing—Canada	363.50971	HD7305
Hospitals—Outpatient services	362.12	RA974-.5	Housing—Central America	363.509728	HD7307-7313
			Housing—China	363.50951	HD7368
Hospitals—Research	362.11072	RA964.5	Housing—Developing countries	363.5091724	HD7391
Hospitals—[By region or country]	362.1109(4-9)	RA980-993	Housing—Europe	363.5094	HD7332-7357.7
Hospitals—Africa	362.11096	RA991	Housing—France	363.50944	HD7338
Hospitals—Arab countries	362.1109174927	RA990.5	Housing—Germany	363.50943	HD7339-.5
Hospitals—Asia	362.11095	RA990	Housing—Great Britain	363.50941	HD7333-7335.5
Hospitals—Australia	362.110994	RA992-.3	Housing—Greece	363.509495	HD7357.5
Hospitals—Canada	362.110971	RA983	Housing—India	363.50954	HD7361
Hospitals—Europe	362.11094	RA985-989	Housing—Iran	363.50955	HD7359.2
Hospitals—Great Britain	362.110941	RA986-988	Housing—Iraq	363.509567	HD7359
Hospitals—New Zealand	362.110993	RA992.5-.7	Housing—Israel	363.5095694	HD7358.45
Hospitals—Oceania	362.11099(5-6)	RA993			

Subject Heading	Dewey	LC	Subject Heading	Dewey	LC
Housing—Italy	363.50945	HD7341	Humanism	144	B821
Housing—Japan	363.50952	HD7367	Humanistic ethics	171.2	BJ1360
Housing—Mexico	363.50972	HD7306	Humanistic Judaism	296.834	BM197.8
Housing—Philippines	363.509599	HD7366	Humanistic psychology	150.198	BF204
Housing—Russia	363.50947	HD7345	Humanitarianism	171.2	BJ1475.3
Housing—South America	363.5098	HD7320-7331	Humidity	551.571	QC915-917
Housing—Spain	363.50946	HD7351	Hummel figurines	738.82	NK4660
Housing—Switzerland	363.509494	HD7353	Humor in education	370.207	LA23
Housing—Turkey	363.509561	HD7358.25	Humorists	808.87092	PN6147
Housing—United States	363.50973	HD7293-7304	Hundred Years War, 1339-1453	944.025	DC96-105
Housing—West Indies	363.509729	HD7314-7319.9	Hungarian language	494.511	PH2001-2800
Houston (Tex.)	976.41411	F394.H8	Hungarian language— Dictionaries	494.5113	PH2625-2693
Howitzers	358.1282	UF560-565	Hungarian language— Grammar	494.5115	PH2097-2410
Howitzers	358.12822	UF470-475	Hungarian language— Lexicography	494.5113028	PH2601-2693
Hsiang dialects	495.17215	PL1861-1870	Hungarian language— Slang	494.5117	PH2800
Hsiung-nu	950.04	DS25	Hungarian literature	894.511	PH3001-3445
Huguenots	284.5	BX9450-9459	Hungarian literature (German)	830	PT3840-3848
Hula (Dance)	792.319969	GV1796.H8	Hungary	939.8	DB901-999
Human acts	241	BV4618	Hungary	943.9	DB901-999
Human anatomy	611	QM	Hungary—Biography	920.0398	DB922
Human anatomy—Atlases	611.0022	QM25	Hungary—Biography	920.0439	DB922
Human anatomy— Laboratory manuals	611.0078	QM34	Hungary—Census	314.39	HA1201-1210
Human anatomy—Variation	611	QM24	Hungary—Civilization	939.8	DB920.5
Human biology	612	QP34-38	Hungary—Civilization	943.9	DB920.5
Human capital	331.11	HD4904.7	Hungary—Description and travel	913.9804	DB906.9-917.3
Human chromosome abnormalities	616.042	RB155.5-.8	Hungary—Description and travel	914.3904	DB906.9-917.3
Human ecology	304.2	GF	Hungary—Gazetteers	913.98003	DB904
Human ecology	304.2	GF1-900	Hungary—Gazetteers	914.39003	DB904
Human ecology—[By region or country]	304.209(4-9)	GF500-895	Hungary—History—To 896	939.8	DB927-928.9
Human ecology—Tropics	304.20913	GF895	Hungary—History—To 896	943.901	DB927-928.9
Human ecology—United States	304.20973	GF503-504	Hungary—History—896-1301	943.902	DB929-.9
Human evolution	599.938	GN281-289	Hungary—History—Charles Robert, 1308-1342	943.903	DB930.2
Human experimentation in medicine	615.50724	R853.H8	Hungary—History—Louis I, 1342-1382	943.903	DB930.3
Human growth	612.6	QP84	Hungary—History— Sigismund, 1387-1437	943.903	DB930.4
Human immunogenetics	616.0796	QR184.2	Hungary—History—Turkish occupation, 1529-1699	943.9041	DB931.94-932.4
Human information processing	153	BF444	Hungary—History—1699-1848	943.9043	DB932.3-934
Human mechanics	612.76	QP301-336	Hungary—History—Francis Joseph, 1848-1916	943.9042	DB940-953
Human physiology	612	QP34-38	Hungary—History—20th century	943.90(43-54)	DB947-957
Human reproduction	612.6	QP251-285	Hungary—History—1918-1945	943.905(1-2)	DB955
Human reproductive technology	618.178	RG133.5-135	Hungary—History—1945-	943.905(3-4)	DB956-957
Human rights	323	JC571-628			
Human rights	342.085	K3236-3268			
Human settlements	307	HT51-65			
Human settlements	307.14	GF101-127			
Human skeleton	611.71	QM101-117			
Human-animal communication	591.59	QL776			
Human-computer interaction	004.019	QA76.9.H85			
Humanism	144	B778			

Subject Heading	Dewey	LC	Subject Heading	Dewey	LC
Hungary—History—Revolution, 1956	943.9052	DB957	Hydraulic motors	621.2	TJ855-857
Hungary—Manufactures	670.9439	TS65.5-66	Hydraulics	532	TC160-179
Hungary—Maps	912.439	G1940-1944	Hydrocarbons	547.41	QD305.H5-.H9
Hungary—Maps	912.439	G6500-6504	Hydrocarbons	547.61	QD341.H9
Hungary—Periodicals	939.8005	DB901	Hydrocephalus	616.858843	RC391
Hungary—Periodicals	943.9005	DB901	Hydrodynamics	532.5	QA911-930
Hunger	612.391	QP141	Hydrodynamics	532.5	QC150-159
Hunt riding	799.23	SF295.65	Hydrodynamics	532.5	TC171-179
Hunters	799.2092	SK15-17	Hydroelectric power plants	621.312134	TK1081-1083
Hunters—Directories	799.292025	SK12	Hydrofoil boats	623.8204	VM362
Hunting	395.5	GT5810-5895	Hydrogen	546.2	QD181.H1
Hunting	799.2	SK	Hydrogen peroxide	614.48	RA766.H9
Hunting, Prehistoric	639.0901	GN799.H84	Hydrographic surveying	551.4607	VK588-597
Hunting—Equipment and supplies	799.2028	SK273-275	Hydrology	551.48	GB651-2998
Hunting—History	799.209	SK21	Hydrometallurgy	669.0283	TN688
Hunting—Museums	799.2074	SK276	Hydrometeorology	551.57	GB2801-2998
Hunting—Periodicals	799.205	SK7	Hydroponics	631.585	SB126.5-.57
Hunting—Societies, etc.	799.206	SK1	Hydrotherapy	615.853	RM801-822
Hunting—[By region or country]	799.29(4-9)	SK40-267	Hygiene	613	RA770.5
Hunting—Africa	799.296	SK251-255	Hygiene	613	RA780
Hunting—North America	799.297	SK40-157	Hygiene, Sexual	613.95	RA788
Hunting—Southern States	799.2975	SK43	Hygienists	613.092	RA424.4-.5
Hunting—United States	799.2973	SK41-145	Hymns	246.75	BV301-530
Hunting—[United States, By state]	799.297(4-9)	SK47-145	Hymns	782.27	M2115-2145
Hunting—West (U.S.)	799.2978	SK45	Hyperbolic navigation	623.89	VK560
Hunting and fishing clubs	799.1206	SH403	Hyperborean languages	494.6	PM1-95
Hunting and fishing clubs	799.206	SK3	Hypertension	616.132	RC685.H8
Hunting customs	394.3	GT5810-5850	Hypnotics	615.782	RM325
Hunting guns	799.20283	SK274	Hypnotism	133.89	BF1111-1156
Hupertrichosis	616.546	RL431	Hypnotism	154.7	RC490-499
Hurdy-gurdy music	787.69	M175.H9	Hypocrisy	241.3	BV4627.H8
Hurricanes	551.552	QC944-948	Hypotension	616.13	RC685.H93
Hussites	284.3	BX4913-4918	Hypothalamic hormones	612.8262	QP572.H9
Hyaline membrane disease	618.922	RJ274	Hypothalamus	611.81	QM455
Hydrants	628.9252	TH9365	Hypothesis	167	BC183
Hydraulic engineering	621.2	TC	Hypothyroidism	616.444	RC657
Hydraulic engineering—[By region or country]	621.109(4-9)	TC21-127	Hysterectomy	618.1453	RG391
Hydraulic engineering—Dictionaries	621.203	TC9	Hysteria	616.8524	RC532
Hydraulic engineering—History	621.209	TC15-20	Ia Drang Valley (Vietnam), Battle of, 1965	959.704342	DS557.8.I
Hydraulic engineering—Periodicals	621.205	TC1	Iatrogenic diseases	615.5	RC90
Hydraulic engineering—Study and teaching	621.1071	TC157-.5	Ice	551.31	GB2401-2597
Hydraulic engineers—Biography	621.2092	TC139-140	Ice-boats	796.97	GV843
Hydraulic fluids	621.20424	TJ844	Ice-breaking vessels	623.828	VM451
Hydraulic jacks	621.2	TJ1435	Ice cream, ices, etc.	641.86(2-3)	TX795
Hydraulic laboratories	621.2072	TC158	Ice fog	551.575	QC929.F7
Hydraulic machinery	621.2	TJ836-935	Ice sheets	551.31	GB2401-2598
Hydraulic mining	622.2927	TN278	Icebergs	551.342	GB2401-2597
			Iceland	949.12	DL301-398
			Iceland—Census	314.912	HA1491-1500
			Iceland—Description and travel	914.91204	DL309-315
			Iceland—Gazetteers	914.912003	DL304
			Iceland—History	949.12	DL351-380
			Iceland—History—To 1262	949.1201	DL357-360

Subject Heading	Dewey	LC	Subject Heading	Dewey	LC
Iceland—History—1918-1945	949.1205	DL375	Illumination of books and manuscripts, Ancient	745.670901	ND2910
Icelandic drama	839.69208	PT7470-7477	Illumination of books and manuscripts, Medieval	745.670902	ND2920-2980
Icelandic drama	839.69209	PT7411	Illumination of books and manuscripts—[By region or country]	745.6709(4-9)	ND3001-3294.5
Icelandic fiction	839.69308	PT7485-7487			
Icelandic fiction	839.69309	PT7413			
Icelandic language	439.69	PD2401-2447	Illumination of books and manuscripts—Exhibitions	745.67074	ND2893
Icelandic language—Dictionaries	439.693	PD2437	Illumination of books and manuscripts—Renaissance	745.6709024	ND2990
Icelandic language—Etymology	439.692	PD2431	Illustration of books	741.6	NC960-995.8
Icelandic language—Grammar	439.695	PD2411-2423	Image processing	621.367	TA1637
			Imagery (Psychology)	153.32	BF367
Icelandic language—Slang	439.697	PD2447	Imaginary wars and battles	355.48	U313
Icelandic language—Study and teaching	439.69071	PD2407	Imaginary wars and battles	359.48	V253
			Imagination	153.32	BF408-426
Icelandic literature	839.69	PT7351-7550	Imagination	701.15	N61-79
Icelandic literature—Study and teaching	839.69071	PT7370-7373	Imaging systems in astronomy	522	QB51.3.I45
Icelandic poetry	839.69108	PT7465-7467	Imitation	153.1523	BF357
Icelandic prose literature	839.69808	PT412-418	Immaculate Conception	232.911	BT620
Icelandic prose literature	839.69808	PT7480-7495	Immanence of God	231	BT124
Iceland—Maps	912.4912	G2060-2064	Immersion method (Language teaching)	407.1	P53.44
Iceland—Maps	912.4912	G6930-6934	Immortality	236.22	BT919-925
Iceland—Periodicals	949.12005	DL301	Immune response	571.964	QR186-.3
Iceland—Politics and government	320.94912	JN7370-7379	Immunization of children	613.0432	RJ240
Ichthyosis	616.544	RL435	Immunodeficiency	571.974	QR188.35
Idaho	979.6	F741-755	Immunogenetics	571.9648	QR184-.4
Idaho—Gazetteers	917.96003	F744	Immunoglobulins	571.967	QR186.7-.85
Idaho—History— 1951-	979.603(3-4)	F750-.22	Immunological deficiency syndromes	616.979	RC606-607
Idaho—Maps	912.796	G4270-4274			
Idaho—National Guard	355.3709796	UA160-169	Immunology	571.96	QR180-189.5
Idaho—Periodicals	979.6005	F741	Immunopharmacology	615.37	RM370-373
Idea (Philosophy)	184	B398.I3	Immunosuppressive agents	615.37	RM373
Idealism	141	B823	Immunotherapy	615.37	RM270-282
Ideals (Algebra)	512.4	QA247	Impasse (Psychotherapy)	616.8914	RC489.I45
Identification	363.258	HV8073-.8	Imperialism	325.32	JC359
Identification cards—Forgeries—United States	364.1630973	HV6679	Impetigo	616.523	RL283
			Implant dentures	617.693	RK667.I45
Identity	111.82	BD236	Imports	382.5	HF1419-1420
Ideology	145	B823.3	Imposition of hands	265.9	BV873.L3
Idols and images—Worship	202.18	BL485	Impotence	616.6922	RC889
Illegitimacy	306.874	HQ998-999	Impotence	616.85832	RC560.I45
Illinois	977.3	F536-550	Impressment	973.525	E357.2-.3
Illinois—Gazetteers	917.73003	F539	Imprinting (Psychology)	591.563	QL763.2
Illinois—History—To 1778	977.30(1-2)	F544	Imprisonment	365	HV8705-8749
Illinois—History—1778-1865	977.30(2-3)	F545	Improvisation (Acting)	792.028	PN2071.I5
			Impulsive personality	616.8584	RC569.5.I46
Illinois—History—1865-	977.304	F546-.4	Inauguration Day	394.40973	JK536
Illinois—History—1951-	977.304(3-4)	F546.2-.4	Inbreeding	636.082	S494
Illinois—Maps	912.773	G4100-4104	Inbreeding	636.082	SF105
Illinois—National Guard	355.3709773	UA170-179	Incandescent lamps	621.326	TK4351-4367
Illinois—Periodicals	977.3005	F536	Incantations	133.44	BF1558
Illumination of books and manuscripts	745.67	ND2889-3416	Incantations	398.45	GR540
			Incarnation	232.1	BT220

Subject Heading	Dewey	LC	Subject Heading	Dewey	LC
Incentives in industry	658.3142	HF5549.5.I5	India—History—Sepoy Rebellion, 1857-1858	954.0317	DS478-.3
Incest	306.877	GN480.3	India—History—Quit India movement, 1942	954.0359	DS480.82
Incest	306.877	HQ71			
Incest	616.85836	RC560.I53	India—History—1947-	954.0(4-5)	DS480.832-481
Incest victims	618.9285836	RC560.I53	India—Manufactures	670.954	TS103-104
Incineration	628.4457	TD796-.2	India—Maps	912.54	G2280-2284
Income	331.21	HB522-715	India—Maps	912.54	G7650-7654
Income tax	336.24	HJ4621-4830	India—Politics and government	320.954	JQ200-620
Income tax—Law and legislation	343.052	K4501-4550	India-Pakistan Conflict, 1947-1949	954.9042	DS385.9
Income tax—Law and legislation—United States	343.73052	KF6351-6499	Indian dance—North America	299.74	E98.D2
Indentured servants	306.363	HD4871-4875	Indian essays	089.97	AC195
Independent Order of Odd Fellows	366.3	HS951-1179	Indiana	977.2	F521-535
			Indiana—Gazetteers	917.72003	F524
Independent Order of Odd Fellows—Periodicals	366.305	HS951-953	Indiana—History—To 1787	977.20(1-2)	F526
Independent Order of Odd Fellows—Directories	366.3025	HS963-975	Indiana—History—1951-	977.204(3-4)	F530-.22
			Indiana—Maps	912.772	G4090-4094
Independent Order of Odd Fellows—History	366.309	HS987-991	Indiana—National Guard	355.3709772	UA180-189
			Indiana—Periodicals	977.2005	F521
Independent Order of Odd Fellows—Rituals	366.3	HS1019-1021	Indianapolis (Ind.)	977.252	F534.I3
Independent Order of Odd Fellows—[By region or country]	366.309(4-9)	HS1041-1051	Indians	970.00497	E51-73
			Indians—Costume	391.08997	E59.C6
			Indians—Folklore	398.08997	E59.F6
Independent Order of Odd Fellows—United States	366.30973	HS1041-1045	Indians—History	970.00497	E58
			Indians of Central America	972.800497	F1434-1435.3
Independent study	371.3943	LB1049	Indians of Central America—Languages	497.9	PM3001-4566
Index theorems	514.74	QA614.92			
Indexes	016	AI	Indians of Mexico	972.00497	F1219-1221
India	934	DS421-486.8	Indians of North America	973.0497	E75-99
India	954	DS421-486.8	Indians of North America—Employment	331.125008997	E98.E6
India—Census	315.4	HA4581-4590			
India—Church history	275.4	BR1150-1156	Indians of North America—Languages	497	PM1-7356
India—Civilization	934	DS421-428.2			
India—Civilization	954	DS421-428.2	Indians of North America—Legal status, laws, etc.	342.730872	KF8201-8228
India—Commerce	381.0954	HF3781-3790			
India—Economic conditions	330.954	HC431-440	Indians of North America—Psychology	155.8497	E98.P95
India—Emigration and immigration	325.(254) or (54)	JV8500-8509	Indians of North America—Religion	299.7	E98.R3
India—History—324 B.C-1000 A.D.	934	DS451-.9	Indians of North America—Social life and customs	390.08997	E98.S7
India—History—324 B.C-1000 A.D.	954.0(2-223)	DS451-.9	Indians of North America—Social life and customs	973.0497	E98.S7
India—History—1000-1765	954.02(23-96)	DS452-462.8	Indians of North America—Wars	973.(1-8)	E81-83.895
India—History—1000-1526	954.02(23-45)	DS457-460	Indians of North America—Wars—1600-1750	973.(1-26)	E82
India—History—British occupation, 1765-1947	954.0(296-4)	DS463-480.83	Indians of North America—Wars—1750-1815	973.(26-53)	E83.(759-813)
India—History—Mysore War, 1790-1792	954.0311	DS474.1	Indians of North America—Wars—1775-1783	975.402	E83.775
India—History—Mysore War, 1799	954.0312	DS475.3	Indians of North America—Wars—1790-1794	973.41	E83.79
India—History—Mutiny, 1809	954.0313	DS475.5	Indians of North America—Wars—1812-1815	973.52	E83.812

Subject Heading	Dewey	LC	Subject Heading	Dewey	LC
Indians of North America—Wars—1815-1875	973.(53-82)	E83.8(17-75)	Indo-European philology—Periodicals	413.028	P501
Indians of North America—Wars—1862-1865	973.7	E83.863	Indo-Iranian languages	491.1	PK
Indians of North America—Wars—1866-1895	973.8(1-7)	E83.866	Indo-Iranian languages	491.1	PK1-9201
Indians of North America—Wars—1868-1869	973.81	E83.869	Indo-Iranian languages—Dictionaries	491.13	PK14
Indians of South America	980.00498	F2229-2290	Indo-Iranian languages—Dictionaries	491.13	PK75-77
Indians of South America—Languages	498	PM5001-7356	Indo-Iranian languages—Grammar	491.15	PK21-41
Indians of the West Indies	972.900497	F1619	Indo-Iranian literature	891.1	PK80-85
Indians of the West Indies—Languages	497	PM5071-5079	Indo-Iranian philology	491.1	PK1-17
Indictments	345.072	K5425	Indo-Iranian philology—Study and teaching	491.1071	PK11-13
Indictments—United States	345.73072	KF9640-9642	Indochina—Maps	912.59	G8000-8198.54
Indigenous peoples	305.8	GN380	Indochina—Religion	294.30959	BQ440-509
Indigestion	616.332	RC827	Indonesia—Census	315.98	HA4601-4610
Indigestion disorders	616.332	RC815.2	Indonesia—Civilization	959.8	DS625
Indirect taxation	336.294	HJ5250-5255	Indonesia—Description and travel	915.9804	DS617-620
Indirect taxation—Law and legislation—United States	343.730526	KF6598-6609	Indonesia—Economic conditions	330.9598	HC446-450
Individualism	141.4	B824	Indonesia—Gazetteers	915.98003	DS614
Individualism	302.54	HM136-146	Indonesia—History	959.8	DS633-644.4
Individualism	323	JC571-605	Indonesia—History—To 1478	959.8012	DS641
Individuality	155.2	BF697-.5	Indonesia—History—1478-1798	959.80(15-21)	DS641.5-642.22
Indo-Aryan languages	491.(2-4)	PK101-2899	Indonesia—History—1798-1942	959.8022	DS643-.22
Indo-Aryan languages, Modern	491.4	PK1501-2845	Indonesia—History—British occupation, 1811-1816	959.8022	DS643
Indo-Aryan languages, Modern—Dialects	491.4(1-9)	PK1550-2899	Indonesia—History—Java War, 1825-1830	959.8022	DS643
Indo-Aryan languages, Modern—Dictionaries	491.13	PK1537	Indonesia—History—Achinese War, 1873-1904	959.8022	DS643
Indo-Aryan languages, Modern—Grammar	491.15	PK1511-1523	Indonesia—History—Japanese occupation, 1942-1945	959.8022	DS643.5
Indo-Aryan philology	491.(2-4)	PK101-119	Indonesia—History—Revolution, 1945-1949	959.8035	DS644
Indo-Aryans	934.02	DS425	Indonesia—History—1950-1966	959.803(5-6)	DS644-.1
Indo-European languages	410	P501-769	Indonesia—History—Coup d'etat, 1965	959.8036	DS644.32
Indo-European languages—Congresses	410.6	P505	Indonesia—History—1966-	959.8036	DS644.4
Indo-European languages—Etymology	412	P721-725	Indonesia—Manufactures	670.9598	TS113.I55
Indo-European languages—Grammar, Comparative	415	P575-769	Indonesia—Maps	912.598	G8070-8074
Indo-European languages—Lexicography	413.028	P761-769	Indonesia—Politics and government	320.9598	JQ760-779
Indo-European languages—Morphology	415	P611-627	Indonesian essays	089.99221	AC168-169
Indo-European languages—Parts of speech	415	P631-663	Indonesian language	499.221	PL5071-5079
Indo-European languages—Phonology	414	P583-610	Indoor games	793	GV1221-1229
Indo-European languages—Syntax	415	P671-675	Indoor gardening	635.965	SB419-.3
			Indoor gardens	635.965	SB419-.3
Indo-European philology	410	P501-769	Induction (Logic)	161	BC80-99
			Induction heating	621.4028	TK4601

Subject Heading	Dewey	LC	Subject Heading	Dewey	LC
Indulgences	264.020866	BX2279-2283	Influence (Psychology)	153.852	BF774
Industrial accidents	363.11	HD7262-.5	Influenza	614.518	RA644.I6
Industrial archaeology	930.1	T37	Influenza	616.203	RC150-.9
Industrial buildings	725.4	NA6396-6589	Information services	025.52	Z674.2-.5
Industrial capacity	338	T58.7-.8	Information technology	303.4833	HC79.I55
Industrial capacity	670.42	T58.7-.8	Information theory	003.54	Q350-390
Industrial districts	333.77	HD1393.5	Infrared astronomy	522.683	QB470
Industrial efficiency	658.515	T58.8	Infrared photography	778.34	TR755
Industrial engineering	670	T55.4-60.8	Infrared radiation—Military applications	623.042	UG487
Industrial engineering—History	670.9	T55.6	Infrared sources	621.362	TA1570
Industrial engineering—Statistical methods	670.21	T57.35	Infrared spectra	535.842	QC457
Industrial engineers	670.92	T56.3	Infrared spectroscopy	535.842	QC457
Industrial hygiene	613.62	RC967	Infrared technology	621.362	TA1570
Industrial hygiene—[By region or country]	613.6209(4-9)	HD7651-7780.8	Inheritance and succession	343.053	K4568
Industrial hygienists	613.62092	RC963	Inheritance and succession	346.052	K805-821
Industrial life insurance	368.362	HG9251-9262	Inheritance and succession—Canada	346.71052	KE806-833
Industrial microbiology	660.62	QR53-.5	Inheritance and succession—England	346.42052	KD1500-1534
Industrial mobilization	355.26	UA18	Inheritance and succession—Ireland	346.415052	KDK360-365
Industrial procurement	658.72	HD39.5	Inheritance and succession—Northern Ireland	346.416052	KDE145-151
Industrial productivity	338.06	HD56-57.5			
Industrial property	346.048	K1500-1578	Inheritance and succession—Scotland	346.411052	KDC462-470
Industrial psychiatry	158.7	RC967.5			
Industrial relations	331	HD6958.5-6976	Inheritance and succession—United States	346.73052	KF753-780
Industrial safety	363.11	T55-.3	Inheritance and transfer tax	336.276	HJ5801-5823
Industrial sociology	306.36	HD6951-6957	Injections	615.6	RM163-176
Industrial toxicology	615.902	RA1229-.5	Injections, Hypodermic	615.6	RM169
Industrialization	338	HD2329	Injunctions	344.01893	K2320
Industries	338	HD2321-4730.9	Ink	667.4	TP946-950
Inequalities (Mathematics)	515.26	QA295	Inland navigation	623.89229	HE617-720
Inertial navigation systems	623.89	VK583.5	Inland navigation	623.89229	TC601-791
Infant baptism	265.12	BV813-.2	Inland navigation—Law and legislation	343.0967	K4182-4194
Infant psychiatry	616.890932	RJ502.5			
Infant psychology	155.422	BF719-720	Inland navigation—[By region or country]	623.89229(4-9)	HE623-720
Infanticide	364.1523	HV6537-6541			
Infantry	356.1	UD	Inland navigation—[By region or country]	627.109(4-9)	TC615-727
Infantry—Equipment	356.118	UD370-375			
Infantry—History	356.109	UD15	Inland navigation—United States	623.8922973	HE623-633
Infantry—Societies, etc.	356.106	UD1			
Infantry drill and tactics	356.1154	UD157-302	Inland navigation—[Other countries]	623.89229(4-9)	HE635-720
Infants	305.232	HQ774			
Infants (Premature)	618.92011	RJ250-.3	Inland waterway vessels	623.82436	VM396
Infants—Care	618.9201	RJ61	Inlets	551.44	GB454.I54
Infants—Care	649.122	RJ101-103	Innate ideas (Philosophy)	121.4	B105.I54
Infants—Development	305.232	HQ774	Inner child	155.2	BF698.35.I55
Infants—Development	612.654	RJ134	Inner cities	307.76	HT156
Infection	616.9	RB153-154	Inorganic acids	546.24	QD167
Infertility	616.692	RC889	Inorganic acids	661.2	TP213-217
Infertility, Female	618.178	RG201-205	Input-output analysis	339.23	HB142
Infertility, Male	616.6921	RC889	Inquiry (Theory of knowledge)	121.6	BD183
Infinite	111.6	BD411			
Infinite	515.24	QA9	Inquisition	272.2	BX1700-1745
Infinite groups	512.3	QA171			
Inflationary universe	523.18	QB991.I54			

Subject Heading	Dewey	LC	Subject Heading	Dewey	LC
Insane, Criminal and dangerous	364.24	HV6133	Inscriptions—South America	411.7098	CN886-888
Insanity	362.2	HV4975-4977	Inscriptions—Spain	411.70946	CN1090-1095
Inscriptions	411.7	CN	Inscriptions—United States	411.70973	CN870-872
Inscriptions, Ancient	411.7	CN120-730	Insect pests	632.7	SB818-945
Inscriptions, Arabic	492.711	PJ7593-7600	Insect rearing	638	SF518
Inscriptions, Aramaic	492.211	PJ5208-5209	Insecticides	632.9517	SB951.5-.54
Inscriptions, Byzantine	487.311	CN455	Insects	398.36957	GR750
Inscriptions, Christian	487.4	CN750-753	Insects	595.7	QL461-599.82
Inscriptions, Etruscan	499.9411	CN479	Insects as carriers of disease	614.432	RA639.5
Inscriptions, Greek	481.1	CN350-455	Insignia	355.14	UC530-535
Inscriptions, Greek	481.1	CN1000-1005	Insignia	359.1342	VC345
Inscriptions, Greek—[By region or country]	481.109(3-9)	CN380-455	Insignia	366.6027	HS159-160
Inscriptions, Greek—Asia	481.1095	CN400	Insignia	929.9	CR4480-4485
Inscriptions, Greek—Crete	481.1094959	CN420	Insomnia	616.84982	RC548-.5
Inscriptions, Greek—Cyprus	481.1095693	CN430	Inspiration	153.3	BF410
Inscriptions, Greek—Egypt	481.10932	CN440-441	Installation (Clergy)	252.7	BV4290
Inscriptions, Greek—Middle East	481.10953	CN440-441	Installment plan	332.743	HG3755.5
Inscriptions, Greek—Turkey	481.109561	CN410-415	Instant photography	770	TR269
Inscriptions, Hebrew	492.411	PJ5034.4-.9	Instinct	591.512	QL781
Inscriptions, Islamic	492.71	CN1153	Institution management	647	TX147
Inscriptions, Japanese	495.611	PL750-751	Institutional care	361.05	HV59-63
Inscriptions, Jewish	492.411	CN745	Instructional materials centers	027.7	LB3044.7-.74
Inscriptions, Korean	495.711	PL969.2-.4	Instrument flying	629.1325214	TL711.B6
Inscriptions, Latin	471	CN510-740	Instrumental music	784	M5-1459
Inscriptions, Semitic	492.0411	PJ3081-3095	Insubordination	355.1334	UB789
Inscriptions—Collectors and collecting	411.7074	CN25-30	Insubordination	359.1334	VB880
Inscriptions—Congresses	411.706	CN15	Insulation (Heat)	621.4024	TH1715-1718
Inscriptions—Dictionaries	411.703	CN70	Insulin	612.34	QP572.I5
Inscriptions—History	411.709	CN55	Insurance	368	HG8011-9999
Inscriptions—Periodicals	411.705	CN1	Insurance, Accident	368.384	HG9301-9343
Inscriptions—Philosophy	411.701	CN40-42	Insurance, Agricultural	368.121	HG9966-9969
Inscriptions—Study and teaching	411.7071	CN50	Insurance, Automobile	368.092	HG9970
Inscriptions—[By region or country]	411.709	CN870-1355	Insurance, Aviation	368.093	HG9972
			Insurance, Burial	368.366	HG9466-9479
Inscriptions—Africa	411.7096	CN1300-1320	Insurance, Business	368.094	HG8059
Inscriptions—Asia	411.7095	CN1150-1230	Insurance, Casualty	368.5	HG9956-9969
Inscriptions—Australia	411.70994	CN1340-1345	Insurance, Child	368.32	HG9271
Inscriptions—Austria	411.709436	CN910-915	Insurance, Disability	368.382	HD7105.2-.25
Inscriptions—Central America	411.709728	CN882-884	Insurance, Disaster	368.122	HG9979
			Insurance, Earthquake	368.1226	HG9981
Inscriptions—China	411.70951	CN1160-1161	Insurance, Fire	368.11	HG9651-9899
Inscriptions—Europe	411.7094	CN900-1130	Insurance, Fire—[By region or country]	368.11009(4-9)	HG9751-9899
Inscriptions—France	411.70944	CN945-948			
Inscriptions—Germany	411.70943	CN950-957	Insurance, Fire—United States	368.1100973	HG9751-9780
Inscriptions—Great Britain	411.70941	CN960-997			
Inscriptions—India	411.70954	CN1170-1175	Insurance, Fire—[Other countries]	368.11009(4-9)	HG9781-9866
Inscriptions—Israel	411.7095694	CN1193-1194			
Inscriptions—Italy	411.70945	CN1010-1015	Insurance, Fire—History	368.11009	HG9660
Inscriptions—Japan	411.70952	CN1180-1181	Insurance, Fire—Law and legislation	346.086	HG9733-9735
Inscriptions—Mexico	411.70972	CN877-878			
Suscriptions—Russia	411.70947	CN1060-1065	Insurance, Fire—Statistics	368.110021	HG9663
			Insurance, Flood	368.1222	HG9983
			Insurance, Government	368.4	HG8205-8220
			Insurance, Group	368.3	HG8058

Subject Heading	Dewey	LC	Subject Heading	Dewey	LC
Insurance, Health	368.382	HG9371-9399	Intelligence tests	153.93	BF431-432.5
Insurance, Hospitalization	368.3827	HG9389	Intelligent control systems	629.89	TJ217.5
Insurance, Inland marine	368.23	HG9903-9905	Intensive care nursing	616.028	RT120.I5
Insurance, Liability	368.5	HG9990	Intensive care units	362.174	RA975.5.I56
Insurance, Life	368.32	HG8751-9271	Intentionality (Philosophy)	128	B105.I56
Insurance, Life—[By region or country]	368.32009(4-9)	HG8941-9200.5	Interactive multimedia	006.7	QA76.76.I59
			Interactive video	006.7	TK6687
Insurance, Life—Law and legislation	346.08632	HG8901-8914	Interactive video	371.334	LB1028.75
			Intercontinental ballistic missiles	358.1754	UG1312.I2
Insurance, Life—Mathematics	368.3200151	HG8779-8793	Intercountry adoption	362.734	HV875.5
Insurance, Malpractice	368.564	HG8053.5-8054.45	Intercropping	631.58	S603.5
			Intercultural communication	303.482	GN345.6
Insurance, Marine	368.22	HE961-971	Intercultural communication	303.482	HM258
Insurance, Marine	368.23	HE961-971			
Insurance, Marine—England	346.420862	KD1845-1847	Interdenominational cooperation	280.042	BV625
Insurance, Maternity	368.424	HG9291-9295	Interest (Psychology)	153.1533	LB1065
Insurance, No-fault automobile	368.5728	HG9970.A4-.A68	Interest (Psychology)	153.1533	BF321.I5
			Interest rates	332.6323	HB531-549
Insurance, Physicians' liability	368.5642	HG8054	Interest rates	332.8	HG1621-1623
			Interface circuits	621.3981	TK7868.I58
Insurance, Products liability	368.562	HG9995	Interfaith marriage	306.843	HQ1031
Insurance, Surety and fidelity	368	HG9997	Interference (Light)	535.47	QC411
			Interferon	571.9644	QR187.5
Insurance, Title	368.88	HG9999	Interferon inducers	571.9644	QR187.5
Insurance, Unemployment	331.2550973	HD7095-7096	Interior architecture	729.24	NA2850-2856
Insurance—[By region or country]	368.9(4-9)	HG8501-8745	Interior decoration	645	TX311-317
			Interior decoration	747	NK1700-3505
Insurance—[Other regions or countries]	368.9(4-9)	HG8550-8740.5	Interior decoration—[By region or country]	747.09(4-9)	NK2000-2096.3
Insurance—United States	368.973	HG8501-8540	Intermediate state	236.4	BT830
Insurance companies	368.0065	HG8075-8107	Internal combustion engines	621.43	TJ751-805
Insurance crimes	364.168	HV6763-6771			
Insurance law	346.086	K1241-1287	Internal medicine	616	RC
Insurance law—Canada	346.71086	KE1141-1220	Internal medicine—Dictionaries	616.003	RC41
Insurance law—England	346.42086	KD1851-1913			
Insurance law—United States	346.73086	KF1146-1238	Internal revenue—United States	336.200973	HJ2361
Insurgency	322.42	JC328.5	Internal revenue law—United States	343.73036	KF6251-6708
Intangible property—England	346.42048	KD1238-1450			
			Internal security—United States	344.7305	KF4850-4856
Integrals	515.4	QA308-311			
Integrals, Generalized	515.4	QA312	International airports	629.136	TL726.15
Integrated logistic support	355.411	U168	International cooperation	327.17	JC362
Integrated optics	621.3693	TA1660	International economic relations	337	HF1351-1532.935
Intellect	153.9	BF431-433			
Intellectual life	306.42	GN451-477.7	International economic relations—[By region or country]	337.(4-9)	HF1451-1647
Intellectual property	346.048	K1401-1578			
Intellectual property—Canada	346.71048	KE2771-2998			
			International finance	332.042	HG3879-4000
Intellectual property—England	346.42048	KD1261-1450	International law	341	K540-5570
			International trade	382	HF1371-1385
Intellectual property—United States	346.73048	KF2971-3193	Internationalism	327.17	JC361-363
			Internet (Computer network)	004.678	TK5105.875.I57
Intellectuals	306.42	HM213			
Intelligence service	359.3432	VB230-250			

Subject Heading	Dewey	LC
Interns (Medicine)	610.695	RA972
Interpersonal communication	158.2	BF637.C45
Interpersonal relations	302	HM132
Interplanetary voyages	629.455	TL789-790
Interpreters (Computer programs)	005.452	QA76.6
Interpreters for the deaf	362.4283	HV2402
Interracial dating	306.73	HQ801.8
Interracial marriage	306.846	HQ1031
Interstate agreements	352.133	JK2441
Interstellar matter	523.1125	QB790-792
Interviewing	158.39	BF761-768
Interviewing in psychiatry	616.8910028	RC480.7
Intestinal absorption	612.38	QP165
Intestines	573.37	QL863
Intestines	611.34	QM345
Intestines	612.33	QP156
Intramural sports	796.042	GV710
Intraocular lenses	617.7524	RE988
Intrauterine contraceptives	613.9435	RG137.3
Intravenous therapy	615.855	RM170-180
Intrenchments	355.44	UG446
Intrenchments	623.1	UG403
Intrusions (Geology)	551.88	QE611-.5
Intuition (Psychology)	153.44	BF315.5
Inuit language	497.12	PM50-64
Inventions	608	T201-339
Inventions—History	609	T15-31
Inventors	609.2	T39-40
Inversions (Geometry)	516.04	QA473
Invertebrates	592	QL360-599
Invertebrates, Fossil	562	QE770-832
Investment clubs	332.6	HG4530
Investments	332.6	HG4501-6051
Investments, Foreign	332.673	HG4538
Investments—[By region or country]	332.609(4-9)	HG4901-5993
Investments—United States	332.60973	HG4905-5131
Investments—[Other countries]	332.609(4-9)	HG5151-5993
Investments—Law and legislation	346.092	K1112-1116
Investments—Law and legislation—Canada	346.71092	KE1060-1089
Investments—Law and legislation—England	346.42092	KD1774-1787
Investments—Law and legislation—United States	346.73092	KF1066-1084
Iodine	546.734	QD181.I1
Ion exchange	541.3723	QD562.I63
Ion rockets	629.4755	TL783.63
Ionian Islands (Greece)	949.55	DF901.I57-.I69
Ionization	530.444	QC701.7-702.7
Ionization	541.3722	QD561-562
Ionization chambers	539.772	QC787.I6
Ionization of gases	530.44	QC702-721
Ionosphere	551.5145	QC881.2.I6
Ions	541.372	QD561-562
Iowa	977.7	F616-630
Iowa—Gazetteers	917.77003	F619
Iowa—History—Civil War, 1861-1865	977.702	E507
Iowa—History—1951-	977.703(3-4)	F625-.42
Iowa—Maps	912.777	G4150-4154
Iowa—National Guard	355.3709777	UA190-199
Iowa—Periodicals	977.7005	F616
Iran	935	DS251-326
Iran	955	DS251-326
Iran Hostage Crisis, 1979-1981	327.730550947	E183.8.I55
Iran—Census	315.5	HA4570.2
Iran—Commerce	381.0955	HF3770.2
Iran—Description and travel	913.504	DS255-259.2
Iran—Description and travel	915.504	DS255-259.2
Iran—Economic conditions	330.955	HC471-480
Iran—Gazetteers	913.5003	DS253
Iran—Gazetteers	915.5003	DS253
Iran—History	935	DS270-318.85
Iran—History	955	DS270-318.85
Iran—History—To 640	935	DS276
Iran—History—Macedonian Conquest, 334-325 B.C.	935.06	D276
Iran—History—640-1500	955.02	DS288-290
Iran—History—640-1256	955.02	DS287.8-288.9
Iran—History—1256-1500	955.02	DS288.95-289.8
Iran—History—16th-18th centuries	955.03	DS292-297
Iran—History—Qajar dynasty, 1794-1925	955.0(4-51)	DS298-316
Iran—History—War with Great Britain, 1856-1857	955.04	DS307.5
Iran—History—1905-1911	955.051	DS313
Iran—History—Paklavi dynasty, 1925-1979	955.05(2-3)	DS316.2-318.7
Iran—History—Mohammed Reza Pahlavi, 1941-1979	955.053	DS318-.7
Iran—History—Revolution, 1979	955.054	DS318.72-.85
Iran—History—1979-	955.054	DS318.72-.85
Iran—Manufactures	670.955	TS107-108
Iran—Maps	912.55	G2255-2259
Iran—Maps	912.55	G7620-7624
Iran—Politics and government	320.955	JQ1780-1789
Iran—Religion	299.155	BL2270-2280
Iranian languages	491.5	PK6001-6996
Iranian languages, Middle	491.53	PK6135
Iranian philology	491.5	PK6001-6996
Iran-Iraq War, 1980-1988	955.0542	DS318.85
Iraq—Antiquities	935	DS69-70.5

Subject Heading	Dewey	LC	Subject Heading	Dewey	LC
Iraq—Census	315.67	HA4569	Iron alloys	669.141	TN756-757
Iraq—Civilization	935	DS70.7	Iron Cross	929.8143	CR5351
Iraq—Civilization	956.7	DS70.7	Iron mines and mining	622.341	TN400-409
Iraq—Commerce	381.09567	HF3770	Iron sculpture	731.2	NB1240.I75
Iraq—Economic conditions	330.9567	HC415.4	Iroquoian languages	497.55	PM1381-1384
Iraq—Gazetteers	913.5003	DS67.8	Iroquois Indians	974.80049755	E99.I7
Iraq—Gazetteers	915.67003	DS67.8	Irrigation	631.587	S612-619
Iraq—History	935	DS70.82-79.66	Irrigation canals and flumes	627.52	TC930-933
Iraq—History	956.7	DS70.82-79.66	Irrigation farming	631.587	S612-619
Iraq—Manufactures	670.9567	TS113.I7	Islam	297	BP
Iraq—Maps	912.567	G2250-2254	Islam	297	BP1-223
Iraq—Maps	912.567	G7610-7614	Islam—Congresses	297.65	BP10-15
Iraq—Politics and government	320.9567	JQ1849	Islam—Dictionaries	297.03	BP40
			Islam—Doctrines	297.2	BP165.5-166.94
Iraq War, 2003	956.70443	DS79.76	Islam—Periodicals	297.05	BP1-9
Ireland—Census	314.15	HA1170.1-.5	Islamic countries—Relations—United States	327.7301767 + 090511	DS35.74.U6
Ireland—Constitutional law	342.415	KDK1200-1350			
Ireland—Description and travel	914.1504	DA969-988			
			Islamic Empire—History—661- 750	956.013	DS38.5
Ireland—Emigration and immigration	325.(2415) or (415)	JV7710-7719	Islamic Empire—History—750- 1258	956.01(3-4)	DS38.6
Ireland—History	936.1	DA900-995	Islamic Empire—History—1258- 1517	956.01(4-5)	DS38.7
Ireland—History	941.5	DA900-995			
Ireland—History—To 1172	936.1	DA930-932.6	Islamic ethics	297.5	BJ1291-1292
Ireland—History—To 1172	941.50(1-2)	DA930-932.6	Islamic law	340.59	BP140-165
Ireland—History—1172-1603	941.50(3-5)	DA933-937.5	Islamic law	340.59	BP140-165
			Islamic preaching	297.37	BP184.25
Ireland—History—17th century	941.506	DA940-946	Islamic religious education	297.77	BP42-48
			Islamic sermons	297.37	BP183.6
Ireland—History—18th century	941.507	DA947-949.5	Islands	551.42	GB471-478
			Islands of the Atlantic—Economic conditions	330.997	HC585-595.5
Ireland—History—19th century	941.5081	DA949.7-958			
			Islands of the Pacific—Economic conditions	330.99(5-6)	HC681-688
Ireland—History—20th century	941.5082	DA959-965			
Ireland—Maps	912.415	G5780-5784	Isolation (Hospital care)	614.45	RA975
Ireland—Periodicals	936.1005	DA900	Isotopes	541.388	QD466.5
Ireland—Periodicals	941.5005	DA900	Israel	933	DS101-151
Ireland—Politics and government	320.9415	JN1405-1571.5	Israel	956.94	DS101-151
			Israel-Arab War, 1948-1949	956.042	DS126.9-.99
Irish language	491.62	PB			
Irish language	491.62	PB1201-1299	Israel-Arab War, 1967	956.046	DS127-.9
Irish language—Etymology	491.622	PB1283-1284	Israel-Arab War, 1973	956.048	DS128.1-.19
Irish language—Grammar	491.625	PB1221-1273	Israel—Census	315.694	HA4560
Irish language—Lexicography	491.623028	PB1287-1295	Israel—Commerce	381.095694	HF3760
			Israel—Description and travel	913.304	DS103-108.5
Irish language—To 1100	491.627	PB1218			
Irish language—Middle Irish, 1100-1550	491.627	PB1218	Israel—Description and travel	915.69404	DS103-108.5
Irish language—Slang	491.627	PB1299	Israel—Economic conditions	330.95694	HC415.25
Irish language—Study and teaching	491.62071	PB1211			
			Israel—History	933	DS114-128.19
Irish literature	891.62	PB1306-1449	Israel—History	956.94	DS114-128.19
Irish literature—To 1100	891.6208001	PB1321	Israel—History—Declaration of Independence, 1948	956.9405	DS126.5
Irish literature—Middle Irish, 1100-1550	891.6208002	PB1322			
Iron	546.621	QE391.I7			

Subject Heading	Dewey	LC	Subject Heading	Dewey	LC
Israel—History—1948-1949	956.94052	DS126.5-126.99	Italy—Commerce	381.0945	HF3581-3590
Israel—Manufactures	670.95694	TS113.I75	Italy—Description and travel	913.704	DG421.5-430.2
Israel—Maps	912.5694	G2235-2239	Italy—Description and travel	914.504	DG421.5-430.2
Israel—Maps	912.5694	G7500-7504	Italy—Directories	945.0025	DG413
Israel—Politics and government	320.95694	JQ1830	Italy—Economic conditions	330.945	HC301-310
Istanbul (Turkey)—History	949.618	DR716-741	Italy—Emigration and immigration	325.(245) or (45)	JV8130-8139
Italian drama	852.09	PQ4133-4160	Italy—Gazetteers	913.7003	DG415
Italian essays	085.1	AC40-45	Italy—Gazetteers	914.5003	DG415
Italian essays	854.09	PQ4183.E8	Italy—Historiography	937.0072	DG465-.7
Italian language	450	PC1001-1977	Italy—Historiography	945.0072	DG465-.7
Italian language—Dialects	457	PC1700-1977	Italy—History	937	DG461-583
Italian language—Dictionaries	453	PC1620-1645	Italy—History	945	DG461-583
Italian language—Etymology	452	PC1571-1580	Italy—History—476-774	945.01	DG503-514.7
Italian language—Grammar	455	PC1099-1400	Italy—History—Gothic War, 535-555	945.02	DG509
Italian language—Lexicography	453.028	PC1620-1693	Italy—History—Carolingian rule, 774-887	945.02	DG515-517
Italian language—Slang	457.09	PC1951-1977	Italy—History—Period of the Italian Kings, 887-962	945.02	DG517.5-518
Italian language—Study and teaching	450.71	PC1065	Italy—History—Germanic rule, 962-1268	945.0(3-4)	DG520-529
Italian letters	856.09	PQ4183.L4	Italy—History—1268-1492	945.0(4-5)	DG530-537.8
Italian literature	850	PQ4001-5999	Italy—History—1492-1870	945.0(5-84)	DG538-551.8
Italian literature—15th century	850.209	PQ4075	Italy—History—16th century	945.0(6-7)	DG539-541.8
Italian literature—16th century	850.409	PQ4079-4080	Italy—History—1789-1815	945.0(7-83)	DG546-549
Italian literature—17th century	850.509	PQ4081-4082	Italy—History—1789-1870	945.0(7-8)	DG550.5-551.8
Italian literature—18th century	850.609	PQ4083-4084	Italy—History—Uprising, 1831	945.083	DG551
Italian literature—19th century	850.709	PQ4085-4086	Italy—History—1849-1870	945.08(3-4)	DG552-554.5
Italian literature—20th century	850.9109	PQ4087	Italy—History—War of 1860-1861	945.083	DG554.5
Italian literature—History and criticism	850.9	PQ4001-4199	Italy—History—1870-1915	945.0(84-91)	DG555-569
Italian literature—Study and teaching	850.71	PQ4013-4023	Italy—History—1914-1945	945.091	DG570-572
Italian periodicals	055.1	PN5241-5250	Italy—History—March on Rome, 1922	945.091	DG571.75
Italian periodicals	055.1	AP37-39	Italy—History—Allied occupation, 1943-1947	945.09(1-24)	DG572
Italian philology	450	PC1001-1977	Italy—History—German occupation, 1943-1945	945.091	DG572
Italian poetry	851.09	PQ4091-4131	Italy—History—Grand Council, 1943	945.091	DG572
Italian prose literature	858.0809	PQ4161-4185	Italy—History—1945-1976	945.09(1-27)	DG577.5-579
Italic languages and dialects	470	PA2420-2915	Italy—History—1976-	945.092(7-9)	DG581-583
Italy	937	DG401-583	Italy—History, Military	355.00945	DG480-484
Italy	945	DG	Italy—Manufactures	670.945	TS79-80
Italy	945	DG401-583	Italy—Maps	912.45	G1983-1989.53
Italy—Biography	920.037	DG463-.8	Italy—Maps	912.45	G6710-6714
Italy—Biography	920.045	DG463-.8	Italy—Periodicals	937.005	DG401
Italy—Census	314.5	HA1361-1379	Italy—Periodicals	945.005	DG401
Italy—Civilization	937	DG441-453	Italy—Politics and government	320.954	JN5201-5690
Italy—Civilization	945.006	DG441-453	Italy—Study and teaching	937.001	DG465.8
Italy—Colonies	325.345	JV2200-2299	Italy—Study and teaching	945.0071	DG465.8

Subject Heading	Dewey	LC	Subject Heading	Dewey	LC
Italy, Central	945.6	DG691-694	Japan—History—Nara period, 710-794	952.01	DS855.7-.73
Italy, Northern	945.(1-3)	DG600-609	Japan—History—Heian period, 794-1185	952.01	DS855.87-856.7
Italy, Southern	945.7	DG819-831	Japan—History—Earlier Nine Years' War, 1051-1062	952.01	DS854
Iwo Jima, Battle of, 1945	940.5426	D767.99.I9
Jacobites	941.10(69-72)	DA813-814
Jaina astrology	133.59444	BF1714.J28
Jaina mantras	294.437	BL1377.3	Japan—History—Later Three Years' War, 1083-1087	952.01	DS856.3
Jaina philosophy	181.044	B162.5
Jainism	294.4	BL1300-1365
Jainism—Doctrines	294.42	BL1356-1375	Japan—History—Kamakura period, 1185-1333	952.021	DS858-861
Jainism—Sacred books	294.482	BL1310-1314.2
Jains	294.4	BL1300-1365	Japan—History—1185-1600	952.02(1-4)	DS856.75-869.6
Jamaica	972.92	F1861-1896
Jamaica—Civilization	972.92	F1874	Japan—History—Jokyu Revolt, 1221	952.021	DS861
Jamaica—Description and travel	917.29204	F1870-1872.2
Jamaica—Gazetteers	917.292003	F1864	Japan—History—Attempted Mongol Invasions, 1274-1281	952.021	DS861
Jamaica—History	972.92	F1878-1887
Jamaica—History—To 1962	972.920(1-5)	F1884-1886	Japan—History—Genko Incident, 1331-1333	952.021	DS861
Jamaica—History—Maroon War, 1795-1796	972.92034	F1884	Japan—History—Kenmu Restoration, 1333-1336	952.02(1-2)	DS863
Jamaica—History—Slave Insurrection, 1831	972.92034	F1886	Japan—History—Muromachi period, 1336-1573	952.02(2-3)	DS863.75-869.6
Jamaica—History—Insurrection, 1865	972.9204	F1886	Japan—History—Period of civil wars, 1480-1603	952.02(3-4)	DS868-869.6
Jamaica—History—1962-	972.9206	F1887
Jamaica—Maps	912.7292	G4960-4964	Japan—History—Tokugawa period, 1600-1868	952.025	DS870-881.84
Jamaica—Periodicals	972.92005	F1861-1896
Jamaica—Politics and government	320.97292	JL630-639	Japan—History—Keicho Peasant Uprising, 1614-1615	952.025	DS871.5
Jameson's Raid, 1895-1896	968.045	DT1889	Japan—History—Ako Vendetta, 1703	952.025	DS871.5
Jansenists	284.84	BX4718.5-4735	Japan—History—19th century	952.025	DS881-.84
Japan	952	DS801-897
Japan—Armed Forces—Management	355.60952	UB105-106	Japan—History—Restoration, 1853-1870	952.025	DS881.2-.84
Japan—Armed Forces—Supplies and stores	355.80952	UC241	Japan—History—1868-	952.0(3-5)	DS881.85-890.3
Japan—History—Meiji period, 1868-1912	952.031	DS881.98-884
Japan—Census	315.2	HA4621-4630	Japan—History—Sakai Incident, 1868	952.025	DS881.4
Japan—Church history	275.2	BR1300-1317
Japan—Civilization	952	DS820.8-827	Japan—History—Civil War, 1868	952.025	DS881.83-.84
Japan—Colonies	325.352	JV5200-5299
Japan—Commerce	381.0952	HF3821-3830	Japan—History—Kobe Incident, 1868	952.031	DS881.4
Japan—Description and travel	915.204	DS807-811	Japan—History—Takehashi Incident, 1878	952.031	DS882.5
Japan—Economic conditions	330.952	HC461-465	Japan—History—Kioizaka Incident, 1878	952.031	DS882.5
Japan—Emigration and immigration	325.(252) or (52)	JV8720-8729	Japan—History—20th century	952.0(31-49)	DS884.5-890.3
Japan—Gazetteers	915.2003	DS805	Japan—History—Taisho period, 1912-1926	952.032	DS885.8-888
Japan—History—To 794	952.01	DS855-.73
Japan—History—To 1185	952.01	DS850-856.72	Japan—History—Showa period, 1926-1989	952.033	DS888.15-890.3
Japan—History—Taika Reform, 645-710	952.01	DS855.6

Subject Heading	Dewey	LC	Subject Heading	Dewey	LC
Japan—History—1926-1945	952.033	DS888.4-.5	Jargon (Terminology)	417.2	P409
Japan—History—March and October Incidents, 1931	952.033	DS888.5	Jason (Greek mythology)	292.13	BL820.A8
			Jaundice	616.3625	RC851
			Jaundice, Neonatal	618.923625	RJ276
Japan—History—May Incident, 1932 (May 15)	952.033	DS888.5	Java man	569.97	GN284.6
			Java Sea, Battle of the, 1942	940.5426	D774.J
Japan—History—February Incident, 1936 (February 26)	952.033	DS888.4-.5	Javanese language	499.222	PL5161-5169
			Javanese literature	899.222	PL5170-5179
Japan—History—1945-	952.0(33-5)	DS888.84-890.3	Jaws	611.716	QM105
Japan—History—Allied occupation, 1945-1952	952.04(4-5)	DS889.16	Jaws	612.92	QP311
			Jazz	781.65	M1366
Japan—History—Heisei period, 1989-	952.0(48-5)	DS890.3	Jealousy	152.48	BF575.J4
			Jehovah's Witnesses	289.92	BX8525-8528
Japan—Manufactures	670.952	TS105-106	Jerusalem	933	DS109-.94
Japan—Maps	912.52	G2355-2359	Jerusalem	956.9442	DS109-.94
Japan—Maps	912.52	G7960-7964	Jerusalem—History	933	DS109.85-.94
Japan—Politics and government	320.952	JQ1600-1699	Jerusalem—History	956.9442	DS109.85-.94
			Jerusalem—History—Siege, 70 A.D.	956.9402	DS122.8
Japan—Religion	299.56	BL2200-2228	Jerusalem—History—Latin Kingdom, 1099-1244	956.944203	D175-195
Japanese drama	895.62008	PL764-769			
Japanese drama	895.62009	PL734-739	Jesus Christ	232	BT198-590
Japanese essays	089.956	AC145-146	Jesus Christ—Biography	232.901	BT300-302
Japanese essays	895.408	PL772-.83	Jesus Christ—Biography—Public life	232.95	BT340-500
Japanese essays	895.6009	PL742-.83			
Japanese fiction	895.63008	PL770-777	Jesus Christ—Character	232.903	BT304-.97
Japanese fiction	895.63009	PL740-747	Jesus Christ—Messiahship	232.1	BT230-245
Japanese language	495.6	PL501-700	Jesus Christ—Miracles	232.955	BT363-367
Japanese language—Dictionaries	495.63	PL674.5-677.6	Jesus Christ—Parables	226.8	BT373-378
			Jesus Christ—Passion	232.96	BT430-470
Japanese language—Grammar	495.65	PL531.3-532.5	Jesus Christ—Person and offices	232.8	BT198-590
Japanese language—To 794	495.67	PL525.2	Jesus Christ—Relics	232.966	BT587
			Jesus Christ—Teachings	232.954	BS2415-2417
Japanese language—Edo period, 1600-1868	495.67	PL525.5	Jesus Christ—Transfiguration	232.956	BT410
Japanese language—Meiji period, 1868-1912	495.67	PL525-.6	Jesus Christ—Words	232	BT306
			Jet lag	616.980213	RC1076.J48
Japanese literature	895.6	PL700-889	Jet stream	551.5183	QC935
Japanese literature	895.608	PL755.12	Jet transports	623.7465	TL685.7
Japanese literature—1185-1600	895.608002	PL790-792	Jewelry	391.7	GT2250-2281
			Jewelry	739.27	NK7300-7695
Japanese literature—Edo period, 1600-1868	895.608003	PL793-799	Jewelry making	739.27	TS740-770
			Jewish cosmology	181.06	B157.C65
Japanese literature—Heian period, 794-1185	895.6108001	PL787-789	Jewish messianic movements	296.336	BM615
Japanese literature—Meiji period, 1868-1912	895.6080042	PL800-820	Jewish periodicals	059.924	AP91-93
			Jewish preaching	296.47	BM730
Japanese literature—Showa period, 1926-1989	895.60800 + (44-5)	PL821-866	Jewish sects	296.8	BM175
			Jewish way of life	296.7	BM723
Japanese literature—To 1185	895.609001	PL726.1185-.1186	Jewish women	305.48696	HQ1172
			Jews	305.8924	GN547
Japanese literature—To 794	895.609001	PL726.12	Jews	933	DS101-151
			Jews	956.94	DS101-151
Japanese poetry	895.61008	PL757-763	Jews—Civilization	933	DS112-113
Japanese poetry	895.61009	PL727-733	Jews—Civilization	956.94	DS112-113
Japanese tea ceremony	394.120952	GT2910-2916			

Subject Heading	Dewey	LC	Subject Heading	Dewey	LC
Jews—Dietary laws	296.73	BM710	Jordan—History—20th century	956.950(3-44)	DS154.5-.55
Jews—Education	296.68	BM70-135	Jordan—History—Intervention, 1958	956.95043	DS154.55
Jews—History—To 1200 B.C.	933.01	DS121	Jordan—Maps	912.5695	G2240-2244
Jews—History—1200-953 B.C.	933.02	DS121.55	Jordan—Maps	912.5695	G7510-7514
Jews—History—To 953 B.C.	933.02	DS121	Jordon—Politics and government	320.95695	JQ1833
Jews—History—953-586 B.C.	933.03	DS121.6	Journalism	070.4	PN4700-5650
Jews—History—Babylonian captivity, 598-515 B.C.	933.03	DS121.65	Journalism—Editing	070.41	PN4778
			Journalism—Exhibitions	070.4074	PN4720
Jews—History—586 B.C.-70 A.D.	933.0(3-5)	DS121	Journalism—Political aspects	070.44932	PN4751
Jews—History—168 B.C.-135 A.D.	933.0(4-5)	DS121.7-.8	Journalism—Social aspects	070.4	PN4749
Jews—History—168 B.C.-135 A.D.	956.9402	DS121.7-.8	Journalism—Study and teaching	070.4071	PN4785-4823
Jews—History—Rebellion, 66-73	933.05	DS122.8	Journalism, Military	359.342	VG500-505
Jews—History—Rebellion, 66-73	956.9402	DS122.8	Journalism, Military—United States	359.3420973	VG503
Jews—History—70-638	956.9402	DS123.5	Judaism	296	BM
Jews—History—Bar Kokhba Rebellion, 132-135	956.9402	DS122.9	Judaism—Congresses	296.67	BM21-30
			Judaism—Customs and practices	296.7	BM650-747
Jews—History—1789-1945	956.940(3-4)	DS124-126	Judaism—Dictionaries	296.03	BM50
			Judaism—Directories	296.025	BM55-65
Jews—Politics and government	320.933	JC67	Judaism—Doctrines	296.3	BM600-603
Jews—Restoration	909.04924	BS649.J5	Judaism—History	296.09	BM150-449
Jew's harp	786.88709	ML1087	Judaism—History—To 70 A.D.	296.09014	BM165-178
Jihad	297.72	BP182	Judaism—History—Medieval and early modern, 425-1789	296.0902	BM180-185
Jitterbug (Dance)	793.33	GV1796.J6			
Job analysis	658.306	HF5549.5.J6	Judaism—History—Modern period, 1750-	296.09033	BM190-199
Job descriptions	658.306	HF5549.5.J613	Judaism—Liturgy	297.38	BM184
Job hunting	650.14	HF5382.7-.75	Judaism—Periodicals	296.05	BM11
Job security	331.2596	HD5708.4-.45	Judaism—Societies, etc.	296.67	BM1
Job stress	158.72	HF5548.85	Judaism—[New Zealand/Australia]	296.099(3 or 4)	BM443-445
Job vacancies	331.124	HD5710.5	Judaism—Afghanistan	296.09581	BM400
Joinery	694.6	TH5662-5663	Judaism—Africa	296.096	BM432-440
Joints	573.78	QL825	Judaism—Arabia	296.0953	BM393-395
Joints	611.72	QM131-142	Judaism—Asia	296.095	BM377-431
Jordan	933	DS153-154.9	Judaism—Austria	296.09436	BM307-309
Jordan	956.95	DS153-154.9	Judaism—Belgium	296.09493	BM310-312
Jordan—Census	315.695	HA4561	Judaism—Bulgaria	296.09499	BM364-366
Jordan—Civilization	933	DS153.4	Judaism—Canada	296.0971	BM227-229
Jordan—Civilization	956.95	DS153.4	Judaism—Central America	296.09728	BM233-247
Jordan—Description and travel	913.304	DS153.2	Judaism—China	296.0951	BM423-425
			Judaism—Denmark	296.09489	BM342-344
Jordan—Description and travel	915.69504	DS153.2	Judaism—Egypt	296.0962	BM434-436
			Judaism—Europe	296.094	BM290-376
			Judaism—Finland	296.094897	BM334-336
Jordan—Economic conditions	330.95695	HC415.26	Judaism—France	296.0944	BM313-315
			Judaism—Germany	296.0943	BM316-318
Jordan—History	933	DS153.7-154.55	Judaism—Great Britain	296.0941	BM292-305
Jordan—History	956.95	DS153.7-154.55	Judaism—Greece	296.09495	BM319-321

Subject Heading	Dewey	LC
Judaism—India	296.0954	BM406-410
Judaism—Iran	296.0955	BM396-398
Judaism—Iraq	296.09567	BM386.4-.6
Judaism—Israel	296.095694	BM390-392
Judaism—Italy	296.0945	BM322-324
Judaism—Japan	296.0952	BM426-428
Judaism—Mexico	296.0972	BM230-232
Judaism—Netherlands	296.09492	BM325-327
Judaism—Norway	296.09481	BM348-350
Judaism—Oceania	296.099(5-6)	BM447-449
Judaism—Palestine	296.095694	BM387-389
Judaism—Poland	296.09438	BM337-339
Judaism—Portugal	296.09469	BM328-330
Judaism—Romania	296.09498	BM370-372
Judaism—Russia	296.0947	BM331-333
Judaism—Scandinavia	296.0948	BM340-353
Judaism—South Africa	296.0968	BM437
Judaism—South America	296.098	BM261-289
Judaism—Spain	296.0946	BM354-356
Judaism—Sweden	296.09485	BM351-353
Judaism—Switzerland	296.09494	BM357-359
Judaism—Syria	296.095691	BM387-389
Judaism—United States	296.0973	BM205-225
Judaism—West Indies	296.09729	BM248-260
Judaism—Yugoslavia	296.094971	BM373-375
Judgment (Logic)	121	BC181
Judgment Day	236.9	BT880-882
Judgment Day (Islam)	297.23	BP166.85
Judgments, Foreign	340.9	K7680
Judgments—United States	347.73077	KF8990-9002
Judicial power	347.012	K3367
Judicial power—United States	347.73012	KF5130
Judicial review	347.012	JF711
Judicial statistics—Canada	347.71013	KE198-206
Judicial statistics—England	347.42013	KD327-332
Judicial statistics—United States	347.73013	KF180-185
Judo	796.8152	GV1114
Junction transistors	621.3815282	TK7871.92
Jungle warfare	355.423	U167.5.J8
Junior colleges	378.1543	LB2328
Junior colleges—United States	378.15430973	LD6501
Junior high schools	373.236	LB1623
Junks	623.810951	VM101
Jupiter (Planet)	523.45	QB384
Jupiter (Planet)	523.45	QB661
Jupiter (Roman deity)	292.2113	BL820.J8
Jurisdiction—United States	347.73051	KF8858-8861
Jury	345.075	K5492
Jury—United States	345.73075	KF9680
Jury—United States	347.730752	KF8971-8984
Justice	320.011	JC578
Justice (Virtue)	241.62	BV4647.J
Justification	234.7	BT763-764.2
Juvenile courts	345.08	K5575-5582
Juvenile delinquency	364.36	HV9051-9230.7
Juvenile delinquency—[By region or country]	364.3609(4-9)	HV9101-9230.7
Juvenile delinquency—United States	364.360973	HV9103-9106
Juvenile delinquency—[Other countries]	364.3609(4-9)	HV9107-9230.7
Juvenile delinquency—Study and teaching	364.36071	HV9068
Juvenile delinquents	364.36	HV9051-9230.7
Kabardian language	499.9624	PK9201.K3
Kabardian literature	899.9624	PK9201.K35-.K39
Kabardians	947.52004	DK34.K13
Kabuki	792.0952	PN2924.5.K3
Kallitype	772.16	TR400
Kalmar War, 1611-1613	948.5034	DL710
Kalmar, Union of, 1397	948.03	DL179
Kalmar, Union of, 1397	948.03	DL485
Kalmar, Union of, 1397	948.5018	DL694
Kalmyks	947.48	DK34.K14
Kannada language	494.814	PL4641-4649
Kansas—Gazetteers	917.81003	F679
Kansas—History	978.1	F676-690
Kansas—History—1854-1861	978.102	F685
Kansas—History—Civil War, 1861-1865	978.1031	E508
Kansas—Maps	912.781	G4200-4204
Kansas—National Guard	355.3709781	UA200-209
Kansas—Periodicals	978.1005	F676
Kaons	539.72162	QC793.5.M42-.M429
Karachay-Balkar language	494.38	PL65.B2
Karaites	296.81	BM185-.4
Karate	796.8153	GV1114.3
Karelian language	494.54	PH501-509
Karen language	495	PL4051-4054
Karma	294.5175	BL2015.K3
Karst	551.447	GB599-609.2
Kashmiri language	491.499	PK7021-7029
Kashmiri literature	891.499	PK7031-7037
Kassr-el-Kebir, Battle of, 1578	946.902	DP614
Kassr-el-Kebir, Battle of, 1578	964.025	DT322
Katyn Forest Massacre, 1940	940.5405	D804.S65
Kayaking	797.1224	GV781-790.3
Kazakhstan	958.45	DK901-909.5
Kearny's Expedition, 1846	973.6242	E405.2
Keewatin—History	971.94	F1106-1110.5
Keewatin—Periodicals	971.94005	F1106.A1
Kelly's Ford (Va.), Battle of, 1863	973.734	E475.3
Kennels	636.70831	SF428

Subject Heading	Dewey	LC	Subject Heading	Dewey	LC
Kentucky—Gazetteers	917.69003	F449	Kinematics	534.5	QC231
Kentucky—History	976.9	F446-460	Kinesiology	613.7	QP303
Kentucky—History—To 1792	976.90(1-2)	F454	Kinetic theory of gases	533.7	QC175-.16
			Kinetic theory of liquids	532.5	QC175.3-.36
Kentucky—History—1792-1865	976.903	F455	Kingdom of God	231.72	BT94
			Kings and rulers	321	JC374-408
Kentucky—History—1865-	976.904	F456-.26	Kings and rulers	352.23	GN492.7
Kentucky—Maps	912.769	G3950-3954	Kings and rulers, Ancient	321.60901	GN495.5
Kentucky—National Guard	355.3709769	UA210-219	Kinship	306.83	GN480-.65
Kentucky—Periodicals	976.9005	F446	Kiribati	996.81	DU615
Kentucky and Virginia resolutions of 1798	973.44	E328	Kiribati—Census	319.681	HA4016.7
			Kiribati—Maps	912.9681	G9480-9484
Kentucky bluegrass	633.21	SB201.K4	Kissing	394	GT2640
Kentucky Derby, Louisville, Ky.	798.400976944	SF357.K4	Kitchens	643.3	TX653-655
			Kites	629.13332	TL759-.7
Kenya—Census	316.762	HA4693	Knitting	746.432	TT819-829
Kenya—Civilization	967.62	DT433.54	Knots and splices	623.8882	VM533
Kenya—Description and travel	916.76204	DT433.527	Knowledge representation (Information theory)	006.332	Q387-.5
Kenya—Economic conditions	330.96762	HC865	Knowledge, Theory of	121	BD143-237
Kenya—Gazetteers	916.762003	DT433.515	Knowledge, Theory of (Religion)	210	BL51
Kenya—History	967.62	DT433.552-.584	Kongo Wars, 1928-1931	967.4103	DT546.37
Kenya—History—To 1963	967.620(1-3)	DT433.565-.577	Koniagmiut Eskimos	979.8004971	E99.E7
Kenya—History—To 1895	967.6201	DT433.565-.567	Koran	297.122	BP100-134
Kenya—History—1895-1963	967.6203	DT433.57-.577	Korea (North)	951.93	DS930-937
			Korea (South)—History—April Revolution, 1960	951.95043	DS922-.42
Kenya—History—1963-	967.6204	DT433.58-.584	Korea (South)—May Revolution, 1961	951.95043	DS922.44
Kenya—Maps	912.6762	G8410-8414			
Keratosis	616.544	RL435	Korea—Census	315.19	HA4630.5-.6
Kerchiefs	687.19	TT657	Korea—Church history	275.19	BR1320-1337
Kerguelen Islands—Census	316.99	HA2309	Korea—Civilization	951.9	DS904
Kerosene	665.5383	TP692.4.K4	Korea—Description and travel	915.1904	DS902.2-.4
Kerosene heaters	697.24	TH7450.5	Korea—Economic conditions	330.9519	HC466-470.2
Kerr black holes	523.8875	QB843.B55			
Kettle Creek (Ga.), Battle of, 1779	973.335	E241.K48	Korea—Gazetteers	915.19003	DS901.8
			Korea—History—To 935	951.901	DS911-.78
Keyboard instruments	786.07	MT180-258	Korea—History—Koryo period, 935-1392	951.901	DS912-.43
Khalsa (Sect)	294.69	BL2018.7.K44			
Khe Sanh, Battle of, 1968	959.704342	DS557.8.K5	Korea—History—Mongolian Invasions, 1231-1270	951.901	DS912.4-.43
Khilji dynasty	954.0234	DS459.2			
Khowar language	491.499	PK7070	Korea—History—Yi dynasty, 1392-1910	951.902	DS913-915.5
Kibbutzim	335.1209694	HX742.2			
Kidnapping	364.154	HV6595-6604	Korea—History—Japanese Invasions, 1592-1598	951.902	DS913-.45
Kidneys	573.496	QL873			
Kidneys	611.61	QM404	Korea—History—Manchu Invasions, 1627-1637	951.902	DS913.615-.675
Kidneys	612.463	QP249			
Kidneys—Diseases	616.61	RC902-918	Korea—History—1864-1910	951.902	DS915-.5
Kidneys—Diseases—Diagnosis	616.61075	RC904-.5			
			Korea—History—20th century	951.90(2-4s)	DS915.56-922.4
Kiev (Ukraine)	947.77	DK508.92-.939			
Kilns	666.43	TP841-842	Korea—History—Japanese occupation, 1910-1945	951.903	DS916.525-.58
Kimonos	391.00952	GT1560			
Kindergarten	372.218	LB1141-1499	Korea—History—1945-	951.904	DS916.6-922.42
Kindness	177.7	BJ1533.K5			
Kinematics	531.112	QA841-842			
Kinematics	532.5	QA913			

Subject Heading	Dewey	LC	Subject Heading	Dewey	LC
Korea—History—Allied occupation, 1945-1948	951.9041	DS917.5-.55	Labor (Obstetrics)—Complications	618.5	RG701-721
Korea—Maps	912.519	G2330-2334.34	Labor, Induced (Obstetrics)	618.4	RG734
Korean Demilitarized Zone (Korea)	951.90422	DS921.7	Labor, Premature	618.397	RG649
Korean drama	895.72008	PL977-979	Labor—[By region or country]	331.09(4-9)	HD8045-8942.5
Korean drama	895.72009	PL962-964	Labor—Afghanistan	331.09581	HD8670.6
Korean fiction	895.73008	PL980-981.5	Labor—Africa	331.096	HD8771-8837
Korean fiction	895.73009	PL965-967	Labor—Australia	331.0994	HD8841-8850
Korean language	495.7	PL901-949	Labor—Benelux countries	331.09492	HD8491-8520.5
Korean language—Dictionaries	495.73	PL935-.6	Labor—Canada	331.0971	HD8101-8110
Korean literature	895.7	PL950-998	Labor—Central America	331.09728	HD8126-8190
Korean poetry	895.71008	PL974-976.4	Labor—China	331.0951	HD8731-8740
Korean poetry	895.71009	PL959-961.4	Labor—Europe	331.094	HD8371-8650.7
Korean War, 1950-1953	951.9042	DS918-921.8	Labor—France	331.0944	HD8421-8440
Korean War, 1950-1953—Aerial operations.	951.904248	DS920.2	Labor—Germany	331.0943	HD8441-8460.5
Korean War, 1950-1953—Armistices	951.90422	DS921.7	Labor—Great Britain	331.0941	HD8381-8400
Korean War, 1950-1953—Atrocities	951.90428	DS920.8-.9	Labor—Greece	331.09495	HD8650.5
Korean War, 1950-1953—Campaigns	951.904242	DS918.2	Labor—India	331.0954	HD8681-8690
			Labor—Iran	331.0955	HD8670.2
Korean War, 1950-1953—History—Prisoners and prisons	951.90427	DS921-.2	Labor—Iraq	331.09567	HD8670
			Labor—Israel	331.095694	HD8660
			Labor—Italy	331.0945	HD8471-8490
Korean War, 1950-1953—Personal narratives, American	951.9042092	DS921.6	Labor—Japan	331.0952	HD8721-8730
			Labor—Mexico	331.0972	HD8111-8120
			Labor—Middle East	331.0956	HD8656-8669
Korean War, 1950-1953—Prisoners and prisons, American	951.90427	DS921	Labor—Philippines	331.09599	HD8711-8720
			Labor—Russia	331.0947	HD8521-8530
			Labor—South America	331.098	HD8251-8370
Korean War, 1950-1953—Search and rescue operations—Korea (North)	951.90428	DS921.5.S4	Labor—Spain	331.0946	HD8581-8590
			Labor—Switzerland	331.09494	HD8601-8610
			Labor—United States	331.0973	HD8051-8085
			Labor—West Indies	331.09729	HD8191-8250
Korea—Politics and government	320.9519	JQ1720-1729.5	Labor contract—Canada	344.710189	KE928-936
Korea—Religion	299.957	BL2230-2240	Labor contract—England	344.4201542	KD1638-1642
Krakow (Poland)	943.86	DK4700-4735	Labor demand	331.123	HD5701-5852
Kristallnacht, 1938	943.086	DS135.G33	Labor laws and legislation	344.01	K1701-1841
Krugerrand (Coin)	737.4968	CJ3948	Labor laws and legislation—England	344.4201	KD3001-3177
Kung fu	796.8159	GV1114.7			
Kuwait—Economic conditions	330.95367	HC415.39	Labor laws and legislation—United States	344.7301	KF3301-3580
Kuwait—Maps	912.5367	G7600-7604	Labor market	331.12	HD5701-5852
Kuwait—Politics and government	320.95367	JQ1848	Labor market—[By region or country]	331.1209(4-9)	HD5723-5851
Kwangju Uprising , Kwangju-si, Korea, 1980	951.95043	DS922.445	Labor market—Afghanistan	331.1209581	HD5812.6
			Labor market—Africa	331.12096	HD5837-5849.3
Kwanzaa	394.26	GT4403	Labor market—Australia	331.120994	HD5850
Kyrgyzstan	958.43	DK911-919.5	Labor market—Benelux countries	331.1209492	HD5785.5-5793.5
Labels—Law and legislation	343.73082	KF1619-1620			
Labels—Law and legislation—Canada	343.71082	KE1616-1618	Labor market—Canada	331.120971	HD5727-5729
			Labor market—Central America	331.1209728	HD5733-5739
Labels—Law and legislation—England	343.42082	KD2208-2209	Labor market—China	331.120951	HD5830
			Labor market—Europe	331.12094	HD5764-5811.84
Labor (Obstetrics)	618.4	RG651-791	Labor market—France	331.120944	HD5773-5776
			Labor market—Germany	331.120943	HD5777-5780.5

Subject Heading	Dewey	LC	Subject Heading	Dewey	LC
Labor market—Great Britain	331.120941	HD5765-5767.5	Lakes	551.482	GB1601-1798.9
			Lakes	578.763	QH98
Labor market—Greece	331.1209495	HD5811.83	Lamanites (Mormon Church)	289.32	BX8627.A3-Z
Labor market—India	331.120954	HD5817-5820			
Labor market—Iran	331.120955	HD5812.56	Lambda calculus	511.35	QA9.5
Labor market—Iraq	331.1209567	HD5812.55	Lambs	636.3	SF376.5
Labor market—Israel	331.12095694	HD5812.2	Laminar flow	532.0525	QA929
Labor market—Italy	331.120945	HD5782-5785	Laminated plastics	668.492	TP1183.L3
Labor market—Japan	331.120952	HD5827	Laminated wood	674.835	TS869
Labor market—Mexico	331.120972	HD5731	Lamps	392.36	GT445
Labor market—Philippines	331.1209599	HD5825	Lances	623.441	U872
Labor market—Russia	331.120947	HD5794-5797	Land banks	332.31	HG2041-2051
Labor market—South America	331.12098	HD5746-5763	Land capability for agriculture	333.76	HD101-1131
Labor market—Spain	331.120946	HD5805-5808	Land capability for agriculture	631.4	S590-599.9
Labor market—Switzerland	331.1209494	HD5810			
Labor market—Turkey	331.1209561	HD5811.93	Land grants—Law and legislation—United States	343.730253	KF5675-5677
Labor market—United States	331.120973	HD5723-5726	Land reform	333.31	HD1332-1333.5
			Land tenure	333.3	HD1241-1339
Labor market—West Indies	331.1209729	HD5740-5745.9	Land tenure—Law and legislation—England	346.420432	KD833-960
Labor movement	331.8	HD4801-4854			
Labor policy	331.12042	HD7795-8013	Land use	333.73	HD101-1131
Labor supply	331.12	HD5701-5852	Land use—Afghanistan	333.7309581	HD860.6
Labor theory of value	335.412	HB206	Land use—Albania	333.73094965	HD810.5
Labor turnover	331.126	HF5549.5.T8	Land use—Algeria	333.730965	HD973
Laboratories	507.2	Q183-.4	Land use—American Samoa	333.73099613	HD1128
Laboratory animals	636.0885	SF405.5-407			
Labors	331	HD4801-8943	Land use—Angola	333.7309673	HD1000
Labrador (Nfld.)—Gazetteers	917.182003	F1135.4	Land use—Anguilla	333.730972973	HD453.2
			Land use—Antigua	333.730972974	HD453.4
Labrador (Nfld.)—History	971.82	F1135-1139	Land use—Arctic regions	333.730998(1-8)	HD1130
Labrador (Nfld.)—Maps	912.7182	G3610-3612	Land use—Argentina	333.730982	HD471-480
Labrador (Nfld.)—Periodicals	971.82005	F1135	Land use—Aruba	333.730972986	HD456.5
			Land use—Australia	333.730994	HD1031-1040
Labyrinth (Ear)	579.89	QL948	Land use—Austria	333.7309436	HD631-640
Labyrinth (Ear)	611.85	QM507	Land use—Azores	333.73094699	HD1028
Labyrinth (Ear)	612.858	QP471-.2	Land use—Bahamas	333.73097296	HD406-410
Labyrinth (Ear)—Diseases	617.882	RF260-275	Land use—Bahrain	333.73095365	HD858
Lace and lace making	746.22	TT800-810	Land use—Bangladesh	333.73095492	HD880.6
Lacquer and lacquering	745.726	NK9900-.7	Land use—Barbados	333.730972981	HD451.5
Lacrimal apparatus—Diseases	617.764	RE201-216	Land use—Belgium	333.7309493	HD691-700
			Land use—Belize	333.73097282	HD336-340
Lacrosse	796.347	GV989	Land use—Benin	333.73096683	HD1012
Lactation	612.664	QP246	Land use—Bermuda Islands	333.73097299	HD1028.3
Lactation disorders	618.71	RG861-866			
Lactose intolerance	616.3998	RC632.L33	Land use—Bhutan	333.73095498	HD880.3
Ladon (Greek mythology)	292.13	BL820.L25	Land use—Bolivia	333.730984	HD481-490
Lagoon ecology	577.63	QH541.5.L27	Land use—Bonaire	333.730972986	HD456.6
Lagoons	551.482	GB2201-2398	Land use—Botswana	333.73096883	HD996
Laity	262.15	BV687	Land use—Brazil	333.730981	HD491-500
Laity—Catholic Church	262.152	BX1920	Land use—Bulgaria	333.7309499	HD811-820
Lake ecology	577.63	QH541.5.L3	Land use—Burkina Faso	333.73096625	HD1018
Lake of the Woods Massacre, 1736	971.018	F1030	Land use—Burma	333.7309591	HD860.7
			Land use—Burundi	333.730967572	HD986
Lake steamers	623.82436	VM460	Land use—Cambodia	333.7309596	HD890.3
Lake-dwellers and lake-dwellings	569.9	GN785-786	Land use—Cameroon	333.73096711	HD1009

Subject Heading	Dewey	LC	Subject Heading	Dewey	LC
Land use—Canada	333.730971	HD311-320	Land use—India	333.730954	HD871-880
Land use—Canary Islands	333.7309649	HD1028.7	Land use—Indonesia	333.7309598	HD891-900
Land use—Cape Verde	333.73096658	HD1028.9	Land use—Iran	333.730955	HD860.2
Land use—Central African Republic	333.73096741	HD1007	Land use—Iraq	333.7309567	HD860
Land use—Chad	333.73096743	HD1008	Land use—Ireland	333.7309415	HD621-630
Land use—Chile	333.730983	HD501-510	Land use—Israel	333.73095694	HD850
Land use—China	333.730951	HD921-930	Land use—Italy	333.730945	HD671-680
Land use—Colombia	333.7309861	HD511-520	Land use—Jamaica	333.73097292	HD431-440
Land use—Comoro Islands	333.7309694	HD1030	Land use—Japan	333.730952	HD911-920
Land use—Congo (Brazzaville)	333.73096724	HD1006	Land use—Jordan	333.73095695	HD851
Land use—Cook Islands	333.73099623	HD1127.5	Land use—Kenya	333.73096762	HD983
Land use—Costa Rica	333.73097286	HD341-350	Land use—Kerguelen Islands	333.7309699	HD1030.7
Land use—Cote d'Ivoire	333.73096668	HD1015	Land use—Kiribati	333.73099681	HD1122.3
Land use—Cuba	333.73097291	HD411-420	Land use—Korea	333.7309519	HD920.5-.6
Land use—Curacao	333.730972986	HD456.7	Land use—Kuwait	333.73095367	HD859
Land use—Cyprus	333.73095693	HD847	Land use—Laos	333.7309594	HD890.4
Land use—Czechoslovakia	333.7309437	HD640.3	Land use—Lebanon	333.73095692	HD849
Land use—Denmark	333.7309489	HD731-740	Land use—Lesotho	333.73096885	HD994
Land use—Djibouti	333.73096771	HD981	Land use—Liberia	333.73096662	HD1025
Land use—Dominica	333.7309729841	HD454.3	Land use—Libya	333.7309612	HD975
Land use—Dominican Republic	333.73097293	HD426-430	Land use—Liechtenstein	333.730943648	HD640.9
Land use—Ecuador	333.7309866	HD521-530	Land use—Luxembourg	333.73094935	HD710.5
Land use—Egypt	333.730962	HD976	Land use—Macao	333.73095126	HD931-935
Land use—El Salvador	333.73097284	HD391-400	Land use—Madagascar	333.7309691	HD989
Land use—England	333.730942	HD601-610	Land use—Madeira Islands	333.73094698	HD1028.5
Land use—Equatorial Guinea	333.73096718	HD1002	Land use—Malawi	333.73096897	HD997
Land use—Ethiopia	333.730963	HD979	Land use—Malaysia	333.7309595	HD890.6
Land use—Falkland Islands	333.7309971	HD1029.5	Land use—Maldives	333.73095495	HD1029.7
Land use—Fiji	333.73099611	HD1126	Land use—Mali	333.73096623	HD1017
Land use—Finland	333.73094897	HD721-725	Land use—Martinique	333.730972982	HD459
Land use—France	333.730944	HD641-650	Land use—Mauritania	333.7309661	HD1020
Land use—French Guiana	333.7309882	HD540.7	Land use—Mauritius	333.73096982	HD1030.3
Land use—French Polynesia	333.7309962	HD1129.5	Land use—Mexico	333.730972	HD321-330
Land use—Gabon	333.73096721	HD1005	Land use—Monaco	333.730944949	HD650.5
Land use—Gambia	333.73096651	HD1024	Land use—Mongolia	333.7309517	HD920.8
Land use—Germany	333.730943	HD651-660.5	Land use—Montserrat	333.730972975	HD453.6
Land use—Ghana	333.7309667	HD1022	Land use—Morocco	333.730964	HD972
Land use—Greece	333.7309495	HD840.5	Land use—Mozambique	333.7309679	HD988
Land use—Greenland	333.7309982	HD1130.5	Land use—Namibia	333.73096881	HD998
Land use—Grenada	333.7309729845	HD454.5	Land use—Nepal	333.73095496	HD860.9
Land use—Guadeloupe	333.730972976	HD458	Land use—Netherlands	333.7309492	HD701-710
Land use—Guam	333.7309967	HD1121.5	Land use—New Caledonia	333.73099597	HD1124
Land use—Guatemala	333.73097281	HD351-360	Land use—New Zealand	333.730993	HD1120.5
Land use—Guinea	333.73096652	HD1016	Land use—Nicaragua	333.73097285	HD371-380
Land use—Guinea Bissau	333.73096657	HD1026	Land use—Niger	333.73096626	HD1014
Land use—Guyana	333.7309881	HD540.3	Land use—Nigeria	333.7309669	HD1021
Land use—Haiti	333.73097294	HD421-425	Land use—Northern Ireland	333.7309416	HD620.5
Land use—History	333.7309	HD113-156	Land use—Norway	333.7309481	HD751-760
Land use—Honduras	333.73097283	HD361-370	Land use—Oman	333.73095353	HD855
Land use—Hong Kong	333.73095125	HD941-945	Land use—Pakistan	333.73095491	HD880.5
Land use—Hungary	333.7309439	HD640.5	Land use—Panama	333.73097287	HD381-385
Land use—Iceland	333.73094912	HD741-750	Land use—Panama Canal Zone	333.730972875	HD386-390
			Land use—Papua New Guinea	333.7309953	HD1122

Subject Heading	Dewey	LC	Subject Heading	Dewey	LC
Land use—Paraguay	333.7309892	HD541-550	Land use—Venezuela	333.730987	HD571-580
Land use—Peru	333.730985	HD551-560	Land use—Vietnam	333.7309597	HD890.5
Land use—Philippines	333.7309599	HD901-910	Land use—Virgin Islands of the United States	333.7309729722	HD450.3
Land use—Poland	333.7309438	HD726-729.5			
Land use—Portugal	333.7309469	HD781-790	Land use—Western Sahara	333.7309648	HD1027
Land use—Puerto Rico	333.73097295	HD441-450	Land use—Yemen	333.7309533	HD854-.5
Land use—Qatar	333.73095363	HD857	Land use—Yugoslavia	333.7309497	HD821-825
Land use—Reunion	333.73096981	HD1030.5	Land use—Zaire	333.73096751	HD1001
Land use—Romania	333.7309498	HD831-840	Land use—Zambia	333.73096894	HD993
Land use—Russia	333.730947	HD711-720	Land use—Zimbabwe	333.7309689	HD992
Land use—Rwanda	333.730967571	HD985	Land, Nationalization of	333.14	HD1301-1339
Land use—Saba (Netherlands Antilles)	333.730972977	HD456.8	Landforms	551.41	GB400-649
			Landing aids (Aeronautics)	629.1351	TL696.L3
Land use—Saint Eustatius (Netherlands Antilles)	333.730972977	HD456.85	Landing operations	355.422	U200
			Landscape	700.42	BH301.L3
Land use—Saint Helena	333.7309973	HD1029	Landscape architecture	712	SB469-476.4
Land use—Saint Kitts and Nevis	333.730972973	HD453.8	Landscape design	712	SB472.45
			Landscape drawing	743.836	NC790-800
Land use—Saint Lucia	333.7309729843	HD454.7	Landscape painting	751.422436	ND2240-2243
Land use—Saint Martin	333.730972977	HD456.9	Landscape painting	758.1	ND1340-1367
Land use—Saint Vincent	333.7309729844	HD454.9	Landscape painting—[By region or country]	758.109(4-9)	ND1351-1367
Land use—Sao Tome and Principe	333.73096715	HD1003	Landscape painting—America	758.109(71-8)	ND1352
Land use—Saudi Arabia	333.7309538	HD853			
Land use—Scotland	333.7309411	HD611-620	Landscape painting—Asia	758.1095	ND1365-.96
Land use—Senegal	333.7309663	HD1019	Landscape painting—Europe	758.1094	ND1353-1364
Land use—Seychelles	333.7309696	HD1029.9			
Land use—Sierra Leone	333.7309664	HD1023	Landscape painting—France	758.10944	ND1356-.6
Land use—Solomon Islands	333.73099593	HD1123			
			Landscape painting—Germany	758.10943	ND1357-.6
Land use—Somalia	333.73096773	HD980			
Land use—South Africa	333.730968	HD991	Landscape painting—Great Britain	758.10941	ND1354-.6
Land use—Spain	333.730946	HD771-780			
Land use—Sri Lanka	333.73095493	HD860.8	Landscape painting—Italy	758.10945	ND1358-.6
Land use—Sudan	333.7309624	HD977	Landscape painting—Spain	758.10946	ND1362-.6
Land use—Surinam	333.7309883	HD540.5	Landscape painting—United States	758.10973	ND1351-.6
Land use—Swaziland	333.73096887	HD995			
Land use—Sweden	333.7309485	HD761-770	Landscape photography	778.936	TR660-.5
Land use—Switzerland	333.7309494	HD791-800	Landslides	551.307	QE599
Land use—Syria	333.73095691	HD848	Language, Universal	401.3	PM8008
Land use—Taiwan	333.730951249	HD936-940	Languages, Artificial	499.99	PM
Land use—Tanzania	333.7309678	HD987	Languages, Artificial	499.99	PM8001-9021
Land use—Thailand	333.7309593	HD890.55	Languages, Secret	417.2	PM9001-9021
Land use—Togo	333.73096681	HD1013	Language acquisition	401.93	P118-.7
Land use—Tonga	333.73099612	HD1127	Language and languages	400	P1-410
Land use—Trinidad and Tobago	333.730972983	HD455	Language and languages—Dictionaries	403	P29
Land use—Tristan da Cunha	333.7309973	HD1029.3	Language and languages—Etymology	412	P321-324.5
Land use—Tunisia	333.7309611	HD974	Language and languages—Grammars	415	P207
Land use—Turkey	333.7309561	HD846.5			
Land use—Uganda	333.73096761	HD984	Language and languages—Periodicals	405	P1-10
Land use—United Arab Emirates	333.73095357	HD856			
			Language and languages—Study and teaching	407.1	P51-59
Land use—United States	333.730973	HD170-279			
Land use—Uruguay	333.7309895	HD561-570	Language arts (Elementary)	372.6	LB1576
Land use—Vanuatu	333.73099595	HD1125	Language disorders	616.855	RC423-428.5

Subject Heading	Dewey	LC	Subject Heading	Dewey	LC
Langue d'oc	449	PC3371-3420	Latin language—Morphology	475	PA2133-2158
Langue d'oc literature	849	PC3381-3420.5	Latin language—Parts of speech	475	PA2161-2281
Lanterns	392.36	GT445	Latin language—Phonology	475	PA2111-2131
Lanterns	398.355	GR950.L4	Latin language—Study and teaching	470.71	PA2061-2067
Laos—Census	315.94	HA4600.4			
Laos—Civilization	959.4	DS555.42	Latin language—Syntax	475	PA2285-2297
Laos—Description and travel	915.9404	DS555.34-.382	Latin literature	870.8001	PA6101-6139
			Latin literature, Medieval and modern	870.900(3-4)	PA8001-8595
Laos—Economic conditions	330.9594	HC443			
Laos—Gazetteers	915.94003	DS555.25	Latin literature—History and criticism	870.9001	PA6001-6098
Laos—History	959.4	DS555.5-86			
Laos—History—1975-	959.4042	DS555.84-.86	Latin philology	470	PA2001-2067
Laos—Maps	912.594	G2374.5-.54	Latin poetry	871.08	PA6121-6135
Laos—Maps	912.594	G8015-8019	Latin poetry	871.09	PA6045-6063
Laos—Politics and government	320.9594	JQ950-959	Latin poetry, Medieval and modern	871.(3-4)08	PA8120-8133
			Latin poetry, Medieval and modern—History and criticism	871.(3-4)09	PA8050-8065
Laparoscopy	618.107545	RG107.5.L34			
Laplace transformation	515.723	QA432			
Lapp language	494.55	PH701-729			
Lapp literature	894.55	PH731-735	Latin prose literature	878.08	PA6138-6139
Lard	664.34	TS1980-1981	Latin prose literature, Medieval and modern	878.08	PA8145-8149
Lard oil	664.34	TP676			
Laryngoscopy	616.2207545	RF514-.5	Latin prose literature, Medieval and modern—History and criticism	878.08	PA8081-8096
Larynx	611.22	QM255			
Larynx	612.2	QP306			
Larynx—Surgery	617.533059	RF516-517	Latin prose literature—History and criticism	878.08	PA6081-6095.5
Lasers	621.366	TA1671-1715			
Last Supper	232.957	BT420	Latitude	526.61	QB231-237
Latent structure analysis	519.535	QA278.6	Latitude	527.1	VK565
Lathes	621.942	TJ1218-1222	Lattice dynamics	530.411	QC176.8.L3
Latin America—Civilization	980	F1408.3-.4	Lattice theory	511.33	QA171.5
Latin America—Description and travel	918.04	F1409-.3	Lattice theory	548.7	QD911-919
			Lattices, Distributive	512.7	QA171.5
Latin America—Gazetteers	918.003	F1406	Latvia	947.96	DK504-.95
Latin America—Periodicals	980.005	F1401	Latvia—Gazetteers	914.796003	DK504.18
Latin drama	872.08	PA6137	Latvia—History	947.96	DK504.37-.79
Latin drama, Medieval and modern	872.(3-4)08	PA8135-8140	Latvia—Maps	912.4796	G7040-7043
			Latvian language	491.93	PG8801-8993
Latin drama, Medieval and modern	872.(3-4)09	PA8073-8079	Latvian literature	891.93	PG8998-9146
			Latvian philology	491.93	PG8801-8993
Latin drama—History and criticism	872.09	PA6067-6075	Launches	623.81	VM340-349
			Launches	797.125	GV835
Latin Empire, 1204-1261	949.504	DF610-629	Laundries	648.1	TT980-999
Latin language	470	PA2001-2995	Lava	552.22	QE461
Latin language, Postclassical	477	PA2300-2309	Law	340-349	K
			Law (Theology)	241.2	BT95-97
Latin language, Preclassical to ca. 100 B.C.	477	PA2510-2519	Law—Dictionaries	340.03	K50-54
			Law—History	340.09	K140-165
Latin language, Vulgar	477	PA2600-2748	Law—Humor	340.0207	K183-184.7
Latin language—Dictionaries	473	PA2361-2390	Law—International unification	341.7	K7051-7054
Latin language—Etymology	472	PA2341-2350	Law—Sources	340.11	K280-286
Latin language—Grammar	475	PA2071-2310	Law—Study and teaching	340.071	K100-103
Latin language—Lexicography	473.028	PA2351-2390	Law—Study and teaching—Canada	349.71071	KE273-322
Latin language—Metrics and rhythmics	871.6	PA2329-2340			

150

Subject Heading	Dewey	LC	Subject Heading	Dewey	LC
Law—Study and teaching—England	349.42071	KD419-452	Law—Germany	349.43	KK
Law, Primitive	340.52	K190-195	Law—Greece	349.495	KKE
Law—Alabama	349.761	KFA0-599	Law—Grenada	349.729845	KGR4000-4499
Law—Alaska	349.798	KFA1200-1799	Law—Guadeloupe	349.72976	KGR5000-5499
Law—Albania	349.4965	KJG	Law—Guatemala	349.7281	KGD
Law—Alberta	349.7123	KEA	Law—Guernsey (Channel Islands)	349.42342	KDG421-440
Law—Anguilla	349.72973	KGJ7000-7499	Law—Haiti	349.7294	KGS
Law—Antigua	349.72974	KGK0-499	Law—Hawaii	349.969	KFH0-599
Law—Argentina	349.82	KHA	Law—Honduras	349.7283	KGE
Law—Arizona	349.791	KFA2400-2999	Law—Hungary	349.439	KKF
Law—Arkansas	349.767	KFA3600-4199	Law—Iceland	349.4912	KKG
Law—Aruba	349.72986	KGK1000-1499	Law—Idaho	349.796	KFI0-599
Law—Austria	349.436	KJJ	Law—Illinois	349.773	KFI1200-1799
Law—Bahamas	349.7296	KGL0-499	Law—Iowa	349.777	KFI4200-4799
Law—Barbados	349.72981	KGL1000-1499	Law—Ireland	349.415	KDK
Law—Belgium	349.493	KJK	Law—Ireland—Dictionaries	349.41503	KDK84
Law—Belize	349.7282	KGA	Law—Isle of Man	349.4279	KDG26-170
Law—Biography	340.092	K170	Law—Italy	349.45	KKH
Law—Bolivia	349.84	KHC	Law—Jamaica	349.7292	KGT0-499
Law—Bonaire	349.72986	KGL2000-2499	Law—Jersey (Channel Islands)	349.42341	KDG220-380
Law—Brazil	349.81	KHD			
Law—British Columbia	349.711	KEB	Law—Kansas	349.781	KFK0-599
Law—British Virgin Islands	349.729725	KGL4000-4499	Law—Kentucky	349.769	KFK1200-1799
Law—Bulgaria	349.499	KJM	Law—Liechtenstein	349.43648	KKJ
Law—California	349.794	KFC0-1199	Law—Louisiana	349.763	KFL0-599
Law—Canada	349.71	KE	Law—Luxembourg	349.4935	KKK0-499
Law—[Canada, By city]	349.71(1-9)	KEZ	Law—Maine	349.741	KFM0-599
Law—Channel Islands	349.4234	KDG	Law—Malta	349.4585	KKK1000-1499
Law—Chile	349.83	KHF	Law—Manitoba	349.7127	KEM
Law—Colorado	349.788	KFC1800-2399	Law—Martinique	349.72982	KGT1000-1499
Law—Columbia	349.861	KHH	Law—Maryland	349.752	KFM1200-1799
Law—Confederate States of America	349.75	KFZ8600-9199	Law—Massachusetts	349.744	KFM2400-2999
Law—Connecticut	349.746	KFC3600-4199	Law—Mexico	349.72	KGF
Law—Costa Rica	349.7286	KGB	Law—Michigan	349.774	KFM4200-4799
Law—Cuba	349.7291	KGN	Law—Minnesota	349.776	KFM5400-5999
Law—Curacao	349.72986	KGP0-499	Law—Mississippi	349.762	KFM6600-7199
Law—Cyprus	349.5645	KJN	Law—Missouri	349.778	KFM7800-8399
Law—Czechoslovakia	349.437	KJP	Law—Monaco	349.44949	KKL
Law—Delaware	349.751	KFD0-599	Law—Montana	349.786	KFM9000-9599
Law—Denmark	349.489	KJR	Law—Montserrat	349.72975	KGT2000-2499
Law—Dominica	349.729841	KGP2000-2499	Law—Nebraska	349.782	KFN0-599
Law—Dominican Republic	349.7293	KGQ	Law—Netherlands	349.492	KKM
Law—Ecuador	349.866	KHK	Law—Netherlands Antilles	349.72986	KGR1000-1499
Law—El Salvador	349.7284	KGC	Law—Nevada	349.793	KFN 600-1199
Law—England	349.42	KD	Law—New Brunswick	349.7151	KEN0-599
Law—England—Dictionaries	349.4203	KD313	Law—New Hampshire	349.742	KFN1200-1799
			Law—New Jersey	349.749	KFN1800-2399
Law—England—History	349.4209	KD530-632	Law—New Mexico	349.789	KFN3600-4199
Law—Falkland Islands	349.9711	KHL	Law—New York (State)	349.747	KFN5000-6199
Law—Finland	349.4897	KJT	Law—Newfoundland	349.718	KEN1200-1799
Law—Florida	349.759	KFF0-599	Law—Nicaragua	349.7285	KGG
Law—France	349.44	KJV	Law—North Carolina	349.756	KFN7400-7999
Law—French Guiana	349.882	KHM	Law—North Dakota	349.784	KFN8600-9199
Law—Georgia	349.758	KFG0-599	Law—Northern Ireland	349.416	KDE
			Law—Norway	349.481	KKN

Subject Heading	Dewey	LC
Law—Nova Scotia	349.716	KEN7400-7999
Law—Ohio	349.771	KFO0-599
Law—Oklahoma	349.766	KFO1200-1799
Law—Ontario	349.713	KEO
Law—Oregon	349.795	KFO2400-2999
Law—Panama	349.7287	KGH
Law—Paraguay	349.892	KHP
Law—Pennsylvania	349.748	KFP0-599
Law—Peru	349.85	KHQ
Law—Poland	349.438	KKP
Law—Portugal	349.469	KKQ
Law—Prince Edward Island	349.717	KEP
Law—Puerto Rico	349.7295	KGV
Law—Quebec	349.714	KEQ
Law—Rhode Island	349.745	KFR0-599
Law—Romania	349.498	KKR
Law—Saba (Netherlands Antilles)	349.72977	KGW0-499
Law—Saint Eustatius (Netherlands Antilles)	349.72977	KGW7000-7499
Law—Saint Kitts and Nevis	349.72973	KGW2000-2499
Law—Saint Lucia	349.729843	KGW3000-3499
Law—Saint Martin	349.72977	KGW8000-8499
Law—Saint Vincent	349.729844	KGW5000-5499
Law—Saskatchewan	349.7124	KES
Law—Scotland	349.411	KDC
Law—Scotland—Dictionaries	349.411003	KDC152
Law—South America	349.8	KH
Law—South Carolina	349.757	KFS1800-2399
Law—South Dakota	349.783	KFS3000-3599
Law—Spain	349.46	KKT
Law—Surinam	349.883	KHS
Law—Sweden	349.485	KKV
Law—Switzerland	349.494	KKW
Law—Tennessee	349.768	KFT0-599
Law—Texas	349.764	KFT1200-1799
Law—Trinidad and Tobago	349.72983	KGX0-499
Law—Turkey	349.561	KKX
Law—United States	349.73	KF
Law—United States—Dictionaries	349.7303	KF156
Law—United States—History	349.7309	KF350-374
Law—United States—Study and teaching	349.73071	KF261-292
numLaw—United States—Territories and possessions	342.730413	KF4635
Law—[United States, By city]	349.7(4-9)	KFX
Law—Uruguay	349.895	KHU
Law—Utah	349.792	KFU0-599
Law—Venezuela	349.87	KHW
Law—Vermont	349.743	KFV0-599
Law—Virgin Islands of the United States	349.729722	KGZ0-499
Law—Virginia	349.755	KFV2400-2999

Subject Heading	Dewey	LC
Law—Wales	349.429	KD9400-9500
Law—Wales—Dictionaries	349.42903	KD9420
Law—Wales—Study and teaching	344.429071	KD9460
Law—Washington	349.797	KFW0-599
Law—Washington, D.C.	349.753	KFD1200-1799
Law—West Indies	349.729	KGJ
Law—West Indies, French	349.72976	KGR3000-3499
Law—West Virginia	349.754	KFW1200-1799
Law—Wisconsin	349.775	KFW2400-2999
Law—Wyoming	349.787	KFW4200-4799
Law—Yugoslavia	349.497	KKZ
Law—Yukon Territory	349.7191	KEY
Law and art—Canada	344.71097	KE3968
Law reporting—United States	348.73041	KF255
Law reports, digests, etc.—Canada	348.71041	KE132-156
Law reports, digests, etc.—England	348.42041	KD187-291
Law reports, digests, etc.—Ireland	348.41504	KDK61-80
Law reports, digests, etc.—Northern Ireland	348.416041	KDE55-60
Law reports, digests, etc.—Wales	348.429041	KD9410-9417
Law School Admission Test	341.0711	KF285
Law schools	340.0711	LC1101-1261
Lawns	635.9647	SB433-.34
Lawyer referral service—United States	340.0973	KF338
Lawyers—Canada	349.71	KE335-355
Lawyers—England	349.42	KD460-472
Lawyers—Ireland	349.415	KDK120-134
Lawyers—Scotland	349.411	KDC225-247
Lawyers—United States	349.73	KF297-338
Laxatives	615.732	RM357
Lay preaching	251	BV4235.L3
Lay readers	262.15	BV677
Layettes	646.4060832	TT637
Le Cateau, Battle of, 1914	940.421	D545.L3
Lead ores	622.344	TN450-459
Leadership	158.4	BF637.L4
Leadership	303.34	HM141
Leadership	355.33041	UB210
Leadership	658.4	HD57.7
Lear jet aircraft	629.133340422	TL686.G
Learned institutions and societies	060	AS
Learned institutions and societies—istory	060.9	AS5
Learning	153.15	LB1060
Learning ability	153.9	LB1134
Learning and scholarship	001.2	AZ
Learning and scholarship—History	001.2090	AZ200-361

Subject Heading	Dewey	LC	Subject Heading	Dewey	LC
Learning and scholarship—History—Medieval, 500-1500	001.20902	AZ321	Lectures and lecturing	080	LC6501-6560.4
Learning and scholarship—Philosophy	001.201	AZ101-111	Leeward Islands (West Indies)	972.97	F2006
Learning and scholarship—Africa	001.2096	AZ800-821	Leeward Islands (West Indies)—Census	317.297	HA866-.9
Learning and scholarship—Asia	001.2095	AZ770-795	Leeward Islands (West Indies)—Maps	912.7297	G5030-5059
Learning and scholarship—Australia	001.2099	AZ850-881	Leeward Islands (West Indies)—Politics and government	320.97297	JL640-649.7
Learning and scholarship—Europe	001.2094	AZ600-765	Left- and right-handedness	152.335	LB1123
Learning and scholarship—Latin America	001.2098	AZ517-588	Leg	573.79	QL950.7
Learning and scholarship—North America	001.2097	AZ501-516	Leg	611.98	QM549
Learning and scholarship—United States	001.20973	AZ503-513	Leg—Abnormalities	616.71043	RD779-789
Learning disabilities	371.9	LC4704-4706	Legal photography	363.24	HV6071
Learning disabled	371.9	LC4818-.53	Legal research—Canada	349.71072	KE250-259
Learning, Psychology of	153.15	BF318-319.5	Legal research—England	349.42072	KD392-400
Learning, Psychology of	153.15	LB1060-1091	Legal research—United States	349.73072	KF240-247
Least squares	511.42	QA275	Legal tender	332.42	HG361-363
Leather	675	TS940-1047	Legends	398.20902	PN683-687
Leatherwork	745.531	NK6200-6210	Legends, Islamic	297.18	BP137-.5
Leatherwork	745.531	TT290	Legislation	328	JF491-619
Leave of absence	331.25763	HD5255-5257.3	Legislation—Canada	328.3771	KE78-125
Leaves	575.57	QK649	Legislation—England	328.3742	KD125-180
Lebanon—Census	315.692	HA4559	Legislation—Ireland	328.37415	KDK38-50
Lebanon—Civilization	939.44	DS80.4	Legislation—Northern Ireland	328.37416	KDE42-50
Lebanon—Civilization	956.92	DS80.4	Legislation—Scotland	328.37411	KDC70-90
Lebanon—Description and travel	913.94404	DS80.2	Legislative bodies	328	JF501-619
Lebanon—Description and travel	915.69204	DS80.2	Legislative bodies—Lower chambers	328.32	JF601-619
Lebanon—Economic conditions	330.95692	HC415.24	Legislative bodies—United States	342.7305	KF4930-5005
Lebanon—Gazetteers	913.944003	DS80.A5	Legislative bodies—Upper chambers	328.31	JF541-549
Lebanon—Gazetteers	915.692003	DS80.A5	Legumes	633.3	SB203-205
Lebanon—History	939.44	DS80.7-87.53	Legumes as food	641.6565	TX558.L4
Lebanon—History	956.92	DS80.7-87.53	Leisure	175	BJ1498
Lebanon—History—635-1516	939.44	DS83	Leisure	790	GV
Lebanon—History—635-1516	956.9203	DS83	Leisure	790.1	GV1-200
Lebanon—History—1516-1918	956.92034	DS84	Lend-lease operations (1941-1945)	940.531	D753.2
Lebanon—History—Civil War, 1975-	956.92044	DS87.5	Lenses	522	QB84.5-135
Lebanon—History—Israeli intervention, 1982-1984	956.92044	DS87.53	Lenses	535.324	QC385
Lebanon—Maps	912.5692	G2225-2229	Lent	263.92	BV85-95
Lebanon—Maps	912.5692	G7470-7474	Leo (Astrology)	133.5266	BF1727.35
Lebanon—Politics and government	320.95692	JQ1828	Leprosy	616.998	RC154-.9
Lectionary preaching	251	BV4235.L43	Leptons (Nuclear physics)	539.7211	QC793.5.L42-.L429
Lecture method in teaching	378.1796	LB2393	Lesbianism	306.7663	HQ75.3-.6
			Lesbianism	616.8583	RC558.5
			Lesotho—Census	316.885	HA4704
			Lesotho—Civilization	968.85	DT2582
			Lesotho—Description and travel	916.88504	DT2572
			Lesotho—Gazetteers	916.885003	DT2554

Subject Heading	Dewey	LC
Lesotho—History	968.85	DT2604-2660
Lesotho—History—To 1966	968.850(1-2)	DT2630-2648
Lesotho—History—1966-	968.8503	DT2652-2660
Lesotho—Maps	912.6885	G8580-8584
Letter writing	395.4	BJ2100-2115
Lettering	745.61	NK3600-3640
Lettering	745.61	TT360
Letters	808.86	PN6130-6140
Letters	809.6	PN4400
Letters, Papal	262.91	BX863
Letters of credit	332.77	HG3745
Leukemia	616.99419	RC643
Levees	627.24	TC337
Levees	627.42	TC533
Levitation	133.92	BF1385
Lexington, Battle of, 1775	973.3311	E241.L6
Libel and slander	364.156	HV6631
Liberalism (Religion)	230.046	BR1615-1617
Liberation theology	230.0464	BT83.57
Liberia—Census	316.662	HA4735
Liberia—Civilization	966.62	DT629
Liberia—Description and travel	916.66204	DT625-627
Liberia—Gazetteers	916.662003	DT623
Liberia—History	966.62	DT630.8-636.53
Liberia—History—To 1847	966.6201	DT633-.3
Liberia—History—1847-1944	966.6202	DT634-.3
Liberia—History—1944-1971	966.62031	DT635-636
Liberia—History—1971-1980	966.62031	DT636.2-.4
Liberia—History—1980-	966.6203(2-3)	DT636.5-.53
Liberia—History—Coup d'etat, 1980	966.62032	DT636.5
Liberia—History—Civil War, 1989-	966.62032	DT636.5
Liberia—Maps	912.6662	G8880-8884
Liberty	323.44	JC585-599
Liberty of conscience	323.442	BV741
Libra (Astrology)	133.5272	BF1727.45
Librarians	020.92	Z720
Librarians	023.2	Z682-.4
Libraries	027	Z662-664
Libraries—Automation	025.3132	Z678.9-.93
Libraries—History	027.009	Z721-871
Library administration	025.1	Z678-.88
Library administrators	023.4	Z682.4.A45
Library catalogs	025.31	Z710
Library consultants	023.2	Z682.4.C65
Library finance	025.11	Z683-.2
Library information networks	021.65	Z674.7-.83
Library legislation—England	344.42092	KD3746
Library legislation—United States	344.73092	KF4315-4319

Subject Heading	Dewey	LC
Library orientation	025.56	Z711.2
Library rules and regulations	025.56	Z704
Library science	020	Z
Library science	020	Z665-720
Library statistics	027.0021	Z683
Library statistics	027.0021	Z711.3
Library use studies	025.58	Z711.3
Librettos	780	ML48-49
Libya	939.74	DT211-239
Libya	961.2	DT211-239
Libya—Census	316.12	HA4685
Libya—Civilization	939.74	DT222
Libya—Civilization	961.2	DT222
Libya—Description and travel	913.97404	DT218-220.2
Libya—Description and travel	916.1204	DT218-220.2
Libya—Economic conditions	330.9612	HC825
Libya—History	939.74	DT223.2-236
Libya—History	961.2	DT223.2-236
Libya—History—To 642	939.74	DT228
Libya—History—642-1551	961.2022	DT229
mLibya—History—1551-1912	961.2024	DT231
Libya—History—1912-1951	961.203	DT235
Libya—History—1951-1969	961.204	DT235.5
Libya—History—1969-	961.2042	DT236
Libya—History—Coup d'etat, 1969	961.2042	DT236
Libya—History—Bombardment, 1986	961.2042	DT236
Libya—Maps	912.612	G8260-8264
Licenses	336.16	HJ5301-5508
Licenses—[By region or country]	336.1609(4-9)	HJ5321-5510
Licenses—United States	336.160973	HJ5321-5374
Lichens	579.7	QK580.7-597.7
Lie algebras	512.482	QA252.3
Lie detectors and detection	363.254	HV8078-.5
Lie groups	512.482	QA387
rin0Liechtenstein	936.3	DB881-898
Liechtenstein	943.648	DB881-898
Liechtenstein—Census	314.3648	HA1210.5
Liechtenstein—Description and travel	913.6304	DB888
Liechtenstein—Description and travel	914.364804	DB888
Liechtenstein—History	936.3	DB891-894
Liechtenstein—History	943.648	DB891-894
Liechtenstein—Maps	912.43648	G6050-6054
Liechtenstein—Periodicals	936.3005	DB881
Liechtenstein—Periodicals	943.648005	DB881

Subject Heading	Dewey	LC
Lieutenant governors—United States	352.2390973	JK2459
Life	113.8	BD430-435
Life (Biology)	570.1	QH325-349
Life (Biology)	570.1	QP81-87
Life-boats	387.29	VK1473
Life-preservers	623.865	VK1477
Life-saving	623.8887	VK1300-1481
Life-saving	797.21	GV838.68-.76
Life-saving apparatus	623.8887	VK1460-1481
Life-saving—[By region or country]	623.888709(4-9)	VK1321-1424
Life-saving—History	623.888709	VK1315
Life on other planets	999	QB54
Life support systems (Space environment)	629.477	TL1500-1575
Ligaments	573.78356	QL827
Ligaments	611.72	QM141
Ligaments	611.72	QM563
Light	535	QC350-467
Light, Colored	615.831	RM835-844
Light, Corpuscular theory of	535.12	QC402
Light, Wave theory of	535.13	QC403
Light—Physiological effect	571.63455	QH651
Light—Physiological effect	615.831	RM838
Light beating spectroscopy	535.843	QC454.L63
Light metals	669.72	TS551-552
Lighthouses	623.8942	VK1000-1246
Lighthouses	627.922	TC375-381
Lighthouses—[By region or country]	623.894209(4-9)	VK1021-1124
Lighthouses—Canada	623.89420971	VK1026-1027
Lighthouses—History	623.894209	VK1015
Lighthouses—United States	623.89420973	VK1023-1025
Lighting	392.36	GT440-445
Lighting	621.32	TH7700-7975
Lighting, Architectural and decorative	729.28	TH7703
Lightning	398.363	GR630
Lightning	551.5632	QC966-.7
Lightning-conductors	693.898	TH9057-9092
Lightning protection	693.898	TH9057-9092
Lightning war	355.422	U167.5.L5
Lightships	623.8943	VK1000-1246
Limanova, Battle of, 1914	940.422	D557.L5
Limbo	235.4	BT850-860
Limericks	808.8175	PN6231.L5
Limited war	355.0215	UA11.5
Lincoln, Abraham, 1809-1865	973.7	E457
Lindy (Dance)	793.33	GV1796.L5
Line geometry	516.183	QA608
Line Islands	996.4	DU650
Line Islands—Maps	912.964	G9530-9534
Line-throwing guns	623.865	VK1481.L55
Line-throwing rockets	623.865	VK1479
Linear accelerators	539.733	QC787.L5
Linear integrated circuits	621.395	TK7874
Linear programming	519.72	T57.74-.79
Linear topological spaces, Ordered	515.73	QA322
Lingerie	687.22	TT669-670
Lingerie industry	338.4739142	HD9948.3
Lingua francas	401.3	PM7801-7895
Linguistic geography	409	P375-381
Linguistic paleontology	417.7	P35
Linguistics	410	P121-143.3
Linguistics, Experimental	417.24	P128.E94
Linguists	410.92	P121-149
Linotype	686.22542	Z253
Lipids	572.57	QP751-752
Lips	573.355	QL857
Lips	611.317	QM306
Liqueurs	663.55	TP611
Liquid crystal displays	621.3815422	TK7872.L56
Liquid fertilizers	631.8	S662-.5
Liquid metal fast breeder reactors	621.4834	TK9203.B7
Liquid propellant rocket—Control systems	629.47522	TL784.C63
Liquidation	658.1	HD2747
Liquids	532	QC141-159
Liquors	663.5	TP589-618
Lisbon (Portugal)	946.9425	DP752-776
Lisbon Expedition, 1589	941.055	DA86.22.D7
Listening	153.68	BF323.L5
Listening	153.733	BF323.L5
Listening (Philosophy)	153.68	B105.L54
Literacy	379.24	LC149-160
Literary agents	070.52	PN163
Literary ethics	174.98	PN154
Literary forgeries and mystifications	098.3	PN171.F6-.F7
Literary movements	809.91	PN597
Literary recreations	790.138	GV1493
Literature	800	PN
Literature, Ancient	809.01	PN611-630
Literature, Medieval	808.8002	PN665-694
Literature, Modern	808.800(3-4)	PN695-779
Literature—Aesthetics	801.93	PN45
Literature—Collections	808	PN6010-6078
Literature—History and criticism	809	PN75-99
Literature—History and criticism	809	PN441-595
Literature—Periodicals	805	PN1-9
Literature—Philosophy	801	PN45
Literature—Societies, etc.	806	PN20-29
Literature—Stories, plots, etc.	808.8024	PN44
Literature—Study and teaching	807.1	PN59-72
Lithographers	763.092	NE2410

Subject Heading	Dewey	LC
Lithography	763	NE2250-2529
Lithography—[By region or country]	763.09(4-9)	NE2301-2396.3
Lithography—19th century	763.09034	NE2297
Lithography—20th century	763.0904	NE2298
Lithography—Catalogs	763.0294	NE2280
Lithography—Exhibitions	763.074	NE2272-2275
Lithography—History	763.09	NE2295-2396.3
Lithuania	947.93	DK505-.95
Lithuania—Gazetteers	914.793003	DK505.18
Lithuania—History	947.93	DK505.37-.79
Lithuanian language	491.92	PG8501-8693
Lithuanian literature	891.92	PG8701-8772
Lithuanian philology	491.92	PG8501-8693
Litter (Trash)	628.44	TD813-870
Little Bighorn, Battle of the, Mont., 1876	978.602	E83.876
Little League baseball	796.357083	GV880.5
Little Red Riding Hood (Tale)	398.245	GR75.L56
Little theater movement	792.02230973	PN2267
Liturgical language	264.02	BX1970
Liturgics	264	BV169-199
Liturgics and Christian union	280.042	BX9.5.L55
Liturgies	264	BV198-199
Liturgies, Early Christian	264.01	BV185
Liver	573.38	QL867
Liver	611.36	QM351
Liver	612.35	QP185
Liver—Diseases	616.362	RC845-848
Liver function tests	616.362075	RC847-.5
Livery	687.16	TT626
Livestock	636	SF1-140
Livestock—Diseases	636.0896	SF600-1100
Livestock brands	636.20812	SF101-103.5
Livestock protection dogs	636.70886	SF428.6
Living room furniture	747.75	NK2117.L5
Livonian language	494.54	PH581-589
Load-line	387.544	VK237
Loans, Personal	332.743	HG3755-3756
Loans—Law and legislation—Canada	346.71073	KE1030-1034
Loans—Law and legislation—England	346.42073	KD1740-1742
Loans—Law and legislation—United States	346.73073	KF1035-1040
Lobbying	328.380973	JK1118
Lobbying	328.38097(4-9)	JK2498
Local area networks (Computer networks)	004.68	TK5105.7-.85
Local church councils	262.5	BV626
Local finance	336.014	HJ9103-9695
Local finance—[By region or country]	336.014(4-9)	HJ9141-9695
Local finance—United States	336.01473	HJ9141-9343
Local finance—[Other countries]	336.014(4-9)	HJ9350-9695
Local finance—Law and legislation	343.03	K4650-4675
Local finance—Law and legislation—England	343.42(1-9)03	KD5710-5752
Local finance—Law and legislation—United States	343.73043	KF6770-6795
Local finance—Periodicals	336.01405	HJ9103
Local government	320.85	JS
Local government—History	352.1409	JS55-67
Local government—Law and legislation—Canada	342.7109	KE4900-4995
Local government—Law and legislation—England	342.4209	KD4746-4840
Local government—Law and legislation—United States	342.7309	KF5300-5332
Local government—Societies, etc.	352.1406	JS42
Local government—Study and teaching	352.14071	JS49
Local government—Africa	351.6	JS7525-7819
Local government—Asia	351.5	JS6950-7520
Local government—Australia	351.94	JS8001-8310
Local government—Austria	351.436	JS4501-4655
Local government—Balkan Peninsula	351.496	JS6899.5-6949.8
Local government—Belgium	351.493	JS6001-6048
Local government—Canada	351.71	JS1701-1800
Local government—Central America	351.728	JS2145-2219
Local government—China	351.51	JS7351-7365
Local government—Denmark	351.489	JS6151-6185
Local government—Europe	351.4	JS3000-6949.8
Local government—France	351.44	JS4801-5250
Local government—Germany	351.43	JS5301-5598
Local government—Great Britain	351.41	JS3001-4295
Local government—Hungary	351.439	JS4661-4696
Local government—India	351.54	JS7001-7090
Local government—Italy	351.45	JS5701-5925
Local government—Japan	351.52	JS7371-7385
Local government—Mexico	351.72	JS2101-2143
Local government—Middle East	351.056	JS7435-7520
Local government—Netherlands	351.492	JS5931-5998
Local government—New Zealand	351.93	JS8331-8399
Local government—Oceania	351.9(5-6)	JS8450-8490

Subject Heading	Dewey	LC	Subject Heading	Dewey	LC
Local government—Philippines	351.599	JS7301-7335	London (England)—History	942.1	DA675-689
Local government—Portugal	351.469	JS6341-6375	Loneliness	155.92	BF575.L7
Local government—Russia	351.47	JS6051-6109	Long distance swimming	797.21	GV838.53.L65
Local government—South America	351.8	JS2300-2778	Long waves (Economics)	338.542	HB3729
Local government—Spain	351.46	JS6301-6335	Long-range weather forecasting	551.6365	QC997
Local government—Sweden	351.485	JS6251-6285	Long-term care facilities	362.16	RA997-999
Local government—Switzerland	351.494	JS6401-6889	Longevity	612.68	QP85
Local government—United States	351.7(4-9)	JS300-1583	Longevity	612.68	RA776.75
Local government—West Indies	351.729	JS1840-2058	Longitude	526.62	QB225-229.5
Local service airlines	387.7	HE9785	Longitude	527.2	VK565-567
Local transit—Law and legislation	343.098	K4080	Looms	677.02854	TS1493
Locks and keys	683.32	TS519-531	Loran	623.8932	VK560-561
Locks and keys	683.32	TH2279	Lord's Supper	264.02036	BX2215-2239
Locks and keys	683.32	TH9735	Lord's Supper	264.03	BX5149.C5
Locksmithing	683.3	TS519-531	Lord's Supper	264.36	BV823-828
Locomotion	612.76	QP301-336	Los Angeles (Calif.)	979.494	F869.L8
Locomotives	625.26	TJ603-695	Loss (Psychology)	155.93	BF575.D35
Log cabins	690.873	TH4840	Loss (Psychology)	155.93	RC455.4.L67
Log cabins	728.73	NA8470	Loss (Psychology) in children	155.93083	BF723.L68
Logarithms	512.922	QA55-59	Lost continents	001.94	GN750-751
Logging	634.98	SD537-538.83	Lotteries	336.17	HG6105-6270.9
Logic	160	BC	Lotteries—Law and legislation—United States	344.730542	KF3992
Logic, Ancient	160	BC25-32	Lotteries—United States	336.170973	HG6126-6134
Logic, Medieval	160	BC34-35	Louisiana	976.3	F366-380
Logic, Modern	160	BC38-39	Louisiana Purchase	973.46	E333
Logic, Symbolic and mathematical	511.3	BC131-135	Louisiana Purchase	976.204	F351-353
Logic, Symbolic and mathematical	511.3	BC131-135	Louisiana—Gazetteers	917.63003	F367
Logic, Symbolic and mathematical	511.3	QA9-10.3	Louisiana—History—To 1803	976.30(1-3)	F372-373
Logic—Congresses	160.6	BC5	Louisiana—History—Revolution, 1775-1783	976.30(2-3)	E263.L
Logic—History	160.9	BC11-39	Louisiana—History—1803-1865	976.30(4-5)	F374
Logic—Methodology	160.1	BC50-57	palphaLouisiana—History—War of 1812	976.304	E359.5.L8
Logic—Periodicals	160.5	BC1	Louisiana—History—Civil War, 1861-1865	976.305	E510
Logic—Study and teaching	160.71	BC59	Louisiana—History—Civil War, 1861-1865	976.305	E565
Logic circuits	621.395	TK7888.4	Louisiana—History—1865-1950	976.306(1-3)	F375
Logic devices	621.395	TK7872.L64	Louisiana—History—1951-	976.306(3-4)	F376-.3
Logic machines	006.3	BC137-138	Louisiana—Maps	912.763	G4010-4014
Logic programming	005.115	QA76.63	Louisiana—National Guard	355.3709763	UA220-229
Logical positivism	146.42	B824.6	Louisiana—Periodicals	976.3005	F366
Logistics	355.411	U168	Love	128.46	BD436
Logistics, Naval	359.411	V179	Love	152.41	BF575.L8
Logos	232.2	BT210	Love	392.4	GT2600-2640
Logs (Nautical instruments)	623.890284	VK581	Low German drama	839.42008	PT4837-4838
Lollards	284.3	BX4900-4906	Low German drama	839.4209	PT4821
Lombards	304.8	D145	Low German language	439.4	PF5601-5844
Lombards	945.01	DG511-514.7	Low German literature	839.4	PT4801-4897
Lombardy (Italy)	945.2	DG651-664.5			

Subject Heading	Dewey	LC	Subject Heading	Dewey	LC
Low German literature—Study and teaching	839.4071	PT4803	Luxembourg—Description and travel	914.93504	DH906-907
Low German literature—To 1500	839.4109	PT4813	Luxembourg—Economic conditions	330.94935	HC330
Low German poetry	839.41008	PT4834-4836	Luxembourg—Emigration and immigration	325.(24935) or (4935)	JV8175
Low German poetry	839.4109	PT4817-4820	Luxembourg—Gazetteers	914.935003	DH903
Low impact aerobic exercises	613.71	RA781.15	Luxembourg—History	949.35	DH908-918.5
Low power television	384.55	HE8700.7-.72	Luxembourg—Periodicals	949.35005	DH901
Low temperature engineering	621.56	TP480-482	Luxembourg—Maps	912.4935	G6020-6024
Low temperature research	536.56072	QC277.9-278.6	Luxembourg (Luxembourg)—History— Siege, 1684	949.3502	DH913
Low temperature research	541.3686072	QD536	Luxuries—Taxation	336.271	HJ5771-5797
Low vision	617.712	RE91	Lying down position	394.12	GT2995
Low-calorie diet	613.25	RM222.2	Lymphatics	573.16	QL841
Low-carbohydrate diet	613.283	RM237.73	Lymphatics	611.42	QM197
Low-Cholesterol diet	613.284	RM237.75	Lymphatics	612.42	QP115
Low-fat diet	613.284	RM237.7	Lymphocytic leukemia	616.99419	RC643
LSD (Drug)	154.4	BF209.L9	Lynchburg (Va.), Battle of, 1864	973.736	E476.65
LSD (Drug)	362.294	HV5822.5.L9	Lynching	364.134	HV6455-6471
LSD (Drug)	615.788	RM666.L88	Lyric poetry	808.14	PN1351-1389
Lubrication and lubricants	621.89	TJ1075-1081	Lyric poetry	808.814	PN691
Lucid dreams	154.63	BF1099.L82	M1 (Tank)	358.1883	UG446.5
Luddites	941.073	DA535	M1 carbine	356.1182425 + 0973	UD395.M17
Lumber	674	TS800-915	Macadamia nut	634.5	SB401.M32
Lumbering	634.98	SD538-557	Macao—Census	315.126	HA4641-4645
Luminescence	535.35	QC476.4-480.2	Macao—Maps	912.5126	G7945-7947
Lunar eclipses	523.38	QB579	Macedonia	949.76	DR2152-2285
Lunar geology	523.3	QB592	Macedonia—History	949.76	DR701.M13-.M14
Lunar soil	523.3	QB592	Macedonia—History—To 168 B.C.	938.0(1-8)	DF233-238
Lunar surface vehicles	629.295	TL480	Macedonia—Karpos Uprising, 1689	949.98	DR2211
Lunar theory	523.3	QB391-399	Macedonian language	491.819	PG1161-1164
Luncheons	641.53	TX735	Macedonian War, 1st, 215-205 B.C.	937.04	DG251
Lungs	573.22	QL848	Macedonian War, 2nd, 200-196 B.C.	937.04	DG251
Lungs	611.24	QM261	Macedonian War, 3rd, 171-168 B.C.	937.04	DG251.6
Lungs	612.2	QP121-125	Machine design	621.815	TJ227-240
Lungs—Cancer	616.99424	RC280.L8	Machine learning	006.31	Q325.5-.78
Lungs-Diseases	616.24	RC756-776	Machine sewing	646.2044	TT713
Lute music	787.83	M140-141	Machine theory	511.35	QA267-268.5
Lutheran Church	284.1	BX8001-8080	Machine translating	418.020285	P307-310
Lutheran Church—Clergy	262.041	BX8071-.2	Machine-guns	358.1282	UF620
Lutheran Church—History	284.109	BX8018-8063	Machine-guns	359.82424	VF410
Lutheran Church—Liturgy	264.041	BX8067	Machine-readable bibliographic data	025.3132	Z699-.5
Lutheran Church—Periodicals	284.104	BX8001	Machine-tools	621.902	TJ1180-1313
Lutheran Church—Sermons	252.041	BX8066	Machinery	621.8	TJ
Lutheran Church—Europe	284.14	BX8020-8040.5	Machinery—Testing	621.80287	TJ148
Lutheran Church—Germany	284.143	BX8020-8023	Machinery—Vibration	621.81	TJ177
Lutheran Church—United States	284.173	BX8041-8061	Machinery industry	338.476218	HD9705-9705.5
Lutherans—Biography	284.1092	BX8079-8080			
Luxembourg	949.35	DH901-925			
Luxembourg—Biography	920.04935	DH904			
Luxembourg—Census	314.935	HA1411-1420			

Subject Heading	Dewey	LC
Macro processors	005.45	QA76.6
Madagascar—Census	316.91	HA4699
Madagascar—Civilization	969.1	DT469.M274
Madagascar—Economic conditions	330.9691	HC895
Madagascar—Gazetteers	916.91003	DT469.M24
Madagascar—History	969.1	DT469.M282-.M345
Madagascar—History—To 1810	969.101	DT469.M31-.M313
Madagascar—History—Hova rule, 1810-1885	969.101	DT469.M32-.M335
Madagascar—History—1885-1960	969.10(1-3)	DT469.M34-.M342
Madagascar—History—Menalamba Rebellion, 1895-1899	969.103	DT469.M34
Madagascar—History—French Invasion, 1895	969.103	DT469.M34
Madagascar—History—Revolution, 1947	969.103	DT469.M34
Madagascar—Maps	912.691	G8460-8464
Madeira Islands—Census	314.698	HA2285
Madeira Islands—Maps	912.4698	G9140-9144
Madeira wine	663.223	TP559.P8
Madrid (Spain)	946.41	DP350-374
Madrigals	782.43	PR1195.M2
Mafia	364.106	HV6441-6453
Magahi language	491.454	PK1821-1824
Magazine design	686.2252	Z253.5
Magi	232.923	BT315
Magic	133.43	BF1585-1623
Magic	133.43	GN475.3
Magic	203	GN475.3
Magic squares	511.64	QA165
Magicians	793.8092	GV1545
Magnanimity	241.4	BV4647.M2
Magnet schools	373.241	LB2818
Magnetic bubble devices	621.39763	TK7872.M25
Magnetic healing	615.8454	RZ422
Magnetic induction	538.4	QC754.2.M33
Magnetic levitation vehicles	625.4	TF1600
Magnetic measurements	538.0287	QC761
Magnetic measurements	538.0287	QC818-849
Magnetic recorders and recording	621.38932	TK7881.6
Magnetic resonance imaging	616.07548	RC78.7.N83
Magnetic separation of ores	622.77	TN530
Magnetic storms	538.744	QC835
Magnetic tapes	621.38234	TK5984
Magnetism	538	QC750-776
Magnetohydrodynamics	538.6	QC718.5.M36
Magnetohydrodynamics	538.6	QC809.M3
Magnetosphere	538.766	QC809.M35
Magnetospheric radio wave propagation	551.514	QC973.4.M33
Magnetrons	621.381334	TK7871.75
Magnets	538.4	QC757
Magyars	943.900494511	DB919
Mah jong	795.34	GV1299.M3
Maharashtri language	491.1	PK1231-1239
Mahayana Buddhism	294.392	BQ7300-7522
Mahican Indians	974.70049734	E99.M12
Mail receiving and forwarding services	383.1	HE5999
Mail-order business	381.142	HF5465.5-5467
Maine—Gazetteers	917.41003	F17
Maine—History	974.1	F16-30
Maine—History—Colonial period, ca. 1600-1775	974.10(1-2)	F23
Maine—History—King William's War, 1689-1697	974.102	F23
Maine—History—King George's War, 1744-1748	974.102	F23
Maine—History—1775-1865	974.10(1-3)	F24
Maine—History—War of 1812	974.103	F24
Maine—Maps	912.741	G3730-3734
Maine—National Guard	355.3709741	UA230-239
Maine—Periodicals	974.1005	F16
Maitreya (Buddhist deity)	294.34211	BQ4690.M3
Maiya language	491.499	PK7045.M3
Majorities	324.63	JF1051-1075
Malabsorption syndromes	616.399	RC862.M3
Malaria	614.532	RA644.M2
Malaria	616.936	RC156-166
Malawi—Census	316.897	HA4707
Malawi—Civilization	968.97	DT3187
Malawi—Description and travel	916.89704	DT3182
Malawi—Gazetteers	916.897003	DT3169
Malawi—History	968.97	DT3194-3237
Malawi—History—To 1891	968.9701	DT3211-3214
Malawi—History—1891-1953	968.9702	DT3216-3225
Malawi—History—Chilembwe Rebellion, 1915	968.9702	DT3225
Malawi—History—1953-1964	968.9703	DT3227-3230
Malawi—History—1964-	968.9704	DT3232-3240
Malawi—Maps	912.6897	G8610-8614
Malay language	499.28	PL5101-5129
Malaya—History	959.5	DS595.8-597.21
Malaya—History—Japanese occupation, 1942-1945	959.503	DS596.6
Malaya—History—Malayan Emergency, 1948-1960	959.504	DS597
Malayalam language	494.812	PL4711-4719

Subject Heading	Dewey	LC	Subject Heading	Dewey	LC
Malaysia—Census	315.95	HA4600.6	Manchuria (China)	951.8	DS781-784.2
Malaysia—Civilization	959.5	DS594	Manchus	951.03	DS753.82-773.6
Malaysia—Description and travel	915.9504	DS592.4-.6	Manchus	951.8	DS781-784.2
			Mandailing dialect	492.37	PJ5401
Malaysia—Gazetteers	915.95003	DS591.5	Mandarin dialects	495.1	PL1891-1900
Malaysia—Maps	912.595	G8030-8034	Mandates	940.31426	D650.T4-651
Maldives—Census	315.495	HA2300	Mandolin music	787.84	M130-134
Maldives—Maps	912.5495	G9215-9219	Manic-depressive psychoses	616.895	RC516
Mali—Census	316.623	HA4727			
Mali—Civilization	966.23	DT551.4	Manicuring	646.727	RL94
Mali—Description and travel	916.62304	DT551.27	Manila Bay, Battle of, 1898	973.895	E717.7
Mali—Gazetteers	916.623003	DT551.15	Manipulation (Therapeutics)	615.82	RD736.M25
Mali—History	966.23	DT551.5-.82			
Mali—History—Coup d'etat, 1968	966.23051	DT551.8	Manipulation (Therapeutics)	615.82	RM724
Mali—Maps	912.6623	G8800-8804	Manitoba—Gazetteers	917.127003	F1061.4
Malnutrition	614.5939	RA645.N87	Manitoba—History	971.27	F1061-1065
Malnutrition	616.39	RC623	Manitoba—Maps	912.7127	G3480-3484
Malnutrition in children	618.9239	RJ399.M26	Manitoba—Periodicals	971.27005	F1061
Malnutrition in pregnancy	618.3	RG580.M34	Manna	222.12	BS1245
Malocclusion	617.643	RK523	Manned undersea research stations	551.46072	GC66
Malta	945.85	DG987-999			
Malta—History	945.85	DG989.8-994.8	Manners and customs	390	GT
Mammal pests	632.69	SB993.5-994	Manpower	355.22	UA17.5
Mammal populations	599.1788	QL708.6	Manpower planning	658.301	HF5549.5.M3
Mammals	599	QL700-739.8	Manual training	372.5	LB1595-1599
Mammals, Fossil	569	QE881-882	Manual training	373.246	TT161-170.7
Mammaplasty	618.19059	RD539.8	Manufactures	338.4767	HD9720-9739
Mammary glands	573.679	QL944	Manufactures	670	TS
Mammary glands	611.49	QM495	Manures	631.861	S655
Mammary glands	612.664	QP188.M3	Manus (Hindu mythology)	294.513	BL1225.M
Man (Christian theology)	233	BT700-745	Manuscripts, Greek (Papyri)	091.09495	PA3301-3371
Man (Hinduism)	294.522	BL1215.M3	Man-woman relationships	306.7	HQ801-.83
Man (Islam)	297.22	BP166.7	Manx language	491.64	PB1801-1847
Man (Theology)	202.22	BL256	Manx literature	891.64	PB1851-1867
Man (Theology)	233	BS661	Many-body problem	521.4	QB362.M3
Man (Theology)	233	BT700-745	Many-body problem	530.144	QC174.17.P7
Man, Prehistoric	569.9	GN700-890	Maori language	499.442	PL6465
Man, Primitive	569.9	GN307-499	Map drawing	526	GA130
Man—Influence of climate	304.25	GF71	Map projection	526.8	GA110-115
Man—Influence of environment	155.9	BF353-.5	Maps	912	G3200-9980
			Maps, Military	355.47	UA985-997
Man—Influence of environment	304.2	GE51-71	Maps, Military	623.71	UG470-474
			Maps, Statistical	310.0223	GA109.8
Man—Migrations	304.8	GN370	Maratha War, 1775-1782	954.0298	DS473
Man—Origin	599.938	GN281-.4	Maratha War, 1816-1818	954.0313	DS475.6
Man-machine systems	621.3984	TA167	Marathi language	491.46	PK2351-2378
Managed care plans (Medical care)	362.104258	RA413-.5	Marathon running	796.4252	GV1065-.23
			Marathon, Battle of, 490 B.C.	938.03	DF225.4
Management	658	HD28-70			
Management—Employee participation	331.0112	HD5650-5660	Marble sculpture	731.2	NB1218
			Marble sculpture, Ancient	732.2	NB69-169
Management science	658	T55.4-60.8	Marble sculpture, Classical	733.3	NB144
Managerial accounting	658.1511	HF5657.4	Marbles (Game)	796.2	GV1213
Managerial economics	338.068	HD30.22	Marches (Band)	784.1897	M1247
Manchu language	494.1	PL471-479	Marches (Band)	784.1897	M1260

Subject Heading	Dewey	LC	Subject Heading	Dewey	LC
Marching	356.114	UD310-315	Marines—Firearms	359.96824	VE350-390
Marching bands	784.8307	MT733.4	Marines—Handbooks, manuals, etc.	359.9633	VE150-155
Marduk (Babylonian deity)	299.21	BL1625.M37	Marines—History	359.9609	VE15
Margarine	664.32	TP684.M3	Marines—Insigna	359.961342	VE345
Marginal utility	330.157	HB201-205	Marines—Uniforms	359.9614	VE400-405
Mari language	494.56	PH801-807	Marines—[By region or country]	359.96309(4-9)	VE21-124
Mariana Islands	996.7	DU640-648			
Mariana Islands—Maps	912.967	G9410-9414	Marines—Africa	359.963096	VE115-119
Mariculture	639.8	SH138	Marines—Asia	359.963095	VE99-113
Marie Galante	972.976	F2076	Marines—Australia	359.9630994	VE121-122
Marihuana	362.295	HV5822.M3	Marines—Canada	359.9630971	VE26-27
Marimba music	786.843	M175.X6	Marines—Central America	359.96309728	VE30-31
Marinas	387.15	VK369-.8	Marines—Europe	359.963094	VE55-96
Marinas	627.38	TC328	Marines—France	359.9630944	VE71-72
Marine algae as feed	636.0855	SF99.M33	Marines—Germany	359.9630943	VE73-74.5
Marine algae as fertilizer	631.87	S661.2.M3	Marines—Great Britain	359.9630941	VE57-64
Marine aquariums	597.177073	SF457.1	Marines—Italy	359.9630945	VE79-80
Marine aquariums, Public	597.073	QL78.5	Marines—Japan	359.9630952	VE105-106
Marine biology	578.77	QH91-95.59	Marines—Mexico	359.9630972	VE28-29
Marine biology—Antarctic Ocean	578.777	QH95.58	Marines—New Zealand	359.9630993	VE122.5
Marine biology—Atlantic Ocean	578.773	QH92-93.9	Marines—Russia	359.9630947	VE85-86
			Marines—Scandinavia	359.9630948	VE86.5
Marine biology—Indian Ocean	578.775	QH94-.7	Marines—South America	359.963098	VE34-54
			Marines—Spain	359.9630946	VE87-88
Marine biology—Pacific Ocean	578.774	QH95-.55	Marines—West Indies	359.96309729	VE32-33
			Marital psychotherapy	616.89156	RC488.5-.6
Marine compressors	623.8501	VM821	Marital status—[By region or country]	306.8109	HB1121-1317
Marine diesel motors	623.87236	VM770			
Marine engineering	623.87	VM595-989	Marital status—United States	306.810973	HB1125-1126
Marine engineering—[By region or country]	623.809(4-9)	VM621-724			
			Marital status—[United States, By city]	306.81097(4-9)	HB1147
Marine engineering—History	623.809	VM615-619	Marital status—[United States, By state]	306.81097(4-9)	HB1145
Marine engineering—Study and teaching	623.8071	VM725-728			
			Marital status—Statistics	306.81021	HB1111-1317
Marine engines	623.87	VM731-779	Maritime Provinces—History	971.5	F1035.8
Marine laboratories	578.77072	QH91.6-.65			
Marine meteorology	551.65162	QC993.83-994.9	Maritime Provinces—Maps	912.715	G3410-3444
Marine microbiology	579.177	QR106-.5	Market surveys	658.83	HF5415.3
Marine mineral resources	333.8509162	TN264	Marketing	381.1	HF5410-5417.5
Marine nuclear reactor plants	623.8728	VM774-777	Marketing (Home economics)	641.31	TX356
Marine painting	751.422437	ND2270-2272	Marketing research	658.83	HF5415.2-.34
Marine painting	758.2	ND1370-1375	Markets	381.18	HF5469.7-5481
Marine parks and reserves	578.77	QH91.75	Markov processes	519.233	QA274.7-.76
Marine photography	778.937	TR670-.5	Marlin spike seamanship	623.88	VM531-533
Marine pollution	363.7394	GC1080-1581	Marquesas Islands	996.31	DU700-701
Marine refrigeration	623.8535	VM485	Marquesas Islands—Maps	912.9631	G9620-9624
Marine resources	333.9164	GC1000-1023	Marriage	265.5	BV835-838
Marine resources conservation	333.916416	GC1018	Marriage	306.81	GN480
			Marriage	306.81	HQ
Marine sediments	551.4686	GC380-399	Marriage	306.81	HQ503-1064
Marine steel	623.81821	VM146	Marriage	392.5	GR465
Marines	359.96	VE	Marriage—History	306.8109	HQ503-518
Marines—Barracks and quarters	359.9671	VE420-425	Marriage, Companionate	306.84	HQ803
			Marriage—History	306.8109	HQ503-518

Subject Heading	Dewey	LC	Subject Heading	Dewey	LC
Marriage—[By region or country]	306.8109(4-9)	HQ531-727.9	Martinique—Politics and government	320.972982	JL830-839
Marriage—Africa	306.81096	HQ691-697.4	Martinis	641.874	TX951
Marriage—Asia	306.81095	HQ663-690.5	Martyrs—Legends	282.0922	BX4654-4662
Marriage—Australia	306.810994	HQ705-706	Marxian economics	335.4	HB97.5
Marriage—Benelux Countries	306.8109492	HQ631-636.5	Mary, Blessed Virgin, Saint	232.91	BT595-680
Marriage—Canada	306.810971	HQ559-560	Mary, Blessed Virgin, Saint—Apparitions and miracles	232.917	BT650-654
Marriage—Central America	306.8109728	HQ563-574			
Marriage—China	306.810951	HQ684	Mary, Blessed Virgin, Saint—Theology	232.91	BT610-660
Marriage—Europe	306.81094	HQ611-662.7			
Marriage—France	306.810944	HQ623-624	Maryland Campaign, 1862	973.7336	E474.61
Marriage—Germany	306.810943	HQ625-626.5	Maryland Campaign, 1864	973.737	E476.66
Marriage—Great Britain	306.810941	HQ613-618.5	Maryland—Gazetteers	917.52003	F179
Marriage—Greece	306.8109495	HQ662.5	Maryland—History	975.2	F176-190
Marriage—India	306.810954	HQ669-670	Maryland—History—Colonial period, ca. 1600-1775	975.20(1-2)	F184
Marriage—Iran	306.810955	HQ666.4			
Marriage—Iraq	306.8109567	HQ666.3	Maryland—History—Revolution, 1775-1783	975.20(2-3)	E263.M3
Marriage—Israel	306.81095694	HQ664			
Marriage—Italy	306.810945	HQ629-630	Maryland—History—War of 1812	975.203	E359.5.M2
Marriage—Japan	306.810952	HQ681-682			
Marriage—Mexico	306.810972	HQ561-562	Maryland—Maps	912.752	G3840-3844
Marriage—Philippines	306.8109599	HQ679-680	Maryland—National Guard	355.3709752	UA240-249
Marriage—Russia	306.810947	HQ637-638	Maryland—Periodicals	975.2005	F176
Marriage—South America	306.81098	HQ588-610	Mascarene Islands	969.8	DT469.M39
Marriage—Spain	306.810946	HQ649-650	Masculinity (Psychology)	155.332	BF692.5
Marriage—Switzerland	306.8109494	HQ653-654	Masks	391.434	GN419.5
Marriage—United States	306.810973	HQ535-557	Masks	391.434	GT1747-1748
Marriage—West Indies	306.8109729	HQ575-587.9	Masks (Sculpture)	731.75	NB1310
Marriage customs and rites	392.5	GT2660-2800	Masochism	616.85835	RC553.M36
Marriage customs and rites, Hindu	294.5441	BL1226.82.M3	Masonry	624.183	TA670-683.94
			Masonry	693.1	TH1199-1301
Marriage customs and rites, Islamic	392.50882971	GT2695.M8	Masonry	693.1	TH5311-5701
			Mass	264.02	BX2230-2234
Marriage customs and rites, Jewish	296.444	BM713	Mass-wasting	551.307	QE598-600.3
			Mass media policy	302.23	P95.8
Marriage customs and rites, Medieval	392.50902	GT2680	Mass suicide	364.1522	HV6547
			Mass transfer	530.475	QC318.M3
Marriage customs and rites—[By country]	392.509(4-9)	GT2701-2796	Massachusetts—Gazetteers	917.44003	F62
Marriage service	264.02085	BX2250-2254	Massachusetts—History	974.4	F61-75
Marriage service	392.5	HQ745	Massachusetts—History—Colonial period, ca. 1600-1775	974.40(1-2)	F67
Marriage with deceased wife's sister	306.84	HQ1028			
Married students	371.82655	LB3613.M3	Massachusetts—History—New Plymouth, 1620-1691	974.402	F68
Mars (Planet)	523.43	QB376			
Mars (Planet)	523.43	QB641	Massachusetts—History—Queen Anne's War, 1702-1713	974.403	E197
Marshall Islands	996.83	DU710			
Marshall Islands—Maps	912.9683	G9460-9464	Massachusetts—History—King George's War, 1744-1748	974.402	E198
Marshes	578.768	QH87.3			
Marshes	627.54	TC975			
Marsyas (Greek deity)	292.2113	BL820.M26	Massachusetts—History—French and Indian War, 1755-1763	974.402	E199
Martial artists	796.8092	GV1113			
Martinique	972.982	F2081			
Martinique—Census	317.2982	HA918.9			
Martinique—Maps	912.72982	G5080-5084			

Subject Heading	Dewey	LC
Massachusetts—History—1775-1865	974.40(2-3)	F69
Massachusetts—History—Revolution, 1775-1783	974.40(2-3)	E263.M4
Massachusetts—History—War of 1812	974.403	E359.5.M3
Massachusetts—History—Civil War, 1861-1865	974.403	E513
Massachusetts—History—1865-	974.404	F70-71
Massachusetts—Maps	912.744	G3760-3764
Massachusetts—National Guard	355.3709744	UA250-259
Massachusetts—Periodicals	974.4005	F61
Massacres—India—Amritsar	954.0357	DS480.5
Massage	615.822	RA780.5
Massage	615.822	RM721-723
Mastectomy	616.99449059	RD667.5
Master of arts degree	378.2	LB2385
Mastoid process—Diseases	617.87	RF235
Masts and rigging	623.862	VM531-533
Masturbation	306.772	HQ447
Matches	662.5	TP310
Materia medica	615.1	RS153-185
Materialization	133.92	BF1378
Materials	620.11	TA401-492
Materials—Creep	620.11233	TA418.22
Materials—Dictionaries	620.1103	TA402
Materials—Periodicals	620.1105	TA401
Materials—Research	620.11072	TA404.2
Materials management	658.7	TS161
Maternal and infant welfare	362.83	HV697-700
Maternity nursing	618.20231	RG951
Mathematical geography	526	GA
Mathematical geography	526	GA1-87
Mathematical geography—Tables	526.021	GA4
Mathematical instruments	510.284	QA71-90
Mathematical physics	530.15	QC19.2-20.85
Mathematical physics—Study and teaching	530.15071	QC20.8-.82
Mathematical statistics	519.5	QA276-280
Mathematicians	510.92	QA28-29
Mathematics	510	QA
Mathematics, Ancient	510.901	QA22
Mathematics, Babylonian	510.935	QA22
Mathematics, Chinese	510.931	QA27.C
Mathematics, Greek	510.938	QA22
Mathematics, Medieval	510.902	QA23
Mathematics, Medieval	510.902	QA32
Mathematics—[By region or country]	510.9(4-9)	QA27
Mathematics—Dictionaries	510.3	QA5
Mathematics—History	510.9	QA21-27
Mathematics—Periodicals	510.5	QA1
Mathematics—Philosophy	510.1	QA8-10.5
Mathematics—Study and teaching	510.71	QA11-20
Mathieu functions	515.54	QA405
Matriarchy	306.859	GN497.5
Matrices	512.9434	QA188-196
Matrix mechanics	530.122	QC174.3-.35
Matter	117	BD331
Matter	117	BD493-708
Matter	530	QC170-197
Maturation (Psychology)	155.51	BF710
Matwork plants	633.58	SB281-283
Mauritania—Census	316.61	HA4730
Mauritania—Civilization	966.1	DT554.4
Mauritania—Description and travel	916.6104	DT554.27
Mauritania—Gazetteers	916.61003	DT554.15
Mauritania—History	966.1	DT554.52-.83
Mauritania—History—1960-	966.105	DT554.8-.83
Mauritania—Maps	912.661	G8820-8824
Mauritius—Census	316.982	HA2305
Mauritius—Civilization	969.82	DT469.M44
Mauritius—Description and travel	916.98204	DT469.M429
Mauritius—Gazetteers	916.982003	DT469.M415
Mauritius—History	969.82	DT469.M45-.M497
Mauritius—History—To 1810	969.8201	DT469.M465-.M467
Mauritius—Maps	912.6982	G9185-9189
Maxima and minima	511.66	QA306
Maxims	398.9	PN6299-6308
May Day	394.2627	GT4945
Mayaguez Incident, 1975	973.925	E865
Mayan languages	497.42	PM3961-3969
Mayors	352.23216	JS143-163
May-pole	394.2627	GT4945
Meadow ecology	577.46	QH541.5.M4
Meadow plants	581.746	QK938.M4
Meadows	633.202	SB199
Meal	664.7207	TS2120-2159
Meaning (Philosophy)	121.68	B105.M4
Measles	614.523	RA644.M5
Measles	616.915	RC168.M4
Measuring instruments	530.7	QC100.5-.8
Measuring-tapes	526.90284	TA579-581
Meat	641.36	TX371-389
Meat	641.36	TX555-556
Mechanical drawing	604.2	T351-385
Mechanical engineering	621	TJ
Mechanical engineering—[By region or country]	621.09(4-9)	TJ21-127
Mechanical engineering—Congresses	621.06	TJ5
Mechanical engineering—History	621.09	TJ15-20

Subject Heading	Dewey	LC
Mechanical engineering—Periodicals	621.05	TJ1-4
Mechanical engineering—Philosophy	621.01	TJ14
Mechanical engineering—Study and teaching	621.071	TJ158-159
Mechanical engineers—Biography	621.092	TJ139-140
Mechanical engineers—Directories	621.025	TJ11-13
Mechanical movements	621.81	TJ181-210
Mechanical organs	786.6609	ML1058
Mechanics	530	QC120-168.86
Mechanics, Analytic	531.01515	QA801-871
Mechanics, Applied	620.1	TA350-359
Mechanotherapy	615.82	RM719-727
Medal of Honor	355.13420973	UB433
Medals	737.22	CJ5501-6661
Medals, Ancient	737.22093	CJ5581-5690
Medals, Greek	737.220938	CJ5625
Medals, Roman	737.220937	CJ5641-5685
Medals—Periodicals	737.2205	CJ5501
Medals—Study and teaching	737.22071	CJ5525
Medals—[By Region or country]	737.2209(4-9)	CJ5795-6661
Medals—Africa	737.22096	CJ6491-6559
Medals—Asia	737.22095	CJ6381-6485
Medals—Australia	737.220994	CJ6561-6569
Medals—Central America	737.2209728	CJ5841-5905
Medals—Europe	737.22094	CJ6091-6380
Medals—United States	737.220973	CJ5801-5812
Medea (Greek mythology)	292.13	BL820.M37
Media programs (Education)	371.33	LB1028.4
Medical assistants	610.737	R728.8
Medical astrology	133.5861	BF1718
Medical bacteriology	616.9201	QR46
Medical climatology	616.988	RA791-954
Medical colleges	610.711	R735-845
Medical economics	338.473621	RA410-415
Medical emergencies	616.025	RC86-88.9
Medical ethics	174.2	R724-726
Medical genetics	616.042	RB155-.8
Medical geography	614.42	RA791-954
Medical geography—[By region or country]	614.42(4-9)	RA801-954
Medical geography—Africa	614.426	RA943-949
Medical geography—Asia	614.425	RA891-934
Medical geography—Australia	614.4294	RA951-952
Medical geography—Canada	614.4271	RA809-810
Medical geography—Central America	614.42728	RA813-814
Medical geography—Europe	614.424	RA845-887
Medical geography—Mexico	614.4272	RA811-812
Medical geography—New Zealand	614.4293	RA952.5
Medical geography—Oceania	614.429(5-6)	RA953-954
Medical geography—South America	614.428	RA817-844
Medical geography—United States	614.4273	RA804-807
Medical geography—West Indies	614.42729	RA815-816
Medical history taking	616.0751	RC65
Medical informatics	610.285	R858-859.7
Medical instruments and apparatus	610.284	R856-858
Medical jurisprudence	614.1	RA1001-1171
Medical jurisprudence—History	614.109	RA1021-1022
Medical jurisprudence—Statistics	614.1021	RA1018.5-.56
Medical jurisprudence—Study and teaching	614.107	RA1027-.5
Medical laboratories	610.72	R860-862
Medical laws and legislation—Canada	344.71041	KE3646-3660
Medical laws and legislation—England	344.4204	KD3395-3413
Medical laws and legislation—Ireland	344.415041	KDK926-932
Medical laws and legislation—Scotland	344.411041	KDC690-695
Medical laws and legislation—United States	344.73041	KF3821-3829
Medical microbiology	616.9041	QR46
Medical microscopy	616.0758	RB43-.6
Medical offices	610.6	R728
Medical parasitology	616.96	QR251-255
Medical personnel—Malpractice	344.0411	RA1056.5
Medical referral	362.172	R727.5
Medical rehabilitation	617.03	RM930-950
Medical screening	362.177	RA427.5-.6
Medical secretaries	651.3741	R728
Medical social work	362.10425	HV687-688
Medical statistics	610.21	RA407-409.5
Medical supplies	355.88	UH440-445
Medical supplies	359.88	VG290-295
Medical thermometers	610.284	RC75
Medicated feeds	636.08557	SF98.M4
Medici, House of	945.05	DG737.42
Medicinal plants	581.634	QK99
Medicinal plants	633.88	SB293-295
Medicinal plants—Encyclopedias	615.32103	RS164
Medicine	610	R
Medicine, Ancient	610.901	R135-138.5
Medicine, Arab	610.089927	R143

Subject Heading	Dewey	LC
Medicine, Botanic	615.53	RV1-9
Medicine, Chronothermal	615.53	RZ414
Medicine, Eclectic	615.53	RV
Medicine, Eclectic	615.53	RV11-431
Medicine, Eclectic—Congresses	615.5306	RV21
Medicine, Eclectic—History	615.5309	RV61
Medicine, Eclectic—Periodicals	615.5305	RV15
Medicine, Eclectic—Study and teaching	615.53071	RV100-181
Medicine, Experimental	616.027	R850-854
Medicine, Industrial	616.9803	RC963-969
Medicine, Medieval	610.902	R141-144
Medicine, Military	355.345	UH201-515
Medicine, Military	616.98023	RC970-971
Medicine, Military—Biography	355.345092	UH341-347
Medicine, Military—Congresses	355.34506	UH205
Medicine, Military—History	355.34509	UH215-324
Medicine, Military—Study and teaching	355.345071	UH398-399
Medicine, Military—Africa	355.345096	UH315-319
Medicine, Military—Argentina	355.3450982	UH236-237
Medicine, Military—Asia	355.345095	UH299-313
Medicine, Military—Australia	355.345094	UH321-322
Medicine, Military—Canada	355.3450971	UH226-227
Medicine, Military—Central America	355.34509728	UH230-231
Medicine, Military—Chile	355.3450983	UH243-244
Medicine, Military—China	355.3450951	UH301-302
Medicine, Military—Colombia	355.34509861	UH245-246
Medicine, Military—Europe	355.345094	UH255-295
Medicine, Military—France	355.3450944	UH271-272
Medicine, Military—Germany	355.3450943	UH273-274
Medicine, Military—Great Britain	355.3450941	UH257-264
Medicine, Military—Greece	355.34509495	UH275-276
Medicine, Military—India	355.3450954	UH303-304
Medicine, Military—Italy	355.3450945	UH279-280
Medicine, Military—Japan	355.3450952	UH305-306
Medicine, Military—Mexico	355.3450972	UH228-229
Medicine, Military—Oceania	355.345099(5-6)	UH323-324
Medicine, Military—Portugal	355.34509469	UH283-284
Medicine, Military—Russia	355.3450947	UH285-286
Medicine, Military—Scandinavia	355.3450948	UH286.5
Medicine, Military—South America	355.345098	UH234-254
Medicine, Military—Spain	355.3450946	UH287-288
Medicine, Military—United States	355.3450973	UH223-224
Medicine, Military—Venezuela	355.3450987	UH254
Medicine, Military—West Indies	355.34509729	UH232-233
Medicine, Naval	359.345	VG
Medicine, Naval	359.345	VG100-475
Medicine, Naval	616.98024	RC981-986
Medicine, Naval—Biography	359.345092	VG226-228
Medicine, Naval—Study and teaching	359.345071	VG230-235
Medicine, Naval—[By region or country]	359.34509(4-9)	VG121-224
Medicine, Naval—Africa	359.345096	VG215-219
Medicine, Naval—Asia	359.345095	VG199-213
Medicine, Naval—Australia	359.3450994	VG221-222
Medicine, Naval—Canada	359.3450971	VG126-127
Medicine, Naval—Central America	359.34509728	VG130-131
Medicine, Naval—Europe	359.345094	VG155-196
Medicine, Naval—France	359.3450944	VG171-172
Medicine, Naval—Germany	359.3450943	VG173-174.5
Medicine, Naval—Great Britain	359.3450941	VG157-164
Medicine, Naval—Italy	359.3450945	VG179-180
Medicine, Naval—Japan	359.3450952	VG205-206
Medicine, Naval—Mexico	359.3450972	VG128-129
Medicine, Naval—New Zealand	359.3450993	VG222.5
Medicine, Naval—Russia	359.450947	VG185-186
Medicine, Naval—Scandinavia	359.3450948	VG186.5
Medicine, Naval—South America	359.345098	VG134-154
Medicine, Naval—Spain	359.3450946	VG187-188
Medicine, Naval—United States	359.3450973	VG123-125
Medicine, Naval—West Indies	359.4509729	VG132-133
Medicine, Oriental	610.95	R581
Medicine, Persian	610.935	R135
Medicine, Physical	615.82	RM695-951
Medicine, Preventive	613	RA421-790
Medicine, Psychosomatic	616.08	RC49-52
Medicine, Tibetan	610.951	R603.T5
Medicine—Formulae, receipts, prescriptions	615.13	RS125-131.9
Medicine—Congresses	610.6	R106
Medicine—Dictionaries	610.3	R121
Medicine—Examinations	616.075	R837.E9
Medicine—History	610.9	R131-684
Medicine—Periodicals	610.5	R5-101
Medicine—Philosophy	610.1	R723-.5
Medicine—Pictorial works	610.222	R120
Medicine—Practice	610.6	R729.5

Subject Heading	Dewey	LC
Medicine—Religious aspects	201.7621	BL65.M4
Medicine—Societies, etc.	610.6	R10-99.7
Medicine—Study and teaching	610.71	R735-845
Medicine—Terminology	610.14	R123
Medicine—[United States, By state]	610.97(4-9)	R155-363
Medicine—Africa	610.96	R651-654
Medicine—Asia	610.95	R581-644
Medicine—Asiatic Russia	610.957	R635-638
Medicine—Australia	610.994	R671-674
Medicine—Austria	610.9436	R499-502
Medicine—Belgium	610.9493	R521-524
Medicine—Canada	610.971	R461-464
Medicine—Central America	610.9728	R469-472
Medicine—China	610.951	R601-604
Medicine—Denmark	610.9489	R539-542
Medicine—Europe	610.94	R484-575
Medicine—France	610.944	R504-507
Medicine—Germany	610.943	R509-512.5
Medicine—Great Britain	610.941	R486-498.4
Medicine—Greece	610.9495	R513-516
Medicine—Iceland	610.94912	R543-546
Medicine—India	610.954	R605-608
Medicine—Indochina	610.959(3-7)	R609-612
Medicine—Indonesia	610.9598	R614-617
Medicine—Iran	610.955	R631-634
Medicine—Ireland	610.9415	R498.6-.9
Medicine—Italy	610.945	R517-520
Medicine—Japan	610.952	R623-626
Medicine—Korea	610.9519	R627-630
Medicine—Mexico	610.972	R465-468
Medicine—Netherlands	610.9492	R526-529
Medicine—New Zealand	610.993	R675-678
Medicine—Norway	610.9481	R547-550
Medicine—Oceania	610.99(5-6)	R681-684
Medicine—Pakistan	610.95491	R604.2-.5
Medicine—Philippines	610.9599	R618-621
Medicine—Poland	610.9438	R535-538
Medicine—Portugal	610.9469	R559-562
Medicine—Russia	610.947	R531-534
Medicine—Saudi Arabia	610.9538	R591-594
Medicine—South America	610.98	R480-483
Medicine—Spain	610.946	R555-558
Medicine—Sri Lanka	610.95493	R608.2-.5
Medicine—Sweden	610.9485	R551-554
Medicine—Switzerland	610.9494	R563-566
Medicine—Turkey	610.9561	R640-643
Medicine—United States	610.973	R151-363
Medicine—West Indies	610.9729	R473-476
Medicine and psychology	601.9	R726.5-.8
Meditation	204.35	BL627
Meditations	248.34	BV4800-4870
Meditations	248.34	BX2177-2198
Mediterranean Region—Historiography	907.201822	DE8-9

Subject Heading	Dewey	LC
Medulla oblongata	573.86	QL933-937
Medulla oblongata	611.81	QM455
Medulla oblongata	612.828	QP377
Meekness	241.4	BV4647.M3
Megarians (Greek philosophy)	183.6	B285
Meiosis	571.845	QH605
Melanesia	995	DU490
Melanesia—Maps	912.95	G2870-2894
Melanesia—Maps	912.95	G9260-9262
Melanesian languages	499.5	PL6201-6209
Melanoma	616.99477	RC280.M37
Melatonin	612.02	QP572.M44
Melodeon music	788.863	M175.M38
Melodrama	808.82527	PN1910-1919
Melody	781.24	ML3834
Melody	781.24	ML3851
Melody	781.2407	MT47
Melons	635.61	SB339
Membrane reactors	660.28424	TP248.25.M45
Membrane separation	660.28424	TP248.25.M46
Memorial Day	394.26973	E642
Memory	153.12	BF370-387
Memory	370.1522	LB1063-1064
Memory	612.82	QP406
Memory (Philosophy)	128.3	BD181.7
Memory disorders	153.12	BF376
Memory disorders	616.83	RC394.M46
Menageries	590.73	QL73
Menarche	612.662	RJ145
Meninges	573.86	QL933-937
Meninges	611.81	QM469
Meningitis	616.82	RC124
Meningitis	616.82	RC376
Meningitis	636.089682	SF799
Mennonites	289.7092	BX8101-8143
Mennonites—Biography	289.7092	BX8141-8143
Mennonites—Canada	289.771	BX8118.5-.7
Mennonites—History	289.709	BX8115-8119
Mennonites—Parties and movements	252.097	BX8129.A1
Mennonites—Sermons	252.097	BX8127
Mennonites—United States	289.773	BX8116-8118
Menominee Indians	977.500497313	E99.M44
Menopause	618.175	RG186
Menorah	296.435	BM657.M35
Men's furnishing goods	646.402	TT570-630
Men's studies	305.31	HQ1088-1090.7
Menstrual cycle	618.172	RG161-186
Menstrual regulation	618.172	RG734
Menstruation disorders	618.172	RG161-186
Mensuration	516.15	QA465
Mensuration	530.8	T50-51
Mental fatigue	152.1886	LB1075
Mental healing	615.851	RZ400-408
Mental health	362.2	RA790-.95

Subject Heading	Dewey	LC	Subject Heading	Dewey	LC
Meteors	523.51	QB740-753	Mexico—Emigration and immigration	325.(272) or (72)	JV7400-7409
Methodism	287	BX8201-8495	Mexico—Gazetteers	917.2003	F1204
Methodist Church	287	BX8201-8495	Mexico—Genealogy	929.1072072	CS100-110
Methodist Church—[Catechisms/Creeds]	238.7	BX8335	Mexico—History—To 1519	972.018	F1228.98
			Mexico—History—To 1810	972.0(1-2)	F1229-1231
Methodist Church—Doctrines	230.7	BX8330-8331.2	Mexico—History—Conquest, 1519-1540	972.02	F1230
Methodist Church—Education	268.87	BX8219-8227	Mexico—History—Spanish colony, 1540-1810	972.02	F1231
Methodist Church—Government	262.07	BX8340-8345.5	Mexico—History—1810-	972.0(3-84)	F1231.5-1236.6
Methodist Church—History	287.09	BX8231-8328	Mexico—History—Wars of Independence, 1810-1821	972.03	F1232
Methodist Church—Liturgy	264.07	BX8337	Mexico—History—1821-1861	972.0(3-6)	F1232-.5
Methodist Church—Sermons	252.7	BX8333	Mexico—History—European intervention, 1861-1867	972.07	F1233
Methodist Church—Societies, etc.	287.06	BX8207	Mexico—History—1867-1910	972.081	F1233.5
Methodist Church—Africa	287.(1-8)6	BX8320-8322	Mexico—History—1910-1946	972.08(16-26)	F1234
Methodist Church—Asia	287.(1-8)5	BX8315-8316	Mexico—History—Revolution, 1910-1920	972.08(16-21)	F1234
Methodist Church—Australia	287.(1-8)94	BX8325-8326	Mexico—History—Decena Tragica, 1913	972.0816	F1234
Methodist Church—Canada	287.(1-8)71	BX8251-8253	Mexico—History—Revolution, 1923-1924	972.0822	F1234
Methodist Church—Europe	287.(1-8)4	BX8275-8310	Mexico—History—1946-1970	972.08(27-31)	F1235-.5
Methodist Church—Great Britain	287.536	BX8276-8293	Mexico—History—1970-1988	972.083(2-4)	F1236
Methodist Church— New Zealand	287.(1-8)93	BX8325-8326	Mexico—History—1988-	972.08(35-41)	F1236
Methodist Church—South America	287.(1-8)8	BX8271-8273	Mexico—Manufactures	670.972	TS28-29
Methodist Church—United States	287.(1-8)73	BX8235-8249	Mexico—Maps	912.72	G1545-1549
			Mexico—Maps	912.72	G4410-4414
Methodist Episcopal Church	287.632	BX8380-8389	Mexico—Periodicals	972.005	F1201
Methodist Episcopal Church	287.633	BX8380-8389	Mexico—Politics and government	320.972	JL1200-1299
Methodists—Biography	287.092	BX8491-8495	Mezzotint engraving	766.2	NE1815-1816.5
Metric spaces	514.325	QA611.28	Mica	622.3674	TN933
Metric system	530.812	QC90.8-94	Michael (Archangel)	235.3	BT968.M5
Metropolitan government—[United States, By state]	352.16097(4-9)	JS422	Michigan	977.4	F561-575
			Michigan—Gazetteers	917.74003	F564
Mexican Americans	973.046872073	E184.M5	Michigan—History—To 1837	977.40(1-3)	F566
Mexican literature	860	PQ7100-7298.36	Michigan—History—1837-1950	977.40(3-4)	F566
Mexican War, 1846-1848	973.62	E401-415.2	Michigan—History—1951-	977.404(3-4)	F570-.2
Mexico	972	F1201-1392	Michigan—Maps	912.774	G4110-4114
Mexico—Armed forces—Supplies and stores	355.80972	UC94-97	Michigan—National Guard	355.3709774	UA260-269
Mexico—Biography	920.072	CT550-558	Michigan—Periodicals	977.4005	F561
Mexico—Census	317.2	HA761-770	Microbial biotechnology	660.6	TP248.27.M53
Mexico—Church history	277.2	BR610-615	Microbial ecology	576.15	QR100-130
Mexico—Civilization	972	F1210	Microbiologists	579.092	QR30-31
Mexico—Climate	551.6972	QC986	Microbiology	579	QR
Mexico—Commerce	381.0972	HF3231-3240	Microbiology—Classification	579.012	QR12
Mexico—Description and travel	917.204	F1211-1216.5			
Mexico—Economic conditions	330.972	HC131-140			

Subject Heading	Dewey	LC	Subject Heading	Dewey	LC
Microbiology—History	579.09	QR21-22	Middle schools	373.236	LB1623
Microbiology—Periodicals	579.05	QR1	Midgets	599.949	GN69.3-.5
Microbiology—Pictorial works	579.0222	QR54	Midrash	296.14	BM511-518
			Midshipmen	359.0071073	V415
Microbiology—Research	579.072	QR61-63	Midway, Battle of, 1942	940.54265933	D774.M5
Microbiology—Technique	579.028	QR65-69	Midwives	618.2	RG950
Microbiology—Terminology	579.014	QR11	Migrant agricultural laborers	331.544	HD1521-1542
Microfilm readers	302.23	TR835			
Micrographics	686.43	Z265	Migrant labor	331.544	HD5855-5856
Micrometeorology	551.66	QC883.7-.86	Migrations of nations	304.8	D135-149
Micronesia	996.5	DU500	Migratory locust	595.726	QL508.A2
Micronesia—Maps	912.965	G2905-2934	Mildew	632.43	SB741.M65
Micronesia—Maps	912.965	G9400-9494	Mile, Nautical	527.015308	VK572
Micronesian languages	499.52	PL6191-6195	Mile, Roman	530.8	G86
Micronesians	305.89952	GN669	Militarism	355.0213	U21
Microorganisms—Evolution	579.138	QR13	Militarism	355.0213	UA10
Microscopes	570.282	QH211-212	Military administration	355.6	UB
Microscopy	570.282	QH201-278.5	Military administration—History	355.609	UB15
Microwave cookery	641.5882	TX832			
Microwave devices	621.3813	TK7876	Military administration—Periodicals	355.605	UB1
Microwave heating	621.4028	TK4601			
Microwave ovens	641.5882	TX657.064	Military architecture	725.18	NA490-497
Microwave transmission lines	621.38131	TK7876	Military art and science	355	U
			Military art and science—Automation	355.40285	UG478
Middle age	305.244	HQ1059.4-.5			
Middle age—Psychological aspects	155.66	BF724.6-.65	Military art and science—Biography	355.0092	U51-55
			Military art and science—Congresses	355.006	U7
Middle Ages	909.07	CB351-355			
Middle Ages—History	940.1	D111-203	Military art and science—Dictionaries	355.003	U24-26
Middle Atlantic States	974	F106			
Middle Atlantic States—Maps	912.74	G3790-3854	Military art and science—Exhibitions	355.0074	U13
			Military art and science—History	355.009	U27-43
Middle class	305.55	HT680-690			
Middle class—[By region or country]	305.5509(4-9)	HT690	Military art and science—History—To 500	355.00901	U29-35
			Military art and science—Officers' handbooks	355	U130-135
Middle ear	573.89	QL948			
Middle ear	611.85	QM507	Military art and science—Soldiers' handbooks	355.5	U110-115
Middle ear	612.854	QP461			
Middle ear—Diseases	617.84	RF220-229	Military bridges	623.67	UG335
Middle East	939.4	DS41-66	Military calls	781.599	UH40-45
Middle East	956	DS41-66	Military ceremonies, honors, and salutes	355.17	U350-365
Middle East—Biography	920.056	CT1870-1919			
Middle East—Commerce	381.0956	HF3756-3770.2	Military currency	332.4	HG353.5
Middle East—Description and travel	913.9404	DS44.98-49.7	Military decorations	355.134	UB430-435
			Military decorations	359.1342	VB330-335
Middle East—Description and travel	915.604	DS44.98-49.7	Military dependents	355.12	UB400-405
			Military discipline	343.014	UB790-795
Middle East—Emigration and immigration	325.(256) or (56)	JV8739-8751	Military education	355.0071	U400-714
			Military education—[By region or country]	355.00710(4-9)	U407-714
Middle East—Gazetteers	913.94003	DS43			
Middle East—Gazetteers	915.6003	DS43	Military education—Africa	355.007106	U670-695
Middle East—History—To 622	939.4	DS38	Military education—Asia	355.007105	U635-660
			Military education—Australia	355.0071094	U700-704
Middle East—Maps	912.56	G7420-7624			
Middle East—Politics and government	320.956	JQ			
Middle East—Religion	200.956	BL660-687			

Subject Heading	Dewey	LC	Subject Heading	Dewey	LC
Military education—Austria	355.00710436	U550-554	Military law—France	343.4401	UB615-619
Military education—Canada	355.0071071	U440-444	Military law—Germany	343.4301	UB620-624
Military education—Central America	355.00710728	U450-454	Military law—Greece	343.49501	UB630-634
			Military law—India	343.5401	UB695-699
Military education—China	355.0071051	U640-644	Military law—Italy	343.4501	UB640-644
Military education—Europe	355.007104	U505-630	Military law—Japan	343.5201	UB700-704
Military education—Germany	355.0071043	U570-574.54	Military law—Mexico	343.7201	UB510-514
			Military law—Oceania	343.9(5-6)01	UB735-736
Military education—Great Britain	355.0071041	U510-549.3	Military law—Portugal	343.46901	UB650-654
			Military law—Russia	343.4701	UB655-659
Military education—India	355.0071054	U645-649	Military law—South America	343.801	UB530-589
Military education—Iran	355.0071055	U655-659			
Military education—Japan	355.0071052	U650-654	Military law—Spain	343.4601	UB660-664
Military education—Mexico	355.0071072	U445-449	Military law—Venezuela	343.8701	UB585-589
Military education—South America	355.007108	U465-499	Military law—West Indies	343.72901	UB520-524
			Military maneuvers	355.4	U250-255
Military education—United States	355.0071073	U408-439	Military maneuvers	356.4	UD460-465
			Military missions	355.032	UA16
Military education—[United States, By state]	355.007107(4-9)	U409	Military museums	355.0074	U13
			Military museums	358.12074	UF6
Military education—West Indies	355.00710729	U455-459	Military music	781.599	M1270
			Military music	781.599	VG30-35
Military engineering	358.22	UG	Military nursing	355.345	UH490-495
Military engineering—[By region or country]	358.2209(4-9)	UG21-124	Military oceanography	359.8	V396-.5
			Military offenses	355.1334	UB780-789
Military engineering—Congresses	358.2206	UG5	Military passes	355.113	UB280-285
			Military pensions	331.25291355	UB370-375
Military engineering—History	358.2209	UG15	Military pensions	362.86	VB280-285
			Military police	355.13323	UB820-825
Military engineering—Societies, etc.	358.2206	UG1	Military police	359.13323	VB920-925
			Military policy	355.0335	UA11
Military engineering—Study and teaching	358.22071	UG157	Military prisons	365.48	UB800-805
			Military prisons	365.48	VB890-895
Military field engineering	358.22	UG360-390	Military railroads	623.63	UG345
Military fireworks	623.452	UF860-880	Military readiness—Law and legislation	343.01	K4720-4760
Military geography	355.47	UA985-997			
Military history	355.009	D25-.4	Military readiness—Law and legislation—Canada	343.7101	KE6800-7240
Military history—Medieval	355.009402	D128			
Military history—Modern	355.00903	D214	Military readiness—Law and legislation—England	343.4201	KD6000-6355
Military hospitals	355.72	UH460-485			
Military hygiene	355.345	UH600-629.5	Military reconnaissance	355.413	U220
Military inspectors general	355.685	UB240-245	Military research	355.07	U390-395
Military intelligence	355.3432	UB250-271	Military reservations	355.7	UB390-395
Military interrogation	355.3432	UB265	Military roads	623.62	UG330
Military law—[By region or country]	343.(4-9)01	UB461-736	Military sealift	359.985	VC530-535
			Military service, Voluntary	355.22362	UB320-325
Military law—Africa	343.601	UB715-729	Military social work	306.27	UH750-769
Military law—Argentina	343.8201	UB530-534	Military statistics	355.0021	UA19
Military law—Asia	343.501	UB685-710	Military supplies	355.8	UC260-267
Military law—Australia	343.9401	UB730-734	Military telecommunication	623.73 (2-3)	UG590-610.5
Military law—Canada	343.7101	UB505-509	Military telegraph	623.732	UG590-613.5
Military law—Central America	343.72801	UB515-519	Military training camps	355.5	U290-295
			Military training camps	359.965	VE430-435
Military law—Chile	343.8301	UB545-549	Military uniforms	355.14	UC480-485
Military law—China	343.5101	UB690-694	Military uniforms	359.81	VC300-345
Military law—Colombia	343.86101	UB550-554	Militia	355.37	UA13
Military law—Europe	343.401	UB590-684	Milk	637.141	SF251-262.5

Subject Heading	Dewey	LC
Mines and mineral resources—Italy	622.0945	TN79-80
Mines and mineral resources—Japan	622.0952	TN105-106
Mines and mineral resources—Mexico	622.0972	TN28-29
Mines and mineral resources—Netherlands	622.09492	TN77-78
Mines and mineral resources—New Zealand	622.0993	TN122.5-.6
Mines and mineral resources—Norway	622.09481	TN81-82
Mines and mineral resources—Pakistan	622.095491	TN104.5-.6
Mines and mineral resources—Paraguay	622.09892	TN51
Mines and mineral resources—Peru	622.0985	TN52
Mines and mineral resources—Philippines	622.09599	TN113.P6
Mines and mineral resources—Portugal	622.09469	TN83-84.5
Mines and mineral resources—Russia	622.0947	TN85-86
Mines and mineral resources—Scandinavia	622.0948	TN88.5
Mines and mineral resources—Spain	622.0946	TN87-88
Mines and mineral resources—Sri Lanka	622.095493	TN104.7-.8
Mines and mineral resources—Surinam	622.09883	TN49
Mines and mineral resources—Sweden	622.09485	TN89-90
Mines and mineral resources—Switzerland	622.09494	TN91-92
Mines and mineral resources—Turkey	622.09561	TN111-112
Mines and mineral resources—United States	622.0973	TN23-25
Mines and mineral resources—Uruguay	622.09895	TN53
Mines and mineral resources—Venezuela	622.0987	TN54
Mines and mineral resources—West Indies	622.09729	TN32-33
Mines and mineral resources—Yugoslavia	622.09497	TN95.Y8
Miniature electronic equipment	621.3810228	TK7870
Miniature horses	636.109	SF293.M56
Miniature objects	745.0228	NK8470-8475
Miniature objects	745.5928	NK492
Miniature weapons	739.70228	NK8475.A7
Minibikes	629.2275	TL443
Minimum wage	331.23	HD4917-4924
Minimum wage—[By region or country]	331.2309(4-9)	HD4918-4924

Subject Heading	Dewey	LC
Mining engineering	622	TN
Mining engineers	622.092	TN139-140
Mining law—Canada	343.71077	KE1790-1802
Mining law—England	343.42077	KD2331-2370
Mining law—United States	343.73077	KF1801-1873
Mining machinery	622.0284	TN345-347
Mining schools and education	622.071	TN165-213
Ministerial responsibility	352.293	JF341
Mink farming	636.97662701	SF405.M6
Minneapolis (Minn.)	977.6579	F614.M5
Minnesota	977.6	F601-615
Minnesota Multiphasic Personality Inventory	155.283	BF698.8.M5
Minnesota Multiphasic Personality Inventory	616.89075	RC473.M5
Minnesota—Gazetteers	917.76003	F604
Minnesota—History—To 1858	977.60(1-4)	F606
Minnesota—History—1858-	977.60(4-5)	F606
Minnesota—Maps	912.776	G4140-4144
Minnesota—National Guard	355.3709776	UA270-279
Minnesota—Periodicals	977.6005	F601
Minorities	323.1	JC312
Minorities—Education	371.829	LC3701-3740
Minorities—Employment	331.6	HD6304
Minotaur (Greek mythology)	292.13	BL820.M63
Minstrel music	791.12	M1365
Minstrels	390.478	GT3650
Mints	332.4	HG321-329
Minuet	793.3	GV1796.M5
Miracles	231.73	BS1199.M5
Miracles	231.73	BS2545.M5
Miracles	231.73	BT97-.2
Mirrors	681.428	TP867
Mirrors	748.8	NK8440-.2
Miscarriage	618.392	RG648
Miscegenation	306.846	E185.62
Miscegenation	306.846	GN254
Missals	264.023	BX2015-2016
Missing link	569.9	GN282.5
Mission of the church	261	BV601.8
Missionaries	266.0092	BV3700-3705
Missions	266	BV2000-3705
Missions—Interdenominational cooperation	266	BV2082.I6
Missions, Medical	362.1	RA390-392
Missions—Africa	266.0096	BV3500-3630
Missions—Asia	266.0095	BV3149-3487
Missions—Australia	266.00994	BV3650-3660
Missions—Canada	266.00971	BV2810-2820
Missions—Europe	266.0094	BV2855-3145
Missions—France	266.00944	BV2940-2945
Missions—Germany	266.00943	BV2950-2957
Missions—Great Britain	266.00941	BV2860-2895
Missions—Japan	266.00952	BV3440-3457

Subject Heading	Dewey	LC	Subject Heading	Dewey	LC
Missions—Oceania	266.0099(3-6)	BV3640-3680	Mogul Empire	954.025	DS461-.9
Missions—Spain	266.00946	BV3120-3127	Mohave Indians	979.004975722	E99.M77
Missions to Jews	266	BV2619-2623	Mohawk Indians	974.7004975542	E99.M8
Missions to lepers	266	BV2637	Mohawk language	497.5542	PM1881-1884
Missions to Muslims	266	BV2625-2626.4	Mohegan Indians	974.600497344	E99.M83
Mississippi	976.2	F336-350	Mohegan language	497.344	PM1885
Mississippi—History—To 1803	976.20(1-4)	F341	Moisture	551.57	QC915-929
Mississippi—History— Civil War, 1861-1865	976.205	E516	Moisture index	551.57	QC915
Mississippi—History—Civil War, 1861-1865	976.205	E568	Moisture index	631.432	S594
Mississippi—Gazetteers	917.62003	F339	Mole (Dermatology)	616.55	RL793
Mississippi—Maps	912.762	G3980-3984	Molecular astrophysics	523.019	QB462.6
Mississippi—National Guard	355.3709762	UA280-289	Molecular biology	572.8	QH506
Mississippi—Periodicals	976.2005	F336	Molecular cloning	660.65	QH442.2
Mississippi River Valley	977	F350.5-358.2	Molecular structure	541.22	QD461
Missouri	977.8	F461-475	Molecular theory	541.2	QD461
Missouri—Gazetteers	917.78003	F464	Molecular weights	541.222	QD463-464
Missouri—History—Civil War, 1861-1865	977.803	E517	Molecules	539.6	QC173
Missouri—History—Civil War, 1861-1865	977.803	E569	Molecules	539.6	QC179
Missouri—Maps	912.778	G4160-4164	Mollusks	594	QL401-432
Missouri—National Guard	355.3709778	UA290-299	Moments of inertia	531.12	QA839
Missouri—Periodicals	977.8005	F461	Moments of inertia	624.25	TG265-267
Missouri compromise	973.7113	E373	Monaco	944.949	DC941-947
Missouri River	978	F598	Monaco—Maps	912.44949	G5980-5984
Miter-gages	694.0284	TH5618	Monarchy	321.6	JC375-393
Mites as carriers of disease	614.433	RA641.M5	Monarchy—Great Britain	342.4106	KD4430-4531
Mitosis	571.844	QH605.2	Monasteries	255.(1-7)	BX2460-2749
Mitral valve insufficiency	616.125	RC685.V2	Monasteries	726.7	NA4850
Mixing	620.1064	TA357.5.M59	Monastic and religious life	255.(1-7)	BX2435
Mnemonics	153.14	BF380-387	Monastic and religious life—History	255.(1-7)009	BX2460-2749
Mobile Bay (Ala.), Battle of, 1864	973.75	E476.85	Monasticism and religious orders	255.(1-7)	BX2400-4560
Mobile home living	643.29	TX1100-1105	Monasticism and religious orders	255.819	BX385
Mobiles (Sculpture)	731.55	NB1315	Monasticism and religious orders	255.819	BX580-583
Mobs	302.33	HM281-283	Monasticism and religious orders for women	255.9(1-7)	BX4200-4563
Mobs	364.143	HV6474-6485	Monasticism and religious orders, Anglican	255.83	BX5970-5974
Moccasins	391.413008997	E98.C8	Monasticism and religious orders, Buddhist	294.3657	BQ6001-6160
Model airplane racing	796.154	GV761.5	Monasticism and religious orders, Hindu	294.5657	BL1238
Model car racing	796.156	GV1570	Monasticism and religious orders, Protestant	255.8	BV4405-4408
Model theory	511.34	QA9.7	Monasticism and religious orders—Rules	255.(1-7)06	BX2436-2437
Modeling	731.42	NB1180-1185	Monasticism and religious orders—Africa	255.(1-7)0096	BX2732-2740
Models (Patents)	608.0228	T324	Monasticism and religious orders—Asia	255.(1-7)0095	BX2677-2731
Models (Persons)	746.92092	HD6073.M7	Monasticism and religious orders—Canada	255.(1-7)00971	BX2527-2529
Models and modelmaking	688.1	TT154-.5	Monasticism and religious orders—Europe	255.(1-7)0094	BX2631-2676
Modems	621.39814	TK7887.8.M63			
Modern dance	792.8	GV1783			
Modernism	273.9	BT82			
Modernism (Art)	700.4112	N6490			
Modesty	179.9	BJ1533.M73			
Modular arithmetic	513.6	QA247.35			
Modular construction	693.97	TH1098			
Modular programming	005.112	QA76.6			

Subject Heading	Dewey	LC
Monasticism and religious orders—Mexico	255.(1-7)00972	BX2530-2532
Monasticism and religious orders—United States	255.(1-7)00973	BX2505-2525
Money	332.4	HG201-1496
Money—[By region or country]	332.49(4-9)	HG451-1496
Money—United States	332.4973	HG451-645
Money—Law and legislation—England	343.42032	KD5284-5286
Money—Law and legislation—United States	343.73032	KF6201-6219
Money—Tables	332.4021	HG3854-3858
Mongolia—Census	315.17	HA4630.8
Mongolia—Maps	912.517	G7895-7899
Mongolian language	494.23	PL401-409
Mongolian languages	494.23	PL400-431
Mongolian literature	894.23	PL410-419
Mongols	305.8942	GN548
Mongols	950.04942	DS19-23
Monitorial system of education	371.39	LB1029.M7
Mon-Khmer languages	495.93	PL4301-4309
Monmouth, Battle of, 1778	973.334	E241.M7
Monologue	808.8245	PN1530
Monologues	808.8245	PN4305.M6
Mononucleosis	616.91122	RC147.G6
Monopolies	338.82	HD2709-2932
Monopolies—United States	343.73072	KF1631-1657
Monorail railroads	625.103	TF694
Monotheism	211.34	BL221
Monotype	686.22542	Z253
Monsoons	551.5184	QC939.M7
Monsters	398.45	GR825-830
Montana	978.6	F726-740
Montana—Gazetteers	917.86003	F729
Montana—History—1951-	978.603(3-4)	F735-.2
Montana—Maps	912.786	G4250-4254
Montana—National Guard	355.3709786	UA300-309
Montana—Periodicals	978.6005	F726
Montenegro	949.745	DR1802-1928
Montenegro—History	949.745	DR1827-1928
Montenegro—Maps	912.49745	G2020-2022
Monterrey (Mexico), Battle of, 1846	973.6242	E406.M7
Montessori method of education	371.392	LB1029.M75
Montserrat	972.975	F2082
Montserrat—Maps	912.72975	G5055-5059
Monuments	725.94	NA9335-9355
Monuments	731.76	NB1330-1685
Monuments—[By region or country]	731.7609(4-9)	NB1501-1685
Moon	523.3	QB580-595
Moon—Maps	912.991	G1000.3-.5
Moon—Maps	912.991	G3195-3199
Moon—Surface	523.3	QB591
Moon—Tables	523.3021	QB399
Moon—Tables	523.3021	VK563-567
Moon worship	202.12	BL438
Moor ecology	577.38	QH541.5.M6
Mooring of ships	387.54044	VK361-365
Moors and heaths	578.738	QH87.5
Moral development	155.25	BF723.M54
Moral education	370.114	LC251-318
Moral re-armament	267.16	BJ10.M6
Morale	355.123	U22
Moravia (Czech Republic)	943.72	DB2300-2421
Moravia (Czech Republic)—Civilization	943.72	DB2335
Moravia (Czech Republic)—Ethnography	943.72004	DB2340-2342
Moravia (Czech Republic)—History	943.72	DB2345-2421
Moravia (Czech Republic)—History—To 906	943.72021	DB2385-2391
Moravians	284.6	BX8551-8593
Moravians—Biography	284.6092	BX8591-8593
Moravians—Education	268.846	BX8561-8564.5
Moravians—History	284.609	BX8565-8569
Moravians—Sermons	252.046	BX8577
Moravians—Societies, etc.	284.606	BX8553
Mordvin language	494.56	PH751-779
Mordvin literature	894.56	PH781-785
Mormon Church	289.3	BX8601-8695
Mormon Church—Education	268.893	BX8610
Mormon Church—History	289.309	BX8611-8617
Mormon Church—Missions	266.93	BX8661
Mormon Church—Sacred books	289.32	BX8621-8631
Mormon Church—Sermons	252.093	BX8639
Mormon cosmology	231.765	BX8643.C68
Mormon temples	246.6	BX8643.T4
Morocco	939.71	DT301-330
Morocco	964	DT301-330
Morocco—Census	316.4	HA4682
Morocco—Civilization	939.71	DT312
Morocco—Civilization	964	DT312
Morocco—Description and travel	913.97104	DT307-310.2
Morocco—Description and travel	916.404	DT307-310.2
Morocco—Economic conditions	330.964	HC810
Morocco—Gazetteers	913.971003	DT304
Morocco—Gazetteers	916.4003	DT304
Morocco—History	939.71	DT313.7-325.92
Morocco—History	964	DT313.7-325.92
Morocco—History—To 647	939.71	DT318
Morocco—History—647-1516	964.02(1-3)	DT319

Subject Heading	Dewey	LC	Subject Heading	Dewey	LC
Morocco—History—1516-1830	964.025	DT321-323.5	Motion pictures—Moral and ethical aspects	175	PN1995.5
Morocco—History—19th century	964.03	DT324	Motion pictures—Religious aspects	791.43682	PN1995.5
Morocco—History—20th century	964.0(4-5)	DT324-325.92	Motion pictures—Reviews	791.4375	PN1995
Morocco—Maps	912.64	G8230-8234	Motion sickness	616.9892	RC103.M6
Morphemics	415	P241-259	Motion study	658.542	T60.7
Morphine	615.7822	RM666.M8	Motivation (Psychology)	153.8	BF199
Morphine habit	362.293	HV5813	Motor vehicles	629.2	TL
Morphine habit	616.8632	RC568.06	Motor vehicles, Amphibious	359.83	V880
Morphology	571.3	QH351	Motor vehicles—Electronic equipment	629.2549	TL272.5-.55
Morphology (Animals)	571.3	QL799-.5	Motor vehicles—Pollution control devices	629.25	TL214.P6
Morrisite War, 1862	979.202	F826			
Mortality	304.64	HB1321-1528	Motorboats	623.81	VM340-349
Mortality—[By region or country]	304.645(4-9)	HB1335-1526	Motorboats	797.125	GV833.5-835.9
			Motorcycles	629.2275	TL439-448
Mortality—Developing countries	304.6451724	HB1528	Motorization, Military	355.83	UC340-345
Mortality—Tables	304.64021	HB1322	Mottoes	929.6	CR73-75
Mortality—Tables	368.3201	HG8783-8785	Mounds	930.1	GN795-796
Mortgage banks	332.32	HG2039.5-2040.5	Mountain climate	551.69143	QC993.6
			Mountain gods	202.12	BL325.M63
Mortgage guarantee insurance	368.852	HG9992	Mountain life	390.09143	GT3490
			Mountain plants	581.7538	QK937
Mortgage loans, Reverse	332.72	HG2039.5-2040.5	Mountain railroads	385.6	HE4051-4071
			Mountain roads	625.709143	TE229.8
Mortgages	332.63244	HG4655	Mountain sickness	616.9893	RC103.A4
Mortgages	332.72	HD1443	Mountain warfare	356.164	UD460-465
Mortgages—England	346.4204364	KD1010-1016	Mountain wave	551.5185	QC939.M8
Mosaics	729.7	NA3750-3860	Mountain worship	202.12	BL447
Mosaics	738.5	NK8500	Mountaineering	796.522	GV199.8-200.3
Mosaics	748.50285	NK5430	Mountains	398.3209143	GR660
Moscow (Russia)	947.31	DK588-609	Mountains	551.432	GB501-555
Moscow, Battle of, 1941-1942	940.5421731	D764.3.M	Mourning customs, Jewish	296.445	BM712
			Mourning etiquette	395.23	BJ2071-2075
Moses (Biblical leader) in the Koran	297.122092	BP133.7.M67	Mouth	573.35	QL857
			Mouth	611.31	QM306
Mosques	726.2	NA4670	Mouth—Cancer	616.99431	RC280.M6
Mosquitoes as carriers of disease	614.4323	RA640	Mouth—Diseases	616.31	RC815-.6
			Mouth—Surgery	617.605	RK529-535
Mosquitoes—Control	614.4323	RA640	Mouth protectors	796.0284	GV749.M6
Mossi languages	496.35	PJ4149	Movement (Philosophy)	573.701	B105.M65
Mother goddesses	202.114	BL325.M6	Movement, Psychology of	152.3	BF295-.5
Mother goddesses	202.114	BL325.M6	Moving target indicator radar	621.3848	TK6592.M67
Mother goddesses, Greek	292.2114	BL820.M65			
Motherhood	306.8743	HQ759-.6	Mowing machines	631.3	S695-697
Mother-of-pearl	639.412	SH377.5	Mozambique—Census	316.79	HA4698
Mothers	306.8743	HQ759-.6	Mozambique—Civilization	967.9	DT3320
Mother's Day	394.2628	HQ759.2	Mozambique—Description and travel	916.7904	DT3308-3312
Motion	531.11	QA801-935			
Motion	531.11	QC122-168	Mozambique—Economic conditions	330.9679	HC890
Motion picture plays	791.437	PN1996-1997			
Motion picture theaters	725.823	NA6845-6846	Mozambique—Gazetteers	916.79003	DT3294
Motion pictures	791.43	PN1993-1999	Mozambique—History	967.9	DT3330-3398
Motion pictures—Editing	778.535	TR899-.5	Mozambique—History—To 1505	967.901	DT3345-3348

Subject Heading	Dewey	LC	Subject Heading	Dewey	LC
Mozambique—History—1505-1698	967.90(1-2)	DT3350-3359	Municipal revenue	336.2014	HJ9115-9123
Mozambique—History—1698-1891	967.902	DT3361-3374	Municipal universities and colleges	378.052	LB2329
Mozambique—History—1891-1975	967.90(2-3)	DT3376-3387	Municipal water supply	628.1	TD201-500
Mozambique—History—War of 1894-1895	967.902	DT3381	Mural painting and decoration	751.73	ND2550-2877
Mozambique—History—Revolution, 1964-1975	967.903	DT3387	Mural painting—[By region or country]	751.7309(4-9)	ND2601-2877
Mozambique—History—1975-	967.905	DT3389-3398	Murder	364.1523	HV6499-6542
			Murder—[By region or country]	364.152309(4-9)	HV6518-6535
Mozambique—Maps	912.679	G8450-8454	Murder—United States	364.15230973	HV6518-6534
Muffins	641.8157	TX770.M83	Murder—[Other regions or countries]	364.152309(4-9)	HV6535
Muffs	391.412	GT2190	Muscles	573.75	QL831
Mugging	364.1552	HV6646-6665	Muscles	611.73	QM151-170
Muhammad, Prophet, d. 632	297.63	BP75-77.5	Muscles	611.73	QM571
			Muscles	612.74	QP321-322
Muhammad, Prophet, d. 632—Miracles	297.63	BP75.8	Muscles—Diseases	616.7	RC925-935
			Muscles—Diseases	616.74	RD688
Mulattoes	305.8044	GN645	Muscles—Diseases	616.74	RD925-927
Mulching	631.451	S661.5	Muscular atrophy	616.74	RC935.A8
Mules	636.183	SF362	Muscular sense	152.182	BF285
Multicultural education	370.117	LC1099-.5	Musculoskeletal banks	362.1783	RD128
Multidimensional Aptitude Battery	153.94	BF432.5.M85	Musculoskeletal system	573.7	QL821-831
			Musculoskeletal system	611.7	QM100-170
Multihull sailboats	797.1246	GV811.53-.58	Musculoskeletal system	612.7	QP301-336
Multilevel marketing	381.1	HF5415.126	Musculoskeletal system—Effect of drugs on	615.773	RM312
Multilinear algebra	512.5	QA199.5			
Multimedia systems	006.7	QA76.575	Musculoskeletal system—Wounds and injuries	617.47044	RD680-688
Multiphase flow	620.1064	TA357.5.M84			
Multiple birth	618.25	RG696-698	Museum conservation methods	069.53	AM141-145
Multiple cropping	631.58	S603.7			
Multiple personality	616.85236	RC569.5.M8	Museum finance	069.0681	AM122
Multiple pregnancy	618.25	RG567	Museums	069	AM
Multiple psychotherapy	616.8914	RC489.M85	Museums—Law and legislation—England	344.42093	KD3736
Multiple sclerosis	614.59834	RA645.M82			
Multiple sclerosis	616.834	RC377	Museums—Law and legislation—United States	344.73093	KF4305
Multiple stars	523.841	QB821-830			
Multiple-choice examinations	371.271	LB3060.32.M85	Museums—Methodology	069.01	AM111-157
			Museums—[By region or country]	069.09	AM10-101
Multiplication	513.213	QA115			
Multiprocessors	004.35	QA76.5	Museums—Africa	069.096	AM80-91
Multipurpose trees	634.99	SB172	Museums—Asia	069.095	AM71-79
Mumps	616.313	RC168.M8	Museums—Australia	069.0994	AM93-95
Munda languages	495.95	PL4501-4509	Museums—Balkan Peninsula	069.09496	AM69
Municipal bonds	332.63233	HG4726			
Municipal buildings	725.13	NA4430-4437	Museums—Canada	069.0971	AM21-22
Municipal engineering	628	TD159-168	Museums—Central America	069.09728	AM25-27
Municipal government by commission	352.250973	JS342-343			
			Museums—China	069.0951	AM72
Municipal government—[United States, By city]	352.16097(4-9)	JS504-1583	Museums—Europe	069.094	AM40-70
			Museums—France	069.0944	AM46-48
Municipal home rule	320.85	JS113	Museums—Germany	069.0943	AM49-51
Municipal officials and employees	352.16092	JS148-155	Museums—Great Britain	069.0941	AM41-43
			Museums—Greece	069.09495	AM52-53
Municipal ownership	352.266	HD4421-4730.9	Museums—Italy	069.0945	AM54-55

Subject Heading	Dewey	LC	Subject Heading	Dewey	LC
Museums—Japan	069.0952	AM77-78	Musical instruments, Ancient	784.1901	ML162-169
Museums—Mexico	069.0972	AM23-24	Musical instruments, Electronic	786.707	MT724
Museums—New Zealand	069.0993	AM96-98			
Museums—Oceania	069.099(5-6)	AM99-100	Musical instruments—Catalogs, Manufacturers'	784.190294	ML155
Museums—Portugal	069.09469	AM66			
Museums—Russia	069.0947	AM60-61	Musical instruments—[By region or country]	784.19(4-9)	ML475-1354
Museums—Scandinavia	069.0948	AM61.5-64			
Museums—South America	069.098	AM33-35	Musical instruments—Africa	784.196	ML544
Museums—Spain	069.0946	AM65	Musical instruments—Asia	784.195	ML525-541
Museums—United States	069.0973	AM11-13	Musical instruments—Australia	784.1994	ML547
Mushrooms, Edible	579.6	QK617			
Mushrooms, Hallucinogenic	579.6	QK600-635	Musical instruments—Austria	784.19436	ML491
Mushrooms, Hallucinogenic	633.88	SB293-295	Musical instruments—Belgium	784.19493	ML496
Mushrooms, Poisonous	581.659	QK617			
Music	780	M	Musical instruments—Canada	784.1971	ML478
Music, Origin of	780.9	ML3800	Musical instruments—Central America	784.19728	ML484
Music—Bibliography	016.78	ML111-158			
Music—Bio-bibliography	780.12	ML105-107	Musical instruments—China	784.195	ML531
Music—Bio-bibliography	780.92	ML385-429	Musical instruments—Czechoslovakia	784.19437	ML493
Music—Dictionaries	780.3	ML100-110			
Music—Examinations, questions, etc.	780.76	MT9	Musical instruments—Denmark	784.19489	ML514
			Musical instruments—Europe	784.194	ML489-522
Music—History and criticism	780.9	ML159-3799			
			Musical instruments—France	784.1944	ML497
Music—Instruction and study	780.7	MT	Musical instruments—Germany	784.1943	ML499-500
Music—Manuscripts	780	ML93-98			
Music—Memorizing	781.426	MT82	Musical instruments—Great Britain	784.1941	ML501
Music—Performance	780.7809	ML457			
Music—Philosophy and aesthetics	780.1	ML3800-3920	Musical instruments—Hungary	784.19439	ML494
			Musical instruments—India	784.1954	ML533
Music—Psychology	781.11	ML3830-3838	Musical instruments—Iran	784.1955	ML539
Music—Societies, etc.	780.6	ML25-28	Musical instruments—Italy	784.1945	ML503
Music—Terminology	780.14	ML108	Musical instruments—Japan	784.1952	ML535
Music—Theory	781	MT6-7			
Music-halls (Variety-theaters, cabarets, etc.)	792.7	PN1960-1969	Musical instruments—Korea	784.19519	ML537
			Musical instruments—Mexico	784.1972	ML482
Music and mythology	780.0398	ML3849			
Music appreciation	781.17	MT90-145	Musical instruments—Netherlands	784.19492	ML505
Music box	786.6509	ML1065-1066			
Music festivals	780.79	ML35-38	Musical instruments—New Zealand	784.1993	ML547
Music in churches	782.3209	ML3001			
Music in prisons	780.0365	ML3920	Musical instruments—Norway	784.19481	ML515
Music in the army	781.599	UH40-45			
Music recorder	788.3609	ML1055	Musical instruments—Oceania	784.199(5-6)	ML547
Music therapy	615.85154	ML3919-3920			
Musical accompaniment	781.4707	MT68	Musical instruments—Portugal	784.19469	ML519
Musical accompaniment	786.14707	MT190			
Musical accompaniment	786.214707	MT239	Musical instruments—Saudi Arabia	784.19538	ML527
Musical dictation	780.14	MT35			
Musical films	791.43657	PN1995.9.M86			
Musical instruments	784.1907	MT170-805S			
Musical instruments	784.1909	ML459-1093			
Musical instruments (Mechanical)	786.607	MT700			

Subject Heading	Dewey	LC
Musical instruments—Scandinavia	784.1948	ML513-516
Musical instruments—South America	784.198	ML486
Musical instruments—Spain	784.1946	ML518
Musical instruments—Sweden	784.19485	ML516
Musical instruments—Switzerland	784.19494	ML520
Musical instruments—United States	784.1973	ML476
Musical instruments—West Indies	784.19729	ML480
Musical intervals and scales	781.246	ML3809
Musical Meter and rhythm	781.22(4 or 6)	ML3850
Musical notation	780.148	MT35
Musical pitch	781.232	ML3807-3809
Musical shorthand	780.1407	MT35
Musical temperament	784.1928	ML3809
Musicals	782.14	M1500-1508
Musicals—History and criticism	782.1409	ML1700-1751
Musicians	780.92	ML385-403
Musicians—Autographs	780.262	ML93-98
Musicians—Salaries, etc.	331.28178	ML3795
Musico-calisthenics	613.714	GV464
Musico-calisthenics	613.714	GV464
Musicology	780.72	ML
Muskogean Indians	975.0049738	E99.M95
Muskogean languages	497.38	PM1971-1974
Muslim converts	297.574	BP170.5
Muslim converts from Christianity	297.574	BP170.5
Muslim converts from Christianity—Biography	297.574092	BP170.5
Muslim pilgrims and pilgrimages	297.35	BP187
Muslim pilgrims and pilgrimages—Saudi Arabia—Mecca	297.352	BP187.3
Muslim saints	297.4092	BP189.33
Muslim teachers	371.100882971	LC905.T42
Muslim women	305.486971	HQ1170
Muslims, Black	297.87	BP62.N4
Mussel fisheries	639.42	SH371-374.52
Mussels	639.42	SH372.5-.52
Mustache	391.5	GT2318
Mustard gas	358.34	UG447.5.M8
Mustard gas	615.91	RA1247.M8
Mustard seed (Parable)	226.8	BT378.M8
Mutagens	576.549	QH465-.5
Mutation (Biology)	576.549	QH460-468
Mutilation	391.65	GN419.2
Mutiny	355.1334	UB787
Mutiny	359.1334	VB860-867
Mutual funds	332.6327	HG4530
Mutual security program, 1951-	355.031	UA12
Mutualism (Biology)	577.852	QH548.3
Mycobacterial diseases	616.92	RC116.M8
Mycoses	616.969	RC117
Myocardial depressants	615.716	RM347
Myocardial infarction	616.1237	RC685.I6
Myocarditis	616.124	RC685.M92
Myocardium	611.12	QM181
Myocardium	612.17	QP113.2
Myocardium—Diseases	616.124	RC685.M9
Mysteries and miracle-plays	809.2527	PN1761
Mysteries of the Rosary	242.74	BT303
Mysticism	149.3	B828
Mysticism	189.5	B728
Mysticism	204.22	BL625
Mysticism	248.22	BV5070-5095
Mysticism—Hinduism	294.5422	BL1215.M9
Mysticism—Islam	297.4	BP189
Mysticism—Jainism	294.4422	BL1378.8
Mysticism in literature	808.804291	PN49
Mystics	248.22	BV5095
Myth in literature	808.8015	PN56.M94
Myth in the Bible	220.68	BS520.5
Myth in the Old Testament	221.68	BS1183
Mythology	201.3	BL300-325
Mythology, Buddhist	294.333	BQ5741-5755
Mythology, Classical	292.13	BL700-820
Mythology, Classical	292.13	BL700-820
Mythology, European	201.3094	BL689-980
Mythology, European	201.3094	BL689-980
Mythology, Indic	294	BL2000-2016
Mythology, Oriental	299.5	BL1000-2370
Mythology, Polynesian	299.924	BL2620.P6
Mythology in literature	808.8037	PN56.M95
N stars	523.88	QB843.N12
Naga languages	495.4	PL3881-3884
Nahuas	972.00497452	F1219.73-.75
Nahuatl Language	497.452	PM4061-4069
Nails (Anatomy)	573.59	QL942
Nails (Anatomy)	611.78	QM488
Nails, Ingrowing	616.547	RD563
Naktong River (Korea), Battle of, 1950	951.904242	DS918.2
Nama language	496.1	PL8541
Names, Personal	929.4	CS2300-3090
Names, Personal—[By region or country]	929.409(4-9)	CS2395-3090
Namibia—Census	316.881	HA4708
Namibia—Civilization	968.81	DT1552
Namibia—Description and travel	916.88104	DT1532-1536
Namibia—Gazetteers	916.881003	DT1514
Namibia—History	968.81	DT1564-1648

Subject Heading	Dewey	LC	Subject Heading	Dewey	LC
Namibia—History—To 1884	968.8101	DT1587-1601	Natural history—Pictorial works	508.0222	QH46
Namibia—History—1884-1915	968.8102	DT1603-1622	Natural history—Study and teaching	508.071	QH51-58
Namibia—History—Herero Revolt, 1904-1907	968.8103	DT1618	Natural history—Terminology	508.014	QH83
Namibia—History—1915-1946	968.8103	DT1625-1636	Natural history—[By region or country]	578.09(4-9)	QH101-199
Namibia—History—1946-1990	968.8103	DT1638-1648	Natural history—Africa	578.096	QH194-195
Namibia—History—1990-	968.8104	DT1648	Natural history—Asia	578.095	QH179-193
Namibia—Maps	912.6881	G8620-8624	Natural history—Australia	578.0994	QH197
Nanking Massacre, Nanjing, Jiangsu Sheng, China, 1937	951.042	DS796.N2	Natural history—Canada	578.0971	QH106-.2
			Natural history—Central America	578.09728	QH108
Nanotechnology	620.5	T174.7	Natural history—Europe	578.094	QH135-178
Naples (Kingdom)—History	945.73	DG845.8-851	Natural history—Mexico	578.0972	QH107
Narcissism	616.85854	RC553.N36	Natural history—South America	578.098	QH111-130
Narcolepsy	616.8498	RC549			
Narcotherapy	616.8918	RC489.N3	Natural history—United States	578.0973	QH104-105
Narcotic habit	362.293	HV5800-5840	Natural history—West Indies	578.09729	QH109
Narcotic habit	616.8632	RC566			
Narcotics	394.14	GT3010	Natural history illustration	508.022	QH46.5
Narcotics	615.7822	RM328	Natural history museums	508.074	QH70
Narration (Rhetoric)	820.8023	PE1425	Natural immunity	571.96	QR185.2
Narrative poetry	808.813	PN6110.N17	Natural landscaping	719	SB439-.26
Narrow gap semiconductors	537.6223	QC611.8.N35	Natural language processing (Computer science)	006.35	QA76.9.N38
Nasopharynx	611.21	QM505			
Nasoscopy	616.21207545	RF345	Natural pesticides	632.95	SB951.145.N37
Natal (South Africa)—Maps	912.684	G8530-8533	Natural products in agriculture	631.86	S587.45
National characteristics	305.8	CB195-197			
National music	781.599	M1627-1853	Natural resources—Law and legislation	346.044	K3478-3486
National music—History and criticism	781.59909	ML3545	Natural resources—Law and legislation—England	346.42046	KD1035
National parks and reserves	363.68	SB481-484	Natural selection	576.82	QH375
			Natural theology	210	BL175-190
National parks and reserves—United States	333.780973	E160	Naturalism	146	B828.2
National socialism	943.086	DD253-256.5	Naturalism in literature	808.8012	PN56.R3
Nationalism	320.54	JC311-314	Naturalism in literature	808.8012	PN601
Native element minerals	549.2	QE389.1	Naturalists	508.092	QH26-35
Native language and education	370.117	LC201.5-.7	Nature (Aesthetics)	700.46	BH301.N3
			Nature conservation	333.7816	QH75-77
Native plant gardening	635.951	SB439-.26	Nature in literature	808.8036	PN48
Natural childbirth	618.45	RG661-662	Nature in the Bible	220.85	BS660-667
Natural disasters	904	GB5018	Nature photography	778.93	TR721-733
Natural family planning	613.9434	RG136.5	Nature study	508.071	QH51-58
Natural foods	641.302	TX369	Nature worship	202.12	BL435-457
Natural gas	622.3385	TN880-884	Naturopaths	615.535092	RZ440
Natural gas	665.7	TP350	Naturopathy	615.535	RZ433-445
Natural gas pipelines	665.744	TN880.5	Nautical almanacs	528	QB8
Natural history	508	QH	Nautical astronomy	527	VK549-587
Natural history—Dictionaries	508.03	QH13	Nautical charts	912.1962	G1059-1061
			Nautical instruments	623.89(2-3)	VK573-587
Natural history—Periodicals	508.06	QH1-7	Nautical training-schools	623.880971	VK525-529
			Navajo Indians	979.10049726	E99.N3

Subject Heading	Dewey	LC	Subject Heading	Dewey	LC
Navajo language	497.26	PM2006-2009	Naval art and science—South America	359.6098	VB34-54
Naval architecture	623.81	VM	Naval art and science—Spain	359.60946	VB87-88
Naval architecture—Study and teaching	623.81071	VM165-276	Naval art and science—United States	359.60973	VB23-25
Naval art and science	359	V	Naval art and science—West Indies	359.609729	VB32-33
Naval art and science	359.6	VB	Naval auxiliary vessels	359.985	V865
Naval art and science—Congresses	359.006	V7	Naval aviation	359.94	VG
Naval art and science—Dictionary	359.003	V23-24	Naval aviation	359.94	VG90-95
Naval art and science—History	359.009	V25-55	Naval battles	359.4	D27
Naval art and science—Periodicals	359.005	V1-5	Naval biography	359.0092	V61-65
Naval art and science—Terminology	359.003	V23-24	Naval ceremonies, honors, and salutes	359.17	V310
Naval art and science—[By region or country]	359.609(4-9)	VB21-124	Naval discipline	343.014	VB840-845
Naval art and science—Africa	359.6096	VB115-119	Naval districts	359	VA
Naval art and science—Argentina	359.60982	VB36-37	Naval education	359.0071	V400-695
Naval art and science—Asia	359.6095	VB99-113	Naval education—[By region or country]	359.00710(4-9)	V411-695
Naval art and science—Australia	359.60994	VB121-122	Naval education—Africa	359.007106	V660-680
Naval art and science—Canada	359.60971	VB26-27	Naval education—Asia	359.007105	V625-650
Naval art and science—Central America	359.609728	VB30-31	Naval education—Australia	359.0071094	V690-694
Naval art and science—Chile	359.60983	VB43-44	Naval education—Canada	359.0071071	V440-444
Naval art and science—China	359.60951	VB101-102	Naval education—Central America	359.00710728	V450-453
Naval art and science—Colombia	359.609861	VB45-46	Naval education—China	359.0071051	V630-634
Naval art and science—Europe	359.6094	VB55-96	Naval education—Confederate States of America	359.0071075	V438
Naval art and science—France	359.60944	VB71-72	Naval education—Europe	359.007104	V500-623
Naval art and science—Germany	359.60943	VB73-74.5	Naval education—Germany	359.0071043	V570-574.54
Naval art and science—Great Britain	359.60941	VB57-64	Naval education— Great Britain	359.0071041	V510-530
Naval art and science—Greece	359.609495	VB75-76	Naval education—India	359.0071054	V635-639
Naval art and science—Italy	359.60945	VB79-80	Naval education—Iran	359.0071055	V645-649
Naval art and science—Japan	359.60952	VB105-106	Naval education—Japan	359.0071052	V640-644
Naval art and science—Mexico	359.60972	VB28-29	Naval education—Mexico	359.0071072	V445-449
Naval art and science—Oceania	359.6099(5-6)	VB123-124	Naval education—South America	359.007108	V465-496
Naval art and science—Portugal	359.609469	VB83-84	Naval education—United States	359.0071073	V411-437
Naval art and science—Russia	359.60947	VB85-86	Naval education—West Indies	359.00710729	V455-458
			Naval history	359.009	D27
			Naval history, Ancient	359.00901	D95
			Naval history, Modern—20th century	359.0094	D436
			Naval hygiene	359.345	VG470-475
			Naval law	343.019	VB350-785
			Naval maneuvers	359.41	V245
			Naval militia—Canada	359.370971	VA402
			Naval museums	359.0074	V13
			Naval museums	359.82074	VF6
			Naval offenses	359.1334	VB850-880
			Naval prints	769.437	NE957-.3
			Naval reconnaissance	359.413	V190

Subject Heading	Dewey	LC
Naval research	359.07	V390-395
Naval reserves	359.37	VA45
Naval strategy	359.42	V160-165
Naval tactics	359.42	V167-178
Navies	359	VA37-42
Navies, Cost of	359.6229	VA20-25
Navies—Officers	359.332	VB310-315
Navigation (Aeronautics)	629.13251	TL586-589
Navigation (Astronautics)	629.453	TL1065-1080
Navigation—Safety measures	623.890289	VK200
Navigation—Study and teaching	623.89071	VK401-529
Navigation—Tables	527.021	VK563-567
Navy Cross (Medal)	355.13420973	VB333
Navy-yards and naval stations	359.7	V230
Navy-yards and naval stations—Great Britain	359.370941	VA460
Navy-yards and naval stations—United States	359.70973	VA66
Neanderthals	569.986	GN285
Near-death experiences	133.9013	BF1045.N4
Nebraska—Gazetteers	917.82003	F664
Nebraska—History	978.2	F661-675
Nebraska—Maps	912.782	G4190-4194
Nebraska—National Guard	355.3709782	UA310-319
Nebraska—Periodicals	978.2005	F661
Necessity (Philosophy)	123.7	BD417
Necessity, Fort, Battle of, 1754	973.26	E199
Neck	611.93	QM535
Necklaces	391.7	GT2260
Necks (Geology)	551.88	QE611-.5
Neckties	391.44	GT2120
Neckties	687.19	TT616
Needlework	746.4	NK8800-9505.5
Needlework	746.4	TT700-845
Negativism	155.232	BF698.35.N44
Negotiable instruments	346.096	K1054-1065
Negotiable instruments—Canada	346.71096	KE980-986
Negotiable instruments—England	346.42096	KD1695-1699
Negotiable instruments—United States	346.73096	KF956-962
Negotiation	158.5	BF637.N4
Negotiation in business	658.4052	HD58.6
Negritos	305.8096	GN664.N3
Neith (Egyptian deity)	299.31	BL2450.N45
Neoclassicism (Architecture)	724.2	NA600
Neo-Confucianism	181.112	B127.N4
Neo-impressionism (Art)	709.0345	N6465.N44
Neon	546.752	QD181.N5
Neon lamps	621.3275	TK4383
Neon tubes	621.3275	TK4383

Subject Heading	Dewey	LC
Neonatal emergencies	618.9201	RJ253.5
Neonatal gastroenterology	618.9201	RJ268.8
Neonatal hematology	618.9215	RJ269.5-271
Neonatal infections	618.929	RJ275
Neonatal intensive care	618.9201	RJ253.5
Neonatology	618.9201	RJ251-325
Neoplatonism	186.4	B517
Neoplatonism	186.4	B645
Neo-Scholasticism	149.91	B839
Nepal—Census	315.496	HA4570.9
Nepal—Civilization	954.96	DS493.7
Nepal—Description and travel	915.49604	DS493.5-.53
Nepal—Economic conditions	330.95496	HC425
Nepal—Gazetteers	915.496	DS493.3
Nepal—History	954.96	DS494.4-495.59
Nepal—History—To 1768	954.96	DS495
Nepal—History—1768-1951	954.96	DS495.3
Nepal—Maps	912.5496	G2295-2299
Nepal—Maps	912.5496	G7760-7764
Nepalese War, 1814-1816	954.0313	DS485.N4
Nepali language	491.495	PK2595-2599
Nephrology	616.61	RC902
Neptune (Planet)	523.481	QB388
Neptune (Planet)	523.481	QB691
Neptune (Planet)—Satellites	523.9881	QB407
Nerve tissue	611.0188	QM575
Nerves	573.85	QL939
Nerves	611.83	QM471
Nerves	612.81	QP361-375.5
Nervous system	573.8	QL921-939
Nervous system	611.8	QM451-471
Nervous system	612.81	QP351-430
Nervous system—Abnormalities	618.928043	RJ290-.5
Nervous system—Diseases	616.8(1-4)	RC346-429
Nervous system—Diseases—Eclectic treatment	616.806	RV241-246
Nervous system—Diseases—Homeopathic treatment	616.806	RX281-301
Nervous system—Surgery	617.48059	RD592.5-596
Nervous system—Tumors	616.9948	RD663
Nervous system—Wounds and injuries	617.48044	RD592.5-596
Nestorian Church	281.8	BX150-159
Nestorians	281.8	BT1440
Netherlands	949.2	DJ
Netherlands—Biography	920.0363	DH103
Netherlands—Biography	920.0363	DJ103-106
Netherlands—Biography	920.0492	DH103
Netherlands—Biography	920.0492	DJ103-106
Netherlands—Census	314.92	HA1381-1390

Subject Heading	Dewey	LC	Subject Heading	Dewey	LC
Netherlands—Civilization	936.3	DH71	Netherlands—History—Batavian Republic, 1795-1806	949.205	DJ211
Netherlands—Civilization	936.3	DJ71			
Netherlands—Civilization	949.2	DH71	Netherlands—History—1815-1830	949.205	DJ241
Netherlands—Civilization	949.2	DJ71			
Netherlands—Description and travel	913.6304	DH31-40	Netherlands—History—1830-1849	949.206	DJ241-251
Netherlands—Description and travel	913.6304	DJ33-41	Netherlands—History—William II, 1840-1849	949.206	DJ251
Netherlands—Description and travel	914.9204	DH31-40	Netherlands—History—William III, 1849-1890	949.206	DJ261
Netherlands—Description and travel	914.9204	DJ33-41	Netherlands—History—Wilhelmina, 1898-1948	949.2071	DJ281-287
Netherlands—Economic conditions	330.9492	HC321-329.5	Netherlands—History—German occupation 1940-1945	949.2071	DJ287
Netherlands—Emigration and immigration	325.(2492) or (492)	JV8150-8159	Netherlands—History—1945-	949.207(1-3)	DJ288-292
Netherlands—Gazetteers	913.63003	DH14	Netherlands—History—Juliana, 1948-1980	949.2072	DJ288-289
Netherlands—Gazetteers	913.63003	DJ14			
Netherlands—Gazetteers	914.92003	DH14	Netherlands—History—Beatrix, 1980-	949.2073	DJ290-292
Netherlands—Gazetteers	914.92003	DJ14			
Netherlands—History	936.3	DH95-207	Netherlands—History, Military	355.009492	DH113
Netherlands—History	936.3	DJ95-292			
Netherlands—History	949.2	DH95-207	Netherlands—History, Military	355.009492	DJ124
Netherlands—History	949.2	DJ95-292			
Netherlands—History—To 1384	936.3	DH141-162	Netherlands—History, Naval	359.009492	DH121
Netherlands—History—To 1384	936.3	DJ151-152	Netherlands—History, Naval	359.009492	DJ130-138
Netherlands—History—To 1384	949.201	DJ151-152	Netherlands—Manufactures	670.9492	TS77-78
Netherlands—History—To 1384	949.201	DH141-162	Netherlands—Maps	912.492	G6000-6004
Netherlands—History—House of Burgundy, 1384-1477	949.201	DH171-177	Netherlands—Periodicals	936.3005	DH1
			Netherlands—Periodicals	936.3005	DJ1
			Netherlands—Periodicals	949.2005	DH1
Netherlands—History—House of Habsburg, 1477-1556	949.202	DJ151-152	Netherlands—Periodicals	949.2005	DJ1
			Netherlands—Politics and government	320.9492	JN5701-5999
Netherlands—History—House of Habsburg, 1477-1556	949.202	DH179-184	Netherlands Antilles—Census	317.2986	HA917-.78
Netherlands—History—Charles V, 1506-1555	949.202	DH182	Network analysis (Planning)	658.4032	T57.85
Netherlands—History—Charles V, 1506-1555	949.202	DJ151-152	Neuengamme (Hamburg, Germany : Concentration camp)	940.531853515	D805.G3
Netherlands—History—Wars of Independence, 1556-1648	949.20(2-3)	DH185-207	Neural computers	006.32	QA76.87
			Neural networks (Computer science)	006.32	QA76.87
Netherlands—History—Twelve Years' Truce, 1609-1621	949.203	DH201	Neural stimulation	616.806	RC350.N48
			Neurasthenia	616.8528	RC552.N5
			Neuritis	616.856	RC416
Netherlands—History—Twelve Years' Truce, 1609-1621	949.203	DJ170	Neuroblastoma	616.9948	RC280.N4
			Neurochemistry	612.8042	QP356.3
			Neurocutaneous disorders	616.5	RL701-751
Netherlands—History—1648-1795	949.204	DJ180-209	Neurologic examination	616.804075	RC348-349
			Neurological intensive care	616.8028	RC350.N49
			Neurological nursing	610.7368	RD596
			Neurological nursing	616.804231	RC350.5

Subject Heading	Dewey	LC	Subject Heading	Dewey	LC
Neurology	616.8(1-4)	RC346-429	New Hampshire—History—Civil War, 1861-1865	974.203	E520
Neuromuscular blocking agents	615.773	RM312	New Hampshire—History—Colonial period, ca. 1600-1775	974.20(1-2)	F37
Neuroophthalmology	617.732	RE725-780	New Hampshire—History—King George's War, 1744-1748	974.202	E198
Neuropharmacology	615.78	RM315-334			
Neuropsychopharmacology	615.78	RM315-334	New Hampshire—History—Revolution, 1775-1783	974.20(2-3)	E263.N4
Neuroses	616.852	RC530-552			
Neutrality, Armed	940.253	D295	New Hampshire—Maps	912.742	G3740-3744
Neutrinos	539.7215	QC793.5.N42-.N429	New Hampshire—National Guard	355.3709742	UA330-339
Neutron bomb	358.428251	UG1282.N48	New Hampshire—Periodicals	974.2005	F31
Neutron counters	539.77	QC787.C6	New Jersey—Gazetteers	917.49003	F132
Neutron sources	539.7213	QC793.5.N4629	New Jersey—History	974.9	F131-145
Neutron stars	523.8874	QB843.N4	New Jersey—History—Colonial period, ca. 1600-1775	974.90(1-2)	F137
Neutrons	539.7213	QC793.5.N462-.N4622			
			New Jersey—History—Revolution, 1775-1783	974.90(2-3)	E263.N5
Nevada	979.3	F836-850			
Nevada—Gazetteers	917.93003	F839	New Jersey—History—1775-1865	974.90(2-3)	F138
Nevada—Maps	912.793	G4350-4354			
Nevada—National Guard	355.3709793	UA320-329	New Jersey—History—War of 1812	974.903	F138
Nevada—Periodicals	979.3005	F836			
New Age movement	299.93	BP605.N48	New Jersey—History—Civil War, 1861-1865	974.903	E521
New Brunswick—Gazetteers	917.151003	F1041.4			
			New Jersey—History—1865-	974.904	F139-140.22
New Brunswick—Maps	912.7151	G3430-3434			
New Brunswick—Periodicals	971.51005	F1041	New Jersey—Maps	912.749	G3810-3814
			New Jersey—National Guard	355.3709749	UA340-349
New Caledonia	995.97	DU720			
New Caledonia—Census	319.597	HA4015	New Jersey—Periodicals	974.9005	F131
New Caledonia—Maps	912.9597	G9340-9344	New Jerusalem Church	289.4	BX8701-8749
New Caledonian literature (French)	840	PQ3998.5.N	New Jerusalem Church—Biography	289.4092	BX8747-8749
New England—Gazetteers	917.4003	F2	New Jerusalem Church—Congresses	289.406	BX8705
New England—History	974	F1-15			
New England—History—Colonial period, ca. 1600-1775	974.0(1-2)	F7-.75	New Jerusalem Church—Education	268.894	BX8714
			New Jerusalem Church—Government	262.094	BX8737
New England—History—French & Indian War, 1755-1763	974.02	E199			
			New Jerusalem Church—History	289.409	BX8715-8719
New England—History—1775-1865	974.0(2-3)	F8			
			New Jerusalem Church—Periodicals	289.405	BX8701
New England—History—Revolution, 1775-1783	974.0(2-3)	F8			
			New Jerusalem Church—Sermons	252.094	BX8724
New England—History—War of 1812	974.03	E357-359			
			New Mexico	978.9	F791-805
New England—Maps	912.74	G3720-3784	New Mexico—Gazetteers	917.89003	F794
New England—Periodicals	974.005	F1	New Mexico—History—To 1848	978.90(1-3)	F799-800
New Guinea	995	DU739-747			
New Guinea—Maps	912.95	G8140-8142	New Mexico—History—1848-	978.90(4-5)	F801-.2
New Hampshire—Gazetteers	917.42003	F32			
New Hampshire—History	974.2	F31-45	New Mexico—History—Civil War, 1861-1865	978.904	E522
New Hampshire—History—1775-1865	974.203	F38			
New Hampshire—History—1951-	974.2043	F40			

Subject Heading	Dewey	LC
New Mexico—History—Civil War, 1861-1865	978.904	E571
New Mexico—Maps	912.789	G4320-4324
New Mexico—National Guard	355.3709789	UA350-359
New Mexico—Periodicals	978.9005	F791
New Orleans (La.)	976.335	F379.N5
New Orleans (La.), Battle of, 1815	973.5239	E356.N5
New Thought	299.93	BF638-648
New towns	307.768	HT169.55-.57
New towns	711.45	NA9053.N
New Year	394.2614	GT4905-4908
New Year sermons	252.68	BV4282
New York (N.Y.)	974.71	F128-.9
New York (State)—Gazetteers	917.47003	F117
New York (State)—History	974.7	F116-130
New York (State)—History—Colonial period, ca. 1600-1775	974.70(1-2)	F122-.1
New York (State)—History—King William's War, 1689-1697	974.702	E196
New York (State)—History—Queen Anne's War, 1702-1713	974.702	E197
New York (State)—History—French and Indian War, 1755-1763	974.702	F123
New York (State)—History—Revolution, 1775-1783	974.70(2-3)	E263.N6
New York (State)—History—1775-1865	974.70(2-3)	F123
New York (State)—History—War of 1812	974.703	E359.5.N6
New York (State)—History—1865-	974.74	F124-125
New York (State)—Maps	912.747	G3800-3804
New York (State)—National Guard	355.3709747	UA360-369
New York (State)—Periodicals	974.7005	F116
New Zealand—Biography	920.0993	CT2880-2888
New Zealand—Census	319.3	HA3171-3190
New Zealand—Civilization	993	DU418
New Zealand—Description and travel	919.304	DU409-413
New Zealand—Economic conditions	330.993	HC661-670
New Zealand—Emigration and immigration	325.(293) or (93)	JV9260-9269
New Zealand—Gazetteers	919.3003	DU405
New Zealand—Genealogy	929.1072093	CS2170-2179
New Zealand—History	993	DU419-422
New Zealand—History—To 1840	993.01	DU420.12-.14

Subject Heading	Dewey	LC
New Zealand—History—1840-1876	993.02(1-2)	DU420.16-.18
New Zealand—History—Maori War, 1845-1847	993.021	DU420.16
New Zealand—History—Taranaki War, 1860-1861	993.022	DU420.22-.34
New Zealand—History—1876-1918	993.0(23-31)	DU420.22-.24
New Zealand—History—1918-1945	993.032	DU420.26-.28
New Zealand—History—1945-	993.0(35-4)	DU420.32-.34
New Zealand—Manufactures	670.993	TS122.5-.6
New Zealand—Maps	912.93	G2795-2799
New Zealand—Maps	912.93	G9080-9084
New Zealand prose literature	828.08	PR9632.2-.6
New Zealand prose literature	828.08	PR9637.25-.92
Newfoundland—Gazetteers	917.18003	F1121.4
Newfoundland—History	971.8	F1121-1124
Newfoundland—Maps	912.718	G3600-3604
Newfoundland—Periodicals	971.8005	F1121
Newsletters	070.175	PN4784.N5
Newspapers	070.172	AN
Newspapers—Indexes	016.07	AI21
Nez Perce Indians	979.7004974124	E99.N5
Nicaragua	972.85	F1521-1537
Nicaragua—Census	317.285	HA831-840
Nicaragua—Civilization	972.85	F1523.8
Nicaragua—Description and travel	917.28504	F1524-.3
Nicaragua—Emigration and immigration	325.(27285) or (7285)	JV7426
Nicaragua—Gazetteers	917.285003	F1522
Nicaragua—History	972.85	F1525.5-1528.22
Nicaragua—History—To 1838	972.850(1-42)	F1526.25
Nicaragua—History—English Invasion, 1780-1781	972.8503	F1526.25
Nicaragua—History—1838-1909	972.850(44-51)	F1526.27
Nicaragua—History—Filibuster War, 1855-1860	972.85044	F1526.27
Nicaragua—History—1909-1937	972.8505(1-2)	F1526.3
Nicaragua—History—Revolution, 1909-1910	972.85051	F1526.3
Nicaragua—History—Revolution of 1912	972.85051	F1526.3
Nicaragua—History—Revolution, 1926-1929	972.85051	F1526.3
Nicaragua—History—1937-1979	972.85052	F1527

Subject Heading	Dewey	LC
Nicaragua—History—Uprising, 1978	972.85052	F1527
Nicaragua—History—1979-1990	972.85053	F1528
Nicaragua—History—Revolution, 1979	972.85052	F1528
Nicaragua—History—1990-	972.85054	F1528
Nicaragua—Maps	912.7285	G4850-4854
Nicaragua—Periodicals	972.85005	F1521
Nicaragua—Politics and government	320.97285	JL1600-1619
Nicaragua—San Carlos Barracks Attack, 1977	972.85052	F1527
Nicaraguan literature	860	PQ7510-7519.2
Nickel	620.188	TA480.N6
Nicknames	929.44	CT108
Nicotine	616.865	RC567
Nicotine	679.7	TS2255
Niger—Census	316.626	HA4724
Niger—Civilization	966.26	DT547.4
Niger—Description and travel	916.62604	DT547.27
Niger—Economic conditions	330.96626	HC1020
Niger—History	966.26	DT547.5-.83
Niger—History—To 1960	966.260(1-3)	DT547.65-.75
Niger—Maps	912.6626	G8770-8774
Niger-Congo languages	496.3	PL8026.N44
Nigeria—Census	316.69	HA4731
Nigeria—Civilization	966.9	DT515.4
Nigeria—Description and travel	916.6904	DT515.27
Nigeria—Economic conditions	330.9669	HC1055
Nigeria—Gazetteers	916.69003	DT515.15
Nigeria—History	966.9	DT515.53-.84
Nigeria—History—To 1851	966.901	DT515.65-.67
Nigeria—History—1851-1899	966.90(1-3)	DT515.7-.72
Nigeria—History—1900-1960	966.903	DT515.7-.77
Nigeria—History—1960-	966.905	DT515.8-.84
Nigeria—History—Coup d'etat, 1966 (January 15)	966.9051	DT515.832
Nigeria—History—Coup d'etat, 1966 (July 29)	966.9051	DT515.832
Nigeria—History—Civil War, 1967-1970	966.9052	DT515.836
Nigeria—History—Coup d'etat, 1983	966.9053	DT515.84
Nigeria—Maps	912.669	G8840-8844
Night fighter planes	358.4303	UG1242.F5
Night flying	629.1325214	TL711.N5
Night photography	778.719	TR610
Night work	331.2574	HD5113-.2
Nightmares	154.63	BF1099.N53
Nihilism	149.8	HX914-917

Subject Heading	Dewey	LC
Nile, Battle of the, 1798	940.27	DC226.N5
Nineteenth century	909.81	CB415-417
Nineteenth century	909.81	D351-400
Nitrates	622.364	TN911
Nitrates	631.842	S651-.3
Nitrates	661.65	TP237-238
Nitrogen	546.711	QD181.N1
Nitrogen fertilizers	631.84	S651-.3
Nitrogen in agriculture	631.84	S587.5.N5
Nitrogen in the body	572.54	QP535.N1
Niumi (Kingdom)	966.3	DT532.23
Niumi (Kingdom)	966.51	DT532.23
No first use (Nuclear strategy)	355.0217	U264
No-tillage	631.5814	S604
Noah's ark	222.11	BL325.D4
Noah's ark	222.1109505	BS658
Nobility	305.522	HT647-653
Nobility, Papal	262.13	CR5547-5577
Nobility—Social life and customs	390.23	GT5010-5090
Nobility—Social life and customs	390.23	GT5350-5490
Noise	152.15	BF205.N6
Noise—Physiological effect	571.444	QP82.2.N6
Noise—Psychological aspects	152.15	BF353.5.N65
Noise barriers	620.23	TD892
Noise pollution	620.23	TD891-893.6
Nomads	305.906918	GN387
Nominations for office	324.273015	JK2063-2075
Nominations for office	324.5	JF2085
Nomography (Mathematics)	518.23	QA90
Non-destructive testing	620.1127	TA417.2-.55
Non-importation agreements, 1768-1769	973.3112	E215.3
Non-insulin-dependent diabetes	616.462	RC660-662.18
Non-timber forest products—United States	634.9870973	SD543.3.U6
Non-Verbal Ability Tests	153.93	BF432.5.N64
Nonarticular rheumatism	616.723	RC927.5.N65
Nonclassical mathematical logic	511.31	QA9.4-.5
Nonets	785.19	M900-986
Nonferrous metals	620.18	TA479.3
Nongraded schools	371.255	LB1029.N6
Nonimpact printing	686.233	Z252.5.N46
Nonionizing radiation	571.45	QP82.2.N64
Nonlethal weapons	363.20284	HV7936.E7
Nonlinear control theory	515.642	QA402.35
Nonlinear functional analysis	515.7248	QA321.5
Nonlinear optics	535.2	QC446.15-.3
Nonlinear programming	519.76	T57.8-.825
Nonlinear wave equations	532.593	QA927

Subject Heading	Dewey	LC	Subject Heading	Dewey	LC
Nonmetallic steel	620.18	TA478	North Dakota—Periodicals	978.4005	F631
Nonmetals	546.7	QD161-169	Northern boundary of the United States	977	F551
Nonparametric statistics	519.5	QA278.8	Northern Hemisphere	910.021813	G912-916
Nonprescription drug industry	338.476151	HD9665-9675	Northern Hemisphere—Maps	912.19813	G1050
Nonprofit organizations—Law and legislation	346.42064	KD2061-2062	Northern Hemisphere—Maps	912.19813	G3210-3212
Nonprofit organizations—Law and legislation	346.73064	KF1388-1390	Northern Ireland—Census	314.16	HA1141-1150
Nonstandard mathematical analysis	515	QA299.82	Northern Ireland—Constitutional law	342.416	KDE410-462
Nontariff trade barriers	382.9	HF1430	Northern Ireland—Maps	912.416	G5790-5794
Nonverbal communication (Psychology)	153.69	BF637.N66	Northern Ireland—Politics and government	320.9416	JN1572
Nonverbal communication in education	370.14	LB1033.5	Northern War, 1700-1721	947.05	DL733-743
Nonverbal intelligence tests	153.93	BF432.5.N65	Northwest Passage	910.0216327	G640-665
Nonwoven fabrics	677.6	TS1828	Northwest Territories—Maps	912.7192	G3530-3564
Noodles	641.822	TX809.N65	Northwest, Canadian	971.92	F1060-.97
Norm-referenced tests	371.271	LB3060.32.N67	Northwest, Old	977	F476-485
North America	970	E31-45	Norway—Biography	920.0363	DL444
North America—Biography	920.07	E36	Norway—Biography	920.0481	DL444
North America—Civilization	970	E40	Norway—Census	314.81	HA1501-1520
North America—Description and travel	917.04	E41	Norway—Civilization	936.3	DL431-433
North America—Gazetteers	917.003	E35	Norway—Civilization	948.1	DL431-433
North America—History	970	E45-46	Norway—Description and travel	913.6304	DL415-419.2
North America—Maps	912.7	G1105-1692	Norway—Description and travel	914.8104	DL415-419.2
North America—Maps	912.7	G3300-4884	Norway—Economic conditions	330.9481	HC361-370
North American language	497	PM	Norway—Emigration and immigration	325.(2481) or (481)	JV8210-8219
North America—Periodicals	970.005	E31	Norway—Gazetteers	913.63003	DL405
North Carolina	975.6	F251-265	Norway—Gazetteers	914.81003	DL405
North Carolina—Gazetteers	917.56003	F252	Norway—Historiography	936.30072	DL445
North Carolina—History—Colonial period, ca. 1600-1775	975.60(1-2)	F257	Norway—Historiography	948.10072	DL445
			Norway—History	936.3	DL401-596
North Carolina—History—Regulator Insurrection, 1766-1771	975.602	F257	Norway—History	948.1	DL401-596
			Norway—History—To 1030	936.3	DL460-478
			Norway—History—To 1030	948.101	DL460-478
North Carolina—History—Revolution, 1775-1783	975.60(2-3)	E263.N8	Norway—History—1030-1397	948.101	DL480-502
North Carolina—History—1775-1865	975.60(2-3)	F258	Norway—History—1397-1814	948.10(1-2)	DL485-502
North Carolina—History—Civil War, 1861-1865	975.603	E524	Norway—History—Christian IV, 1588-1648	948.102	DL490
North Carolina—History—Civil War, 1861-1865	975.603	E573	Norway—History— Scottish Expedition, 1612	948.102	DL490
North Carolina—History—1865-	975.604	F259-260.42	Norway—History—Hannibal's War, 1644-1645	948.102	DL490
North Carolina—Maps	912.756	G3900-3904			
North Carolina—National Guard	355.3709756	UA370-379	Norway—History—Frederick III, 1648-1670	948.102	DL490
North Carolina—Periodicals	975.6005	F251	Norway—History—Christian V, 1670-1699	948.102	DL495-.8
North Dakota	978.4	F631-645			
North Dakota—Gazetteers	917.84003	F634	Norway—History—War of 1807-1814	948.102	DL499
North Dakota—Maps	912.784	G4170-4174			
North Dakota—National Guard	355.3709784	UA380-389			

Subject Heading	Dewey	LC
Norway—History—1814-1905	948.103	DL503-526
Norway—History—Christian Frederick, 1814	948.10(2-3)	DL500-502
Norway—History—1905-1940	948.1041	DL530-532
Norway—History—Separation from Sweden, 1905	948.1041	DL525
Norway—History—German Occupation, 1940-1945	948.1041	DL532
Norway—History—1945-	948.10(43-5)	DL533
Norway—Manufactures	670.9481	TS81-82
Norway—Maps	912.481	G2065-2069
Norway—Maps	912.481	G6940-6944
Norway—Periodicals	936.3005	DL401-403
Norway—Periodicals	948.1005	DL401-403
Norway—Politics and government	320.9481	JN7401-7695
Norwegian drama	839.82208	PT8699-8718
Norwegian drama	839.82209	PT8500-8534
Norwegian fiction	839.82308	PT8720-8722
Norwegian fiction	839.82309	PT8555-8567
Norwegian language	439.82	PD2571-2699
Norwegian language—Dialects	439.827	PD2696-2699
Norwegian language—Dictionaries	439.823	PD2688-2695
Norwegian language—Etymology	439.822	PD2683-2684
Norwegian language—Grammar	439.825	PD2619-2673
Norwegian language—Lexicography	439.823028	PD2687-2695
Norwegian language—Slang	439.827	PD2699
Norwegian language—Study and teaching	439.82071	PD2611-2612
Norwegian literature	839.82	PT8301-9155
Norwegian literature (Nynorsk)	839.82	PT9000-9094
Norwegian literature—Study and teaching	839.82071	PT8340-8344
Norwegian philology	439.82	PD2501-2999
Norwegian poetry	839.82108	PT8675-8695
Norwegian poetry	839.82109	PT8460-8490
Norwegian prose literature	839.82808	PT8540-8567
Norwegian prose literature	839.82808	PT8719-8722
Nose	612.86	QP458
Nose—Diseases	616.21	RF341-437
Nose—Diseases—Eclectic treatment	617.52306	RV341-347
Nose—Diseases—Homeopathic treatment	617.52306	RX451
Note-taking	378.170281	LB2395
Nothing (Philosophy)	111.5	BD398
Notices to mariners	623.8922	VK798
Nova Scotia—Gazetteers	917.16003	F1036.4

Subject Heading	Dewey	LC
Nova Scotia—History	971.6	F1036-1040
Nova Scotia—Maps	912.716	G3420-3424
Nova Scotia—Periodicals	971.6005	F1036
Nowcasting (Meteorology)	551.6362	QC997.75
Nozzles	532.52	TC173
Nubian languages	496.5	PL8571-8574
Nuclear astrophysics	523.019	QB463-464.2
Nuclear chemistry	541.38	QD601-608
Nuclear counters	539.77	QC787.C6
Nuclear crisis stability	355.0217	U263
Nuclear energy	539.7	QC791.9-792.8
Nuclear energy	621.48	TK9001-9401
Nuclear engineering	621.48	TK9001-9401
Nuclear engineering—Periodicals	621.4805	TK9001
Nuclear engineering—Safety measures	621.480289	TK9152-.16
Nuclear fission	539.762	QC789.7-790.8
Nuclear fuel rods	621.4833	TK9207
Nuclear fuels	621.4833	TK9360
Nuclear fusion	539.764	QC790.95-791.8
Nuclear industry	333.7924	HD9698-.5
Nuclear magnetic resonance	538.362	QC762
Nuclear medicine	616.07575	R895-920
Nuclear physics	539.7	QC770-798
Nuclear power plants	621.483	TK1078
Nuclear power plants—Instruments	621.480284	TK9178-9183
Nuclear propulsion	621.485	TK9230
Nuclear reactors	621.483	QC786.4-786.8
Nuclear reactors	621.483	TK9202-9230
Nuclear reactors—Computer programs	621.4830285	QC783.3-.4
Nuclear reactors—Cooling	621.48336	TK9212
Nuclear rockets	629.4753	TL783.5
Nuclear saline water conversion plants	628.16723	TD479.6
Nuclear ships	623.8728	VM317
Nuclear ships	623.8728	VM774-777
Nuclear structure	539.74	QC793.3.S8
Nuclear submarines	359.93834	V857.5
Nuclear terrorism—United States	303.625073	HV6432
Nuclear warfare	355.0217	U263
Nuclear weapons	355.825119	U264
Nucleic acids	572.8	QP620-625
Nucleotide sequence	572.8633	QP625.N89
Nude in art	704.9421	N7572
Nudism	613.194	GV450
Nudist camps	613.19406	GV451-.4
Nullification	973.561	E384.3
Number concept	512.7	QA141.15
Number theory	512.7	QA241-247.5
Numbers, Divisibility of	512.72	QA242
Numbers, Prime	512.723	QA246
Numeration	513.5	QA141-.8

Subject Heading	Dewey	LC	Subject Heading	Dewey	LC
Numerical analysis	518	QA297-299.4	Object-oriented programming (Computer science)	005.117	QA76.64
Numerical calculations	518	QA297			
Numerical differentiation	518.53	QA355			
Numerical functions	512	QA246	Object constancy (Psychoanalysis)	616.8917	RC489.024
Numerical integration	518.54	QA299.3-.4			
Numerical weather forecasting	551.634	QC996	Object relations (Psychoanalysis)	616.8917	RC489.025
Numerology	133.335	BF1623.P9	Objective tests	371.271	LB3060.32.035
Numismatics	737	CJ	Objectivity	121.4	BD220
Nunamiut Eskimos	979.8004971	E99.E7	Obligations (Law)	346.02	K830-968
Nurse and patient	610.730699	RT86.3	Oboe	788.5207	MT360-378
Nurse and physician	610.730699	RT86.4	Oboe music	788.52	M65-69
Nurse practitioners	610.730692	RT82.8	Obsessive-compulsive disorders	616.85227	RC533
Nurseries (Horticulture)	635	SB118.48-.75			
Nursery rhymes	398.8	PN6110.C4	Obstacles (Military science)	358.22	UG375
Nursery rhymes	398.8	PZ8.3	Obstetrical emergencies	618.3025	RG571-591
Nurses	610.73092	RT34-37	Obstetrical extraction	618.82	RG741
Nurses—Directories	610.73025	RT25	Obstetrical forceps	618.20284	RG739
Nurses' aides	610.730698	RT84	Obstetricians	618.2092	RG509-510
Nursing	610.73	RT	Obstetricians—Directories	618.20025	RG504-505
Nursing—[By region or country]	610.7309(4-9)	RT4-17	Obstetrics	618.2	RG
			Obstetrics, Eclectic	618.206	RV361-365
Nursing—Congresses	610.7306	RT3	Obstetrics, Homeopathic	618.206	RX476
Nursing—Data processing	610.730285	RT50.5	Obstetrics—Apparatus and instruments	618.200284	RG545
Nursing—History	610.7309	RT31			
Nursing—Philosophy	610.7301	RT84.5	Obstetrics—Case studies	618.209	RG529
Nursing—Practice	610.73069	RT86.7-.75	Obstetrics—History	618.209	RG511-518
Nursing—Psychological aspects	610.73019	RT86	Obstetrics—Research	618.20072	RG155
			Obstetrics—Surgery	618.8	RG725-791
Nursing—Research	610.73072	RT81.5	Occasional sermons	252	BV4254.2
Nursing—Societies, etc.	610.7306	RT1	Occasional services	265.9	BV199
Nursing—Study and teaching	610.73071	RT71-81	Occupational training	370.113	HD5715-.5
			Occluded fronts (Meteorology)	551.5512	QC880.4.F7
Nursing assessment	610.73069	RT48-.6			
Nursing diagnosis	610.73069	RT48.6	Occultism	133	BF1404-2050
Nursing ethics	174.2	RT85	Occultism—[By region or country]	133.09(4-9)	BF1434
Nursing homes	362.16	RA997-999			
Nursing schools	610.730711	RT71-81	Occultism—Congresses	133.06	BF1404
Nutation	521.9	QB165	Occultism—Dictionaries	133.03	BF1407
Nutrition	363.8	TX341-641	Occultism—Directories	133.025	BF1409
Nutrition	612.3	QP141-185.3	Occultism—History	133.09	BF1421-1429
Nutrition	613.2	RA784	Occultists	133.092	BF1408-.2
Nutrition—Study and teaching	363.8071	TX364-365	Occupational dermatitis	616.5	RL241
			Occupational health services	613.62	RC968-969
Nutrition disorders	614.5939	RA645.N87			
Nutrition disorders	616.39	RC620-627	Occupational neuroses	616.8521	RC552.03
Nutrition disorders in animals	636.089639	SF851-855	Occupational therapy	615.8515	RM735-.7
			Occupational therapy	616.89165	RC487
Nutritionally induced diseases	614.5939	RA645.N87	Occupations—Folklore	398.355	GR890-910
			Occupations—Statistics	331.7	HB2581-2787
Nutritionally induced diseases	616.39	RC622	Ocean-atmosphere interaction	551.5246	GC190-.5
Nuts	634.5	SB401	Ocean bottom	551.4683	GC87-.6
Oaths	394	GT3085	Ocean circulation	551.462	GC228.5-.6
Ob-Ugric languages	494.51	PH1251-1254	Ocean currents	551.462	GC229-299
Obesity	616.398	RC628-.5	Ocean engineering	620.4162	TC1501-1800

Subject Heading	Dewey	LC	Subject Heading	Dewey	LC
Ocean engineering—Congresses	620.416206	TC1505	Office buildings	725.23	NA6230-6234
Ocean engineering—Periodicals	620.416205	TC1501	Office equipment and supplies	651.2	HF5548-.115
Ocean temperature	551.4653	GC160-177	Office Management	651.3	HF5546-5548
Ocean travel	910.45	G540-550	Office practice—Automation	651.8	HF5548.125-.6
Ocean wave power	621.20422	TC147	Offshore support vessels	623.826	VM466.035
Ocean waves	551.463	GC205-226	Ogallala Indians	978.0049752	E99.O3
Oceania	990	DU	Ohio	977.1	F486-500
Oceania—Biography	920.099(5-6)	CT2900-3090	Ohio River Valley	977	F516-520
Oceania—Church history	279.9(5-6)	BR1490-1495	Ohio—Gazetteers	917.71003	F489
Oceania—Description and travel	919.(5-6)04	DU19-23.5	Ohio—History—To 1787	977.10(1-2)	F495
Oceania—Emigration and immigration	325.29(5-6) or 9(5-6)	JV9290-9470	Ohio—History—Revolution, 1775-1783	977.102	E263.O
Oceania—Gazetteers	919.(5-6)003	DU10	Ohio—History—1787-1865	977.103	F495
Oceania—Genealogy	929.107209(5-6	CS2191-2209	Ohio—History—War of 1812	977.103	E359.5.O2
Oceania—History	995-996	DU28.11-66	Ohio—History—Civil War, 1861-1865	977.103	E525
Oceania—Manufactures	670.99(5-6)	TS123-124	Ohio—History—1865-	977.104	F496-.2
Oceania—Politics and government	320.99(5-6)	JQ5995-6651	Ohio—Maps	912.771	G4080-4084
Oceania—Religion	299.92	BL2600-2630	Ohio—National Guard	355.3709771	UA390-399
Oceanographic instruments	551.460284	GC41	Ohio—Periodicals	977.1005	F486
Oceanographic research ships	623.8226	VM453	Oil-shales	662.3383	TN858-859
Oceanographic submersibles	387.2045	GC67	Oil burners	697.044	TH7466.06
Oceanography	551.46	GC	Oil fields—Production methods	622.338	TN870
Oceanography—Antarctic Ocean	551.4617	GC461-462	Oil filters	621.890284	TJ1081
Oceanography—Arctic Ocean	551.46132	GC401-455	Oil gasification	665.773	TP759
Oceanography—Atlantic Ocean	551.4613	GC481-711	Oil hydraulic machinery	621.20424	TJ843
Oceanography—Indian Ocean	551.4615	GC721-761	Oil industries	338.476655	HD9490-.5
Oceanography—Pacific Ocean	551.4614	GC771-871	Oil pollution of soils	628.55	TD879.P4
Oceanography—Research	551.46072	GC57-59	Oil pollution of water	628.16833	TD427.P4
Octets	785.18	M800-886	Oil reservoir engineering	622.3382	TN871
Ocular pharmacology	617.7061	RE994	Oil storage tanks	665.542	TP692.5
Odes	808.8143	PN6110.O4	Oil well drilling	622.3381	TN871.2-.3
Odessa (Ukraine), Battle of, 1941	940.5421772	D764.3	Oil well drilling rigs	622.3381	TN871.5
O'Donnell Camp (Philippines : Concentration camp)	940.5317599	D805.P5	Oil well drilling, Submarine	622.33819	TN871.3
			Oils and fats	664.3	TP669-699
Odors	152.166	BF271	Oilseed plants	633.85	SB298-299
Odors	612.86	QP458	Ointments	615.19	RS201.O3
Offenses against property	364.16	HV6635-6700	Ojibwa Indians	977.00497333	E99.C6
Offenses against property—United States	345.73026	KF9350-9379	Ojibwa language	497.333	PM851-854
			Oklahoma	976.6	F691-705
Offenses against public safety	364.142	HV6419-6433	Oklahoma—Gazetteers	917.66003	F692
			Oklahoma—History—Land Rush, 1889	976.604	F699
Offenses against the person	364.15	HV6493-6633	Oklahoma—History—Land Rush, 1893	976.604	F699
Offenses against the person—United States	345.73025	KF9304-9329	Oklahoma—Maps	912.766	G4020-4024
			Oklahoma—National Guard	355.3709766	UA400-409
			Oklahoma—Periodicals	976.6005	F691
			Old age	362.6	HV1450-1493
			Old age	612.67	QP86
			Old age homes	362.16	HV1454-.2
			Old age pensions	331.252	HD7105.3-.35

Subject Heading	Dewey	LC	Subject Heading	Dewey	LC
Old growth forests	333.75	SD387.043	Operation Restore Hope, 1992-1993	967.73053	DT407.42
Old Norse language	439.6	PD2201-2392	Operational art (Military science)	355.4	U161-163
Old Norse language—Dialects	439.67	PD2387-2392	Operator algebras	512.556	QA326
Old Norse Language—Dialects	439.67	PD2483-2489	Operetta	782.1209	ML1900
Old Norse language—Etymology	439.62	PD2361-2369	Ophthalmic drugs	617.7061	RE994
Old Norse language—Grammar	439.65	PD2229-2331	Ophthalmic lenses	617.7522	RE961-962
			Ophthalmic nursing	617.70231	RE88
Old Norse language—Lexicography	439.63028	PD2376-2385	Ophthalmologic emergencies	617.7026	RE48
Old Norse literature	839.6	PT7101-7338	Ophthalmologists	617.70232	RE31-36
Old Norse literature—Study and teaching	839.6071	PT7135-7139	Ophthalmologists—Directories	617.70025	RE22
Old Norse philology	439.6	PD2201-2392	Ophthalmology	617.7	RE
Old Norse poetry	839.6108	PT7230-7252	Ophthalmology—Congresses	617.7006	RE11
Old Norse Poetry	839.6109	PT7170-7175	Ophthalmology—History	617.709	RE26-30
Old Norse prose literature	839.6808	PT7177-7211	Ophthalmology—Instruments	617.700284	RE73
Old Norse prose literature	839.6808	PT7255-7262			
Old Order Mennonites	289.7092	BX8129.043	Ophthalmology—Periodicals	617.7005	RE6
Old Persian inscriptions	491.5111	PK6128	Ophthalmology—Societies, etc.	617.7006	RE1
Old Persian language	491.51	PK6121-6129			
Old Saxon language	439.4	PF3992-4000	Ophthalmology—Study and teaching	617.70071	RE56
Old Turkic language	494.31	PL31	Ophthalmology—Terminology	617.70014	RE20
Oligarchy	321.5	JC419			
Oligopolies	338.82	HD2757-2768	Opioid habit	616.8632	RC568.058
Olympia (Greece : Ancient sanctuary)	938.8	DF261.05	Opium	633.75	SB295.06
			Opium habit	362.293	HV5816
Olympics—Records	796.48	GV721.8	Opium habit	616.8632	RC568.06
Oman—Census	315.353	HA4565	Opium poppy	633.75	SB295.065
Oman—Economic conditions	330.95353	HC415.35	Opposition (Political science)	328.369	JF518
Oman—Maps	912.5353	G7560-7564	Ops (Roman deity)	292.2113	BL820.06
Oman—Politics and government	320.95353	JQ1843	Optic nerve	573.88	QL949
			Optic nerve	611.84	QM511
Omens	133.334	BF1777	Optical communications	621.3827	TK5103.59
Oncogenic DNA viruses	579.2569	QR372.058	Optical gyroscopes	629.1352	TL589.2.06
Oncology	616.994	RC254-282	Optical instruments	535.028	QC370.5-379
Onions	635.25	SB341	Optical instruments	616.700284	RE73
Online data processing—Downloading	005.7	QA76.55-.57	Optical measurements	535.0284	QC367
			Optical storage devices	621.39767	TK7895.M4
Ontario—Gazetteers	917.13003	F1056.4	Opticians	681.4092	RE940-981
Ontario—History	971.3	F1056-1059.7	Optics	535	QC350-467
Ontario—Maps	912.713	G3460-3464	Optimism	149.5	B829
Ontario—Periodicals	971.3005	F1056	Optimism	155.232	BF698.35.057
Ontology	111	BD300-450	Optimism	155.232	BJ1477
Opals	549.68	QE394.07	Optimum ship routing	387.52	VK570
Open-hearth furnaces	669.1422	TN740-742	Optometry	617.75	RE940-981
Open and closed shop	331.8892	HD6488-.2	Oracles	133.3248	BF1745-1779
Open plan schools	371.256	LB1029.06	Oracles	203.2	BL613
Opera	782.1	ML3858	Oracles, Greek	133.32480938	DF125
Operant conditioning	153.1526	BF319.5.06	Oral contraceptives	613.94322	RG137.5
Operas	782.1	M1500-1508	Oral interpretation	808.54	PN4145-4151
Operating systems (Computers)	005.43	QA76.76.063	Oral medication	615.6	RM162

Subject Heading	Dewey	LC	Subject Heading	Dewey	LC
Oral medicine	616.31	RC815-.6	Ordnance, Naval—History	359.8209	VF15
Oral reading	372.452	LB1573.5	Ordnance, Naval—Societies, etc.	359.8206	VF1
Oratorios	782.23	M2000-2007			
Oratory	808.85	PN4001-4355	Ordnance, Naval—[By region or country]	359.8209(4-9)	VF21-124
Oratory, Ancient	885.108	PA3479-3842			
Oratory—History	809.5	PN4021-4055	Ordnance, Naval—Africa	359.82096	VF115-119
Orbiting astronomical observatories	522.29	QB500.267-.268	Ordnance, Naval—Argentina	359.820982	VF36-37
Orbits	521.3	QB355-357	Ordnance, Naval—Asia	359.82095	VF101-113
Orbs	929.7	CR4485.07	Ordnance, Naval—Australia	359.820994	VF121-122
Orchards	634	SB354-402	Ordnance, Naval—Canada	359.820971	VF26-27
Orchestra	784.209	ML1200-1251	Ordnance, Naval—Central America	359.8209728	VF30-31
Orchestral music	784.2	M1000-1075			
Orchestral music—Analysis, appreciation	784.2117	MT125	Ordnance, Naval—Chile	359.820983	VF43-44
			Ordnance, Naval—Colombia	359.8209861	VF45-46
Order (Philosophy)	117	B105.07			
Orders of knighthood and chivalry	929.71	CR4501-6305	Ordnance, Naval—Europe	359.82094	VF55-96
			Ordnance, Naval—France	359.820944	VF71-72
Orders of knighthood and chivalry, Papal	255.7	CR5547-5575	Ordnance, Naval—Germany	359.820943	VF73-74.5
Orders of knighthood and chivalry, Papal	255.791	CR4701-4731	Ordnance, Naval—Great Britain	359.820941	VF57-64
Orders of knighthood and chivalry—[By region or country]	929.7(2-9)	CR4801-6305	Ordnance, Naval—Italy	359.820945	VF79-80
			Ordnance, Naval—Japan	359.820952	VF105-106
			Ordnance, Naval—Mexico	359.820972	VF28-29
Orders of knighthood and chivalry—Austria	929.736	CR4951-5005	Ordnance, Naval—New Zealand	359.820993	VF122.5
Orders of knighthood and chivalry—France	929.74	CR5025-5085	Ordnance, Naval—Portugal	359.8209469	VF83-84
			Ordnance, Naval—Russia	359.820947	VF85-86
Orders of knighthood and chivalry—Germany	929.73	CR5100-5475	Ordnance, Naval—Scandinavia	359.820948	VF86.5
Orders of knighthood and chivalry—Great Britain	929.72	CR4801-4917	Ordnance, Naval—South America	359.82098	VF34-54
Orders of knighthood and chivalry—Greece	929.795	CR5485-5489	Ordnance, Naval—Spain	359.820946	VF87-88
Orders of knighthood and chivalry—Italy	929.75	CR5500-5580	Ordnance, Naval—Turkey	359.8209561	VF111-112
			Ordnance, Naval—United States	359.820973	VF23-25
Orders of knighthood and chivalry—Poland	929.738	CR5713-5737	Ordnance, Naval—West Indies	359.8209729	VF32-33
Orders of knighthood and chivalry—Portugal	929.769	CR5900-5925	Ordnance, Rapid-fire	358.128	UF560-565
Orders of knighthood and chivalry—Russia	929.77	CR5657-5703	Ore carriers	623.8245	VM457
			Oregon	979.5	F871-885
Orders of knighthood and chivalry—Scandinavia	929.78	CR5745-5809	Oregon—Gazetteers	917.95003	F874
Orders of knighthood and chivalry—Spain	929.76	CR5819-5889	Oregon—History—To 1859	979.50(1-3)	F879-880
			Oregon—History—1859-	979.504	F881-.35
Ordinary-language philosophy	149.94	B828.36	Oregon—History—1951-	979.504(3-4)	F881.2-.35
			Oregon—Maps	912.795	G4290-4294
Ordination	262.14	BV685	Oregon—National Guard	355.3709795	UA410-419
Ordination	262.14	BV830	Oregon—Periodicals	979.5005	F871
Ordination—Catholic Church	264.02084	BX2240	Oregon Trail	979.503	F880
			Ores	622.34	TN400-580
Ordination of women	262.14	BV676	Organ	786.509	ML550-649
Ordnance	358.1282	UF520-780	Organ—Instruction and study	786.507	MT180
Ordnance testing	358.1280287	UF890			
Ordnance testing	359.80287	VF540	Organ donors	362.1783092	RD129.5
Ordnance, Naval	359.82	VF	Organ music	786.5	M6-14
			Organic acids	661.86	TP247.2

Subject Heading	Dewey	LC	Subject Heading	Dewey	LC
Organic compounds	661.8	TP247-248	Orthodox Eastern Church—Austria	281.9436	BX630-639
Organic compounds—Synthesis	547.2	QD262	Orthodox Eastern Church—Greece	281.9495	BX610-619
Organic farming	631.584	S605.5	Orthodox Eastern Church—Hungary	281.9439	BX630-639
Organic fertilizers	631.86	S654	Orthodox Eastern Church—Russia	264.01947	BX560-563
Organic gardening	635.0484	SB453.5			
Organic semiconductors	537.6223	QC611.8.07	Orthopedic apparatus	617.9	RD755-757
Organic solid state chemistry	541.0421	QD478	Orthopedic emergencies	616.7025	RD750
Organic wastes as feed	636.0855	SF99.W34	Orthopedic hospitals	362.11	RD705-706
Organic wastes as fertilizer	631.86	S654	Orthopedic hospitals—United States	362.110973	RD705.5
Organic water pollutants	628.1682	TD427.07	Orthopedic implants	617.470592	RD755.5-.7
Organizational behavior	658.019	HD58.7	Orthopedic nursing	616.70231	RD753
Organizational change	658.406	HD58.8	Orthopedic shoes	616.70284	RD757.S45
Organized crime investigation	363.25906	HV8079.073	Orthopedic slings	617.9	RD757.S5
Organometallic compounds	547.05	QD410-412.5	Orthopedic surgery	617.47	RD701-789
Oriental antiquities	709.31	N5343-5345	Orthopedic traction	617.9	RD736.T7
Oriental antiquities	950	DS11	Orthopedics	616.7	RD701-811
Oriental drama	895.2008	PJ371	Orthopedics—Diagnosis	616.70754	RD734-.5
Oriental languages	490	PJ	Orthopedics—History	616.709	RD725-726
Oriental languages	490	PL	Orthopedics—Periodicals	616.7005	RD711
Oriental languages—Etymology	490.2	PJ183	Orthopedics—Pictorial works	617.300222	RD733.2
Oriental languages—Grammar	490.5	PJ120-171	Orthopedists	616.70232	RD727-728
Oriental languages—Lexicography	490.3028	PJ187	Osage Indians	977.8004975254	E99.08
Oriental languages—Study and teaching	490.071	PJ65-69	Oscillations	531.32	QA865-867.5
			Oscillators, Electric	621.38412	TK6565.07
Oriental literature	895	PJ306-489	Osiris (Egyptian deity)	299.31	BL2450.07
Orientation (Psychology)	152.1882	BF299.07	Osmosis	541.3415	QD543
Orienteering	796.58	GV200.4	Osteitis	616.712	RC931.064
Origami	736.982	TT870	Osteoarthritis	616.7223	RC931.067
Oriya language	491.45	PK2561-2569	Osteopathic hospitals	362.11	RZ302-304
Ornamental evergreens	635.97715	SB435	Osteopathic medicine	615.533	RZ
Ornamental grasses	635.9	SB431.7	Osteopathic medicine	615.533	RZ301-397.5
Ornamental trees	635.977	SB435-437	Osteopathic medicine—Congresses	615.53306	RZ313
Ornithology	598	QL671-699	Osteopathic medicine—History	615.53309	RZ321-325
Orphanages	362.732	HV959-1420.5			
Orphanages—[By region or country]	362.73209(4-9)	HV971-1420.5	Osteopathic medicine—Periodicals	615.53305	RZ311
Orphanages—United States	362.7320973	HV971-995	Osteopathic medicine—Societies, etc.	615.53306	RZ301
Orphans	362.73	HV959-1420.5	Osteopathic medicine—Study and teaching	615.533071	RZ337-338
Orthodonic appliances	617.64300284	RK527-528	Osteopathic medicine—Vocational guidance	615.533023	RZ336
Orthodontics	617.643	RK520-528	Osteopathic physicians—Biography	615.533092	RZ331-332
Orthodontics, Corrective	617.643	RK527-528	Osteopathic physicians—Directories	615.533025	RZ333
Orthodox Eastern Church	281.9	BX200-754			
Orthodox Eastern Church	281.947	BX460-605	Osteopathic schools	615.5330711	RZ337-338
Orthodox Eastern Church—Government	262.01947	BX520-558	Osteoporosis	616.716	RC931.073
Orthodox Eastern Church—History	281.94709	BX485-492	Osteosarcoma	616.9947	RC280.B6
Orthodox Eastern Church—Liturgy	264.019	BX350-376	Otolaryngologic examination	617.51075	RF48-.5

Subject Heading	Dewey	LC	Subject Heading	Dewey	LC
Otolaryngological nursing	617.80231	RF52.5	Packet switching (Data transmission)	621.38216	TK5105
Otolaryngologists	617.51092	RF37-38	Packhorse camping	796.54	GV199.7
Otolaryngologists—Directories	617.510025	RF28	Paddle steamers	387.2044	HE566.P3
Otolaryngology	617.51	RF	Paddle tennis	796.346	GV1006
Otolaryngology, Operative	617.51059	RF51-52	Paddleball	796.34	GV1003.2
Otolaryngology—Congresses	617.51006	RF16	Pageants	394.5	GT3980-4099
Otolaryngology—Diagnosis	617.51075	RF48-.5	Pageants	791.62	PN3202-3299
Otolaryngology—History	617.5109	RF25-26	Pagodas	720.951	NA1540-1547
Otolaryngology—Periodicals	617.51005	RF11	Pagodas—Design and construction	690.61	TH4224
Otolaryngology—Societies, etc.	617.51006	RF1	Pahari languages	491.49	PK2591-2610
Otolaryngology—Study and teaching	617.80071	RF62	Pain	612.88	QP401
			Pain	616.0472	RB127
Otolaryngology—Wounds and injuries	617.51044	RF50	Pain	616.0472	RC73-.2
			Paint	667.6	TP934-937.5
Otology	617.8	RF110-320	Paint mixing	667.0283	TT310
Outdoor cookery	641.578	TX823	Painting	750	ND
Outdoor education	371.384	LB1047	Painting—Biography	759	ND34-38
Outdoor furniture	684.18	TT197.5.09	Painting—Catalogs	750.294	ND40-45
Outdoor life	796.5	GV191.2-200.56	Painting—Conservation and restoration	751.6	ND1630-1662
Outdoor medical emergencies	616.98	RC88.9.095	Painting—History	759	ND49-813
Outdoor photography	778.71	TR659.5	Painting—Study and teaching	750.71	ND1115-1120
Outlaws	364.3	HV6441-6453	Painting—[By region or country]	759.(1-9)	ND204-1113
Outlet stores	381.15	HF5429.2-.215			
Outline maps	912	GA101-130	Painting—Afghanistan	759.9581	ND992-.3
Outrigger canoes	386.229	GN440.2	Painting—Africa	759.96	ND1080-1099
Ovaries	573.665	QL881	Painting—Africa, East	759.9676	ND1097-.6
Ovaries	611.65	QM421	Painting—Africa, Southern	759.968	ND1091.7-1096.6
Overhead projection	371.335	LB1043.5	Painting—Africa, West	759.966	ND1098-1099
Overlay dentures	617.692	RK656-666	Painting—Algeria	759.965	ND1088-.3
Overtime	331.2572	HD5111	Painting—Argentina	759.982	ND330-339
Overtures	784.18926	M1004	Painting—Asia	759.95	ND960-1070.3
Oxidation	547.23	QD281.09	Painting—Asiatic Russia	759.957	ND992.4-999
Oxygen	546.721	QD181.01	Painting—Australia	759.994	ND1100-1105.3
Oxygen	661.0721	TP245.09	Painting—Austria	759.36	ND501-511.6
Oxygen therapy	615.836	RM666.08	Painting—Bahamas	759.97296	ND300-302
Oxygen—Physiological effect	572.53	QP913.01	Painting—Bolivia	759.984	ND340-349
			Painting—Brazil	759.981	ND350-359
Oyster fisheries	639.41	SH371	Painting—Burma	759.9591	ND1012-.3
Oyster shell	639.41	SH379.5	Painting—Cambodia	759.9596	ND1015-.3
Ozone layer	551.5142	QC881.2.09	Painting—Canada	759.11	ND240-249.5
Pacemaker, Artificial (Heart)	617.4120645	RC684.P3	Painting—Central America	759.9728	ND260-290
			Painting—Chile	759.983	ND360-369
Pacific Coast Indians, Wars with, 1847-1865	979.02	E83.84	Painting—China	759.951	ND1040-1049.6
			Painting—Colombia	759.9861	ND370-379
Pacific Island literature	899	PN849.026	Painting—Costa Rica	759.97286	ND273-275
Pacific Ocean—Maps	912.1964	G2860-2867	Painting—Cuba	759.97291	ND303-305
Pacific railroads	385.0979	HE1062	Painting—Denmark	759.89	ND711-723.3
Pacific railroads	385.0979	HE2763	Painting—Ecuador	759.9866	ND380-389
Pacific railroads—Early projects	385.0979	HE2763	Painting—Egypt	759.962	ND1081-1085.3
			Painting—El Salvador	759.97284	ND288-290
Pacific States—Maps	912.79	G4230-4232	Painting—Ethiopia	759.963	ND1086-.3
Pack transportation	358.25	UC300-305	Painting—Europe	759.(2-8)	ND450-955
Packaging	688.8	TS195-198.8	Painting—Finland	759.897	ND955.F5

Subject Heading	Dewey	LC	Subject Heading	Dewey	LC
Painting—France	759.4	ND541-553.3	Painting, Iraqi	759.9567	ND967-969
Painting—French Guiana	759.9882	ND397	Painting, Islamic	750.882971	ND146
Painting—Germany	759.3	ND568-589	Painting, Japanese	759.952	ND1050-1059.6
Painting—Great Britain	759.2	ND461-481	Painting, Korean	759.9519	ND1060-1070.3
Painting—Greece	759.3	ND591-603.3	Painting, Medieval	759.02	ND140-146
Painting—Guatemala	759.97281	ND276-278	Painting, Modern	759.06	ND160-196
Painting—Guyana	759.9881	ND395	Painting, Modern—17th century	759.04	ND180-182
Painting—Haiti	759.97294	ND306-308	Painting, Modern—18th century	759.04	ND186-188
Painting—Honduras	759.97283	ND279-281			
Painting—Hungary	759.39	ND512-522.6	Painting, Modern—19th century	759.05	ND190-192
Painting—India	759.954	ND1001-1010.3			
Painting—Indonesia	759.9598	ND1026-.8	Painting, Modern—20th century	759.06	ND195-196
Painting—Iran	759.955	ND980-989			
Painting—Israel	759.95694	ND977-979	Painting, Renaissance	759.03	ND170-172
Painting—Italy	759.5	ND611-623.3	Paired-association learning	153.1526	BF319.5.P34
Painting—Jamaica	759.97292	ND309-311	Pakistan—Census	315.491	HA4590.5
Painting—Japan	759.952	ND1050-1059.6	Pakistan—Civilization	934	DS379
Painting—Jordan	759.95695	ND979-.8	Pakistan—Civilization	954.91	DS379
Painting—Korea	759.9519	ND1060-1070.3	Pakistan—Description and travel	913.404	DS377
Painting—Laos	759.9594	ND1016-.3			
Painting—Lebanon	759.95692	ND976.6-.8	Pakistan—Description and travel	915.49104	DS377
Painting—Libya	759.9612	ND1089-.3			
Painting—Malaysia	759.9595	ND1025-.8	Pakistan—Economic conditions	330.95491	HC440.5
Painting—Mexico	759.972	ND250-259			
Painting—Morocco	759.964	ND1090-.3	Pakistan—Gazetteers	915.491003	DS376.8
Painting—New Zealand	759.993	ND1106-1108	Pakistan—Gazetteers	934.003	DS376.8
Painting—Nicaragua	759.97285	ND282-284	Pakistan—History	934	DS381.7-388.2
Painting—Norway	759.81	ND761-773.3	Pakistan—History	954.91	DS381.7-388.2
Painting—Oceania	759.99(5-6)	ND1110-1113	Pakistan—Manufactures	670.95491	TS104.5-.6
Painting—Pakistan	759.95491	ND1010.7-.73	Pakistan—Maps	912.5491	G2270-2274
Painting—Panama	759.97287	ND285-287	Pakistan—Maps	912.5491	G7640-7644
Painting—Paraguay	759.9892	ND400-409	Pakistan—Politics and government	320.95491	JQ629
Painting—Peru	759.985	ND410-419			
Painting—Philippines	759.9599	ND1027-1029	Pakistan—Religion	299.14122	BL2035
Painting—Poland	759.38	ND999.P6	Palaces	728.82	NA7710-7786
Painting—Portugal	759.69	ND821-833.3	Palaces	728.8209376	NA320
Painting—Puerto Rico	759.97295	ND312-314	Palaces	728.820938	NA277
Painting—Russia	759.7	ND681-699	Paleobotany—Africa	561.196	QE947
Painting—Saudi Arabia	759.9538	ND970-972	Paleobotany—Antarctic regions	561.19989	QE950
Painting—Scandinavia	759.8	ND701-793.3			
Painting—South America	759.98	ND320-439	Paleobotany—Arctic regions	561.1998(1-8)	QE934
Painting—Spain	759.6	ND801-813.3			
Painting—Sri Lanka	759.95493	ND1010.6-.63	Paleobotany—Asia	561.195	QE946
Painting—Surinam	759.9883	ND396	Paleobotany—Australia	561.1994	QE948
Painting—Sweden	759.85	ND781-793.3	Paleobotany—Canada	561.1971	QE938
Painting—Syria	759.95691	ND989.6-.8	Paleobotany—Central America	561.19728	QE941
Painting—Thailand	759.9593	ND1021-1023			
Painting—Tunisia	759.9611	ND1091-.3	Paleobotany—Europe	561.194	QE943-945
Painting—Turkey	759.9561	ND861-873.3	Paleobotany—Mexico	561.1972	QE939
Painting—United States	759.13	ND205-238	Paleobotany—New Zealand	561.1993	QE948.2
Painting—Uruguay	759.9895	ND420-429	Paleobotany—Oceania	561.199(5-6)	QE949
Painting—Venezuela	759.987	ND430-439	Paleobotany—South America	561.198	QE942
Painting—Vietnam	759.9597	ND1014-.63			
Painting—West Indies	759.9729	ND291-315	Paleobotany—United States	561.1973	QE936-937
Painting, Ancient	759.01	ND70-130			
Painting, Industrial	667.6	TT300-380	Paleobotany—West Indies	561.19729	QE940

Subject Heading	Dewey	LC	Subject Heading	Dewey	LC
Paleoclimatology	551.69	QC884-.2	Pali language—Etymology	491.372	PK1083-1086
Paleogeography	551.7	QE501.4.P3	Pali language—Grammar	491.375	PK1017-1073
Paleography	411.7	Z105-115.5	Pali language—Lexicography	491.373028	PK1087-1093
Paleolithic period, Lower	930.12	GN771	Pali literature	891.37	PK4501-4681
Paleomagnetism	538.727	QE501.4.P35	Pali philology	491.37	PK1001-1095
Paleontology	560	QE701-996.5	Palm frond weaving	746.41	TT877.5
Paleontology—Periodicals	560.5	QE701	Palm Sunday	263.92	BV53
Paleontology—Cambrian	560.1723	QE726	Palmistry	133.6	BF910-940
Paleontology—Cenozoic	560.178	QE735-741.3	Palms	635.9345	SB413.P17
Paleontology—Cretaceous	560.177	QE734	Palpitation	616.128	RC685.A65
Paleontology—Devonian	560.174	QE728	Pan (Greek deity)	292.2113	BL820.P2
Paleontology—Eocene	560.1784	QE737	Panama	972.87	F1561-1577
Paleontology—Jurassic	560.1766	QE733	Panama—Census	317.287	HA851-854
Paleontology—Mesozoic	560.176	QE731-734	Panama—Civilization	972.87	F1563.8
Paleontology—Miocene	560.1787	QE739	Panama—Description and travel	917.28704	F1564-.3
Paleontology—Oligocene	560.1785	QE738	Panama—Emigration and immigration	325.(27287) or (7287)	JV7429
Paleontology—Paleozoic	560.172	QE725-730	Panama—Gazetteers	917.287003	F1562
Paleontology—Precambrian	560.171	QE724	Panama—History	972.87	F1565.5-1567
Paleontology—Africa	560.96	QE757	Panama—History—To 1903	972.870(1-3)	F1566.45
Paleontology—Antarctic regions	560.9989	QE760	Panama—History—1903-1946	972.87051	F1566.5
Paleontology—Arctic regions	560.9981	QE744	Panama—History—Revolution, 1903	972.87051	F1566.5
Paleontology—Asia	560.95	QE756	Panama—History—1946-1981	972.8705(1-3)	F1566.5-1567
Paleontology—Australia	560.994	QE758	Panama—History—Coup d'etat, 1968	972.87051	F1566.5
Paleontology—Canada	560.971	QE748	Panama—History—1981-	972.87053	F1567
Paleontology—Central America	560.9728	QE751	Panama—History—American Invasion, 1989	972.87053	F1567
Paleontology—Europe	560.94	QE753-755	Panama—Maps	912.7287	G4870-4874
Paleontology—Mexico	560.972	QE749	Panama—Periodicals	972.87005	F1561
Paleontology—South America	560.98	QE752	Panamanian literature	860	PQ7520-7529.2
Paleontology—United States	560.973	QE746-747	Panarabism	320.5409174927	DS38
Paleontology—West Indies	560.9729(9)	QE750	Panbabylonism	299.21	BL1625.P3
Palestine—History—70-638	956.9402	DS123.5	Pancakes, waffles, etc.	641.815	TX770.P34
Palestine—History—638-1917	956.9403	DS124-125.5	Pancreas	573.377	QL866
Palestine—History—1799-1917	956.94034	DS125	Pancreas	611.37	QM353
Palestine—History—1917-1948	956.9404	DS125.5-126.4	Pancreas	612.34	QP188.P26
Palestine—History—Arab riots, 1920	956.9404	DS126	Pancreas—Diseases	616.37	RC857-858
Palestine—History—1929-1948	956.9404	DS126-.4	Pancreas—Secretions	612.34	QP195
Palestine—History—Arab riots, 1929	956.9404	DS126	Pandora (Greek mythology)	292.13	BL820.P
Palestine—History—Arab rebellion, 1936-1939	956.9404	DS126	Panhandle culture	976.481	E99.P244
Palestine—History—Proposed partition, 1937	956.9404	DS126	Panic disorders	616.85223	RC535
Palestine—History—Partition, 1947	956.9404	DS126.4	Panjabi language	491.42	PK2631-2639
Pali language	491.37	PK1001-1095	Pannonia Region	939.8	DJK77
Pali language—Dictionaries	491.373	PK1089-1095	Panoramas	745.8	N7436.5-.53
			Panoramas	751.74	ND2880-2881
			Pantheism	211.2	BL220
			Pantomimes	792.3	PN6120.P3-.P4
			Paoli Massacre, 1777	973.333	E241.P2
			Papacy	262.13	BX950-961

Subject Heading	Dewey	LC
Papacy—History—To 1309	262.13090 (1-23)	BX965-1263
Papacy and Christian union	280.042	BX9.5.P29
Papal decorations	255.791	CR5547-5577
Papal States	945.6	DG791-800
Papal States—History	945.6	DG796-800
Papal visits	262.13	BX958.V7
Paper	676	TS1080-1268
Paper	676	Z247
Paper-cutting machines	686.20284	Z249
Paper airplanes	745.592	TL778
Paper coatings	676.235	TS1118.F5
Paper finishing	676.234	TS1118.F5
Paper money	332.4044	HG348-353.5
Paper products	676	TS1080-1268
Paper sculpture	731.2	NB1270.P3
Paperhanging	698.6	TH8441
Papermaking	676	TS1080-1268
Papermaking—History	676.09	TS1090-1096
Paperweights	748.84	NK5440.P3
Papillomavirus diseases	571.992445	QR201.P26
Papovaviruses	579.2445	QR406-.2
Papua New Guinea	995.3	DU740
Papua New Guinea—Census	319.53	HA4013
Papuan languages	499.12	PL6601-6621
Papuans	305.89912	GN664.P2
Parabola	516.152	QA485
Parachute troops	356.166	UD480-485
Parachutes	629.134386	TL750-758
Parachutes—Rigging	629.134386	TL753
Parachuting	629.134386	TL750-758
Parachuting	797.56	GV769.5-770.2
Parades	394.5	GT3980-4096
Paradise	236.24	BT844-849
Paradise (Islam)	297.23	BP166.87
Paradox	165	BC199.P2
Paraguay	989.2	F2661-2699
Paraguayan literature	860	PQ8250-8259
Paraguay—Census	318.92	HA1041-1050
Paraguay—Civilization	989.2	F2670
Paraguay—Description and travel	918.9204	F2671-2676
Paraguay—Economic conditions	330.9892	HC221-225
Paraguay—Emigration and immigration	325.(2892) or (892)	JV7500-7509
Paraguay—Gazetteers	918.92003	F2664
Paraguay—History	989.2	F2679.35-2689.23
Paraguay—History—To 1811	989.20(1-3)	F2683-2684
Paraguay—History—Revolution of the Comuneros, 1721-1735	989.203	F2683
Paraguay—History—War of Independence, 1810-1811	989.203	F2683

Subject Heading	Dewey	LC
Paraguay—History—1811-1870	989.20(4-5)	F2686-2687
Paraguay—History—1870-1938	989.20(6-71)	F2688-.5
Paraguay—History—Revolution, 1904	989.2071	F2688
Paraguay—History—Revolution, 1922-1923	989.2071	F2688
Paraguay—History—Revolution, 1936	989.2071	F2688
Paraguay—History—1938-1989	989.207(1-3)	F2689
Paraguay—History—Revolution, 1947	989.2072	F2689
Paraguay—History—20th century	989.207	F2688
strightParaguay—History—1989-	989.2073	F2689.2-.23
Paraguay—History—Coup d'etat, 1989	989.2073	F2689.2
Paraguay—Manufactures	670.9892	TS51
Paraguay—Maps	912.892	G5380-5384
Paraguay—Periodicals	989.2005	F2661
Paraguay—Politics and government	320.9892	JL3200-3299
Parallel computers	004.35	QA76.5
Paralysis	618.92842	RJ301
Paralysis	618.92842	RJ496.P2
Paralytic shellfish poisoning	615.954	SH177.R4
Paranoid schizophrenia	616.898	RC514
Paraplegics	617.58	RC406.P3
Parapsychology	133	BF1001-1389
Parapsychology—Biography	133.092	BF1026-1027
Parapsychology—Congresses	133.06	BF1021
Parapsychology—Dictionaries	133.03	BF1025
Parapsychology—History	133.09	BF1028-.5
Parapsychology—Periodicals	133.05	BF1001-1008
Parapsychology—Study and teaching	133.071	BF1040.5
Parasites	591.65	QL757
Parasitic diseases	614.55	RA643-644
Parasitic diseases	616.96	RC119-.7
Parasitic plants	632.52	SB610-615
Parasitology	591.65	QL757
Parathyroid glands	612.44	QP188.P3
Parcel post	383.125	HE6171-6173
Parcel post—United States	383.1250973	HE6471-6473
Pardon	364.65	HV8692
Pardon—United States	345.73077	KF9695
Parent-teacher conferences	371.103	LC225.5
Parent and adult child	306.874084	HQ755.86
Parent and teenager	306.874	HQ799.15
Parental behavior in animals	591.563	QL762
Parental leave	331.25763	HD6065-.5

Subject Heading	Dewey	LC	Subject Heading	Dewey	LC
Parenteral solutions	615.19	RS201.P37	Pastoral art	700.421734	N8205
Parenteral solutions	615.855	RM149	Pastoral counseling	253.5	BV4012.2
Parenteral therapy	615.855	RM149	Pastoral counseling (Judaism)	296.61	BM652.5
Parenthood	306.874	HQ755.7-759.92	Pastoral counseling centers	253.5	BV4012.25
Parenting	306.874	HQ755.7-759.92	Pastoral medicine	253	BV4335
Parents' and teachers' associations	371.19206	LC230-235	Pastoral prayers	264.13	BV250-254
Parents of exceptional children	306.8740879	HQ759.913	Pastoral psychology	253.52	BV4012-.3
Parents of handicapped children	306.874087	HQ759.913	Pastoral systems	636.0845	SF140.P38
Paris (France)	944.36	DC701-790	Pastoral theology	253	BV4000-4470
Parish missions	269.6	BX2375	Pastoral theology (Islam)	297.61	BP184
Parkinsonism	616.833	RC382	Pastry	641.8659	TX773
Parkinsonism, Symptomatic	616.833	RC382	Pastures	633.202	SB199
Parks	363.68	SB481-485	Patchwork	746.46	NK9100-9499
Parks—United States	363.680973	SB482-483	Patent laws and legislation—England	346.420486	KD1361-1413.3
Parks—[Other countries or regions]	363.6809(4-9)	SB484-485	Patent laws and legislation—United States	346.730486	KF3091-3193
Parks—Management	363.68068	SB481-485	Patent medicines	615.1	RM671-.5
Parmesan cheese	637.354	SF272.P3	Patents	608	T201-342
Parodies	808.87	PN6110.P3	Patents—History	608.7	T221-323.7
Parody	808.87	PN6149.P3	Pathogenic bacteria	579.3	QR201
Parole	364.63	HV9278	Pathogenic fungi	571.995	QR245-248
Parsees	295	BL1500-1590	Pathogenic microorganisms	579.165	QR201
Part-songs	783.1	M1578-1600	Pathology	616.07	RB
Part-time employment	331.25727	HD5110-.2	Pathology—Congresses	616.0706	RB3
Parthian War, 113-117	937.07	DG294	Pathology—History	616.0709	RB15-.2
Partial dentures	617.692	RK664-666	Pathology—Periodicals	616.0705	RB1
Partial dentures, Removable	617.692	RK665	Pathology—Study and teaching	616.07071	RB123-124
Partial differential operators	515.7242	QA329.42	Patience	179.9	BJ1533.P3
Partial sums (Series)	515.243	QA295	Patient compliance	615.5	R727.43
Particle accelerators	539.73	QC787.P3	Patient education	615.507	RT90-.3
Particle accelerators	539.73	TK9340	Patio gardening	635.9671	SB473.2
Particle beams	539.73	QC793.3.B4	Patios	728.93	NA8375
Particles (Nuclear physics)	539.72	QC793-.5	Patriarchs (Bible)	222.110922	BS573
Parties to actions—United States	347.73052	KF8890-8896.5	Patriarchs and patriarchate	262.13	BX400-440
Partitions (Mathematics)	512.73	QA165	Patriarchy	321.1	GN479.6
Partnership—England	346.420682	KD2049-2054	Patriotic societies	369	HS2301-2460.7
Parts of speech	415	P270-288	Patriotic societies—United States	369.1	HS2321-2330
Party decorations	745.5941	TT900.P3	Patriotism—United States	323.60973	JK1758-1759
Parvovirus infections	571.99247	QR201.P33	Patriots' Day	394.26973	E231
Parvoviruses	579.247	QR408-.2	Pattern perception	006.4	Q327
Paschal mystery	263.93	BV55	Pattern perception	152.1423	BF311
Passenger ships	623.8243	VM381-383	Pattern perception	152.1423	QP360
Passion-plays	792.16	PN3203-3299	Pavements	625.8	TE250-278.8
Passivity (Psychology)	155.232	BF698.35.P36	Pavements, Asphalt	625.85	TE266-276
Passover	296.437	BM675.P3	Pavements, Concrete	625.84	TE278-.8
Passover	296.437	BM695.P3	Pavements, Mosaic	729.7	NA3750-3860
Passover cookery	641.5676437	TX739.2.P37	Pavements, Wooden	625.83	TE253
Passover sermons	296.4737	BM747.P3	Pawnbroking	332.34	HG2070-2106
Passports—United States	342.73082	KF4794-.5	Pawnee Indians	978.200497933	E99.P3
Pasta products	641.822	TX394.5	Pay equity	331.2153	HD6061-.2
Pastel drawing	741.235	NC880	Pearl fisheries	639.412	SH375-377
			Pearl Harbor (Hawaii), Attack on, 1941	940.5428	D767.92

Subject Heading	Dewey	LC
Pearl of great price (Parable)	226.8	BT378.P
Peasantry	331.763	HD1521-1542
Peasantry	333.32	HD1336-1339
Peasantry	391.024	GT1850
Peasantry—Social life and customs	390.24	GT5650-5680
Peat soils	631.826	S592.85
Pedantry	155.232	BF698.35.P43
Peddlers and peddling	381.092	HF5457-5459
Pediatric anesthesia	617.960083	RD139
Pediatric cardiology	618.9212	RJ421-426
Pediatric clinics	362.12	RJ27-28
Pediatric clinics—United States	362.110973	RJ27.2-.3
Pediatric emergencies	618.920025	RJ370
Pediatric endocrinology	618.924	RJ418-420
Pediatric gastroenterology	618.9233	RJ446-456
Pediatric hematology	618.9215	RJ411-416
Pediatric intensive care	618.920028	RJ370
Pediatric neurology	618.928	RJ486-496
Pediatric nursing	618.9200231	RJ245-247
Pediatric ophthalmology	618.920977	RE48.2.C5
Pediatric oral medicine	618.9231	RJ460-463
Pediatric pharmacology	615.1083(2-4)	RJ560-570
Pediatric respiratory diseases	618.922	RJ431-436
Pediatric urology	618.926	RJ466-478.5
Pediatricians	618.9200092	RJ43
Pediatricians—Directories	618.9200025	RJ29
Pediatricians—Societies, etc	618.920006	RJ1
Pediatrics	618.92	RJ
Pediatrics—Congresses	618.920006	RJ21
Pediatrics—History	618.920009	RJ36-42
Pediatrics—Periodicals	618.920005	RJ16
Pediatrics—Practice	618.920232	RJ33.5-.8
Pediatrics—Psychosomatic aspects	618.9200019	RJ47.5-.53
Pedodontics	617.645	RK55.C5
Peer counseling of students	371.4047	LB1027.5
Pegasus (Greek mythology)	292.13	BL820.P4
Peking man	569.97	GN284.7
Pelvic bones—Fractures	617.158	RD549-.5
Pelvic inflammatory disease	618.142	RG411
Pelvic pain	618.1	RG483.P44
Pelvis—Diseases	617.55	RC946
Pelvis—Diseases—Eclectic treatment	617.5506	RV297
Pen-based computers	004.16	QA76.89
Pen drawing	741.26	NC905
Penal colonies	365.34	HV8935-8962
Penance	264.02086	BX2260-2283
Penance	265.6	BV840-850
Penance (Jainism)	294.434	BL1375.P
Pencil drawing	741.24	NC890-895
Pendulum	531.324	QA862.P4
Penetration mechanics	620.1126	TA354.5
Penicillin	615.3295654	RM666.P35
Penicillin	615.3295654	RS165.P38
Peninsular Campaign, 1862	973.73(1-3)	E473.6-.68
Peninsular War, 1807-1814	940.27	DC231-233.5
Penis	611.64	QM416
Penis—Diseases	616.66	RC896
Penmanship	372.634	LB1536
Penmanship	372.634	LB1590
Penmanship	652.1	Z43-45
Pennsylvania—Gazetteers	917.48003	F147
Pennsylvania—History	974.8	F146-160
Pennsylvania—History—Colonial period, ca. 1600-1775	974.80(1-2)	F152-.2
Pennsylvania—History—1865-	974.804	F154-155.3
Pennsylvania—Maps	912.748	G3820-3824
Pennsylvania—National Guard	355.3709748	UA420-429
Pennsylvania—Periodicals	974.8005	F146
Pennsylvania Dutch	974.8004310748	F160.G3
Pens	681.6	TS1262-1266
Pentecost	263.94	BT122.5
Pentecost Festival	263.94	BV60
Pentecost Festival	394.266	GT4995.P45
Pentecost season	263.94	BV61-63
Pentecostal churches	289.94	BX8762-8780
Pentecostalism	270.82	BR1644-.5
People (Constitutional law)	342.08	K3224-3229
People (Constitutional law)	342.08	K3290-3304
People (Constitutional law)—United States	342.7308	KF4881-4921
Peptic ulcer	616.343	RC821
Peptide hormones	572.65	QP572.P4
Peptides	547.756	QD431-.7
Peptides	572.65	QP552.P4
Perceptual-motor learning	152.334	BF295-.5
Percussion drilling	622.23	TN279
Percussion drilling	628.114	TD412
Percussion instruments	786.809	ML1030-1040
Percussion music	786.8	M146
Perennials	635.932	SB434
Perfectionism (Personality trait)	155.232	BF698.35.P47
Performance contracts in education	371.393	LB2806.2
Performance practice (Music)	781.4409	ML457
Performing arts	790.2	PN1560-1590
Performing arts—History	790.209	PN1581
Performing arts—Law and legislation—England	344.42097	KD3720-3731
Perfumes	391.63	GT2340

Subject Heading	Dewey	LC	Subject Heading	Dewey	LC
Pericardium	611.11	QM181	Perspective	604.245	T369
Pericardium	616.11	RC685.P5	Perspective	742	NC749-750
Perinatal cardiology	618.3261	RG618	Perspiration	612.7921	QP221
Perinatal death	618.32	RG631-633	Perturbation (Astronomy)	521.4	QB361-407
Perinatology	618.32	RG600-650	Perturbation (Mathematics)	515.392	QA871
Periodic law	546.8	QD467	Peru	985	F3401-3619
Periodicals	050	AP	Peru—Census	318.5	HA1051-1070
Periodicals	050	PN4700-5650	Peru—Civilization	985	F3410
Periodicals—Indexes	050	AI11	Peru—Description and travel	918.504	F3410.5-3425
Periodontal disease	617.632	RK361-450	Peru—Economic conditions	330.985	HC226-230
Periodontics	617.645	RK361-450	Peru—Emigration and immigration	325.(285) or (85)	JV7510-7519
Periodontitis	617.632	RK450.P4	Peru—Gazetteers	918.5003	F3404
Peripheral vascular diseases	616.131	RC694	Peru—History	985	F3430.3-3448.4
Peritoneum	611.38	QM367	Peru—History—To 1548	985.0(1-2)	F3442
Peritonitis	618.7	RC867.5	Peru—History—Conquest, 1522-1548	985.02	F3442
Perjury	364.134	HV6326	Peru—History—1548-1820	985.0(2-4)	F3444
Permaculture	631.58	S494.5.P47	Peru—History—Insurrection of Tupac Amaru, 1780-1781	985.033	F3444
Permic languages	494.53	PH1001-1004			
Permutations	511.64	QA165			
Perpetual calendars	529.3	CE91-92	Peru—History—To 1820	985.0(1-4)	F3442-3444
Persecution	272	BR1600-1609	Peru—History—War of Independence, 1820-1829	985.0(4-5)	F3446
Persephone (Greek deity)	292.2114	BL820.P7			
Perseus (Greek mythology)	292.13	BL820.P5	Peru—History—1829-1919	985.0(5-631)	F3447
Persian cat	636.832	SF449.P4			
Persian drama	891.552009	PK6421-6422	Peru—History—Spanish question, 1864	985.05	F3447
Persian Gulf War, 1991	956.70442	DS79.72			
Persian Gulf War, 1991—Prisoners and prisons	956.704427	DS79.74	Peru—History—Revolution of 1872	985.061	F3447
			Peru—History—1919-1968	985.063(1-2)	F3448
Persian language	491.55	PK6201-6399			
Persian literature	891.55	PK6400-6599	Peru—History—Revolution, 1930	985.0632	F3448
Persian poetry	891.551009	PK6416-6420			
Persian prose literature	891.55808	PK6423	Peru—History—1968-1980	985.0633	F3448.2
Persian prose literature	891.55808	PK6443			
Personal archives	027.1	CD977	Peru—History—Coup d'etat, 1968	985.0633	F3448.2
Personal property	346.047	K783-793			
Personal property—Canada	346.71047	KE765-781	Peru—History—1980-	985.06(4-5)	F3448.2
Personal property—England	346.42047	KD1205-1465	Peru—Manufactures	670.985	TS52
Personal property—United States	346.73047	KF701-720	Peru—Maps	912.85	G5310-5314
			Peru—Periodicals	985.005	F3401
Personalism	141.5	B828.5	Peru—Politics and government	320.985	JL3400-3499
Personality	126	BD331			
Personality	158.1	BF698-.9	Peruvian literature	860	PQ8300-8498.36
Personality assessment	155.28	BF698.4-.8	Pessimism	149.6	B829
Personality development	155.41825	BF723.P4	Pessimism	155.232	BF698.35.P49
Personality disorders	616.858	RC554-569.5	Pesticidal plants	633.898	SB292
Personality questionnaires	155.283	BF698.8.P48	Pesticide residues in feeds	636.0855	SF98.P46
Personnel management	658.3	HF5549-.5	Pesticide resistance	632.95042	SB957
Persons (Canon law)	262.932	BX1939.P47	Pesticides	632.95	SB950.9-970.4
Persons (Law)—Canada	346.71012	KE498-606	Pesticides—Application	632.94	SB952.8-955
Persons (Law)—England	346.42012	KD723-785	Pesticides—Government policy	344.04633	SB970-.4
Persons (Law)—Ireland	346.415012	KDK185-205			
Persons (Law)—Northern Ireland	346.416012	KDE90-98	Pesticides—Physiological effect	571.49	QP801.P38
Persons (Law)—Scotland	346.411012	KDC350-378			
Persons (Law)—United States	346.73012	KF465-553			

Subject Heading	Dewey	LC	Subject Heading	Dewey	LC
Pests	632.(6-7)	SB599-1100	Pharmacopoeias	615.11	RS139-141.9
Pests—Biological control	632.96	SB975-989	Pharmacy	615.1	RS
Pests—Control	632.9	SB950-989	Pharmacy	636.08951	SF915-918
Pet boarding facilities	636.0887	SF414.3	Pharmacy, Homeopathic	615.532	RX671-675
Pet grooming salons	636.70833	SF427.55	Pharmacy, Military	355.345	UH420-425
Pet shows	636.0811	SF411.5	Pharmacy, Military	359.345	VG270-275
Petit mal epilepsy	616.853	RC374.5	Pharmacy—Congresses	615.106	RS3
Petition, Right of	323.48	JC609	Pharmacy—History	615.109	RS61-68
Petition, Right of	323.480973	JK1731	Pharmacy—Laboratory manuals	615.1078	RS93
Petrified forests	561.16	QE991	Pharmacy—Periodicals	615.105	RS21
Petroleum	622.3382	TN860-879	Pharmacy—Research	615.10724	RS122
Petroleum	665.5	TP690-692.5	Pharmacy—Societies, etc.	615.106	RS1
Petroleum—Prospecting	622.1828	TN271.P4	Pharmacy—Study and teaching	615.1071	RS101-121
Petroleum—Refining	665.53	TP690-692.5	Pharmacy—Study and	615.10710(4-9)	RS110-121
Petroleum—Storage	665.542	TP692.5	teaching—[By region or		
Petroleum as fuel	665.5	TP355	country]		
Petroleum pipelines	665.544	TN879.5-.6	Pharmacy—Terminology	615.1014	RS55
Petroleum products	665.5	TP690-692.5	Pharmacy management	615.1068	RS100-.4
Petroleum waste	628.16836	TD899.P4	Pharmacy technicians	615.1092	RS122.95
Petroleum waste	628.16837	TD800	Pharynx	611.32	QM331
Petrology	552	QE420-499	Pharynx—Diseases	616.32	RF481-499
Petrology—Periodicals	552.005	QE420	Pharyngitis	616.32	RF485
Petrology—Africa	552.096	QE453	Phase rule and equilibrium	541.392	QD503
Petrology—Antarctic regions	552.09989	QE456.5	Phase transformations (Statistical physics)	530.474	QC175.16.P5
Petrology—Arctic regions	552.09981	QE456	Phase-transfer catalysts	541.395	QD505
Petrology—Asia	552.095	QE452	Pheasant shooting	799.246	SK325.P5
Petrology—Australia	552.0994	QE453.5-454	Pheasants	598.625	QL696.G27
Petrology—Canada	552.00971	QE445.5-446	Phenology	578.42	QH544
Petrology—Central America	552.09728	QE447	Phenols	547.632	QD341.P5
Petrology—Europe	552.0094	QE451	Phenomenalism	142.7	BD352
Petrology—Mexico	552.00972	QE446.5-.6	Phenomenological	150.192	BF204.5
Petrology—New Zealand	552.0993	QE454.5-.6	psychology		
Petrology—Oceania	552.099(5-6)	QE455	Phenomenology	142.7	B829.5
Petrology—South America	552.098	QE449	Philadelphia (Pa.)	974.811	F158.1-.9
Petrology—United States	552.00973	QE444-445	Philippine languages	499.21	PL5501-6135
Petrology—West Indies	552.09729	QE448	Philippine literature	860	PQ8700-8899
Pets	636.0887	SF411-459	Philippine literature	899.21	PL5530-5547
Pets—Housing	636.0887	SF414.2	Philippines	959.9	DS651-689
Petting zoos	590.73	QL76-77.5	Philippines—Census	315.99	HA4611-4620
Pews and pew rights	247.1	BV863.P4	Philippines—Civilization	959.9	DS663-664
Pewter	739.533	NK8400-8420	Philippines—Commerce	381.09599	HF3811-3820
Phantom limb	617.58	RD553	Philippines—Description and travel	915.9904	DS658-660
Pharisees	296.812	BM175.P4	Philippines—Economic conditions	330.9599	HC451-460
Pharmaceutical arithmetic	615.10151	RS57			
Pharmaceutical chemistry	615.19	RS400-431	Philippines—Emigration and immigration	325.(2599) or (599)	JV8685
Pharmaceutical ethics	174.2	RS100.5			
Pharmaceutical museums	615.1074	RS123	Philippines—Gazetteers	915.99003	DS654
Pharmaceutical technology	615.19	RS192-210	Philippines—History—To 1521	959.901	DS673.8
Pharmacists	615.1092	RS71-73			
Pharmacists—Directories	615.1025	RS74-76	Philippines—History— 1521-1812	959.902	DS674
Pharmacognosy	615.321	RS160-167			
Pharmacokinetics	615.7	RM301.5	Philippines—History— 1521-1898	959.90(22-312)	DS674-.9
Pharmacology	615.1	RM300-671.5			
Pharmacology, Experimental	615.10724	RM301.25-.27			

Subject Heading	Dewey	LC	Subject Heading	Dewey	LC
Philippines—History—1812-1898	959.902	DS675	Philosophy, Iranian	181.5	B150-153
Philippines—History—Cavite Mutiny, 1872	959.902	DS675.5	Philosophy, Islamic	181.07	B740-753
Philippines—History—Coup d'etat, 1989	959.9047	DS686.6	Philosophy, Israeli	181.3	B5055-5059
Philippines—History—Insurrection, 1896-1898	959.9027	DS676	Philosophy, Italian	195	B3551-3656
			Philosophy, Japanese	181.12	B135-138
Philippines—History—Insurrection, 1899-1901	959.9031	DS679	Philosophy, Japanese	181.12	B5243-5244
			Philosophy, Jewish	181.06	B154-157
Philippines—History—Japanese occupation, 1942-1945	959.9035	DS686.4	Philosophy, Jewish	181.3	B755-759
			Philosophy, Korean	181.119	B139.1-.4
			Philosophy, Medieval	189	B720-785
Philippines—History—1946-1986	959.904(1-6)	DS686.5-.6	Philosophy, Mexican	199.72	B1015-1019
			Philosophy, Middle Eastern	181.3	B5025-5099
Philippines—History—1986-	959.904(7-8)	DS686.614	Philosophy, Middle Eastern	181.(6-8)	B5025-5099
			Philosophy, Modern	190	B790-5739
Philippines—History—Revolution, 1986	959.9047	DS686.62	Philosophy, Norwegian	198.1	B4411-4445
			Philosophy, Oriental	181	B121-162.7
Philippines—History—Attempted coup, 1987	959.9047	DS686.6	Philosophy, Oriental	181	B5000-5295
			Philosophy, Polish	199.438	B4687-4691
Philippines—Manufactures	670.9599	TS113.P6	Philosophy, Portuguese	196.9	B4591-4598
Philippines—Maps	912.599	G8060-8064	Philosophy, Renaissance	190	B770-785
Philippines—Politics and government	320.9599	JQ1250-1419	Philosophy, Romanian	199.498	B4821-4825
			Philosophy, Russian	197	B4201-4279
Philology	400	P	Philosophy, Shinto	181.09561	B162.6
Philosophers	109.22	B104	Philosophy, South American	199.8	B1030-1084
Philosophical anthropology	128	BD450			
Philosophical theology	230.01	BT40-55	Philosophy, Spanish	196.1	B4561-4568
Philosophy	100	B	Philosophy, Swedish	198.5	B4455-4495
Philosophy	100	BD	Philosophy, Swiss	199.494	B4628-4651
Philosophy, African	199.6	B5300-5320	Philosophy, Taoist	181.114	B163
Philosophy, American	191	B850-945	Philosophy, Turkish	199.561	B4871-4875
Philosophy, Ancient	180	B108-708	Philosophy, West Indian	199.729	B1028-1029
Philosophy, Ancient	189	B630-708	Philosophy—Congresses	106	B20
Philosophy, Arab	181.92	B740-753	Philosophy—Dictionaries	103	B40-48
Philosophy, Arab	181.92	B5295	Philosophy—History	109	B69-4695
Philosophy, Babylonian	181.6	B145-148	Philosophy—Periodicals	105	B1-8
Philosophy, Belgian	199.493	B4151-4175	Philosophy—Societies, etc.	106	B11-18
Philosophy, Buddhist	181.043	B162	Philosophy—Study and teaching	107.1	B52-.65
Philosophy, Canadian	191	B981-995			
Philosophy, Central American	199.728	B1025-1026	Philosophy—Terminology	103	B49-50
			Philosophy of mind	128.2	BD418-.5
Philosophy, Chinese	181.11	B125-128	Philosophy of nature	113	BD581
Philosophy, Chinese	181.11	B5230-5234	Phlebitis	616.142	RC696
Philosophy, Confucian	181.112	B127.C65	Phobias	616.85225	RC535
Philosophy, Czech	199.437	B4801-4805	Phobias in children	618.9285225	RJ506.P38
Philosophy, Danish	198.9	B4325-4395	Phoenician antiquities	939.44	DS80.3
Philosophy, Dutch	199.492	B4041-4095	Phoenician language	492.6	PJ4171-4187
Philosophy, Egyptian	181.2	B140-143	Phoenicians	381.093944	HF370
Philosophy, English	192	B1111-1674	Phoenicians	939.44	DS81-89
Philosophy, Finnish	198.8	B4711-4800	Phoenix (Ariz.)	979.173	F819.P57
Philosophy, French	194	B1801-2430	Phoenix Islands (Kiribati)	996.81	DU790
Philosophy, German	193	B2521-3396	Phonetic alphabet	421	PE1151
Philosophy, Greek (Modern)	199.495	B3500-3515	Phonetic spelling	421	PE1151
			Phonetics	414.8	P221-232
Philosophy, Hungarian	199.439	B4811-4815	Phonograph	780.26609	ML1055
			Phosphate minerals	549.72	QE389.64

Subject Heading	Dewey	LC	Subject Heading	Dewey	LC
Phosphate mines and mining	622.364	TN913-914	Photography—Plates	771.5322	TR281
Phosphatic fertilizers	631.85	S647	Photography—Printing processes	772.774	TR330-333
Phosphorus	546.712	QD181.P1	Photography—Processing	772.774	TR287-500
Photobiochemistry	572.435	QP517.P45	Photography—Studios and dark rooms	771.1	TR550-581
Photochemistry	541.35	QD701-731			
Photoconductivity	537.54	QC612.P5	Photography—Study and teaching	770.71	TR161
Photocopying	686.4	TR824-835			
Photoelasticity	620.11295	TA418.12	Photography—Tables	770.21	TR151
Photoelectric cells	621.381542	TK8300-8360	Photography—Wastes, Recovery of	771.47	TR225
Photoelectric multipliers	621.381542	TK8314			
Photoelectricity	537.54	QC611	Photography—[By region or country]	770.9(4-9)	TR21-127
Photoemission	537.54	QC715.15			
Photoengraving	686.2327	TR970-977	Photography—Africa	770.96	TR115-119
Photoengraving—Halftone process	686.2327	TR975	Photography—Argentina	770.982	TR36-37
			Photography—Asia	770.95	TR99-113
Photogrammetry	526.982	TA593	Photography—Asiatic Russia	770.957	TR109-110
Photogrammetry	526.982	TR693-696			
Photograph collections	779.074	N4000-4042	Photography—Australia	770.994	TR121-122
Photographers	770.92	TR139	Photography—Austria	770.9436	TR65-.2
Photographic chemicals	771.5	TR212	Photography—Bolivia	770.984	TR38-39
Photographic chemistry	771.5	TR210-212	Photography—Brazil	770.981	TR41-42
Photographic interpretation (Military science)	623.72	UG476	Photography—Canada	770.971	TR26-27
			Photography—Central America	770.9728	TR30-31
Photographic lenses	771.352	TR270-271			
Photographic reproduction of plans, drawings, etc.	686.4	TR920-923	Photography—Chile	770.983	TR43-44
			Photography—China	770.951	TR101-102
Photographic surveying	526.982	TA592-593.9	Photography—Colombia	770.9861	TR45-46
Photographs— Conservation and restoration	770.288	TR465	Photography—Ecuador	770.9866	TR47
			Photography—Egypt	770.962	TR117-118
			Photography—Europe	770.94	TR55-95
Photographs—Trimming, mounting, etc.	771.44	TR340	Photography—France	770.944	TR71-72.5
			Photography—Germany	770.943	TR73-74.5
Photography	770	TR	Photography—Great Britain	770.941	TR57-64
Photography, Artistic	770	TR183	Photography—Greece	770.9495	TR75-76
Photography, Artistic	770	TR640-688	Photography—India	770.954	TR103-104
Photography, High-speed	778.37	TR593	Photography—Iran	770.955	TR107-108
Photography, Military	623.72	TR785	Photography—Ireland	770.9415	TR59-60
Photography, Panoramic	778.36	TR661	Photography—Italy	770.945	TR79-80
Photography, Pinhole	771	TR268	Photography—Japan	770.952	TR105-106
Photography—Artificial light	778.72	TR600	Photography—Mexico	770.972	TR28-29
Photography—Biography	770.92	TR139-140	Photography—Netherlands	770.9492	TR77-78
Photography—Congresses	770.6	TR5	Photography—New Zealand	770.993	TR122.5-.6
Photography—Developing and developers	771.49	TR295	Photography—Norway	770.9481	TR81-82
			Photography—Oceania	770.99(5-6)	TR123-124
Photography— Encyclopedias	770.3	TR9	Photography—Paraguay	770.9892	TR51
			Photography—Peru	770.985	TR52
Photography—Enlarging	771.44	TR475	Photography—Russia	770.947	TR85-86
Photography—Enlarging	771.44	TR905	Photography—Spain	770.946	TR87-88
Photography—Equipment and supplies	771	TR196-199	Photography—Sweden	770.9485	TR89-90
			Photography—Switzerland	770.9494	TR91-92
Photography—Exhibitions	770.74	TR6	Photography—Turkey	770.9561	TR111-112
Photography—Films	771.5324	TR283	Photography—United States	770.973	TR22-25
Photography—History	770.9	TR15			
Photography—Lighting	778.72	TR590-620	Photography—Uruguay	770.9895	TR53
Photography—Negatives	771.43	TR290-312	Photography—Venezuela	770.987	TR54
Photography—Periodicals	770.5	TR1	Photography—West Indies	770.9729	TR32-33

Subject Heading	Dewey	LC	Subject Heading	Dewey	LC
Photography of sports	070.49796	TR821	Physically handicapped—[Other countries]	362.4809(4-9)	HV3024
Photogravure	686.2327	TR980	Physically handicapped—Services for	362.48	HV3011-3024
Photojournalism	070.49	TR820			
Photolithography	686.2325	TR940-950	Physician and patient	610.696	R727.3-.45
Photomechanical processes	686.232	TR925-997	Physicians	355.345092	UH400
			Physicians	610.695	R707-.4
Photometry	535.220287	QC391	Physicians—Biography	610.92	R134-.5
Photon beams	539.7217	QC173	Physicians—Directories	610.695025	R711-713.97
Photon rockets	629.4754	TL783.57	Physicists	530.092	QC15-16
Photonics	621.36	TA1501-1820	Physics	530	QC
Photons	539.7217	QC793.5.P42-.P429	Physics—Congresses	530.06	QC1
			Physics—Encyclopedias	530.03	QC5
Photonuclear reactions	539.756	QC794.8.P4	Physics—History	530.09	QC6.9-9
Photosensitivity disorders	616.5	RL247	Physics—Laboratory manuals	530.078	QC35-37
Photosynthesis	572.46	QK882			
Photostat	686.45	TR470	Physics—Philosophy	530.01	QC5.56-6.4
Phototherapy	615.831	RM835-844	Physics—Study and teaching	530.071	QC30-48
Phototypesetting	686.22544	TR1010			
Phrenology	139	BF866-885	Physics—Vocational guidance	530.071	QC29
Physical anthropology	599.9	GN49-298			
Physical diagnosis	616.0754	RC76-.5	Physiognomy	138	BF839.8-861
Physical distribution of goods	381.1	HF5415.6-.9	Physiological apparatus	571.0284	QP55
			Physiology	571	QP
Physical education and training	796.07	GV201-555	Physiology, Comparative	571.1	QP31-33
			Physiology, Pathological	571.9	RB113
Physical education and training, Military	355.5	U320-325	Physiology—Periodicals	571.05	QP1
			Physiology—Study and teaching	571.071	QP39-47
Physical education for children	613.7042	GV443			
			Physiology—Terminology	571.014	QP13
Physical fitness—Testing	613.70287	GV436	Phytogeography	581.9	QK101-474.5
Physical fitness centers	613.706	GV428-433	Piano	786.209	ML649.8-747
Physical geography	910.02	GB	Piano—Instruction and study	786.207	MT220-255
Physical geology	551	QE28.2			
Physical instruments	530.7	QC53-55	Piano music	786.2	M20-39
Physical laboratories	530.072	QC51	Piccolo	788.3309	ML935-937
Physical metallurgy	669.9	TN690	Piccolo music	788.33	M110.P5
Physical optics	535.2	QC392-449.5	Picketing	331.8927	HD5468
Physical sciences	500.2	Q	Picnicking	394.15	GT2955
Physical therapists	615.82092	RM699.5-.7	Picture-writing, Indian	497	E98.P6
Physical therapists—Directories	615.82025	RM697	Picture books	741.6	NC965.85
			Picture frames and framing	684	N8550-8553
Physical therapy	615.82	RM695-893	Pictures	750	ND1142-1146
Physical therapy—Congresses	615.8206	RM696	Pictures—Copying	702.872	N8580
			Pictures in education	371.3352	LB1043.67
Physical therapy—Societies, etc.	615.8206	RM695	Pidgin English	427.9	PM7891
			Pidgin languages	417.22	PM7801-7895
Physical therapy—Study and teaching	615.82071	RM706-707	Piece-work	331.2164	HD4928.P5
			Piece of eight	737.4946	CJ3189
Physically handicapped children—Education	371.91	LC4201-4580	Piers	627.31	TC357
			Pietism	273.7	BR1650-1653
Physically handicapped children—Vocational education	370.113087	LC4219.7	Piety	241.4	BV4647.P5
			Pig Latin	427	PE3729.U
			Pigments	622.3662	TN948.P5
Physically handicapped—[By region or country]	362.4809(4-9)	HV3023-3024	Pigments	667.29	TP934-937.5
			Pigments	751.2	ND1510
Physically handicapped—United States	362.480973	HV3023	Pigments (Biology)	572.59	QP670-671

Subject Heading	Dewey	LC	Subject Heading	Dewey	LC
Plants, Ornamental	635.9	SB403-450.87	Platonic love	184	B398.L9
Plants, Potted	635.986	SB415	Plato's cave (Allegory)	184	B398.C34
Plants, Protection of	632.9	SB950-989	Play (Philosophy)	790.01	B105.P54
Plants, Sex in	575.6	QK658-659	Play behavior in animals	591.563	QL763.5
Plants, Sex in	575.6	QK827-830	Player-piano music	786.66	M20-32
Plants, Useful	581.63	QK98.4	Playgrounds	796.068	GV421-433
Plants—Absorption of water	575.76	QK871	Playgrounds—Equipment and supplies	796.0680284	GV426-.5
Plants—Collection and preservation	580.75	QK61	Plazas	711.55	NA9070-9072
Plants—Disease and pest resistance	632.95042	SB750	Pleading—United States	347.73072	KF8866-8885
			Pleasure	152.42	BF515
Plants—Evolution	581.38	QK980-989	Pleurisy	616.25	RC751
Plants—Frost resistance	632.11	QK756	Plots (Drama, novel, etc.)	809.924	PN3378
Plants—Habitat	577	QK900-938	Plows	631.3	S683-685
Plants—Metabolism	572.42	QK881-897	Plumbing	696.1	TH6101-6729
Plants—Nutrition	572.42	QK867-898	Plumbing—Repairing	696.10288	TH6681-6685
Plants—Reproduction	575.6	QK825-830	Pluralism	147.4	BD394
Plants—Respiration	572.472	QK891	Plush	677.617	TS1680
Plants for land reclamation	631.64	S621.5.P59	Pluto (Planet)	523.482	QB701
Plants for soil conservation	631.45	S627.P55	Plywood	674.834	TS870
Plasma (Ionized gases)	530.44	QC717-.8	Pneumatic machinery	621.51	TJ950-1030
Plasma astrophysics	523.019	QB462.7-.72	Pneumatic presses	621.98	TJ1465
Plasma chemistry	541.0424	QD581	Pneumatic tools	621.904	TJ1005-1007
Plasma exchange (Therapeutics)	615.39	RM175-176	Pneumatics	533	QC161-166.5
			Pneumonia	616.241	RA644.P8
Plasma exchange (Therapeutics)	616.99406	RC271.P54	Pneumonia	616.241	RC771-772
			Poaching	799.2028	SK36.7
Plasma rockets	629.4755	TL783.6	Podiatry	617.585	RD563
Plaster	693.6	TH8135-8139	Poetics	808.1	PN1039-1049
Plaster casts	731.452	NB1190	Poetry	808.1	PN1010-1525
Plastic analysis (Engineering)	620.11233	TA652	Poetry, Medieval	808.82	PN688-691
			Poetry—Collections	808.108	PN6099-6110
Plastic foams	668.493	TP1183.F6	Poetry—History and criticism	809.1	PN1105-1279
Plastic sculpture	731.2	NB1270.P5			
Plasticity	531.385	QA931-939	Poetry—Study and teaching	808.81071	PN1101
Plasticity	531.385	QC191			
Plastics	620.1923	TA455.P5-.P55	Poisoning	364.1791	HV6549-6555
Plastics	668.4	TP1101-1185	Poisoning	615.9	RA1190-1270
Plastics—Congresses	668.406	TP1105	Poisoning, Accidental, in children	615.90083	RA1225
Plastics—Encyclopedias	668.403	TP1110			
Plastics—Extrusion	668.413	TP1175.E9	Poisonous animals	591.65	QL100
Plastics—History	668.409	TP1116-1118	Poisonous fishes	597.165	QL618.7
Plastics—Molding	668.412	TP1150	Poisonous plants	581.659	QK100
Plastics—Patents	668.4027	TP1114	Poisonous snakes—Venom	615.942	RA1242.S53
Plastics—Periodicals	668.405	TP1103	Poisons	615.9	RA1190-1270
Plastics—Societies, etc.	668.406	TP1101	Poker	795.412	GV1251-1255
Plastics—Study and teaching	668.4071	TP1127-1129	Poland	943.8	DK4010-4800
			Poland—Biography	920.0438	DK4130-4138.5
Plastics—Welding	668.415	TP1160	Poland—Census	314.38	HA1451-1460
Plastics craft	745.572	TT297-.5	Poland—Civilization	943.8	DK4110-4115
Plastics in building	624.18923	TA668	Poland—Congresses	943.8006	DK4018
Plastics machinery	668.41	TP1135	Poland—Description and travel	914.3804	DK4047-4081
Plate tectonics	551.8	QE511.4-.48			
Plateaus	551.434	GB571-578	Poland—Economic conditions	330.9438	HC340.3
Plating	671.732	TS213			
Plating	671.732	TS662-693	Poland—Emigration and immigration	325.(2438) or (438)	JV8195

Subject Heading	Dewey	LC
Poland—Gazetteers	914.38003	DK4030
Poland—Historiography	943.80072	DK4139-.25
Poland—History—To 960 (ca.)	943.8022	DK4210-.7
Poland—History—Piast period, 960-1386	943.8022	DK4211-4249.5
Poland—History—Mieszko II, 1025-1034	943.8022	DK4222
Poland—History—Casimir I, 1040-1058	943.8022	DK4223
Poland—History—1138-1305	943.8022	DK4227-4246.5
Poland—History—Mongol Invasion, 1241	943.8022	DK4245.7
Poland—History—Jagellons, 1386-1572	943.8023	DK4249.7-4289
Poland—History—To 1572	943.802(2-3)	DK4186-4289
Poland—History—16th century	943.802(3-4)	DK4276
Poland—History—Elective monarchy, 1572-1763	943.802(4-5)	DK4289.5-4328
Poland—History—Partition period, 1763-1796	943.8025	DK4328.9-4348
Poland—History—Stanislaus II Augustus, 1764-1795	943.8025	DK4330-4348
Poland—History—Revolution of 1794	943.8025	DK4338-4345
Poland—History—To 1795	943.802(2-5)	DK4186-4348
Poland—History—18th century	943.80(25-3)	DK4314.5
Poland—History—Revolution, 1830-1832	943.8032	DK4359-4363
Poland—History—Partisan Campaign, 1833	943.8032	DK4363.2
Poland—History—Revolution, 1846	943.8032	DK4364
Poland—History—Revolution, 1863-1864	943.8033	DK4366-4378
Poland—History—1864-1918	943.8033	DK4379.5-4395
Poland—History—Revolution, 1905-1907	943.8033	DK4383-4389
Poland—History—German occupation, 1914-1918	943.8033	DK4390-4395
Poland—History—Austrian occupation, 1915-1918	943.8033	DK4394-4395
Poland—History—1918-1945	943.804(4-53)	DK4397-4420
Poland—History—Wars of 1918-1921	943.804	DK4404-4409
Poland—History—Coup d'etat, 1926	943.804	DK4409.4
Poland—History—Occupation, 1939-1945	943.8053	DK4410-4415
Poland—History—1945-	943.805(4-7)	DK4429-4442
Poland—History—1980-1989	943.8056	DK4443
Poland—History—1989-	943.8057	DK4442
Poland—Maps	912.438	G1950-1954
Poland—Maps	912.438	G6520-6524
Poland—Periodicals	943.8005	DK4010
Poland—Politics and government	320.9438	JN6750-6769
Polar regions	910.0211	G575-597
Polar regions—Maps	912.191	G1054-1055
Polar regions—Maps	912.191	G3260-3272
Polarization (Light)	535.52	QC440-446
Police	363.2	HV7551-8280.7
Police, Private	363.289	HV8290-8291
Police, Rural	363.2091734	HV7965-7985
Police—History	363.209	HV7903-7909
Police—Job stress	363.22019	HV7936.J63
Police—Study and teaching	363.2071	HV7923
Police—[By region or country]	363.209(4-9)	HV8130-8280.7
Police—Africa	363.2096	HV8267-8279.3
Police—Asia	363.2095	HV8241.85-8263
Police—Australia	363.20994	HV8280
Police—Benelux countries	363.209492	HV8215.5-8223.5
Police—Canada	363.20971	HV8157-8160
Police—Central America	363.209728	HV8163-8169
Police—China	363.20951	HV8260
Police—Directories	363.2025	HV7900
Police—Drug testing	363.2	HV7936.D78
Police—Europe	363.2094	HV8194-8261.84
Police—France	363.20944	HV8203-8206
Police—Germany	363.20943	HV8207-8210
Police—Great Britain	363.20941	HV8195-8197.5
Police—Greece	363.209495	HV8241.83
Police—India	363.20954	HV8247-8250
Police—Italy	363.20945	HV8212-8215
Police—Japan	363.20952	HV8257
Police—Mexico	363.20972	HV8161
Police—Middle East	363.20956	HV8241.9-8242.56
Police—Philippines	363.209599	HV8255
Police—Portugal	363.209469	HV8239
Police—Russia	363.20947	HV8224-8227
Police—South America	363.2098	HV8176-8193
Police—Spain	363.20946	HV8235-8238
Police—United States	363.20973	HV8130-8148
Police—West Indies	363.209729	HV8170-8175.9
Police administration	353.36	HV7935-8025
Police artists	363.258	HV8073.4
Police chiefs	363.22	HV8012
Police communication systems	363.24	HV7936.C8
Police divers	363.22	HV8080.D54
Police dogs	636.70886	HV8025
Police patrol—Field interrogation	363.232	HV8080.P2
Police patrol—Surveillance operations	363.232	HV8080.P2
Police power	342.0418	JK371.P7-.P8

Subject Heading	Dewey	LC	Subject Heading	Dewey	LC
Police power—Canada	342.710418	KE5006-5010	Polling places	324.65	JF1125
Police power—United States	342.730418	KF4695	Pollution	628.5	TD172-193.5
			Pollution—History	628.509	TD179
Police power—United States	342.730418	KF5399-.5	Pollution—Physiological effect	571.49	QP82.2.P6
Police psychiatrists	363.22	HV7936.P75	Pollution—Research	628.5072	TD178.5-.7
Police psychologists	363.22	HV7936.P75	Pollution—[By region or country]	628.509(4-9)	TD179.5-191
Police reports	363.24	HV7936.R53	Pollution—Africa	628.5096	TD188-.5
Police social work	363.22	HV8079.2-.3	Pollution—Arctic regions	628.50998	TD190-.5
Police stations	725.18	NA4490-4497	Pollution—Asia	628.5095	TD187-.5
Policewomen	363.22082	HV8023	Pollution—Australia	628.50994	TD189.5.A8
Poliomyelitis	616.835	RC180-181	Pollution—Canada	628.50971	TD182-.4
Poliomyelitis—Nursing	616.8350231	RC180.8	Pollution—Europe	628.5094	TD186-.5
Polish language	491.85	PG6001-6790	Pollution—Mexico	628.50972	TD182.6-.7
Polish language—Dialects	491.857	PG6700-6790	Pollution—New Zealand	628.50993	TD189.5.N4
Polish language—Lexicography	491.853028	PG6625-6638	Pollution—South America	628.5098	TD185-.5
			Pollution—United States	628.50973	TD180-181
Polish literature	891.85	PG7001-7446	Pollution control equipment	628.5028	TD192
Polish philology	491.85	PG6001-6790	Poltergeists	133.142	BF1483
Polishes	667.72	TP940	Polyandry	306.8423	GN480.6
Political anthropology	306.2	GN492-495	Polycarbonates	668.423	TP1180.P57
Political clubs	324.3	JF2101	Polyester fibers	677.4743	TS1548.7.P58
Political conventions	324.2730156	JK2255-2261	Polyesters	668.4225	TP1180.P6
Political corruption	324.66	JF1081-1083	Polygamy	306.8423	GN480.33-.36
Political crimes and offenses	364.131	HV6254-6322.7	Polygamy	306.8423	HQ981-996
Political customs and rites	398.27	GN492.3	Polyglot glossaries, phrase books, etc.	413	P361
Political geography	320.12	JC319-323	Polyglot glossaries, phrase books, etc.	418	PB73
Political parties	324.2	JF2011-2112			
Political parties—Great Britain	324.241	JN1111-1129	Polygons	516.154	QA482
			Polygraph operators	363.254092	HV8078
Political parties—United States	342.73087	KF4788	Polymerization	547.28	QD281.P6
			Polymerization	668.92	TP156.P6
Political persecution	323.044	JC585-599	Polymers	547.7	QD380-388
Political rights—Great Britain	323.0941	JN900-1088	Polymers	620.192	TA455.P58
			Polynesia	996	DU510
Political rights—United States	323.0973	JK1717-2217	Polynesia—Maps	912.96	G2970-2984
			Polynesia—Maps	912.96	G9500-9652
Political science	320	B65	Polynesian languages	499.4	PL6401-6551
Political science	320	HM33	Polytheism	211.32	BL217
Political science	320	J	Ponies	636.16	SF315
Political science	320	JA	Pontoon bridges	623.67	UG335
Political science—Congresses	320.06	JA35.5	Pontoon bridges	624.24	TG450
			Pool (Game)	794.733	GV891-899
Political science—History	320.09	JA81-84	Poor	362.5	HV4023-4470.7
Political science—Periodicals	320.05	JA1-26	Poor—[By region or country]	362.509(4-9)	HV4041-4173
Political science—Periodicals	320.05	JA51	Poor—Africa	362.5096	HV4157-4169.3
			Poor—Asia	362.5095	HV4131.85-4156.5
Political science—Societies, etc.	320.06	JA27-34			
Political science—Study and teaching	320.071	JA86-88	Poor—Australia	362.50994	HV4170
			Poor—Benelux countries	362.509492	HV4105.5-4113.5
Polka (Dance)	793.31	GV1796.P55			
Pollen	571.845	QK658	Poor—Canada	362.50971	HV4047-4050
Pollination	571.8642	QK926	Poor—Central America	362.509728	HV4053-4059
Pollination	575.65	QK828	Poor—China	362.50951	HV4150

Subject Heading	Dewey	LC
Poor—Developing countries	362.5091724	HV4173
Poor—Europe	362.5094	HV4084-4131.84
Poor—France	362.50944	HV4093-4096
Poor—Germany	362.50943	HV4097-4100.5
Poor—Great Britain	362.50941	HV4085-4087.5
Poor—India	362.50954	HV4137-4140
Poor—Italy	362.50945	HV4102-4105
Poor—Japan	362.50952	HV4147
Poor—Mexico	362.50972	HV4051
Poor—Russia	362.50947	HV4114-4117
Poor—South America	362.5098	HV4066-4083
Poor—Spain	362.50946	HV4125-4128
Poor—United States	362.50973	HV4043-4046
Poor—West Indies	362.509729	HV4060-4065.9
Popcorn	635.677	SB191.P64
Popes	262.13	BX1001-1378
Popes	262.13	BX1805-1810
Popes—Abdication	262.13	BX958.A23
Popes—Infallibility	262.131	BX1806
Popular instrumental music	784.16309	ML3469-3541
Popular music	781.63	M1627-1844
Popular music	781.6309	ML3469-3541
Population	304.6	HB848-3697
Population—History	304.609	HB851-853
Population assistance	363.96091724	HB884.5
Population biology	577.88	QH352
Population density	304.61	HB1953
Population genetics	576.58	QH455
Population geography—Afghanistan	304.609581	HB2096.6
Population geography—Albania	304.6094965	HB2086.5
Population geography—Algeria	304.60965	HB2121.4
Population geography—American Samoa	304.6099613	HB2153.7
Population geography—Angola	304.609673	HB2124.4
Population geography—Anguilla	304.60972973	HB2016.72
Population geography—Antigua	304.60972974	HB2016.74
Population geography—Arctic regions	304.60998	HB2155
Population geography—Argentina	304.60982	HB2019-2020
Population geography—Aruba	304.60972986	HB2017.35
Population geography—Australia	304.60994	HB2135-2136
Population geography—Austria	304.609436	HB2051-2052
Population geography—Azores	304.6094699	HB2127.5
Population geography—Bahamas	304.6097296	HB2007-2008
Population geography—Bahrain	304.6095365	HB2095.9
Population geography—Bangladesh	304.6095492	HB2100.6
Population geography—Barbados	304.60972981	HB2016.57
Population geography—Belgium	304.609493	HB2063-2064
Population geography—Belize	304.6097282	HB1995-1996
Population geography—Benin	304.6096683	HB2125.7
Population geography—Bermuda Islands	304.6097299	HB2128
Population geography—Bhutan	304.6095498	HB2100.3
Population geography—Bolivia	304.60984	HB2021-2022
Population geography—Bonaire	304.60972986	HB2017.36
Population geography—Botswana	304.6096883	HB2123.9
Population geography—Brazil	304.60981	HB2023-2024
Population geography—Bulgaria	304.609499	HB2087-2088
Population geography—Burkina Faso	304.6096625	HB2126.4
Population geography—Burma	304.609591	HB2096.7
Population geography—Burundi	304.60967572	HB2122.8
Population geography—Cambodia	304.609596	HB2104.3
Population geography—Cameroon	304.6096711	HB2125.4
Population geography—Canada	304.60971	HB1989-1990
Population geography—Canary Islands	304.609649	HB2129
Population geography—Cape Verde	304.6096658	HB2129.5
Population geography—Central African Republic	304.6096741	HB2125.2
Population geography—Chad	304.6096743	HB2125.3
Population geography—Chile	304.60983	HB2025-2026
Population geography—China	304.60951	HB2114
Population geography—Colombia	304.609861	HB2027-2028
Population geography—Comoro Islands	304.609694	HB2132.5
Population geography—Congo (Brazzaville)	304.6096724	HB2125
Population geography—Cook Islands	304.6099623	HB2153.65

Subject Heading	Dewey	LC	Subject Heading	Dewey	LC
Population geography—Costa Rica	304.6097286	HB1997-1998	Population geography—Guadeloupe	304.60972976	HB2017.7
Population geography—Cote d'Ivoire	304.6096668	HB2126	Population geography—Guam	304.609967	HB2152.7
Population geography—Cuba	304.6097291	HB2009-2010	Population geography—Guatemala	304.6097281	HB1999
Population geography—Curacao	304.60972986	HB2017.37	Population geography—Guinea	304.6096652	HB2126.2
Population geography—Cyprus	304.6095693	HB2093.5	Population geography—Guinea-Bissau	304.6096657	HB2127.3
Population geography—Czechoslovakia	304.609437	HB2052.3	Population geography—Guyana	304.609881	HB2032.3
Population geography—Denmark	304.609489	HB2071-2072	Population geography—Haiti	304.6097294	HB2011
Population geography—Djibouti	304.6096771	HB2122.3	Population geography—Honduras	304.6097283	HB2000
Population geography—Dominica	304.609729841	HB2016.93	Population geography—Hong Kong	304.6095125	HB2117
Population geography—Dominican Republic	304.6097293	HB2012	Population geography—Hungary	304.609439	HB2052.5
Population geography—Ecuador	304.609866	HB2029-2030	Population geography—Iceland	304.6094912	HB2073-2074
Population geography—Egypt	304.60962	HB2121.7	Population geography—India	304.60954	HB2099-2100
Population geography—Salvador	304.6097284	HB2004	Population geography—Indonesia	304.609598	HB2107-2108
Population geography—England and Wales	304.60942(9)	HB2045-2046	Population geography—Iran	304.60955	HB2096.4
Population geography—Equatorial Guinea	304.6096718	HB2124.6	Population geography—Iraq	304.609567	HB2096.3
Population geography—Ethiopia	304.60963	HB2122	Population geography—Ireland	304.609415	HB2049-2050
Population geography—Falkland Islands	304.6099711	HB2131	Population geography—Israel	304.6095694	HB2094
Population geography—Fiji	304.6099611	HB2153.5	Population geography—Italy	304.60945	HB2059-2060
Population geography—Finland	304.6094897	HB2068.3	Population geography—Jamaica	304.6097292	HB2013-2014
Population geography—France	304.60944	HB2053-2054	Population geography—Japan	304.60952	HB2111-2112
Population geography—French Guiana	304.609882	HB2032.7	Population geography—Jordan	304.6095695	HB2094.3
Population geography—French Polynesia	304.609962	HB2153.9	Population geography—Kenya	304.6096762	HB2122.5
Population geography—Gabon	304.6096721	HB2124.9	Population geography—Kerguelen Islands	304.609699	HB2134
Population geography—Gambia	304.6096651	HB2127	Population geography—Kiribati	304.6099681	HB2152.9
Population geography—Germany	304.60943	HB2055-2056	Population geography—Korea	304.609519	HB2112.5-.6
Population geography—Ghana	304.609667	HB2126.8	Population geography—Kuwait	304.6095367	HB2096
Population geography—Greece	304.609495	HB2092.5	Population geography—Laos	304.609594	HB2104.4
Population geography—Greenland	304.609982	HB2156	Population geography—Lebanon	304.6095692	HB2093.9
Population geography—Grenada	304.609729845	HB2016.95	Population geography—Lesotho	304.6096885	HB2123.7

Subject Heading	Dewey	LC	Subject Heading	Dewey	LC
Population geography—Liberia	304.6096662	HB2127.2	Population geography—Oman	304.6095353	HB2095.3
Population geography—Libya	304.609612	HB2121.6	Population geography—Pakistan	304.6095491	HB2100.5
Population geography—Liechtenstein	304.60943648	HB2052.9	Population geography—Panama	304.6097287	HB2002-2003
Population geography—Luxembourg	304.6094935	HB2066.5	Population geography—Papua New Guinea	304.609953	HB2152.8
Population geography—Macao	304.6095126	HB2115	Population geography—Paraguay	304.609892	HB2033-2034
Population geography—Madagascar	304.609691	HB2123.2	Population geography—Peru	304.60985	HB2035-2036
Population geography—Madeira Islands	304.6094698	HB2128.5	Population geography—Philippines	304.609599	HB2109-2110
Population geography—Malawi	304.6096897	HB2124	Population geography—Poland	304.609438	HB2068.7
Population geography—Malaysia	304.609595	HB2104.6	Population geography—Portugal	304.609469	HB2081-2082
Population geography—Maldives	304.6095495	HB2131.5	Population geography—Qatar	304.6095363	HB2095.7
Population geography—Mali	304.6096623	HB2126.3	Population geography—Reunion	304.6096981	HB2133.5
Population geography—Martinique	304.60972982	HB2017.9	Population geography—Romania	304.609498	HB2091-2092
Population geography—Mauritania	304.609661	HB2126.6	Population geography—Russia	304.60947	HB2067-2068.2
Population geography—Mauritius	304.6096982	HB2133	Population geography—Rwanda	304.60967571	HB2122.7
Population geography—Mexico	304.60972	HB1991-1992	Population geography—Saint Eustatius (Netherlands Antilles)	304.60972977	HB2017.385
Population geography—Mongolia	304.609517	HB2112.8	Population geography—Saint Helena	304.609973	HB2130
Population geography—Montserrat	304.60972975	HB2016.76	Population geography—Saint Lucia	304.609729843	HB2016.97
Population geography—Morocco	304.60964	HB2121.3	Population geography—Saint Martin	304.60972977	HB2017.39
Population geography—Mozambique	304.609679	HB2123	Population geography—Saint Vincent	304.609729844	HB2016.99
Population geography—Namibia	304.6096881	HB2124.2	Population geography—Saudi Arabia	304.609538	HB2094.7
Population geography—Nepal	304.6095496	HB2096.9	Population geography—Scotland	304.609411	HB2047-2048
Population geography—Netherlands	304.609492	HB2065-2066	Population geography—Senegal	304.609663	HB2126.5
Population geography—New Caledonia	304.6099597	HB2153.3	Population geography—Seychelles	304.609696	HB2132
Population geography—New Zealand	304.60993	HB2152.5	Population geography—Sierra Leone	304.609664	HB2126.9
Population geography—Nicaragua	304.6097285	HB2001	Population geography—Solomon Islands	304.6099593	HB2153
Population geography—Niger	304.6096626	HB2125.9	Population geography—Somalia	304.6096773	HB2122.2
Population geography—Nigeria	304.609669	HB2126.7	Population geography—South Africa	304.60968	HB2123.4
Population geography—Northern Ireland	304.609416	HB2048.5	Population geography—Spain	304.60946	HB2079-2080
Population geography—Norway	304.609481	HB2075-2076	Population geography—Sri Lanka	304.6095493	HB2096.8

Subject Heading	Dewey	LC	Subject Heading	Dewey	LC
Population geography—St. Kitts and Nevis	304.60972973	HB2016.78	Population geography—Zambia	304.6096894	HB2123.6
Population geography—Sudan	304.609624	HB2121.8	Population policy	363.9	HB883.5
Population geography—Surinam	304.609883	HB2032.5	Population Research	304.6072	HB850-.5
Population geography—Swaziland	304.6096887	HB2123.8	Porcelain	738.2	NK4370-4584
Population geography—Sweden	304.609485	HB2077-2078	Porches	721.84	NA7125
Population geography—Switzerland	304.609494	HB2083-2084	Pornography	363.47	HQ471-472
Population geography—Syria	304.6095691	HB2093.7	Pornography	704.9428	NX650.E7
Population geography—Taiwan	304.60951249	HB2116	Pornography—Social aspects	363.47	HQ471
Population geography—Tanzania	304.609678	HB2122.9	Port wine	663.223	TP559.P8
Population geography—Thailand	304.609593	HB2104.55	Portfolio management	332.6	HG4529.5
Population geography—Togo	304.6096681	HB2125.8	Portland cement	624.1833	TA680-683.94
Population geography—Tonga	304.6099612	HB2153.6	Portrait miniatures	704.942	N7616
Population geography—Trinidad and Tobago	304.60972983	HB2017	Portrait miniatures	757.7	ND1329.8-1337
Population geography—Tristan da Cunha	304.609973	HB2130.5	Portrait painting	751.42242	ND2200-2202
Population geography—Tunisia	304.609611	HB2121.5	Portrait painting	757	ND1300-1337
Population geography—Turkey	304.609561	HB2093.4	Portrait painting—15th century	757.090(24-31)	ND1308
Population geography—Uganda	304.6096761	HB2122.6	Portrait painting—16th century	757.09031	ND1308
Population geography—United States	304.60973	HB1965-1987	Portrait painting—17th century	757.09032	ND1309.3
Population geography—[United States, By state]	304.6097(4-9)	HB1985	Portrait painting—18th century	757.09033	ND1309.4
Population geography—[United States, By city]	304.6097(4-9)	HB1987	Portrait painting—19th century	757.09034	ND1309.5
Population geography—Uruguay	304.609895	HB2037-2038	Portrait painting—20th century	757.0904	ND1309.6
Population geography—Vanuatu	304.6099595	HB2153.4	Portrait painting—Biography	759	ND1328-1329
Population geography—Venezuela	304.60987	HB2039-2040	Portrait painting—Asia	757.095	ND1325-1326.8
Population geography—Vietnam	304.609597	HB2104.5	Portrait painting—Europe	757.094	ND1313-1324
Population geography—Western Sahara	304.609648	HB2127.4	Portrait painting—France	757.0944	ND1316-.6
Population geography—Western Samoa	304.6099614	HB2153.8	Portrait painting—Germany	757.0943	ND1317-.7
Population geography—Yemen	304.609533	HB2094.9-2095	Portrait painting—Great Britain	757.0941	ND1314-.6
Population geography—Yugoslavia	304.609497	HB2088.5	Portrait painting—Italy	757.0945	ND1318-.6
Population geography—Zaire	304.6096751	HB2124.5	Portrait painting—Netherlands	757.09492	ND1319-.6
			Portrait painting—Russia	757.0947	ND1320-.6
			Portrait painting—Spain	757.0956	ND1322-.6
			Portrait painting—United States	757.0973	ND1311-.9
			Portrait photography	778.92	TR575-581
			Portrait photography	778.92	TR680-681
			Portrait sculpture	731.82	NB1293-1310
			Portraits	704.942	N7575-7649
			Portugal	946.9	DP
			Portugal—Biography	920.0366	DP536
			Portugal—Biography	920.0469	DP536
			Portugal—Census	314.69	HA1571-1580
			Portugal—Civilization	936.6	DP532-.7
			Portugal—Civilization	946.9	DP532-.7
			Portugal—Colonies	325.3469	JV4200-4299
			Portugal—Description and travel	913.6604	DP520-526.5

Subject Heading	Dewey	LC	Subject Heading	Dewey	LC
Portugal—Description and travel	914.6904	DP520-526.5	Portugal—History—Revolution, 1640	946.902	DP628
Portugal—Economic conditions	330.9469	HC391-394.5	Portugal—History—John IV, 1640-1656	946.9032	DP634-.8
Portugal—Emigration and immigration	325.(2469) or (469)	JV8260-8269	Portugal—History—Alfonso VI, 1656-1683	946.9032	DP635
Portugal—Gazetteers	913.66003	DP514	Portugal—History—Peter II, 1683-1706	946.9032	DP636-.8
Portugal—Gazetteers	914.69003	DP514	Portugal—History—John V, 1706-1750	946.9032	DP638
Portugal—Historiography	936.60072	DP536.8-.96	Portugal—History—Joseph I, 1750-1777	946.9033	DP639-641.9
Portugal—Historiography	946.90072	DP536.8-.96	Portugal—History—Maria I, 1777-1816	946.903(3-4)	DP642-644.9
Portugal—History	936.6	DP501-900	Portugal—History—John VI, 1816-1826	946.903(4-5)	DP650-651
Portugal—History	946.9	DP501-900	Portugal—History—Conspiracy of 1817	946.9034	DP650
Portugal—History—To 1385	936.6	DP558-618	Portugal—History—Revolution, 1820	946.9035	DP650
Portugal—History—To 1385	946.90(1-2)	DP558-618	Portugal—History—1826-1853	946.903(5-6)	DP653-660
Portugal—History—Alfonso Henriques, 1139-1185	946.90(1-2)	DP570	Portugal—History—Civil War, 1846-1847	946.9035	DP659
Portugal—History—Sancho I, 1185-1211	946.902	DP571	Portugal—History—Uprising, 1846	946.9035	DP659
Portugal—History—Alfonso II, 1211-1223	946.902	DP572	Portugal—History—Peter V, 1853-1861	946.9036	DP665-.5
Portugal—History—Sancho II, 1223-1248	946.902	DP573	Portugal—History—Charles I, 1889-1908	946.9036	DP668-669
Portugal—History—Alfonso III, 1248-1279	946.902	DP574	Portugal—History—Revolution, 1891	946.9036	DP662
Portugal—History—Denis, 1279-1325	946.902	DP575-.3	Portugal—History—20th century	946.904	DP670-682.2
Portugal—History—Alfonso IV, 1325-1357	946.902	DP576	Portugal—History—1910-1974	946.904(1-3)	DP675-680.5
Portugal—History—Pedro I, 1357-1367	946.902	DP577	Portugal—History—Revolution, 1910	946.9041	DP674-682.2
Portugal—History—Fernando, 1367-1383	946.902	DP578	Portugal—History—Revolution, 1926	946.9042	DP680
Portugal—History—Interregnum, 1383-1385	946.902	DP580	Portugal—History—1974-	946.9044	DP680
Portugal—History—John I, 1385-1433	946.902	DP585-590	Portugal—History—Revolution, 1974	946.9044	DP681
Portugal—History—Period of discoveries, 1385-1580	946.902	DP582-618	Portugal—History—Coup d'etat, 1975	946.9044	DP681
Portugal—History—Edward, 1433-1438	946.902	DP592-594	Portugal—History, Military	355.009469	DP547
Portugal—History—Alfonso V, 1438-1481	946.902	DP596-598	Portugal—History, Naval	359.009469	DP550-551
Portugal—History—John II, 1481-1495	946.902	DP600-602	Portugal—Manufactures	670.9469	TS83-84.5
Portugal—History—Manual, 1495-1521	946.902	DP604-606	Portugal—Maps	912.469	G1975-1979
Portugal—History—John III, 1521-1557	946.902	DP608-610	Portugal—Maps	912.469	G6690-6694
Portugal—History—Sebastian, 1557-1578	946.902	DP612-616	Portugal—Periodicals	936.6005	DP501
Portugal—History—Henry I, 1578-1580	946.902	DP618	Portugal—Periodicals	946.9005	DP501
Portugal—History—Modern, 1580-	946.90(2-4)	DP620-682.2	Portugal—Politics and government	320.9469	JN8423-8661
Portugal—History—Spanish dynasty, 1580-1640	946.902	DP622-629	Portuguese drama	869.208	PQ9164-9170
			Portuguese drama	869.209	PQ9083-9095
			Portuguese language	469	PC5001-5498

Subject Heading	Dewey	LC	Subject Heading	Dewey	LC
Portuguese language—Dialects	469.7	PC5350-5498	Postnatal care	618.7	RG801-871
Portuguese language—Dictionaries	469.3	PC5325-5348	Postoperative pain	617.919	RD98.4
Portuguese language—Etymology	469.2	PC5301-5315	Postpartum depression	618.76	RG852
Portuguese language—Grammar	469.5	PC5061-5231	Postpartum psychiatric disorders	618.76	RG850-852
Portuguese language—Lexicography	469.3028	PC5320-5348	Posture	599.947	GN231-232
Portuguese language—Slang	469.709	PC5498	Posture	613.78	RA781.5
Portuguese language—Study and teaching	469.0071	PC5035-5039	Posture disorders	616.7	RD762
Portuguese literature	869	PQ9000-9999	Potassium salts	622.3636	TN919
Portuguese literature—Foreign countries	869	PQ9421	Potters	738.092	NK4200-4210
Portuguese literature—Study and teaching	869.071	PQ9008-9009.5	Pottery	666.3	TP785-842
Portuguese periodicals	056.9	PN5321-5330	Pottery	738	NK3700-4695
Portuguese philology	469	PC5001-5041	Pottery, Ancient	738.0901	NK3800-3855
Portuguese poetry	869.108	PQ9149-9163	Pottery, Medieval	738.0902	NK3870-3885
Portuguese poetry	869.109	PQ9061-9081	Pottery—[By region or country]	738.09(4-9)	NK4001-4184
Portuguese prose literature	869.80808	PQ9172-9188	Pottery—Collectors and collecting	738.075	NK4230
Portuguese prose literature	869.80809	PQ9097-9119	Potting soils	631.4	S589.8-.85
Position-finders	623.46	UF853	Poultry—Breeding	636.5082	SF492-493
Positivism	146.4	B831	Poultry—Diseases	636.50896	SF995-.4
Possession (Law)—England	346.420437	KD810-815	Poultry—Feeding and feeds	636.508(4-5)	SF494
Post-traumatic stress disorder	616.8521	RC552.P67	Poultry—Hatcheries	636.5082	SF495-497
Post office buildings	725.16	NA4450-4457	Poverty	339.46	HC79.P6
Postage stamps	383.23	HE6182-6228	Poverty	362.5	HV1-4630
Postage-stamp albums	769.56075	HE6221	Powder metallurgy	671.37	TN695-697
Postal rates	383.23	HE6125-6148	Powders (Pharmacy)	615.19	RS201.P8
Postal savings banks	332.22	HG1951-1956	Power-plants	621.3121	TJ164
Postal service	355.693	UH80-85	Power-plants	690.54	TH4581-4591
Postal service	359.34	VG60-65	Power (Mechanics)	621	TJ163.6-.95
Postal service	383.1	HE6000-7500	Power of attorney—England	346.42029	KD2022
Postal service—[By region or country]	383.49(4-9)	HE6300-7496	Power transmission	621.85	TJ1045-1119
Postal service—United States	383.4973	HE6300-6500	Power transmission	631.372	S711-713
Postal service—[Other countries]	383.49(4-9)	HE6651-7496	Powwows	394.2608997	E98.P86
Postal service—Biography	383.492	HE6061	Practical nursing	610.730693	RT62
Postal service—Directories	383.1025	HE6031	Practical theology	230	BV
Postal service—History	383.49	HE6041-6055	Pragmatics	144.3	B831.5
Postal service—Law and legislation	343.0992	K4245-4254	Pragmatics	401.9	P99.4.P72
Postal service—Study and teaching	383.1071	HE6036	Pragmatism	144.3	B832
Postal service—Unclaimed mail	383.1	HE6149	Prague (Czech Republic)	943.712	DB2600-2650
Postcards	383.122	HE6184.P65	Prairie ecology	577.44	QH541.5.P7
Postcards	741.683	NC1870-1879	Prairie Provinces—Maps	912.712	G3470-3504
Posters	659.132	HF5843-.5	Prairies	551.453	GB571-578
Posters	741.674	NC1800-1850	Prairies	581.744	QK938.P7
Postmarks	383.1	HE6182-6228	Prakrit languages	491.3	PK1201-1429
			Prakrit languages—Dictionaries	491.33	PK1223-1225
			Prakrit languages—Grammar	491.35	PK1206-1215
			Prakrit literature	891.308	PK5003-5009
			Prakrit literature	891.309	PK4990-5001.8
			Prayer	204.3	BL560
			Prayer—Buddhism	294.3443	BQ5595-5630
			Prayer—Christianity	264.13	BV205-287
			Prayer—Islam	297.382	BP178
			Prayer—Judaism	296.45	BM669

Subject Heading	Dewey	LC	Subject Heading	Dewey	LC
Prayer groups	242.2	BV287	Presbyterian Church in the U.S.A.	285.1	BX8950-8958
Prayer-books	242.8	BV245-283	Presbyterianism	285.(1-2)	BX8901-9225
Prayers	204.3	BL560	Presbyterians—Biography	285.092	BX9220-9225
Prayers	264.13	BV228-284	Preschool children	305.233	HQ774.5
Pre-trial procedure—United States	347.73072	KF8900-8902	Preschool teachers	372.21	LB1775.5
Preaching	251	BV4200-4317	Prescription writing	615.14	RM139
Preaching—History	251.009	BV4207-4208	Presidents	352.23	JF255
Precedence	929.7	CR3575	Presidents—Election	324.63	JF285
Precious metals	332.4042	HG258-312	Presidents—Messages	352.238	J80-82
Precious metals	622.342	TN410-439	Presidents—United States	352.230973	JK511-609
Precious stones	622.38	TN980-997	Presidents—United States—Election	324.0973	JK524-529
Precious stones	739.27	NK7650-7690	Presidents—United States—Messages	352.2380973	J82
Precious stones, Artificial	666.88	TP873-.5	Presidents—United States—Mistresses	321.80420973	E176.4
Precipitation (Meteorology)	551.577	QC929	Press	070.172	PN4700-5650
Precipitation gauges	551.5770284	QC926	Pressing of garments	648.1	TT583
Precipitation hardening	669.8	TN672	Pressure cookery	641.587	TX840.P7
Predestination	234.9	BT809-810.2	Pressure gages	621.185	TJ370-372
Predestination—Islam	297.227	BP166.3	Pressure vessels	681.76041	TS283
Prefabricated houses	643.2	TH4819.P7	Pressure welding	671.529	TS228.9
Pregnancy	618.2	RG551-591	Prestressed concrete construction	624.183412	TA683.9-.94
Pregnancy—Nutritional aspects	618.24	RG559	Prestressed construction	624.183412	TA665
Pregnancy—Psychological aspects	618.20019	RG560	Pretheological education	230.071	BV4163
Pregnancy—Signs and diagnosis	618.2075	RG563-564	Preventive dentistry	617.601	RK60.7-.8
Premenstrual syndrome	618.172	RG165	Price cutting	338.52	HF5417
Prenatal diagnosis	618.32075	RG628-.3	Price fixing	658.816	HF5417
Prenatal influences	618.24	RJ91	Price maintenance	658.816	HF5417
Preparatory schools	373.222	LC58-.7	Price regulation—England	343.42083	KD2215
Presbyterian Church	285	BX8901-9225	Prices	332.41	HG229-.5
Presbyterian Church—Education	268.85	BX8917-8925	Prices	338.52	HB221-236
Presbyterian Church—Government	262.05	BX9190-9195	Prices	338.52	HD6977-7080
Presbyterian Church—History	285.(1-2)09	BX8930-9169	Prices—Government policy	338.526	HB236
Presbyterian Church—Liturgy	264.05	BX9185-9187	Pricing	658.816	HF5416.5-5417
Presbyterian Church—Sermons	252.05	BX9178	Pride and vanity	179.8	BJ1535.P9
Presbyterian Church—Societies, etc.	285.(1-2)06	BX8905	Priests	206.1	BL635
Presbyterian Church—Africa	285.(1-2)6	BX9160-9162	Priests	262.03	BX5175-5182.5
Presbyterian Church—Asia	285.(1-2)5	BX9150-9151	Priests	262.14	BV659-683
Presbyterian Church—Canada	285.(1-2)71	BX9001-9003	Priests	262.142	BX1912-1914.5
Presbyterian Church—Europe	285.(1-2)4	BX9050-9140	Priests, Buddhist	294.361	BQ5140-5355
Presbyterian Church—Great Britain	285.(1-2)41	BX9052-9105	Priests, Jewish	221.92	BS1199.P7
Presbyterian Church—Latin America	285.(1-2)8	BX9011-9043	Primaries	324.2730154	JK2071-2077
			Primaries	324.54	JF2085
Presbyterian Church in the U.S.	285.1	BX8960-8968	Primary commodities	381.4	HF1040-1054
			Primary nursing	610.733	RT90.7
			Primates	599.8	QL737.P9-.P968
			Primates, Fossil	569.8	QE882.P7
			Prime ministers—Canada	342.7106	KE4730
			Prime ministers—Great Britain	342.4106	KD4462
			Primitivism in art	700.4145	ND1267
			Prince Edward Island—History	971.7	F1046-1049.7

Subject Heading	Dewey	LC	Subject Heading	Dewey	LC
Prince Edward Island—Maps	912.717	G3440-3444	Prisons—History	365.09	HV8497-8654
Prince Edward Island—Periodicals	971.7005	F1046	Prisons—Social aspects—Poland	365.9438	HV9715.7
Print finishing processes	686.2	Z244	Prisons—Statistics	365.021	HV8482-8488
Printed circuits	621.381531	TK7868.P7	Prisons—[By region or country]	365.9(4-9)	HV9441-9649
Printers	686.2092	Z231-234	Prisons—Africa	365.96	HV9836-9868.5
Printers' marks	686.20278	Z235-236	Prisons—Australia	365.994	HV9871-9875
Printing	686.2	Z	Prisons—Benelux countries	365.9492	HV9696-9710.5
Printing	686.2	Z116.A2-265.5.A5	Prisons—Canada	365.971	HV9501-9510
Printing	686.225	Z242.9-264	Prisons—Central America	365.9728	HV9516-9550
Printing—History	686.09	Z124-242	Prisons—China	365.951	HV9816-9820
Printing—Layout	686.2252	Z246	Prisons—Europe	365.94	HV9636-9775.7
Printing—Specimens	686.224	Z250	Prisons—France	365.944	HV9661-9670
Printing—Study and teaching	686.071	Z122-.5	Prisons—Germany	365.943	HV9671-9680.5
Printing-press	681.62	Z249-.4	Prisons—Great Britain	365.941	HV9641-9650
Printing industry—Estimates	686.20299	Z245	Prisons—Greece	365.9495	HV9776-831
Printing ink	667.4	Z247	Prisons—India	365.954	HV9791-9795
Prints	769	NE	Prisons—Italy	365.945	HV9686-9695
Prints—[By region or country]	769.9(4-9)	NE501-794.5	Prisons—Japan	365.952	HV9811-9815
Prints—Catalogs	769.0294	NE63-75	Prisons—Mexico	365.972	HV9511-9515
Prints—Collectors and collecting	769.12	NE880-885	Prisons—Middle East	365.956	HV9776.5-9785.2
Prints—Conservation and restoration	769.0288	NE380	Prisons—Philippines	365.9599	HV9806-9810
Prints—Encyclopedias	769.03	NE20	Prisons—Russia	365.947	HV9711-9715
Prints—History	769.9	NE400-773	Prisons—South America	365.98	HV9576-9635
Prints—Marketing	381.45769	NE62	Prisons—Spain	365.946	HV9741-9745
Prints—Periodicals	769.05	NE1	Prisons—United States	365.973	HV9456-9481
Prints—Private collections	769.12	NE57-59	Prisons—West Indies	365.9729	HV9551-9575.95
Prints—Technique	760.28	NE830-835	Private banks	332.123	HG1978-2031
Prisms	516.156	QA491	Private duty nursing	610.732	RT104
Prisms	535.420284	QC425	Private investigators	363.289	HV8081-8099
Prison administration	365.068	HV8756-8763	Private masses	264.02036	BX2231.7
Prison discipline	365.643	HV8766-8778	Private revelations	248.29	BV5091.R4
Prison homicide	365.64	HV9025	Private schools	371.02	LC47-57
Prison industries	365.65	HV8888-8931	Private security services	363.289	HV8290-8291
Prison libraries	027.665	Z675.P8	Prize contests in advertising	659.17	HF6146.P75
Prison nurses	365.66	HV8833-8844	Probabilities	121.63	BC141
Prison physicians	365.66	HV8833-8844	Probabilities	519.2	QA273-274.8
Prison psychology	155.962	HV6089	Probation	364.63	HV9278
Prison reformers	365.7	HV8971-8978	Problem-solving therapy	616.8914	RC489.P68
Prison sentences	365	HV8708-8719	Procedure (Law)	347.05	K2100-2385
Prison violence	365.6	HV9025	Procedure (Law)—Canada	347.7105	KE8341-8605
Prison visits	365.6	HV8884	Procedure (Law)—England	347.4205	KD6850-7640
Prisoners, Transportation of	365.64	HV8935-8962	Procedure (Law)—Ireland	347.41505	KDK1580-1713
Prisoners—Russia (Federation)	364.130947	HV9715.15	Procedure (Law)—Northern Ireland	347.41605	KDE510-530
Prisoners of war—Japan—Diaries	940.547252092	D805.J3	Procedure (Law)—Scotland	347.41105	KDC840-915
Prisoners of war—United States	365.480973	UB803	Procedure (Law)—United States	347.7305	KF8700-9075
Prisons	365	HV8301-9960	Processes, Infinite	515.24	QA295
			Processions	394.5	GT3980-4099
			Proctology	616.35	RC864-866
			Producer cooperatives	334.6	HD3120-3260.9
			Producer cooperatives—[By region or country]	334.609(4-9)	HD3131-3260.9
			Product coding	381	HF5416
			Product management	658.5	HF5415.15-.157

Subject Heading	Dewey	LC	Subject Heading	Dewey	LC
Product recall	363.19	HF5415.9	Property tax—Law and legislation—United States	343.73054	KF6525-6558
Product safety—Law and legislation—United States	344.73042	KF3945-3965	Prophets	224	BS1501-1675.5
Production (Economic theory)	338	HD	Prophets (Mormon theology)	231.745	BX8643.P7
Production control	658.5	T56	Prophets, Pre-Islamic	297.246	BP166.4
Profession (Buddhist monastic orders)	294.3657	BL1478	Proportion (Anthropometry)	599.949	GN66-69
Professional education	378.013	LC1051-1071	Proportion (Art)	741.018	NC745
Professional employees	331.71	HD8038	Proportional representation	328.3347	JF1071-1075
Professional ethics	174	BJ1725	Proposition (Logic)	160	BC181
Professions	395.52	GT6110-6390	Proprietary libraries	027.2	Z675.P85
Professions—Law and legislation	344.01712	K4360-4375	Prospecting	622.18	TN270-271
Professions—Law and legislation—United States	344.7301712	KF2900-2940	Prostate	573.658	QL878
Profit	338.516	HB601	Prostate	611.63	QM416
Profit	338.516	HC79.P7	Prostate—Diseases	616.65	RC899
Profit-sharing	331.2164	HD2970-3110.9	Prosthesis	617.9	RD130
Profit-sharing—[By region or country]	331.216409(4-9)	HD2981-3110.9	Prosthodontics	617.69	RK641-667
Progesterone	612.405	QP572.P7	Prostitution	306.74	HQ101-440.7
Prognosis	616.075	RC80	Prostitution—[By region or country]	306.7409(4-9)	HQ141-270.7
Program music	781.56	ML3855	Prostitution—History	306.7409	HQ111-117
Program music	781.5609	ML3300-3354	Protective clothing	363.1172	HD7395.C5
Programmed instruction	371.334	LB1028.5	Protective coatings	667.9	TA418.76
Programming (Electronic computers)	005.1	QA76.6-.66	Protective coloration (Biology)	591.472	QL767
Programming (Mathematics)	519.7	QA402.5	Proteins	547.75	QD431-.7
Programming languages (Electronic computers)	005.13	QA76.7-.73	Protest songs	781.592	M1977.P75
Progress	303.44	CB155	Protestant church buildings	726.58(1-9)	NA4828.5
Progress	303.44	HM101-121	Protestant churches	280.4	BX4800-9999
Progressive taxation	336.293	HJ2326-2327	Protestant churches—Missions	266	BV2350-2595
Projectiles	358.1282513	UF750-770	Protestant churches—Missions—History	266.009	BV2400-2595
Projectiles	359.8251	VF480-500	Protestant churches—Relations	280.4	BX4818-.3
Projectiles, Aerial	358.128251	UF767	Protestant churches—Asia	280.4095	BX4857
Projection	516.5	QA501-521	Protestant churches—Central America	280.409728	BX4833.5-4834
Projection	604.245	T362-369	Protestant churches—Europe	280.4094	BX4837-4854
Projective techniques	155.284	BF698.7	Protestant churches—France	280.40944	BX4843
Projective techniques	616.890028	RC473.P7	Protestant churches—Germany	280.40943	BX4844-.5
Prolactin	612.405	QP572.P74	Protestant churches—Great Britain	280.40941	BX4838-4840
Proletariat	331.11	HD4801-8943	Protestant churches—Italy	280.40945	BX4847
Promises	177.3	BJ1500.P7	Protestant churches—Mexico	280.40972	BX4833
Promotions	658.31424	HF5549.5.P7	Protestant churches—South America	280.4098	BX4836
Proof theory	511.36	QA9.54	Protestant churches—Spain	280.40946	BX4851
Proofreading	686.2255	Z254	Protestant churches—West Indies	280.409729	BX4835
Propaganda	303.375	HM263	Protestantism	280.4	BX4800-4946
Propellers	623.873	VM753-757	Protestantism—History	280.409	BX4804-4807
Propellers, Aerial	629.13436	TL705-708	Protestantism—Periodicals	280.405	BX4800
Property	330.17	HB701-715			
Property tax	336.22	HJ4101-4936			
Property tax—[By region or country]	336.2309(4-9)	HJ4120-4460			
Property tax—Law and legislation	343.054	K4560-4564			

Subject Heading	Dewey	LC	Subject Heading	Dewey	LC
Protestants	280.4092	BX4800-9890	Prussia (Germany)— History— Revolution, 1848-1849	940.284	DD424
Protohistory	930	CB305			
Protozoa	579.4	QL366-369.2			
Protozoan diseases	616.936	RC118.7	Prussia (Germany)— History—William I, 1861-1888	943.0(76-83)	DD425-446
Provencal language	449	PC3201-3299			
Provencal language— Dialects	449.77	PC3296			
			Prussia (Germany)— History—1870-	943.08(2-8)	DD446-454
Provencal language— Etymology	449.2	PC3283-3286	Prussia (Germany)— History, Military	355.00943	DD354
Provencal language— Grammar	449.5	PC3219-3273	Prussia (Germany)— History, Naval	359.00943	DD358
Provencal language— Lexicography	449.3028	PC3287-3295	Prussia (Germany)— Periodicals	936.3005	DD301
Provencal language—Slang	449.7	PC3299	Prussia (Germany)— Periodicals	943.005	DD301
Provencal literature	849	PC3301-3359			
Proverbs	398.9	PN6400-6525	Prussia(Germany)— Gazetteers	914.3003	DD308
Providence and government of God	231.5	BT95-96.2	Prussian language	491.91	PG8201-8208
Providence and government of God	231.5	BT135	Prussian language—Dictionaries	491.913	PG8206
Prudence	179.9	BJ1533.P9	Pseudomonas	579.332	QR82.P78
Prussia (Germany)	936.3	DD301-491	Psoriasis	616.526	RL321
Prussia (Germany)	943	DD301-491	Psychiatric aides	616.890092	RC440.5
Prussia (Germany)— Biography	920.043	DD343-.8	Psychiatric day treatment	616.891	RC439.2
			Psychiatric emergencies	616.89025	RC480.6
Prussia (Germany)— Civilization	936.3	DD331	Psychiatric ethics	174.2	RC455.2.E8
			Psychiatric hospitals— Emergency service	362.2881	RC480.6
Prussia (Germany)— Civilization	943	DD331			
Prussia (Germany)— Description and travel	913.6304	DD314-320	Psychiatric nursing	616.890231	RC440
			Psychiatric referral	362.172	RC455.2.R43
Prussia (Germany)— Description and travel	914.304	DD314-320	Psychiatric social work	362.20425	HV689-690
			Psychiatry, Comparative	616.89	RC455.4.C6
Prussia (Germany)— Gazetteers	913.63003	DD308	Psychiatry—Differential therapeutics	616.891	RC480.52
Prussia (Germany)— Historiography	936.30072	DD345	Psychiatry—Methodology	616.89001	RC455.2.M4
			Psychoanalysis	150.195	BF173-175.5
Prussia (Germany)— Historiography	943.0072	DD345	Psychoanalysis	616.8917	RC500-510
			Psychoanalytic counseling	150.195	BF175.4.C68
Prussia (Germany)—History	936.3	DD341-454	Psychodiagnostics	616.89075	RC469-473
Prussia (Germany)—History	943	DD341-454	Psychodrama	616.891523	RC489.P7
Prussia (Germany)— History—1640-1740	943.0(41-52)	DD394-399.8	Psychohistory	901.9	D16.16
			Psychokinesis	133.88	BF1371-1389
Prussia (Germany)— History—Frederick William I, 1713-1740	943.052	DD399-.8	Psycholinguistics	401.9	P37
			Psychological child abuse	616.858223	RC569.5.P75
			Psychological consultation	158.3	BF637.C56
Prussia (Germany)— History—1740-1789	943.05(3-7)	DD406-413.2	Psychological literature	808.066	BF76.7
			Psychological literature	808.066	BF76.7
Prussia (Germany)— History—Frederick II, 1740-1786	943.053	DD401-413.2	Psychological tests	150.287	BF176-.5
			Psychological warfare	355.3434	UB275-277
			Psychologists	150.92	BF109
Prussia (Germany)— History—Frederick William II, 1786-1797	943.06	DD414-416	Psychologists— Professional ethics	174.915	BF76.4
			Psychology	150	BF
Prussia (Germany)— History—Frederick William IV, 1840-1861	943.07	DD424-.9	Psychology, Applied	158	BF636-637
			Psychology, Comparative	156	BF660-685
			Psychology, Forensic	614.15	RA1148

Subject Heading	Dewey	LC	Subject Heading	Dewey	LC
Psychology, Industrial	158.7	HF5548.7-.85	Public health—[By region or country]	614.09(4-9)	RA442-558
Psychology, Military	355.0019	U22.3	Public health—Africa	614.096	RA545-552
Psychology, Pathological	616.89	RC435-571	Public health—Asia	614.095	RA525-541
Psychology, Religious	201.615	BL53	Public health—Canada	614.0971	RA449-450
Psychology, Religious	201.615	BL53	Public health—Central America	614.09728	RA453-454
Psychology—Congresses	150.6	BF20	Public health—Developing countries	614.091724	RA441.5
Psychology—Dictionaries	150.3	BF31			
Psychology—History	150.9	BF81-105	Public health—Europe	614.094	RA483-523
Psychology—Methodology	150.1	BF38.5-39.8	Public health—Mexico	614.0972	RA451-452
Psychology—Periodicals	150.5	BF1-8	Public health—North America	614.097	RA443-450
Psychology—Research	150.72	BF76.5-.6			
Psychology—Study and teaching	150.71	BF77-80.7	Public health—South America	614.098	RA457-482
Psychology—Terminology	150.14	BF32	Public health—United States	614.0973	RA445-448.5
Psychopharmacology	615.78	RM315-334			
Psychoses	616.89	RC512-528	Public health—West Indies	614.09729	RA455-456
Psychosexual development	155.3	BF723.S4	Public health laws	344.04	K3566-3597
Psychosexual disorders	616.8583	RC556-560	Public health laws—Canada	344.71041	KE3575-3635
Psychosurgery	617.481	RD594-.15			
Psychotherapists—Professional ethics	174.2	RC455.2.E8	Public health laws—England	344.4204	KD3351-3375
Psychotherapy	616.8914	RC475-489	Public health laws—United States	344.7304	KF3775-3816
Psychotherapy—Failure	616.8914	RC489.F27			
Psychotherapy—Moral and ethical aspects	616.8914	RC455.2.E8	Public health nursing	610.734	RT97
			Public health surveillance	614.42	RA652.2.P82
Psychotherapy—Termination	616.8914	RC489.T45	Public hospitals	362.11	RA960-996
			Public hospitals—Outpatient services	362.12	RA974-.5
Psychotherapy patients—Abuse of	616.89140092	RC455.2.A28			
			Public housing—Law and legislation	344.063635	K3550-3553
Psychotropic drugs	615.788	RM315-334			
Pteridophyta	587	QK520-532	Public law	342	K3150
Puberty	612.661	QP84.4	Public libraries	027.5	Z675.C8
Public administration	350	JF	Public opinion	303.38	HM261
Public administration—Decision making	352.33	JF1525.D4	Public opinion polls	303.380723	HM261
			Public policy (Law)	342.041	K3220-3225
Public administration—Canada	351.71	JL1-500	Public relations	659.2	HD59-.6
			Public school closings	379.1535	LB2832.2
Public administration—Great Britain	351.41	JN309-678	Public schools	371.01	LC
			Public service employment	352.63	HD5713.5-.6
Public administration—United States	353	JK404-1685	Public speaking	808.851	PN4121-4130
			Public utilities	363.6	HD2763-2768
Public administration—[United States, By state]	352.1309(4-9)	JK2443-2525	Public utilities—Law and legislation	343.09	K3978-3990
			Public utilities—Law and legislation—Canada	343.7109	KE2020-2061
Public architecture	725	NA9050.5			
Public buildings	725	NA4170-5095	Public utilities—Law and legislation—England	343.4209	KD2535-2560
Public buildings—[By region or country]	725.09(4-9)	NA4201-4385			
			Public welfare	361.6	HV
Public buildings—United States	725.0973	NA4205-4228.3	Public welfare—Law and legislation	344.0316	K1960-2000
Public buildings—Access for the physically handicapped	725.087	NA2545.P5	Public welfare—Law and legislation	344.420316	KD3291-3315
			Public welfare—Law and legislation–United States	344.730316	KF3720-3745
Public contracts	346.023	HD3860-3861			
Public defenders	345.7301	JK1548.P8			
Public domain	343.02	K3476-3558			
Public health	614	RA			
Public health—Research	614.072	RA440.85-.87	Public works	363	HD3840-4420.8

Subject Heading	Dewey	LC
Public works—Law and legislation—England	343.420256	KD1195
Public works—Law and legislation—United States	344.7306	KF5865
Public worship	264	BV5-25
Publishers and publishing	070.5	Z278-550
Publishers and publishing—[By region or country]	070.509(4-9)	Z289-550
Puddings	641.8644	TX773
Pueblo Indians	978.9004974	E99.P9
Pueblo Indians—Antiquities	978.9004974	E78
Puerperal convulsions	618	RG831
Puerperal disorders	618.7	RG801-871
Puerperal psychoses	618.76	RG851
Puerto Rican literature	860	PQ7420-7440
Puerto Rico	972.95	F1951-1983
Puerto Rico—Census	317.295	HA901-910
Puerto Rico—Civilization	972.95	F1960
Puerto Rico—Description and travel	917.29504	F1961-1965.3
Puerto Rico—Emigration and immigration	325.(27295) or (7295)	JV7380-7389
Puerto Rico—Gazetteers	917.295003	F1954
Puerto Rico—History	972.95	F1970-1976.3
Puerto Rico—History—To 1898	972.950(1-4)	F1973
Puerto Rico—History—Insurrection, 1868	972.9504	F1973
Puerto Rico—History—1898- 1952	972.950(4-52)	F1975
Puerto Rico—History—Nationalist Insurrection, 1950	972.95052	F1975
Puerto Rico—History—1952-	972.95053	F1976-.3
Puerto Rico—Maps	912.7295	G4970-4974
Puerto Rico—Periodicals	972.95005	F1951
Puerto Rico—Politics and government	320.97295	JL1040-1059
Pulleys	621.85	TJ1103
Pullman cars	625.23	TF457
Pulmonary artery	611.13	QM191
Pulmonary circulation	612.2	QP107
Pulmonary embolism	616.249	RC776.P85
Pulmonary function tests	616.2075	RC734.P84
Pulmonary pharmacology	615.72	RM388-.7
Pulse	612.14	QP101
Pumping machinery	621.69	TJ899-927
Pumping stations	628.144	TD485-487
Punic War, 1st, 264-241 B.C.	937.04	DG243-244
Punic War, 2nd, 218-201 B.C.	937.04	DG247-249.4
Punic War, 3rd, 149-146 B.C.	937.04	DG252.6
Punishment	364.6	HV7231-9960
Pupil (Eye)	573.88	QL949
Pupil (Eye)	611.84	QM511
Pupil (Eye)	612.84	QP476
Puppets	791.53	PN1970-1979
Puppies	636.707	SF421-435
Purchasing power	332.41	HG229-.5
Pure Land Buddhism	294.3926	BQ8500-8769
Purgatory	236.5	BT840-842
Puritans	285.9	BX9301-9359
Puritans	974.02008825	F7
Puritans—[By region or country]	285.909(4-9)	BX9331-9359
Purity, Ritual—Islam	297.38	BP184.4
Puzzles	793.73	GV1491-1507
Pyramids	932.01	DT63-.5
Pyromania	616.85843	RC569.5.P9
Pyrometers	536.520287	QC277
Qatar—Census	315.363	HA4567
Qatar—Economic conditions	330.95363	HC415.37
Qatar—Maps	912.5363	G7580-7584
Qatar—Politics and government	320.95363	JQ1845
Quadrant	522.4	QB105
Quadrant	623.890284	VK583
Quadruliance, 1815	940.27	D383
Quadruple Alliance, 1718	940.253	D287.5
Quadruplets	306.875	GN63.6
Quakers—Biography	289.6092	BX7790-7795
Quality circles	658.4013	HD66-.2
Quality control	658.562	TS156-.6
Quality of life	306	HN25
Quality of work life	306.361	HD6951-6957
Quantity (Philosophy)	119	B105.Q34
Quantity cookery	641.57	TX820
Quantity theory of money	332.401	HG226.6
Quantum chemistry	541.28	QD462-464
Quantum electrodynamics	530.1433	QC679-680.5
Quantum electronics	537.5	QC685-689.55
Quantum field theory	530.143	QC174.45-.52
Quantum statistics	530.133	QC174.4-.43
Quantum theory	530.12	QC173.96-174.52
Quarantine	614.46	RA655-758
Quarantine—[By region or country]	614.4609(4-9)	RA664-758
Quarantine—Africa	614.46096	RA753-755
Quarantine—Asia	614.46095	RA738-751
Quarantine—Australia	614.460994	RA756
Quarantine—Canada	614.460971	RA671
Quarantine—Central America	614.4609728	RA675
Quarantine—Europe	614.46094	RA700-737
Quarantine—Mexico	614.460972	RA673
Quarantine—North America	614.46097	RA664-677
Quarantine—Oceania	614.46099(5-6)	RA758
Quarantine—South America	614.46098	RA678-699

Subject Heading	Dewey	LC	Subject Heading	Dewey	LC
Quarantine—United States	614.460973	RA665-667	Radar in speed limit enforcement	363.23320284	HV8079.5
Quarantine—West Indies	614.4609729	RA677	Radar meteorology	551.6353	QC973.45-.8
Quarks	539.72167	QC793.5.Q252-.Q2529	Radar transmitters	621.38483	TK6587
Quarreling	241.3	BV4627.Q	Radar—Military applications	623.7348	UG612-.5
Quarries and quarrying	622.292	TN277	Radiation	539.2	QC474-492
Quarries and quarrying—Safety measures	622.8	TN277	Radiation—Dosage	615.842	RM845-862.5
Quartets	785.14	M400-486	Radiation—Safety measures	621.480289	TK9152-.16
Quartz	549.68	QE391.Q2	Radiation carcinogenesis	616.994	RC268.55
Quasars	523.115	QB860	Radiation chemistry	541.382	QD625-655
Quasi contracts	346.029	K920	Radiation preservation of food	664.0288	TP371.8
Quasi contracts—England	346.42029	KD1924	Radiation sources	539.2	QC476.S6
Quasi contracts—United States	346.73029	KF1244-.5	Radiation sterilization	614.48	RA766.R2
Quebec (Province)—Gazetteers	917.14003	F1051.4	Radiators	697.507	TH7480-7495
Quebec (Province)—History	971.4	F1051-1055	Radicals (Chemistry)	541.224	QD471
Quebec (Province)—Maps	912.714	G3450-3454	Radio	621.384(1-5)	TK6540-6571.5
Quebec (Province)—Periodicals	971.4005	F1051	Radio—Antennas	621.384135	TK6565.A6
Queries (Authorship)	381.45808	PN161	Radio—Equipment and supplies	621.384 (1-5) + 0284	TK6560-6565
Queuing theory	519.82	QA274.8	Radio—Installation on ships	623.8932	VK397
Queuing theory	658.4034	T57.9	Radio—Interference	621.38411	TK6553
Quietism	248.47	BV5099	Radio—Periodicals	621.38405	TK6540
Quilting	746.46	TT835	Radio—Receivers and reception	621.38418	TK6563-6564
Quinine	633.88393	RS165.C3	Radio—Repairing	621.384 (1-5) + 0288	TK6553
Quintets	785.15	M500-586	Radio—Transmitters and transmission	621.384131	TK6561-6562
Quintuplets	306.875	GN63.6			
Quotation	808.882	PN171.Q6	Radio astronomy	522.682	QB475-479.55
Quotations	808.882	PN6080-6095	Radio beacons	621.384191	TL696.B4
Quotations, English	820.802	PN6081-6084	Radio broadcasting	384.54	HE8690-8699
Quotations, French	840.802	PN6086-6089	Radio broadcasting	791.44	PN1991-.9
Quotations, German	830.802	PN6090-6093	Radio comedies	791.44617	PN1991.8.C65
Rabbinical literature	296.1	BM495-532	Radio compass	623.8932	VK577
Rabbis	296.092	BM652	Radio compass	629.1352	TL696.C7
Rabbits	636.9322	SF451-455	Radio direction finders	629.1352	TL696.D5
Rabies	614.563	RA644.R3	Radio in aeronautics	629.1355	TL693-696
Rabies	616.953	RC148	Radio in education	371.3331	LB1044.5-.6
Race	270.089	BT734-.3	Radio in navigation	623.8932	VK397
Race	305.8	HT	Radio meteorology	551.635	QC972.6-973.8
Race	305.8	HT1501-1595	Radio music	781.544	M176.5
Race	909.04	CB195-281	Radio on boats	623.85641	VM325
Race—Religious aspects	200.8	BL65.R3	Radio plays	808.8222	PN6120.R2
Race—Religious aspects—Christianity	270.089	BT734-.3	Radio plays—Technique	808.222	PN1991.73
Race relations	305.8	GN496-498	Radio telescopes	522.682	QB479.2
Race relations	305.8	HT1501-1595	Radio waves	537.534	QC676-678.6
Race relations—History	305.8009	HT1507	Radio waves—Polarization	537.534	QC665.P6
Racetracks (Automobile racing)	796.72068	TE305	Radio, Military	623.7341	UG611-.5
Racetracks (Horse-racing)	798.40068	SF324-.4	Radioactive dating	551.701	QE508
Racing	796	GV1018	Radioactive pollution of the atmosphere	628.535	TD887.R3
Radar	621.3848	TK6573-6595			
Radar in astronomy	522.68	QB480	Radioactive pollution of water	628.1685	TD427.R3

Subject Heading	Dewey	LC	Subject Heading	Dewey	LC
Radioactive substances	549.528	QE364.2.R3	Railroads, Local and light— [By region or country]	388.4209(4-9)	HE3651-4043
Radioactive substances— Toxicology	616.9897	RA1231.R2	Railroads, Local and light— Periodicals	388.4205	HE3601
Radioactive substances in rivers, lakes, etc.	628.1685	TD427.R3	Railroads, Narrow-gage	385.52	TF675
Radioactive waste disposal	628.42	TD812-.4	Railroads—Baggage handling	385.22	HE2556
Radioactivity	539.752	QC794.95-798	Railroads—Baggage handling	625.23	TF656
Radioactivity—Instruments	539.770284	QC785.5-787	Railroads—Cars	385.37	HE1830
Radiochemistry	541.38	QD601-608	Railroads—Cars	625.2	TF371-499
Radioecology	577.277	QH543.5-.6	Railroads—Congresses	625.1006	TF5
Radiography, Medical	616.07572	RC78-.5	Railroads—Continuous rails	625.15	TF262
Radiotherapy	615.842	RM845-862.5	Railroads—Crossings	385.312	HE1617-1618
Radium—Therapeutic use	615.8423	RM859	Railroads—Crossings	625.163	TF263
Radon	546.756	QD181.R2	Railroads—Design and construction	625.1	TF200-320
Raeto-Romance language	459.9	PC901-949	Railroads—Design and construction—Costs	625.11299	TF193
Raeto-Romance language—Dialects	459.97	PC941-949	Railroads—Directories	385.025	HE1009
Raeto-Romance language—Dictionaries	459.93	PC937	Railroads—Directories	625.10025	TF12
Raeto-Romance language—Etymology	459.92	PC931	Railroads—Earthwork	625.12	TF220-226
Raeto-Romance language—Grammar	459.95	PC911-923	Railroads—Electrification	621.33	TF858-859
Raeto-Romance language—Slang	459.97	PC949	Railroads—Employees	331.761385	HE1741-1759
Raeto-Romance language—Study and teaching	459.9071	PC907	Railroads—Employees	385.092	HD8039.R1-.R45
			Railroads—Equipment and supplies	625.100284	TF340-499
Raeto-Romance literature	859.9	PC951-986	Railroads—Fares	385.22	HE1951-2100
Rafts	623.8202	VM352	Railroads—Finance	385.1	HE2231-2261
Ragtime music	781.645	M1366	Railroads—Freight	385.24	HE2301-2547
Raids (Military science)	355.422	U167.5.R34	Railroads—Freight	625.24	TF662-667
Railroad accidents	363.122	HE1779-1795	Railroads—Freight-cars	625.24	TF470-481
Railroad conductors	385.092	HE1811	Railroads—History	385.09	HE1021
Railroad engineering	625.1	TF	Railroads—History	625.1009	TF15-20
Railroad engineering— Tables	625.10021	TF205	Railroads—Livestock transportation	385.24	HE2321.L7
Railroad engineers	625.10092	TF139-140	Railroads— Maintenance and repair	625.100288	TF530-548
Railroad law	343.095	K4061-4070	Railroads—Management	385.068	HE1621-1813
Railroad museums	625.10074	TF6	Railroads—Models	625.19	TF197
Railroad stations	385.314	HE1613-1614	Railroads—Passenger traffic	385.22	HE2561-2591
Railroad terminals	625.18	TF300-308	Railroads—Passenger traffic	385.22	TF653
Railroads	385	HE1001-5600	Railroads—Passenger-cars	625.23	TF455-461
Railroads	625.1	TF	Railroads—Periodicals	385.05	HE1001
Railroads, Cable	625.5	TF835	Railroads—Periodicals	625.1005	TF1-4
Railroads, Elevated	388.44	HE4201-5300	Railroads—Rails	625.15	TF258-262
Railroads, Elevated	625.44	TF840-841	Railroads—Research	625.10072	TF171-183
Railroads, Elevated—[By region or country]	388.4409(4-9)	HE4401-5260	Railroads—Safety measures	625.100289	TF610
Railroads, Elevated— United States	388.440973	HE4401-4491	Railroads—Signaling	625.165	TF615-640
Railroads, Elevated— [Other countries]	388.4409(4-9)	HE4500-5260	Railroads—Snow-plows	625.100288	TF542
Railroads, Industrial	385.54	TF677	Railroads—Societies, etc.	385.06	HE1003
Railroads, Local and light	388.42	HE3601-4043	Railroads—Specifications	625.100212	TF195
Railroads, Local and light	625.(4-6)	TF670-1124	Railroads—Statistics	385.021	HE2271-2273
			Railroads—Surveying	625.11	TF210-217

Subject Heading	Dewey	LC	Subject Heading	Dewey	LC
Railroads—Switching	625.163	TF592	Railroads—Ireland	385.09415	HE3041-3050
Railroads—Track	675.14	TF240-268	Railroads—Italy	385.0945	HE3091-3100
Railroads—Traffic	385.2	HE1821-2591	Railroads—Japan	385.0952	HE3351-3360
Railroads—Yards	625.18	TF590-593	Railroads—Kenya	385.096762	HE3419
Railroads—[By region or country]	385.09(4-9)	HE2701-3560	Railroads—Korea	385.09519	HE3360.5
			Railroads—Laos	385.09594	HE3320.4
Railroads—[By region or country]	625.1009(4-9)	TF21-127	Railroads—Lesotho	385.096885	HE3429
			Railroads—Liberia	385.096662	HE3457
Railroads—Algeria	385.0965	HE3412	Railroads—Libya	385.09612	HE3414
Railroads—Angola	385.09673	HE3433	Railroads—Madagascar	385.09691	HE3425
Railroads—Argentina	385.0982	HE2901-2910	Railroads—Malawi	385.096897	HE3432
Railroads—Australia	385.0994	HE3461-3550	Railroads—Malaysia	385.09595	HE3321-3330
Railroads—Austria	385.09436	HE3051-3059.2	Railroads—Mali	385.096623	HE3449
Railroads—Bangladesh	385.095492	HE3300.6	Railroads—Mauritania	385.09661	HE3452
Railroads—Belgium	385.09493	HE3111-3120	Railroads—Mexico	385.0972	HE2811-2820
Railroads—Belize	385.097282	HE2825.5	Railroads—Morocco	385.0964	HE3411
Railroads—Benin	385.096683	HE3444	Railroads—Mozambique	385.09679	HE3424
Railroads—Bolivia	385.0984	HE2911-2920	Railroads—Namibia	385.096881	HE3432.3
Railroads—Botswana	385.096883	HE3431	Railroads—Netherlands	385.09492	HE3121-3130
Railroads—Brazil	385.0981	HE2921-2930	Railroads—New Zealand	385.0993	HE3550.5
Railroads—Bulgaria	385.09499	HE3231-3240	Railroads—Nicaragua	385.097285	HE2846-2850
Railroads—Burkina Faso	385.096625	HE3450	Railroads—Niger	385.096626	HE3446
Railroads—Burundi	385.0967572	HE3422	Railroads—Nigeria	385.09669	HE3453
Railroads—Cameroon	385.096711	HE3442	Railroads—Norway	385.09481	HE3171-3180
Railroads—Canada	385.0971	HE2801-2810	Railroads—Pakistan	385.095491	HE3300.5
Railroads—Chad	385.096743	HE3441	Railroads—Paraguay	385.09892	HE2966-2970
Railroads—Chile	385.0983	HE2931-2940	Railroads—Peru	385.0985	HE2971-2980
Railroads—China	385.0951	HE3281-3290	Railroads—Philippines	385.09599	HE3341-3350
Railroads—Colombia	385.09861	HE2941-2950	Railroads—Poland	385.09438	HE3060.5
Railroads—Congo (Brazzaville)	385.096724	HE3439	Railroads—Portugal	385.09469	HE3201-3210
			Railroads—Romania	385.09498	HE3251-3260
Railroads—Costa Rica	385.097286	HE2831-2835	Railroads—Russia	385.0947	HE3131-3140.2
Railroads—Cote d'Ivoire	385.096668	HE3447	Railroads—Rwanda	385.0967571	HE3421
Railroads—Czechoslovakia	385.09437	HE3059.3	Railroads—Sao Tome and Principe	385.096715	HE3436
Railroads—Denmark	385.09489	HE3151-3160			
Railroads—Ecuador	385.09866	HE2951-2960	Railroads—Saudi Arabia	385.09538	HE3380.3
Railroads—Egypt	385.0962	HE3401-3410	Railroads—Senegal	385.09663	HE3451
Railroads—El Salvador	385.097284	HE2851-2855	Railroads—Sierra Leone	385.09664	HE3455
Railroads—Equatorial Guinea	385.096718	HE3435	Railroads—Somalia	385.096773	HE3417
			Railroads—South Africa	385.0968	HE3426
Railroads—Ethiopia	385.0963	HE3416	Railroads—South America	385.098	HE2891-3000
Railroads—France	385.0944	HE3061-3070	Railroads—Spain	385.0946	HE3191-3200
Railroads—French Guiana	385.09882	HE2964	Railroads—Sri Lanka	385.095493	HE3300.3
Railroads—Gabon	385.096721	HE3438	Railroads—Sudan	385.09624	HE3415
Railroads—Gambia	385.096651	HE3456	Railroads—Surinam	385.09883	HE2963
Railroads—Germany	385.0943	HE3071-3080.5	Railroads—Swaziland	385.096887	HE3430
Railroads—Ghana	385.09667	HE3454	Railroads—Sweden	385.09485	HE3181-3190
Railroads—Great Britain	385.0941	HE3011-3040	Railroads—Switzerland	385.09494	HE3211-3220
Railroads—Guatemala	385.097281	HE2836-2840	Railroads—Tanzania	385.09678	HE3423
Railroads—Guinea	385.096652	HE3448	Railroads—Togo	385.096681	HE3445
Railroads—Guinea-Bissau	385.096657	HE3458	Railroads—Tunisia	385.09611	HE3413
Railroads—Guyana	385.09881	HE2962	Railroads—Uganda	385.096761	HE3420
Railroads—Honduras	385.097283	HE2841-2845	Railroads—United States	385.0973	HE2704-2791
Railroads—Hungary	385.09439	HE3059.5	Railroads—Uruguay	385.09895	HE2981-2990
Railroads—Iceland	385.094912	HE3161-3170	Railroads—Venezuela	385.0987	HE2991-3000
Railroads—India	385.0954	HE3291-3300	Railroads—Vietnam	385.09597	HE3320.3
Railroads—Indonesia	385.09598	HE3331-3340			

Subject Heading	Dewey	LC	Subject Heading	Dewey	LC
Railroads—West Indies	385.09729	HE2856-2889	Reading (Kindergarten)	372.4	LB1181.2
Railroads—Western Sahara	385.09648	HE3458.2	Reading (Preschool)	372.4	LB1140.5.R4
Railroads—Yugoslavia	385.09497	HE3241-3245	Reading (Primary)	372.4	LB1525-.8
Railroads—Zaire	385.096751	HE3434	Reading comprehension	372.47	LB1050.45
Railroads—Zambia	385.096894	HE3428	Reading disability and crime	364.25	HV6166
Railway mail service	383.143	HE6175-.5			
Railway mail service—United States	383.1430973	HE6475-.3	Reading machines	372.40284	LB1050.37
			Reading readiness	372.414	LB1050.43
Rain-making	551.68	QC928.6	Real-time data processing	004.33	QA76.54-.545
Rain-water (Water-supply)	628.11	TD418	Real estate business	333.33	HD1361-1395.5
Rain and rainfall	551.577	QC924.5-926.2	Real property	333.30973	HD251-279
Rain forest ecology	577.34	QH541.5.R27	Real property—Canada	346.71043	KE625-754
Rain gauges	551.5770284	QC926	Real property—England	346.42043	KD821-1195
Rainbow	551.567	QC976.R2	Real property—United States	346.73043	KF566-698
Rajasthani language	491.479	PK2701-2709			
Ramadan sermons	297.362	BP183.6	Realism	149.2	B835
Raman effect	535.846	QC454.R36	Realism in literature	808.8012	PN56.R3
Random access memory	621.3973	TK7895.M4	Reality	111	BD331
Random noise theory	621.38224	TK5101	Rearguard action (Military science)	355.422	U215
Range-finding	359.422	VF550			
Range-finding	623.46	UF850-857	Reasoning	160	BC177
Range ecology	577.4	QH541.5.R3	Reasoning (Psychology)	153.43	BF442
Range management	636.0845	SF84.82-98	Recall	324.68	JF247.R4
Rangelands	633.202	SB193-.55	Recall	324.680973	JK1533
Rangelands	636.0845	SF84.82-85.6	Recall	324.680973	JS344.R4
Rape	364.1532	HV6558-6569	Receivers	332.75	HG3773
Rape—Investigation	363.259532	HV8079.R35	Recidivism	364.3	HV6049
Rape trauma syndrome	616.8521	RC560.R36	Recipes	641.5	TX151-162
Rape victims	362.883	RC560.R36	Reciprocating pumps	621.65	TJ915
Rappelling	796.522	GV200.19.R34	Reciprocity	382.9	HF1721-1733
Rare birds	597.168	QL676.7	Recitation (Education)	371.37	LB1039
Rare breeds	636.082	SF105.27-.275	Recitations	808.54	PN4199-4355
Rare earth metals	546.41	QD172.R2	Reclamation of land	627.5	TC801-937
Rare mammals	599.168	QL706.8-.83	Reclamation of land	627.5	TC970-978
Rationalism	149.7	B833	Reclamation of land	627.54	TC343-345
Rationalism	211.4	BL2700-2790	Reclamation of land	631.6	S604.8-621.5
Rationalism	239.7	BT1209-1211	Reclamation of land—[By region or country]	627.509(4-9)	TC815-927
Rationing	381.3	HF5415			
Raw food diet	613.26	RM237.5	Recognition (Psychology)	153.124	BF378.R4
Raw materials	381.43	HF1051-1054	Recoilless rifles	358.1282	UF656
Rayon	677.46	TS1688	Recombinant blood proteins	615.39	RM171.4
Razors	646.7240284	TT967			
Reactor fuel reprocessing	621.4838	TK9360	Reconnaissance aircraft	358.45	UG1242.R4
Read-only memory	621.3973	TK7895.M4	Reconstruction (1914-1939)	940.5 (1-2)	D652-659
Readers	428.6	PE1117-1130			
Readers	428.6	PE1417	Reconstruction (1939-1951)	940.53144	D824-829
Reading	372.4	LB1050			
Reading	808.54509	PN83	Recorder music	788.36	M110.R4
Reading—Ability testing	372.48	LB1050.46	Recording instruments	530.7	QC53
Reading—Phonetic method	372.465	LB1573.3	Recording instruments	621.373	TK393
Reading—Remedial teaching	372.43	LB1050.5	Recreation	790	GV
			Recreation centers	790.068	GV182-.5
Reading (Elementary)	372.4	LB1525	Recreation leadership	790.092	GV14.5
Reading (Elementary)	372.4	LB1573	Recreational therapy	615.85153	RM736.7
Reading (Elementary)—Whole-word method	372.462	LB1573.37	Recreational therapy	616.891653	RC489.R4
			Recruiting and enlistment	355.223	UB320-345
			Recruiting and enlistment	359.2236	VB260-275

223

Subject Heading	Dewey	LC	Subject Heading	Dewey	LC
Recycling (Waste, etc.)	628.4458	TD794.5	Reformed Presbyterian Church	285.136	BX8990-8998.38
Red Brigades	323.0440951	HV6335.C	Refraction, Astronomical	522.9	QB155-156
Red Cross	361.77	UH535-537	Refraction, Double	535.324	QC425
Red Cross	361.77	VG457	Refrigeration and refrigerating machinery	621.56	TP490-497
Red Cross	361.77	HV560-583	Refrigerator cars	625.24	TF477
Red Cross—[By region or country]	361.7709(4-9)	HV575-580	Refrigerator ships	623.8245	VM459
Red dwarfs	523.88	QB843.R4	Refrigerators	621.57	TP496-497
Red fescue	633.28	SB413.R43	Refugees	362.87	HV640-.5
Red giants	523.88	QB843.R42	Refugees, Political	362.87	HV640-.5
Red tide	639.964	SH177.R4	Refuse and refuse disposal	628.44	TD785-812.5
Redemption	234.3	BT775	Refuse and refuse disposal, Rural	628.744	TD929-930.4
Reducing diets	613.25	RM222.2	Refuse and refuse disposal—Research	628.44072	TD793.3
Reduction (Chemistry)	541.393	QD63.R4			
Redwood	634.9758	SD397.R3	Refuse collection	628.442	TD794
Reed-organ	786.5509	ML597	Refuse collection—United States	628.440973	TD788-.4
Reed-organ music	786.55	M15-17			
Reed-organ—Methods—Self-instruction	786.5507	MT208	Refuse collection—[Other countries]	628.4409(4-9)	TD789
Reefs	551.424	GB461-468	Refutation (Logic)	184	B491.R44
Reference books	028.7	Z711	Regattas	797.14	GV775
Referendum	328.23	JF491-497	Regeneration (Biology)	571.889	QH499
Reflecting telescopes	522.2	QB88	Regeneration (Botany)	571.8892	QK840
Reflection (Optics)	535.323	QC385	Regeneration (Theology)	234.4	BT790
Reflection (Optics)	535.323	QC425	Regional planning	711.3	NA9000-9428
Refloating of ships	363.3481	VK1259	Regional planning—[By region or country]	307.1209(4-9)	HT392-395
Reforestation	634.956	SD409			
Reformation	270.6	BR300-420	Regional planning—United States	307.120973	HT392-394
Reformation—Causes	270.6	BR307			
Reformation—Early movements	270.6	BR295	Regional planning—Law and legislation	346.045	K3531-3544
Reformatories	365.34	HV9051-9230.7	Regional planning—Law and legislation—Canada	346.71045	KE5258-5284
Reformatories for women	365.34082	HV8738			
Reformed Church	284.2	BX9401-9640	Regular Baptists	286.1	BX6388.3-.38
Reformed Church—Doctrines	230.42	BX9420-9422.2	Rehabilitation counselors	362.0425	HD7255-7256
			Rehabilitation technology	617.03	RM950
Reformed Church—Government	262.042	BX9425	Reincarnation	202.37	BL515
Reformed Church—History	284.209	BX9415	Reincarnation	299.934	BP573.R5
Reformed Church—Liturgy	264.042	BX9427-.5	Reinforced concrete construction	624.18341	TA683-683.94
Reformed Church—Sermons	252.042	BX9426			
			Reinforced concrete construction	693.54	TH1501
Reformed Church—Societies, etc.	284.206	BX9403			
			Reinforcement (Psychology)	153.85	BF319.5.R4
Reformed Church—Africa	284.26	BX9618-9640			
Reformed Church—Asia	284.25	BX9615	Reinforcement learning (Machine learning)	006.31	Q325.6
Reformed Church—Canada	284.271	BX9596-9598			
Reformed Church—Europe	284.24	BX9430-9480	Reining (Horsemanship)	798.2028	SF296.R4
Reformed Church—France	284.244	BX9450-9459	Relapsing fever	616.9244	RC182.R3
Reformed Church—Netherlands	284.2492	BX9470-9479	Relationism	111	B836
			Relativity (Physics)	530.11	QC173.5-.65
Reformed Church—Switzerland	284.2494	BX9430-9439	Relaxation	613.792	RA785
			Relics	235.2	BV890
Reformed Church—United States	284.273	BX9495-9593	Relics	235.2	BX577
			Relics	235.2	BX2315
Reformed Church in the United States	285.733	BX9551-9593	Religion	200	BL

Subject Heading	Dewey	LC	Subject Heading	Dewey	LC
Religion	200	BL48-50	Representation (Philosophy)	324.6301	B105.R4
Religion and civilization	201.7	BL55	Representations of groups	512.22	QA176
Religion and culture	201.7	BL65.C8	Representative government and representation	324.63	JF1051-1075
Religion and ethics	205	BJ47	Reproduction	571.8	QH471-489
Religion and justice	205.22	BL65.J87	Reproduction	612.6	QP251-285
Religion and law	201.72	BL65.L33	Reproduction (Psychology)	153.123	BF365-395
Religion and politics	201.72	BL65.P7	Reproduction, Asexual	571.89	QH475-479
Religion and science	201.65	BL239-265	Reptiles	398.36979	GR740
Religion and sociology	201.7	BL60	Reptiles	597.9	QL641-669
Religion and state	201.72	BL65.S8	Republics	321.86	JC421-458
Religion in the public schools	379.28	LC107-120	Requiems	782.3238	M2010-2014
Religion, Prehistoric	201.42	GN799.R4	Requisitions, Military	355.28	UC15
Religion—Directories	200.25	BL35	Rescue dogs	636.70886	SF428.55
Religion—Periodicals	200.5	BL1-10	Research	507.2	Q180
Religion—Philosophy	210	BL51	Research	607.2	T65
Religions	230-299	BL74-98	Research—Law and legislation	344.09	K3770
Religion—Societies or Congresses	206	BL11-21	Research aircraft	629.130072	TL567.R47
Religion—Study and teaching	200.71	BL41	Research natural areas	508.072	QH75-77
Religious calendars—Judaism	296.43	BM690	Research, Industrial	607.2	T175-178
Religious communities	206.5	BL632	Research, Industrial—Laboratories	660.072	TP187-197
Religious education—Audio-visual aids	268.635	BV1535	Reservoir sedimentation	628.132	TD396
Religious education—Home training	249	BV1590	Reservoirs	627.86	TC167
Religious education—Teaching methods	268.6	BV1534-1536	Reservoirs	628.132	TD395-397
Religious ethics	205	BJ1188-1295	Residents (Medicine)	610.695	RA972
Religious life	204	BL624-627	Respiration	612.2	QP121-125
Religious life—Buddhism	294.3444	BQ5360-5680	Respiratory agents	615.72	RM388-.7
Religious life—Hinduism	294.544	BL1228	Respiratory allergy	616.202	RC589-596
Religious life—Islam	297.57	BP188	Respiratory infections	616.2	RC740
Religious medals	737.224	CJ5793.R34	Respiratory insufficiency in children	618.922	RJ312
Religious tolerance	241.4	BR1610	Respiratory organs	573.2	QL845-855
Remarriage	306.84	HQ1018-1019	Respiratory organs	611.2	QM251-265
Remedial teaching	374.012	LB1029.R4	Respiratory organs	612.2	QP121-125
Reminiscing	153.123	BF378.R44	Respiratory organs—Diseases	616.2	RC705-779
Remote handling (Radioactive substances)	621.4835	TK9151.6-.7	Respiratory organs—Diseases—Eclectic treatment	616.206	RV261-266
Remote submersibles	623.8205	TC1662	Respiratory organs—Diseases—Homeopathic treatment	616.206	RX321-326
Remount service	357.2	UC600-695	Respiratory organs—Diseases—Nursing	616.20231	RC735.5
Renaissance	808.80024	PN715-749	Respiratory organs—Foreign bodies	616.244	RD137
Renaissance	909.08	CB351-369	Respiratory organs—Obstructions	616.24	RC776.03
Renal anemia	616.152	RC641.7.R44	Respiratory therapy	615.836	RC735.I5
Renal hypertension	616.132	RC918.R38	Respiratory therapy	615.836	RM161
Renewable energy sources	621.042	TJ807-830	Respiratory therapy for children	615.542	RJ434
Rent	333.5	HB401	Responsive worship	265	BV199.R5
Rent	339.21	HB401	Rest	613.79	RA785
Rental libraries	027.3	Z675.R4			
Repairing	745.50288	TT151			
Reparation	342.03288	K970			
Repentance	234.5	BT800			
Reporters and reporting	070.43	PN4781			

Subject Heading	Dewey	LC	Subject Heading	Dewey	LC
Rest periods	331.2576	HD5112	Rhetoric, Ancient	808.0481	PA3265
Restaurants	647.95	TX945-.5	Rhetorical criticism	809	PN4096
Restaurants—Personnel management	647.950683	TX911.3.P4	Rheumatic fever	616.991	RC182.R4
Restorationism	289.134	BX9901-9996	Rheumatism	616.723	RC927-.5
Resumes (Employment)	650.14	HF5383	Rheumatoid arthritis	616.7227	RC933
Resurrection	202.3	BL503	Rhode Island—Gazetteers	917.45003	F77
Resurrection	236.8	BT870-872	Rhode Island—History	974.5	F76-90
Resurrection (Islam)	297.23	BP166.83	Rhode Island—History—Colonial period, ca. 1600-1775	974.50(1-2)	F82
Resuscitation	615.025	RC87			
Retail trade	381.1	HF5428-5429.6	Rhode Island—History—King George's War, 1744-1748	974.502	E198
Retaining walls	624.164	TA760-772			
Retaining walls	624.257	TG325			
Retina	573.88	QL949	Rhode Island—History—Revolution, 1775-1783	974.50(2-3)	E263.R4
Retina	611.84	QM511			
Retina	612.843	QP479	Rhode Island—History—Civil War, 1861-1865	974.503	E528
Retina—Diseases	617.735	RE551-661			
Retinal detachment	617.735	RE603	Rhode Island—Maps	912.745	G3770-3774
Retirement age	331.252	HD7105-7108.4	Rhode Island—National Guard	355.3709745	UA430-439
Retreats	269.6	BV5068.R4			
Retreats—Catholic Church	269.6	BX2375-2376	Rhode Island—Periodicals	974.5005	F76
Retroviruses	579.2569	QR414.5-.6	Rhythm	153.753	BF475
Reunion—Census	316.981	HA2307	Ribosomes	571.658	QH603.R5
Reunion—Civilization	969.81	DT469.R37	Ribs	599.947	GN70
Reunion—Description and travel	916.98104	DT469.R35	Ribs	611.712	QM113
			Rice	641.3318	TX558.R5
Reunion—Gazetteers	916.981003	DT469.R32	Rich man and Lazarus (Parable)	226.8	BT378.D5
Reunion—History	969.81	DT469.R42-.R458			
			Rickets	618.92395	RJ396
Reunion—History—To 1764	969.8102	DT469.R44-.R443	Rickettsia	571.99327	QR353.5.R4
			Riddles	808.882	PN6366-6377
Reunion—History—1764-1946	969.8102	DT469.R45-.R453	Rider-gods	299.15	BL1590.R5
			Ridesharing	388.413212	HE5620.R53
Reunion—History—British occupation, 1810-1815	969.8102	DT469.R45	Ridgway's revolving battery	359.820973	VF440
			Riding clubs	798.2306	SF310-.5
Reunion—History—1946-	969.8104	DT469.R455-.R458	Riding schools	798.23071	SF310.4
			Riemann surfaces	515.93	QA333-337
Reunion—Maps	912.6981	G9190-9194	Rif language	493.3	PJ2377
Revelation	228	BS646	Rifle practice	799.31	GV1177
Revelation	231.74	BT126-127.5	Rifles	356.1182425	UD390-395
Revelation	248.29	BV5091.R4	Rifles	359.82425	VD370
Revelation (Islam)	297.2115	BP166.6	Rifles	799.202832	SK274.2-.4
Revelation (Mormon theology)	231.74	BX8643.R4	Rifles, Bolt action	683.422	TS536.6.B6
			Right and wrong	170	BJ1410-1418
Revenge	241.3	BV4627.R4	Right to labor	331.8892	HD4903-.5
Revenue	336.02	HJ2240-7395	Right to life	342.085	K3252
Revenue-stamps	336.272	HJ5315	Rings	391.7	GT2270
Revivals	269.24	BV3750-3799	Rings	739.2782	NK7440-7459
Revolutions	303.64	HM281-283	Rings	739.2782	TS720-770
Revolutions	321.094	JC491	Rings (Algebra)	512.4	QA247
Revolvers	356.1182436	UD410-415	Rings (Gymnastics)	613.714	GV539
Revolvers	359.82436	VD390	Ringworm	616.57	RL780
Revolvers	683.436	TS537	Rio de la Plata, Battle of the, 1939	940.5428	D772.G7
Revues	782.14	M1500-1508			
Reward (Psychology)	153.85	BF505.R48	Riot helmets	363.20284	HV7936.E7
Rhetoric	808	P301-.5	Riots	303.623	HM281-283
Rhetoric	808	PN171.4-229	Riots	355.351	U230

Subject Heading	Dewey	LC	Subject Heading	Dewey	LC
Riots	364.143	HV6474-6485	Robots	629.892	TJ210.2-211.49
Risk	338.5	HB615	Rock-drills	621.952	TA745-747
Risk (Insurance)	368	HG8054.5	Rock-drills	622.23	TN279-281
Risk management	658.155	HD61	Rock climbing	796.5223	GV200.2
Rites and ceremonies	203.8	BL600-619	Rock deformation	551.8	QE604
Rites and ceremonies	203.8	GN473	Rock excavation	624.152	TA740-747
Rites and ceremonies	264	BV169-199	Rock gardens	635.9672	SB459
Ritual	203.8	BL600-619	Rock glaciers	551.312	GB641-648
Ritualism	264	BV180-181	Rock music	784.16609	ML3533.8-3534
Ritualism	264.03	BX5123	Rockabilly music	784.16609	ML3535
River boats	623.82436	VM461-.5	Rockets (Aeronautics)	629.475	TL780-785.8
River engineering	628.112	TC401-558	Rockets (Aeronautics)—	629.433	TL784.C63
River engineering—[By	628.109(4-9)	TC415-527	Guidance systems		
region or country]			Rockets (Aeronautics)—	621.43560228	TL844
River steamers	623.82436	VM461-.5	Models		
Rivers	398.32091693	GR680	Rockets (Ordnance)	358.1282356	UF767
Rivers	551.483	GB1201-1399.5	Rocks	398.365	GR800
Rivers	628.112	TC401-558	Rocks	552	QE420-499
Riviera (France)	944.9	DC608.1-.9	Rocks, Carbonate	552.58	QE471.15.C3
Riviera (Italy)	945.18	DG975.R6	Rocks, Igneous	552.1	QE461-462
RNA	572.88	QP623-.5	Rocks, Metamorphic	552.4	QE475
RNA viruses	579.25	QR395	Rocks, Sedimentary	552.5	QE471-.15
Road-rollers	625.70284	TE223-227	Rockslides	551.307	QE599
Road drainage	625.734	TE215	Rocky Mountains	978	F721-722
Road machinery	625.70284	TE223-227	Rodeos	791.84	GV1834
Road materials	625.8	TE200-205	Roll-mill	671.32	TS340
Roads	388.1	HE331-380	Roll-on/roll-off ships	387.5442	HE566.R64
Roads, Brick	625.82	TE255	Roll-on/roll-off ships	623.8245	VM393.R64
Roads, Concrete	625.84	TE278-.8	Roller-skating	796.21	GV858.2-859.7
Roads, Earth	625.74	TE230	Roller bearings	621.822	TJ1071
Roads, Gravel	625.82	TE233	Rollers (Printing)	686.20284	Z256
Roads, Macadamized	625.86	TE243	Rolling (Aerodynamics)	629.132364	TL574.M6
Roads, Plank	625.83	TE245	Roman emperors	937.0099	DG124
Roads, Roman	388.10937	DG28-29	Romance fiction	808.80145	PN816
Roads—[By region or	625.709(4-9)	TE21-127	Romance languages	440	PC
country]			Romance languages—	440.05	PC1-5
Roads—Congresses	625.706	TE5	Periodicals		
Roads—Design and	625.725	TE175	Romance languages—	440.071	PC35-39
construction			Study and teaching		
Roads—Foundations	625.733	TE210-212	Romance literatures	840	PQ
Roads—History	625.709	TE15-19	Romania	939.8	DR201-296
Roads—Location	625.7	TE206-209.5	Romania	949.8	DR
Roads—Maintenance and	625.76	TE220-.63	Romania	949.8	DR201-296
repair			Romania—Census	314.98	HA1641-1650
Roads—Periodicals	625.705	TE1-4	Romania—Civilization	939.8	DR212
Roads—Specifications	625.70212	TE180	Romania—Civilization	949.8	DR212
Roads—Study and	625.7071	TE191	Romania—Description and	913.9804	DR207-210
teaching			travel		
Roads—Surveying	625.723	TE209-.5	Romania—Description and	914.9804	DR207-210
Roadside ecology	577.55	QH541.5.R62	travel		
Roadside improvement	625.77	TE177	Romania—Economic	330.9498	HC405
Roadside marketing	381.41	S571.5	conditions		
Roadside rest areas	625.77	TE178.8	Romania—Gazetteers	914.98003	DR204
Roadsteads	387.12	VK321	Romania—Historiography	939.80072	DR216.7-.92
Roasting (Cookery)	641.71	TX690	Romania—Historiography	949.80072	DR216.7-.92
Robbery investigation	363.259552	HV8079.R62	Romania—History	939.8	DR215-267.5
Robotics	629.892	TJ210.2-211.49	Romania—History	949.8	DR215-267.5

Subject Heading	Dewey	LC	Subject Heading	Dewey	LC
Rome—History—Theodosians, 379-455	937.0(8-9)	DG330-338	Rule of law—United States	340.11	KF382
Rome—History—Romulus Augustulus, 475-476	937.09	DG365	Rule of the road at sea	623.8884	VK371
			Rum	663.59	TP607.R9
Rome—Periodicals	937.005	DG11	Rummy (Game)	795.418	GV1295.R8
Rome—Politics and government	320.9376	JC81-89	Running	796.42	GV1061-1069
			Runways (Aeronautics)	629.1363	TL725.3.R8
Rome—Religion	292.07	BL800-820	Rural-urban migration	307.24	HB1955
Rome—Religion	292.07	BL800-820	Rural aged	305.26091734	HQ1060-1064
Rome—Study and teaching	937.0071	DG206.5	Rural aged	362.6091734	HV1450-1494
Roof gardening	635.9671	SB419.5	Rural churches	250.91734	BV638-.8
Roofing	690.15	TH2431-2459	Rural free delivery—United States	383.1450973	HE6455-6456
Roofs	690.15	TH2391-2495			
Roofs, Open-timbered	721.5	NA2900	Rural geography	910.021734	GF127
Roofs, Shell	690.15	TH2416-2417	Rural health	613.091734	RA771-.7
Root crops	635.1	SB209-211	Rural hospitals	362.11091734	RA975.R87
Root crops	635.1	SB351.R65	Rural libraries	027.091734	Z675.V7
Roots (Botany)	575.54	QK644	Rural population	304.6091734	HB2371-2578
Roots (Botany)	581.498	QK776	Rural roads	388.12091734	HE336.R85
Roots, Numerical	513.23	QA119	Rural roads	625.7091734	TE229-.9
Rope	677.71	TS1784-1787	Russia	947	DK1-290.3
Rorschach Test	155.2842	BF698.8.R5	Russia	947	DK510-651
Rorschach Test	616.89075	RC473.R6	Russia (Federation)—History—Revolution, 1917-1921	947.084	DK265.8.R85
Rosary	242.74	BX2310.R7			
Rose gardens	635.933734	SB411			
Roses	635.933734	SB410.9-411.7	Russia, Soviet Union	943.8	DK
Rosh ha-Shanah	296.4315	BM695.N5	Russia, Soviet Union	947	DK
Rotary converters	621.313	TK2796	Russia—Armed Forces—Management	355.60947	UB85-86
Rotary drilling	622.23	TN281.5			
Rotary pumps	621.66	TJ917	Russia—Census	314.7	HA1431-2-1450.12
Rotating masses of fluid	532.5	QA913			
Roulette	795.23	GV1309	Russia—Church history	274.7	BR930-939
Route choice	388.1	HE336.R68	Russia—Civilization	947	DK32-.7
Route surveying	526.9	TA625	Russia—Commerce	381.0947	HF3621-3630
Roving vehicles (Astronautics)	629.295	TL475-480	Russia—Congresses	947.006	DK2.5
			Russia—Description and travel	914.7(04)	DK19-29
Row houses	728.312	NA7520			
Rowing	797.123	GV790.9-807.5	Russia—Economic conditions	330.947	HC331-340
Royal houses	321.03094	D352.1			
Royal houses	321.03094	D412.7	Russia—Emigration and immigration	325.(247) or (47)	JV8180-8189
Royal houses	321.6	D226.7			
Royal Psalms	223.2	BS1445.M4	Russia—Gazetteers	914.7003	DK14
Rubber bands	678.35	TS1920	Russia—Genealogy	929.1072047	CS840-869
Rubber bearings	621.822	TJ1073.R8	Russia—History	947	DK65-290.3
Rubber industry and trade	678.2	TS1870-1935	Russia—History—To 1533	947.0(1-42)	DK70-104
Rubber plants	633.8952	SB289-291	Russia—History—Ivan IV, 1533-1584	947.043	DK106-107
Rubber, Artificial	678.72	TS1925-1927			
Rubbing	760	NC915.R8	Russia—History—Time of Troubles, 1598-1613	947.045	DK111-112
Rubella	614.524	RA644.R8			
Rubella	616.916	RC182.R8	Russia—History—1613-1689	947.04(6-9)	DK112.8-126
Ruby lasers	621.366	TA1705			
Rugby football	796.333	GV945	Russia—History—1613-1917	947.0(47-83)	DK112.8-264.8
Rugs	747.5	NK2775-2898			
Rugs—Private collections	747.5074	NK2790	Russia—History—Aleksei Mikhailovich, 1645-1676	947.048	DK116-122.5
Rugs, Braided	746.73	TT850			
Rugs, Islamic	746.70882971	NK2809.I8	Russia—History—Rebellion of Stenka Razin, 1667-1671	947.048	DK118.5
Rugs, Oriental	746.75095	NK2808-2810			

Subject Heading	Dewey	LC	Subject Heading	Dewey	LC
Russia—History—Sofia Alekseevna, 1682-1689	947.049	DK125	Russo-Finnish War, 1939-1940	948.97032	DL1095-1105
Russia—History—Peter I, 1689-1725	947.05	DK128-148	Russo-Japanese War, 1904-1905	952.031	DS516-517.9
Russia—History—Streltsy Revolt, 1698	947.05	DK133	Rwanda—Census	316.7571	HA4695
			Rwanda—Civilization	967.571	DT450.22
Russia—History—Rebellion of Pugachev, 1773-1775	947.063	DK183	Rwanda—Description and travel	916.757104	DT450.2
Russia—History—Catherine II, 1762-1796	947.063	DK168-183	Rwanda—Economic conditions	330.967571	HC875
Russia—History—1801-1917	947.0(72-83)	DK188-264.8	Rwanda—Gazetteers	916.7571003	DT450.115
Russia—History—Alexander I, 1801-1825	947.072	DK190-201	Rwanda—History	967.571	DT450.26-.437
Russia—History—December Uprising, 1825	947.073	DK212	Rwanda—History—Civil War, 1994	967.571043	DT450.435
Russia—History—Nicholas I, 1825-1855	947.073	DK209-215.97	Rwanda—Maps	912.67571	G8430-8434
			Ryukyu Islands—History	952.29	DS895.R97
Russia—History—Alexander II, 1855-1881	947.081	DK219-223	Saba (Netherlands Antilles)	972.977	F2088
Russia—History—Alexander III, 1881-1894	947.082	DK234-243	Sabbatarians	296.82092	BX9680.S3
			Sabbath	296.41	BM685
Russia—History—Nicholas II, 1894-1917	947.083	DK251-264.8	Sabbathaians	296.82	BM199.S3
			Sabbatical year (Judaism)	296.4391	BM720.S2
Russia—History—Revolution, 1905-1907	947.083	DK263-264.7	Sabers	355.8241	U850-863
			Sabers	357.0482	UE420-425
Russia—History—February Revolution, 1917	947.0841	DK265.19	Sabotage	331.893	HD5473
			Sacramentals	264.0209	BX2295-2310
Russia—History, Naval	359.00947	DK55-59	Sacramentals	264.9	BV875-885
Russia—Manufactures	670.947	TS85-86	Sacramentaries	264.023	BX2037
Russia—Maps	912.47	G2110-2193	Sacraments	265	BV800-873
Russia—Maps	912.47	G7060-7342	Sacraments (Liturgy)	264.0208	BX2200-2292
Russia—Periodicals	947.005	DK1	Sacraments—Adventists	264.06708	BX6124.3-.6
Russia—Politics and government	320.947	JN6500-6598	Sacraments—Church of England	264.035	BX5148-5149
Russian language	491.7	PG2001-2847	Sacraments—Congregational churches	264.05808	BX7238-7239
Russian language—Dialects	491.77	PG2700-2850	Sacraments—Lutheran Church	264.04108	BX8072-8073.5
Russian language—Dictionaries	491.73	PG2625-2693	Sacraments—Methodist Church	264.0708	BX8338
Russian language—Etymology	491.72	PG2571-2591	Sacraments—Mormon Church	264.09308	BX8655-.3
Russian language—Grammar	491.75	PG2097-2127	Sacraments—New Jerusalem Church	264.09408	BX8736
Russian language—Lexicography	491.73028	PG2601-2693	Sacraments—Orthodox Eastern Church	264.019	BX377-378
Russian language—Morphology	491.75	PG2171-2197	Sacraments—Presbyterian Church	264.05	BX9188-9189
Russian language—Parts of speech	491.75	PG2199-2321	Sacraments—Unitarianism	264.0913308	BX9854
Russian language—Phonology	491.715	PG2131-2161	Sacraments—Universalism	264.0913408	BX9954
Russian language—Slang	491.7709	PG2850	Sacred books	208.2	BL70-71
Russian language—Study and teaching	491.7071	PG2065-2069	Sacred meals	203.6	BL619.S3
			Sacred vocal ensembles	782.221438	M2018-2019.5
Russian literature	891.7	PG2900-3580	Sacred vocal music	782.2209	ML2900-3275
Russian periodicals	059.9171	PN5271-5280	Sacred vocal music	782.3	M1999-2199
Russian philology	491.7	PG2001-2069	Sacrifice	203.4	BL570
			Sacrifice	294.534	BL1236.76.S23
			Sacrilege	241.3	BV4726.S2
			Saddlery	685.1	TS1030-1035

Subject Heading	Dewey	LC
Sadducees	296.813	BM175.S2
Sadism	306.775	HQ79
Sadomasochism	306.775	HQ79
Sadomasochism	616.85835	RC560.S23
Safaris	916.04	G516
Safe-deposit boxes	332.178	HG2251-2256
Safety-lamps	622.473	TN307
Safety appliances	363.107	HD7273
Safety factor in engineering	624.10289	TA656.5
Sagas	839.6308	PT7261-7262
Sagas	839.6309	PT7181-7193
Sagittarius (Astrology)	133.5274	BF1727.6
Sahara	966	DT331-346
Sahara—Description and travel	916.604	DT333
Sailboat living	643.2	GV811.65
Sailboats	623.8223	VM351-361
Sailing	623.88203	VK543
Sailing	797.124	GV811
Sailing ships—Models	623.8201043	VM298
Sailing, Single-handed	797.124	GV811
Sailors	359.0092	VD
Sailors	387.5092	HD8039.S4
Sailors—[By region or country]	359.0092	VD21-124
Sailors—History	359.0092	VD15
Sailors—Services for	362.858	HV3025-3163
Sailors—United States	359.009	VD23-25
Sails	623.862	VM532
Saint Bartholomew's Day, Massacre of, France, 1572	944.029	DC118
Saint Croix (V.I.)	972.9722	F2096
Saint Eustatius (Netherlands Antilles)	972.977	F2097
Saint Helena—Census	319.73	HA2291
Saint Helena—Maps	912.973	G9170-9174
Saint John (V.I.)	972.9722	F2098
Saint Kitts (Island)—Maps	912.72973	G5040-5044
Saint Kitts and Nevis	972.973	F2091
Saint Louis (Mo.)	977.866	F474.S2
Saint Lucia	972.9843	F2100
Saint Lucia—Maps	912.729843	G5110-5114
Saint Martin	972.976	F2103
Saint Patrick's Day	394.262	GT4995.P3
Saint Thomas (V.I.)	972.9722	F2105
Saint Vincent—Maps	912.729844	G5120-5124
Saintes Islands (Guadeloupe)	972.976	F2070
Saints	235.2	BT683-694
Salad dressing	641.814	TX819.S27
Salads	641.83	TX740
Salads	641.83	TX807
Sales executives	381.092	HF5439.25-.8
Sales meetings	658.8106	HF5438.8.M4
Sales personnel	381.092	HF5439.25-.8
Sales presentations	658.82	HF5438.8.P74
Sales tax	336.2713	HJ5711-5721
Saline water conversion	628.167	TD478-480.7
Saline water conversion—Electrodialysis process	628.1674	TD480.5
Saline water conversion—Reverse osmosis process	628.16744	TD480.4
Salinity	551.4664	GC121-127
Saliva	612.313	QP191
Salivary glands	611.316	QM325-371
Salivary glands	612.313	QP188.S2
Salmon fishing	799.1755	SH684-686.7
Salmonellosis	616.927	RC182.S12
Salon-orchestra music	784.4	M1350
Salt	394.12	GT2870
Salt	622.3632	TN900-909
Salt—Physiological effect	572.5238224	QP913.N2
Salt-free diet	613.285	RM237.8
Salt lake ecology	577.639	QH541.5.S22
Salt mines and mining	622.3632	TN900-909
Salts	546.34	QD189-193
Saltwater fishing	799.16	SH457-.5
Salutations	394	GT3050
Salvadoran literature	860	PQ7530-7539.2
Salvage	387.55	VK1491
Salvage	387.55	HE971
Salvation	234	BT750-810.2
Salvation Army	287.96	BX9701-9743
Salvation Army	287.96	HV4330-4470.7
Salvation outside the Catholic Church	234	BT755
Salvation outside the church	234	BT759
Samaria Region	933	DS110.S3
Samaria Region	956.953	DS110.S3
Samaritan Aramaic language	492.29	PJ5271-5279
Samaritan theology	296.3	BM945
Samoan Islands	996.1(3-4)	DU810-819
Samoan Islands—Maps	912.961(3-4)	G9555-9557
Samoan question	996.1(3-4)	DU817
Sampling (Statistics)	310.0723	HA31.2
Sampling (Statistics)	519.52	QA276.6
San Francisco (Calif.)	979.461	F869.S3
Sanatoriums	362.16	RA960-993
Sand	622.3622	TN939
Sand and gravel plants	622.3622	TN939
Sand Creek Massacre, Colo., 1864	978.802	E83.863
Sand dune ecology	577.583	QH541.5.S26
Sand dune planting	631.64	S621.5.S3
Sand dunes	551.375	GB631-638
Sand waves	551.375	GB649.S3
Sandstone	552.5	QE471.15.S25
Sandstone	622.353	TN957
Sandwich construction	624.1779	TA492.S25
Sandwiches	641.84	TX818
Sanitary engineering	628	TD

Subject Heading	Dewey	LC	Subject Heading	Dewey	LC
Sanitary engineering—[By region or country]	628.09(4-9)	TD21-127	Saudi Arabia—Civilization	939.49	DS215
Sanitary engineering—History	628.09	TD15-20	Saudi Arabia—Civilization	953.8	DS215
			Saudi Arabia—Description and travel	913.94904	DS204.5-208
Sanitary engineering—Periodicals	628.05	TD1-4	Saudi Arabia—Description and travel	915.3804	DS204.5-208
Sanitary engineers—Biography	628.092	TD139-140	Saudi Arabia—Economic conditions	330.9538	HC415.33
Sanitary engineers—Directories	628.025	TD12	Saudi Arabia—History	939.49	DS221-244.63
Sanitary landfills	628.44564	TD795-.7	Saudi Arabia—History	953.8	DS221-244.63
Sanitation, Household	392.36	GT472	Saudi Arabia—Maps	912.538	G2249.3-.34
Sanitation, Household	648	TH6014-7696	Saudi Arabia—Maps	912.538	G7530-7534
Sanitation, Rural	628.7	TD920-931	Saudi Arabia—Politics and government	320.9538	JQ1841
Sanskrit language	491.2	PK401-976	Savanna ecology	577.48	QH541.5.P7
Sanskrit language—Dictionaries	491.23	PK925-969	Savannas	551.453	GB561-568
Sanskrit language—Etymology	491.22	PK901-919	Savannas	578.748	QH87.7
			Saving and thrift	332.0415	HG7920-7933
Sanskrit language—Grammar	491.25	PK501-811	Savings accounts	332.1752	HG1660
			Savings and loan associations	332.32	HG2121-2156
Sanskrit language—Lexicography	491.23028	PK920-969	Savings banks	332.21	HG1881-1966
Sanskrit literature	891.2	PK3591-4485	Sawmills	674.2	TS850
Sanskrit philology	491.2	PK401-418	Saws	621.934	TJ1233-1255
Sao Tome and Principe—Census	316.715	HA4713	Saws	674.0284	TS850-851
			Saxons	941.017	DA150-162
Sao Tome and Principe—History	967.15	DT615.5-.8	Saxony (Germany)—History	943.21	DD801.S31-.S59
			Saxophone music	788.7	M105-109
Sao Tome and Principe—Maps	912.6715	G8675-8679	Scabies	616.57	RL764.S28
			Scaffold burial	393.4	GT3350
Sapphires	622.384	TN997.S24	Scale insects	632.752	SB939
Sardine fisheries	639.2745	SH351.S3	Scales (Fishes)	597.1477	QL639
Saskatchewan—Gazetteers	917.124003	F1070.4	Scales (Weighing instruments)	530.7	QC107
Saskatchewan—History	971.24	F1070-1074.7	Scalping	399.08997	E98.W2
Saskatchewan—Maps	912.7124	G3490-3494	Scandinavia	948	DL
Saskatchewan—Periodicals	971.24005	F1070	Scandinavia—Biography	920.048	CT1240-1328
Sasquatch	001.944	QL89.2.S2	Scandinavia—Church history	274.8	BR970-1019
Satanism	133.422	BF1546-1550			
Satanism	202.16	BL480	Scandinavia—Civilization	936.3	DL30-33
Satellite master antenna television	384.555	HE8700.7-.72	Scandinavia—Civilization	948	DL30-33
			Scandinavia—Congresses	936.3006	DL1.5
Satellites	523.98	QB401-407	Scandinavia—Congresses	948.006	DL1.5
Sati	393.9	GT3370	Scandinavia—Description and travel	913.6304	DL6.7-11.5
Satin	677.39	TS1640-1688			
Satire	808.87	PN6231.S2	Scandinavia—Description and travel	914.804	DL6.7-11.5
Satis (Egyptian deity)	299.31	BL2450.S27			
Saturn (Planet)	523.46	QB671	Scandinavia—Economic conditions	330.948	HC341-380
Saturn (Planet)	523.46	QB384	Scandinavia—Gazetteers	913.63003	DL4
Saturn (Planet)—Orbit	623.263	QB384	Scandinavia—Gazetteers	914.8003	DL4
Saturn (Planet)—Ring system	523.986	QB405	Scandinavia—Genealogy	929.1072048	CS890-939
			Scandinavia—History	936.3	DL43-87
Saturn (Roman deity)	292.2113	BL870.S29	Scandinavia—History	948	DL43-87
Sauces	641.814	TX819	Scandinavia—History—15th century	948.03	DL61-65
Saudi Arabia	939.49	DS201-248			
Saudi Arabia	953.8	DS201-248			
Saudi Arabia—Census	315.38	HA4563			

Subject Heading	Dewey	LC	Subject Heading	Dewey	LC
Scandinavia—History—The Count's War, 1534-1536	948.04	DL75-81	School choice	379.111	LB1027.9
			School closings	379.1535	LB2823.2
Scandinavia—History—20th century	948.08	DL83-87	School discipline	371.5	LB3011-3095
			School districts	379.1535	LB2817-.5
Scandinavia—Manufactures	670.948	TS88.5	School employees	371.201	LB2831.5-.585
Scandinavia—Maps	912.48	G6910-6963	School employees—Legal status, laws, etc.—United States	344.7307	KF4192-.5
Scandinavia—Periodicals	936.3005	DL1			
Scandinavia—Periodicals	948.005	DL1			
Scandinavia—Politics and government	320.948	JN7011-7066	School enrollment	371.219	LC130-139
			School facilities	371.6	LB3205-3325
Scandinavian languages	439.(5-6)	PD1501-5929	School field trips	371.384	LB1047
Scandinavian languages—Dialects	439.(5-6)7	PD1850-1893	School grounds	371.61	LB3251
			School health services	371.71	LB3401-3495
Scandinavian languages—Etymology	439.(5-6)2	PD1801-1819	School hygiene	371.71	LB3401-3495
			School integration	379.263	LC214-.3
Scandinavian languages—Grammar	439.(5-6)5	PD1559-1701	School libraries	027.8	Z675.S3
			School management and organization	371.2	LB3011-3095
Scandinavian languages—Lexicography	439.(5-6)3028	PD1823			
			School management and organization	378.1	LB2801-2997
Scandinavian languages—Study and teaching	439.(5-6)071	PD1535-1539			
			School management teams	371.2	LB2806.3
Scandinavian literature	839.5	PT7001-9999	School milk programs	371.716	LB3473-3479
Scandinavian literatures	839.5	PT	School personnel management	371.201	LB2831.5-2844.4
Scandinavian literature—Study and teaching	839.5071	PT7035-7039			
			School photography	371.897	TR818
Scandinavian periodicals	058	PN5280.5-5310	School principals	371.2012	LB2831.9-.976
Scandinavian philology	439.(5-6)	PD1501-1541	School psychology	371.713	LB1027.55
Scarabs	736.20932	NK5561	School safety patrols	363.1257	LB2865
Scarlatina	616.92987	RC182.S2	School social work	371.46	LB3013.4
Scattering (Physics)	539.758	QC794.6.S3	School sports	796.042	GV346
Scattering amplitude (Nuclear physics)	539.758	QC794.6.S3	School superintendents	371.2011	LB2831.7-.776
			School supervision	371.203	LB2806.4
Scene painting	751.75	ND2885-2888	School vandalism	371.58	LB3249
Schism, The Great Western, 1378-1417	284.8	BX1301	School violence	371.78	LB3013.3
			School year	371.23	LB3034
Schizophrenia	616.898	RC514	School-age child care	305.234	HQ778.6
Scholarly publishing	070.594	Z286.S37	Schools	371	L
Scholarships	371.223	LB2848-2849	Schools	371	LB
Scholarships	378.34	LB2338-2339	Schools—Centralization	379.1535	LB2861
Scholasticism	149.91	B839	Schools—Decentralization	379.1535	LB2862
Scholasticism	149.91	BD125	Schools—Furniture, equipment, etc.	371.63	LB3261-3281
Scholasticism	189.4	B734			
School accidents	363.119371	LB2864.6.A25	Schools—Prayers	242.2	BV283.S3
School administrators	371.2011	LB2831.8-.876	Schools—United States	371.00973	LD
School attendance	371.294	LB3081-3087	Sciatica	616.856	RC420
School attendance	371.294	LC142-148.5	Science	500	Q
School boards	379.1531	LB2831	Science and astrology	133.585	BF1729.S34
School bonds	379.13	LB2824-2830	Science fiction	808.838762	P96.S34
School bonds	379.130973	HG4951-4953	Science fiction	808.838762	PN3433-.8
School breakfast programs	371.716	LB3473-3479	Science fiction	808.838762	PN6120.95.S33
School buildings	371.6	LB3205-3295	Science projects	507.8	Q182.3
School children—Food	371.716	LB3473-3479	Science, Ancient	509.01	Q124.95
School children—Substance use	362.290834	HV4999.C45	Science, Medieval	509.02	Q124.97
			Science, Renaissance	509.0(24-31)	Q125.2
School children—Transportation	371.872	LB2864	Science—[By region or country]	509.(4-9)	Q127-.2
			Science—Data processing	502.85	Q183.9

Subject Heading	Dewey	LC	Subject Heading	Dewey	LC
Science—Dictionaries	503	Q123	Screen doors	690.1822	TH2278
Science—Exhibitions	507.4	Q105	Screen process printing	686.2316	TT273
Science—History	509	Q124.6-127.2	Screens	749.3	NK2910
Science—Methodology	501	Q174-175.32	Screws	621.882	TJ1338-1340
Science—Nomenclature	501.4	Q179	Scribes, Jewish	296.4615	BM659.S3
Science—Periodicals	505	Q1-9	Scrotum—Diseases	616.67	RC897
Science—Philosophy	501	Q174-175.32	Sculptors	730.92	NB1115
Science—Social aspects	303.483	Q175.5	Sculpture	730	NB
Science—Societies, etc.	506	Q10-99	Sculpture, Ancient	732.2	NB69-169
Science—Study and teaching	507.1	Q181-183.4	Sculpture, Byzantine	734.224	NB172
Science—Terminology	501.4	Q179	Sculpture, Chinese	730.951	NB1040-1049.6
Scientific apparatus and instruments	502.84	Q184-185.7	Sculpture, Gothic	734.25	NB180
Scientific illustration	502.2	Q222	Sculpture, Greek	733.3	NB90-105
Scientific surveys	508	Q148-149	Sculpture, Japanese	730.952	NB1050-1059.6
Scientists—Biography	509.2	Q141-143	Sculpture, Medieval	734	NB170-180
Scientists—Directories	502.5	Q145	Sculpture, Modern	735	NB185-198.5
Scintillation counters	539.775	QC787.S34	Sculpture, Prehistoric	732	GN799.S4
Sclera—Diseases	617.719	RE328	Sculpture, Primitive	732.2	NB62-64
Scleroderma (Disease)	616.544	RL451	Sculpture, Renaissance	735.21	NB190
Scones	641.815	TX770.B55	Sculpture, Rococo	735.21	NB193
Scorpio (Astrology)	133.5273	BF1727.5	Sculpture, Roman	733.5	NB115-120
Scotland	936.1	DA750-890	Sculpture—Appreciation	730.11	NB1142.5
Scotland	941.1	DA750-890	Sculpture—Catalogs	730.216	NB35
Scotland—Census	314.11	HA1151-1160	Sculpture—Conservation and restoration	731.48	NB1199
Scotland—Constitutional law	342.411	KDC750-785	Sculpture—Exhibitions	730.74	NB16-17
Scotland—Description and travel	914.1104	DA850-878	Sculpture—History	730.9	NB60-615
Scotland—Emigration and immigration	325.(2411) or (411)	JV7700-7709	Sculpture—Periodicals	730.5	NB1
Scotland—History—To 1057	941.101	DA777-778.9	Sculpture—Technique	731.028	NB1170-1195
Scotland—History—1057-1603	941.10(2-5)	DA779-790	Sculpture—[By region or country]	730.9(4-9)	NB201-1114
Scotland—History—1649-1660	941.1063	DA803.8	Sculpture—Afghanistan	730.9581	NB992-.3
Scotland—History—18th century	941.10(69-73)	DA809-814.5	Sculpture—Africa	730.96	NB1080-1099
			Sculpture—Africa, East	730.9676	NB1097-.6
Scotland—History—19th century	941.1081	DA815-818	Sculpture—Africa, Southern	730.968	NB1091.7-1096.6
Scotland—History—20th century	941.1082	DA821-826	Sculpture—Africa, West	730.966	NB1098-1099
Scotland—Maps	912.411	G5770-5774	Sculpture—Algeria	730.965	NB1088.3
Scotland—Periodicals	936.1005	DA750	Sculpture—Argentina	730.982	NB330-339
Scotland—Periodicals	941.1005	DA750	Sculpture—Asia	730.95	NB960-1070.3
Scotland—Politics and government	320.9411	JN1187-1371	Sculpture—Asiatic Russia	730.957	NB992.4-999
Scots language	427.9411	PE2101-2364	Sculpture—Australia	730.994	NB1100-1105.3
Scottish deerhound	636.7532	SF429.S39	Sculpture—Austria	730.9436	NB501-511.6
Scottish literature	820	PR8631-8644	Sculpture—Bahamas	730.97296	NB300-302
Scottish literature	820.9	PR8510-8553	Sculpture—Belgium	730.9493	NB661-673.3
Scouts and scouting	355.413	U190	Sculpture—Bolivia	730.984	NB340-349
Scrap metals	363.7288	TS214	Sculpture—Brazil	730.981	NB350-359
Scrapers (Earthmoving machinery)	624.1520284	TA725	Sculpture—Burma	730.9591	NB1012-.3
			Sculpture—Cambodia	730.9596	NB1015-.3
			Sculpture—Canada	730.971	NB240-249.5
			Sculpture—Central America	730.9728	NB260-290
			Sculpture—Chile	730.983	NB360-369
			Sculpture—Colombia	730.9861	NB370-379
			Sculpture—Costa Rica	730.97286	NB273-275
			Sculpture—Cuba	730.97291	NB303-305
			Sculpture—Czechoslovakia	730.9437	NB523-534.5

Subject Heading	Dewey	LC	Subject Heading	Dewey	LC
Sculpture—Denmark	730.9489	NB711-723.3	Sculpture—Switzerland	730.9494	NB841-853.3
Sculpture—Ecuador	730.9866	NB380-389	Sculpture—Syria	730.95691	NB989.6-.8
Sculpture—Egypt	730.962	NB1081-1085.3	Sculpture—Thailand	730.9593	NB1021-1023
Sculpture—El Salvador	730.97284	NB288-290	Sculpture—Tunisia	730.9611	NB1091.6
Sculpture—Ethiopia	730.963	NB1086.3	Sculpture—Turkey	730.9561	NB861-873.3
			Sculpture—United States	730.973	NB205-238
Sculpture—Europe	730.94	NB450-955	Sculpture—Uruguay	730.9895	NB420-429
Sculpture—Finland	730.94897	NB955.F5	Sculpture—Venezuela	730.987	NB430-439
Sculpture—France	730.944	NB541-553.3	Sculpture—Vietnam	730.9597	NB1014-.63
Sculpture—French Guiana	730.9882	NB397	Sculpture—West Indies	730.9729	NB291-315
Sculpture—Germany	730.943	NB561-589	Sculpture—Yugoslavia	730.9497	NB941-953.3
Sculpture—Great Britain	730.941	NB461-481	Sea-floor spreading	551.136	QE511.7
Sculpture—Greece	730.9495	NB591-603	Sea-walls	627.24	TC335
Sculpture—Guatemala	730.97281	NB276-278	Sea breeze	551.5185	QC939.L37
Sculpture—Guyana	730.9881	NB395	Sea ice drift	551.343	GB2401-2598
Sculpture—Haiti	730.97294	NB306-308	Sea Islands Creole dialect	427.9	PM7875.G8
Sculpture—Honduras	730.97283	NB279-281	Sea kayaking	797.1224	GV788.5
Sculpture—Hungary	730.9439	NB512-522.6	Sea songs	782.421595	M1977.S2
Sculpture—Iceland	730.94912	NB741-753.3	Seafaring life	387.54044	VK149
Sculpture—India	730.954	NB1001-1010.3	Seafaring life	910.45	G540-550
Sculpture—Indonesia	730.9598	NB1026-.8	Seafood	641.392	TX385-388
Sculpture—Iran	730.955	NB980-989	Seafood gathering	639.22	SH400-.8
Sculpture—Iraq	730.9567	NB967-969	Seafood poisoning	615.954	RA1242.S48
Sculpture—Israel	730.95694	NB977-979	Seagrasses	639.89	SH393
Sculpture—Italy	730.945	NB611-623.3	Sealing	639.29	SH360-363
Sculpture—Jamaica	730.97292	NB309-311	Seals	737.6	CD
Sculpture—Jordan	730.95695	NB979.6-.8	Seals (Numismatics)	737.6	CD5001-6471
Sculpture—Korea	730.9519	NB1060-1070.6	Seals (Numismatics)	929.(82 or 92)	JC345-347
Sculpture—Laos	730.9594	NB1016-.3	Seals (Numismatics)— Biography	737.6092	CD5051-5052
Sculpture—Lebanon	730.95692	NB976.6-.8			
Sculpture—Libya	730.9612	NB1089.3	Seals (Numismatics)— Congresses	737.606	CD5009
Sculpture—Malaysia	730.9595	NB1025-.8			
Sculpture—Mexico	730.972	NB250-259	Seals (Numismatics)— Exhibitions	737.6074	CD5017-5018
Sculpture—Morocco	730.964	NB1090.3			
Sculpture—Netherlands	730.9492	NB641-653.3	Seals (Numismatics)— History	737.609	CD5049
Sculpture—New Zealand	730.993	NB1106-1108			
Sculpture—Nicaragua	730.97285	NB282-284	Seals (Numismatics)— Periodicals	737.605	CD5001
Sculpture—Norway	730.9481	NB761-773.3			
Sculpture—Oceania	730.99(5-6)	NB1110-1113	Seals (Numismatics)— Societies, etc.	737.606	CD5005
Sculpture—Pakistan	730.95491	NB1010.7-.73			
Sculpture—Panama	730.97287	NB285-287	Seals (Numismatics)— Study and teaching	737.6071	CD5045
Sculpture—Paraguay	730.9892	NB400-409			
Sculpture—Peru	730.985	NB410-419	Seals (Numismatics)— Techniques	737.6028	CD5085-5175
Sculpture—Philippines	730.9599	NB1027-1029			
Sculpture—Poland	730.9438	NB955.P6	Seals (Numismatics)—[By region or country]	737.609(4-9)	CD5592-6471
Sculpture—Portugal	730.9469	NB821-833.3			
Sculpture—Puerto Rico	730.97295	NB312-314	Seals (Numismatics)— Canada	737.60971	CD5619
Sculpture—Romania	730.9498	NB921-933.3			
Sculpture—Russia	730.947	NB681-699	Seals (Numismatics)— Central America	737.609728	CD5621-5700
Sculpture—Saudi Arabia	730.9538	NB970-972			
Sculpture—Scandinavia	730.948	NB701-793.3	Seals (Numismatics)— Mexico	737.60972	CD5620
Sculpture—South America	730.98	NB320-439			
Sculpture—Spain	730.946	NB801-813.3	Seals (Numismatics)— United States	737.60973	CD5601-5617
Sculpture—Sri Lanka	730.95493	NB1010.6-.63			
Sculpture—Surinam	730.9883	NB396	Seamanship	623.88	VK541-547
Sculpture—Sweden	730.9485	NB781-793.3	Seaplane bases	629.1361	TL725.6
			Seaplanes	629.133347	TL684-.3

Subject Heading	Dewey	LC	Subject Heading	Dewey	LC
Search-lights	623.852	VM493	Sedimentology	552.5	QE471-.15
Search and rescue operations	363.3481	TL553.8	Sedition	364.131	HV6285
			Seduction	364.153	HV6584-6589
Search and rescue operations—United States	363.34810973	UG854.A4	Seed adulteration and inspection	631.521	SB114
Search dogs	636.70886	SF428.73	Seed crops	633	SB183-187
Searches and seizures—United States	345.730522	KF9630	Seed technology	631.521	SB113.2-118.45
			Seedlings—Transplanting	631.536	SB121
Seashore	551.458	GB451-460	Seeds	631.521	SB113.2-118.45
Seashore ecology	577.69	QH541.5.S35	Segregation in education	379.26	LC212.5-.73
Seasonal unemployment	331.137044	HD5855-5856	Seismology	551.22	QE531-541
Seasons	398.33	GR930	Seismometry	551.220287	QE541
Seasons	525.5	QB637.2-.8	Selection (Plant breeding)	631.52	SB123-.25
Seattle (Wash.)	979.7772	F899.S4	Self	155.2	BF697-.5
Seawater	551.465	GC100-103	Self-actualization (Psychology)	158.1	BF637.S4
Seawater—Distillation	623.854	VM505			
Secession	342.73042	JK310-331	Self-confidence	155.232	BF575.S39
Secession—Southern States	973.713	E458-459	Self-control	153.8	BF632
			Self-control	179.9	BJ1533.D49
Second-born children	306.87	HQ777.22	Self-control in children	155.4138	BF723.S25
Second Advent	236.9	BT885-886	Self-defense	613.66	GV1111
Second language acquisition	401.93	P118.2	Self-denial	241.4	BV4647.S4
			Self-destructive behavior	616.8582	RC569.5.S45
Secondary recovery of oil	622.3382	TN871.37	Self-destructive behavior in children	618.928582	RJ506.S39
Secret service	363.283	HV7961			
Secret societies	366.(1-5)	GN495.2	Self-efficacy	153.8	BF611
Secret societies	366.(1-5)	HS101-330.7	Self-esteem	158.1	BF697.5.S46
Secret societies—[By region or country]	366.(1-5)09(4-9)	HS201-330.7	Self-help groups	361.4	HV547
			Self-injurious behavior	616.8582	RC569.5.S48
Secret societies—United States	366.(1-5)0973	HS203-206	Self-insurance	368	HG8082
			Self-interest	171.9	BJ1474
Secret societies—[Other countries]	366.(1-5)09(4-9)	HS207-330.7	Self-mutilation	616.8582	RA1146
			Self-mutilation	616.8582	RC552.S4
Secret societies—Congresses	366.(1-5)06	HS110	Self-organizing systems	003.7	Q325-390
			Self-presentation	155	BF697.5.S44
Secret societies—Directories	366.(1-5)03	HS121-123	Self-reliance	179.9	BJ1533.S27
			Self in children	155.4182	BF723.S24
Secret societies—History	366.(1-5)09	HS125-148	Self psychology	155.2	BF697-.5
Secret societies—Periodicals	366.(1-5)05	HS101-106	Selling	381.1	HF5438-5439
			Selling—Automobiles	381.45388342	HF5439.A8
Secret societies—Rituals	366.(1-5)	HS155-158	Selling—Drugs	381.456151	HF5439.D75
Secretion	612.4	QP190-246.5	Semantics	401.43	P325-.5
Secular Franciscans	255.3	BX3651-3653	Semantics, Historical	401.4309	P325.5.H57
Secularism	211.6	BL2700-2790	Semen	612.61	QP255
Securities	332.632	HG4650-4930.5	Semiconductor storage devices	621.39732	TK7895.M4
Securities—Canada	346.71092	KE1042-1056			
Securities fraud	364.168	HV6763-6771	Semiconductor wafers	621.38152	TK7871.85-.99
Securities theft	364.168	HV6763-6771	Semiconductors	537.6226	QC610.9-611.8
Security (Law)	346.092	K1100-1108	Seminars	378.177	LB2393.5
Security (Law)—United States	346.73092	KF1046-1062	Seminary extension	230.0711	BV4164
			Seminole Indians	975.9004973859	E99.S28
Sedatives	615.782	RM325	Seminole War, 1st, 1817-1818	975.903	E83.817
Seder	296.437	BM695.P35			
Sediment transport	551.353	TC175.2	Seminole War, 2nd, 1835-1842	975.904	E83.835
Sedimentary structures	552.5	QE472			
Sedimentation and deposition	551.303	QE571-597	Semiotics	401.41	P99-.4
			Semites	305.892	GN547

Subject Heading	Dewey	LC	Subject Heading	Dewey	LC
Semites—Religion	299.2	BL1600-1710	Serbia—History—1804-1918	949.7101(4-5)	DR2006-2032
Semitic languages	492	PJ3001-9278	Serbia—History—Insurrection, 1804-1813	949.71014	DR343
Semitic languages, Northwest	492.047	PJ4121-4129	Serbia—History—Milos Obrenovic, 1814-1839	949.71014	DR2016
Semitic languages—Dictionaries	492.043	PJ3004	Serbia—History—Revolt, 1883	949.71015	DR2026.8
Semitic languages—Etymology	492.042	PJ3065	Serbia—History—1918-	949.710(2-3)	DR2033-2047
Semitic languages—Grammar	492.045	PJ3021-3041	Serbia—History—1918-1945	949.7102	DR2033-2040
Semitic languages—Lexicography	492.043028	PJ3071-3075	Serbia—History—1945-1992	949.710(2-3)	DR2041-2047
Semitic languages—Study and teaching	492.04071	PJ3011-3013	Serbia—History—1992-	949.7103	DR2047
Semitic literature	892.009	PJ3097	Serbia—Maps	912.4971	G2015-2017
Senegal—Census	316.63	HA4729	Serbia—Maps	912.4971	G6850-6853
Senegal—Civilization	966.3	DT549.4	Serbo-Croatian language	491.82	PG1224-1399
Senegal—Description and travel	916.6304	DT549.27	Serbo-Croatian language—Dictionaries	491.823	PG1374-1384
Senegal—Gazetteers	916.63003	DT549.15	Serbo-Croatian language—Grammar	491.825	PG1229-1313
Senegal—History	966.3	DT549.47-.83			
Senegal—History—To 1960	966.30(1-3)	DT549.7-.73	Serbo-Croatian language—Slang	491.827	PG1399
Senegal—History—1960-	966.305	DT549.8-.83	Serbo-Croatian philology	491.82	PG1201-1223
Senegal—History—Coup d'etat, 1962	966.3051	DT549.8	Serfdom	306.365	HT751-815
Senegal—Maps	912.663	G8810-8814	Serfdom—[By region or country]	306.36509(4-9)	HT781-815
Senile dementia	616.83	RC524	Serfdom—Austria	306.36509436	HT803
Seniority, Employee	658.312	HF5549.5.S4	Serfdom—France	306.3650944	HT785
Sense organs	573.87	QL945-949	Serfdom—Germany	306.3650943	HT791-801
Sense organs	611.8	QM501-511	Serfdom—Great Britain	306.3650941	HT781
Senses and sensation	121.35	BD214	Serfdom—Russia	306.3650947	HT807-809
Senses and sensation	152.1	BF231-299	Sericulture	638.2	SF541-560
Senses and sensation	612.8	QP431-495	Series, Infinite	515.243	QA295
Sensory stimulation in newborn infants	155.42221	BF720.S45	Serigraphy	764.8	NE1843-1844
Sentences (Criminal procedure)	345.0772	K5510-5560	Sermon on the mount	226.9	BT380-.2
Separation of powers	320.404	JF229	Sermons	252	BV4239-4316
Separation of powers	342.73044	JK305	Serotherapy	615.37	RM270-282
Separation of powers—England	342.42044	KD4000-4010	Serpent worship	202.12	BL441
Separation of powers—United States	342.73044	KF4565-4579	Service industries	338.4	HD9980-9990
			Service stations	629.286	TL153
September 11 Terrorist Attacks, 2001	973.931	HV6432.7	Service, Compulsory non-military	331.1173	HD4871-4875
Septets	785.17	M700-786	Service, Compulsory non-military	331.1173	HD4905.5
Septic tanks	628.742	TD778	Setters (Dogs)	636.7526	SF429.S5
Sepulchral monuments	736.5	NB1800-1895	Seven Days' Battles, 1862	973.732	E473.68
Serbia	949.71	DR1932-2125	Seven Years' War, 1756-1763	940.2534	DD409-412.8
Serbia—History	949.71	DR343	Seventeenth century	909.6	D242-283.5
Serbia—History—To 1456	949.71013	DR1977-1999.5	Seventh-Day Adventists	286.732	BX6151-6155
Serbia—History—1456-1804	949.71013	DR2000-2005	Seventh-Day Baptists	286.3	BX6390-6408
Serbia—History—Great Emigration, 1690	949.71013	DR2004.8	Severance pay	331.216	HD4928.D5
			Sewage	628.3	TD730-737
Serbia—History—Insurrection, 1788	949.71013	DR2005	Sewage	631.869	S657
			Sewerage, Rural	628.742	TD929-930.4

Subject Heading	Dewey	LC	Subject Heading	Dewey	LC
Sewerage—[By region or country]	628.309(4-9)	TD521-627	Sex role in mass media	305.3	P96.S5
Sewerage—History	628.309	TD515-520	Sexadecimal system	513.5	QA141.8.S4
Sewage—Purification	628.3	TD745-758.5	Sexism in communication	305.3	P96.S48
Sewage disposal	628.36	TD741-780	Sexism in religion	200.8	BL458
Sewage disposal, Rural	628.742	TD929-930.4	Sexism in textbooks	379.156	LB3045.66
Sewage irrigation	628.3623	TD760	Sexology—Research	613.9072	HQ60
Sewage lagoons	628.351	TD746.5	Sextant	623.890284	VK583
Sewage sludge—Conditioning	628.364	TD769.7	Sextets	785.16	M600-686
			Sexual animosity	155.3	BF692.15
Sewage sludge—Incineration	628.37	TD770-.3	Sexual aversion disorders	616.8583	RC560.S45
			Sexual behavior in animals	591.562	QL761
Sewer design	628.2	TD678-688	Sexual disorders in children	618.92098	RJ476.5-478.5
Sewerage	628.3	TD511-780	Sexual ethics	176	HQ31-64
Sewers, Concrete	628.2	TD682	Sexual ethics for teenagers	176.0835	HQ35
Sewing	646.2	TT700-715	Sexual ethics for women	176.082	HQ46
Sewing machines	646.2044	TJ1501-1519	Sexual instinct	306.7	HQ19-30.7
Sex	306.7	HQ	Sexual selection in animals	591.562	QL761
Sex	306.7	HQ12-449	Sexually abused children	618.9285836	RJ507.S49
Sex (Psychology)	155.3	BF692-.5	Sexually transmitted diseases	614.547	RA644.V4
Sex—Folklore	398.354	GR462			
Sex—Religious aspects—Christianity	233.5	BT708	Sexually transmitted diseases	616.951	RC200-203
			Sexually transmitted diseases—Prevention	614.547	RA644.V4
Sex—Religious aspects—Islam	297.577	BP190.5.S4			
			Seychelles—Census	316.96	HA2301
Sex addition	616.8583	RC560.S43	Seychelles—Civilization	969.6	DT469.S44
Sex crimes	364.153	HQ71-72	Seychelles—Description and travel	916.9604	DT469.S427
Sex crimes	364.153	HV6558-6569			
Sex crimes—Investigation	363.25953	HV8079.S48	Seychelles—Gazetteers	916.96003	DT469.S415
Sex customs	306.73	HQ12-18	Seychelles—History	969.6	DT469.S452-.S483
Sex customs	392.6	GN484.3			
Sex discrimination in education	379.26	LC212.8-.83	Seychelles—History—Coup d'etat, 1977	969.6	DT469.S48
			Seychelles—History—Coup d'etat, 1981	969.6	DT469.S48
Sex discrimination in employment	331.4133	HD6060-.5			
			Seychelles—Maps	912.696	G9200-9204
Sex distribution (Demography)	305.3	HB1741-1948	Shade-tolerant plants	635.9543	SB434.7
			Shades and shadows	742	NC755
Sex distribution (Demography)—United States	305.30973	HB1755-1777	Shadow prices	338.52	HB143
			Shadow shows	791.53	PN1979.S5
			Shaft sinking	622.25	TN283
Sex distribution (Demography)—[United States by city]	305.3097(4-9)	HB1777	Shakers	289.8	BX9751-9793
			Shakers—Biography	289.8092	BX9791-9793
Sex distribution (Demography—[United State by state]	305.3097(4-9)	HB1775	Shakers—Congresses	289.806	BX9755
			Shakers—Education	268.898	BX9761-9764
			Shakers—Government	262.098	BX9776
Sex in the Bible	220.83067	BS680.S5	Shakers—History	289.809	BX9765-9769
Sex instruction	613.9071	HQ56-59	Shakers—Sermons	252.098	BX9777
Sex instruction for boys	613.9071	HQ41	Shakers—[By region or country]		
Sex instruction for children	613.9071	HQ53			
Sex instruction for girls	613.9071	HQ51	Shakers—United States	289.80973	BX9766-9768
Sex instruction for the aged	613.9071	HQ55	Shakespeare, William, 1564-1616	822.33	PR2750-3112
Sex instruction for the handicapped	613.9071	HQ54-.4			
			Shaktism	294.5514	BL1282.2-.292
Sex offenders	364.153	HQ71-72	Shale	552.5	QE471.15.S5
Sex role	305.3	HQ1075-.5	Shamanism	201.44	BF1585-1623
Sex role in children	155.3	BF723.S42	Shamanism	201.44	BL2370.S5

Subject Heading	Dewey	LC	Subject Heading	Dewey	LC
Shampoos	646.7240284	TT969	Shipment of goods	658.788	HF5761-5780
Sharecropping	333.335563	HD1478	Shipping	387.5	HE561-971
Shareware (Computer software)	005.3	QA76.76.S46	Shipping—Congresses	387.506	HE562
			Shipping—Finance	387.54	HE603-605
Sharpshooting (Military science)	356.114	UD330-335	Shipping—Periodicals	387.505	HE561
			Shipping—Rates	387.54	HE594
Shaving	646.724	TT970	Shipping—Societies, etc.	387.506	HE564
Shaving (Jewish law)	340.18	BM523.5.S53	Shipping bounties and subsidies	387.50681	HE740-743
Shawnee Indians	976.800497317	E99.S35			
Sheep-shearing	636.30833	SF379	Ships	359.83	VK
Sheep	636.3	SF371-379	Ships	387.2	GN440.1
Sheet-metal	671.823	TS250	Ships	623.81	VM
Shell money	332.4	GN435.7-450.5	Ships, Concrete	623.81833	VM148
Shell money	332.4	HG235	Ships, Iron and steel	623.81821	VM146-147
Shellcraft	745.55	NK8643	Ships, Medieval	623.821	VM17
Shellcraft	745.55	TT862	Ships, Wooden	623.8184	VM142-144
Shellfish	594	QL401-445.2	Ships—Cargo	387.245	VK235-237
Shellfish culture	639.4	SH365-380.92	Ships—Electric equipment	623.8503	VM471-479
Shellfish culture—[By region or country]	639.409(4-9)	SH365-367	Ships—Electronic equipment	623.8504	VM480-.5
Shellfish gathering	639.4	SH400.4-.8	Ships—Equipment and supplies	623.86	VM781-861
Shells	591.477	QL401-432			
Shells, Concrete	624.1834	TA683.5.S4	Ships—Fires and fire prevention	623.8886	VK1250-1294
Shelving (Furniture)	749.3	NK2740			
Shenandoah Valley Campaign, 1862	973.732	E473.7	Ships—Fuel	623.874	VM779
			Ships—Heating and ventilation	623.853	VM481-482
Shenandoah Valley Campaign, 1864 (August-November)	973.737	E477.33	Ships—Lighting	623.852	VM491-493
			Ships—Manning	359.32092	VK221
			Ships—Measurement	623.810287	VM155
Shenandoah Valley Campaign, 1864 (May-August)	973.73(6-7)	E476.66	Ships—Water-supply	623.8542	VM503-505
			Ships' lights	623.852	VM815
			Ships of the line	358.32	V795
Shenandoah Valley Campaign, 1865	973.738	E477.65	Shipworms	594.4	TC201
			Shipwrecks	363.123	VK1250-1299
Sherman's March to the Sea	973.7378	E476.69	Shipwrecks	910.452	G521-539
			Shipwrecks—[By region or country]	363.12309(4-9)	VK1270-1294
Shields	623.441	GN498.S5			
Shields	739.752	NK6808	Shipwrecks—Pacific Ocean	910.45209164	G530.H82
Shields	929.6	CR91-93	Shock	616.047	RB150.S5
Shift systems	331.25725	HD5111.5-.6	Shoemakers	685.310092	HD8039.B7-.B72
Shifting cultivation	631.5818	S602.87	Shoes	685.31	TS989-1025
Shiite shrines	297.35	BP194.6	Shooting	799.21	SK37-39.5
Shiites	297.82	BP193	Shooting	799.31	GV1151-1181.3
Shiloh, Battle of, 1862	973.731	E473.54	Shooting, Military	356.11547	UD330-335
Shinto	299.561	BL2216-2227.8	Shooting contests	799.31	GV1167-1172
Shinto—Rituals	299.56138	BL2224.2	Shooting preserves	799.206	SK317
Shinto—Sacred books	299.56182	BL2217-.5	Shoots (Botany)	575.49	QK645-650
Shinto devotional calendars	299.56136	BL2224.3	Shop fronts	725.21	NA6225
Shinto shrines	299.56135	BL2224.9-2225.3	Shop mathematics	670.420151	TJ1165
Ship-railroads	625.39	TC771-772	Shopping centers	381.11	HF5429.7-5430.6
Ship burial	393.1	GT3380	Shopping malls	381.11	HF5429.7-5430.6
Ship captains	387.5092	VK205	Shore protection	627.24	TC330-340
Ship models	623.8201	VM298	Shoring and underpinning	624.152	TH5281
Ship models in bottles	745.5928	VM298.3	Short-term memory	153.12	BF378.S54
Ship registers	387.20216	HE565-566	Short rotation forestry	634.92	SD387.S52
Shipbuilding industry	338.4762382	VM298.5-301	Short stories, German	833.0108	PT1337-1340
Shipbuilding subsidies	623.820681	VM299.5-.7			

Subject Heading	Dewey	LC	Subject Heading	Dewey	LC
Short story	809.31	PN3373	Signatures (Writing)	929.88	Z41-42
Shorthand	653	Z53-104.5	Signs and symbols	246.55	BV150-168
Shoshonean Indians	979.0049745	E99.S39	Sikh sects	294.69	BL2018.7
Shoshonean languages	497.4574	PM2321	Sikhism	294.6	BL2017-2018.7
Shoshoni Indians	979.6004974574	E99.S4	Sikhism—Sacred books	294.682	BL2017.2-.4
Shoshoni Indians—Wars, 1863-1865	978.701	E83.863	Sikhs	294.6	BL2020.S5
Shoshoni Indians—Wars, 1863-1865	979.202	E83.863	Silage	633.2	SB195
Shoshoni Indians—Wars, 1863-1865	979.602	E83.863	Silent film music	781.542	M176
Shotguns	799.202834	SK274.5	Silent films—Musical accompaniment	781.54207	MT737
Shoulder joint—Dislocation	617.16	RD557.5	Silent reading	418.4	LB1050.55
Show-windows	659.157	HF5845-5849	Silesia, Lower (Poland and Germany)	943.85	DK4600.S44
Show dogs	636.70811	SF425.3	Silesia, Upper (Poland and Czech Republic) History	943.72	DK4600.S46
Show horses	636.10811	SF295.185-.187	Silesia, Upper (Poland and Czech Republic) History	943.85	DK4600.S46
Show riding	798.24	SF295.2	Silhouettes	741.7	NC910-.5
Showers (Plumbing fixtures)	696.182	TH6492	Silicone rubber	668.4227	TS1927.S55
Shrines	203.5	BL580-586	Silk	638.2	SF541-560
Shrubland ecology	577.38	QH541.5.S55	Silk	677.39	TS1546
Shuffleboard	796.2	GV1099	Silk	677.39	TS1640-1688
Shuttle cars (Mine haulage)	622.6	TN342	Silk-printing	686.2316	TP901
Siberia (Russia)	957	DK751-781	Silkworms	638.2	SF541-560
Sibling rivalry	155.443	BF723.S43	Silkworms, Non-mulberry	638.2	SF559.5-560
Sibyls	133.3248	BF1745-1779	Silos	690.892	TH4935
Sicily (Italy)—History	945.8	DG861-875	Silva Mind Control	615.851	RZ403.S56
Sicily (Italy)—Maps	912.458	G6760-6763	Silver	332.4223	HG301-309
Sick	362.1	HV687-694	Silver	620.18923	TA480.S5
Sick leave	331.25762	HD5115.5-.6	Silver flatware	739.2383	NK7234-7235
Sickles	631.3	S695-697	Silver mines and mining	339.27421	HD9536
Siddurim	296.45	BM675.D3	Silver mines and mining	622.3423	TN430-439
Sidecar motorcycle racing	796.75	GV1060.14	Silverpoint drawing	741.25	NC900-902
Sidesaddle riding	798.23	SF309.27	Silverwork	739.23	NK7100-7695
Sidewalk art exhibitions	707.4	N8665	Silvicultural systems	634.95	SD392
Sidewalks	625.88	TE280-295	Simulated environment (Teaching method)	371.397	LB1029.S5
Siege warfare	355.44	UG443-449	Sin	233.14	BT715-722
Sierra Leone—Census	316.64	HA4733	Sin	241.3	BV4625
Sierra Leone—Civilization	966.4	DT516.4	Sin (Islam)	297.22	BP166.75
Sierra Leone—Description and travel	916.6404	DT516.2	Sin (Judaism)	296.32	BM630
Sierra Leone—Gazetteers	916.64003	DT516.15	Sin, Original	233.14	BT720
Sierra Leone—History	966.4	DT516.5-.82	Sin, Unpardonable	241.3	BT721
Sierra Leone—History—To 1896	966.40(1-2)	DT516.65-.72	Sin, Venial	241.31	BV4625.6-.7
Sierra Leone—Maps	912.664	G8860-8864	Sindhi language	491.41	PK2781-2794
Sight-reading (Music)	781.42307	MT236	Singapore—Maps	912.5957	G8040-8044
Sight-singing	782.042307	MT870	Singing—Methods	782.001	MT825-850
Sign language	419	E98.S5	Singing—Methods	782.001	MT882
Sign painting	667.6	TT360	Single people	306.815	HQ800-.4
Signal generators	621.381548	TK7872.S5	Single women	306.8153	HQ800.2
Signal lights	629.040289	TA1250	Single-session psychotherapy	616.8914	RC480.55
Signals and signaling	358.24	UG570-613.5	Sinking-funds	336.363	HJ8052
Signals and signaling	384	HE9723-9737	Sinkholes	551.447	GB609.2
Signals and signaling	623.8561	V280-285	Sino-Indian Border Dispute, 1957-	954.042	DS480.85
Signals and signaling	623.8561	VK381-397	Sino-Tibetan languages	495	PL3521-3529

Subject Heading	Dewey	LC
Sins	241.3	BV4625-4627
Sisterhoods	255.9(1-7)	BX4200-4556
Sisterhoods	255.983	BX5185
Sitar music	787.82	M142.S5
Sitting customs	392	GT3005.3-.4
Sixteenth century	909.5	CB367-401
Sizing (Textile)	677.028	TS1488
Skating	796.91	GV848.9-852
Skeet shooting	799.3132	GV1181.3
Skeleton	573.76	QL821-827
Skeleton	599.947	GN70
Skeleton	611.71	QM101-117
Skepticism	121.2	BD201
Skepticism	149.73	B779
Skepticism	149.73	B837
Skepticism	211.4	BL2700-2790
Skeptics (Greek philosophy)	186	B525
Ski racing	796.935	GV854.9.R3
Ski resorts	796.93068	GV854.35
Ski troops	356.164	UD470-475
Skin	573.5	QL941-943
Skin	599.945	GN191-199
Skin	611.77	QM481-484
Skin—Cancer	616.99477	RC280.S5
Skin—Care and hygiene	613.4	RL87
Skin—Inflammation	616.5	RL231-241
Skin-grafting	617.4770592	RD121
Skin divers	797.23092	GV837.9-838
Skipjacks	623.8226	VM331
Skirmishing	355.422	U210
Skis and skiing	796.93	GV854
Skull	599.948	GN71-131
Skull	611.715	QM105
Skull—Abnormalities	616.71043	RD763
Skull—Fractures	617.155	RD529
Skydiving	797.56	GV769.5-770
Slabs	624.1772	TA660.S6
Slander	177.3	BJ1535.S6
Slander	241.3	BV4627.S6
Slang	417.2	P409-410
Slaughtering and slaughter-houses	664.9029	TS1960-1967
Slave-trade	381.44	HT975-1445
Slave labor	331.11734	HD4861-4865
Slavery	306.362	HT851-1444
Slavery	973.711	E441-453
Slavery—History	306.362090 (1-5)	HT863-867
Slavery—Africa	306.362096	HT1321-1427
Slavery—Asia	306.362095	HT1240.5-1315
Slavery—Australia	306.3620994	HT1431
Slavery—Benelux countries	306.36209492	HT1196-1203
Slavery—Canada	306.3620971	HT1051-1052
Slavery—Central America	306.36209728	HT1055-1056
Slavery—China	306.3620951	HT1241-1244
Slavery—Europe	306.362094	HT1155-1240
Slavery—France	306.3620944	HT1176-1180
Slavery—Germany	306.3620943	HT1181
Slavery—Great Britain	306.3620941	HT1161-1165
Slavery—Greece	306.36209495	HT1234
Slavery—Italy	306.3620945	HT1191-1194
Slavery—Japan	306.3620952	HT1276
Slavery—Mexico	306.3620972	HT1053-1054
Slavery—Philippines	306.36209599	HT1271
Slavery—Russia	306.3620947	HT1206-1209
Slavery—South America	306.362098	HT1121-1152
Slavery—Spain	306.3620946	HT1216-1220
Slavery—Switzerland	306.36209494	HT1227-1228
Slavery—West Indies	306.36209729	HT1071-1119
Slavery and the church	261.8	HT910-921
Slaves—Emancipation	326.8	HT1025-1037
Slavic languages	491.8	PG
Slavic languages	491.8	PG1-9198
Slavic languages—Dialects	491.877	PG350-400
Slavic languages—Dictionaries	491.83	PG331-335
Slavic languages—Etymology	491.8042	PG301-319
Slavic languages—Grammar	491.8045	PG59-97
Slavic languages—Lexicography	491.8043028	PG320-335
Slavic languages—Slang	491.877	PG400
Slavic languages—Study and teaching	491.8071	PG35-39
Slavic literature	891.8	PG500-585
Slavic philology	491.8	PG1-41
Sled dog racing	798.83	SF440.15
Sled dogs	636.70886	SF428.7
Sleep	154.6	BF1068-1073
Sleep	612.821	QP425-427
Sleep	613.794	RA786-.3
Sleep-wake cycle	571.77	QP84.6
Sleep disorders	616.8498	RC547-549
Sleep positions	154.6	BF1073.S56
Sleeping customs	392	GT3000.3-.5
Sleeping-cars (Railroads)	625.23	TF459
Sleeptalking	154.64	BF1073.S58
Slide-rule	510.284	QA73
Slides (Photography)	778.2	TR504-508
Slings	623.441	GN498.S55
Slopes (Physical geography)	551.43	GB448
Slot machines	688.752	TJ1570
Slovak language	491.87	PG5201-5399
Slovak language—Dictionaries	491.873	PG5375-5384
Slovak language—Grammar	491.875	PG5231-5325
Slovak literature	891.87	PG5400-5546
Slovak philology	491.87	PG5201-5223
Slovakia	943.73	DB2700-3150
Slovakia—Civilization	943.73	DB2735

Subject Heading	Dewey	LC	Subject Heading	Dewey	LC
Slovakia—Description and travel	914.37304	DB2718-2722	Smoking	394.14	GT3020
			Smoking	616.865	RC567
Slovakia—Gazetteers	914.373003	DB2707	Smoking—[By region or country]	362.29609(4-9)	HV5755-5770
Slovakia—History	943.73	DB2744-3000			
Slovakia—History—To 1526	943.7302	DB2795-2791	Smoking—United States	362.2960973	HV5755-5768
			Smoking—[Other countries]	362.29609(4-9)	HV5770
Slovakia—History—1526-1800	943.73023	DB2795-2801			
			Smugglers	364.133	HJ6619
Slovakia—History—1800-1918	943.7302(34-4)	DB2795-2801	Smugglers—United States	364.1330973	HJ6690-6710
			Snake cults (Holiness churches)	289.9	BX7990.H6
Slovakia—History—1918-1993	943.730(3-5)	DB2805-2841			
			Snakes	597.96	QL666.06-.694
Slovakia—History—Uprising, 1944	943.73033	DB2822	Snare drum	786.9409	ML1038.S
			Snare drum music	786.94	M146
Slovakia—History—Intervention, 1968	943.73042	DB2842	Sniping (Military science)	356.114	UD330-335
			Snow	551.5784	QC929.S7
Slovenia	939.8	DR1352-1485	Snow and ice climbing	796.52	GV200.3
Slovenia	949.73	DR1352-1485	Snow camping	796.54	GV198.9
Slovenia—History	939.8	DR1376-1450	Snow loads	624.172	TA654.4
Slovenia—History	949.73	DR1376-1450	Snow loads	624.252	TG304
Slovenia—History—1945-1990	949.7302	DR1444-1450	Snow loads	690.21	TH895
			Snow removal	625.22	TF542
Slovenia—History—1990-	949.7303	DR1452-1457.5	Snow removal	625.763	TD868-870
Slovenia—Maps	912.4973	G6875-6878	Snow White (Tale)	398.21	GR75.S6
Slovenian language	491.84	PG1801-1899	Snowboarding	796.95	GV857.S57
Slovenian language—Dictionaries	491.843	PG1888-1894.5	Snowmobiling	796.94	GV857.S6
			Snowshoes and snowshoeing	796.92	GV853
Slovenian language—Grammar	491.845	PG1819-1881			
			Snuff	394.14	GT3030
Slovenian language—Lexicography	491.843028	PG1887-1894.5	Soap	668.12	TP990-992.5
			Soap box derbies	796.6	GV1029.7
Slovenian literature	891.84	PG1900-1962	Soap operas	791.446	PN1991.8.S4
Slovenian philology	491.84	PG1801-1813	Soap operas	791.456	PN1992.8.S4
Slow learning children	371.926	LC4661-4700.4	Soccer	796.334	GV943-944
Slow pitch softball	796.3578	GV881	Soccer—Tournaments	796.33464	GV943.45-.54
Slow virus diseases	616.91	RC114.6	Soccer referees	796.3343	GV942.7
Sluice gates	627.882	TC553	Social adjustment	302.14	RC455.4.S67
Slums	307.3364	HV4023-4170.7	Social change	303.4	HM101-121
Small business—Finance	338.6420681	HG4027.7	Social classes	305.5	HT
Small business—Law and legislation—United States	343.7307	KF1659-.1	Social classes	305.5	HT601-1444
			Social classes—History	305.509	HT607
Small churches	250	BV637.8	Social classes—Research	305.5072	HT608
Small painting	751.77	ND1159	Social contract	320.11	JA81-84
Small presses	070.592	Z231.5.L5	Social contract	320.11	JC336
Smallpox	616.912	RC183-.9	Social ecology	304.2	HM206-208
Smaze	363.7392	QC882	Social ethics	303.372	HM216
Smell	152.166	BF271	Social group work	361.4	HV45
Smell	612.86	QP458	Social groups	305	HM131-134
Smell disorders	616.856	RF341	Social hierarchy in animals	591.56	QL775
Smelting furnaces	669.0282	TN677-.5	Social influence	303.34	HM259
Smocking	746.44	TT840.S66	Social interaction	302.3	HM291
Smog	614.59	RA576	Social interaction	302.4	HM291
Smoke	614.59	TD884	Social legislation	344	K1701-2000
Smoke plumes	363.7392	QC882.6	Social legislation—Canada	344.71	KE3098-3542
Smoke prevention	628.532	TD884	Social legislation—England	344.42	KD3000-3315
Smoke screens	355.41	UG447.7	Social legislation—Ireland	344.415	KDK800-895
Smoking	362.296	HV5725-5770			

Subject Heading	Dewey	LC	Subject Heading	Dewey	LC
Social legislation—Northern Ireland	344.416	KDE320-348	Social structure	305	GN478-491.7
Social legislation—Scotland	344.411	KDC635-674	Social surveys	361.10723	HN29
			Social work education	361.3071	HV11-.8
Social legislation—United States	344.73	KF3300-3771	Social work with criminals	361.3	HV7428
			Social work with gays	361.308664	HV1449
Social norms	306	GN493.3	Social work with juvenile delinquents	364.6	HV9051-9230.7
Social perception	302.12	BF323.S63			
Social problems	361.1	HN	Social workers—Supervision of	361.3092	HV40.54
Social problems—Congresses	361.106	HN3			
			Socialism	335	HX
Social problems—History	361.109	HN8-19	Socialism	335	HX1-550
Social problems—Periodicals	361.105	HN1	Socialism, Christian	335.7	HX51-54
			Socialism—[By region or country]	335.009(4-9)	HX80-517.5
Social psychology	302	HM251-291			
Social responsibility of business	658.408	HD60-.5	Socialism—History	335.009	HX21-54
			Socialism—Study and teaching	335.0071	HX19-.2
Social sciences	300	H			
Social sciences—Biography	300.92	H57-59	Socialist ethics	171.7	BJ1388
Social sciences—Congresses	300.6	H21-29	Socialization	303.32	GN510
			Socialization	303.32	HQ783
Social sciences—Experiments	300.724	H62	Socially handicapped children—Education	371.82694	LC4051-4100
Social sciences—History	300.9	H51-53			
Social sciences—Methodology	300.1	H61-.4	Societies	366	HS
			Societies—Congresses	366.006	HS5
Social sciences—Periodicals	300.5	H1-8	Societies—Directories	366.0025	HS17
			Societies—Encyclopedias	366.003	HS12
Social sciences—Research	300.72	H62-.5	Societies—History, organization, etc.	366.009	HS25-35
Social sciences—Study and teaching	300.71	H62-.5			
			Societies—Periodicals	366.005	HS1
Social security	368.4	HD7088-7250.7	Society, Primitive	301.7	GN406-498
Social security—[By region or country]	368.4009	HD7121-7250.7	Society Islands	996.21	DU870
			Society Islands—Maps	912.9621	G9640-9644
Social security—Law and legislation	344.05242	K1861-1929	Society of Friends	289.605	BX7601-7795
			Society of Friends—Congresses	289.606	BX7606.5-7608
Social security—Law and legislation—England	343.4205242	KD3241-3250			
			Society of Friends—Education	268.896	BX7619-7627
Social security—United States	343.7305242	KF3641-3664			
			Society of Friends—Government	262.096	BX7740-7746
Social security—United States	368.400973	HD7123-7126			
			Society of Friends—History	289.609	BX7630-7728
Social service	361	HV1-696	Society of Friends—Periodicals	289.605	BX7601
Social service, Rural	361.91734	HV67			
Social service—[By region or country]	361.9(4-9)	HV85-520.5	Society of Friends—Sermons	252.096	BX7733
			Society of Friends—Africa	289.66	BX7720-7723
Social service—United States	361.973	HV85-99	Society of Friends—Asia	289.65	BX7715-7716
Social service—[United States, By state or city]	361.97(4-9)	HV98-99	Society of Friends—Australia	289.694	BX7725-7726
			Society of Friends—Canada	289.671	BX7650-7653
Social service—[Other countries]	361.9(4-9)	HV101-520.5			
			Society of Friends—Europe	289.64	BX7675-7710
Social service—Directories	361.025	HV7	Society of Friends—Great Britain	289.641	BX7676-7693
Social service—History	361.709	HV16-25			
Social service—Societies, etc.	361.006	HV6	Society of Friends—South America	289.68	BX7671-7673
			Society of Friends—United States	289.673	BX7635-7649
Social service—Vocational guidance	361.3023	HV10.5			
			Sociobiology	304.5	GN365.9

Subject Heading	Dewey	LC	Subject Heading	Dewey	LC
Sociolinguistics	306.44	P40	Soil microbiology	579.1757	QR111-113
Sociological jurisprudence	340.115	K368-380	Soil moisture	631.432	S594
Sociology	301	HM	Soil pollution	363.7396	TD878-880
Sociology, Biblical	220.8301	BS670	Soil pollution	613.1	RA571
Sociology, Christian	261.5	BT738-.5	Soil protection	628.5	TD878-880
Sociology, Hindu	294.517	BL1215.S64	Soil science	631.4	S590-599.9
Sociology, Islamic	297.27	BP173.25-.45	Soil surveys	625.732	TE208-.5
Sociology, Rural	307.72	HT401-485	Soil surveys	631.47	S592.14-.147
Sociology, Rural—History	307.72090 (1-5)	HT415	Soils	631.4	S590-599.9
Sociology, Urban	307.76	HT101-395	Soils, Irrigated	631.587	S599-.9
Sociology, Urban—History	307.7609	HT111-150	Soils—Agricultural chemical content	631.41	S592.6.A34
Sociology, Urban—Research	307.76072	HT110	Soils—Analysis	631.4	S593
Sociology, Urban—Africa	307.76096	HT148	Soils—Pesticide content	628.55	TD879.P37
Sociology, Urban—Asia	307.76095	HT147	Solar activity	523.72	QB524-526
Sociology, Urban—Australia	307.760994	HT149	Solar cells	621.31244	TK2960
Sociology, Urban—Canada	307.760971	HT127	Solar collectors	621.472	TJ812
Sociology, Urban—Central America	307.7609728	HT128	Solar compass	522	QB105
Sociology, Urban—Developing countries	307.76091724	HT149.5	Solar cosmic rays	539.7223	QC485
Sociology, Urban—Europe	307.76094	HT131-145	Solar cycle	523.73	QB526.C9
Sociology, Urban—France	307.760944	HT135	Solar eclipses	523.78	QB541-545
Sociology, Urban—Germany	307.760943	HT137	Solar energy	621.47	TJ809-812.8
Sociology, Urban—Great Britain	307.760941	HT133	Solar energy industries	333.7923	HD9681
Sociology, Urban—Mexico	307.760972	HT127.7	Solar energy—Research	621.47072	TJ811-.5
Sociology, Urban—South America	307.76098	HT129	Solar engines	621.473	TJ812.5
Sociology, Urban—United States	307.760973	HT123-.5	Solar flares	523.75	QB516.F6
Sociology—Congresses	301.06	HM13	Solar greenhouses	631.583	SB415-416.3
Sociology—Dictionaries	301.03	HM17	Solar heating	697.78	TH7413-7414
Sociology—History	301.09	HM19-22	Solar houses	697.78	TH7414
Sociology—Methodology	301.01	HM24-37	Solar magnetic fields	523.72	QB539.M23
Sociology— Periodicals	301.05	HM1-7	Solar noise storms	523.72	QB539.N6
Sociology—Study and teaching	301.071	HM45-47	Solar power plants	621.31244	TK1085-1087
Sociometry	302.015195	HM253	Solar power plants	621.31244	TK1545
Sofia (Bulgaria)	949.99	DR97	Solar radiation	523.72	QB531
Softball	796.3578	GV881-.4	Solar radiation	551.5271	QC910.2-911.82
Software compatibility	005	QA76.76.C64	Solar saline water conversion plants	628.16725	TD479.7
Software documentation	005.3	QA76.76.D63	Solar system	523.2	QB500.5-785
Software engineering	005.1	QA76.758	Solar wind	523.58	QB529
Software maintenance	005.16	QA76.76.S64	Soldiers	355.0092	U1-145
Software protection	005.8	QA76.76.P76	Soldiers	355.0092	U750-773
Soil acidity	631.42	S592.575	Soldiers—Billeting	355.71	UC410
Soil biochemistry	631.417	S592.7-.85	Soldiers—Education, Non-military	355.5071	U715-717
Soil biology	578.757	QH84.8	Soldiers' monuments	725.94	NA9325-9355
Soil chemistry	631.41	S592.5-.6	Soldiers of fortune	355.354	G539
Soil conservation	631.45	S622-627	Solid fuel reactors	621.4834	TK9203.S65
Soil conservation projects	631.45	S627.P76	Solid propellants	629.47524	TL785
Soil ecology	577.57	QH541.5.S6	Solid state chemistry	541.0421	QD478
Soil management	631.4	S590-592	Solid state physics	531	QC176-.9
Soil mechanics	624.15136	TA710-711.5	Solidification	536.42	QC303
			Solo instrument music	785	M175.5
			Solo man	569.9	GN284.4
			Solomon Islands	995.93	DU850
			Solomon Islands—Census	319.593	HA4014
			Solomon Islands—Maps	912.9593	G9280-9284

Subject Heading	Dewey	LC	Subject Heading	Dewey	LC
Solubility	541.342	QD543	South Africa—Census	316.8	HA4701
Solution (Chemistry)	541.34	QD541-549	South Africa—Civilization	968	DT1752
Solutions (Pharmacy)	615.19	RS201.S6	South Africa—Description and travel	916.804	DT1730-1738
Solvents	661.807	TP247.5	South Africa—Economic conditions	330.968	HC905
Somali language	493.54	PJ2531-2534			
Somalia	967.73	DT401-409	South Africa—Gazetteers	916.8003	DT1714
Somalia—Census	316.773	HA4690	South Africa—History	968	DT1772-1969
Somalia—Civilization	967.73	DT402.2	South Africa—History—To 1836	968.0(2-42)	DT1807-1845
Somalia—Description and travel	916.77304	DT401.8	South Africa—History—Frontier Wars, 1811-1878	968.0(3-45)	DT1837
Somalia—Economic conditions	330.96773	HC850	South Africa—History—1836-1909	968.04(2-9)	DT1848-1922
Somalia—Gazetteers	916.773003	DT401.2	South Africa—History—Great Trek, 1836-1840	968.044	DT1853
Somalia—History	967.73	DT402.5-407.3	South Africa—History—Xhosa Cattle-Killing, 1856-1857	968.045	DT1863
Somalia—History—1960-1991	967.7305(1-2)	DT407-.3			
Somalia—History—1991-	967.73053	DT407	South Africa—History—Usutu Uprising, 1888	968.045	DT1888
Somalia—Maps	912.6773	G8350-8354	South Africa—History—1906-1961	968.0(49-58)	DT1924-1941
Somatization disorder	616.8524	RC552.S66			
Somatotypes	599.949	GN66	South Africa—History—Rebellion, 1914-1915	968.052	DT1933
Son of Man	232.9	BT232	South Africa—History—1961-	968.06	DT1945-1970
Sonar	623.8938	VK388			
Sonar	623.8938	VK560	South Africa—History—Soweto Uprising, 1976	968.0627	DT1959
Sonata	784.18307	MT62			
Song cycles	782.47	M1621.4	South Africa—Maps	912.68	G8500-8504
Songbooks	782.42	M1977.C5	South America	980	F2201-3799
Songhai Empire	966.23	DT551.45.S	South America—Armed Forces—Supplies and stores	355.8098	UC106-154
Songs—Accompaniment	781.4707	MT68			
Songs—History and criticism	782.4209	ML2500-2862			
			South America—Biography	920.08	CT640-758
Sonnet	808.8142	PN1514	South America—Church history	278	BR660-730
Sontay Raid, 1970	959.704342	DS557.8.S6			
Sophists (Greek philosophy)	183.1	B288	South America—Climate	551.698	QC988
			South America—Commerce	381.098	HF3371-3480
Sopono (Cult)	299.6869	BL2480.Y6			
Sorbian languages	491.88	PG5631-5698	South America—Economic conditions	330.98	HC161-239.5
Sorbian literature	891.88	PG5661-5698			
Sotho language	496.3977	PL8689	South America—Genealogy	929.107208	CS270-409
Soul	128.1	BD419-428	South America—History	980	F2201-2239
Soul	202.22	BL290	South America—Maps	912.8	G1700-1779
Soul	233.5	BT740-743	South America—Maps	912.8	G5200-5668
Soul (Hinduism)	294.522	BL1215.S8	South America—Politics and government	320.98	JL
Soul (Islam)	297.225	BP166.73			
Sound	534	QC220-246	South America—Religion	299.8	BL2580-2592
Sound—Equipment and supplies	534.0284	QC228.3	South American periodicals	079.8	PN5000-5106
			South Atlantic States—Maps	912.75	G3870-3933
Sound—Measurement	534.0287	QC243			
Sound production by animals	591.594	QL765	South Carolina—Gazetteers	917.57003	F267
			South Carolina—History	975.7	F266-280
Sound recordings—Album covers	741.66	NC1882-1883.3	South Carolina—History—Colonial period, ca. 1600-1775	975.70(1-2)	F272
Sound-waves—Damping	534.208	QC235			
Sound-waves—Damping	534.208	QC243			
Sounding and soundings	623.8938	VK584.S6			
Soundproofing	693.834	TH1725			
Source reduction (Waste management)	628.44	TD793.95			

Subject Heading	Dewey	LC	Subject Heading	Dewey	LC
South Carolina—History—Queen Anne's War, 1702-1713	975.702	E197	Soviet Union—Periodicals	947.084005	DK266.A2
			Sowing	631.531	SB121
South Carolina—History—1775-1865	975.70(2-3)	F273	Space and time	114-115	BD620-655
			Space and time	153.752	BF467-475
South Carolina—History—Civil War, 1861-1865	975.703	E471.1	Space and time	530.11	QC173.59.S65
			Space astronomy	520	QB136
South Carolina—History—Civil War, 1861-1865	975.703	E529	Space biology	571.0919	QH327-328
			Space cabin atmospheres	629.477	TL1530
South Carolina—History—Civil War, 1861-1865	975.703	E577	Space colonies	629.442	TL795.7
			Space flight	629.41	TL790
South Carolina—History—1865-	975.704	F274-275.42	Space flight—Physiological effect	612.0145	RC1150-1151
South Carolina—Maps	912.757	G3910-3914	Space flight to Jupiter	629.4555	TL799.J8
South Carolina—National Guard	355.3709757	UA440-449	Space flight to Mars	629.4553	TL799.M3
			Space flight to the moon	629.454	TL799.M6
South Carolina—Periodicals	975.7005	F266	Space flight to Venus	629.4552	TL799.V45
			Space flight training	629.45071	TL1085
South Dakota	978.3	F646-660	Space industrialization	338.0999	TL797
South Dakota—Gazetteers	917.83003	F649	Space law	341.47	K4135
South Dakota—Maps	912.783	G4180-4184	Space medicine	616.980214	RC1120-1160
South Dakota—National Guard	355.3709783	UA450-459	Space microbiology	579.17	QR130
			Space perception	153.752	BF469
South Dakota—Periodicals	978.3005	F646	Space photography	778.35	TR713
Southern Hemisphere	910.021814	G918-922	Space sciences	500.5	QB495-500.268
Southern Hemisphere—Maps	912.19814	G1052	Space ships	629.47	TL795-.5
			Space stations	629.442	TL797
Southern Hemisphere—Maps	912.19814	G3220-3222	Space suits	629.4772	TL1550
			Space surveillance	358.8	UG1500-1530
Southern States—History	975	F206-220	Space tools	629.450284	TL1098
Southwest, New	979	F786-790	Space vehicle accidents	363.124	TL867
Southwest, Old	976	F396	Space vehicles—Batteries	629.47445	TL1102.B3
Sovereignty	320.15	JC327	Space vehicles—Electric equipment	629.474	TL1100-1102
Soviet literature	891.708004	PN849.R9-.R92			
Soviet Union—Historiography	947.0840072	DK266.A33	Space vehicles—Electronic equipment	629.474	TL3000-3285
Soviet Union—History—Revolution, 1917-1921	947.0841	DK265-.95	Space vehicles—Materials	629.472	TL950-954
			Space vehicles—Piloting	629.458	TL1090-1095
Soviet Union—History—1917-1936	947.084(1-2)	DK265-272.7	Space vehicles—Specifications	629.40212	TL869
Soviet Union—History—Allied intervention, 1918-1920	947.0841	DK266-.5	Space vehicles—Sterilization	629.4774	TL945
Soviet Union—History—1925-1953	947.0842	DK267-273	Space vehicles—Tracking	629.437	TL4030
			Space vehicles—Tracking	629.457	TL4030
Soviet Union—History—1939-1945	947.0842	DK273	Space vehicles—Water-supply	629.4773	TL1565
Soviet Union—History—German occupation, 1941-1944	947.0842	DK273	Space warfare	358.8	UG1530
			Spain	936.6	DP1-402
			Spain	946	DP
Soviet Union—History—1953-1985	947.085	DK274-282	Spain	946	DP1-402
			Spain—Biography	920.0366	DP58
Soviet Union—History—1985-1991	947.0854	DK285-290.3	Spain—Biography	920.046	DP58
			Spain—Census	314.6	HA1541-1560
Soviet Union—History—Attempted coup, 1991	947.086	DK285-290.3	Spain—Church history	274.6	BR1020-1029
			Spain—Civilization	936.6	DP48-.9
Soviet Union—History, Military	355.00947	DK50-54	Spain—Civilization	946	DP48-.9
			Spain—Colonies	325.346	JV4000-4099
			Spain—Commerce	381.0946	HF3681-3690

Subject Heading	Dewey	LC	Subject Heading	Dewey	LC
Spain—Congresses	936.6006	DP2	Spain—History—Revolution, 1820-1823	946.072	DP215
Spain—Congresses	946.006	DP2	Spain—History—Isabella II, 1833-1868	946.072	DP216-220
Spain—Description and travel	913.6604	DP27-43.2	Spain—History—Carlist War, 1833-1840	946.072	DP219-.2
Spain—Description and travel	914.604	DP27-43.2	Spain—History—Revolution, 1854	946.072	DP217
Spain—Directories	946.0025	DP11	Spain—History—Revolutionary period, 1868-1875	946.073	DP222-232.6
Spain—Economic conditions	330.946	HC381-390	Spain—History—Carlist War, 1873-1876	946.07(3-4)	DP228-231.5
Spain—Emigration and immigration	325.(246) or (46)	JV8250-8259	Spain—History—Republic, 1873-1875	946.073	DP230-231.5
Spain—Gazetteers	913.66003	DP12	Spain—History—Alfonso XII, 1875-1885	946.074	DP232-.6
Spain—Gazetteers	914.6003	DP12	Spain—History—Alfonso XIII, 1886-1931	946.074	DP233-272.4
Spain—Historiography	936.60072	DP63-.83	Spain—History—Dictatorship, 1923-1930	946.074	DP247
Spain—Historiography	946.0072	DP63-.83	Spain—History—Republic, 1931-1939	946.081	DP250-269.9
Spain—History—To 711	936.6	DP91-96	Spain—History—Revolution, 1931	946.08	DP250
Spain—History—To 711	946.01	DP91-96	Spain—History—Civil War, 1936-1939	946.081	DP269.A1-.9
Spain—History—Roman period, 218 B.C.-414 B.C.	936.603	DP94-95	Spain—History—1939-1975	946.082	DP270-271
Spain—History—Gothic period, 414-711	946.01	DP96	Spain—History—1975-	946.083	DP272-.4
Spain—History—711-1516	946.0(2-3)	DP97.3-160.8	Spain—History—Coup d'etat, 1981	946.083	DP272
Spain—History—Ferdinand and Isabella, 1479-1516	946.03	DP161.5-166	Spain—History, Military	355.00946	DP76-78
Spain—History—Charles I, 1516-1556	946.042	DP172-175	Spain—History, Naval	359.00946	DP80-81
Spain—History—House of Austria, 1516-1700	946.04	DP170-189	Spain—Manufactures	670.946	TS87-88
Spain—History—Philip II, 1556-1598	946.043	DP176-181	Spain—Maps	912.46	G1965-1969
Spain—History—Philip III, 1598-1621	946.051	DP182-183.9	Spain—Maps	912.46	G6560-6564
Spain—History—Philip IV, 1621-1665	946.052	DP184-185.9	Spain—Periodicals	936.6005	DP1
Spain—History—Charles II, 1665-1700	946.053	DP186-189	Spain—Periodicals	946.005	DP1
Spain—History—Bourbons, 1700-	946.054	DP192-200.8	Spain—Politics and government	320.946	JN8101-8399
Spain—History—18th century	946.054	DP194-200.8	Spanish and Portuguese essays	086.(1 or 9)	AC70-75
Spain—History—Louis I, 1724	946.055	DP195	Spanish drama	862.08	PQ6217-6241
Spain—History—Ferdinand VI, 1746-1759	946.056	DP198-.7	Spanish drama	862.09	PQ6099-6129
Spain—History—Charles III, 1759-1788	946.057	DP199-.9	Spanish fiction	863.08	PQ6251-6257
Spain—History—Charles IV, 1788-1808	946.058	DP200-.8	Spanish fiction	863.09	PQ6138-6147
Spain—History—19th century	946.0(58-7)	DP201-232.6	Spanish language	460	PC4001-4977
Spain—History—Napoleonic Conquest, 1808-1813	940.27	DP204-208	Spanish language—Dialects	467	PC4700-4941
Spain—History—Ferdinand VII, 1813-1833	946.072	DP214-215.9	Spanish language—Dictionaries	463	PC4620-4645
Spain—History—Bourbon Restoration, 1814-1868	946.072	DP212-220	Spanish language—Etymology	462	PC4571-4580
			Spanish language—Grammar	465	PC4099-4400
			Spanish language—Lexicography	463.028	PC4620-4693

Subject Heading	Dewey	LC	Subject Heading	Dewey	LC
Spanish language—Slang	467.09	PC4951-4977	Speeches, addresses, etc., American	815.09	PS400-408
Spanish language—Study and teaching	460.71	PC4065	Speeches, addresses, etc., English	825.08	PR1321-1329
Spanish literature	860	PQ6001-8929	Speeches, addresses, etc., English	825.09	PR901-907
Spanish literature—To 1500	860.(1-2)09	PQ6057-6060	Speeches, addresses, etc., French	845.08	PQ1281-1283
Spanish literature—Classical period, 1500-1700	860.(2-3)09	PQ6063-6072	Speeches, addresses, etc., German	835.009	PT801
Spanish literature—Foreign countries	860	PQ7020-8921	Speeches, addresses, etc., German	835.08	PT1344-1345
Spanish literature—History and criticism	860.9	PQ6022-6167	Speechwriting	808.5	PN4142
Spanish literature—Study and teaching	860.71	PQ6013-6020	Spellers	428.1	PE1144-1146
			Spelling ability	372.632	LB1574
Spanish periodicals	056.1	PN5317.P4	Spent reactor fuels	621.48335	TK9360
Spanish philology	460	PC4001-4071	Spermicides	613.9432	RG137.2
Spanish poetry	861.08	PQ6174.95-6215	Spherical astronomy	522.7	QB140-237
			Spherical trigonometry	516.244	QA535
Spanish poetry	861.09	PQ6075-6098	Spice plants	633.8(3-4)	SB305-307
Spanish prose literature	868.0808	PQ6247-6264	Spice trade	381.41383	HD9210-9211
Spanish prose literature	868.0809	PQ6131-6153	Spices	394.12	GT2870
Spanish Succession, War of, 1701-1714	940.2526	D281-283.5	Spices	641.3383	TX406-407
			Spies	355.3432092	UB270-271
Spanish Succession, War of, 1701-1714	940.2526	DP196	Spies	359.3432092	VB250
			Spillways	627.883	TC555
Spatial analysis (Statistics)	310.1	HA30.6	Spin excitations	539.725	QC794.6.E9
Spatial behavior	153.752	BF469	Spinal adjustment	616.73062	RZ265.S64
Spears	623.441	GN498	Spinal canal	611.711	QM111
Special districts—United States	324.973	JS426	Spinal cord	573.869	QL938.S6
			Spinal cord	611.82	QM465
Special education	371.9	LC3950-3990.4	Spinal cord	612.83	QP370-375
Special forces (Military science)	356.16	UG633	Spinal cord—Diseases	616.856	RC400-406
			Spinal cord—Surgery	617.482059	RD594.3
Special forces (Military science)—United States—History	356.160973	U262	Spine	611.711	QM111
			Spine	612.83	QP330
Special libraries	026	Z675.A2	Spine—Abnormalities	616.73043	RD768-771
Special operations (Military science)	356.16	U262	Spine—Instability	616.73	RD771.I58
			Spine—Wounds and injuries	617.482044	RD533
Specific gravity	531.14	QC111-114			
Specifications	620.00212	TA180-181	Spinning	677.02822	TS1480-1487
Spectroscope	535.84	QC465	Spinning	677.02822	GN432
Spectrum analysis	543.5	QC450-467	Spires	721.5	NA2930
Spectrum analysis	543.5	QD95-96	Spirits	235	BT960-962
Spectrum analysis—Instruments	535.840284	QC451	Spirits (Islam)	297.21	BP166.89
			Spiritual direction	253.53	BV5053
Speculation	332.645	HG6001-6051	Spiritual direction	253.53	BX382.5
Speech	153.6	BF455-463	Spiritual direction	253.53	BX2350.7
Speech	153.6	LB1139.L3	Spiritual healing	234.131	BT732.5-.56
Speech	612.78	QP306	Spiritual life—Zen Buddhism	294.3444	BQ9288
Speech disorders	616.855	RC423-428.8			
Speech synthesis	621.399	TK7882.S65	Spiritual works of mercy	241.4	BV4647.M4
Speech therapy	616.85506	RC423-428.8	Spiritualism	133.9	BF1228-1389
Speeches, addresses, etc.	808.85	PN6121-6129	Spiritualism (Philosophy)	110	BD331
Speeches, addresses, etc., American	815.08	PS660-668	Spiritualism (Philosophy)	133.9	B841
			Spirituals (Songs)	782.253	M1670-1671
			Spithead Mutiny, 1797	941.073	DA87.7 1797

Subject Heading	Dewey	LC	Subject Heading	Dewey	LC
Spleen	573.1555	QL868	Sri Lanka—Maps	912.5493	G7750-7754
Spleen	611.41	QM371	Sri Lanka—Politics and government	320.95493	JQ650-659
Spleen	612.41	QP187	Stability	515.392	QA871
Sponges	593.4	QL370.7-374.2	Stability of airplanes	629.13236	TL574.S7
Spontaneous generation	576.83	QH325	Stability of ships	623.81	VM159
Spores (Botany)—Dispersal	571.847	QK929	Stadiums	725.827	NA6860-7010
Sporting goods	796.0284	GV743-749	Stadiums	796.068	GV415-416
Sporting guns	799.20283	SK274	Staff rides	355.4(8)	U280-285
Sporting prints	769.49796	NE960-.3	Staff, Pastoral	254	BV168.S7
Sports	306.483	GN454-455	Staffs (Sticks, canes, etc.)	391.44	GT2220
Sports	796	GV561-1198.995	Stains and staining (Microscopy)	570.2827	QH237
Sports—Economic aspects	796.0681	GV716	Staircases	690.1832	TH5667-5680
Sports—Law and legislation—England	344.42099	KD3525	Stairs	721.832	NA3060
Sports—Law and legislation—United States	344.73099	KF3989	Stalingrad, Battle of, 1942-1943	940.5421721	D764.3.S7
Sports administration	796.06	GV713	Stamp collecting	769.56	HE6187-6230
Sports facilities	796.068	GV401-433	Standardbred horse	636.13	SF293.S72
Sports for the handicapped	796.087	GV709.3	Standardization	658.562	T59-.2
Sports journalism	070.449796	PN4784.S6	Standardization	658.562	HD62
Sports medicine	617.1027	RC1200-1245	Standards, Engineering	620.00218	TA368
Spotsylvania Court House, Battle of, Va., 1864	973.736	E476.52	Standards, Military	355.15	UC590-595
Spraying and dusting in agriculture	632.94	SB953	Staphylococcal infections	571.99353	QR201.S68
			Staphylococcal infections	616.92	RC116.S8
Spring festivals	394.262	GT4504-.995	Starch	664.2	TP415-416
Springboard diving	797.24	GV838.67.S65	Stars	398.362	GR625
Springs	551.498	GB1198-.4	Stars	523.8	QB799-903
Springs (Mechanism)	621.824	TJ210	Stars, New	523.88	QB841
Springs—Folklore	398.364	GR690	Stars, New	523.88	QB895
Squall lines	551.55	QC880.4.S65	Stars—Atlases	520.223	QB65
Squalls	551.55	QC880.4.S65	Stars—Catalogs	523.80216	QB6
Square root	513.23	QA49	Stars—Clusters	523.85	QB851-855.9
Square root	513.23	QA119	Stars—Evolution	523.88	QB806
Squatter sovereignty	346.043	JK318	Stars—Formation	523.88	QB806
Squatter sovereignty	973.711	E415.7	Stars—Masses	523.81	QB814
Sri Lanka	954.93	DS488-490	Stars—Observations	523.8	QB6
Sri Lanka—Census	315.493	HA4570.8	Stars—Photographic measurements	523.87	QB121
Sri Lanka—Description and travel	915.49304	DS489-.15	Stars—Radiation	523.82	QB817
Sri Lanka—Economic conditions	330.95493	HC424	Stars—Rotation	523.83	QB810
			Starvation	616.39	RA1116
Sri Lanka—Gazetteers	915.493003	DS488.9	State aid to private schools	379.32	LB2828
Sri Lanka—History	954.93	DS489.5-490	State bankruptcy	336.368	HJ8061
Sri Lanka—History—To 1505	954.9301	DS489.6-.63	State departments of education	379.152	LB2809
Sri Lanka—History—1505-1948	954.930(1-2)	DS489.7-.73	State farms	334.683	HD1493-.5
Sri Lanka—History—Rebellion, 1818	954.9302	DS489.7	State governments—United States	352.130973	JK2403-9593
Sri Lanka—History—Rebellion, 1848	954.9302	DS489.7	State governments—[United States, By state]	352.1309(4-9)	JK2701-9593
Sri Lanka—History—1948-	954.9303	DS489.8-.86	State universities and colleges	378.053	LB2329.5
Sri Lanka—History—Rebellion, 1971	954.93031	DS489.8	State, The	320.011	JC
			State, The—Origin	320.11	GN492.6
Sri Lanka—Manufactures	670.95493	TS104.7-.8	States rights	342.73042	JK311-325
Sri Lanka—Maps	912.5493	G2290-2294	States, Small	321.06	JC365

Subject Heading	Dewey	LC	Subject Heading	Dewey	LC
Statics	531.12	QA821-835	Stellar oscillations	523.83	QB812
Stationery	676.2823	TS1228-1268	Stencil work	745.73	TT270-273
Stations of the Cross	264.0274	BX2040	Step aerobics	613.71	GV501.5
Statistical astronomy	520.21	QB149	Stepfathers	306.8742	HQ756
Statistical consultants	310.92	QA276.17	Steppes	551.453	GB571-578
Statistical mechanics	530.13	QC174.7-175.36	Sterilization of women	618.12059	RG138
Statistical weather forecasting	551.633	QC996.5	Sterilization reversal	617.463	RD585.5
			Sterilization reversal	618.12059	RG138
Statistics	310	HA	Sterilization reversal	618.145	RD585
Statistics—Graphic methods	001.4226	HA31	Sterilization, Eugenic—Law and legislation—United States	344.73048	KF3832
Statistics—History	310.9	HA19			
Statistics—Methodology	310.1	HA29-32	Stethoscopes	616.0754028	RC76.3
Statistics—Periodicals	310.5	HA1	Stevedores	387.5092	HD8039.L8
Statistics—Research	310.72	HA35	Stewardship, Christian	248.6	BV772
Status offenders	365.6	HV9051-9230.7	Stews	641.73	TX693
Statutes	348.022	K7010-7011	Still-life painting	751.422435	ND2290-2305
Statutes—England	348.42022	KD125-150	Still-life painting	758.4	ND1390-1400
Statutes—England	349.42	KD8850-9355	Still-life photography	778.935	TR656.5
Statutes—London	342.421	KD8996-9142	Stillbirth	618.4	RG631-633
Statutes—United States	348.73022	KF50-70	Stimulants	615.785	RM332-.3
Statutes—Wales	348.429022	KD9407	Stir frying	641.774	TX689.5
Stealth aircraft	385.4183	UG1240	Stochastic processes	519.23	QA274-.8
Steam	621.1	TJ268-280.7	Stock-exchanges	332.642	HG4551-4598
Steam-boilers	621.183	TJ281-393	Stock companies	338.86	HD2709-2932
Steam-boilers, Marine	623.8722	VM741-750	Stock index futures	332.63228	HG6043
Steam-boilers—Safety appliances	621.1830289	TJ350-357	Stock options	332.63228	HG6042
			Stockbrokers	332.62	HG4621
Steam-engines	621.1	TJ461-740	Stockholm (Sweden)	948.73	DL976
Steam-heating	697.5	TH7561-7599	Stocks	332.6322	HG4661
Steam-heating, Low pressure	697.5	TH7570-7578	Stoics	188	B528
			Stomach	573.36	QL862
Steam-pipe coverings	621.185	TJ427	Stomach	611.33	QM341
Steam-pipes	621.185	TJ415-444	Stomach	612.32	QP151
Steam-turbines	621.165	TJ735-740	Stomach—Diseases	616.33	RC816-840
Steam as a disinfectant	614.48	RA766.S8	Stomach—Secretions	612.32	QP193
Steam engineering	621.1	TJ268-748	Stomach—Surgery	617.553059	RD540.5-.57
Steam generating heavy water reactors	621.483	TK9203.H4	Stone	622.35	TN950-997
			Stone age	930.1(2-4)	GN775-768
Steam power plants	621.312132	TJ395-444	Stone carving	731.463	NB1208-1210
Steamboat disasters	363.123	VK1250-1299	Stone money	332.4	GN436.2
Steamboat lines	387.2044	HE945	Stone walls	690.12	TH2249
Steamboats—Passenger accommodation	387.2044	HE599-601	Stonemasonry	693.1	TH5401-5440
			Stoneware	738.3	NK4360-4367
Steaming (Cookery)	641.73	TX691	Storage batteries	621.31242	TK2941
Steel, Galvanized	620.17	TA472-473	Stores or stock-room keeping	381.1	HF5495
Steel, Stainless	620.16	TA479.S7			
Steel, Structural	624.1821	TA684-695	Storm sewers	628.212	TD665
Steel—Fatigue	620.176	TA473	Storm surges	551.463	GC225-226
Steel-works	669.142	TN755	Storms	363.3492	HV635.5-636
Steel-works	672	TS300-360	Storms	551.55	QC940.6-959
Steel boats	359.82	V880	Storytelling	372.677	LB1042
Steel boats	623.843	VM320-361	Storytelling	808.543	GR72.3
Steel houses	728	NA7180	Stoves	641.5028	TX657.S3-.S8
Steel I-beams	624.17723	TA660.S67	Stoves	697.22	TH7435-7458
Steeplechasing	798.45	SF359-.7	Stoves, Coal	697.22	TH7443-7446
Steering-gear	623.862	VM841-845			

Subject Heading	Dewey	LC	Subject Heading	Dewey	LC
Surface chemistry	541.33	QD506-509	Surrealism (Literature)	808.801163	PN56.S87
Surface tension	530.427	QC183	Surrogate mothers	306.8743	HQ759.5
Surfaces	516.352	QA571-573	Surveying	526.9	TA501-625
Surfaces	516.36	QA631-638	Surveying—Instruments	526.90284	TA562-581
Surfaces	516.36	QA641-672	Surveying—Study and teaching	526.9071	TA535-538
Surgery	617	RD			
Surgery—Complications	617.919	RD98-.4	Surveyors	526.9	TA515-531
Surgery, Homeopathic	617	RX366-376	Surveyors' chains	526.90284	TA579
Surgery, Military	617.99	RD151-498	Surveys	526.3	QB301-328
Surgery, Military—Africa	617.99096	RD481-489	Surveys	526.9	GA51-87
Surgery, Military—Asia	617.99095	RD445-476	Surveys	551.0723	QE61-350
Surgery, Military—Australia	617.990994	RD493	Surveys—Plotting	526.9	TA611
Surgery, Military—Canada	617.990971	RD216	Survival after airplane accidents, shipwrecks, etc.	613.69	TL553.7
Surgery, Military—Central America	617.9909728	RD224-225			
Surgery, Military—Europe	617.99094	RD268-441	Survival swimming	797.21	GV838.76
Surgery, Military—Mexico	617.990972	RD221	Suspension bridges	624.23	TG400
Surgery, Military—New Zealand	617.990993	RD493.5	Swahili language	496.392	PL8701-8704
			Swamp camping	796.54	GV198.95
Surgery, Military—Oceania	617.99099(5-6)	RD498	Swamp ecology	577.68	QH541.5.S9
Surgery, Military—South America	617.99098	RD235-267	Swamps	551.41	GB621-628
			Swamps	578.768	QH87.3
Surgery, Military—United States	617.990973	RD200-214	Swastika	203.7	BL604.S8
			Swaziland—Census	316.887	HA4705
Surgery, Military—West Indies	617.9909729	RD231-232	Swaziland—Civilization	968.87	DT2742
			Swaziland—Description and travel	916.88704	DT2732
Surgery, Minor	617.024	RD111-114			
Surgery, Naval	617.99	RD151-498	Swaziland—Economic conditions	330.96887	HC925
Surgery, Plastic	617.952	RD118-120.5			
Surgery, Primitive	617.0901	GN477.5-.7	Swaziland—Gazetteers	916.887003	DT2714
Surgery, Primitive	617.0901	GN477.5-.7	Swaziland—History	968.87	DT2754-2806
Surgical dressings	617.93	RD113-.4	Swaziland—Maps	912.6887	G8590-8594
Surgical nursing	617.0231	RD99-.35	Swearing	179.5	BJ1535.S9
Surgical wound infections	617.919	RD98.3	Swearing	241.3	BV4627.S9
Surinam	988.3	F2401-2431	Swearing	394	GT3080
Surinam—Census	318.83	HA1035	Sweatshops	331.117	HD2337-2339
Surinam—Civilization	988.3	F2409.8	Sweden—Biography	920.0363	DL644
Surinam—Description and travel	918.8304	F2410-2413	Sweden—Biography	920.0485	DL644
			Sweden—Census	314.85	HA1521-1540
Surinam—Gazetteers	918.83003	F2404	Sweden—Civilization	936.3	DL631-635
Surinam—History	988.3	F2420.3-2425.23	Sweden—Civilization	948.5	DL631-635
Surinam—History—To 1814	988.301	F2423	Sweden—Description and travel	913.6304	DL614.55-619.5
Surinam—History—1814-1950	988.30(1-31)	F2424	Sweden—Description and travel	914.8504	DL614.55-619.5
Surinam—History—1950-	988.303(1-2)	F2425-.23	Sweden—Economic conditions	330.9485	HC371-380
Surinam—History—Coup d'etat, 1980	988.3032	F2425	Sweden—Emigration and immigration	325.(2485) or (485)	JV8220-8229
Surinam—History—Coup d'etat, 1982	988.3032	F2425	Sweden—Gazetteers	913.63003	DL605
			Sweden—Gazetteers	914.85003	DL605
Surinam—Manufactures	670.9883	TS49	Sweden—Historiography	936.30072	DL645
Surinam—Maps	912.883	G5260-5264	Sweden—Historiography	948.50072	DL645
Surinam—Periodicals	988.3005	F2401	Sweden—History	936.3	DL601-991
Surinam—Politics and government	320.9883	JL780-789	Sweden—History	948.5	DL601-991
			Sweden—History—To 1397	936.3	DL660-700.9
Surplus military property	355.62137	UC260-267			
Surrealism	709.04062	NX600.S9			

Subject Heading	Dewey	LC	Subject Heading	Dewey	LC
Sweden—History—To 1397	948.501	DL660-700.9	Swedish drama	839.7208	PT9605-9625
			Swedish drama	839.7209	PT9415-9449
Sweden—History—Magnus II Ericksson, 1319-1363	948.501	DL689	Swedish fiction	839.7308	PT9627-9630
			Swedish fiction	839.7309	PT9480-9492
Sweden—History—1397-1523	948.5018	DL696-700.9	Swedish language	439.7	PD5001-5929
Sweden—History—1523-1718	948.503(2-4)	DL701-879	Swedish language—Dialects	439.77	PD5700-5929
Sweden—History—Gustavus I Vasa, 1523-1560	948.5032	DL703	Swedish language—Dictionaries	439.73	PD5625-5693
Sweden—History—Eric XIV, 1560-1568	948.5032	DL703.8	Swedish language—Etymology	439.72	PD5571-5599
Sweden—History—17th century	948.503	DL704.6-.7	Swedish language—Grammar	439.75	PD5101-5400
Sweden—History—Charles IX, 1604-1611	948.5032	DL704.8	Swedish language—Lexicography	439.73028	PD5611-5693
Sweden—History—Gustavus II, Adolphus, 1611-1632	948.5034	DL705.A2-715	Swedish language—Study and teaching	439.7071	PD5065
			Swedish literature	839.7	PT9201-9999
Sweden—History—Charles X Gustavus, 1654-1660	948.5034	DL725.7	Swedish philology	439.7	PD5001-5071
			Swedish poetry	839.7108	PT9580-9599
Sweden—History—Charles XI, 1660-1697	948.5034	DL727-729	Swedish poetry	839.7109	PT9375-9405
			Swedish prose literature	839.7808	PT9460-9499
Sweden—History—Charles XII, 1697-1718	948.5034	DL730-743	Swedish prose literature	839.7808	PT9626-9639
Sweden—History—1718-1814	948.50(36-4)	DL747-805	Swimming	797.21	GV837
			Swimming—Crawl stroke	797.21	GV838.52.C73
Sweden—History—Ulrika Eleonora, 1718-1720	948.5036	DL753	Swimming—Records	797.21	GV838.5
			Swine	636.4	SF391-397.4
Sweden—History—Frederick I, 1720-1751	948.5036	DL755-759	Swine plague	636.408969	SF977.P5
			Swiss literature (French)	840	PQ3870-3888
Sweden—History—Insurrection, 1743	948.5036	DL757	Swiss literature (German)	830	PT3860-3878
			Switching circuits	621.381537	TK7868.S9
Sweden—History—Gustavus III, 1771-1792	948.503(6-8)	DL766-770	Switzerland	949.4	DQ
			Switzerland—Biography	920.0364	DQ52-.7
Sweden—History—Revolution, 1772	948.503(6-8)	DL766	Switzerland—Biography	920.0494	DQ52-.7
			Switzerland—Census	314.94	HA1591-1610
Sweden—History—1814-1905	948.50(3-4)	DL807-859	Switzerland—Civilization	936.4	DQ36-39
			Switzerland—Civilization	949.4	DQ36-39
Sweden—History—20th century	948.505	DL860-879	Switzerland—Commerce	381.09494	HF3701-3710
			Switzerland—Congresses	936.4006	DQ2
Sweden—History—Gustavus V, 1907-1950	948.505(1-3)	DL867-870	Switzerland—Congresses	949.4006	DQ2
			Switzerland—Description and travel	913.6404	DQ20-26
Sweden—History—Farmers' Demonstration, 1914	948.5051	DL868	Switzerland—Description and travel	914.9404	DQ20-26
Sweden—History—Gustavus VI Adolphus, 1950-1973	948.505(3-4)	DL872-876	Switzerland—Economic conditions	330.9494	HC395-400
			Switzerland—Emigration and immigration	325.(2494) or (494)	JV8280-8289
Sweden—History—Carl XVI Gustav, 1973-	948.50(54-6)	DL877-879	Switzerland—Gazetteers	913.64003	DQ14
Sweden—Manufactures	670.9485	TS89-90	Switzerland—Gazetteers	914.94003	DQ14
Sweden—Maps	912.485	G2070-2074	Switzerland—Historiography	936.40072	DQ52.8-.95
Sweden—Maps	912.485	G6950-6954	Switzerland—Historiography	949.40072	DQ52.8-.95
Sweden—Periodicals	936.3005	DL601	Switzerland—History—To 1648	936.4	DQ79-84
Sweden—Periodicals	948.5005	DL601	Switzerland—History—To 1648	949.40(1-3)	DQ79-84
Sweden—Politics and government	320.9485	JN7721-7995			

Subject Heading	Dewey	LC	Subject Heading	Dewey	LC
Switzerland—History—To 1032	936.4	DQ85-87	Sympathetic nervous system	573.85	QL939
Switzerland—History—To 1032	949.401	DQ85-87	Sympathetic nervous system	611.83	QM471
Switzerland—History—1032-1499	949.40(1-2)	DQ88-110	Symphonies	784.184	M1001
Switzerland—History—Perpetual League, 1291	949.402	DQ90-91	Symptomatology	616.047	RC69
			Synagogue architecture	726.3	NA4690
Switzerland—History—1499-1648	949.403	DQ104-118	Synagogue music	781.76	M2099.5
			Synagogue music	781.76	M2114.3
Switzerland—History—1648-1798	949.404	DQ111-123	Synagogue music	781.76	M2186-2187
Switzerland—History—1789-1815	949.40(4-5)	DQ131-151	Synagogues	296.65	BM653-655
			Synchrotrons	539.735	QC787.S9
Switzerland—History—Helvetic Republic, 1798-1803	949.405	DQ131-151	Syndicalism	335.82	HD6477
			Synthesizer music	786.74	M1473
			Synthetic fabrics	677.4	TS1688
Switzerland—History—19th century	949.40(5-6)	DQ124	Syphilis	616.9513	RC201-.9
			Syriac language	492.3	PJ5701-5809
Switzerland—History—1815-	949.40(6-74)	DQ154-191	Syriac language—Dictionaries	492.33	PJ5490-5493
Switzerland—History—1815-1830	949.4062	DQ154	Syriac language—Etymology	492.32	PJ5483
Switzerland—History—1830-1848	949.4062	DQ156	Syriac language—Grammar	492.35	PJ5419-5471
			Syriac literature	892.3	PJ5601-5695
Switzerland—History—Sonderbund, 1845-1847	949.4062	DQ158-161	Syriac philology	492.3	PJ5401-5411
			Syria—Census	315.691	HA4558
Switzerland—History—1848-	949.40(63-74)	DQ171-210	Syria—Civilization	939.43	DS94.6
			Syria—Civilization	956.91	DS94.6
Switzerland—History—20th century	949.407	DQ201-210	Syria—Description and travel	913.94304	DS94
Switzerland—History, Military	355.009494	DQ59	Syria—Description and travel	915.69104	DS94
			Syria—Economic conditions	330.95691	HC415.23
Switzerland—Manufactures	670.9494	TS91-92			
Switzerland—Maps	912.494	G1895-1899	Syria—Gazetteers	913.943003	DS92.6
Switzerland—Maps	912.494	G6040-6044	Syria—Gazetteers	915.691003	DS92.6
Switzerland—Periodicals	936.4005	DQ1	Syria—History	939.43	DS94.9-98.3
Switzerland—Periodicals	949.4005	DQ1	Syria—History	956.91	DS94.9-98.3
Switzerland—Politics and government	320.9494	JN8701-9599	Syria—Maps	912.5691	G2220-2224
			Syria—Maps	912.5691	G7460-7464
Sword-dance	793.35	GV1796.S9	Syria—Politics and government	320.95691	JQ1826
Swordplay	355.4	U865			
Swordplay	796.86	GV1143-1150.6	Syrups	615.19	RS201.S8
Swords	355.8241	U850-872	Syrups	664.1	TP375-414.5
Swords	356.118241	UD420-425	System analysis	003	QA402-.37
Swords	357.048241	UE420-425	System theory	003.01	Q295
Swords	739.722	NK6700-6799	Systems engineering	620.001171	TA168
Symbolic play	155	BF720.P56	Systems software	005.43	QA76.76.S95
Symbolism	133.33	BF1623.S9	T cells	571.966	QR185.8.T2
Symbolism	203.7	BL600-620	T-ball	796.3578	GV881.5
Symbolism	246.55	BV150-168	T-shirts	687.21	TT675
Symbolism in art	704.946	N7740-7745	Tabla music	786.93	M146
Symbolism in literature	808.8015	PN56.S9	Table	642	TX871-885
Symbolism in the Bible	220.64	BS477	Table-moving (Spiritualism)	133.92	BF1375
Symbolism of numbers	133.3359	BF1623.P9	Table etiquette	395.54	BJ2041
Symmetry	539.725	Q172.5.S95	Table setting and decoration	642.7	TX871-885
Symmetry (Physics)	539.725	QC174.17.S9			
Symmetry (Physics)	539.725	QC793.3.S9	Table tennis	796.346	GV1005

Subject Heading	Dewey	LC
Tables	684.13	TS880
Tables	684.13	TT197.5.T3
Tablets (Medicine)	615.19	RS201.T2
Taboo	390	GN494
Tactics	355.42	U164-167.5
Tagalog language	499.211	PL6051-6059
Tagalog literature	899.211	PL6058
Tahiti	996.211	DU870
Tahitian language	499.444	PL6515
Tailoring	687.044	TT570-630
Taiwan—Census	315.1249	HA4646-4650
Taiwan—Civilization	931	DS799.4
Taiwan—Civilization	951.249	DS799.4
Taiwan—Description and travel	913.104	DS799.15-.24
Taiwan—Description and travel	915.124904	DS799.15-.24
Taiwan—Economic conditions	330.951249	HC430.5
Taiwan—Emigration and immigration	325.(251249) or (51249)	JV8710-8719
Taiwan—Gazetteers	915.1249003	DS798.96
Taiwan—Gazetteers	931.003	DS798.96
Taiwan—History	931	DS799.99-.833
Taiwan—History	951.249	DS799.99-.833
Taiwan—History—To 1895	931	DS799.64-.66
Taiwan—History—To 1895	951.2490(2-3)	DS799.64-.66
Taiwan—History—Insurrection, 1895	951.24904	DS799.69
Taiwan—History—1895-1945	951.2490(3-4)	DS799.69-.72
Taiwan—History—1945-	951.24905	DS799.77-.833
Taiwan—History—February Twenty Eighth Incident, 1947	951.24905	DS799.823
Taiwan—History—1975-	951.24905	DS799.83-.833
Taiwan—History—Kaohsiung Incident, 1979	951.24905	DS799.834
Taiwan—Maps	912.51249	G2340-2344
Taiwan—Politics and government	320.951249	JQ1520-1539
Tajikistan	958.6	DK921-929.5
Tales	398.2	GR74-76
Talismans	133.44	BF1561
Talismans	398.45	GR600
Tall buildings	690	TH6057.T23
Tall buildings	720.483	NA6230-6234
Talmud	296.12	BM500-509
Tambourine music	786.95	M175.T
Tamil language	494.811	PL4751-4759
Tank engineers	358.22092	UG127-128
Tankers	387.245	HE566.T3
Tankers	623.8245	VM455
Tanks (Military science)	358.1883	UG446.5
Tannaim	296.120092	BM177
Tanning	675.23	TS940-1047
Tantrism	294.5514	BL1141.2-1142.6
Tanzania—Census	316.78	HA4697
Tanzania—Civilization	967.8	DT442.5
Tanzania—Description and travel	916.7804	DT439-440.5
Tanzania—Economic conditions	330.9678	HC885
Tanzania—Gazetteers	916.78003	DT437
Tanzania—History	967.8	DT443.5-448.25
Tanzania—History—To 1964	967.80(1-3)	DT443.5-448.25
Tanzania—Maps	912.678	G8440-8444
Taoism	299.514	BL1900-1940
Taoist ethics	299.5145	BL1290.8
Taos Indians	978.900497496	E99.T2
Tap dancing	792.78	GV1794
Tapa	641.812	GN432
Tapestry	677.64	TS1780
Tapestry	746.3	NK2975-3049
Taps and dies	621.984	TJ1335
Tarawa, Battle of, 1943	940.5426	D767.917
Target practice	358.125	UF340-345
Target practice	359.547	VF310-315
Tariff	382.7	HF1701-2701
Tariff—[By region or country]	382.709(4-9)	HF1745-2580.9
Tariff—United States	382.70973	HF1750-1757
Tariff—[Other regions or countries]	382.709(4-9)	HF1761-2580.9
Tariff—Law and legislation	343.056	K4600-4640
Tariff—Law and legislation—England	343.42056	KD5641-5694
Tariff—Law and legislation—United States	343.73056	KF6651-6708
Tariff preferences	382.7	HF1721-1733
Tarot	133.32424	BF1879.T2
Tartar emetic	615.73	RM666.T2
Taste	152.167	BF261
Taste	612.87	QP456
Tatar language	494.387	PL65.T3
Tatar literature	894.387	PL65.T35-.T39
Tatars	950.0494387	DS25
Tatting	746.436	TT840.T38
Taurus (Astrology)	133.5263	BF1727.2
Tautomerism	541.2252	QD471
Tax assessment	336.2	HJ3241
Tax evasion—United States	345.730233	KF6334
Tax exemption	336.206	HJ2336-2337
Tax exemption—Law and legislation—United States	343.7304	KF6329-6330
Tax incidence	336.294	HJ2321-2323
Tax revenue estimating	336.20015195	HJ2351.4
Taxation	336	HJ2240-7395
Taxation (Roman law)	343.37604	KJA3210
Taxation—[By region or country]	336.2009(4-9)	HJ2361-3192.7
Taxation—United States	336.200973	HJ2361-2442

Subject Heading	Dewey	LC
Taxation—[United States, By state]	336.20097(4-9)	HJ2391-2442
Taxation—[Other regions or countries]	336.2009(4-9)	HJ2449-3192.7
Taxation—History	336.2009	HJ2250-2279
Taxation—Law and legislation	343.04	K4456-4590
Taxation—Law and legislation—England	343.4204	KD5351-5605
Taxation—Law and legislation—United States	343.7304	KF6271-6636
Taxation of personal property	336.23	HJ4581-4601
Taxicabs	388.34232	HE5601-5725
Taxidermy	590.752	QL63
Tea	394.12	GT2905-2916
Tea tax (American colonies)	973.3115	E215.7
Teacher-student relationships	371.1023	LB1033
Teacher exchange programs	370.1163	LB2283-2285
Teachers	370.92	LA2301-2397
Teachers	371.1	LB2832-2844.47
Teachers	371.11	LB1755-1779
Teachers, Part-time	371.14	LB2844.1
Teachers, Probationary	371.144	LB2844.1.P7
Teachers—Certification	371.12	LB1771-1773
Teachers—In-service training	370.711	LB1731
Teachers—Leaves of absence	371.104	LB2843.L4
Teachers—Legal status, laws, etc.—United States	344.73078	KF4175-4190
Teachers—Salaries, etc.	331.2813711	LB2842-2844
Teachers—Tenure	371.104	LB2836
Teachers—Training of	370.711	LB1705-2286
Teachers—Workload	371.1412	LB2844.1.W6
Teachers colleges	370.711	LB1805-2151
Teachers' unions	331.88113711	LB2844.52-.53
Teaching	371.1	LB1025-1050.7
Teaching	371.1	LB1775-1785
Teaching	371.102	LB
Teaching machines	371.334	LB1029.A85
Teaching, Freedom of	371.104	LC72-.5
Team learning approach in education	371.148	LB1032
Team nursing	610.73028	RT90.5
Tear gas munitions	363.20284	HV7936.E7
Technical education	370.113	LC1041-1047
Technical education	607.1	T61-173
Technical education—[By region or country]	607.10(4-9)	T71-170
Technical illustration	602.2	T11.8
Technological forecasting	601.12	T174
Technological unemployment	331.137042	HD6331-.2
Technology	600	T
Technology—Abbreviations	601.48	T8
Technology—Congresses	606	T6
Technology—Dictionaries	603	T9-10
Technology—History	609	T14.7-33
Technology—Language	601.4	T11-.3
Technology—Periodicals	605	T1-5
Technology—Philosophy	601	T14
Technology—Social aspects	303.483	T14.5
Technology—Sociological aspects	306.46	HM221
Technology—Terminology	601.4	T9-10
Technology assessment	303.483	T174.5
Technology transfer	338.926	T174.3
Teddy bears	790.133	GV1220.7
Teenage girls	305.235	HQ798
Teenage mothers	306.87430835	HQ759.4
Teenage parents	306.8740835	HQ759.64
Teenage pregnancy	618.200835	RG556.5
Teenagers—Growth	612.661	RJ140
Teeth	573.356	QL858
Teeth	599.943	GN209
Teeth	611.314	QM311
Teeth—Care and hygiene	617.601	RK61
Teeth—Diseases	617.63	RK301-493
Teeth—Diseases—Diagnosis	617.630754	RK308-310
Teeth—Extraction	617.66	RK531-.5
Teeth—Polishing	617.601	RK60.7
Teeth—Transplantation	617.60592	RK533
Teeth—Wounds and injuries	617.6044	RK490-493
Telecommunication	621.382	TK5101-5105.9
Telecommunication—Law and legislation	343.0994	K4301-4339
Telecommuting	658.3128	HD2331-2336.35
Telegraph	384.1	HE7601-8635
Telegraph	621.383	TK5105-5865
Telegraph, Wireless	384.52	HE8660-8688
Telegraph, Wireless	621.3842	TK5700-5865
Telegraph, Wireless—Installation on ships	623.85642	VK397
Telegraph, Wireless—Marconi system	621.3842	TK5811-5865
Telegraph—[By region or country]	384.109(4-9)	HE7761-8630.7
Telegraph—Directories	384.1025	HE7621
Telegraph—Periodicals	621.38305	TK5107
Telegraph—Rates	384.13	HE7681-7691
Telegraph—Societies, etc.	384.106	HE7603
Telegraph—United States	384.10973	HE7761-7798
Telegraph lines	384.15	TK5301-5481
Telemarketing	381.142	HF5415.1265
Teleology	124	BD530-595
Telepathy	133.82	BF1161-1171
Telephone	384.6	HE8701-9685
Telephone	621.385	TK6001-6571.5

Subject Heading	Dewey	LC	Subject Heading	Dewey	LC
Telephone—Directories	621.385025	TK6011	Temptation	241.3	BT725
Telephone—Periodicals	621.38505	TK6001	Ten commandments	222.16	BS1281-1285.5
Telephone answering services	338.4765173	HD9999.T34-.T344	Ten commandments	241.52	BV4655-4710
			Tender offers (Securities)	332.6322	HG4028.T4
Telephone cables	621.38784	TK6381-6383	Tendonitis	616.76	RC935.T4
Telephone companies	384.6	HE8701-9685	Tendons	611.74	QM170
Telephone companies—[By region or country]	384.609(4-9)	HE8801-9685	Tennessee	976.8	F431-445
			Tennessee—Gazetteers	917.68003	F434
Telephone companies—United States	384.60973	HE8801-8846	Tennessee—History—Civil War, 1861-1865	976.804	E531
Telephone companies—[Other countries]	384.609(4-9)	HE8861-9685	Tennessee—History—Civil War, 1861-1865	976.804	E579
Telephone etiquette	395.59	BJ2195	Tennessee—Maps	912.768	G3960-3964
Telephone lines	621.38784	TK6201-6285	Tennessee—National Guard	355.3709768	UA460-469
Telephone switchboards	621.385	TK6391-6397			
Telephone switching systems, Electronic	621.3857	TK6397	Tennessee—Periodicals	976.8005	F431
			Tennis	796.342	GV990-1005
Telephone systems	621.387	TK6401-6505	Tension headache	616.84914	RB128
Telephone wire	621.38784	TK6381-6383	Tents	355.81	UC570-575
Telescopes	358.128	UF845	Term loans	332.1753	HG1641-1643
Telescopes	522.2	QB88	Terminal care	616.029	R726.8
Telescopic sights	623.46	UF855	Terminal care	616.029	RT87.T45
Television	621.388	TK6630-6720	Terminally ill	616.029	R726.8
Television, Master antenna	621.38835	TK6676	Terminals (Transportation)	388.47	TA1225
Television—Equipment and supplies	621.38800284	TK6650-6655	Terra-cotta sculpture	731.2	NB145-159
			Terra-cotta sculpture	731.2	NB1265
Television—Periodicals	621.388005	TK6630.A1	Terrariums	635.9824	QH68
Television actors and actresses	791.45028092	PN1992.4	Terrestrial radiation	551.5272	QC809.T4
			Terrorism—Prevention	363.32	HV6431
Television advertising	659.143	HF6146.T42	Terrorism—United States—Prevention	303.6250973	HV6432
Television broadcasting	384.55	HE8700-.95			
Television comedies	791.45617	PN1992.8.C66	Terrorists—Saudi Arabia—Biography	303.62509538	HV6430.B55
Television in education	371.3358	LB1044.7			
Television programs	384.5532	PN1992-.92	Testing	530.8	QC100-111
Television programs—Rating	384.5532	HE8700.65-.66	Testing	620.110287	TA401-492
			Testing-machines	620.11260287	TA413-.5
Television weathercasting	551.632	QC877.5	Testosterone	612.405	QP572.T4
Telugu language	494.827	PL4771-4779	Tetanus	616.9318	RC185
Temper	152.47	BF575.A5	Teton Indians	978.0049752	E99.T34
Temper tantrums in children	155.41247	BF723.A4	Teutonic Knights	255.7914	CR4759-4775
			Teutonic Knights	255.7914	DK4600.P77
Temperament	155.26	BF795-811	Teutonic race	305.83	GN549.T4
Temperance	362.2926	HV5001-5720	Texas	976.4	F381-395
Temperance (Virtue)	241.4	BV4647.T4	Texas—Gazetteers	917.64003	F384
Temperance—History	362.292609	HV5020-5025	Texas—History—To 1846	976.40(1-4)	F389-390
Temperance—Societies, etc.	362.292606	HV5006	Texas—History—1810-1821	976.402	F389
			Texas—History—1846-1950	976.40(5-63)	F391
Temperature measurements	536.50287	QC270-278.6	Texas—History—Revolution, 1835-1836	976.403	F390
Tempering	671.36	TS320			
Temples	726.1	NA4610-4710	Texas—History—Republic, 1836-1846	976.404	F390
Temples, Buddhist	294.3435	BQ5130-5137			
Temples, Buddhist—Dedication	294.3435	BL1477.8.D4	Texas—History—Civil War, 1861-1865	976.405	E532
Temples, Hindu	294.535	BL1243.72-.78	Texas—History—Civil War, 1861-1865	976.405	E580
Tempo (Music)	781.2207	MT42			
Temporary marriage	306.84	HQ803			

Subject Heading	Dewey	LC	Subject Heading	Dewey	LC
Texas—History—1951-	976.406(3-4)	F391.2-.4	Theodicy	231.8	BT160-162
Texas—Maps	912.764	G4030-4034	Theological seminaries	230.0711	BV4019-4160
Texas—National Guard	355.3709764	UA470-479	Theological virtues	241.4	BV4635-4639
Texas—Periodicals	976.4005	F381	Theology, Doctrinal	231-239	BT65-84
Text processing (Computer science)	005	QA76.9.T48	Theology, Doctrinal—History	230.09	BT20-30
Textbook bias	371.32	LB3045.6	Theology, Practical	240-248	BV1-4
Textbooks	371.32	LB3045-3048	Theology—History	270	BT1313-1480
Textbooks	371.32	LT	Theology—Study and teaching	230.071	BV4019-4180
Textile chemistry	677	TP890-933	Theory of distributions (Functional analysis)	515.7	QA324
Textile crafts	746	TT699-854.5	Theosophy	299.934	BP500-585
Textile design	746	NK8800-9505.5	Therapeutics	615.5	RM
Textile fabrics	677	TS1300-1865	Therapeutics, Experimental	615.5072	RM111
Textile fibers	677	TS1540-1549	Therapeutics, Physiological	615.82	RM695-931
Textile finishing	677.02825	TS1510	Therapeutics, Suggestive	616.89162	RC490-499
Thai language	495.91	PL4111-4251	Therapeutics—Congresses	615.506	RM21
Thai literature	895.911	PL4200-4209	Therapeutics—History	615.509	RM41-47
Thailand—Census	315.93	HA4600.55	Therapeutics—Periodicals	615.505	RM16
Thailand—Civilization	959.3	DS568	Therapeutics—Societies, etc.	615.506	RM1
Thailand—Description and travel	915.9304	DS564-566.2	Therapeutics—Study and teaching	615.5071	RM108-.5
Thailand—Economic conditions	330.9593	HC445	Therapeutics—Terminology	615.5014	RM38
Thailand—Gazetteers	915.93003	DS563	Theravada Buddhism	294.391	BQ7100-7285
Thailand—History	959.3	DS570.95-586	Thermal analysis	543.26	QD79.T38
Thailand—Maps	912.593	G2375-2379	Thermal analysis	543.26	QD117.T4
Thailand—Maps	912.593	G8025-8029	Thermal stresses	620.1121	TA418.58
Thailand—Politics and government	320.9593	JQ1740-1749	Thermochemistry	541.36	QD510-536
Thallium	546.678	QD181.T7	Thermodynamics	536.7	QC310.15-319
Thanatology	306.9	HQ1073-.5	Thermodynamics	621.4021	TJ265
Thanksgiving cookery	641.568	TX739.2.T45	Thermoelectricity	537.65	QC621-625
Thanksgiving Day	263.97	BV75	Thermometers	536.50287	QC270-278.6
Thanksgiving Day	394.2649	GT4975	Thermonuclear fuels	621.484	TK9360
The Grenadines	972.9844	F2061	Thermotherapy	615.832	RM865-868.5
Theater	792	PN2000-3299	Thieves	364.162	HV6653
Theater, Open-air	792.022	PN2219.08	Thin films	530.4175	QC176.82-.9.R37
Theater—History	792.09	PN2100-2193	Thirst	612.391	QP139
Theater—History—To 500	792.0901	PN2131-2145	Thirteen (The number)	398.41	GR933
Theater—History—Medieval, 500-1500	792.0902	PN2152-2160	Thirty Years' War, 1618-1648	940.24	D251-271
Theater—History—18th century	792.09033	PN2171-2179	Thought and thinking	153.42	BF441-449.5
Theater—History—20th century	792.09034	PN2181-2193	Thought and thinking	153.42	LB1590.3-.5
			Thrace	949.61	DR50-.84
Theater—China	792.0951	PN2870-2878	Thread	677.02862	TS1590
Theater—Greece	792.09495	PN2660-2668	Threshing machines	631.3	S699-701
Theater—Japan	792.0952	PN2920-2928	Throat	611.32	QM535
Theater architecture	725.822	NA6820-6846	Throat—Diseases	616.31	RF460-547
Theaters	725.822	NA6820-6845	Throat—Examination	616.31075	RF476
Theaters—Accidents	792.028	PN2091.A	Throat—Wounds and injuries	617.531044	RF547
Theaters—Stage-setting and scenery	792.025	PN2091.S8	Thrombosis	617.74	RE651
Theater—United States	792.0973	PN2220-2298	Thunderstorms	398.363	GR630
Theism	211.3	BD555	Thunderstorms	551.554	QC968-.2
Theism	211.3	BL200	Thyroid gland	611.44	QM371
Theocracy	321.5	JC20-89	Thyroid gland—Diseases	616.44	RC655-657

Subject Heading	Dewey	LC	Subject Heading	Dewey	LC
Tibet (China)—Description and travel	915.15	DS785	Tobogganing	796.95	GV856
			Toddlers	305.232	HQ774.5
Tibetan language	495.4	PL3601-3651	Toenails	573.59	QL942
Tibetan literature	895.4	PL3701-3775	Toes	611.98	QM549
Tibeto-Burman languages	495.4	PL3551-4001	Toes—Abnormalities	617.585043	RD786-789
Tick-borne diseases	614.433	RA641.T5	Tofu	641.35655	TX401.2.S69
Ticonderoga, Battle of, 1758	973.26	E199	Togo—Census	316.681	HA4723
			Togo—Civilization	966.81	DT582.4
Tidal currents	551.464	GC308-309	Togo—Description and travel	916.68104	DT582.27
Tidal power	621.20422	TC147			
Tidal power-plants	621.312134	TK1081	Togo—Gazetteers	916.681003	DT582.15
Tide pool ecology	577.69	QH541.5.S35	Togo—History	966.81	DT582.5-.82
Tides	551.464	GC300-376	Togo—History—1922-1960	966.8103	DT582.75
Tigers	599.756	QL737.C23			
Tile construction	693.3	TH1077-1083	Togo—Maps	912.6681	G8760-8764
Tiles	721.0443	NA3705	Toilets	392.36	GT476
Tillage	631.51	S604	Toilets	696.182	TH6498
Timber	338.17498	SD430-557	Tokelau	996.15	DU910
Timber	620.12	TA419-424.6	Tokelau—Maps	912.9615	G9550-9554
Timberline	581.73	QK938.F6	Tokens	737.3	CJ4801-5450
Time	115	BD638	Tokens—[By region or country]	737.309(4-9)	CJ4901-5336
Time	529	QB209-224			
Time, Equation of	529.1	QB217	Tokens—United States	737.30973	CJ4901-4906
Time—Systems and standards	529.0218	QB223	Tokens—Exhibitions	737.3074	CJ4805-4808
			Tokens—Museums	737.3074	CJ4805-4806
Time-series analysis	519.55	QA280	Tokens—Periodicals	737.305	CJ4801
Time measurements	529.7	QB213	Toll roads	388.122	HE336.T64
Time perception	153.753	BF468	Tomatoes	635.642	SB349
Time study	658.5421	T60.4-.47	Tombs	726.8	NA6120-6199
Timpani music	786.93	M146	Tombs—[By region or country]	726.809	NA6149-6199
Tin	620.185	TA480.T5			
Tin mines and mining	622.3453	TN470-479	Tomography	616.0757	RC78.7.T6
Tin ores	622.3453	TN470-479	Tone (Phonetics)	414.8	P223
Tires, Rubber	678.32	TS1912	Tonga	996.12	DU880
Tissue banks	362.1783	RD127-128.5	Tonga—Census	319.612	HA4017
Tissue-integrated prostheses	617.69	RK667.T57	Tonga—Maps	912.9612	G9570-9574
			Tonga language (Tonga Islands)	499.48	PL6531
Tissues	611.018	QM551-575			
Tissues	611.018	QP88-.6	Tongue	573.357	QL946
Titanium	620.18932	TA480.T54	Tongue	611.313	QM503
Titans (Mythology)	292.13	BL820.T6	Tonnage	387.2	HE565
Tithes	248.6	BX5165	Tonsillectomy	617.531059	RF484.5
Tithes	254.8	BV771	Tonsillitis	616.314	RF491
Tithes—Mormon Church	248.6	BX8643.T5	Tonsils	611.32	QM331
Titles of honor and nobility	929.7	CR3499-4420	Tonsils	612.312	QP146
Toasts	808.851	PN6340-6348	Tonsils—Diseases	616.32	RF481-499
Tobacco	394.14	GT3020-3030	Tools	621.9	GN436.8-437
Tobacco	633.71	SB273-278	Tools	621.9	TJ1180-1313
Tobacco—Physiological effect	616.865	RC567	Toothpicks	394.12	GT2952
			Topaz	549.62	QE391.T6
Tobacco—Physiological effect	616.865	RM666.T6	Topical preaching	251	BV4235.T65
			Topographical drawing	526.98	TA616
Tobacco-pipes	688.42	TS2270	Topographical surveying	526.3	TA590
Tobacco habit	362.296	HV5725-5770	Topology	514	QA611-614.97
Tobacco habit	616.865	RC567	Torah scrolls	296.4615	BM657.T6
Tobacco industry	336.27863371	HD9130-9149	Tories, English	324.24102	JN1129.T7
Tobacco industry	679.7	TS2220-2283	Tornadoes	551.553	QC955-.5

Subject Heading	Dewey	LC	Subject Heading	Dewey	LC
Torpedo-boats	359.3258	V830-840	Traditional farming	630	GN407.4-.8
Torpedoes	359.82517	V850-855	Traditional medicine	615.88	GN477-.7
Torts	346.03	K923-968	Traditional medicine	615.88	GR880
Torts—Canada	346.7103	KE1232-1309	Trafalgar, Battle of, 1805	941.073	DA88.5 1805
Torts—England	346.4203	KD1941-1980	Traffic accidents	363.125	RA772.T7
Torts—Ireland	346.41503	KDK450-469	Traffic accidents	613.69	RC1040-1045
Torts—United States	346.7303	KF1246-1329	Traffic circles	625.7	TE176.5
Torture	364.67	HV8593-8599	Traffic congestion	388.314	HE336.C64
Total hip replacement	617.4720592	RD549	Traffic police	363.2332	HV8079.5-.55
Total knee replacement	617.5820592	RD561	Traffic regulations	388.312	HE369-373
Total quality management	658.4013	HD62.15	Traffic safety	363.125	HE5613.5-5614.6
Totalitarianism	321.9	JC480-481	Traffic surveys	388.310723	HE369-373
Totemism	202.11	GN489	Traffic violations	364.147	HV6422-6425
Totems	202.11	GN491	Tragedy	808.820512	PN6111-6120
Touch	152.182	BF275	Trail riding	798.23	SF309.28
Touch	612.88	QP451	Trails	625.88	TE303
Tourist camps, hostels, etc.	910.466	TX901-941	Trails	625.88	TE304
Tourist trade	338.4791	G154.9	Training-ships	359.50973	V435-436
Tournaments	790.134	GV1191-.75	Tramps	362.5	HV4480-4630
Tournaments	929.6	CR4553	Trance	248.29	BV5090-5091
Towboats	623.8232	VM464	Tranquilizing drugs	615.7882	RM333
Towers	690.15	TH2180	Transactional analysis	616.89145	RC489.T7
Towers	721.5	NA2930	Transcendental Meditation	158.125	BF637.T68
Toxemia of pregnancy	618.7	RG575-576	Transcendentalism	141.3	B823
Toxicity testing	615.907	RA1199-.5	Transcendentalism (New England)	141.3	B905
Toxicological emergencies	615.908	RA1224.5	Transfer factor (Immunology)	615.37	RM282.T7
Toxicology	615.9	RA1190-1270			
Toxicology—Research	615.90072	RA1199-.5	Transfer of training	153.154	LB1059
Toxicology—Study and teaching	615.90071	RA1198-.3	Transfer RNA	572.886	QP623.5.T73
			Transference (Psychology)	154.2	RC489.T73
Toys	394.3	GN454-456	Transfiguration (Spiritualism)	133.9	BF1389.T7
Toys	745.592	TT174-.5			
Toys	790.1330901	GN799.T75	Transformations (Mathematics)	516.1	QA601-608
Trace elements in the body	572.515	QP534			
Tracheotomy	617.533059	RF517	Transgenic plants	631.5233	SB123.57
Track system (Education)	371.25	LB3061.8	Transients (Electricity)	621.31921	TK3226
Track-athletics	796.42	GV1060.5-1098	Transistor amplifiers	621.381535	TK7871.2-.58
Tracked landing vehicles	623.7472	UG615-620	Transition metal compounds	546.6	QD172.T6
Traction-engines	629.2252	TL233-.8			
Trade-unions	331.88	HD6350-6940.7	Transits	523.9	QB175-185
Trade-unions—[By region or country]	331.8809(4-9)	HD6500-6940.7	Transliteration	411	P226
			Transmigration	202.1	BL525
Trade-unions—United States	331.880973	HD6500-6519	Transnational crime	364.135	HV6252
			Transpersonal psychology	150.198	BF204.7
Trade-unions—History	331.8809	HD6451-6481.2	Transplantation of organs, tissues, etc.	617.954	RD120.6-129.8
Trade-unions—Organizing	331.8912	HD6490.O7			
Trade-unions—Recognition	331.8912	HD6490.R4	Transport theory	530.138	QC175.2-.25
Trade associations—Law and legislation—England	346.4206	KD2228	Transportation	388	HE
			Transportation	394.53	GT5220
Trade associations—Law and legislation—United States	346.73064	KF1661	Transportation, Military	355.83	UH500-505
			Transportation, Military	358.25	UC
			Transportation, Military	358.25	UC270-360
Trade regulation	343.08	K3842-3862	Transportation, Military	359.83	VC
Trade regulation—Canada	343.7108	KE1591-1660	Transportation, Military	359.985	VC550-580
Trade regulation—England	343.4208	KD2204-2231	Transportation—Biography	388.092	HE151.4-.5
Trade winds	551.5183	QC939.T7	Transportation—Congresses	388.06	HE11
Trademarks	602.75	T325			

Subject Heading	Dewey	LC	Subject Heading	Dewey	LC
Transportation—History	388.09	HE159-181	Trees in cities	635.977	SB436
Transportation—Law and legislation	343.093	K4021-4025	Trench mortars	358.1282	UF563.A77
			Trestles	624.2	TG365-370
Transportation—Law and legislation—Canada	343.71093	KE2071-2649	Trial practice (Canon law)	262.934	BX1939.T65
Transportation—Law and legislation—England	343.42093	KD2571-2838	Trial practice—United States	347.73075	KF8911-8925
			Trials	345.075	K5460-5492
Transportation—Law and legislation—United States	343.73093	KF2161-2654	Trials	347.07	K540-546
			Trials (Bribery)—United States	345.7302	KF221.B74
Transportation—Periodicals	388.05	HE1-8	Trials (Conspiracy)—United States	345.730207	KF221.C6
Transportation—Rates	388.042	HE1831-2220	Trials—Canada	347.7107	KE225-237
Transportation—Rates	388.049	HE195.4-.5	Trials—England	347.4207	KD370-379.5
Transportation—Statistics	388.021	HE191.4-.5	Trials—Ireland	347.41507	KDK102-106
Transportation—Study and teaching	388.071	HE191.9-192	Trials—Scotland	347.41107	KDC184-188
			Trials—United States	345.7307	KF219-224
Transportation—Theory	388.01	HE147.5-149	Trials—United States	347.7307	KF8910-8986
Transportation engineering	629.04	TA1001-1280	Trials—Wales	345.42907	KD9423
Transportation engineering—[By region or country]	629.0409(4-9)	TA1021-1127	Triangle	516.154	QA482
			Triangle music	786.8842	M175.T
Transportation engineering—United States	629.040973	TA1023-1025	Triangulation	526.33	QB311
			Triangulation	526.33	TA583
Transportation engineering—History	629.0409	TA1015	Tribes	305.8	GN492.5
			Trick photography	778.8	TR148
Transportation engineering—Periodicals	629.0405	TA1001-1004	Trick riding	798.23	SF296.T75
			Tricks	793.8	GV1541-1561
Transportation engineering—Study and teaching	629.04071	TA1163	Tricycles	796.6(2-4)	GV1040-1058
			Trigonometry	516.24	QA531-538
Transportation medicine	616.9802	RC1030-1035	Trigonometry—Tables	516.24021	QA55
Transportation noise	620.23	TD893.6.T7	Trinidad and Tobago	972.983	F2116-2123
Transports	355.83	UC320-325	Trinidad and Tobago—Census	317.2983	HA867
Transsexualism	305.3	HQ77.7-.95			
Transubstantiation	264.02036	BX2220	Trinidad and Tobago—Maps	912.72983	G5150-5162
Transvaal—Maps	912.682	G8540-8543			
Transvestites	306.778	HQ76.97-77.2	Trinidad and Tobago—Politics and government	320.972983	JL650-659
Transylvania (Romania)	949.84	DR279-280.74			
Trapping	799.2	SK283-.6	Trinity	231.044	BT109-115
Trapshooting	799.3132	GV1181-.3	Trios	785.13	M300-386
Trauma centers	362.18	RA975.5.T83	Tripitaka	294.382	BQ1100-3340
Travel	394.53	GT5220-5285	Triple Entente, 1907	940.288	D443
Travel	910	G149-180	Triple Entente, 1907	940.288	D511
Travel—Guidebooks	910.202	G153	Triplets	306.875	GN63.6
Travel—Health aspects	613.68	RA783.5	Triumphal arches	725.96	NA9360-9380
Travel etiquette	395.5	BJ2137-2156	Trolley buses	629.22233	TL232
Travel posters	741.674	NC1849.T68	Trolls	398.45	GR555
Travelers	910.92	G200-336	Trombone music	788.93	M90-94
Traveling sales personnel	381.092	HF5441-5444	Tropical crops	631.913	SB111
Treadmill exercise tests	616.12075	RC683.5.E94	Tropical medicine	616.9883	RC960-962
Treason	323.6	JC328	Tropical plants	581.748	QK936
Treason	364.131	HV6275	Tropics	910.0213	G905-910
Tree crops	634.99	SB170-171	Tropics—Climate	551.6913	QC993.5
Tree planting	634.9565	SD391	Tropics—Maps	912.193	G1053
Tree planting	635.977	SB435-437	Tropics—Maps	912.193	G3240-3241
Tree worship	202.12	BL444	Troposphere	551.513	QC881.2.T75
Trees	582.16	QK474.8-494	Troubadours	390.478	GT3650
Trees	634.9	SD391-535	Troubadours	849.104	PC3304-3330
Trees—Folklore	398.368216	GR785			

Subject Heading	Dewey	LC	Subject Heading	Dewey	LC
Trousers	687.113	TT605	Tunisia—History—1516-1881	961.103	DT261-263.76
Trout fishing	799.1755	SH687-688	Tunisia—History—Expedition of Charles V, 1535	961.103	DT262
Truck drivers	629.224092	TL230.3
Trucking	388.324	HE5601-5725
Trucking—[By region or country]	388.32409(4-9)	HE5623-5725	Tunisia—History—Conquest, 1573	961.103	DT262
Trucks	629.224	TL230-.5	Tunisia—History—French occupation, 1881-1956	961.104	DT263.9-264.3
Trumpet-calls	781.599	UH40-45
Trumpet-calls	788.92	M1270	Tunisia—History—1956-	961.105	DT264.35-.49
Trumpet music	788.92	M85-89	Tunisia—Maps	912.611	G8250-8254
Truncheons	363.20284	HV7936.E7	Tunneling	622.26	TN285
Trusses	624.1773	TA660.T8	Tunneling	623.68	UG340
Trust companies	332.26	HG4301-4480.9	Tunneling	624.19	TA800-820
Trust companies—Directories	332.26025	HG4307	Tunneling (Physics)	530.416	QC174.1
			Tupi languages	498.3829	PM7171-7179
Trust companies—History	332.2609	HG4311	Turbines	621.406	TJ266-267.5
Trust companies—[By region or country]	332.2609(4-9)	HG4341-4480.9	Turbomachines	621.406	TJ266-267.5
			Turbulence	532.59	QA913
Trust companies—United States	332.260973	HG4341-4356	Turfgrasses	635.9642	SB433-.34
			Turkey	956.1	DR
Trust companies—[Other countries]	332.2609(4-9)	HG4357-4480.9	Turkey—Census	315.61	HA4556.5
			Turkey—Civilization	939.2	DR432
Truth	121	BC171	Turkey—Civilization	956.1	DR432
Truthfulness and falsehood	177.3	BJ1420-1428.3	Turkey—Description and travel	913.9204	DR421-429.4
Tsetse-flies	614.4322	RA641.T7
Tuba music	788.98	M95-99	Turkey—Description and travel	915.6104	DR421-429.4
Tuberculin test	616.995075	RC311.2
Tuberculosis	614.542	RA644.T7	Turkey—Economic conditions	330.9561	HC491-495
Tuberculosis	616.995	RC306-320.5
Tuberculosis—Chemotherapy	616.995061	RC311.3.C45	Turkey—Gazetteers	939.2003	DR414
			Turkey—Gazetteers	956.1003	DR414
Tuberculosis—Diet therapy	616.9950654	RC311.D5	Turkey—Historiography	939.20072	DR438.8-.95
Tuberculosis—Hospitals	362.196995	RC309-.5	Turkey—Historiography	956.10072	DR438.8-.95
Tuberculosis—Vaccination	614.542	RA644.T7	Turkey—History	939.2	DR436-603
Tugboats	623.8232	VM464	Turkey—History	956.1	DR436-603
Tumors	616.994	RC254-282	Turkey—History—To 1453	939.2	DR481
Tumors	616.994	RD651-678	Turkey—History—To 1453	956.101	DR481
Tungsten ores	549.74	QE390.2.T85	Turkey—History—Ottoman Empire, 1288-1918	956.101(4-5)	DR485-486
Tungus-Manchu languages	494.1	PL450
Tunisia	939.73	DT241-269	Turkey—History—1288-1453	956.101(4-5)	DR493-502
Tunisia	961.1	DT241-269
Tunisia—Census	316.11	HA4684	Turkey—History—Bayezid I, 1389-1403	956.1015	DR496
Tunisia—Civilization	939.73	DT252
Tunisia—Civilization	961.1	DT252	Turkey—History—Invasion of Timur, 1402	956.1015	DR496
Tunisia—Description and travel	913.97304	DT248-250.2
			Turkey—History—Mehmed II, 1451-1481	956.10152	DR501-.7
Tunisia—Description and travel	916.1104	DT248-250.2
			Turkey—History—1453-1683	956.1015(2-3)	DR502-536
Tunisia—Economic conditions	330.9611	HC820
			Turkey—History—Bayezid II, 1481-1512	956.10152	DR503
Tunisia—Gazetteers	913.973003	DT244
Tunisia—Gazetteers	916.11003	DT244	Turkey—History—Suleyman I, 1520-1566	956.10152	DR505-506
Tunisia—History	939.73	DT253.4-264.49
Tunisia—History	961.1	DT253.4-264.49	Turkey—History—Wars with Persia, 1576-1639	956.10153	DR523
Tunisia—History—To 647	939.73	DT258
Tunisia—History—647-1516	961.102	DT259	Turkey—History—Mehmed III, 1595-1603	956.10153	DR525

Subject Heading	Dewey	LC
Turkey—History—Murad IV, 1623-1640	956.10153	DR529
Turkey—History—Mehmed IV, 1648-1687	956.10153	DR534-536.5
Turkey—History—1683-1829	956.1015(3-4)	DR536-562
Turkey—History—Suleyman II, 1687-1691	956.10153	DR537
Turkey—History—Mustafa II, 1695-1703	956.10153	DR541.3
Turkey—History—Rebellion, 1703	956.10153	DR542
Turkey—History—Ahmed III, 1703-1730	956.10153	DR542-545
Turkey—History—Mahmud I, 1730-1754	956.10153	DR547-548
Turkey—History—Mustafa III, 1757-1773	956.10153	DR551-553
Turkey—History—Abdul Hamid I, 1774-1789	956.10154	DR555
Turkey—History—Selim III, 1789-1807	956.10154	DR559-.5
Turkey—History—Mahmud II, 1808-1839	956.10154	DR562-564
Turkey—History—1829-1878	956.10154	DR564-573.7
Turkey—History—Tanzimat, 1839-1876	956.10154	DR565
Turkey—History—1878-1909	956.10154	DR573.7-584.5
Turkey—History—Revolution, 1909	956.10154	DR583
Turkey—History—Mehmed V, 1909-1918	956.10154	DR583-588
Turkey—History—Mehmed VI, 1918-1922	956.1023	DR589
Turkey—History—Revolution, 1918-1923	956.1023	DR589
Turkey—History—1918-1960	956.10(23-36)	DR589-590
Turkey—History—Revolution, 1960	956.1036	DR593
Turkey—History—1960-	956.10(36-4)	DR593-603
Turkey—History—Coup d'etat, 1971	956.1037	DR600
Turkey—History—Coup d'etat, 1980	956.1038	DR601
Turkey—History, Military	355.009561	DR448
Turkey—History, Naval	359.009561	DR451
Turkey—Manufactures	670.9561	TS111-112
Turkey—Maps	912.561	G2210-2214
Turkey—Maps	912.561	G7430-7434
Turkey—Politics and government	320.9561	JQ1800-1809
Turkeys	636.592	SF507
Turkic languages	494.3	PL21-29
Turkic languages, Northeast	494.37	PL41-45
Turkic languages, Northwest	494.37	PL61-65
Turkic languages, Southeast	494.357	PL51-56
Turkish drama	894.352008	PL237-238
Turkish drama	894.352009	PL221
Turkish language	494.35	PL
Turkish language	494.35	PL101-199
Turkish literature	894.35	PL201-272
Turkmen language	494.364	PL331-334
Turkmenistan	958.5	DK931-939.5
Turnover tax	336.27	HJ5711-5715
Turpentine	665.332	TP977-979.5
Turquoise	549.72	QE394.T8
Turtle fisheries	639.392	SH399.T9
Tuscany (Italy)	945.5	DG731-759.3
Tutors and tutoring	371.394	LC41
Twelfth century	909.1	CB353
Twelfth century	909.1	D201.7-.8
Twentieth century	909.82	CB425-430
Twentieth century	909.82	D410-893
Twentieth century—Forecasts	003.20904	CB160-161
Twins	306.875	GN63.6
Twins—Psychology	155.444	BF723.T9
Two-body problem	521.4	QB362.T9
Two-dimensional echocardiography	616.1207543	RC683.5.U5
Two-tier wage payment systems	331.216	HD4928.T93
Tympanic membrane—Diseases	617.85	RF210
Typewriters	652.3	Z49-50.5
Typhoid fever	614.5112	RA644.T8
Typhoid fever	616.9272	RC187-197
Typhoid fever—Vaccination	614.5112	RA644.T8
Typhoon modification	551.68	QC948
Typhoons	551.552	QC948
Typhus fever	616.9222	RC199-.9
Typology (Theology)	220.64	BS478
Typology (Theology)	232.1	BT225
Uganda—Census	316.761	HA4694
Uganda—Civilization	967.61	DT433.24
Uganda—Description and travel	916.76104	DT433.227
Uganda—Economic conditions	330.96761	HC870
Uganda—Gazetteers	916.761003	DT433.215
Uganda—History	967.61	DT433.252-.287
Uganda—History—To 1890	967.6101	DT433.265-.267
Uganda—History—1890-1962	967.610(1-3)	DT433.27-.273
Uganda—History—1971-1979	967.61042	DT433.282
Uganda—History—1979-	967.6104(2-4)	DT433.284-.286
Uganda—Maps	912.6761	G8420-8424

Subject Heading	Dewey	LC
Ugaritic language	492.67	PJ4150
Ukraine	947.7	DK508-.95
Ukrainian language	491.79	PG3801-3899
Ukrainian language—Grammar	491.795	PG3819-3881
Ukrainian language—Dictionaries	491.793	PG3888-3894.5
Ukrainian language—Lexicography	491.793028	PG3887-3894.5
Ukrainian literature	891.79	PG3900-3987
Ukulele music	787.89	M142.U5
Ultrasonic encephalography	616.8047543	RC386.6.U45
Ultrasonic testing	620.11274	TA417.4
Ultrasonic waves	534.55	QC244
Ultrasonic waves—Therapeutic use	615.83	RM862.7
Ultrasonics in medicine	616.07543	R857.U48
Ultrasonics in obstetrics	618.207543	RG527.5.U48
Ultraviolet radiation	535.014	QC459-.5
Ultraviolet spectroscopy	535.844	QC459-.5
Umbilical cord—Prolapse	618.5	RG719
Umbrellas and parasols	391.44	GT2210
Underemployment	331.13	HD5709-.2
Underground architecture	720.473	NA2542.7
Underground construction	624.19	TA712
Underground electric lines	621.31923	TK3251-3261
Underground railroad	973.7115	E450
Undertakers and undertaking	363.75	HD9999(.U5-.U54)
Undertakers and undertaking	363.75	RA622-623.6
Underwater acoustics	534.23	QC242-.5
Underwater archaeology	930.102804	CC77.U5
Underwater childbirth	618.4	RG663
Underwater construction	627.7	TC195-201
Underwater demolition teams	359.984	VG86-88
Underwater demolition teams—United States	359.9840973	VG87
Underwater drilling	627.75	TC193
Underwater exploration	551.4607	GC65-78
Underwater photography	778.73	TR800
Underwater pipelines	627.7	TC1800
Underwater welding and cutting	623.8432	VM965
Underwear	391.42	GT2073
Underwear	687.2	TT669-678
Unemployed	331.137	HD5707.5-5710.2
Unemployment	331.137	HD5707.5-5710.2
Uneven parallel bars	613.714	GV536
Unicorns	398.469	GR830.U6
Unidentified flying objects	001.942	TL789-.6
Unified operations (Military science)	366.46	U260
Uniform state laws	348.7(4-9)	KF165
Unincorporated societies—Canada	346.71064	KE1351-1361
Unincorporated societies—England	346.42064	KD2046-2054
Unincorporated societies—United States	346.73064	KF1361-1381
Unit method of teaching	371.36	LB1029.U6
Unitarian Universalist churches	289.1	BX9801-9869
Unitarian Universalist churches—Congresses	289.106	BX9805-9807
Unitarian Universalist churches—Education	268.891	BX9817-9823
Unitarian Universalist churches—Government	262.091	BX9850
Unitarian Universalist churches—History	289.109	BX9831-9835
Unitarian Universalist churches—Sermons	252.091	BX9843
Unitarianism	289.133	BX9801-9869
Unitarianism—[By region or country]	289.1(4-9)	BX9833-9835
Unitarianism—United States	289.173	BX9833
Unitarians	289.1092	BX9867-9869
United Arab Emirates—Census	315.357	HA4566
United Arab Emirates—Economic conditions	330.95357	HC415.36
United Arab Emirates—Politics and government	320.95357	JQ1844
United States	973	E151-887
United States. Air Force	358.400973	UG633-634.5
United States. Air Force—History	358.400973	UG633
United States. Air Force—Non-commissioned officers—History	358.413380973	UG823
United States. Army	355.30973	UA24-39
United States. Army—Airborne troops	940.541273	D769.346
United States. Army—Appropriations and expenditures	355.30973	UA24.A7
United States. Army—Artillery	358.120973	UA32-33
United States. Army—Artillery	358.120973	UF23
United States. Army—Artillery—Drill and tactics	358.1240973	UF160-162
United States. Army—Cavalry	357.10973	UA30-31
United States. Army—Commissariat	355.620973	UC40-44
United States. Army—Equipment	355.80973	UC523
United States. Army—Field service	355.350973	U173

Subject Heading	Dewey	LC	Subject Heading	Dewey	LC
United States. Army—Handbooks, manuals, etc.	355.5470973	U113	United States. Marine Corps—Drill and tactics	359.9650973	VE160-162
United States. Army—History	355.00973	E181	United States. Navy	359.80973	VC20-65
United States. Army—History	355.30973	UA23-25	United States. Navy—Accounting	359.6220973	VC503
United States. Army—Infantry	356.10973	UA28-29	United States. Navy—Appropriations and expenditures	359.6220973	VA53
United States. Army—Infantry	356.10973	UD23	United States. Navy—Aviation	359.940973	VG93
United States. Army—Inspection	355.6850973	UB243	United States. Navy—Barracks and quarters	359.710973	VC423
United States. Army—Maneuvers	355.40973	U253	United States. Navy—Boats	359.3220973	V880
United States. Army—Medals, badges, decorations	355.13420973	UC533	United States. Navy—Boatswains	359.3380973	VG953
United States. Army—Officers	355.3320973	UB412-414	United States. Navy—Chaplains	359.3470973	VG23
United States. Army—Ordnance and ordnance stores	355.80973	UF523-563	United States. Navy—Communication systems	359.9830973	VG73
United States. Army—Parachute troops	940.541273	D769.347	United States. Navy—Draftsmen	359.3380973	VG913
United States. Army—Pay, allowances, etc.	355.640973	UC70-75	United States. Navy—Field service	359.350973	V175
United States. Army—Physical training	355.50973	U323	United States. Navy—Fire control technicians (Missile)	359.98170973	VF347
United States. Army—Procurement	355.62120973	UC263	United States. Navy—Firearms	359.8240973	VD360-390
United States. Army—Records and correspondence	355.60973	UB163	United States. Navy—Firearms	359.8240973	VF350-420
United States. Army—Recruiting, enlistment, etc.	355.2230973	UB323	United States. Navy—History	359.30973	E182
United States. Army—Registers	355.309730216	U11	United States. Navy—Inspection	359.6850973	VB223
United States. Army—Special Forces—History	356.160973	UA34.S64	United States. Navy—Intelligence specialists	359.34320973	VG1020
United States. Army—Transportation	358.250973	UC273	United States. Navy—Machinist's mates	359.3380973	VG803
United States. Coast Guard	359.9709073	V437	United States. Navy—Maneuvers	359.410973	V245
United States. Coast Guard	359.970973	VG53	United States. Navy—Officers	359.3320973	VB313-314
United States. Congress	328.73	JK1012-1432	United States. Navy—Officers' handbooks	359.3320973	V133
United States. Congress. House	328.320973	JK1308-1432	United States. Navy—Ordnance and ordnance stores	359.80973	VF353-420
United States. Congress. Senate	328.310973	JK1154-1259	United States. Navy—Organization	359.30973	VA49-395
United States. Congress—Directories	328.73025	JK1012	United States. Navy—Pay, allowances, etc.	359.80973	VC50-65
United States. Congress—History	342.730509	JK1033-1059	United States. Navy—Personnel management	359.610973	VB258
United States. Continental Army—History	973.34(4-5)	E259	United States. Navy—Petty officers' handbooks	359.3320973	V123
United States. Dept. of Defense	355.60973	UA23.2-.6	United States. Navy—Physical training	359.50973	V263
United States. Marine Corps	359.9630973	VE23-25			

Subject Heading	Dewey	LC	Subject Heading	Dewey	LC
United States. Navy—Postal service	359.340973	VG63	United States—Capital and capitol	725.110973	NA4411-4413
United States. Navy—Procurement	359.62120973	VC260-267	United States—Census	317.3	HA201-730
United States. Navy—Recruiting, enlistment, etc.	359.22360973	VB263	United States—Civilization	973	E162-168
			United States—Civilization	973	E169.1-.12
United States. Navy—Safety measures	359.00289	V383	United States—Climate	551.6973	QC983-984
United States. Navy—Sailors' handbooks	359.3380973	V143-144	United States—Commerce	381.0973	HF3000-3163
			United States—Defenses	355.450973	UA23
United States. Navy—Sailors' handbooks	359.3380973	VD150-155	United States—Description and travel	917.304	E161.5-169.04
United States. Navy—Small-boat service	359.310973	VD403	United States—Directories	973.025	E154.5-.7
United States. Navy—Songs and music	782.421599	VG33	United States—Economic conditions	330.973	HC101-110
United States. Navy—Submarine forces	359.9330973	V858	United States—Emigration and immigration	325.(273) or (73)	JV6403-7127
United States. Navy—Supplies and stores	359.80973	VC263	United States—Ethnic relations	305.8073	E184.A1
United States. Navy—Transportation	359.9850973	VC553	United States—Gazetteers	917.3003	E154
United States. Navy—Weapons systems	359.820973	VF347	United States—Genealogy	929.1072073	CS42-71
United States. Navy—Yeomen	359.3380973	VG903	United States—Historical geography— Maps	911.73	G3701
United States—Antiquities	973.1	E75-99	United States—Historiography	973.072	E175-.7
United States—Antiquities	973.1	E159.5	United States—History	973	E171-183.9
United States—Appropriations and expenditure	352.530973	HJ2050-2053	United States—History—Colonial period, ca. 1600-1775	973.(1-2)	E186-199
United States—Armed Forces—Afro-Americans	355.008996073	E185.63	United States—History—King William's War, 1689-1697	973.25	E196
United States—Armed Forces—Airborne troops	356.1660973	UD483	United States—History—Queen Anne's War, 1702-1713	973.25	E197
United States—Armed Forces—Headquarters	355.306073	UB233	United States—History—King George's War, 1744-1748	973.26	E198
United States—Armed Forces—Management	355.60973	UB23-25	United States—History—French and Indian War, 1755-1763	973.26	E199
United States—Armed Forces—Messes	355.3410973	UC723	United States—History—Revolution, 1775-1783	973.3	E201-298
United States—Armed Forces—Officers' clubs	355.3460973	U56-59	United States—History—Revolution—1775-1783—Campaigns	973.33	E230-241
United States—Armed Forces—Parachute troops	356.1660973	UD483	United States—History—1783-1865	973.3	E301-655
United States—Armed Forces—Procurement	355.62120973	UC260-267	United States—History—Confederation, 1783-1789	973.318	E303-309
United States—Armed Forces—Reserves	355.370973	UA42-560	United States—History—Constitutional period, 1789-1809	973.4	E310-337
United States—Armed Forces—Reserves, [United States, By state]	355.37097(4-9)	UA50-549	United States—History—1801-1809	973.4(6-8)	E331-337
United States—Armed Forces—Warrant officers	355.3320973	UB408-.5	United States—History—Tripolitan War, 1801-1805	973.47	E335
United States—Armed Forces—Warrant officers	359.3320973	VB308	United States—History—1815-1861	973.(51-68)	E338
United States—Armed Forces—Women's reserves	355.3480973	UA45	United States—History—1809-1817	973.5(1-4)	E341-370
United States—Biography	920.073	E176			

Subject Heading	Dewey	LC	Subject Heading	Dewey	LC
United States—History—War of 1812	973.52	E351-364.9	United States—Politics and government	320.973	JK
United States—History—War with Algeria, 1815	973.53	E365	United States—Politics and government—To 1775	320.9730903	JK54-103
United States—History—1817-1825	973.54	E371-375	United States—Politics and government—1861-1865	320.97309034	JK320
United States—History—1825-1829	973.55	E376-380	United States—Politics and government—1865-1877	320.97309034	JK321
United States—History—1849-1877	973.(63-82)	E415.6-680	United States—Race relations	305.8073	E184-185.98
United States—History—1849-1877	973.(63-82)	E671-680	United States—Religion	277.3	BR513-569
United States—History—Civil War, 1861-1865	973.7	E461-656	United States—Seal	737.60973	CD5610
			United States—Social conditions	973	HN51-90
United States—History—Civil War, 1861-1865—Cartography	973.70223	E468.9	United States—Statistics	317.3	HA201-214
			United States—Statistics, Vital	317.3	HA201-214
United States—History—1865-1898	973.8(1-8)	E660-735	United States—Territorial expansion	973	E179.5
United States—History—1865-1921	973.(8-913)	E660-783	United States—Territories and possessions	320.120973	JK2556
United States—History—1865-	973.(8-9)	E660-887	United States—Territories and possessions	325.373	JV500-599
United States—History—20th century	973.91	E740-887	United States—Territories and possessions—Maps	912.73	G3690-3691
United States—History—1901-1909	973.911	E740-760	Universalism	289.134	BX9901-9969
United States—History—1909-1913	973.912	E761-765	Universalism—Congresses	289.13406	BX9905-9907
			Universalism—Education	268.89134	BX9917-9923
United States—History—1913-1921	973.913	E766-783	Universalism—History	289.13409	BX9931-9935
United States—History—1919-1933	973.91(3-6)	E784-805	Universalism—Sermons	252.09134	BX9943
			Universalists	289.134092	BX9967-9969
United States—History—1933-1945	973.917	E806-812	Universities and colleges	378	LB2300-2411
United States—History—1945-1953	973.918	E813-816	Universities and colleges—Accreditation	353.88284	LB2331.6-.615
United States—History—1953-1961	973.921	E835-837.7	Universities and colleges—Admission	378.161	LB2351-2359
United States—History—1961-1969	973.92(2-3)	E838-851	Universities and colleges—Curricula	378.199	LB2361-2365
United States—History, Military	355.00973	E181	Universities and colleges—Entrance requirements	378.1617	LB2351-2360
United States—History, Naval	359.00973	E182	Universities and colleges—Examinations	378.1662	LB2353
United States—Manufactures	670.973	TS23-25	Universities and colleges—Examinations	378.1662	LB2367
United States—Manufactures— Law and legislation	343.73078	KF1875-1893	Universities and colleges—Faculty	378.12	LB2331.7-.74
United States—Maps	912.73	G1200-1534.24	Universities and colleges—Finance	378.106	LB2342
United States—Maps	912.73	G3690-4383	Universities and colleges—Graduate work	378.155	LB2371
United States—Militia	355.370973	UA42-560	Universities and colleges—Africa	378.6	LG401-690
United States—National Guard	355.370973	UA42-560	Universities and colleges—Asia	378.5	LG21-320
United States—Officials and employees—Salaries, etc.	352.630973	JK771-794	Universities and colleges—Australia	378.94	LG715-720
United States—Periodicals	973.05	E151	Universities and colleges—Canada	378.7	LE3-5

Subject Heading	Dewey	LC	Subject Heading	Dewey	LC
Universities and colleges—Caribbean Area	378.729	LE15-17	Urdu literature	891.439	PK2030-2058
Universities and colleges—Central America	378.728	LE11-13	Uremia	616.635	RC915
Universities and colleges—Europe	378	LF	Urethra—Diseases	616.62	RC892
Universities and colleges—Mexico	378.72	LE7-9	Urinary organs	573.49	QL872-881
Universities and colleges—Middle East	378.56	LG331-370	Urinary organs	611.61	QM401-413
			Urinary organs	612.46	QP247-250.8
Universities and colleges—New Zealand	378.93	LG741-745	Urinary organs—Calculi	616.622	RC916
Universities and colleges—Oceania	378.9(5-6)	LG961	Urinary organs—Diseases	616.6	RC900-923
			Urinary organs—Examination	616.6075	RC901
Universities and colleges—South America	378.8	LE21-78	Urinary tract infections	616.6	RC901.8
Universities and colleges—United States	378.73	LD13-7251	Urination disorders	616.6	RC901.75
University cooperation	378.104	LB2331.5	Urology	616.6	RC870-923
University extension	378.175	LC6201-6401	Uruguay	989.5	F2701-2799
Unmarried fathers	362.8294	HV700.7	Uruguayan literature	860	PQ8510-8519
Unmarried mothers	362.8394	HV700.5	Uruguay—Census	318.95	HA1071-1090
Unsteady flow (Aerodynamics)	629.13232	TL574.U5	Uruguay—Civilization	989.5	F2710
			Uruguay—Description and travel	918.9504	F2711-2715
Unsteady flow (Fluid dynamics)	620.1064	TA357.5.U57	Uruguay—Economic conditions	330.9895	HC231-235
Upland game bird shooting	799.246	SK323-325	Uruguay—Emigration and immigration	325.(2895) or (895)	JV7520-7529
Upland game bird shooting—[By region or country]	799.24609(4-9)	SK324	Uruguay—Gazetteers	918.95003	F2704
			Uruguay—History	989.5	F2720-2729.52
Uranium	546.431	QD181.U7	Uruguay—History—To 1810	989.50(1-3)	F2723
Uranium	661.0431	TP245.U7	Uruguay—History—1810-1830	989.504	F2725
Uranus (Planet)	523.47	QB387	htUruguay—History—1830-1875	989.505	F2726
Uranus (Planet)	523.47	QB681	Uruguay—History—Great War, 1843-1852	989.505	F2726
Urban agriculture	630.91732	S494.5.U72	Uruguay—History—1875-1904	989.50(5-61)	F2726
Urban anthropology	307.76	GN395	Uruguay—History—Revolution, 1886	989.5061	F2726
Urban climatology	551.691732	QC981.7.U7	Uruguay—History—Revolution, 1897	989.5061	F2726
Urban ecology	577.56	HT241-243			
Urban ecology (Biology)	577.56	QH541.5.C6	Uruguay—History—1904-1973	989.506(1-5)	F2728
Urban economics	330.91732	HT321-325	Uruguay—History—Revolution, 1935	989.5063	F2728
Urban geography	910.021732	GF125	Uruguay—History—1973-1985	989.5066	F2729
Urban health	613.091732	RA566.7	Uruguay—History—Coup d'etat, 1973	989.5066	F2729
Urban homesteading	363.5091732	HD7289.4-.42	Uruguay—History—1985-	989.5067	F2729
Urban poor	362.5091732	HV4023-4470.7	Uruguay—Manufactures	670.9895	TS53
Urban renewal	307.3416	HT170-178	Uruguay—Maps	912.895	G5370-5374
Urban renewal—United States	307.34160973	HT175-177	Uruguay—Periodicals	989.5005	F2701
Urban renewal—[Other countries]	307.341609(4-9)	HT178	Uruguay—Politics and government	320.9895	JL3600-3699
Urban runoff	628.21	TD657-.5	User interfaces (Computer systems)	005.437	QA76.9.U83
Urban schools	370.91732	LC5101-5143			
Urban transportation	388.4	HE305-311	Usury	332.83	HB551
Urban transportation	388.4	TA1205-1207	Utah	979.2	F821-835
Urban universities and colleges	378.052	LB2328.4	Utah—Gazetteers	917.92003	F824
Urban-rural migration	307.26	HB1956-2157			
Urban-rural migration	307.26	HT381			
Urdu language	491.439	PK1975-1987			

Subject Heading	Dewey	LC
Utah—History—Civil War, 1861-1865	979.202	E532.95
Utah—Maps	912.792	G4340-4344
Utah—National Guard	355.3709792	UA480-489
Utah—Periodicals	979.2005	F821
Ute Indians	978.8004974576	E99.U8
Ute language	497.4576	PM2515
Uterine hemorrhage	618.54	RG580.H5
Uterine hemorrhage	618.54	RG711
Uterine hemorrhage	618.54	RG821
Uterus	573.667	QL881
Uterus	611.66	QM421
Uterus, Pregnant	618.2	RG519-520
Uterus—Diseases	618.14	RG301-391
Uterus—Diseases—Diagnosis	618.1075	RG304-.5
Uterus—Rupture	618.14	RG361
Utilitarianism	144.6	B843
Utilities (Computer programs)	005.43	QA76.6.U84
Utopian socialism—[By region or country]	335.1209(4-9)	HX651-780.7
Utopian socialism—History	335.1209	HX626-632
Utopias	321.07	HX
Utopias	321.07	HX806-811
Uvea—Diseases	617.72	RE350-355
Uzbekistan	958.7	DK941-949.5
V symbol	203.7	BL604.V2
Vacation homes	690.872	TH4835
Vacation homes	728.7	NA7574-7579
Vacation schools, Religious	268	BV1585
Vacations, Employee	331.2576	HD5260-5267
Vaccination	614.47	RA638
Vaccination	615.372	RM281
Vaccines	615.372	QR189-.5
Vacuum	533.5	QC166-.5
Vacuum-gages	533.50284	QC166
Vacuum-tubes	621.381512	TK7872.V3
Vacuum-tubes	621.384132	TK6565.V3
Vacuum pumps	621.55	TJ940.5
Vacuum technology	621.55	TJ940-.5
Vagina—Diseases	618.15	RG268-272
Vagrancy	364.148	HV4480-4630.7
Valentine decorations	745.59416	TT900.V34
Valleys	551.442	GB561-568
Valuation	332.63221	HG4028.V3
Valuation	657.73	HF5681.V3
Value	332.41	HG223
Value	338.521	HB201-206
Value-added tax	336.2714	HJ5711-5715
Values	121.8	BD232
Values	121.8	BD430-435
Values	153.45	BF778
Vampires	133.423	BF1556
Vampires	398.45	GR830.V3
Van Allen radiation belts	538.766	QC809.V3
Vandal language	439.9	PD1270

Subject Heading	Dewey	LC
Vandalism	364.164	HV6666-6669
Vandals	304.808939	D139
Vans	629.2234	TL230
Vanuatu	995.95	DU760
Vanuatu—Census	319.595	HA4015.5
Vanuatu—Maps	912.9595	G9295-9297
Variable stars	523.844	QB833-841
Variation (Biology)	576.54	QH401-411
Variation (Music)	781.825	ML3845
Varicose veins	616.143	RC695-697
Vasculitis	616.131	RC694.5.I53
Vasectomy	617.463	RD585.5
Vasoactive intestinal peptides	572.65	QP572.V28
Vasomotor system	612.18	QP109
Vaudeville	792.7	PN1960-1969
Vaulting	796.434	GV1079-1080
Vaulting (Horsemanship)	798.25	SF296.V37
Vector analysis	515.63	QA433
Vector control	614.43	RA639.3
Vedas	294.5921	BL1112.2
Vedic language	491.29	PK201-379
Vedic language—Dictionaries	491.293	PK375-379
Vedic language—Etymology	491.292	PK361-369
Vedic language—Grammar	491.295	PK231-313
Vedic literature	891.29	PK2911
Vegetable gardening	635	SB320-353.5
Vegetable juices	641.35	TX391
Vegetable oils	665.3	TP680-684
Vegetable trade	381.415	HD9220-9235
Vegetables	635	SB320-353.5
Vegetables—Drying	664.805	TP443-444
Vegetarian cookery	641.5636	TX837-838
Vegetarianism	613.262	RM236
Vegetarianism	613.262	TX392-.8
Vegetarianism	641.5636	TX837-838
Vegetation mapping	580.223	QK63
Vegetation surveys	580.723	QK62
Veils	391.43	GT2112
Veins	573.186	QL835
Veins	611.14	QM191
Veins (Geology)	551.88	QE611-.5
Veins—Diseases	616.14	RC695-697
Veins—Puncture	617.414059	RM182-190
Vellum printed books	096.2	Z1030
Velvet	677.617	TS1675
Venda language	496.397	PL8771
Vendetta	364.256	HV6441-6453
Vending machines	629.82	TJ1560
Veneers and veneering	674.83	TS870
Veneration of saints and Christian union	280.042	BX9.5.V45
Venezuela	987	F2301-2349
Venezuela—Census	318.7	HA1091-1100
Venezuela—Civilization	987	F2310

Subject Heading	Dewey	LC
Venezuela—Description and travel	918.704	F2311-2315
Venezuela—Economic conditions	330.987	HC236-239.5
Venezuela—Emigration and immigration	325.(287) or (87)	JV7530-7539
Venezuela—Gazetteers	918.7003	F2304
Venezuela—History	987	F2319.5-2328.52
Venezuela—History—To 1556	987.0(1-3)	F2322
Venezuela—History—To 1810	987.0(1-3)	F2322
Venezuela—History—1556-1810	987.03	F2322
Venezuela—History—Insurrection of the Comuneros, 1781	987.03	F2322
Venezuela—History—Miranda's Expedition, 1806	987.03	F2322
Venezuela—History—1810-	987.0(4-6)	F2322.8
Venezuela—History—1810-1830	987.0(4-5)	F2324
Venezuela—History—War of Independence, 1810-1823	987.0(4-5)	F2324
Venezuela—History—1830-1935	987.061	F2325
Venezuela—History—Federal Wars, 1858-1863	987.062	F2325
Venezuela—History—Anglo German Blockade, 1902	987.0631	F2325
Venezuela—History—Revolution, 1902-1903	987.0631	F2325
Venezuela—History—1908-1935	987.06313	F2325
Venezuela—History—1935-1958	987.063(14-2)	F2326
Venezuela—History—1935-1974	987.063(1-3)	F2326-2327
Venezuela—History—Revolution, 1945	987.0632	F2326
Venezuela—History—Coup d'etat, 1948	987.0632	F2326
Venezuela—History—Revolution, 1958	987.0633	F2326
Venezuela—History—1974-	987.063(3-4)	F2328-.52
Venezuela—History—Attempted coup, 1992 (February 4)	987.064	F2328
Venezuela—History—Attempted coup, 1992 (November 27)	987.064	F2328
Venezuela—Manufactures	670.987	TS54
Venezuela—Maps	912.87	G5280-5284
Venezuela—Periodicals	987.005	F2301
Venezuela—Politics and government	320.987	JL3800-3899
Venezuelan literature	860	PQ8530-8550.36
Venice (Italy)	945.31	DG670-684.72
Ventilation	697.92	TH7647-7699
Ventricular fibrillation	616.128	RC685.V43
Ventriloquism	793.89	GV1557
Venus (Planet)	523.42	QB372
Venus (Planet)	523.42	QB621
Venus (Planet), Transit of	523.423	QB509-513
Venus (Planet)—Orbit	523.423	QB372
Venus (Planet)—Surface	523.42	QB621
Veps language	494.54	PH541-549
Verdun, Battle of, 1914	940.421	D545.V25
Verdun, Battle of, 1916	940.4272	D545.V3
Verdun, Battle of, 1940	940.54214	D756.5.V3
Vermont—Gazetteers	917.43003	F47
Vermont—History	974.3	F46-60
Vermont—History—To 1791	974.303	F52
Vermont—History—Revolution, 1775-1783	974.30(2-3)	E263.V5
Vermont—History—War of 1812	974.303	E359.5.V3
Vermont—History—Civil War, 1861-1865	974.303	E533
Vermont—Maps	912.743	G3750-3754
Vermont—National Guard	355.3709743	UA490-499
Vermont—Periodicals	974.3005	F46
Versification	808.1	P311
Versification	808.1	PN1031-1035
Vertebrae	611.711	QM111
Vertebrates	596	QL605-739.8
Vertebrates, Fossil	566	QE841-899
Vertically rising aircraft	629.13335	TL685
Vestals	292.61	BL815.V4
Vestibular apparatus	612.858	QP471
Veterans, Disabled	362.408697	UB360-366
Veterans—Education	371.82697	UB356-359
Veterans—Employment	331.52	UB356-359
Veterans—Medical care	362.108697	UB368-369.5
Veterinarians	636.089092	SF612-613
Veterinarians—Directories	636.089025	SF611
Veterinarians—Professional ethics	174.2	SF756.39
Veterinary acupuncture	636.0895892	SF914.5
Veterinary anatomy	636.0891	SF761-767
Veterinary anesthesia	636.089796	SF914
Veterinary autopsy	636.08960759	SF769
Veterinary bacteriology	636.0896014	SF780.3
Veterinary cardiology	636.089612	SF811
Veterinary colleges	636.0890711	SF756.3-.37
Veterinary critical care	636.0896028	SF778
Veterinary disinfection	636.089448	SF757.15
Veterinary emergencies	636.0896025	SF778
Veterinary epidemiology	636.08944	SF780.9

Subject Heading	Dewey	LC	Subject Heading	Dewey	LC
Veterinary genetics	636.0821	SF756.5	Video tapes in education	371.33523	LB1044.75
Veterinary hospitals	636.089	SF604.4-.7	Videocassette recorders	621.38833	TK6655.V5
Veterinary hygiene—Law and legislation	344.049	K3615-3617	Videodisc players	384.558	TK6685
			Vienna (Austria)	943.613	DB841-860
Veterinary hygiene—Law and legislation—England	344.42049	KD3420-3422	Vietnam	959.7	DS556-559.916
			Vietnam—Census	315.97	HA4600.5
Veterinary hygiene—Law and legislation—United States	344.73049	KF3835-3838	Vietnam—Civilization	959.7	DS556.42
			Vietnam—Description and travel	915.9704	DS556.34-.39
Veterinary medicine	636.089	SF600-1100	Vietnam—Economic conditions	330.9597	HC444
Veterinary medicine—Congresses	636.08906	SF605	Vietnamese Conflict, 1961-1975	959.7043	DS557-559.8
Veterinary medicine—Diagnosis	636.0896075	SF771-774	Vietnamese Conflict, 1961-1975—Regimental histories—United States	959.7043	DS558.4
Veterinary medicine—History	636.08909	SF615-724			
Veterinary medicine—Societies, etc.	636.08906	SF600-604	Vietnamese Conflict, 1961-1975—Prisoners and prisons	959.70437	DS559.4
Veterinary medicine—Terminology	636.089014	SFS610			
Veterinary nursing	636.089073	SF774.5	Vietnamese language	495.922	PL4371-4379
Veterinary obstetrics	636.08982	SF887	Vietnamese literature	895.922	PL4378
Veterinary oncology	636.0896992	SF910.T8	Vietnamese literature (French)	840	PQ3960-3979
Veterinary orthopedics	636.08967	SF910.5			
Veterinary physiology	636.0892	SF768-.2	Vietnamese reunification question (1954-1976)	959.704(2-44)	DS556.9-.93
Veterinary prescriptions	636.08951	SF916.5			
Veterinary public health	636.0894	SF740	Vietnam—Gazetteers	915.97003	DS556.25
Veterinary service, Military	355.345	UH650-655	Vietnam—History—To 939	959.703	DS556.6-.63
Veterinary surgery	636.0897	SF911-914.4	Vietnam—History—Later Le dynasty, 1428-1787	959.703	DS556.7-.73
Veterinary vaccines	636.0895372	SF918.V32			
Veterinary virology	636.08960194	SF780.4	Vietnam—History—19th century	959.70(3-4)	DS556.8-.83
Vibraphone music	786.843	M175.X6			
Vibration	531.32	QA935-939	Vietnam—History—August Revolution, 1945	959.703	DS556.815
Vibration	534.5	QC235-241			
Vibration (Aeronautics)	629.132362	TL574.V5	Vietnam—Maps	912.597	G2370-2374
Vicars apostolic	262.142	BX1910	Vietnam—Maps	912.597	G8020-8024
Vicars-general	262.142	BX1910	Vietnam—Politics and government	320.9597	JQ800-899
Vice	179.8	BJ1534-1535			
Vice	241.3	BV4630-4647	Viking ships	359.3220948	V46
Vice (Buddhism)	294.35	BQ4425-4430	Vikings	948.5014	DL65
Vice-Presidents—United States	352.2390973	JK609.5	Viol music	787.6	M59
			Viola music	787.3	M45-49
Vice control	364	HV8067	Violence	303.6	HM281-283
Viceroyalty	353.15092	JV431	Violence	616.8582	RC569.5.V55
Vices	179.8	BJ1534-1535	Violence in mass media	303.6	P96.V5
Vices	241.3	BV4625-4627	Violence in psychiatric hospitals	362.21	RC439.4
Victims of crimes	362.88	HV6250-.4			
Victims of crimes—United States	344.7303288	KF9763	Violetta d'amore music	787.66	M59.V
			Violin	787.209	ML800-897
Victims of crimes surveys	362.880723	HV6250	Violin music	787.2	M40-44
Victims of terrorism—United States—Biography	364.154092273	HV6432	Violoncello music	787.4	M50-54
			Viral carcinogenesis	616.994071	RC268.57
Video games	794.8	GV1469.3	Viral pollution of water	628.168	TD427.V55
Video recordings	791.45	PN1992.95	Virgin birth	232.921	BT317
Video recordings for the hearing impaired	362.4283	HV2503	Virgin Islands of the United States	972.9722	F2136
Video tapes	371.33523	LB1044.75			

272

Subject Heading	Dewey	LC
Virgin Islands of the United States—Census	317.29722	HA911-915
Virgin Islands of the United States—History—1775-1783	972.9722	E263.W5
Virgin Islands of the United States—History—1775-1793	972.9722	E263.W5
Virgin Islands of the United States—Maps	912.729722	G5010-5014
Virginia—Gazetteers	917.55003	F224
Virginia—History	975.5	F221-235
Virginia—History—Colonial period, ca. 1600-1775	975.50(1-2)	F229
Virginia—History—1775-1865	975.50(2-3)	F230
Virginia—History—Revolution, 1775-1783	975.50(2-3)	E263.V8
Virginia—History—War of 1812	975.503	E359.5.V8
Virginia—History—Civil War, 1861-1865	975.503	E534
Virginia—History—Civil War, 1861-1865	975.503	E581
Virginia—Maps	912.755	G3880-3884
Virginia—National Guard	355.3709755	UA500-509
Virginia—Periodicals	975.5005	F221
Virginity	241.66	BV4647.C5
Virgo (Astrology)	133.5267	BF1727.4
Virtue	179.9	BJ1518-1691
Virtue	241.4	BV4630-4647
Virtues	241.4	BV1518-1533
Virtues	241.4	BV4625-4627
Virtues (Buddhism)	294.35	BQ4401-4430
Virus diseases	614.57	RA644.V55
Virus diseases	616.91	RC114-.7
Virus diseases in children	618.92925	RJ401-406
Viruses	579.2	QR355-502
Viscosity	531.1134	QC189-.2
Vision	612.84	QP474-495
Vision, Monocular	617.712	RE95
Vision disorders	617.75	RE91-95
Visions	232.917	BT650-660
Visions	248.29	BV5091.V6
Visiting nurses	610.7343	RT98
dctlparVisiting teachers	371.46	LB3013.5
Visual aids	371.335	LB1043.5-1044
Visual learning	153.152	LB1067.5
Visual perception	152.14	BF241
Visually handicapped—Means of communication	362.418	HV1631.5
Vital statistics	310	HA154-4737
Vitamin therapy	615.328	RM259
Vitamins	613.286	TX553.V5
Vitreous body—Diseases	617.746	RE501
Vocabulary	401.4	P305-.18

Subject Heading	Dewey	LC
Vocal cords—Diseases	616.22	RF526
Vocal ensembles	782.0438	M1528-1529.5
Vocal music	782	M1495-5000
Vocal music—History and criticism	782.009	ML1400-3275
Vocational education	370.113	LC1041-1047
Vocational guidance	331.702	HF5381-5382.5
Voice	591.594	QL765
Voice	612.78	QP306
Voice disorders	616.855	RF510-540
Volcanic ash, tuff, etc.	552.23	QE461-462
Volcanic gases	551.23	QE545
Volcanoes	551.21	QE521.5-527.5
Volleyball	796.325	GV1015-.57
Voltameter	621.3743	QC615
Voltameter	621.3744	TK331
Voltmeter	621.3743	TK321
Volumetric analysis	543.24	QD111
Voluntarism	302.14	HN49.V64
Volunteer workers in long-term care facilities	362.16092	RA997-998
Voodooism	299.675	BL2490
Vortex-motion	532.59	QA925
Vortex-motion	532.595	QC159
Votic language	494.54	PH561-569
Voting	324.62	JF825-1141
Voting, Compulsory	324.62	JF1031
Voting-machines	324.65	JF1128
Voting age	324.62	JF841
Voyages and travels	910	G149-922
Voyages around the world	910.41	G420-445
Voyeurism	616.8583	RC560.V68
Vulcanization	678.24	TS1891
Vulva—Diseases	618.16	RG261-266
Wages	331.21	HD4909-5100.7
Wages—Tables	658.32021	HF5705-5707
Wages—Canada	331.2971	HD4977-4980
Wages—Central America	331.29728	HD4983-4989
Wages—Developing countries	331.291724	HD4967
Wages—Europe	331.294	HD5014-5061.84
Wages—Mexico	331.2972	HD4981
Wages—South America	331.298	HD4996-5013
Wages—United States	331.2973	HD4973-4976
Wages—West Indies	331.29729	HD4990-4995.9
Wagons	388.341	HD9709.5
Wake Island, Battle of, 1941	940.542665	D767.99.W3
Wake services	264.02085	BX2045.W34
Wakes (Fluid dynamics)	532.593	QA913
Waldenses	284.4	BX4872-4883
Wales	942.9	DA700-745
Wales—Biography	920.0429	DA710
Wales—Census	314.29	HA1161-1170
Wales—Civilization	942.9	DA711.5
Wales—Description and travel	914.2904	DA725-731.2

Wales—History	942.9	DA714-722.1
Wales—Maps	912.429	G5760-5764
Wales—Periodicals	942.9005	DA700
Wales—Politics and government	320.9429	JN1150-1159
Walking (Sports)	796.51	GV1071
Wall hangings	746.3	NK2910
Wall hangings	746.3	TT850.2
Wall Street	332.64273	HG4571-4575.3
Wallis and Futuna Islands	996.16	DU920
Wallis and Futuna Islands—Maps	912.9616	G9515-9517
Wallpaper	676.2848	TH8461-8463
Wallpaper	747.3	NK3375-3496.3
Walls	690.12	TH2201-2251.5
Walls	721.2	NA2940-2942
Waltz	793.33	GV1761
Wampum	332.4089973	E98.M7
War	355.02	U
War	359	V
War, Cost of	355.622	UA17
War—Casualties (Statistics, etc.)	355.345021	UH215-325
War—Relief of sick and wounded	355.345	UH
War—Relief of sick and wounded	355.345	UH201-551
War and civilization	909	CB481
War and crime	364.2	HV6189
War and emergency legislation—United States	343.7301	KF5900-6075.5
War correspondents	070.4333092	PN4823
War crimes	364.13809041	D625-626
War games	355.48	U310
War games, Naval	359.48	V250
War horses	357.2	UE460-475
War memorials	725.94	NA9325-9330
War neuroses	616.8521	RC550
War on Terrorism, 2001-	363.320973	HV6432.7
War relief	363.34988	HV639
War wounds	617.044	RD156
Warehouses	381	HF5484-5495
Warehouses	725.35	NA6340-6343
Warehouses—Design and construction	690.535	TH4451-4499
Wars of Liberation, 1813-1814	940.27	DC236-238.5
Warsaw (Poland)	943.84	DK4610-4645
Warsaw, Battle of, 1945	940.5421384	D765.2.W3
Warships	359.32	V750-995
Warships—Camouflage	359.41	V215
Warships—Turrets	359.32	VF440
Warts	616.544	RL471
Wharves	627.31	TC357
Washington (D.C.)	975.3	F191-205
Washington (D.C.)—Gazetteers	917.53003	F192

Washington (D.C.)—History—Capture by the British, 1814	975.302	E356.W3
Washington (D.C.)—Maps	912.753	G3850-3854
Washington (D.C.)—National Guard	355.3709753	UA120-129
Washington (D.C.)—Periodicals	975.3005	F191
Washington (State)	979.7	F886-900
Washington (State)—Gazetteers	917.97003	F889
Washington (State)—History—To 1889	979.70(1-3)	F891
Washington (State)—History—1889-	979.704	F891
Washington (State)—Maps	912.797	G4280-4284
Washington (State)—National Guard	355.3709797	UA510-519
Washington (State)—Periodicals	979.7005	F886
Washington's Birthday	394.26973	E312.6
Waste lands	333.73137	HD1665-1671
Waste products	658.567	TP995-996
Watchdogs	636.70886	SF428.8
Watchmen	363.289	HV8290-8291
Water	546.22	QD169.W3
Water	551.48	GB651-2998
Water	551.57	QC920
Water—Aeration	628.165	TD458
Water—Analysis	546.22	QD142
Water—Distribution	628.144	TD481-493
Water—Law and legislation—England	346.4204691	KD1070
Water—Pollution	628.168	TD419-428
Water—Purification	628.162	TD429.5-477
Water-electrolyte imbalances	616.3992	RC630
Water-pipes	628.15	TD491
Water-power	621.20422	TC147
Water-power	621.21	TJ840-890
Water-supply	551.48	GB651-2998
Water-supply	628.1	TD201-500
Water-supply, Rural	628.72	TD927
Water-supply—[By region or country]	628.109(4-9)	TD221-327
Water-supply—History	628.109	TD215-220
Water-supply—Law and legislation	343.0924	K3496-3501
Water-wheels	621.21	TJ860-880
Water chemistry	546.22	GB855
Water conservation	628.13	TD388-.5
Water conservation projects	628.13	TD388-.5
Water gardens	635.9674	SB423
Water hammer	620.1064	TC174
Water heaters, Gas	696.6	TH6561
Water in landscape architecture	714	SB475.8

Subject Heading	Dewey	LC	Subject Heading	Dewey	LC
Water in the body	572.539	QP535.H1	Weapons—Law and legislation—United States	344.730533	KF3941-3942
Water jets	532.52	TC173	Weather	551.6	QC980-999
Water mills	621.21	TJ859	Weather—Periodicals	551.605	QC980
Water quality	628.16	TD370-375	Weather—Physiological effect	571.49	QP82.2.C5
Water quality management	628.16	TD365-.5	Weather—Psychological aspects	155.915	BF353.5.W4
Water resources development	333.91	HD1690-1702	Weather broadcasting	551.632	QC877.5
Water resources development	627	TC401-558	Weather control	551.68	QC926.6-928.74
Water resources development—Law and legislation—United States	346.7304691	KF5551-5590	Weather control—Law and legislation—United States	344.730655168	KF5594
Water reuse	628.162	TD429	Weather forecasting	551.63	QC994.95-999
Water skiing	797.35	GV840.S5	Weather radar networks	551.6353	QC973.8.W
Water towers	628.13	TD489	Weather reporting, Radio	551.632	QC877.5
Water towers	628.9252	TH9332-9334	Weather, Influence of the moon on	551.5	QC883-.2
Water treatment plants	628.162	TD434	Weathering	551.302	QE570
Water waves	532.59	TC172	Weavers	677.028242092	GN432
Watercolor painting	751.422	ND1700-2495	Weavers	677.028242092	HD8039.T4
Watercolor painting—Study and teaching	751.422071	ND2110-2115	Weaving	677.028242	TS1490-1500
Waterfalls	551.484	GB1401-1597	Weaving	677.028242	GN432
Waterfowl	799.244	SK331-335	Wedding anniversaries	394.2	GT2800
Watergate Affair, 1972-1974	973.924	E860	Wedding cakes	392.5	GT2797
			Wedding decorations	745.926	SB449.5.W4
Watergate Trial, Washington, D.C., 1973	345.730231	KF224.W	Wedding etiquette	395.22	BJ2051-2065
			Weddings, Military	355.17	U350-355
Waterloo, Battle of, 1815	940.27	DC241-244.7	Weeds	632.5	SB610-615
Waterproofing of fabrics	677.682	TS1520	Weeds—Control	632.5	SB610-615
Watersheds	551.45	GB561-568	Week-day church schools	371.071	BV1580-1583
Waterspouts	551.553	QC957	Weekly rest-day	331.2576	HD5114
Waterways	386	HE380.8-560	Weighing-machines	530.7	QC107
Waterways—Canada	386.0971	HE399-401.25	Weight lifting	613.713	GV546.3
Waterways—Latin America	386.098	HE401.5-402	Weights and measures	530.81	QC81-114
Waterways—United States	386.0973	HE392.8-398	Weights and measures—History	530.8109	QC83-86
Waterways—[Other countries]	386.09(4-9)	HE403.5-520.9	Weights and measures—Law and legislation—United States	343.73075	KF1665-1666
Waterproofing	693.892	TH9031			
Wave-motion, Theory of	531.33	QA935	Welding	671.52	TS227-228.96
Wave-motion, Theory of	532.593	QA927	Wells	398.364	GR690
Wave guides	621.381331	QC661	Wells	628.114	TD405-414
Wave makers	532.59	TC172	Welsh language	491.66	PB2101-2199
Wave mechanics	530.124	QC174.2-.26	Welsh literature	891.66	PB2206-2499
Wavelets (Mathematics)	515.2433	QA403.3	West (U.S.)—History	978	F590.3-596.3
Waves	532.593	QC157	West (U.S.)—History—To 1848	978.0(1-2)	F592-.7
Waves	551.463	GC211-222			
Waves	551.463	GC211.2	West (U.S.)—History—1848-1860	978.02	F593
Waxes	665.1	TP669-695			
Weak interactions (Nuclear physics)	539.7544	QC794.8.W4	West (U.S.)—History—1860-1890	978.02	F594
Weapons	355.8	U800-897	West (U.S.)—History—Civil War, 1861-1865	978	E470.9
Weapons	739.7	NK6600-6999			
Weapons, Prehistoric	623.441	GN799.W3	West (U.S.)—History—1890-1945	978.0(2-32)	F595
Weapons—Law and legislation	344.0533	K3661			
Weapons—Law and legislation—England	344.420533	KD3492	West (U.S.)—History—1945-	978.033	F595-.3

Subject Heading	Dewey	LC	Subject Heading	Dewey	LC
West (U.S.)—Maps	912.78	G4050-4052	Whole and parts (Philosophy)	111.82	BD396
West Indian literature (French)	840	PQ3940-3949	Wholesale trade	381.2	HF5419-5422
West Indies	972.9	F1601-1629	Whooping cough	614.543	RA644.W6
West Indies—Biography	920.0729	CT329-448	Whooping cough	616.204	RC204
West Indies—Civilization	972.9	F1609.5	Wide area networks (Computer networks)	004.67	TK5105.87-.888
West Indies—Climate	551.69729	QC987	Wide gap semiconductors	537.6223	QC611.8.W53
West Indies—Commerce	381.09729	HF3311-3369	Wide-screen processes (Cinematography)	778.53	TR855
West Indies—Description and travel	917.2904	F1610-1613	Widow suicide	393.9	GT3370
West Indies—Economic conditions	330.9729	HC151-158.6	Widowers	306.882	HQ1058-.5
West Indies—Emigration and immigration	325.(2729) or (729)	JV7320-7397	Widows	306.883	HQ1058-.5
West Indies—Gazetteers	917.29003	F1604	Wife abuse	364.15553	HV6626-.23
West Indies—Genealogy	929.10720729	CS200-261	Wife abuse	616.85822	RC569.5.F3
West Indies—History	972.9	F1620-1623	Wife abuse—Investigation	363.2595553	HV8079.S67
West Indies—Manufactures	670.9729	TS32-33	Wigs	391.5	GT2310
West Indies—Maps	912.729	G1600-1692	Wigs	646.7248	TT975
West Indies—Maps	912.729	G4900-5184	Wild men	305.3899	GN372
West Indies—Periodicals	972.9005	F1601	Wild plants, Edible	581.632	QK98.5
West Virginia	975.4	F236-250	Wild women	305.48969	GN372
West Virginia—Gazetteers	917.54003	F239	Wildcat strikes	331.892	HD5311
West Virginia—History—Civil War, 1861-1865	975.403	E536	Wilderness survival	796.5	GV200.5-.56
West Virginia—History—Civil War, 1861-1865	975.403	E582	Wildlife cinematography	778.53859	TR893.5
West Virginia—History—1951-	975.404(3-4)	F245-.42	Wildlife conservation	333.95416	QL81.5-84.7
West Virginia—National Guard	355.3709754	UA520-529	Wildlife management—Congresses	639.906	SK352
West Virginia—Periodicals	975.4005	F236	Wildlife management areas	639.9	SK351-579
West Virginia—Maps	912.754	G3890-3894	Wildlife management areas—[By region or country]	639.909(4-9)	SK361-579
Western Hemisphere—Maps	912.19812	G1100-1779	Wildlife management areas—Africa	639.9096	SK571-575
Western riding	798.23	SF309.3	Wildlife management areas—Asia	639.9095	SK553-567
Western saddle	636.13037	SF309.9	Wildlife management areas—Australia	639.90994	SK577
Western Sahara—Census	316.48	HA4737	Wildlife management areas—Canada	639.90971	SK470-471
Western Samoa	996.14	DU819.A2	Wildlife management areas—Central America	639.909728	SK475
Western swing (Music)	784.16409	ML3541	Wildlife management areas—Europe	639.9094	SK503-543
Wetland conservation	333.91816	QH75-77	Wildlife management areas—Great Britain	639.90941	SK505-511
Wetland ecology	577.68	QH541.5.M3	Wildlife management areas—Mexico	639.90972	SK473
Wetlands	578.768	QH87.3	Wildlife management areas—South America	639.9098	SK479-501
Whaling	639.28	SH381-385	Wildlife management areas—United States	639.9097(3-9)	SK361-465
Whaling	910.45	G545	Wildlife management areas—West Indies	639.909729	SK477
Wheat-free diet	613.26	RM237.87	Wildlife managers	639.9092	SK354
Wheelchairs	617.9	RD757.W4	Wildlife photography	778.932	TR729.W54
Wheels	621.81	TJ181.5	Wildlife rehabilitation	333.95416	SF996.45
Whiskey	663.52	TP605	Wildlife reintroduction	333.95416	QL83.4
Whiskey Rebellion, Pa., 1794	973.43	E315	Wildlife rescue	636.0832	QL83.2
Whistling	782.98	MT949.5			
White collar crime investigation	363.25968	HV8079.W47			
White collar workers	331.792	HD8039.M39			
White dwarfs	523.887	QB843.W5			

Subject Heading	Dewey	LC	Subject Heading	Dewey	LC
Wildlife watching—Africa, Eastern	590.72309676	QL337.E25	Women—History	305.409	HQ1121-1172
			Women—Psychology	155.633	HQ1206-1216
Will	153.8	BF608-635	Women—Services for	362.83	HV1442-1448
Will	153.8	LB1071	Women—Sexual behavior	306.7082	HQ29
Wind ensembles	785.43	M955-959	Women—Social conditions	305.42	HQ1121-1870.5
Wind erosion	551.372	QE597	Women—Socialization	302.32082	HQ1201-1216
Wind forecasting	551.6418	QC931	Women—Societies and clubs	367.082	HQ1871-2030.7
Wind instrument music	788	M111			
Wind instruments	788.09	ML929-990	Women—Suffrage	324.623	JF847-855
Wind power	621.45	TJ820-828	Women—United States	305.40973	HQ1402-1439
Windlasses	621.864	VM811	Women—Vocational education	370.113082	LC1500-1506
Windmills	621.453	TJ823-828			
Window gardening	635.9678	SB419-.3	Women clergy	262.14	BV676
Windows	690.1823	TH2261-2276	Women physicians	610.82	R692
Windows	721.823	NA3000-3030	Women's rights	323.34	HQ1236-.5
Winds	551.518	QC930.5-959	Women's studies	305.407	HQ1180-1186
Winds aloft	551.518	QC935	Wood—Chemistry	674.386	TS932-934
Windsurfing	797.33	GV811.63.W56	Wood-carving	736.4	NK9700-9799
Windward Islands	972.98	F2011	Wood-engraving	761.2	NE1000-1325
Windward Islands—Maps	912.7298	G5090-5184	Wood-engraving—[By region or country]	761.209(4-9)	NE1101-1196.3
Wine and wine making	663.2	TP544-559			
Winter grain	633.1	SB188-192	Wood-engraving—Exhibitions	761.2074	NE1010-1012
Winter sports	796.9	GV841-857			
Winter warfare	355.423	U167.5.W5	Wood-engraving—History	761.209	NE1030-1196.3
Wisconsin	977.5	F576-590	Wood-engraving—15th century	761.209024	NE1050-1075
Wisconsin—Gazetteers	917.75003	F579			
Wisconsin—History—To 1848	977.50(1-3)	F584	Wood-engraving—16th century	761.209031	NE1050-1075
			Wood-engraving—17th century	761.209032	NE1050-1075
Wisconsin—History—1848-	977.50(3-4)	F586-.42			
			Wood-engraving—18th century	761.209033	NE1085-1088
Wisconsin—History—Civil War, 1861-1865	977.503	E537			
			Wood-engraving—19th century	761.209034	NE1090-1093
Wisconsin—Maps	912.775	G4120-4124			
Wisconsin—National Guard	355.3709775	UA530-539	Wood-engraving—20th century	761.20904	NE1095-1097
Wisconsin—Periodicals	977.5005	F576			
Wit and humor	808.87	PN6147-6231	Wood-engraving—Periodicals	761.205	NE1000
Wit and humor, Pictorial	857.00222	PC1300-1766			
Witchcraft	133.43	BF1562.5-1584	Wood-pulp	676.12	TS1171-1177
Witchcraft	398.45	GR530	Woodlots	634.99	SD387.W6
Witness bearing (Christianity)	248.5	BV4520	Woodwind ensembles	785.8	M955-959
			Woodwork	745.51	NK9600-9955
Wok cookery	641.589	TX724.5.C	Woodwork	745.51	TT180-203.5
Wok Cookery	641.589	TX840.W65	Wool	677.31	TS1547
Wolf ritual	299.7138	E98.R2	Woolen and worsted manufacture	677.31	TS1600-1631
Woman (Buddhism)	294.3378344	BQ4570.W6			
Woman (Christian theology)	233	BT704	Word of God (Islam)	297.211	BP166.2
Women	305.4	HQ1101-2030.7	Word processing	005.52	HF5548.115
Women	390.082	GT2520-2540	Work	158.7	BF481
Women, Prehistoric	569.9	GN799.W66	Work	174	BJ1498
Women—[By region or country]	305.409(4-9)	HQ1400-1870.5	Work	331	HD4801-8943
			Work—Psychological aspects	158.7	BF481
Women—Biography	920.72	CT3200-3830			
Women—Crimes against	362.88082	HV6250.4.W65	Work environment	331.25	HD7260-7780.8
Women—Diseases	618	RC48.6	Work environment	616.9803	RC963-969
Women—Education	371.822	LC1401-2571	Work ethic	306.3613	HD4905-.3
Women—Education (Higher)	378.19822	LC1551-1651	Work groups	658.402	HD66-.2

Subject Heading	Dewey	LC
Work sharing	331.257277	HD5110.5-.6
Workhouses	365.34	HV8748-8749
Working animals	636.0886	SF170-180
Working class	331.11	HD4801-8943
Working class women—[By region or country]	331.409(4-9)	HD6091-6220.7
Working class—Education	371.82623	LC5001-5060
Working class—Religious life	248.88	BV4593
Working dogs	636.73	SF428.2
Working mothers	306.8743	HQ759.48
Workshops	684.08	TT152-153.7
World history	909	D17-24.5
World maps	912	G1001-1046
World politics	909	D31-34
World War, 1914-1918	940.3	D501-680
World War, 1914-1918—Aerial operations	940.44	D600-607
World War, 1914-1918—Atrocities	940.405	D625-626
World War, 1914-1918—Biography	940.3092	D507
World War, 1914-1918—Campaigns	940.4(2-3)	D529-578
World War, 1914-1918—Campaigns—Western front	940.4(2-3)	D530-549.5
World War, 1914-1918—Campaigns—Belgium	940.4(2-3)	D541-542
World War, 1914-1918—Campaigns—Eastern front	940.4(2-3)	D550-569.5
World War, 1914-1918—Campaigns—France	940.4(2-3)	D544-545
World War, 1914-1918—Campaigns—France	940.4(2-3)	D548-549.5
World War, 1914-1918—Campaigns—Germany	940.4(2-3)	D531-538.5
World War, 1914-1918—Campaigns—Italy	940.4(2-3)	D569
World War, 1914-1918—Campaigns—Turkey	940.4(2-3)	D566-568.9
World War, 1914-1918—Naval operations	940.454	D580-589
World War, 1914-1918—Peace	940.439	D613-614
World War, 1914-1918—Peace	940.439	D642-651
World War, 1914-1918—Prisoners and prisons	940.472	D627
World War, 1914-1918—Prisoners and prisons, Russian	940.47247	D627.R8
World War, 1914-1918—Registers of dead	940.467	D609
World War, 1939-1945	940.53	D731-838
World War, 1939-1945—Aerial operations	940.544	D785-792
World War, 1939-1945—Armistice	940.5312	D812
World War, 1939-1945—Atrocities	940.5405	D803-804.35
World War, 1939-1945—Biography	940.53092	D736
World War, 1939-1945—Blockades	940.5452	D770-784
World War, 1939-1945—Campaigns	940.542	D755-769.87
World War, 1939-1945—Campaigns—Pacific Ocean	940.5426	D767-.99
World War, 1939-1945—Campaigns—Africa, North	940.5423	D766.82
World War, 1939-1945—Campaigns—Burma	940.5425	D767.6
World War, 1939-1945—Campaigns—Eastern front	940.5425	D764-766.7
World War, 1939-1945—Campaigns—France	940.54214	D761-762
World War, 1939-1945—Campaigns—Germany	940.54213	D757-.9
World War, 1939-1945—Campaigns—Great Britain	940.54211	D759-760.8
World War, 1939-1945—Campaigns—Greece	940.5421495	D766.3-.32
World War, 1939-1945—Campaigns—Japan	940.54252	D767.2-.25
World War, 1939-1945—Campaigns—Japan—Okinawa Island	940.5425229	D767.99.045
World War, 1939-1945—Campaigns—Poland	940.542138	D765-.2
World War, 1939-1945—Campaigns—Western front	940.5421	D756-763
World War, 1939-1945—Campaigns—Yugoslavia	940.5421497	D766.6-.62
World War, 1939-1945—Caricatures and cartoons	940.5400222	D745-.7
World War, 1939-1945—Casualties	940.5467	D797
World War, 1939-1945—Casualties	940.548	D797
World War, 1939-1945—Causes	940.5311	D741
World War, 1939-1945—Civilian relief	940.5477	D808-809
World War, 1939-1945—Diplomatic history	940.532	D748-754
World War, 1939-1945—Jews	940.5318	D810.J4
World War, 1939-1945—Medical care	940.5475	D806-807
World War, 1939-1945—Naval operations	940.545	D770-784
World War, 1939-1945—Naval operations—Submarine	940.5451	D780-784

Subject Heading	Dewey	LC
World War, 1939-1945—Occupied territories	940.5336	D802.A2
World War, 1939-1945—Personal narratives	940.548(1-2)	D811-.5
World War, 1939-1945—Pictorial works	940.5300222	D743.2
World War, 1939-1945—Prisoners and prisons	940.5472	D805
World War, 1939-1945—Prisoners and prisons, Japanese	940.547252	D805.J3
World War, 1939-1945—Propaganda	940.5488	D810.P6-.P7
World War, 1939-1945—Refugees	940.5308691	D808-809
World War, 1939-1945—Registers of dead	940.5467	D797
World War, 1939-1945—Reparations	940.531422	D818-819
World War, 1939-1945—Secret service—Great Britain	940.548641	D810.S7
World War, 1939-1945—Tank warfare	940.541	D793
World War, 1939-1945—Underground movements	940.5336	D802
World War, 1939-1945—Underground movements—France—Biography	940.53440922	D802.F8
Worms	592.3	QL386-394
Worry	152.46	BF575.W8
Worship	203	BL550-620
Worship	203	GN470-474
Worship	248.3	BV5-530
Worship (Hinduism)	294.53	BL1226
Worship (Islam)	297.3	BP184.2
Worship (Jainism)	294.43	BL1376-1380
Worship (Judaism)	296.4	BM656-685
Worship—History	248.309	BV5-8
Worship—History—Early church, ca. 30-600	248.30901	BV6
Wounded Knee Massacre, S.D., 1890	978.303	E99.D1
Wounded Knee Massacre, S.D., 1890	978.3031	E83.89
Wounds and injuries	617.1	RA1121
Wounds and injuries	617.1	RC87
Wounds and injuries—Chiropractic treatment	617.1062	RZ270-275
Wrestling	796.812	GV1195
Writing	652.1	Z40-104.5
Writing—Identification	363.2565	HV8074-8076
Wu dialects	495.172	PL1931-1940
Wyoming	978.7	F756-770
Wyoming—Gazetteers	917.87003	F759
Wyoming—Maps	912.787	G4260-4264
Wyoming—National Guard	355.3709787	UA540-549
Wyoming—Periodicals	978.7005	F756
Xenon	546.755	QD181.X1
X-ray astronomy	522.6863	QB472-473
X-ray spectroscopy	537.5352	QC482.S6
X-rays	539.7222	QC480-482.3
Xylophone music	786.843	M175.X6
Yacht racing	797.14	GV826.5-832
Yachting	797.1246	GV811.8-833
Yachts	623.82023	VM331-333
Yama (Buddhist deity)	294.34211	BQ4750.Y35
Yao language	496.397	PL8801-8804
Yarn	677.02862	TS1550-1590
Yarn	677.02862	TS1600-1631
Yawing (Aerodynamics)	629.132364	TL574.M6
Yearbooks	050	AY
Yeast	579.562	QR151
Yeast as feed	636.0855	SF99.Y4
Yellow fever	614.541	RA644.Y4
Yellow fever	616.91854	RC206-216
Yellowstone National Park	978.752	F722
Yemen—Census	315.33	HA4564
Yemen—Economic conditions	330.9533	HC415.34
Yemen—Maps	912.533	G7550-7554
Yemen—Politics and government	320.9533	JQ1842
Yiddish essays	083.91	AC103-104
Yiddish language	439.1	PJ5111-5119
Yiddish language—Dictionaries	439.13	PJ5117
Yiddish language—Grammar	439.15	PJ5115-5116.5
Yiddish literature	839.09	PJ5120-5192
Yoga	181.45	B132.Y6
Yoga (Jainism)	294.4436	BL1375.Y63
Yom Kippur	296.432	BM675.A8
Yom Kippur	296.432	BM695.A8
Young adults	305.235	HQ799.5-.9
Young adults—Sexual behavior	306.70835	HQ27-.5
Young American Medal for Bravery	929.8173	CR6253.Y
Young men	362.7083	HV1423
Young Men's Christian associations	267.3	BV1000-1220
Young women	362.7083	HV1425
Young Women's Christian associations	267.5	BV1300-1393
Youth	305.235	HQ793-799.9
Youth, Buddhist—Conduct of life	294.35	BJ1289.5.Y6
Youth, Muslim—Religious life	297.57	BP188.3.Y6
Youth—[By region or country]	305.23509(4-9)	HQ799
Youth—Crimes against	362.88083	HV6250.4.Y68
Youth—Employment	331.34	HD6270-6276

Subject Heading	Dewey	LC	Subject Heading	Dewey	LC
Youth—Physiology	612.661	RJ140-145	Yukon Territory—Periodicals	971.91005	F1091.A1
Youth—Religious life	248.83	BV4530-4579			
Youth—Societies and clubs	367.4	HS3250-3270	Yupik Eskimos	979.8004971	E99.E7
Youth—Substance use	362.29083	HV4999.Y68	Zaire—Census	316.751	HA4711
Youth—Travel	910.83	G156.5.Y6	Zaire—Civilization	967.51	DT649
Youth hostels	910.466	TX907-910	Zaire—Description and travel	916.75104	DT645-647.5
Youth in church work	258.0835	BV4427-4430			
Youth in missionary work	266.0083	BV2617	Zaire—Economic conditions	330.96751	HC955
Youth in the ecumenical movement	280.0420835	BX9.5.Y68	Zaire—History	967.51	DT650.2-663
Youth sermons	252.55	BV4310	Zaire—History—To 1908	967.510(1-22)	DT654-655.2
Youthfulness	155.5	BF724-.3	Zaire—History—1908-1960	967.51024	DT657-.2
Youths' periodicals	050.835	AP200-230			
Yugoslavia	939.8	DR1202-2285	Zaire—History—1960-	967.5103	DT658-.25
Yugoslavia	949.7	DR1202-2285	Zaire—History—Civil War, 1960-1965	967.51031	DT658
Yugoslavia—Biography	920.0398	DR1233-1235			
Yugoslavia—Biography	920.0497	DR1233-1235	Zaire—History—Shaba Invasion, 1977	967.51033	DT658.25
Yugoslavia—Census	314.97	HA1631-1635			
Yugoslavia—Civilization	939.8	DR1228	Zaire—History—Shaba Uprising, 1978	967.51033	DT658.25
Yugoslavia—Civilization	949.7	DR1228			
Yugoslavia—Congresses	939.8006	DR1205	Zaire—Maps	912.6751	G8650-8654
Yugoslavia—Congresses	949.7006	DR1205	Zambia—Census	316.894	HA4703
Yugoslavia—Description and travel	913.9804	DR1218-1224	Zambia—Civilization	968.94	DT3052
			Zambia—Description and travel	916.89404	DT3050
Yugoslavia—Description and travel	914.9704	DR1218-1224			
			Zambia—Economic conditions	330.96894	HC915
Yugoslavia—Economic conditions	330.9497	HC407			
			Zambia—Gazetteers	916.894003	DT3037
Yugoslavia—Gazetteers	913.98003	DR1209	Zambia—History	968.94	DT3064-3119
Yugoslavia—Gazetteers	914.97003	DR1209	Zambia—History—To 1890	968.9401	DT3079-3089
Yugoslavia—Historiography	939.80072	DR1239-1243	Zambia—History—1890-1924	968.9402	DT3091-3101
Yugoslavia—Historiography	949.70072	DR1239-1243			
Yugoslavia—History	939.8	DR1232-1321	Zambia—History—1924-1953	968.9402	DT3103-3106
Yugoslavia—History	949.7	DR1232-1321			
Yugoslavia—History—1918-1945	949.70(2-3)	DR1281-1312	Zambia—History—1953-1964	968.9403	DT3108-3111
			Zambia—History—1964-	968.9404	DT3113-3119
Yugoslavia—History—Axis occupation, 1941-1945	949.7022	D802.Y8	Zen Buddhism	294.3927	BQ9250-9519
			Zen Buddhism—Psychology	294.3375	BL1493
Yugoslavia—History—Coup d'etat, 1941	949.7022	DR1297-1298	Zimbabwe—Census	316.89	HA4702
			Zimbabwe—Civilization	968.91	DT2908
Yugoslavia—History—1945-1980	949.7023	DR1300	Zimbabwe—Description and travel	916.89104	DT2900-2904
Yugoslavia—History—1980-1992	949.7024	DR1306-1313.8	Zimbabwe—Economic conditions	330.9689	HC910
Yugoslavia—History—1992-	949.7103	DR1306-1312	Zimbabwe—Gazetteers	916.891003	DT2884
			Zimbabwe—Guidebooks	916.8910451	DT2886
Yugoslavia—History, Military	355.009497	DR1250-1251	Zimbabwe—History	968.91	DT2914-3000
			Zimbabwe—History—1890-1965	968.910(2-4)	DT2959-2979
Yugoslavia—History, Naval	359.300497	DR1252-1253			
Yugoslavia—Manufactures	670.9497	TS95.Y8	Zimbabwe—History—Shona Insurrection, 1896-1897	968.9102	DT2970
Yugoslavia—Maps	912.497	G6840-6844			
Yugoslavia—Periodicals	939.8005	DR1202			
Yugoslavia—Periodicals	949.7005	DR1202	Zimbabwe—History—Ndebele Insurrection, 1896	968.9102	DT2968
Yukon Territory—Gazetteers	917.191003	F1092			
Yukon Territory—History	971.91	F1091-1095.5			
Yukon Territory—Maps	912.7191	G3520-3524	Zimbabwe—History—1965-1980	968.9104	DT2981-2994

Subject Heading	Dewey	LC	Subject Heading	Dewey	LC
Zimbabwe—History—Chimurenga War, 1966-1980	968.9104	DT2988	Zoology, Economic—[Other countries]	591.609(4-9)	SB993.34
Zimbabwe—History—1980-	968.9105	DT2996-3000	Zoology—[By region or country]	590.9(4-9)	QL155-339
Zionism	320.54095694	DS149-151	Zoology—Arctic regions	590.98	QL105
Zither music	787.7	M135-137	Zoology—Experiments	590.724	QL52.6
Zither—Instruction and study	787.707	MT620-634	Zoology—Pictorial works	590.222	QL46
			Zoology—Societies, etc.	590.6	QL1
Zodiac	523	QB15-26	Zoology—Study and teaching	590.71	QL51-58
Zodiac	523	QB802			
Zoning	333.7717	HT169.6-.9	Zoology—Terminology	590.14	QL10
Zoning law—England	346.42045	KD1125-1162	Zoonoses	614.56	RA639-641
Zoogeography	590.9(4-9)	QL101-345	Zoonoses	616.959	RC113.5
Zoological museums	590.74	QL71	Zoonoses	636.0896959	SF740
Zoologists	591.5092	QL26-31	Zoos	590.73	QL76-77.5
Zoology	590	QL	Zoroastrianism	295	BL1500-1590
Zoology, Economic	591.6	SB922-998	Zoroastrianism—Sacred books	295.82	BL1510-1525
Zoology, Economic—[By region or country]	591.609(4-9)	SB993.3-.34	Zulu language	496.3986	PL8841-8844
			Zulu War, 1879	968.045	DT1875-1882
Zoology, Economic—United States	591.60973	SB993.3-32	Zuni Indians	979.100497994	E99.Z9
			Zuni language	497.994	PM2711

About the Author

After working in the fields of teaching and counseling, Ms. Scott earned her Masters in Library and Information Sciences summa cum laude from Catholic University, specializing in library automation.

In Federal Libraries, Ms. Scott has been the Head of Cataloging at the U.S. Bureau of the Census Library, Systems Librarian at the Judges' Library for the U.S. Court of Appeals in Washington, and Head of Technical Services and Systems at the NASA Goddard Space Flight Center Library. She also directed cataloging projects for the National Library of Medicine, National Oceanic and Atmospheric Administration, and NASA Langley.

Ms. Scott automated the library at the Harvard Center for Hellenic Studies, and a special military library at Ft. Belvoir, Virginia, and organized a digitization project for the architectural drawings used in the Pentagon Renovation Program.

Ms. Scott's interests are in providing information to users remotely through digitization and automation, and the arrangement of materials in manners most useful to the end user. Reflecting these interests, she provided access to needed materials for a special military library's branch sites scattered around the country utilizing a website, a customized web-based OPAC with pre-configured searches, and linking fields in cataloging records. She also developed a classification system reflecting the Agency's information needs and the type of materials in a special collection within the military library.